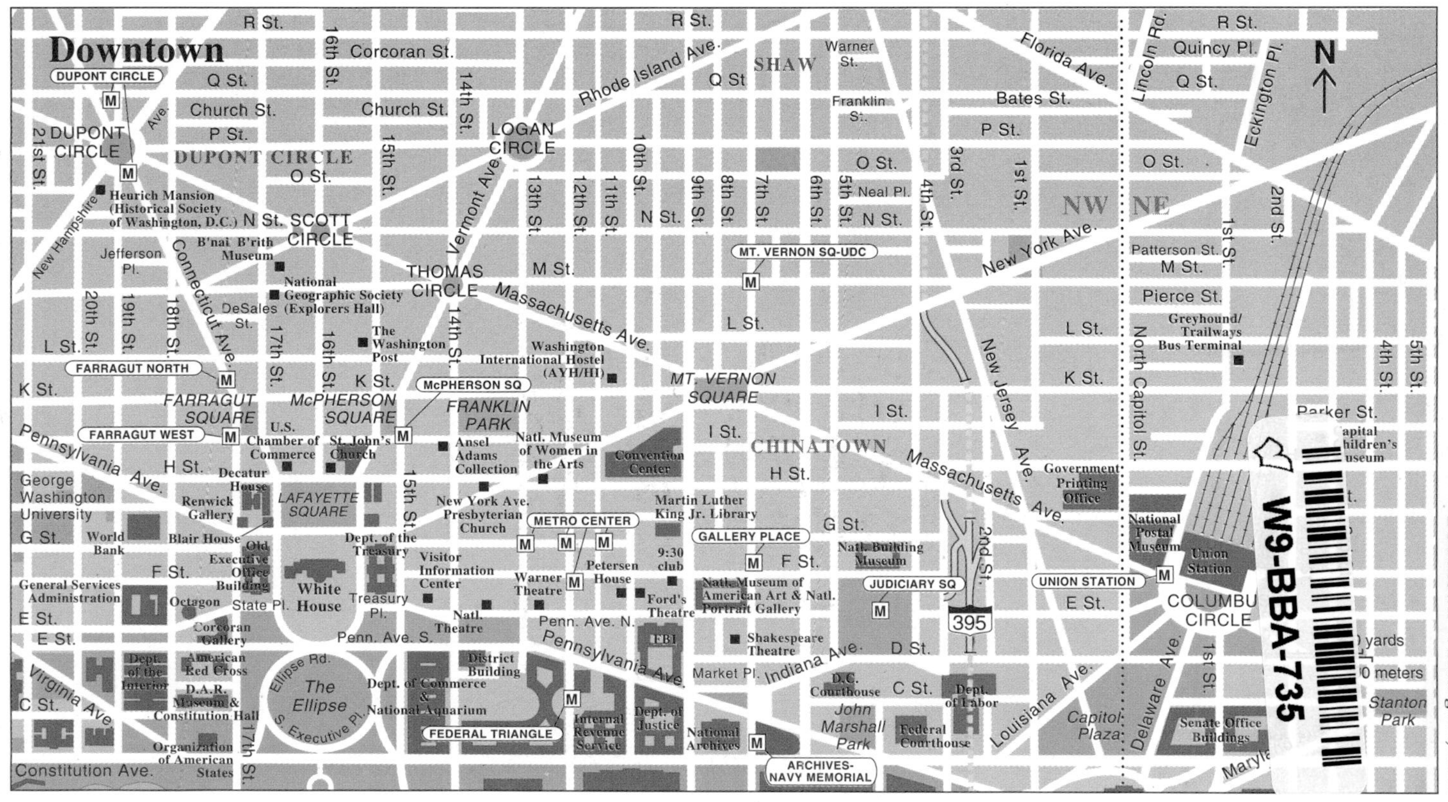
Downtown
N
DUPONT CIRCLE
DUPONT CIRCLE
SCOTT CIRCLE
THOMAS CIRCLE
LOGAN CIRCLE
SHAW
CHINATOWN
MT. VERNON SQUARE
McPHERSON SQUARE
FARRAGUT SQUARE
FRANKLIN PARK
LAFAYETTE SQUARE
John Marshall Park
The Ellipse
Capitol Plaza
Stanton Park
COLUMBU CIRCLE
NW
NE
FARRAGUT NORTH
FARRAGUT WEST
McPHERSON SQ
METRO CENTER
GALLERY PLACE
JUDICIARY SQ
UNION STATION
MT. VERNON SQ-UDC
ARCHIVES-NAVY MEMORIAL
FEDERAL TRIANGLE
Heurich Mansion (Historical Society of Washington, D.C.)
B'nai B'rith Museum
National Geographic Society (Explorers Hall)
DeSales St.
The Washington Post
Washington International Hostel (AYH/HI)
Natl. Museum of Women in the Arts
Ansel Adams Collection
New York Ave. Presbyterian Church
U.S. Chamber of Commerce
St. John's Church
Decatur House
Renwick Gallery
Blair House
Old Executive Office Building
White House
Dept. of the Treasury
Visitor Information Center
Natl. Theatre
Warner Theatre
Petersen House
Ford's Theatre
9:30 club
Martin Luther King Jr. Library
Convention Center
Natl. Building Museum
Natl. Museum of American Art & Natl. Portrait Gallery
Shakespeare Theatre
FBI
Dept. of Justice
Internal Revenue Service
National Archives
District Building
Dept. of Commerce & National Aquarium
Octagon
Corcoran Gallery
American Red Cross
D.A.R. Museum & Constitution Hall
Organization of American States
Dept. of the Interior
World Bank
General Services Administration
George Washington University
D.C. Courthouse
Federal Courthouse
Dept. of Labor
Government Printing Office
National Postal Museum
Union Station
Senate Office Buildings
Greyhound/Trailways Bus Terminal
Connecticut Ave.
Massachusetts Ave.
Rhode Island Ave.
Vermont Ave.
New Hampshire Ave.
Pennsylvania Ave.
Virginia Ave.
Constitution Ave.
New York Ave.
New Jersey Ave.
Florida Ave.
Louisiana Ave.
Indiana Ave.
Delaware Ave.
Maryla
Lincoln Rd.
Eckington Pl.
Quincy Pl.
North Capitol St.
Penn. Ave. N.
Penn. Ave. S.
Market Pl.
Ellipse Rd.
S. Executive Pl.
State Pl.
Treasury Pl.
Jefferson Pl.
Patterson St.
Pierce St.
Parker St.
Neal Pl.
Warner St.
Franklin St.
Bates St.
Corcoran St.
Church St.
R St.
Q St.
P St.
O St.
N St.
M St.
L St.
K St.
I St.
H St.
G St.
F St.
E St.
D St.
C St.
1st St.
2nd St.
3rd St.
4th St.
5th St.
6th St.
7th St.
8th St.
9th St.
10th St.
11th St.
12th St.
13th St.
14th St.
15th St.
16th St.
17th St.
18th St.
19th St.
20th St.
21st St.
395
yards
meters

Central Washington, D.C.

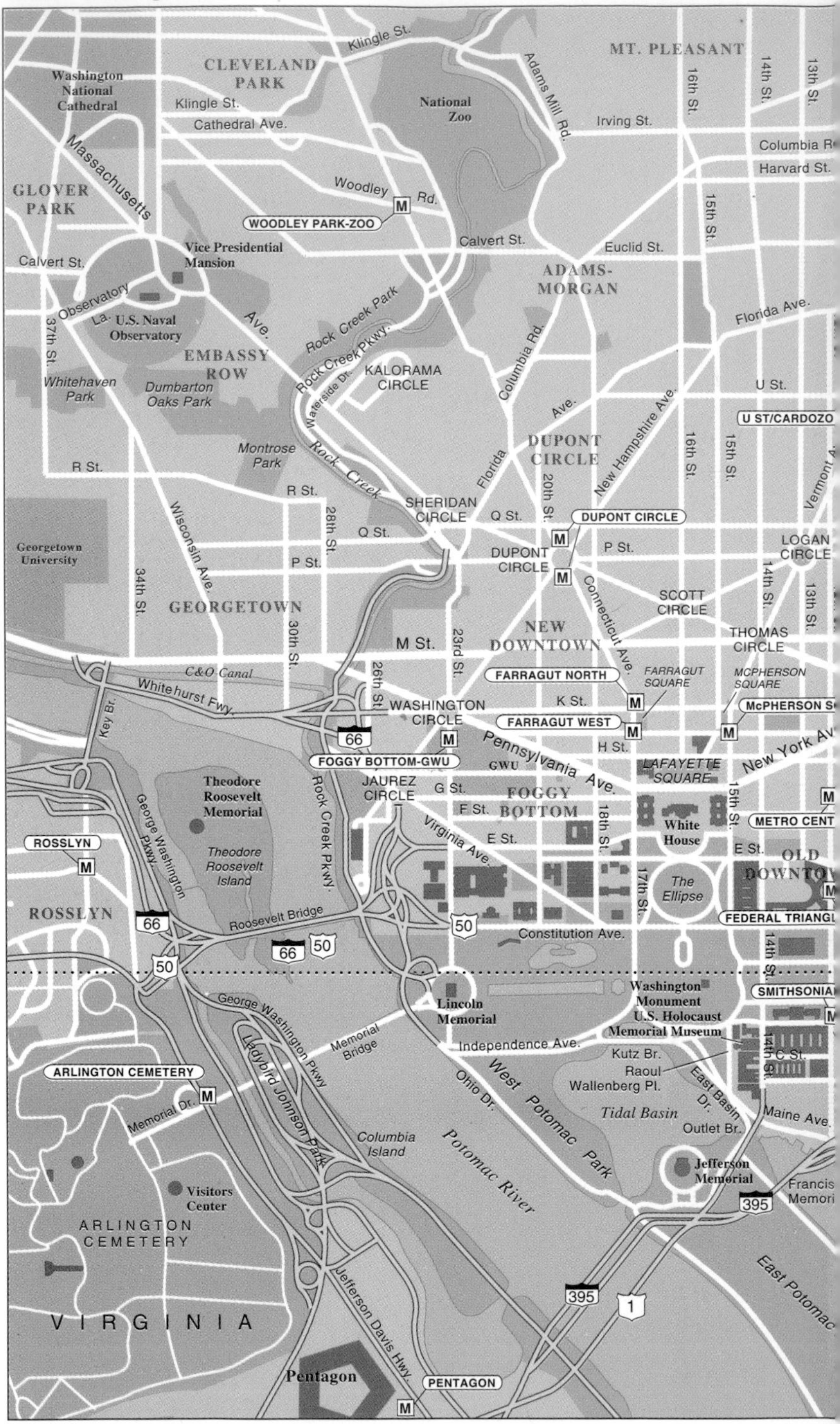

Klingle St.
MT. PLEASANT
CLEVELAND PARK
Washington National Cathedral
Klingle St.
Cathedral Ave.
National Zoo
Adams Mill Rd.
Irving St.
16th St.
14th St.
13th St.
Columbia Rd.
Harvard St.
Massachusetts
GLOVER PARK
Woodley Rd.
WOODLEY PARK-ZOO
15th St.
Calvert St.
Euclid St.
Vice Presidential Mansion
Calvert St.
ADAMS-MORGAN
Observatory La.
U.S. Naval Observatory
Ave.
Rock Creek Park
Rock Creek Pkwy.
Florida Ave.
37th St.
EMBASSY ROW
Waterside Dr.
KALORAMA CIRCLE
Columbia Rd.
Whitehaven Park
Dumbarton Oaks Park
U St.
New Hampshire Ave.
U ST/CARDOZO
Ave.
DUPONT CIRCLE
Montrose Park
Rock Creek
Florida
16th St.
15th St.
Vermont Ave.
R St.
R St.
SHERIDAN CIRCLE
Q St.
20th St.
DUPONT CIRCLE
Wisconsin Ave.
28th St.
Q St.
P St.
LOGAN CIRCLE
Georgetown University
P St.
DUPONT CIRCLE
34th St.
Connecticut Ave.
SCOTT CIRCLE
14th St.
13th St.
GEORGETOWN
30th St.
NEW DOWNTOWN
THOMAS CIRCLE
M St.
23rd St.
C&O Canal
FARRAGUT NORTH
FARRAGUT SQUARE
MCPHERSON SQUARE
Whitehurst Fwy.
26th St.
K St.
McPHERSON SQ
Key Br.
WASHINGTON CIRCLE
FARRAGUT WEST
66
Pennsylvania Ave.
H St.
New York Ave.
FOGGY BOTTOM-GWU
GWU
LAFAYETTE SQUARE
Theodore Roosevelt Memorial
Rock Creek Pkwy.
JAUREZ CIRCLE
G St.
FOGGY BOTTOM
F St.
18th St.
15th St.
METRO CENTER
ROSSLYN
George Washington Pkwy.
Virginia Ave.
E St.
White House
E St.
OLD DOWNTOWN
Theodore Roosevelt Island
17th St.
The Ellipse
ROSSLYN
66
Roosevelt Bridge
50
FEDERAL TRIANGLE
Constitution Ave.
66
50
50
14th St.
Washington Monument
SMITHSONIAN
Lincoln Memorial
U.S. Holocaust Memorial Museum
George Washington Pkwy
Memorial Bridge
Independence Ave.
14th St.
C St.
Kutz Br.
Raoul Wallenberg Pl.
Ladybird Johnson Park
ARLINGTON CEMETERY
Ohio Dr.
West Potomac Park
East Basin Dr.
Memorial Dr.
Tidal Basin
Maine Ave.
Outlet Br.
Columbia Island
Potomac River
Jefferson Memorial
Visitors Center
Francis Memorial
395
ARLINGTON CEMETERY
East Potomac
395
1
VIRGINIA
Jefferson Davis Hwy.
Pentagon
PENTAGON

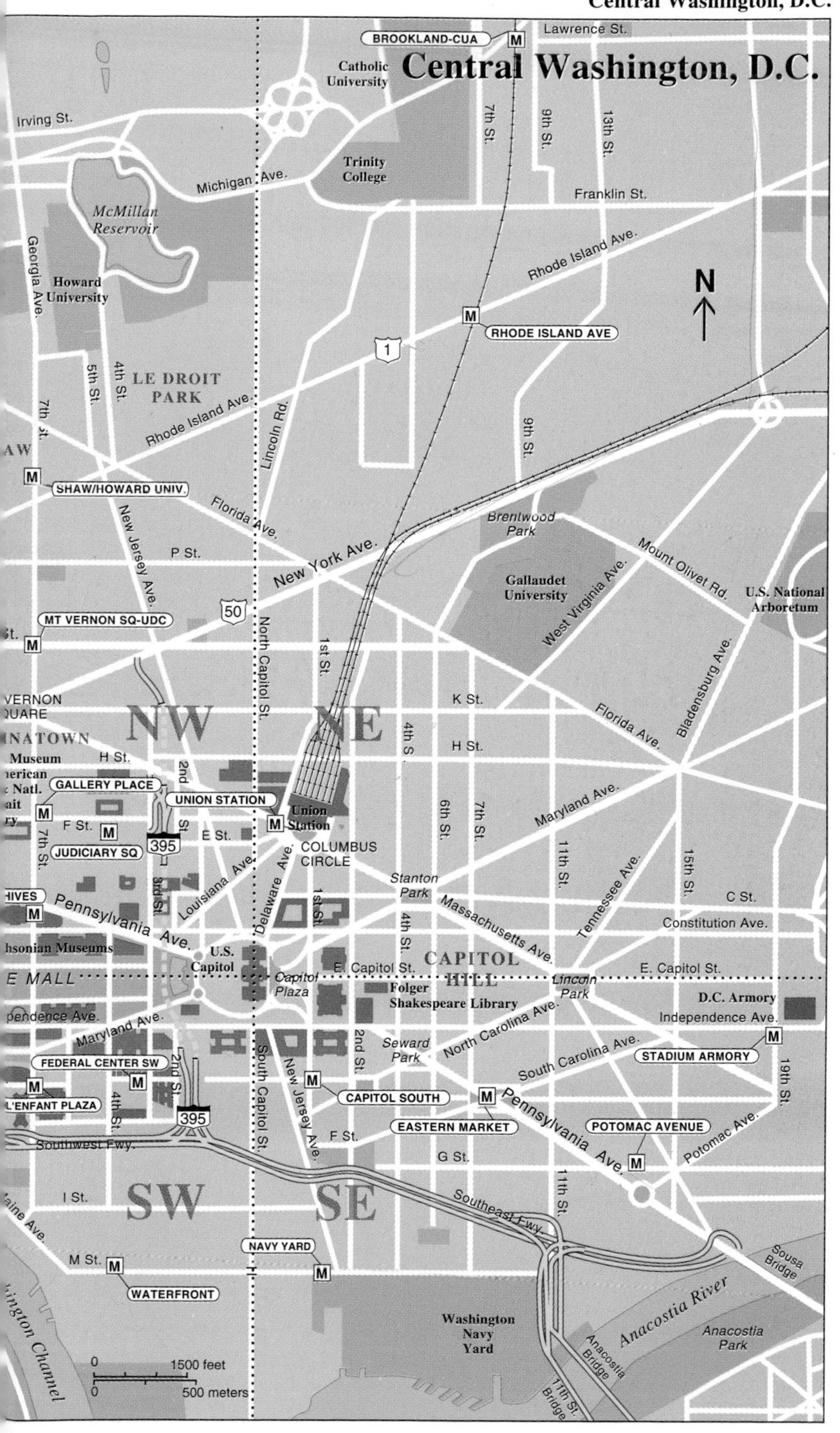
Central Washington, D.C.
BROOKLAND-CUA
Lawrence St.
Catholic University
Trinity College
Irving St.
Michigan Ave.
McMillan Reservoir
Howard University
Georgia Ave.
7th St.
9th St.
13th St.
Franklin St.
Rhode Island Ave.
RHODE ISLAND AVE
N
LE DROIT PARK
5th St.
4th St.
Lincoln Rd.
SHAW/HOWARD UNIV.
Florida Ave.
New Jersey Ave.
P St.
New York Ave.
Brentwood Park
Mount Olivet Rd.
Gallaudet University
West Virginia Ave.
U.S. National Arboretum
MT VERNON SQ-UDC
North Capitol St.
1st St.
Bladensburg Ave.
K St.
NW
NE
H St.
GALLERY PLACE
UNION STATION
Union Station
F St.
JUDICIARY SQ
E St.
395
COLUMBUS CIRCLE
Louisiana Ave.
Delaware Ave.
Maryland Ave.
6th St.
11th St.
15th St.
Tennessee Ave.
Stanton Park
Massachusetts Ave.
C St.
Constitution Ave.
Pennsylvania Ave.
U.S. Capitol
E. Capitol St.
CAPITOL HILL
Capitol Plaza
Folger Shakespeare Library
Lincoln Park
D.C. Armory
Independence Ave.
North Carolina Ave.
Seward Park
South Carolina Ave.
STADIUM ARMORY
19th St.
FEDERAL CENTER SW
L'ENFANT PLAZA
South Capitol St.
CAPITOL SOUTH
EASTERN MARKET
POTOMAC AVENUE
Potomac Ave.
Southwest Fwy.
F St.
G St.
I St.
SW
SE
Southeast Fwy.
NAVY YARD
M St.
WATERFRONT
Washington Navy Yard
Anacostia River
Anacostia Park
Sousa Bridge
Anacostia Bridge
11th St. Bridge
0
1500 feet
500 meters

The Mall Area, Washington, D.C.

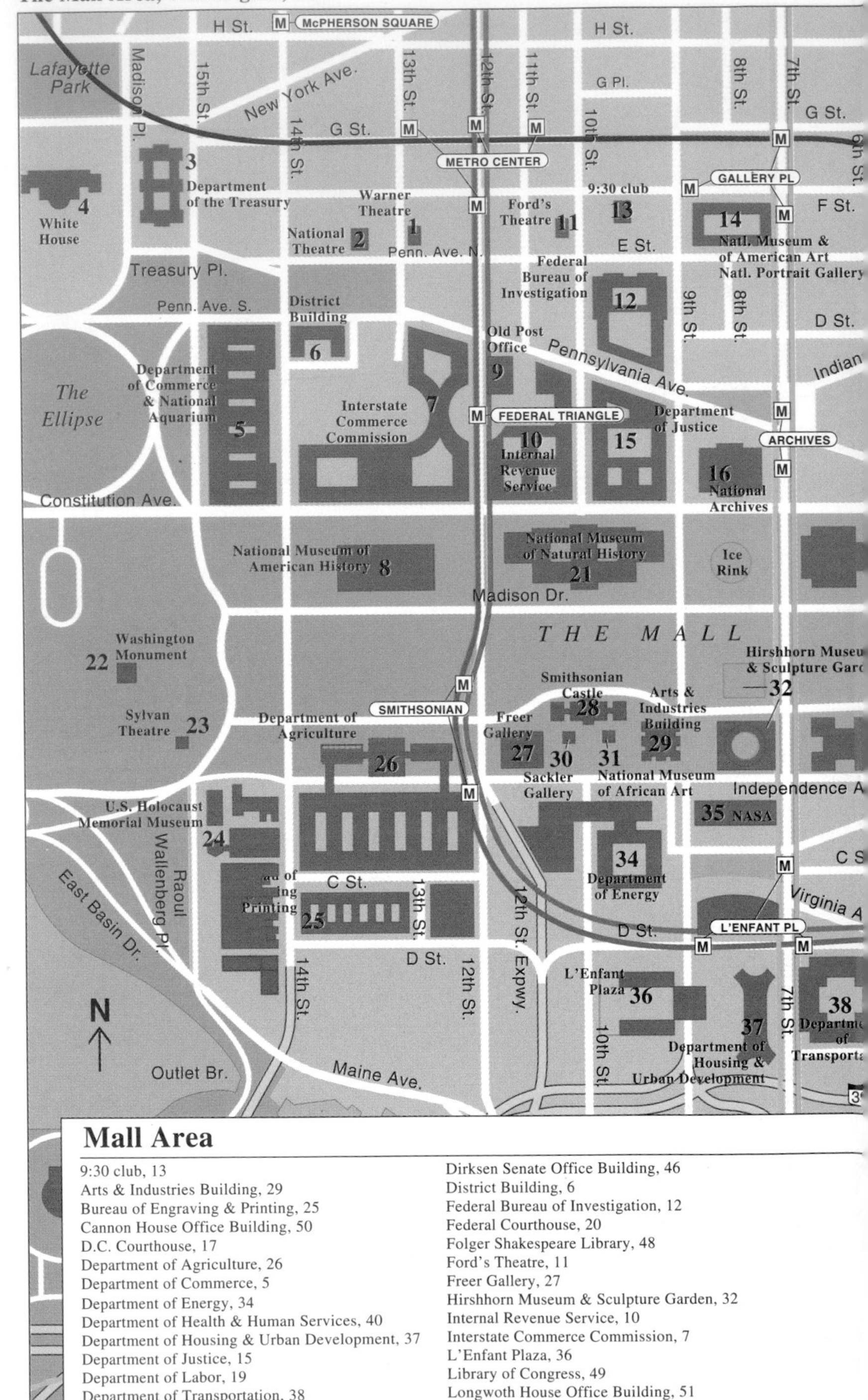

Mall Area

9:30 club, 13
Arts & Industries Building, 29
Bureau of Engraving & Printing, 25
Cannon House Office Building, 50
D.C. Courthouse, 17
Department of Agriculture, 26
Department of Commerce, 5
Department of Energy, 34
Department of Health & Human Services, 40
Department of Housing & Urban Development, 37
Department of Justice, 15
Department of Labor, 19
Department of Transportation, 38
Department of the Treasury, 3
Dirksen Senate Office Building, 46
District Building, 6
Federal Bureau of Investigation, 12
Federal Courthouse, 20
Folger Shakespeare Library, 48
Ford's Theatre, 11
Freer Gallery, 27
Hirshhorn Museum & Sculpture Garden, 32
Internal Revenue Service, 10
Interstate Commerce Commission, 7
L'Enfant Plaza, 36
Library of Congress, 49
Longwoth House Office Building, 51
National Aquarium, 5

The Mall Area, Washington, D.C.

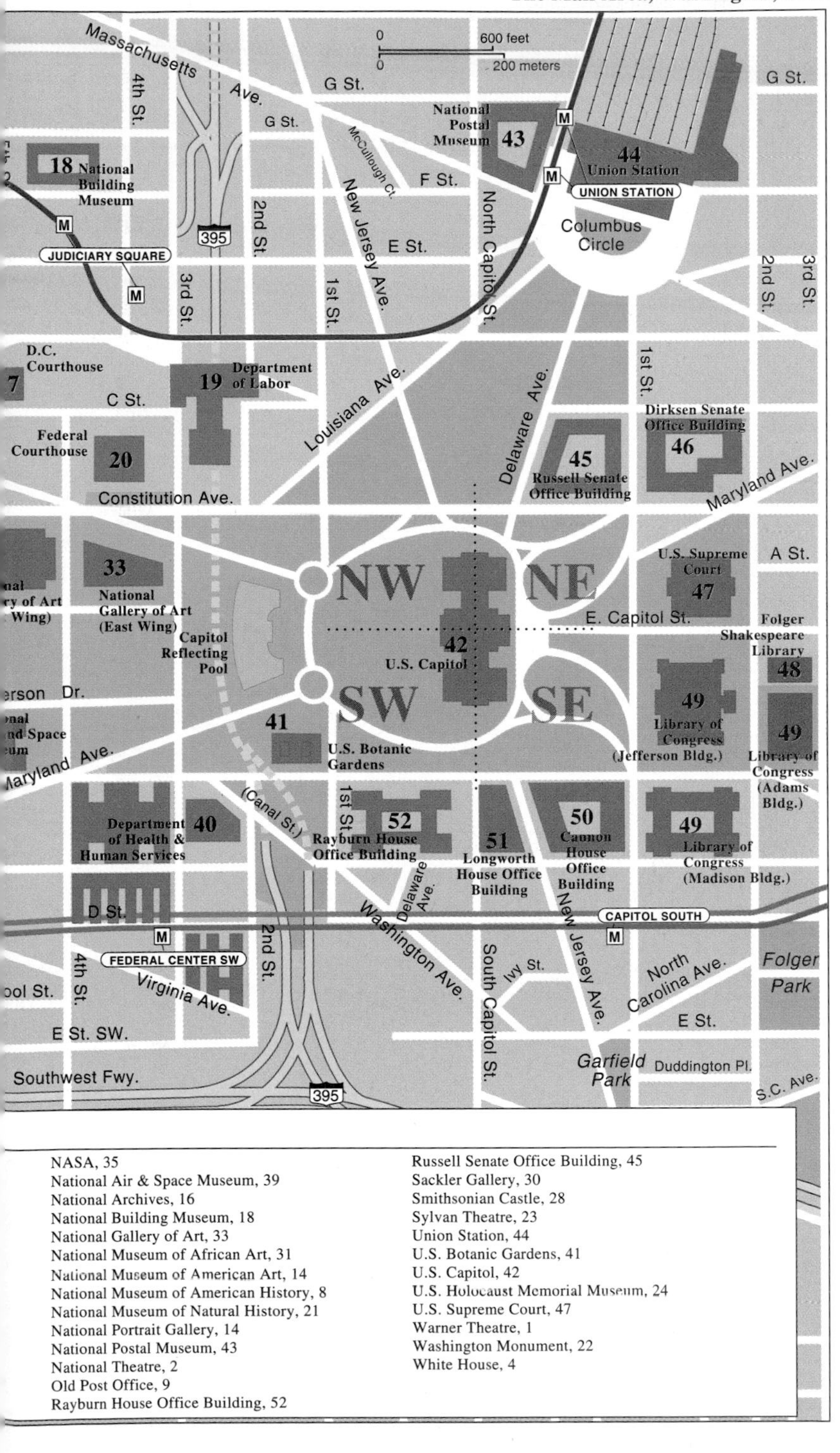

NASA, 35
National Air & Space Museum, 39
National Archives, 16
National Building Museum, 18
National Gallery of Art, 33
National Museum of African Art, 31
National Museum of American Art, 14
National Museum of American History, 8
National Museum of Natural History, 21
National Portrait Gallery, 14
National Postal Museum, 43
National Theatre, 2
Old Post Office, 9
Rayburn House Office Building, 52
Russell Senate Office Building, 45
Sackler Gallery, 30
Smithsonian Castle, 28
Sylvan Theatre, 23
Union Station, 44
U.S. Botanic Gardens, 41
U.S. Capitol, 42
U.S. Holocaust Memorial Museum, 24
U.S. Supreme Court, 47
Warner Theatre, 1
Washington Monument, 22
White House, 4

White House Area, Foggy Bottom, and Nearby Arlington

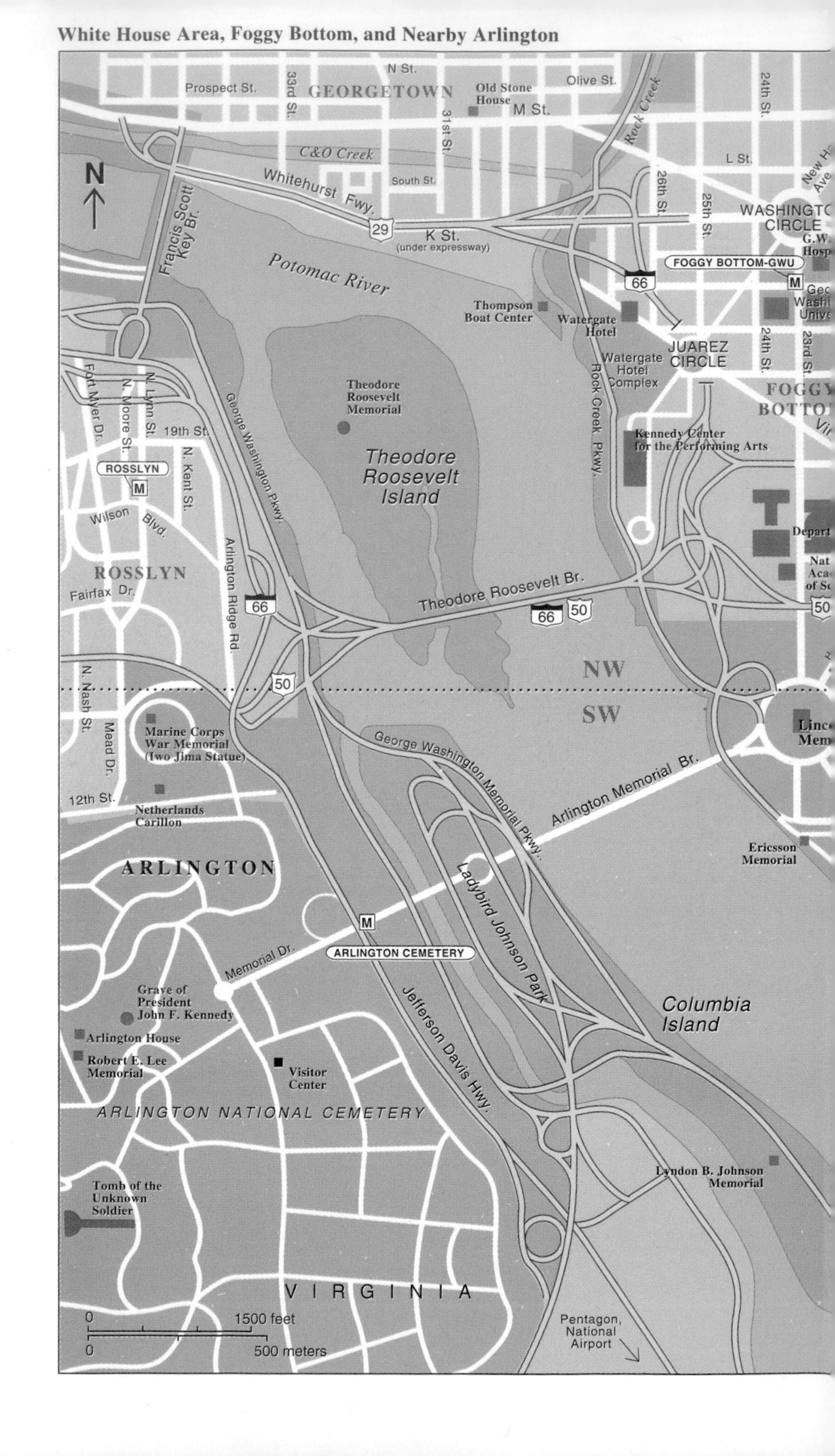

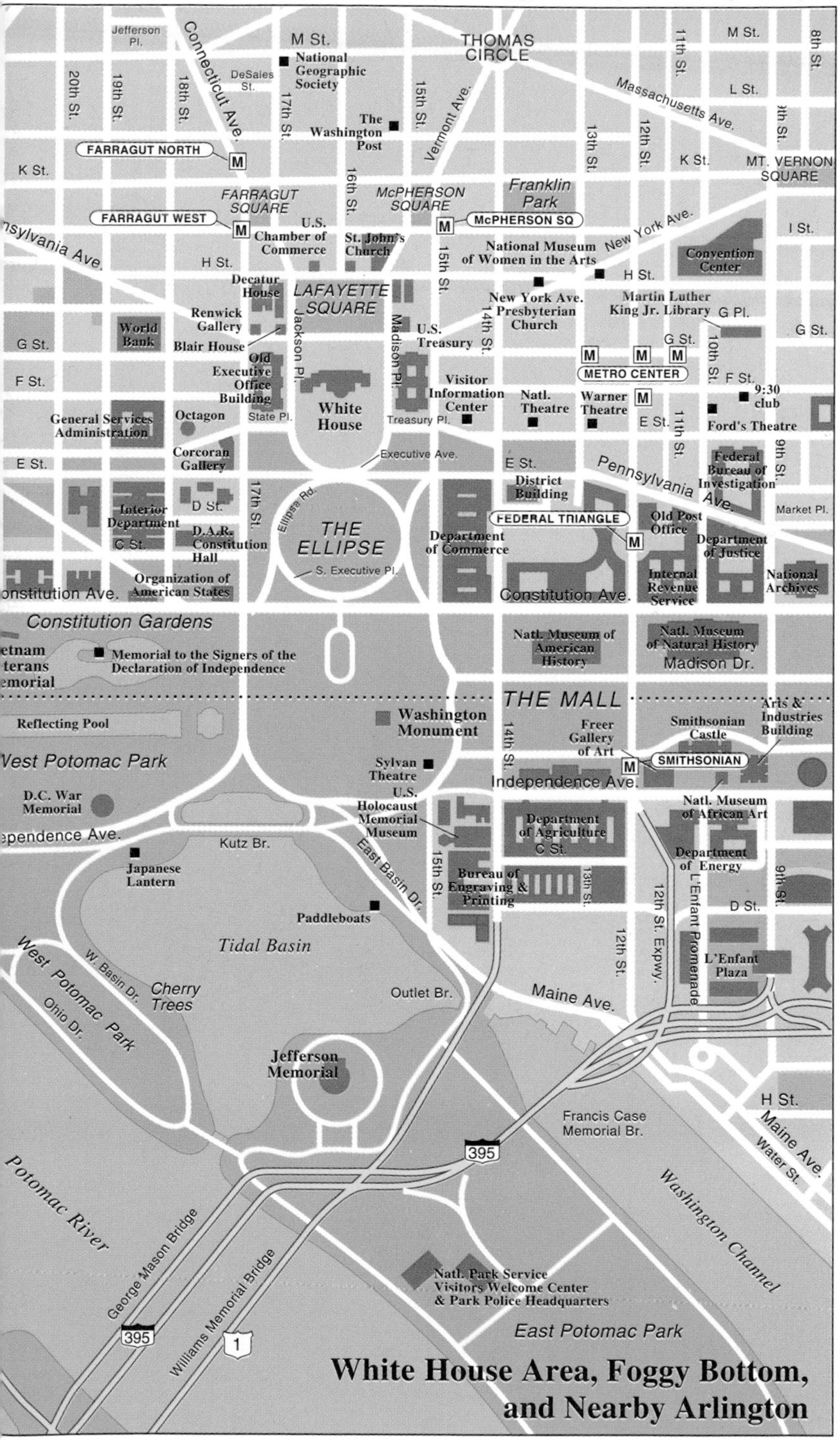

Jefferson Pl.
M St.
Connecticut Ave.
DeSales St.
National Geographic Society
THOMAS CIRCLE
11th St.
M St.
8th St.
20th St.
19th St.
18th St.
17th St.
15th St.
Vermont Ave.
Massachusetts Ave.
L St.
9th St.
The Washington Post
FARRAGUT NORTH
13th St.
12th St.
K St.
MT. VERNON SQUARE
K St.
FARRAGUT SQUARE
16th St.
McPHERSON SQUARE
Franklin Park
FARRAGUT WEST
U.S. Chamber of Commerce
McPHERSON SQ
New York Ave.
I St.
Pennsylvania Ave.
St. John's Church
National Museum of Women in the Arts
Convention Center
H St.
H St.
Decatur House
LAFAYETTE SQUARE
15th St.
New York Ave. Presbyterian Church
Martin Luther King Jr. Library
Renwick Gallery
Jackson Pl.
Madison Pl.
14th St.
G Pl.
World Bank
U.S. Treasury
G St.
G St.
Blair House
10th St.
G St.
Old Executive Office Building
METRO CENTER
F St.
F St.
Visitor Information Center
Natl. Theatre
Warner Theatre
9:30 club
White House
General Services Administration
Octagon
State Pl.
Treasury Pl.
E St.
11th St.
Ford's Theatre
Corcoran Gallery
Executive Ave.
E St.
Pennsylvania Ave.
Federal Bureau of Investigation
E St.
9th St.
17th St.
District Building
Interior Department
D St.
Ellipse Rd.
Market Pl.
FEDERAL TRIANGLE
Old Post Office
C St.
D.A.R. Constitution Hall
THE ELLIPSE
Department of Commerce
Department of Justice
Organization of American States
S. Executive Pl.
Internal Revenue Service
National Archives
Constitution Ave.
Constitution Ave.
Constitution Gardens
Natl. Museum of American History
Natl. Museum of Natural History
Vietnam Veterans Memorial
Memorial to the Signers of the Declaration of Independence
Madison Dr.
THE MALL
Arts & Industries Building
Reflecting Pool
Washington Monument
Freer Gallery of Art
Smithsonian Castle
14th St.
West Potomac Park
Sylvan Theatre
SMITHSONIAN
Independence Ave.
U.S. Holocaust Memorial Museum
D.C. War Memorial
Natl. Museum of African Art
Department of Agriculture
Independence Ave.
C St.
Kutz Br.
East Basin Dr.
Department of Energy
Japanese Lantern
15th St.
Bureau of Engraving & Printing
13th St.
12th St. Expwy.
L'Enfant Promenade
9th St.
D St.
Paddleboats
12th St.
Tidal Basin
L'Enfant Plaza
West Potomac Park
W. Basin Dr.
Cherry Trees
Outlet Br.
Maine Ave.
Ohio Dr.
Jefferson Memorial
H St.
Francis Case Memorial Br.
Maine Ave.
Water St.
395
Potomac River
Washington Channel
George Mason Bridge
Williams Memorial Bridge
Natl. Park Service Visitors Welcome Center & Park Police Headquarters
395
1
East Potomac Park

White House Area, Foggy Bottom, and Nearby Arlington

Metrorail System, Washington, D.C.

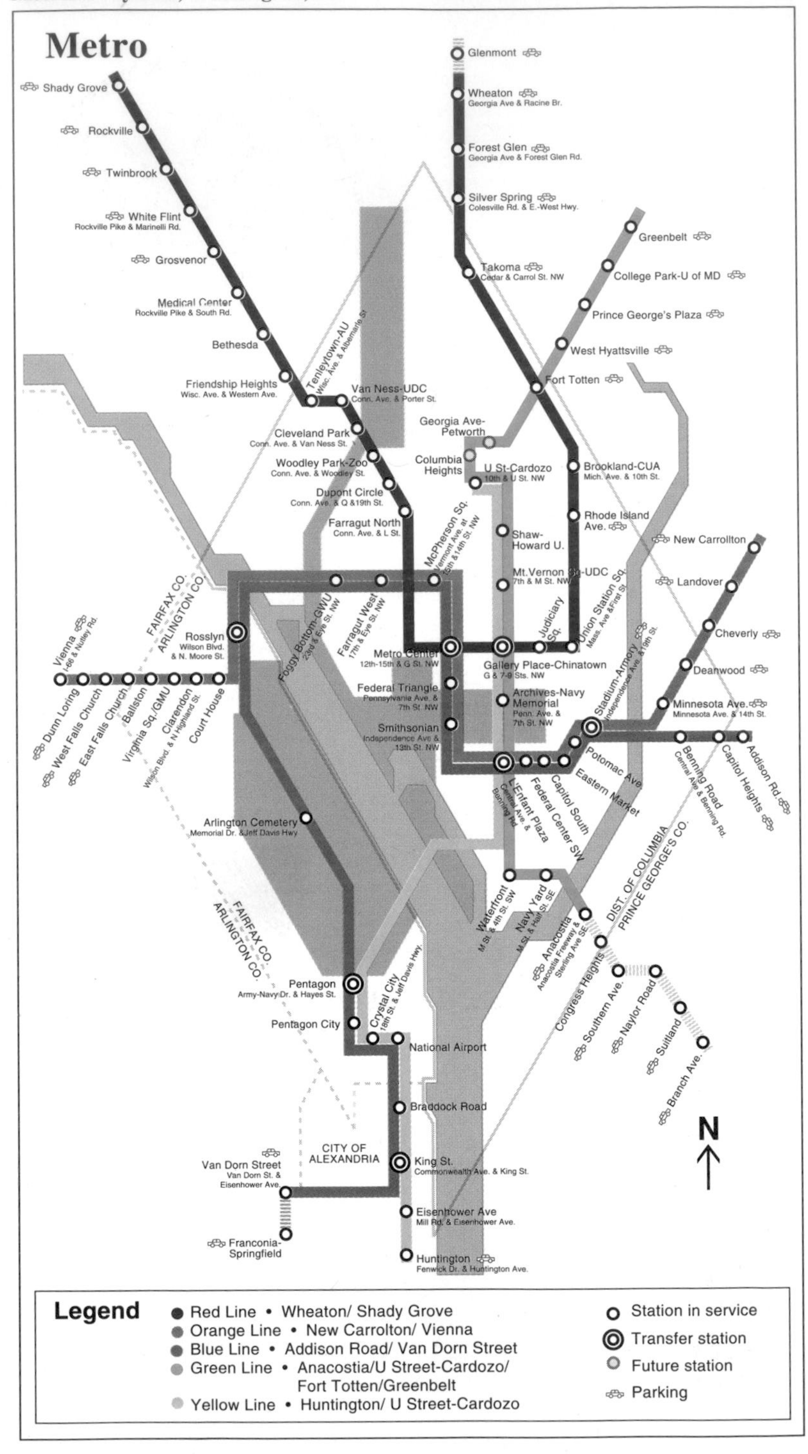

LET'S GO:

WASHINGTON, D.C.

is the best book for anyone traveling on a budget. Here's why:

▪ No other guidebook has as many budget listings.

In Washington, D.C. we list over 2,500 budget travel bargains. We tell you the cheapest way to get around, and where to get an inexpensive and satisfying meal once you've arrived. We give hundreds of money-saving tips that anyone can use, plus invaluable advice on discounts and deals for students, children, families, and senior travelers.

▪ Let's Go researchers have to make it on their own.

Our Harvard-Radcliffe researcher-writers travel on budgets as tight as your own—no expense accounts, no free hotel rooms.

▪ Let's Go is completely revised each year.

We don't just update the prices, we go back to the place. If a charming café has become an overpriced tourist trap, we'll replace the listing with a new and better one.

▪ No other guidebook includes all this:

Honest, engaging coverage of the city and beyond; up-to-the-minute prices, directions, addresses, phone numbers, and opening hours; in-depth essays on local culture, history, and politics; comprehensive listings on transportation between and within regions and cities; straight advice on work and study, budget accommodations, sights, nightlife, and food; detailed maps; and much more.

▪ Let's Go is for anyone who wants to see Washington, D.C. on a budget.

LET'S GO PUBLICATIONS

Let's Go: Alaska & The Pacific Northwest
Let's Go: Britain & Ireland
Let's Go: California
Let's Go: Central America
Let's Go: Eastern Europe
Let's Go: Europe
Let's Go: France
Let's Go: Germany
Let's Go: Greece & Turkey
Let's Go: Ireland
Let's Go: Israel & Egypt
Let's Go: Italy
Let's Go: London
Let's Go: Mexico
Let's Go: New York City
Let's Go: Paris
Let's Go: Rome
Let's Go: Southeast Asia
Let's Go: Spain & Portugal
Let's Go: Switzerland & Austria
Let's Go: USA
Let's Go: Washington, D.C.

Map Guides (coming March 1996)

Let's Go: Boston
Let's Go: London
Let's Go: New York City
Let's Go: Paris
Let's Go: San Francisco
Let's Go: Washington, D.C.

LET'S GO

The Budget Guide to

WASHINGTON, D.C.

1996

Stephen P. Janiak
Editor

St. Martin's Press New York

HELPING LET'S GO

If you want to share your discoveries, suggestions, or corrections, please drop us a line. We read every piece of correspondence, whether a postcard, a 10-page e-mail, or a coconut. All suggestions are passed along to our researcher-writers. Please note that mail received after May 1996 may be too late for the 1997 book, but will be retained for the following edition. Address mail to:

Let's Go: Washington, D.C.
One Story Street
Cambridge, MA 02138
USA

Visit Let's Go in the travel section of **http://www.americanexpress.com/student/**, or send e-mail to:

LetsGo@delphi.com
Subject: "Let's Go: Washington, D.C."

In addition to the invaluable travel advice our readers share with us, many are kind enough to offer their services as researchers or editors. Unfortunately, the charter of Let's Go, Inc. enables us to employ only currently enrolled Harvard-Radcliffe students.

Map revisions pp. 2-3, 118, 155, 159, 183, 242-3 by Let's Go, Inc.

Distributed outside the USA and Canada by Macmillan.

ISBN: 0-312-13558-0

First edition
10 9 8 7 6 5 4 3 2 1

Let's Go: Washington, D.C. is written by Let's Go Publications, One Story Street, Cambridge, MA 02138, USA.

Printed in the USA on recycled paper with biodegradable soy ink.

Contents

Maps

Color Maps

About Let's Go

THIRTY-SIX YEARS OF WISDOM

Back in 1960, a few students at Harvard University banded together to produce a 20-page pamphlet offering a collection of tips on budget travel in Europe. This modest, mimeographed packet was offered to passengers as an extra on their student charter flights to Europe. The following year, students traveling to Europe researched the first full-fledged edition of *Let's Go: Europe*, a pocket-sized book featuring irreverent write-ups of sights and a decidedly youthful slant. Throughout the 60s, our guides reflected the times; one section of the 1968 *Let's Go: Europe* discussed "Street Singing in Europe on No Dollars a Day," which we said "has very little to do with music." The 1969 guide to America led off with sound advice on San Francisco's Haight-Ashbury ("dig the scene"). During the 70s and 80s, we gradually added regional and city guides, and expanded coverage into the Middle East, Central America, and Asia.

We've seen a lot in 36 years. *Let's Go: Europe* is now the world's best-selling international guide, translated into seven languages. And our guides are still researched, written, and produced entirely by students who know first-hand how to see the world on the cheap. As the budget travel world expands, so does Let's Go. The first editions of *Let's Go: Central America* and *Let's Go: Southeast Asia* hit the shelves this year, and *Let's Go: India & Nepal* is right on their heels. Our useful new series of map guides combine concise city coverage with vivid fold-out maps. Our new guides bring our total number of titles, with their spirit of adventure and their honesty, accuracy, and editorial integrity, to 28.

HOW WE DO IT

Each guide is completely revised and updated every year by a well-traveled set of 200 students, who work on all aspects of each guide's development. Every winter, we recruit over 110 researchers and 50 editors to write our books anew. After several months of training, Researcher-Writers hit the road for seven weeks of exploration, from Anchorage to Ankara, Estonia to El Salvador, Iceland to Indonesia. Those hired possess a rare combination of budget travel sense, writing ability, stamina, and courage. Train strikes, stolen luggage, food poisoning, and irate tourist officials are all part of a day's work. Editors work from spring to fall, massaging copy written on Himalayan bus rides into witty yet informative prose. A student staff of typesetters, cartographers, publicists, and managers keeps our lively and sophisticated team together. In September, the collected efforts of the summer are delivered to our printer, who turns them into books in record time. And even as you read this, work on next year's editions is well underway.

WHY WE DO IT

At Let's Go, our goal is to give you a great vacation. We don't think of budget travel as the last recourse of the destitute; we believe that it's the only way to travel. Living cheaply and simply brings you closer to the real people and places you've been saving up to visit. Our book will ease your anxieties and answer your questions about the basics—to help you get off the beaten track and explore. Once you learn the ropes, we encourage you to put Let's Go away now and then to strike out on your own. As any seasoned traveler will tell you, the best discoveries are often those you make yourself. When you find something worth sharing, drop us a line. We're Let's Go Publications, One Story Street, Cambridge, MA 02138, USA (e-mail: LetsGo@delphi.com).

HAPPY TRAVELS!

Acknowledgments

Special (!) thanks to Abby Rezneck. A cheerful and sprightly intern, Chutrudee "Joy" Somberg obsessed over the notorius careers of Washington mayors and the book is all the better for it. Cherubic Karlene Rosera came to my aid when I had the Bawlmer blues. James Bronzan was the biggest help for finding me Carrie Mallonee, who covered accommodations in Baltimore with an enthusiasm disturbing to all of us who've been there. Marios Broustas found me Tara Arden-Smith, a reporter for the *Washington Post* who provided the inside scoop about the paper's nixing of Nixon. Tom Moore cleaned up after me like no one ever has or ever will. Will you marry me, Tom? The two Tims (Hiçyılmaz and Perlstein) were there when I needed to talk. Emily Tucker was godsend for GI help. SoRelle Braun, my late-night buddy, I know there's a full moon in your future. Dan O. Williams and David Fagundes, always in my corner (whether they liked it or not!), provided the humor that kept me laughing the entire summah. I will forever cherish memories of Pat Morita, nocturnal emissions, and putrid pungent swamps. Stuff It, guys. Statue of David, when I felt beaten and battered by the text, one look at you in your buff and naked glory was all I needed to get me going. Working here has been a blast. I'll miss the seething passion and latent desire that was the Domestic Room. Long live Let's Go, and don't forget to boldly split infinitives.

The book is dedicated to my Grandpa and Nana, George Rossetti (1906-1989) and Fannie Rossetti. Happily married for 58 years, they loved each other through good and bad. I hope someday to achieve a relationship half as wonderful. **—S.P.J.**

Researcher-Writers

Abigail Rezneck *Washington, D.C., Annapolis, MD*
A fount of creativity and enthusiam issued forth from Abby, a delight and a savior to her editor. Her mission: to seek the hip, the hot, and the gay. Commencing in Annapolis, Abby discovered the secret rituals of U.S. Navy plebes. After marvelling over a sweaty hoarde of men stripped to their boxers attempting to mount a greased pole, she fled to Old Downtown for a more tame testament to the Navy's prowess. Barely making it out of FBI Headquarters alive (or is it awake?) with her *Let's Go* notes intact, she put on her funkiest dress and headed over to the Farragut nightclubs. The stunning Ms. Rezneck accumulated admirers at places like 15 Minutes, Zei, and The Crow Bar as quickly as D.C. accumulates debt. Wandering north, Abby went Down Under to research gay nightlife in and around The Circle, learning the essential vocabulary ("cruisy," "stand-and-model," "RuPaul," "track lighting") along the way. The Shaw/ U District revitilization is evident by the revitalization of our listings, thanks to Abby finding bar after club after mall. After worshipping the institution of dance at her favorite club, Tracks (in Southeast), Abby headed home to her native Upper Northwest to report (with tongue planted firmly in cheek) on the sex lives of Hsing-Hsing and Ling-Ling. Seeing a portrait of Richard Nixon etched on a piece of rice at the Archives, Abby aspired to have a similar memorial. Sports fanatic and art gallery guru, our heroine's itinerary ended with a fantasy-come-true tour of the Metro Center accommodations. Abby's thorough research and thoughtful prose, her detailed marginalia and constant good cheer, buoyed our spirits and made us smile. She covered her regions with depth and panache, and performed above and beyond the call of duty.

Julie Zikherman *Washington, D.C., Baltimore, MD, Fairfax, VA*
Intially a skeptic, Julie found beauty and charm as well as urban sophistication as she fell under Washington's spell. A sports bar zealot, Julie did a lovely job covering the rowdy and randy beer guzzling joints of Georgetown. When the heat of D.C.'s sultry summer got to her, she retreated to the air-conditioned oasis that was her room at Georgetown University to do her research. Particularly partial to libraries and interns, Julie got the scoop on D.C. from intellectual bookworms and the gophers of the political elite. Intolerant of bombast, Julie skipped the Senate and House visits in favor of the less touristy and more local. She discovered ethnic hipness in Adams-Morgan, eating at some of the best restaurants in the city and hangin' in some of the coolest bars and clubs. She found the Smithsonian perfection of a week at the Mall, determining (like thousands of tourists before her) that the view from the top of the Washington Monument is not worth the wait. She reveled in the concrete-and-glass boxes of impersonal big-business Rosslyn, then paid her respects at the National Cemetery, becoming particularly fond of the ship's mast rising out of the ground. Julie resolved to sort out the urban complexity of Alexandria and the quaint, small-town order in Old Town, which she highly recommends. Terminally carless and a proud pedestrian, she basked in the glow of Great Falls Park, and then packed herself up and moved to Baltimore. Julie's attention to her work and level of excitement were evident in her captivating copybatches, which provided endless hours of fun for us back at the office.

Bridget Flynn *Shenandoah National Park, Richmond, Charlottesville, Williamsburg, James River Plantations, Jamestown, Yorktown, Virginia Beach, Delaware Seashore, Harper's Ferry.*

How To Use This Book

Let's Go gives you an inside understanding of the capital, whether you want to explore the inner workings of Congress, see world-class art, or party hard. We give you the scoop on the city's history and how to see it for yourself. We help you budget your time and money, telling you where to go and what to expect when you get there. We help you navigate the city by Metro, bus, taxi, car, bike, and on foot.

An Introduction fills you in on history, politics, people, and architecture, and features an expanded visual and print media section. **Essentials** tells you how to get to D.C. for cheap, how to get to and from the airports, and discusses everything from Internet resources to kosher dining. It provides a new quick glance Metro chart plus an expanded and detailed section on government internships. **Accommodations** are listed in order of value, based on price, location, safety, and comfort. **Food** includes reviews of over 200 restauraunts cross-referenced by type of food, price, and hours. **Sights** allows you to guide yourself around the city, telling you when to look up, when to pay an entrance fee, and when to just say no. **Museums & Galleries** is your guide to the Smithsonian and all of the other major collections in D.C.; this year it includes a new section on Washington's art gallery district. **Nightlife & Entertainment** provides the most up-to-date information you're likely to find about the hippest watering holes, live music venues, jazz and blues bars, and dance clubs. We also set the record straight about classical music, pool halls, and theater. An expanded and in-depth **Sports & Recreation** chapter details Washington-area spectator sports from football to college basketball and participatory sports from swimming to rollerblading to horseback riding. **Shopping** tells you where the mawls are, and where to buy music, a good book, or that bagpipe you've always wanted. **Bisexual, Gay and Lesbian D.C**. is comprehensive coverage of Washington's gay subculture. We tell you where to stay, eat, drink, dance, shop, and work out. Ironically, we also help you get out of the District: in **Daytripping** you'll find Annapolis, Baltimore, Richmond, expanded coverage of beaches and historic Virginia, and more. Check out the **Appendix** for more than 60 annual events that take place in or around D.C.

Most sections are organized according to preference (the others are alphabetical), and where coverage is geographical, areas are presented clockwise beginning with Capitol Hill, the symbolic center of Washington. Several sections feature **Let's Go Picks**—these are the places too good to miss. Sporadic grayboxes contain infobites about particularly quirky or spectacular items of note.

Use this book as your personal tour guide, your Yellow Pages, and your traveling companion. But no visit to D.C. would be complete without following your instincts and discovering the city for yourself.

A NOTE TO OUR READERS

The information for this book is gathered by Let's Go researchers during the summer months. Each listing is derived from the assigned researcher's opinion based upon his or her visit at a particular time. The opinions are expressed in a candid and forthright manner. Other travelers might disagree. Those traveling at a different time may have different experiences since prices, dates, hours, and conditions are always subject to change. You are urged to check beforehand to avoid inconvenience and surprises. Travel always involves a certain degree of risk, especially in low-cost areas. When traveling, especially on a budget, you should always take particular care to ensure your safety.

Washington, D.C.: An Introduction

Most travelers come to Washington to be impressed and slightly intimidated by its elaborate monuments, museums, and monolithic edifices. But while it would take days to see the entire Smithsonian complex, never venturing beyond the pomp and gloss of Federal Washington is a terrible mistake. There's a reason D.C.'s street plan is actually two networks of roads. Beneath the broad avenues radiating from the white-domed Capitol and the White House, a grid of local streets suggests the presence of a separate city, a thriving commercial and residential metropolis with its own sights, treasures, and protocol.

Two discrete cities, then, Federal Washington and local D.C. coexist in the diamond shaped District without much conflict or contradiction. Just blocks from the tourist-infested Mall in every direction, D.C. communities—yuppie, gay, Latino, black—dwell and prosper, separate from the goings-on of government. From the bars and businesses around Dupont Circle and the ethnic delights of Adams-Morgan to the college crowds in Georgetown and Foggy Bottom, Washington's second city has more to offer than downtown can display and more to see than any tour guide will show you.

But there is a dark side to the city's duality. D.C. runs a budget deficit which rivals that of the federal government and local officials have neither the funds nor the prestige to keep the city afloat. The recent loss of home rule in the District increased the irony of the juxtaposition of the two bureaucracies: one powerful, the other powerless. And the city's impoverished population braces itself against a barrage of crime, drugs, and broken families. The squalor endures, largely because the transient policy wonks—who return after work to the suburban plushness of Maryland and Virginia—have little interest in cleaning it all up.

Despite its difficult urban problems, Washington's strange experiment—an infant nation building a capital from scratch—has matured into one of America's most interesting, and consequently most visited, cities. Somewhere between political powerhouse, sleepy Southern town, decaying metropolis, and vigorous urban center lies D.C.'s impressive, intimidating, but entertaining and ultimately distinctive character.

HISTORY

FOUNDING AND EARLY YEARS

No nation had ever before the opportunity offered them of deliberately deciding on the spot where their Capital City should be fixed.

—Pierre L'Enfant, letter to George Washington (1789)

Like many a young adult fresh out of college, the Continental Congress after the Revolutionary War realized that independence meant little without a place to stay. While the weak Articles of Confederation governed the new United States, the Congress convened in Philadelphia in 1783 and tried to decide where to park itself for good. Kingston, NY, Nottingham, NJ, and Williamsburg, then the capital of Virginia, were all candidates for the honor. Before the Congress could make a decision, a mob of Continental Army veterans converged on Philadelphia demanding back pay, and the scared legislators hightailed it to Princeton, NJ, Annapolis, MD, Trenton, NJ, and finally to New York City, where George Washington's inauguration (socialists take note) took place on Wall Street. By this point, the Congress had two pressing questions: where to put the permanent capital and whether the U.S. should fund

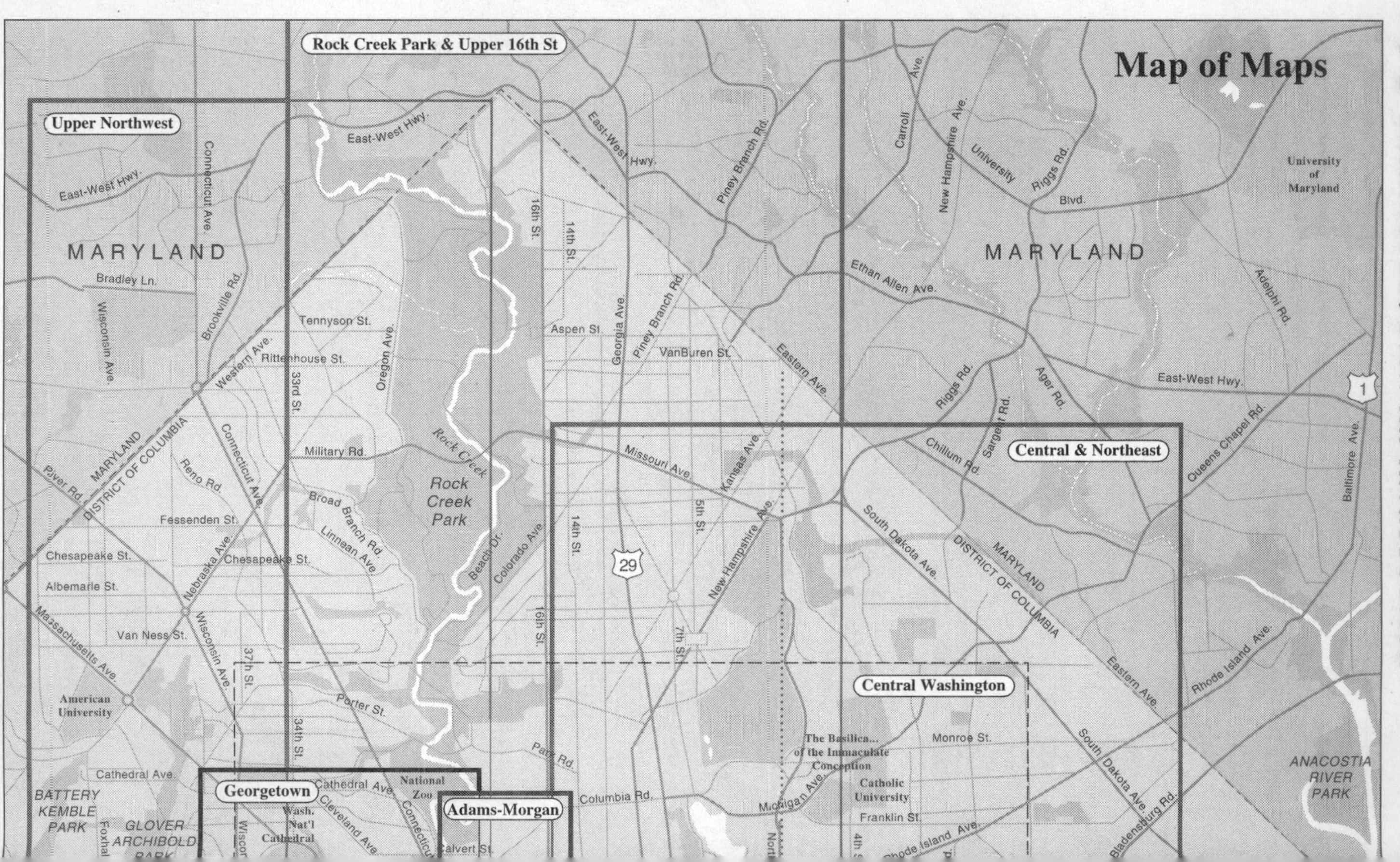
Map of Maps
Rock Creek Park & Upper 16th St
Upper Northwest
Central & Northeast
Central Washington
Georgetown
Adams-Morgan
MARYLAND
MARYLAND
DISTRICT OF COLUMBIA
University of Maryland
Rock Creek Park
Rock Creek
American University
National Zoo
Wash. Nat'l Cathedral
The Basilica... of the Immaculate Conception
Catholic University
BATTERY KEMBLE PARK
GLOVER ARCHIBOLD PARK
ANACOSTIA RIVER PARK
East-West Hwy.
Connecticut Ave.
Bradley Ln.
Wisconsin Ave.
Brookville Rd.
Western Ave.
River Rd.
Reno Rd.
Fessenden St.
Chesapeake St.
Albemarle St.
Nebraska Ave.
Massachusetts Ave.
Van Ness St.
Cathedral Ave.
Foxhall
Tennyson St.
Rittenhouse St.
33rd St.
Oregon Ave.
Military Rd.
Broad Branch Rd.
Linnean Ave.
37th St.
34th St.
Porter St.
Cleveland Ave.
Calvert St.
Beach Dr.
Colorado Ave.
16th St.
14th St.
Aspen St.
Georgia Ave.
Piney Branch Rd.
VanBuren St.
Eastern Ave.
Missouri Ave.
Kansas Ave.
5th St.
7th St.
New Hampshire Ave.
29
Park Rd.
Columbia Rd.
Michigan Ave.
Monroe St.
Franklin St.
Rhode Island Ave.
Carroll Ave.
University Blvd.
Riggs Rd.
Ethan Allen Ave.
Sargent Rd.
Ager Rd.
Chillum Rd.
Adelphi Rd.
Queens Chapel Rd.
Baltimore Ave.
1
South Dakota Ave.
Bladensburg Rd.

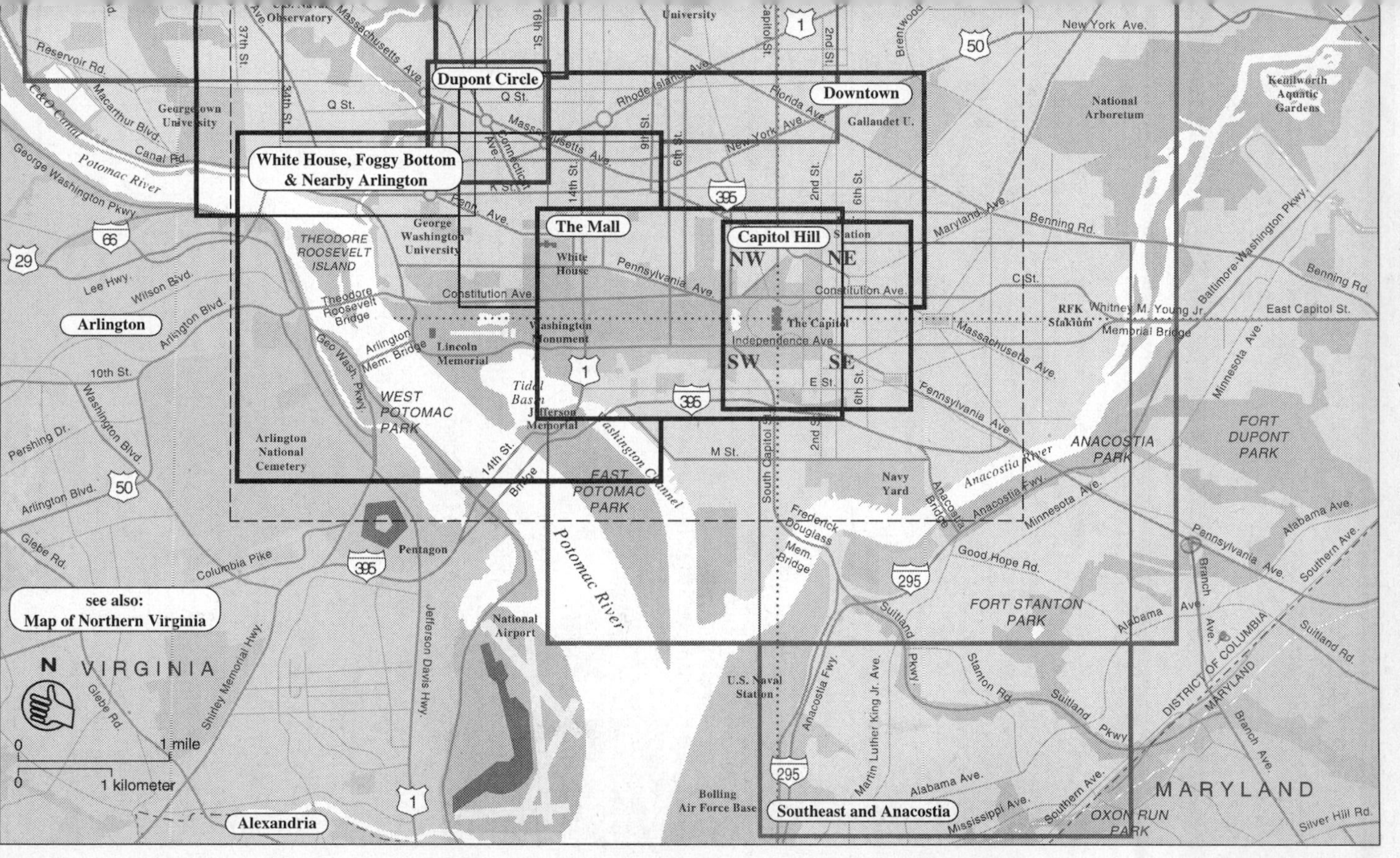

Dupont Circle
Downtown
White House, Foggy Bottom & Nearby Arlington
The Mall
Capitol Hill
NW
NE
SW
SE
Southeast and Anacostia
Arlington
Alexandria
see also: Map of Northern Virginia
Kenilworth Aquatic Gardens
National Arboretum
Gallaudet U.
Georgetown University
George Washington University
THEODORE ROOSEVELT ISLAND
Theodore Roosevelt Bridge
Arlington Mem. Bridge
White House
Washington Monument
Lincoln Memorial
The Capitol
Tidal Basin
Jefferson Memorial
WEST POTOMAC PARK
EAST POTOMAC PARK
Arlington National Cemetery
Pentagon
National Airport
Potomac River
Washington Channel
RFK Stadium
Whitney M. Young Jr. Memorial Bridge
ANACOSTIA PARK
Anacostia River
FORT DUPONT PARK
FORT STANTON PARK
Navy Yard
Anacostia Bridge
Frederick Douglass Mem. Bridge
U.S. Naval Station
Bolling Air Force Base
OXON RUN PARK
VIRGINIA
MARYLAND
DISTRICT OF COLUMBIA
N
New York Ave.
Rhode Island Ave.
Florida Ave.
Massachusetts Ave.
Connecticut Ave.
Pennsylvania Ave.
Constitution Ave.
Independence Ave.
Maryland Ave.
Benning Rd.
Baltimore-Washington Pkwy.
East Capitol St.
C St.
E St.
M St.
K St.
Q St.
16th St.
14th St.
9th St.
6th St.
2nd St.
34th St.
37th St.
South Capitol St.
Minnesota Ave.
Alabama Ave.
Southern Ave.
Suitland Rd.
Suitland Pkwy.
Branch Ave.
Good Hope Rd.
Anacostia Fwy.
Martin Luther King Jr. Ave.
Stanton Rd.
Mississippi Ave.
Silver Hill Rd.
Reservoir Rd.
Macarthur Blvd.
Canal Rd.
C&O Canal
George Washington Pkwy.
Geo Wash. Pkwy.
Lee Hwy.
Wilson Blvd.
Arlington Blvd.
10th St.
Washington Blvd.
Pershing Dr.
Glebe Rd.
Columbia Pike
Jefferson Davis Hwy.
Shirley Memorial Hwy.
14th St. Bridge
1 mile
1 kilometer
50
1
395
295
66
29

the states' leftover war debt. Politicians from the mercantile northern states, led by the wily Alexander Hamilton, wanted the capital for themselves, but also yearned for debt relief. The prosperous, agrarian South didn't want to subsidize the North, but also sought the capital. As a compromise, the Congress assumed the states' obligations but decided on a southern capital, instructing George Washington to pick a spot "no more than ten miles square" along the Potomac River. George chose the Potomac's intersection with the Anacostia River, since the point was closest to Mount Vernon, his home, but also ideal (in theory) for a port. Maryland and Virginia together agreed to donate a diamond-shaped parcel of 100 sq. mi. ("ten miles square"), French engineer Pierre L'Enfant was hired to design Washington City, and the real fun began.

L'Enfant was enchanted by stately Paris and wanted to make Washington the French capital's more rational cousin. The "L'Enfant Plan" laid out central Washington in a grid pattern with an overlay of diagonal avenues, named for states and radiating (mostly) from the Capitol and White House to an effusion of monumental squares. The plan covered only what was then called "Washington City," not Georgetown, Alexandria, or the miles of farmland around their edges. L'Enfant planned a central canal and port facilities, but his real love seemed to be the public spaces and wide avenues of his design. The plan had already offended the area's landed gentry by seizing more land for roads than they expected, and L'Enfant's exacting "artistic temperament" hardly endeared him to political superiors. When L'Enfant tore down an aristocrat's porch (it stood in the way of New Jersey Ave. SE), not even his friend George W. could save him from the wrath of the rich. L'Enfant was fired; his deputies Benjamin Banneker and Andrew Ellicott replaced him. (Banneker, an accomplished astronomer, may have been America's first African-American intellectual. He supervised the city's construction for three months before poor health forced him to quit.) The ousted Pierre refused to take Congress's offered sum, then spent the first part of the 19th century wandering around Washington trying to get paid.

The "city of magnificent distances" (D.C.'s 19th-century nickname) was far from magnificent and far from a city. In 1800 the capital village held scattered wooden buildings, dirt roads, and only 3244 residents, with 123 free African-Americans and over 500 slaves. (The nickname really meant there was very little between the public buildings.) Early "improvements" didn't help matters: Tiber Creek was diverted and dammed to form the Washington Canal, whose stagnant water proved a boon to mosquitoes and bred the enduring, but false, legend that Washington was "built on a swamp." The paint was barely dry on the original Capitol before the War of 1812 brought British troops here in August 1814 to burn the city down (in a civilized way, of course). The government buildings bit the dust, and Dolly Madison (the fourth President's wife) made a name for herself by carrying from the flaming White House one of Gilbert Stuart's many portraits of George Washington. Washingtonians have fled in August ever since.

Though rain put out the blaze the Brits lit, Congress was almost ready to throw in the towel; a postwar vote on a proposal to move the capital lost by only eight votes. The capital stayed, but so did the problems. As a port city between two plantation states, the District made a logical first stop for slave traders, whose shackled cargo awaited sale in crowded pens on the Mall and near the White House. Foreign diplomats were properly disgusted, deeming D.C. definitely "Southern." Between the slave trade and the swamp air, elected officials understandably decided D.C. was no place for families: America's elected elite lived in all-male boarding houses, chewed tobacco, and fought frequent duels in a famous valley near Bladensburg, MD. National politics became an affair of personalities: after one debate on the Senate floor, a South Carolina representative clobbered aged anti-slavery Massachusetts senator Charles Sumner with a cane. Another senator's marriage to Peggy Eaton, the beautiful daughter of a tavern-keeper, began a chain of social snubs and reactions that caused the resignation of Andrew Jackson's Vice President John Calhoun, who would later become a fire-breathing secessionist.

Though subject to severe racial prejudice, a town-within-the-town of free African-Americans was growing faster than the rest of the city. By 1850 Washington held 2000 slaves, 8000 free blacks, and 30,000 whites. White fear of uprisings had already given rise to discriminatory laws and social unrest (like the Snow Riots of 1835), but the thriving community close to the "upper South" plantations continued to draw African-American migrants. Black residents established 15 schools in Georgetown and Washington City before the Civil War.

During the 1830s and 40s British travelers felt compelled to publish their Washington journals, which make delightful reading—a long record of unpaved streets, courteous officials, half-erected buildings, broad vistas, and horrifying slave traffic. Charles Dickens, who dropped by in 1842, called D.C. "the City of Magnificent Intentions":

> *Spacious avenues, that begin in nothing, and lead nowhere; streets, mile-long, that only want houses, roads and inhabitants; public buildings that need but a public...One might fancy the season over, and most of the houses gone out of town forever with their masters.*

CIVIL WAR TO WORLD WAR I

"Such as it is, it is likely to remain," began Dickens's next paragraph. He hadn't counted on the War Between the States, whose outbreak in 1861 turned all military eyes on Washington and turned the capital from the Union's appendix to its jugular vein. The city's social elite brought picnic baskets to the First Battle of Bull Run, but an unexpected Confederate victory forced the Union military to harden up the capital. Soon forts encircled the city, and soldiers slept in government offices and overran the Mall. (Military Rd. NW still links some of these forts.) While Abraham Lincoln sent troops to keep Maryland loyal, D.C. society turned out to help the Union, and the President himself attended a skirmish in his trademark stovepipe hat. (When he stood for a better view of the battle, a Union officer shouted "Get down, you fool!") Though every other building seemed full of troops, Lincoln directed that work continue on the Capitol dome: "It is a sign," he reasoned, "that the Union shall go on." An 1862 *Harper's* magazine cover showed "Convalescent Troops Passing Through Washington," an everyday sight in the overcrowded wartime capital.

The Civil War and Reconstruction sent tens of thousands of former slaves north for a better life; for a time, they found a worse death instead in spontaneous shanty towns like Murder Bay, a few blocks from the White House. After Lincoln's assassination in 1865, the postwar Republican ascent spelled better times for black people. The five years after 1868 were called the "Golden Age of Black Washington," with new and enforced civil-rights laws, black senators and congressmen, a black public-school system, an African-American at the helm of Georgetown University, and the founding of Dunbar High School and Howard University, for 50 years a two-step path into D.C.'s black elite. President Grant appointed former slave and abolitionist Frederick Douglass the District's recorder of deeds. With Sella Martin, Douglass edited the aptly named *New Era;* his 1877 "Lecture on the Nation's Capital" angered Congressmen and still makes good reading.

In May 1870, Congress gave Washington the right to choose a mayor. Holdover official Sayles J. Bowen kicked off a program of public works with a boneheaded move: paving Pennsylvania Ave. with wooden blocks that sank in the mud. Deputy Mayor Alexander "Boss" Shepherd took *de facto* charge in 1871; protected by his friendship with President Grant, Boss Shepherd resurfaced the streets, planted trees, and employed thousands of laborers in his super-efficient city improvement plan, just as L'Enfant would have wished. He tore down decrepit buildings, built sewers, parks, and new roads, and installed streetlights. Of course, all this cost money; the controversial, fast-acting Shepherd sent the city into record-breaking debt, and the federal bailout that followed reattached control of the city to Congress and robbed D.C. of self-government for over 100 years.

As D.C. temporarily prospered, federal Washington floundered. The political patronage system plus the corruption of the Grant years led a torrent of office-seekers to Washington, bombarding executives and grinding down congressmen with persistent requests for favors and jobs. Charles J. Guiteau, universally described as a "disgruntled office seeker," shot President James A. Garfield in 1881. Not long afterward, in 1885, new President Grover Cleveland (by most accounts the first honest Chief since Lincoln) stayed up all night reading job applications patronage-seekers had hand-delivered; it was time for a change, and Cleveland made one by enforcing the 1882 Civil Service Act, setting in place the not-entirely-partisan federal bureaucracy we know and love today. Cleveland struggled through his early-1890s second term, as national depression brought strikes to Chicago and Coxey's Army of 300 unemployed workers to Washington in search of relief. It was D.C.'s first big protest march, and Cleveland dithered while federal police crushed the encampments.

Washington had more or less turned modern, with apartment houses, telephones, and electric streetcars. But the capital was hardly a place of beauty. Vigorous President Theodore Roosevelt, who charged in in 1901, appointed the McMillan Commission to give the adolescent city a shave and a haircut. The commission—architects Daniel Burnham and Charles McKim, sculptor Augustus Saint-Gaudens, and landscape bigshot Frederick Law Olmsted—was the principal planner of D.C.'s current public spaces and monuments, and it shares responsibility for the "feel" of the city with L'Enfant. The commission decided to make the muddy Mall a permanent lawn, build a memorial to Lincoln at one end, designate land elsewhere for parks, erect Memorial Bridge, and build Union Station (among other things).

Meanwhile D.C.'s African-Americans were losing economic power, even as their numbers (and artistic achievements) increased. As employment segregation tightened, most became obliged to work in service industries (driving taxis, catering); the gains of Reconstruction were long gone. Roosevelt himself listened to the black community, but Georgia-born Woodrow Wilson supported a segregation so thorough that black leader "Lady Mollie" Mary Church Terrell couldn't get young poet Langston Hughes considered for a job at the Library of Congress—not even as a page. Newspapers fanned white "Negrophobia" into the race riots of 1919. Cafeterias and even public parks became segregated facilities; at the 1922 dedication of the Lincoln Memorial, world-famous educator Booker T. Washington was made to sit in a "colored" section. Though activists tried to increase hiring, "more federal jobs meant more messengers and janitors," in the words of historian David Lewis. Black Washington in these years was almost an autonomous city, with its own movie houses, theaters, shops, social clubs, political leaders, and demographic patterns. The city-within-a-city was hardly unified, though; middle-class black people in LeDroit Park had little to do with the impoverished "alley dwellings" in SW and SE.

FDR and WWII

After the stock market crash of 1929, President Hoover responded to the Great Depression with platitudes instead of money. The "Bonus Army" of unemployed veterans marched to the Mall to demand new benefits but got dispersed by the National Guard instead. The election of Franklin Delano Roosevelt in 1932 gave the country a New Deal: to D.C., it brought a herd of idealistic liberals anxious to make the "Alphabet Soup" of new agencies and relief programs work. NRA, WPA, AAA, YCC, FHA, and SEC were just a few of the novel acronyms FDR's "try-anything" philosophy spawned; his liberal ideas enraged Washington's old-money "cave dwellers," who snubbed the government from 16th St. and Dupont Circle while newcomers with Ph.D.s moved into Georgetown. The influx began to transform the city from a "sleepy Southern town" into an expanding young metropolis eternally envious of New York's sophistication.

As professionals continued to move into Washington, Nazi Germany began invading its neighbors, and D.C. had to prepare for war. In 1940 and '41, the President tried discreetly to persuade a country still scarred by World War I to help Great Britain save Europe. With the national government swollen to its post-Depression size and international conflict taking center stage, Washington became the hub of patriotism and the focus of protest. Isolationist pickets surrounded the White House,

Nazi puppet ambassadors showed up along Massachusetts Ave., and Congress, as late as 1941, decided to renew the military draft by only one vote. After Japan attacked Pearl Harbor on December 7, 1941, and the U.S. entered the war, Washington's bureaucracy ballooned. Soldiers on leave filled Washington's ballrooms, FDR's handpicked coordinators (like Leon Henderson and Donald Nelson) tried to straighten out the wartime economy, the War Department seized hotels for office space, and civilians of both sexes poured into D.C. as war-related clerical jobs opened up daily. A 1943 guidebook called the District "the Cinderella City."

Black Washington was changing too, but more slowly, and persistent prejudice sparked protest in many forms. The city's segregation came to national attention when the Daughters of the American Revolution barred African-American opera star Marian Anderson from singing at Constitution Hall. Anderson sang instead, on Easter Sunday, 1939, on the steps of the Lincoln Memorial to an audience of 75,000. It had, unfortunately, only a symbolic effect on segregation in Washington. Black labor leader A. Phillip Randolph threatened to organize a march on Washington unless Roosevelt demanded fair federal hiring; he got what he asked for, but the decree did little good. The "alley dwelling" problem was worse than ever; a federal agency "cleared" the slums by kicking out the poor and creating (as a brochure actually announced) "Low-Income Housing for White Families." The tradition of the sit-in began in the 40s when Howard University students entered Thompson's Restaurant and refused to leave until they were served. (Mary Church Terrell led a more successful sit-in there years later.)

FDR's successor, Harry S. Truman, dropped a bomb on Washington's racism when his appointed commission released its 1947 report. The Supreme Court's 1953 "Lost Laws" ruling (that civil rights laws from 1872 could still be enforced) essentially desegregated most of the city. Paradoxically, the integration of movie theaters, stores, and eating establishments destroyed many black-owned businesses, and the African-American commercial districts north of Massachusetts Ave. began to deteriorate. In a similar vein, Dunbar High School—so good that black families moved here from the Deep South just to send their children—became nothing special after 1954's *Brown v. Board of Education* Supreme Court decision integrated America's schools.

Sen. Joseph McCarthy's witch hunts for Communists terrorized the bureaucracy in the early 1950s, but the government and its city kept getting bigger. (McCarthy finally disgraced himself in the famous, televised Army-McCarthy hearings of 1954.) A crew of Cold Warriors conducted affairs of state throughout the 50s and 60s; John F. Kennedy's narrow victory in 1960 enchanted the press and brought a new cultural savvy to the still-provincial capital. His Texan successor, Lyndon Johnson, once the Senate's shrewd Majority Leader, stampeded the Congress into civil rights action, then steered the nation deep into the Vietnam War. The District had meanwhile grown beyond its borders—the area's population doubled from 1950 to 1970, but much of the increase came in suburbs, where the 50s bourgeoisie loved to live.

THE LAST FEW DECADES

During the turbulent, politicized 1960s, Washington was the nation's March Central, hosting one demonstration after the next. Martin Luther King, Jr. led two of the most important. The 1963 March on Washington, site of his "I Have a Dream" speech, gathered 250,000 people of all races on the Mall. The '63 marchers, black and white, middle-class and poor, demanded an end to legal segregation, while those who came to D.C. in the 1968 Poor Peoples' Campaign demanded economic empowerment. When news of King's assassination (April 4, 1968) reached Washington, days of riots destroyed parts of D.C.; as in the Los Angeles Watts riots, desperate African-Americans burned down their own communities, especially the commercial corridors along 14th St., 7th St., H St., and U St. NW.

Goings-on around Washington held the nation rapt during the Watergate years of 1973-4, when the break-ins he authorized and the White House audiotapes he made brought disgrace and resignation to President Richard Nixon. The U.S. bicentennial in 1976 drew tourists in record numbers to the capital. The Carter administration (1977-81) brought in Democratic outsiders from Georgia, while the Reagan administration (1981-89) imported conservative outsiders and smooth operators, many from his native California. The two Reagan inaugurals were the most expensive ever. Not surprisingly, the federal deficit tripled in the first three years of the Reagan era. During these years, conservative appointees clashed with more moderate federal workers, pro-business attitudes paralyzed regulators, and the Pentagon's $1000 toilet seats became the stuff of legend. While the "Teflon President's" popularity cowed Congress for several years, the Iran-Contra scandals of 1986-88 demonstrated either astounding disregard for the law or incredible ignorance at the top. President Bush's administration bore witness to the passing of communism in Eastern Europe and the Soviet Union, and fought a high-profile war in the Middle East. Amid the pomp and circumstance of the victory parade, scandals—ranging from the very small (the House banking scandal) to the very large (the B.C.C.I. scandal)—sent voter confidence plummeting.

With Fleetwood Mac's "Don't Stop Thinkin' About Tomorrow" playing in the background, Democrat Bill Clinton headed to the White House in early 1993 with a mandate to cut the U.S. deficit and improve the nation's health care system. Since then, the President has fought an uphill battle; the administration's plan for health-care reform was scuttled by a Congress too timid to ask employers to pay for universal health care coverage. Minor foreign policy victories buoyed his sinking reputation; he supervised (but did not really catalyze) the Israeli-Arab peace agreements and spontaneously normalized U.S. relations with Vietnam. After the 1994 Congressional election turned both houses overwhelmingly Republican, Clinton has vacillated between cooperation with the demanding Congress and insistence on a stricter breed of liberalism. Attempts at compromise on a balanced budget plan are evidence of the former; the Chief's hard line in favor of affirmative action (following the '95 Court ruling) move him more staunchly into the liberal camp. Clinton suffered another defeat when the House failed to pass his comprehensive crime bill, which would have banned certain types of assault weapons and helped cities hire additional police officers, among other provisions.

Downtown developers kept the economy moving from the late 70s to the late 80s, though often at the expense of residential areas. While the city's population dropped to 617,000 in 1988, the suburbs ballooned, producing pseudo-urban areas like Rockville, Maryland—the state's second largest city. The burgeoning black middle class lived in the city on 16th St. NW and in parts of NE or fled to the suburbs, where anti-discrimination laws unlocked homeowning opportunities and lower taxes increased the appeal. D.C.'s population in 1988 was 70% black, today it's 75%. The white population in the District itself tends to live west of Rock Creek Park; some white residents are moneyed, many are not. While the 70s produced flight to suburban outposts, the 80s lured many back to the townhouses of formerly rundown or blue-collar neighborhoods in the controversial process of gentrification. And hopeful immigrants keep arriving in city and suburbs, especially in Mount Pleasant, Adams-Morgan, Arlington, and Montgomery County. All these groups together fuel the metropolitan area with plenty of cultural and commercial vitality. But a large (and more publicized) segment of Washington sees fewer reasons for optimism: the mid-80s advent of crack, a cheap, condensed, smokeable form of cocaine, incapacitated thousands of addicts ("pipeheads"). Teens without functional families or schools saw crack as their only career opportunity; dealers' turf wars, often fought with machine guns, made the body count higher than ever. As the long rise in crack use seems to be halting, despair and easy access to guns keep some areas dangerous and bleak.

A century of rule-by-Congressional-committee came largely to an end in 1973, when Congress passed the Home Rule Act, giving D.C. an elected mayor, a city council, and a non-voting delegate in Congress. The first mayor, Walter Washington, represented the native, middle-class black establishment; the second one, Marion Barry, grew up in rural North Carolina. Elected in 1978 by a multi-racial coalition,

Barry was known as a 60s civil-rights leader. Though he promised reforms, his first term was noted mostly for attracting business to the city. In the 80s, though, the shine wore off. Barry hadn't reformed the city, and some members of his administration were accused of misusing city funds and other forms of corruption. The mayor himself was caught smoking crack (some say entrapped) by undercover federal agents in January 1990. Political outsider Sharon Pratt Kelly, who campaigned with a broom in her hand, was elected mayor in November 1990. She was subsequently voted out of office in 1994, replaced by Marion Barry himself. For more on Barry and Kelly, see below.

The Illustrious Mayors of D.C.—Marion Barry and Sharon Pratt Kelly

In 1978, Marion S. Barry was voted into office for the first time. At the end of his first term, Barry's actions as mayor were denounced by critic after critic. Barry was reelected anyway. In the middle of his second term, Barry was accused of buying drugs from Karen Johnson, a convicted drug dealer and former city employee. The charge was denied by Barry, although he admitted to having had an earlier "personal relationship" with Johnson.

By 1985 Barry had justified the early Home Rule advocates who insisted D.C. was able to manage its affairs without the interference of Congress and the White House. He had straightened out the city's most serious financial problems. Later the Mayor would push new office construction to record levels, propelling property taxes to over $700 million annually.

In 1986, additional corruption charges surfaced. It was alleged that Mayor Barry had billed the city for personal trips and political travels. Again, Barry was reelected. In 1987, Karen Johnson told a government informant that she had sold cocaine to the mayor on numerous occasions. Also in 1987, Barry's chief financial aide revealed that Barry's office was unable to locate records concerning two years of spending from the Mayor's discretionary accounts.

On Jan. 18, 1990, Barry was arrested on a narcotics charge, having been caught on film using crack at a downtown hotel. Seeking leniency in sentencing by the federal court judge, Barry admitted on television to being a drug addict. After a lengthy trial process, Barry was convicted of cocaine possession and sentenced to six months in prison.

With the fall of Barry, Sharon Pratt Kelly rose to power in Sept. 1990. She won the Democratic primary with 35% of the vote, then the general election with 86% of the vote.

In Aug. 1992, Kelly's campaign committee returned $4000 it had received illegally from D.C.'s Housing Finance Agency. A year later, Kelly's reelection committee gave back $2000 it had accepted from the Embassy of Saudi Arabia, in violation of federal laws prohibiting political contributions by foreign nationals.

Complaints about the Kelly administration were mounting. Kelly spent $65 per hour for professional make-up services, and she moved into a fancy new eleventh-floor office with bulletproof glass, gas fireplace, granite bathroom countertops, and a raised-beam ceiling. While Kelly's administration was having its own problems, stunned federal officials looked on as Barry was elected to the City Council, only months after he finished serving his prison sentence.

In 1994, Barry made one of the most incredible comebacks in history, winning a fourth term in office. There he will remain until 1998.

WHAT'S HAPPENIN' NOW

The big news in Washington last year was the **1994 Election.** In response to what many a Democrat as well as many a Republican have considered a mediocre President, Republicans swept elections across the country, sending masses of fresh faces to D.C. and erasing the huge majority that Democrats had enjoyed in both the House and Senate for over 50 years. Democratic policies and bureaucracy have changed almost overnight. The once little-known **Newt Gingrich** became one of America's most popular magazine cover stories. The Republicans were propelled into power by their **"Contract with America,"** a document outlining the things in government that the Republicans would change if elected. The new Congress has held firm to its promises—it has slashed social programs to trim the deficit. Sensing possible political doom for the Democratic party, five Democrats had converted to Republicanism by August 1995. The Presidential Election in November 1996 promises to be a heated battle—one that will either limit the losses of the Democrats, or solidify the Republicans' stranglehold on America.

On the local level, former crack-smoking **Marion Barry,** claiming a need for redemption, was reelected Mayor of D.C. He inherited a deficit of around $700 million, but he won't have to worry about it too much: after a 12-year failed trial period of autonomy, the **Washington Home Rule Charter** was revoked. Today, Barry and his bureaucracy have to answer to a Congressionally-appointed (and GOP-allied) financial control board. The control board tells the City Council how much money needs to be cut, and the Council gets to figure out where to cut. This arrangement will be in place until the city is back in the black.

■ U.S. GOVERNMENT AND POLITICS

The structure of the U.S. government is mostly dictated by the **Constitution,** a document penned by smart 18th-century aristocrats (mostly by James Madison) and designed to prevent the twin horrors of executive tyranny and mob rule. The Constitution divides power between the U.S. government and the 50 states; there's a list of powers delegated to Congress and to the President, an "elastic clause" letting Congress do other things, and an Amendment (the 10th) giving all the leftover powers to the states. The federal government has three branches: **legislative, executive,** and **judicial,** each of which limits the power of the others (the "checks and balances" system). **Congress** drafts and votes on **bills;** the **President** (the Chief Executive) can sign them (making them **laws**) or veto them. A vetoed bill returns to Congress, which has to vote for it by a two-thirds majority the second time around to override the Prez and make the bill law. (If Congress is soon to adjourn, the President can ignore a bill and make it go away—a "pocket veto.") The **federal court system,** topped by the **Supreme Court,** interprets federal laws; the Supremes interpret the Constitution and throw out laws that violate it (even state laws).

Congress is a bicameral legislature and consists of the 435-member **House of Representatives** and the 100-member **Senate.** House Members are popularly elected and serve two-year terms, representing numbered **districts** of about 575,000 people within a state (which are redrawn every 10 years after the Census). 1992 saw new seats created in growing states like California, and incumbents running against other incumbents in declining states like Michigan and Pennsylvania. Senators serve six-year terms; each state, even tiny Delaware, gets two. Until the Seventeenth Amendment was added to the Constitution in 1913, most senators were chosen by state legislatures; now state voters elect them. As the original "representative" chamber, only the House may initiate bills that change taxes. Originally the elite chamber, the Senate gives "advice and consent" to Presidential appointments like federal judges, Supreme Court justices, Cabinet secretaries, and ambassadors. In practice this means the Senate must **confirm** them before they can officially assume their jobs; lower-level nominees are often taken "hostage" by senators who block their confirmations pending some favor from the executive branch.

Though the whole House or Senate can meet to debate and vote on a bill, almost all their work gets done in **standing committees;** the House has 22, the Senate 16. These committees consider facts and write and edit bills; each one has separate staffers whose job is to be more informed than the members on whatever issues the committee deals with. **Select** or **special** committees are convened to hold investigations (as for the Iran-Contra scandal), administer Congressional affairs (like the House gym), and make members look good (e.g., the Select Committee on Aging).

Especially powerful standing committees are the **House Ways and Means Committee** and the **Senate Rules Committee,** which decide when and how a bill will be debated when it gets "reported" from the committee to the House or Senate floor. Most Members have urgent desires to sit on committees related to their state or district (forestry for Oregon, transportation for Michigan). Most also yearn for powerful committees, especially House Appropriations or Senate Finance, which get to mark up and vote on all budgets. Low-status committees, especially Ethics, are near-powerless.

The **party leadership,** the top Democrats and Republicans in each chamber, decides who gets to sit on what committee; all the committees are led by chairpersons from the majority party and ranking minority members from the other side. Both houses have **majority** and **minority leaders** and **whips** (deputy leaders). While the **Speaker of the House,** chosen from the majority party, presides *de jure* and *de facto* over that chamber, the official head of the Senate is the Vice President, who has little real power and only votes to break ties. Speaker of the House (now Newt Gingrich, R-Georgia) and Senate Majority Leader (currently the caustic Bob Dole, R-Kansas) are therefore roughly equivalent jobs. Both men argue that their influence is equivalent to that of the Prez himself. (The House Majority Leader is Richard Armey, R-Texas; the Minority Leader is Richard Gephardt, D-Missouri. The Senate Minority Leader is Thomas Daschle, D-South Dakota.) These guys also coordinate and orchestrate each party's legislative agenda. The whole setup depends on the **two-party system,** and America's split into Democrats and Republicans prevents splinter groups and minor parties from holding the influence they sometimes wield in parliamentary systems like Italy's or Israel's.

President Bill Clinton, besides signing off on laws, is Commander-in-Chief of the armed forces and head of the Executive Branch. (That's why the oath of office made him promise to "take care that the laws will be faithfully executed.") Al Gore, his **Vice President,** presides over the Senate (but only votes in case of a tie) and serves as the President's emissary (unless the President dies or gets too sick to do his job, in which case the Veep takes the office of the President). Presidents are elected for four-year terms; the 22nd Amendment, a reaction to Franklin Roosevelt's death during his fourth term, has banned presidents since from serving more than two. The President is the summit of the complex pyramid of federal bureaucracy, where those near the top are political appointees, those lower down career civil servants. Fourteen **departments** together do most of the government's work; their Secretaries together make up the **Cabinet.** The State Department, now run by Warren Christopher (who is the Secretary of State), conducts foreign policy; the Treasury Department, run by former Goldman-Sachs exec. Robert Rubin, formulates economic policy and collects taxes and fees (through the IRS). The Defense Department, headed by William Perry, presides over military matters. The Attorney General (currently the 6'3" Janet Reno) steers the Justice Department, which acts as the government's law firm, representing the executive branch in civil and criminal cases. Independent **regulatory agencies,** like the Environmental Protection Agency and the Food and Drug Administration, enforce their designated laws outside the purview of government departments. The White House also has its own **executive staff** (which Clinton shrank by 25%), which writes the President's speeches, draws up his schedules, and digs up information for him; the supposedly advisory National Security Council was a favorite tool for illegal covert action in the mid-80s.

In what was largely interpreted by the national press as an attempt to restore (or at least create the image of) order and direction to a floundering administration, Bill Clinton chose July of 1994 to announce the most dramatic reshuffling of his White House staff to date. His long-time friend and kindergarten classmate Thomas "Mack" McLarty was removed as Chief of Staff and replaced by Clinton's former budget director Leon Panetta. Erstwhile Republican spin-meister David Gergen, who had been earlier hired by Clinton as a special presidential advisor in the area of "communications," moved from the White House to new office space in the State Department to assume a more prominent role in the formulation and mass-marketing of the administration's foreign policy initiatives. Political consultant Dick Morris, regarded suspiciously by many Democrats for his work with their Republican rivals, has now filled Gergen's shoes as Clinton's unofficial advisor.

The real wheels of the government are oiled by more than just elected officials. Thousands of **staffers** grind away each day researching for Congressfolk, communicating with constituents, and running campaigns. And millions of civil-service bureaucrats spread funds and forms around the nation.

The **Supreme Court's** nine justices are appointed for life by the President, but must be confirmed by the Senate. The current Chief Justice is the conservative William Rehnquist. The justices hear and vote on cases involving Constitutional issues; because they interpret the law rather than decide facts, no jury is involved in their deliberations. The court is the ultimate guarantor of civil liberties and civil rights, the protections from government intrusion contained in or implied chiefly by the Bill of Rights (the first ten Constitutional amendments) and the Fourteenth Amendment. The First Amendment promises freedom of speech, press, assembly, and religion; the Fourth stops warrantless searches and seizures; the Fifth, Sixth, Seventh, and Eighth regulate trials and punishments; and the Fourteenth guarantees no deprivation of life, liberty, or property without due process of law—just one of its several wondrous provisions. The Supreme Court accepts cases for review from federal appellate courts or state supreme courts; it only takes about 5% of the ones it's asked to hear, though. Presidents understandably try to appoint justices who share their philosophies, but they've often been unpleasantly surprised; Eisenhower said the worst mistake he made as President was appointing the groundbreakingly liberal Chief Justice Earl Warren. (Even the Reaganauts have had smaller surprises, like the reluctance of David Souter and Anthony Kennedy to go all-out for the conservative agenda.)

Throughout the Bush administration, the Court became increasingly conservative as Reagan and Bush nominees replaced justices from the 60s and 70s who died or retired in ill health; the court slowly rolled back the broad civil liberties created and guaranteed in recent decades, issued muddy rulings on civil rights and racial issues, took the government's side against criminal defendants, curtailed the right to privacy, made the death penalty easier to impose, and edged toward overturning the watershed 1973 *Roe v. Wade* abortion-rights decision. Most recently, centrists Ruth Bader Ginsburg and Stephen G. Breyer were appointed to the nation's top judicial body by striving-to-be-centrist President Clinton. Bader Ginsburg, previously a noted feminist appellate judge, brings to the court her vigorous support for women's rights and strong committment to preserving a woman's constitutional right to an abortion. Breyer, a Harvard law professor confirmed in August of 1994, is an articulate consensus-builder often criticized by liberals for his allegedly pro-business leanings. Since these appointments the Court has kept up its trend toward centrism with several close and controversial rulings: in 1994, it upheld *Roe* by a narrow 5-4 margin, but in 1995, by the same margin, it called for stricter scrutiny of affirmative action laws.

Elected officials want to be reelected. Swarms of **interest groups** are happy to help them, for a price: "lobbies" for specific corporations, industries (like tobacco or steel), and constituencies (like small businesses, gun owners, or teachers) contribute to the campaigns of Congresspeople and other elected officials, generally as a reward or an incentive for certain votes or positions. These organizations, especially the non-corporate ones who can't compete in the contribution race, can pull their members together and swamp Congressional offices with calls, letters, and reasons to favor their cause. In the mid-70s, concern over the power of rich people and corporations led to a law limiting individual giving; the law, in turn, led to **Political Action Committees** (PACs), organizations that collect and disperse contributions. Congressional incumbents (especially in the House) are more likely than not to get reelected, so PACs like to give to them rather than to their challengers; this in turn widens incumbents' financial edge, making them even more likely to win again.

■ ARTS AND CULTURE

ARCHITECTURE

Pierre L'Enfant aimed to make central Washington a unified work of art; you may have to look at a map to know it, though. The L'Enfant plan makes the Capitol building D.C.'s architectural focus; low government buildings with similar façades were supposed to flank the broad avenues, making most of Washington's vistas converge on the Congress and the dome above it. L'Enfant also expected—and got—plenty of trees all over the city (and that's not counting Rock Creek Park). The Mall was to be a central promenade, leading from the Capitol to some sort of Washington Monument, with trees on either side.

Early D.C. architects were self-consciously designing for a republic—in their eyes, the most important one since the Romans; their Federal style unapologetically echoed Athens and Rome with columns, pediments, friezes, and marble, marble, marble. Many of these designs—William Thornton's original Capitol and James Hoban's White House, for example—were selected in anonymous competitions entered mostly by amateur builders. The mid-1800s saw the advent of the professional architect; the new breed was more interested in modern European than in ancient Greek models, and many of their works were homes or churches. The outstanding designer among these was Benjamin Latrobe, whose St. John's Church and Decatur House (near the White House) were models of sophistication.

Boss Shepherd (in charge 1871-74) sunk megabucks into new sewers, paved roads, and trees. He also paved the road to Victorian excess by authorizing A.B. Mullet's State, War, and Navy Building (now the Old Executive Office Building); the gingerbread windows delight tourists now, but the severe Neoclassicists of the early 1900s were understandably underwhelmed, and kept trying to get the building demolished. Where the O.E.O. building goes overboard on ornaments, the Smithsonian's Arts and Industries Building is a garish flood of contrasting colors—fun to look at but hard to imagine wanting to build. The Library of Congress's Jefferson Building, the magnificent Pension building (now the National Building Museum), and the Old Post Office are more dignified examples of Victorian style.

The budget-inspired freeze on building that followed Boss Shepherd's fall from power thawed around the turn of the century, when Daniel Burnham brought the Beaux Arts style to Washington. The McMillan Commission revamped Washington's public spaces and commissioned Burnham's Union Station. The Commission also proposed the Lincoln Memorial, which heralded a return to Neoclassicism, though this time bigger and sparer. John Russell Pope, the undisputed emperor of 30s and 40s pseudo-Greco-Roman building, made his masterpiece the domed West Building of the National Gallery of Art on the Mall.

When the dust of World War II cleared, European avant-garde architects had settled in America and brought with them the International-style office building, unaffectionately nicknamed the "glass box." As always, Washington was about a decade behind New York City in the adoption of new architectural trends. D.C. firms strived to blend international modernism's clean lines and brutal simplicity with the monumental marbleness of already-extant buildings; the Kennedy Center and the National Geographic building are two fairly successful examples. I.M. Pei's popular 1978 East Wing (of the National Gallery of Art) obeys the letter of modernist dictates (big planes, no ornaments, no paint, exposed structural elements) but certainly violates its spirit—the quite beautiful array of glass and white triangles was emphatically not designed for efficiency. In this it heralded the postmodern architecture that moved here in earnest from New York in the late 80s. Postmodern buildings rewrite old styles in modernism's plainer, planar vocabulary, with unusually shaped windows (for example) set into two-color blocks of sheer granite; the Canadian embassy, which puts Greek elements where the Greeks would never think to put them, is certainly the best "postmodern" building now standing in D.C. A few especially nice postmodern offices stand among mediocre older buildings at 20th and M St. NW (at the northwest corner) and along K St.

A few considerations make Washington's urban plan unusual. The most obvious is the height limit—roughly the elevation of the Capitol dome and the Washington monument, or about 13 stories. On one hand, this means that truly big office buildings nearly always turn out sprawling and ugly; on the other hand, you can always see the sky—and the Capitol—downtown, and many feel it's worth the trade. A number of 20th-century buildings have had to occupy awkward acute angles where avenues and circles or numbered or lettered streets intersect; there are as many answers to this as there are angles, though the East Wing and the otherwise boring office building at the corner of Dupont Circle, Connecticut, and P St. NW provide two interesting solutions. Architects of new embassies have to decide how much the building should fit into Washington, and how much to reflect the style and culture of the relevant nation instead; the Canadian Embassy succeeds at the first, the British and Japanese at the second. Finally, there's the omnipresent Classical vocabulary (you've noticed if you've read this far) of domes, columns, long steps, and such; every Washington architect has to adjust to the inevitable monumental atmosphere and the overriding Roman grid plan of the capital city.

VISUAL ARTS

The body politic's craze to commemorate has burdened D.C. with a profusion of public art. Eagles squint from cornices, workers labor heroically from the neo-Hellenic friezes above public buildings, and generals and statesmen gesture from horseback in almost every traffic circle. Most public statues date from between the 1870s, when public art remembered Civil War figures, and World War II, when the government found more urgent ways to spend its money. Though few of these statues are worthy of a Phidias, many still merit interest: some bear curious anecdotes (like Gen. Scott in Scott Circle or Benito Juarez on Virginia Ave. NW), others have curious inscriptions (like the modern memorial on Roosevelt Island), and still others might actually teach you some history. Aesthetic delights may be had in Lafayette Park and from the Grant Memorial near the Capitol, the statue of Robert Emmet near Dupont Circle, and the hard-to-get-to Adams Memorial in Rock Creek Cemetery.

The public memorial as its own art form, half sculpture and half architecture, may have reached its zenith in Washington. Though they're really an outgrowth of the same old outdoor statue idea, memorials give designers more room to innovate and viewers more space to contemplate. (Though he ordered trees removed to watch the Jefferson Memorial being built, FDR said he wanted his own monument to be no bigger than his desk.) D.C.'s monuments reach their highest concentration west of the Mall, where the Washington Monument and the Lincoln and Jefferson memorials lurk; designs range from copycat Greek to the spare self-reflection of the Vietnam Veterans Memorial, the simplest and most affecting piece of outdoor art in Washington. Since 1986, the government has laid down the law on future monuments: the honoree must have been dead for at least 25 years, three commissions must say yes to the project, and the construction must not use federal funds.

Collector Duncan Phillips's museum was showing off modern art while New York's MoMA was still just a building fund, but D.C. had no indigenous painters of note until a generation later, when Kenneth Noland's clean-lined abstractions, Gene Davis's parallel stripes, and the experimental canvases of critics' darling Morris Louis were said to form the Washington Color School. Look for Color Schoolers in the Hirshhorn and the Phillips, though there's no guarantee you'll see them even there.

Though it's not a hotbed of visual innovation, Washington still boasts world-class museum collections. The West Wing of the National Gallery of Art is filled to the brim with masters everybody should know, from Giotto to Raphael to Vermeer. Twentieth-century and touring exhibitions go up in the Gallery's Pei-faced East Wing. The Hirshhorn's one cylinder is powered by two engines: contemporary art and 20th-century sculpture, one indoors, the other outside in the adjacent Sculpture Garden. Away from the Mall, check out the Phillips Collection, the Corcoran Gallery (for 19th-century American and 1980s art), the Renwick (for American crafts), and the National Museum of American Art.

MUSIC

Music in Washington began inauspiciously with John Philip Sousa, who led the Marine Corps Marching Band from the 1880s to the 1900s. The peppery Sousa taught the band to play, then initiated the bevy of military brass concerts and parades that toot, stomp, and honk near the Mall to this day. Later, things began to swing: the Howard Theater and other jazz venues nurtured a string of Washington artists, most notably the immortal Duke Ellington. Jazz songstresses from D.C. include Roberta Flack and Shirley Horne; the latter still performs in Washington clubs. Classical music-related performances took off with the building of the Kennedy Center, which gave the National Symphony Orchestra, the Washington Ballet, and many lesser musical groups a home as shiny and multi-chambered as a nautilus shell.

D.C. didn't go far in rock-and-roll until punk touched down in the early 80s; then, inspired by charismatic (and short-lived) bands like Minor Threat, "straightedge" punks shaved their heads and drew Xs on their hands to parade their abstinence from drugs and alcohol. Where rock elsewhere affected combativeness with leather, studs, and long-winded guitar fuzz, D.C. punks, some as young as 13, packaged honest teen angst in two-minute songs. As the decade wore on they combined their no-nonsense attitude with real political activism: all-ages shows in rented halls to benefit the likes of the Washington Free Clinic and the American Civil Liberties Union are the best place to take in what's left of "hard core," as the music is and was called. The winnowing of the punk moment has made space for a profusion of new trends and sounds: bratty feminist girl-rockers and unrepentant old-time punks have taken to heavy percussion (often performed at outdoor festivals at monuments or on the Supreme Court steps), while a new generation of bands is quietly reinventing the New Wave, running record labels out of their basements (most notably Tsunami and the Simple Machines label), and sparring with Olympia, Washington, and Providence, Rhode Island, for the title of capital of the International Pop Underground. The city recoiled when d.c. space, a punk-friendly fixture of the D.C. scene, closed down on New Year's Day, 1992. The 9:30 Club and The Black Cat pick up some of the slack; after a show there, you can follow the performers to their 3am snacks at Dante's on 14th St. The new 200-seat Capitol Ballroom promises to expand the size and scale of the D.C. scene. Record-hunters should seek out Dischord Records vinyl by Scream, Gray Matter, or Rites of Spring, or LPs by Government Issue; important bands still around include Wingtip Sloat, Circus Lupus, Unrest, and nationally known (to their regret) Fugazi.

Though rap music is as strong here as in most urban centers (Basehead lives in SE), the indigenous dance sound of D.C. is go-go. Repeated efforts to turn go-go music from a D.C. thing into a national craze have failed; some say producers and promoters have failed to do it justice, while others maintain that the experience of live go-go just can't be copied on vinyl. The best go-go bands blend African percussion and instrumental virtuosity with the trimmings of rap; some have over ten performers. One premier act, E.U. (once known as Experience Unlimited), went national with their dance hit "Da Butt." Other perennials include Rare Essence and Chuck Brown and the Soul Searchers. Hear live go-go outdoors at festivals like Malcolm X Day, Marvin Gaye Day, or Adams-Morgan Day, or call CJ the TJ (telephone jockey), at 543-GOGO for chill recorded listings of the week's performances.

THEATER AND FILM

Washington has had professional theater for a long time, and that's not counting Congress or the President. The "Washington Theatre" in 1821 and the National Theater in 1835 started a trend that flowered over a hundred years later, when Zelda Fichandler's Arena Stage gave birth to the American regional-theater movement. Mounting new productions with its own repertory company, Arena succeeded hundreds of miles from Broadway, launching (among other shows) Lorraine Hansberry's *Raisin in the Sun*. The elegant Warner Theater has gone from vaudeville to rap to Sondheim-type stage productions (after renovations and under new management) over the past century. While the multi-performing-art Kennedy Center allures, the cup of small-stage innovation has passed to the theater district of 14th St. NW, where several young companies experiment their hearts out.

The **movies** haven't passed D.C. by either: Jimmy Stewart (*Mr. Smith Goes to Washington*) tried to make it honest, Klaatu (*The Day the Earth Stood Still*) landed a spaceship in it, the journalists of *Broadcast News* seemed to ooze right through the city, and *Dave* took over for the look-alike President. Clint Eastwood played out what should have happened on November 22, 1963, in a classic of Monday-morning filmmaking (*In the Line of Fire*). Other recent favorites include *No Way Out* starring Kevin Costner and John Grisham's *Pelican Brief*.

Haunted Hangout

The Exorcist, featuring Linda Blair as a teen possessed by the Devil (imagine that!), was filmed in Georgetown, and the steep set of stairs which saw several of the movie's most gruesome scenes (a few priests were thrown from the ledge) remain haunted— by local college students.

LITERATURE

> *The White House of future poems, of dreams, of dramas, there in the soft and copious moon—*
>
> —*Walt Whitman,* Specimen Days

More than a pit stop but less than Parnassus, D.C. has briefly inspired and housed many of America's famous writers. Though British novelists like Dickens and Trollope have left vitriolic records of their visits to Washington, the first 1st-class scribbler to settle in the capital was poet Walt Whitman, whose years of volunteer work as a Union Army nurse are recorded in his memoir *Specimen Days.* Whitman's Lincoln elegies and his Civil War poems (collectively titled *Drum-Taps*) were surely influenced by his D.C. days, when cattle milled about the Washington Monument and Union encampments filled the avenues. (Contemporaries recall the poet as skilled and tender in his care of the wounded.) Frederick Douglass lived in Anacostia when he finished his autobiography in the 1870s and 80s. Initially ignored by the masses, the book has been studied as literature in recent years. It records the trials and experiences of the former slave, abolitionist, orator, and diplomat. The historian and grumpy belletrist Henry Adams "took it for granted" (in his own words) that he would someday live in the White House, just like his grandpa John Quincy Adams; he didn't get the White House, but he did get a well-appointed house nearby where he and his wife gathered diplomats and historians such as Henry Cabot Lodge and George Bancroft in a turn-of-the-century literary salon.

More poetry, and perhaps better writing, emanated from the African-American community in the early 20th century, when the famous Harlem Renaissance established a D.C. outpost around U St., through Shaw and in LeDroit Park. Ballad-poet Paul Dunbar's move to D.C. was emulated by Langston Hughes and Jean (*Cane*) Toomer. The MuSoLit club gave black intelligentsia a gathering place. Later poems of black Washington emanated from residents Sterling Brown and E. Ethelbert Miller and native daughter Elizabeth Alexander. Other poets made strange pilgrimages to see *Cantos* verse-maker Ezra Pound, who was confined in St. Elizabeth's for criminal insanity. Literary lions and doves converged on the city for the 1968 March on the Pentagon, led by novelist Norman Mailer and by Robert Lowell, whose poem "July in Washington" may be the best ever written about the city. Since World War II, the Library of Congress has attracted important poets for the two-year job of Poetry Consultant; in the mid-80s the title changed to Poet Laureate (held now by Pulitzer Prize winner Rita Dove). The post has made the LoC the only place for consistently high-class literary events in Washington. More demotic art forms have found Washington more congenial: popular interest in the machinations of government spawned its very own genre, the "Washington novel."

If, like the ancient Greeks and Romans, English-speaking peoples counted persuasive writing as literature, we'd have to admit that Washington has produced a whole genre of American writing. The memorable line (now known as the soundbite) has flourished here at least since Daniel Webster's toast "Liberty and Union, now and forever, one and inseparable." Today's equivalents sound more folksy than sonorous, but Presidents and their speechwriters still specialize in the ringing aphorism. FDR said "We have nothing to fear but fear itself" when he promised Americans a New Deal. Truman convinced Congress to send millions in postwar aid to Europe partly by invoking the name of its planner, General George Marshall. Martin Luther King, Jr., came to D.C. to tell the world he had a dream. The past two decades of political follies have brought a new irony to political talk; though more dough than ever goes to media gurus, the most memorable lines are the ones that ring false, from Nixon's laughable "I am not a crook" to Reagan's summary of Iran-contra: "Mistakes were made." Two more recent entries, Bush's "This will not stand" (referring to the Iraqi invasion of Kuwait) and President Clinton's "I feel your pain," have, at least, the virtue of honesty. No matter what you think the U.S. stands for, Washington has always been *the* place in which to scribble a speech, stand up, and be heard.

■ INTERNATIONAL WASHINGTON

Though it once experienced a British Invasion, D.C. didn't start out very international. German-Americans worked in Foggy Bottom, Chinese-Americans hung onto Chinatown, and the African-American community, of course, maintained its Washington presence. Nineteenth-century embassies served a social function: a diplomat succeeded by impressing Americans and moving in senators' circles. (Some embassies did other things, too, like espionage.) One legend maintains that European governments classed D.C. as a "hardship post," akin to tropical Asia, where diplomats could dress informally and received higher pay. Ambassadors, especially the British and French, were automatically social lions; since embassies are technically foreign territory, they lasted through Prohibition as legal speakeasies. (Underage Georgetown University students rent them out for similar reasons.) Though ambassadorial business has become more complicated and more official, diplomatic Washington still adheres to old-school rules, gathering socialites and officeholders in decorated mansions and seating them by arcane rules only the State Department understands. (The *Washington Post* Style section can tell you more than you possibly want to know about the embassy party scene.) The "dean" of the diplomatic corps is the one who's been in D.C. the longest. You can see, if not touch, diplomatic D.C. by looking for the foreign flags or national crests that hang outside almost all embassies; Embassy Row, around Massachusetts Ave. near and west of Dupont Circle, holds an especially high concentration.

Another kind of international Washington can be seen in the D.C.-area neighborhoods that immigrants have imbued with their cultures. A large Hispanic community anchors itself in Adams-Morgan and Mount Pleasant, along with a substantial first-generation African and Afro-Caribbean culture. Southeast Asian immigrants have ringed D.C., establishing communities in the suburbs and around Arlington's "Little Saigon." (See the write-ups of these neighborhoods for more on D.C.'s ethnic communities.)

■ THE STATEHOOD DEBATE

> *It is not easy to ever estimate the influence of the people of the District of Columbia. Aside from American women, they are now the only people in the Republic denied the elective franchise.*
>
> *—Frederick Douglass, "Lecture on the Nation's Capital" (1877)*

Although District residents have been able to vote for Presidential electors since 1961 and enjoyed limited home rule from 1973 to 1995, many Washingtonians feel that they are being denied the rights due to them as American citizens. Although they must pay an income tax imposed by Congress, District residents have no representation in the Senate and only a non-voting delegate, Eleanor Holmes Norton (D), in the House. Congress is still able, and frequently willing, to meddle in Washington's local affairs, blocking, for example, changes in D.C.'s sex laws and preventing the District from imposing a tax on commuters from Virginia and Maryland. That Congress is mostly white and the District population mostly black casts additional doubt on the justice of the arrangement.

Some Washingtonians feel that the only sure path to equality is for most of the current District to become the 51st state, leaving a small enclave of federal buildings as the Constitutionally-mandated federal district. Sure, the new state would be kind of puny, but there are more people living in the District than in the full-fledged states of Alaska or Wyoming. Thinking along these lines, members of the small Statehood Party have advocated statehood since 1969. Their efforts peaked in the early 1980s when D.C. voters called for a convention to write a constitution for the proposed state and later approved the resulting document. Since then, however, scandals in the D.C. government, a declining population, the recent loss of home rule, and dwindling interest among Washingtonians have lessened the chances that a 51st star will be added to the flag anytime soon.

Financial Woes

Since the beginning of Home Rule in 1973, the job of running Washington has been a financial matter. The city has had a budget deficit since the first years under the Home Rule Charter, when a ban on taxing commuters made two thirds of the salaries paid within the District untaxable. During the mid-1970s, Mayor Marion Barry used deep cuts and later extravagant spending to balance the city budget and create surpluses. A combination of factors, however, turned his financial solutions into more serious problems. Barry's expansionary fiscal policy of increasing the number of workers and contractors on the government payroll would have worked if those beneficiaries had remained within the city limits and paid income tax on their salaries. Taking advantage of the commuter tax ban and the cheaper real estate in the suburbs, most made the move across the District line into Maryland and Virginia, taking any hopes of a broader tax base with them.

Barry's spending became less responsible throughout the 1980s, and his successor, Sharon Pratt Kelly, took office with the promise that she would undo the financial damage Barry had done. Her spending record, however, was no better than Barry's. At last count (in 1994) the city deficit hovered around an unprecedented $700 million. With the loss of Home Rule in 1995, and the obvious fact that D.C. can't support itself financially, the vision of statehood for the District is looking even dimmer.

■ THE MEDIA

As a rule, the newspaper correspondents in Washington were unfriendly, and the lobby sceptical.

—*Henry Adams,* The Education of Henry Adams *(1902)*

Where industrial cities might depend on oil or ore, Washington depends on information. Politicians prepare proposals, release reactions, and seek soundbites for newspapers and TV before scouring the next day's news to find out how they look. Ambitious bureaucrats and White House insiders conduct their in-fighting through press statements, unattributed quotations, "leaks," and surreptitious traffic with journalists ("Sources close to the President said today..."). And the government needs hard facts on everything from rutabagas to rent rates just to make its regulations and mete out funds. All this makes D.C. a veritable ant farm of journalists.

READ ALL ABOUT IT

Washington papers began as political organs for individual politicians. President Woodrow Wilson got hip to the power of the press in the 1910s and began to take reporters' questions at semi-regular conferences. FDR wowed reporters with weekly conferences and regular access, though he also bypassed them and addressed America directly in his radio "fireside chats." JFK coddled reporters (and consequently improved his press), but journalism became more adversarial as race riots, youth movements, and the Vietnam War began to fracture America. Nixon spewed venom at the liberal press via Vice President Spiro Agnew and appointed inquisitional White House "plumbers" to stop the leaks. Perhaps driven by indignation, investigative reporting reached new heights. In 1970, Daniel Ellsberg and the *New York Times* published the famous "Pentagon Papers," which exposed government duplicity about Vietnam. A few years later, *Washington Post* reporters Bob Woodward and Carl Bernstein forced President Nixon out of office with their revelation of the Watergate scandal. The White House's latest inhabitant, Bill Clinton, had a reputation for wowing reporters until he took office, at which point media relations soured.

Today's Washington journalists often stay close to the government even as they try to dig up its dirt. Reporters must cultivate well-placed sources to hear the latest inside news; some say this makes the press inevitably partial. Op-ed pundits are as much a part of the sprawling permanent government as Congressional staffers or Pentagon bureaucrats. Televised press conferences let the President reward friendly journalists by calling on them for questions, though the Chief is sometimes tripped up by a sharp, unknown reporter. During and after the Reagan years, pundits worried that video charisma and sophisticated advertising would make political journalism irrelevant. And reporters complained of Pentagon "manipulation" during the bloody-on-one-side Persian Gulf war. Yet alongside the designer media firms, the made-for-TV statements, and non-events, the old-time religion of investigative journalism holds on to a mission and no small following.

In this town of news junkies, the **Washington Post** is the ubiquitous opiate, a newspaper of record with comprehensive, if not always incisive, political, national, and international coverage. (Though the liberal *Post* hopes someday to repeat its Watergate glory days, its most obvious influence of late has been local. Disgraced mayor Marion Barry rode to power on the white votes the *Post's* endorsement brought him in 1978; as if to make up for it, a *Post* endorsement spurred the 1991 election of relative underdog Sharon Pratt Kelly as the new mayor of D.C. In the most recent Mayoral election, the Post backed Kelly in the primary and she lost; they then committed the liberal sin of backing Republican candidate Carol Schwartz in the election–all to avoid showing support for guess who? Alas, Barry is back in power.)The Metro section covers local news, festivals, and shootings. Style is a Washington institution all by itself, a definitive fluffy gossip sheet that is read religiously by all in the know. Sunday's *Outlook* bursts with political opinion, while Friday's Weekend section helps readers (especially families) decide what to do with the next two days.

The Washington **City Paper** (Baltimore has one too) is a thick, free, "alternative" weekly distributed (on Fri.) to vending machines and cool stores all over town, with excellent local investigative reporting, feature stories, and more comprehensive listings of the arts in D.C. (especially theater and popular music) than the staid *Post* seems able to provide. (Use the *Post's* movie listings, but rely on *City Paper's* movie reviews and club listings.) Look through the paper for occasional special coupons for clubs. *City Paper* also has a Classifieds section—including the city's best personals (if you're into that) and a large number of apartment and roommate listings.

The **Washington Times,** a conservative daily left over from the early 80s "Reagan Revolution," has since lost respectability due to staff shake-ups, hard-right columnists, and widespread awareness that Rev. Sun Myung Moon's Unification Church funds the paper (hence its nickname, *The Moonie Times*). But once in a blue moon, the *Times* does find local stories the *Post* has missed.

Some national news-and-views magazines base themselves in Washington. The best known is the highly respected (and ultra-snide) weekly **The New Republic,** which once carried the standard for American liberalism and now devotes a fair share of its pages to mounting a passive-aggressive campaign against the President and favorite son Al Gore. *TNR* prints news analysis and arts pieces from all over, including a roving "Diarist" column and a by-line by Michael Kinsley.

The smaller, more wonkish **Washington Monthly** likes to boast that it broke famous stories, like Mayor Barry's corruption, National Security Council misdeeds, and design flaws in the space shuttle, years before better-known pages got hold of them. The scrappy *Monthly* is a favorite of aspiring policymakers; the mag keeps tabs on the bureaucracy, but not always on the city as a whole.

Away from the bright lights of national news, Washington's communities run their own papers. The daily **Washington Afro-American** covers black D.C. in a friendly, interested way, with attention to individual citizens' achievements. The well-written, free weekly **Washington Blade,** stacked in various stores (especially around Dupont Circle), is the strong gay and lesbian community's paper, with articles, listings, an events calendar, and a directory of gay professionals.

If it's Congress you're interested in, read **Roll Call,** which prints gossip, news, and an events calendar for members of the House, the Senate, and their lucky staffers twice a week. Free **Intermission** serves Washington's smaller theaters. Monthly **Washingtonian** is almost the neighborhood magazine of the affluent suburbs; plenty of articles on celebrities and real estate mix with interesting D.C. trivia, surprising, money-saving tidbits, and lots of lists ("top 10 delis," etc.). **Regardie's** magazine mixes business news with gossip and satire.

The Capitol Hill neighborhood cleans up weekly with **Hill Rag,** an area paper distributed all over downtown. The **In Towner** covers local issues (zoning and crime, for example) for Dupont Circle, Adams-Morgan, and points east (Scott and Logan Circles) and west (Cleveland Park). The **Georgetowner** does the same for its namesake. The monthly **Old Town Crier** runs news and restaurant and gallery listings for Old Town Alexandria. Events listings of interest to the tourist community congregate in **Go** and **Where,** slick, free magazines distributed at downtown hotels, where even a scruffy budget traveler can pick one up. Or stop by one of the friendly neighborhood D.C. libraries:

Martin Luther King, Jr. Public Library, 901 G St. NW (727-1111). Metro: Metro Center. The main branch of D.C.'s public-library system. Call 727-0321 for additional branches. Open Mon.-Thurs. 9am-9pm, Fri.-Sat. 9am-5:30pm, Sun. 1-5pm. Longer hours in the summer.

Library of Congress, 1st St. SE (707-5000, recorded events schedule 707-8000), between East Capitol and Independence Ave. Metro: Capitol South. The vast collection, including rare items, is open to anyone of college age or older with a legitimate research purpose. It's a closed-stack library, so they'll bring the books to you. It's also a non-circulating library, so you must do your reading there. Most reading rooms open Mon., Wed., and Thurs. 8:30am-9:30pm, Tues., Fri., and Sat. 8:30am-5pm. For further information call 707-6400.

Folger Shakespeare Library, 201 East Capitol St. SE (544-4600). Houses the world's largest collection of Shakespeareana, and hosts exhibits related to Shakespeare and his culture. To see the books, you need to be working on a Ph.D. thesis. Exhibits open Mon.-Sat. 10am-4pm; library open Mon.-Fri. 8:45am-4:45pm.

Up-and-Coming

A hip, bold, funny, informative, and opinionated new paper, **Generation Next** is nothing short of a brilliant representation of twentysomething interests and concerns. Search for a free copy at establishments all over Dupont Circle; your quest will be well rewarded.

ON THE RADIO (AND TV)

Not all points can be made in print, and in a city where image is everything, visual media matter as much or more than the written word. Due to their proximity to government activity, local television networks and radio stations sometimes beat national ones to newsworthy stories.

National TV shows filmed in Washington are not usually the studio audience type. Political programs like MacNeil/Lehrer's hour of interviews and the McLaughlin Group's heated discussions aren't exactly the spectator sort, and besides, if you really want to know what's going on in Congress, you can tune in to the nonstop CNN and C-SPAN coverage for play-by-play at most Capitol Hill area bars and restaurants. (Or, you can go and sit in on Congress yourself.)

D.C. radio is conspicuously missing a Top-40 station. If you can get over this slight, try these Washington favorites: **AM:** 630, **WMAL** (news/talk/sports); 730, **WBZS** (financial news); 1260, **WWDC** (big band/original hits); 1300, **WJFK** (talk/jazz; FM 106.7); 1500, **WTOP** (news); 1580, **WPGC** (hip hop; FM 95.5). **FM:** 88.5, **WAMU** (NPR; news/talk/music); 97.1, **WASH** (adult contemporary); 98.7, **WMZQ** (country); 99.1, **WHFS** (modern rock); 99.5 **WGAY** (soft adult contemporary); 100.3 **WBIG** (oldies); 103.5, **WGMS** (classical); 107.3, **WRQX** (70s, 80s, and 90s mix).

Washington's TV stations and affiliations are: Channel 4, **WRC/NBC;** Channel 5, **WTTG/Fox;** Channel 7, **WJLA/ABC;** Channel 9, **WUSA/CBS;** Channel 20, **WDCA/Ind.;** Channel 26, **WETA/PBS.**

Essentials

An elegant urban space with an impeccable public-transit system, D.C. is hardly a mysterious city. With the exception of government, Washington's primary business is tourism; visitors are barraged with an overwhelming amount of free information from travel offices, tourist information centers, and special-interest organizations.

PLANNING YOUR TRIP

WHEN TO GO

CLIMATE

Washington weather can be sub-zero (rarely), pleasantly mild (most of the time) or unbearably hot and humid (July and August, sometimes June). The summer humidity, in fact, is legendarily repellent; a French foreign minister blamed the heat when he killed himself here in the 1890s (the suicide note explained his aversion to iced drinks, one he shared with President Zachary Taylor, who died of a massive brain embolism upon drinking a mint julep one fateful day in 1850).

	Average High	Average Low
January	42°F	27°F
February	46°	29°
March	57°	38°
April	67°	46°
May	76°	57°
June	85°	71°
July	89°	71°
August	87°	70°
September	80°	63°
October	69°	50°
November	58°	41°
December	47°	32°

—courtesy of the National Oceanic and Atmospheric Administration

U.S. HOLIDAYS

Martin Luther King, Jr.'s Birthday is celebrated on the third Monday in January (Jan. 15 in 1996), **Presidents Day** on the third Monday in February (Feb. 19). **Memorial Day,** falling on the last Monday of May (May 27), honors all U.S. citizens who have died in wars and signals the unofficial start of summer. Halfway through summer, **Independence Day** explodes on July 4. Americans celebrate their independence from England with barbecues and fireworks. Summer unofficially ends with another long weekend, **Labor Day,** on the first Monday of September (Sept. 2). **Columbus Day** comes on the second Monday in October (Oct. 14). **Thanksgiving,** the fourth Thursday of November (Nov. 28), celebrates the arrival of the Pilgrims in New England in 1620. The holiday season peaks at **Christmas** (Dec. 25) and runs through **New Year's Day** (Jan. 1). Most public agencies and offices and many businesses close on these holidays.

■■■ JUST THE FACTS, MA'AM

GOVERNMENT INFORMATION OFFICES

United States Tourist Offices, found in many countries, can provide you with armloads of free literature. If you can't find a U.S. Tourist Office in your area, write the **U.S. Travel and Tourism Administration,** Department of Commerce, 14th St. and Constitution Ave. NW, Rm. 1860, Washington, D.C. 20230 (482-4003). For general tourist information, you may want to inquire at state and city tourist offices.

HITTING THE BOOKS

When planning your itinerary, scrutinize the publications that specialize in Washington-area travel. The **U.S. Government Printing Office,** 710 N. Capitol St., NW (Metro: Union Station) offers a number of helpful bibliographies and publications, including the pamphlet *Travel and Tourism,* a useful bibliography on U.S. travel; call or write ahead if you have time (Superintendent of Documents, U.S. Government Printing Office, Washington, D.C. 20402; 512-1800). The **United States Travel and Tourism Administration,** Department of Commerce, Rm. 1860, 14th and Constitution Ave. NW, Washington, D.C. 20230 (482-4003) also provides abundant free literature.

GETTIN' IT ON-LINE :^)

We've come a long way since the world of Tron. In researching your trip to the Greater Washington area, you should be aware that there is a vast amount of information available through the international computer network known as the **Internet.** Some commercial providers, such as America On-line, CompuServe, and Prodigy, offer sophisticated services like **on-line airline reservations.** Even the most basic mode of access can provide an overabundance of information. Most universities and many businesses offer students and employees Internet access. Commercial gateways provide Internet access for a monthly fee (usually $20-30).

Internet Services

One primary means of transmitting and discussing information across the Internet are forums known collectively as Usenet, and individually as **newsgroups.** There are thousands of newsgroups accessible by users all over the world; sometimes, they're your best source for up-to-the-minute information. New groups are always poppin' up; unfortunately, not all groups are available from all systems, although your system administrator can usually add new groups on request. A basic news-reading program can be accessed on most UNIX systems by typing "rn" for "read news" or "tin." A caveat: most newsgroups are unmoderated, so the quality of conversation and the reliability of information posted within them is not always certain.

There are several "hierarchies" of newsgroups. One, the "soc" groups, primarily addresses social issues and socializing; subscribe to **soc.culture.usa.**. The "alt" prefix stands for "alternative" and the groups are less formalized. A good example is **alt.politics.usa.** "Rec" groups, such as **rec.travel.air** are oriented toward the arts, hobbies, and recreation. (In general, you can insert almost any country name into soc and alt groups: for instance, **rec.travel.usa.**) Some systems also provide access to the "ClariNet" newsgroups, read-only (copyrighted) groups which compile the latest wire service news.

Three of the other services available on the Internet are **FTP** (file transfer protocol), **gopher,** and **World Wide Web;** each can be used to obtain files and other information stored in areas of other computer systems accessible to the public. Thousands of such archives exist, including many with information on travel. A particularly useful archive is **rec-travel** at ftp.cc.umanitoba.ca; it includes travelogues, U.S. State Department Advisories, and a plethora of other useful info. Use your WWW browser to check out the handy CIA World Factbook; point to "http://www.ic.gof/94fact/fb94toc/fb94toc.html". Another good source of information is the **Yahoo** directory, a thorough subject listing of Web pages. The URL is "http://www.yahoo.com". The "Student and Budget Travel Resource Guide" lists a wide variety of on-line travel information. It is available through the WWW at "http://asa.ugl.lib.umich.edu/chdocs/travel/travel-guide.html"; or, send e-mail to "travel-guide@umich.edu".

Learning how to navigate the Internet to these sites is not extraordinarily complex, but somewhat beyond the scope of this book; ask a system manager or computer-using friend, or check out any one of the many comprehensive guides to the Internet now available in most bookstores.

■■■ DOCUMENTS AND FORMALITIES

Foreign visitors who wish to travel to the United States should plan early so they can complete all the necessary paperwork in time. All foreign visitors are required to have a **passport, visitor's visa,** and **proof of intent to leave** (i.e., a round-trip airline ticket). You should probably file all applications several weeks or months in advance of your planned departure date. Remember—you're relying on government agencies to complete these transactions.

PASSPORTS

As a precaution in case your passport is lost or stolen, be sure before you leave to **photocopy** your passport. Carry this photocopy in a safe place apart from your passport, perhaps with a travel companion, and leave another copy at home. Better yet, carry a photocopy of all the pages of the passport, including all visa stamps. These measures will facilitate the issuing of a new passport. If you do need a new passport while in the U.S., go to your consulate or embassy.

British citizens, British Dependent Territories citizens, and British Overseas citizens may apply for a **full passport.** Residents of the U.K., the Channel Islands and the Isle of Man also have the option of applying for a more restricted **British Visitor's Passport.** For a full passport, valid for 10 years (five years if under 16), apply in person or by mail to a passport office, located in London, Liverpool, Newport, Peterborough, Glasgow, or Belfast. Application forms are also available from main post offices (in Northern Ireland from any local office of the DSS). The fee is UK£18. Children under 16 may be included on a parent's passport. Processing by mail usually takes four to six weeks. Along with the application and fee you must submit (1) a birth certificate and marriage certificate (if applicable), (2) two identical recent photographs signed by a guarantor, and (3) the expired passport. The London office offers same-day walk-in rush service; arrive early. A Visitor's Passport, valid for one year in some Western European countries and Bermuda only (but not for purposes of employment nor for a visit of longer than three months in any one country), is available from main post offices in England, Scotland, and Wales, and from passport offices in Northern Ireland, the Channel Islands, and the Isle of Man. The fee is UK£12.

Irish citizens can apply for a passport by mail to either the Department of Foreign Affairs, Passport Office, Setanta Centre, Molesworth St., Dublin 2 (tel. (01) 671 16 33), or the Passport Office, 1A South Mall, Cork (tel. (021) 627 25 25). Use the new Passport Express service, which offers a two-week turn-around and is available through post offices for an extra IR£3. You can also obtain an application form at a local Garda station. Passports cost IR£45 and are valid for 10 years. Citizens under 18 or over 65 can request a three-year passport that costs IR£10.

Australian citizens must apply for a passport in person at a Post Office, a Passport Office, or an Australian diplomatic mission overseas. An appointment may be necessary. Passport offices are located in Adelaide, Brisbane, Canberra City, Darwin, Hobart, Melbourne, Newcastle, Perth, and Sydney. A parent may file an application for a child who is under 18 and unmarried. Application fees are adjusted frequently.

To obtain a passport, one must fill out an Australian Passport Application including the Proof of Identity section. Evidence of Australian citizenship can be either an Australian passport issued after November 22, 1984 or one of the following three items: Full Australian Birth Certificate (photocopies or extracts are not acceptable), Australian Citizenship Certificate, or an Australian Registration of Birth Overseas and Birth Certificate. Minors require both a Full Birth Certificate and an Australian Citizenship Certificate. Evidence of change of name may also be necessary. Proof of identity can be a driver's license, employment ID with photo, etc. When applicable, an Alien Registration Card (green card) is required. Two passport photos in color or black and white and endorsed as stated in the application form are necessary. Payment may be made by cash, certified check or money order made out to: Australian Government Imprest Account. Personal checks are not accepted. For more information, call toll free (in Australia) 131 232.

Applicants for **New Zealand** passports must contact their local Link Centre, travel agent, or New Zealand Representative for an application form, which they must complete and mail to the New Zealand Passport Office, Documents of National Identity Division, Department of Internal Affairs, Box 10-526, Wellington (tel. (04) 474 81 00). The application fee is NZ$80 for an application submitted in New Zealand and can vary greatly abroad. Standard processing time is ten working days from receipt of completed application. Overseas citizens should send the passport application to the nearest embassy, high commission, or consulate.

South African citizens can apply for a passport at any Home Affairs Office. Two photos, either a birth certificate or an identity book, and the SAR38 fee must accompany a completed application. For further information, contact the nearest Department of Home Affairs Office.

U.S. EMBASSIES

Canada: 100 Wellington St. Ottawa, Ontario K1P 5T1 (tel. (613) 238-5335; fax 238-5720).

England: 24/31 Grovenor Sq., London W1A 1AE (tel. (44171) 499 90 00; fax 409 16 37).

Ireland: 42 Elgin Rd., Ballsbridge, Dublin (tel. (3531) 668 71 22; fax 668 99 46).

Australia: Moonah Place, Canberra, A.C.T. 2600 (tel. (616) 270 50 00; fax 270 59 70).

New Zealand: 29 Fitzherbert Terrace, Thorndon, Wellington (tel. (644) 472 20 68; fax 471 23 80).

South Africa: 877 Pretoria ST., Arcadia 0083 (tel. (2712) 342 10 48; fax 342 22 44).

VISAS

To acquire a visa for entrance to the U.S., you will need your passport and proof of intent to leave the U.S. Most visitors obtain a B-2 or "pleasure tourist" visa, valid for six months. Contact the nearest U.S. consulate in your home country to obtain yours. Upon arrival, the I-94 form (an arrival/departure certificate) will be attached to your visa; if you lose this, replace it at the nearest **U.S. Immigration and Naturalization Service (INS)** office. The INS also grants extensions for visas (max. 6 months), which require form I-539 as well as a $70 fee. For a list of local offices, travelers outside the D.C. area may write or call the INS Central Office, 425 I St. NW #5044, Washington, D.C. 20536 (514-4316).

Visitors from certain nations may enter the U.S. without visas through the **Visa Waiver Pilot Program.** Travelers qualify as long as they are traveling for business or pleasure, are staying for 90 days or less, have proof of intent to leave and a completed I-94W form, and enter aboard particular air or sea carriers. Participating countries include the U.K. Contact the nearest U.S. consulate for more information.

Canadian citizens do not need a visa or passport, but must carry proof of citizenship (a driver's license, birth certificate, or voter registration card). Canadian citizens under 16 need notarized permission from both parents. Naturalized citizens should have their naturalization papers with them; occasionally officials will ask to see them. **Mexican citizens** may cross into the U.S. with an I-186 form.

Non-Tourist Visas For Work And Study

If you are not a citizen of the U.S. and hope to **work** in this country, there are numerous rules of which you must be aware. The place to start getting specific information on visa categories and requirements is your nearest U.S. Embassy or Consulate or the Educational Advisory Service of the Fulbright Commission (a U.S. embassy-affiliated organization). You can also write to organizations such as Council, which have work-abroad programs. The alphabet soup of obtaining a worker's visa may seem complex, but it's critical that you go through the proper channels, particularly in California, where sentiment against undocumented workers is virulent. Above all, do not try to give your consular officer any monkey-business. Working or studying in the U.S. with only a B-2 visa is grounds for deportation; if the U.S. consulate suspects that you may be trying to enter the country as a worker under the aegis of a pleasure trip, you will be denied a visa altogether.

Foreign students who wish to **study** in the United States must apply for either a J-1 visa (for exchange students) or an F-1 visa (for full-time students enrolled in an academic or language program). To obtain a J-1, you must fill out an IAP-66 eligibility form, issued by the program in which you will enroll. Both are valid for the duration of stay, which includes the length of your particular program and a brief grace period thereafter. In order to extend a student visa, submit an I-538 from 15 to 60 days before the original departure date.

If you are studying in the U.S., you can take any on-campus job to help pay the bills once you have applied for a social security number and have completed an Employment Eligibility Form (I-9). If you are studying full-time in the U.S. on an F-1 visa, you can take any on-campus job provided you do not displace a U.S. resident. On-campus employment is limited to 20 hours per week while school is in session, but you may work full-time during vacation if you plan to return to school. For further information, contact the international students office at the institution you will be attending.

CUSTOMS: ENTERING THE U.S.

Customs restrictions should not impose an undue burden on budget travelers. You may bring the following into the U.S. duty free: 200 cigarettes, 50 cigars, or 2 kilograms of smoking tobacco; $100 in gifts; and personal belongings such as clothing and jewelry. Articles imported in excess of your exemption will be subject to varying duty rates, to be paid upon arrival. In general, customs officers ask how much money you're carrying and your planned departure date in order to ensure that you'll be able to support yourself while here. Carry prescription drugs in labeled containers and have a written prescription or doctor's statement ready to show the customs officer. Women especially should be aware that certain prescription drugs are illegal in the U.S. For more information, including the helpful pamphlet *U.S. Customs Hints for Visitors (Nonresidents),* contact a U.S. embassy or write the U.S. Customs Service, P.O. Box 7407, Washington, D.C. 20004 (927-2095).

CUSTOMS: GOING HOME

Canadian citizens who remain abroad for at least one week may take back up to CDN$300 worth of goods duty-free once every calendar year; this amount can not be combined from various trips. Canadian citizens or residents who travel for a period between 48 hours and six days can take back up to CDN$100 with the exception of tobacco and alcohol. You are permitted to ship goods except tobacco and alcohol home under this exemption as long as you declare them when you arrive. Citizens over the legal age (which varies by province) may import in-person up to 200 cigarettes, 50 cigars, 400gof loose tobacco or tobacco sticks, 1.14L wine or alcohol, and 24 355mL cans/bottles beer; the value of these products is included in the CDN $300. For more information, write to Canadian Customs, 2265 St. Laurent Blvd., Ottawa, Ontario, K1G 4K3 (tel. (613) 993-0534). Or, from within Canada, call (800) 461-9999.

British citizens must declare any goods in excess of the following allowances: (1) 200 cigarettes, 100 cigarillos, 50 cigars, or 250 g tobacco; (2) still table wine (2 liters); (3) strong liqueurs over 22% volume (1 liter), or fortified or sparkling wine, other liqueurs (2 liters); (4) perfume (60 cc/ml); (5) toilet water (250 cc/ml); and (6) £136 worth of all other goods including gifts and souvenirs. You must be over 17 to import liquor or tobacco. For more information about U.K. customs, contact Her Majesty's Customs and Excise, Custom House, Nettleton Road, Heathrow Airport, Hounslow, Middlesex, TW6 2LA (tel. (0181) 910-3744; fax (0181) 910-3765).

Irish citizens and visitors to Ireland must declare everything in excess of the following allowances for goods obtained outside the EC or duty and tax free in the EC: (1) 200 cigarettes, or 100 cigarillos, or 50 cigars, or 250g tobacco; (2) 1 liter of alcoholic drinks exceeding 22% vol. or 2 liters of alcoholic drinks not exceeding 22% vol.; (3) Two liters of still wine; (4) 50g of perfume; (5) toilet water (1/4 liter); (6) IR£142 of other goods per adult traveler (£73 per traveler under 15 years of age). A maximum of 25 liters of beer may be imported as a part of, but not in addition to, the adult allowance. Goods obtained duty-free and tax paid in another EC country, within certain limits set out for personal use, will not be subject to additional customs duty. Travelers under 17 are not entitled to any allowance for tobacco or alcoholic products. For more information, contact The Revenue Commissioners, Dublin Castle (tel. (01) 679-2777) or The Collector of Customs and Excise, The Custom House, Dublin 1.

There is no limit on the amount of **Australian** and/or foreign cash that may be brought into or taken out of Australia. However, amounts of AUS$5000 or more, or the equivalent in foreign currency, must be reported. A duty/tax free allowance of AUS$400 (under 18, AUS$200) is available for goods intended as gifts. For further information, contact the Australian Customs Service, 5 Constitution Ave., Canberra, ACT 2601 (tel. (6) 275 62 55; fax 275 69 89).

New Zealand citizens may bring home up to NZ$700 worth of goods (not including cigarettes/cigars/tobacco, liquor, and perfume; contact the organization listed below for specific quantities) duty-free if they are for personal use or are unsolicited gifts. You must be over 17 to import liquor and tobacco. Consult the *New Zealand Customs Guide for Travelers,* available from customs offices, or contact New Zealand Customs, 50 Anzac Avenue, Box 29, Auckland (tel. (09) 377 35 20; fax 309 29 78).

Each **South African** citizens may import duty-free: 400 cigarettes, 50 cigars, 250g tobacco, 2L wine, 1L of spirits, 250mL toilet water, 50mL perfume, and other items up to a value of R500. Amounts exceeding this limit but not SAR10, 000 are dutiable at 20%. Goods acquired abroad and sent to the Republic as unaccompanied baggage do not qualify for any allowances. You may not export or import South African bank notes in excess of SAR500. Persons who require specific information or advice concerning customs and excise duties can address their inquiries to: The Commissioner for Customs and Excise, Private Bag X47, Pretoria, 0001. This agency distributes the pamphlet, *South African Customs Information,* for visitors and residents who travel abroad. South Africans in the U.S. should contact: South African Mission to the IMF/World Bank, 3201 New Mexico Ave. Rm. 380, NW, Washington, DC 20016 (tel. (202) 364-8320/1; fax 364-6008).

IDENTIFICATION

All visitors to Washington, D.C. should carry at least two **forms of identification,** one of which should be a **photo ID.** Banks in particular will require more than one form of identification whenever you cash a traveler's check. Before you leave, **photocopy** your important documents as well as your credit cards, and leave these copies with someone you can contact easily.

In the world of budget travel, youth has its privileges. **Students** should bring proof of their status to get discounts on sights and transportation. A current **univer-**

sity ID card will generally suffice for U.S. students. International students should consider obtaining the **International Student Identity Card (ISIC),** the most widely accepted form of student identification. The card, which is sponsored by the International Student Travel Confederation (ISTC), can get you discounts galore; ask about discounts even when none are advertised. The perks include access to student airfares through **Council Travel,** sickness and accident insurance of up to $3000 as well as $100 per day for in-hospital care for up to 60 days, and a toll-free 24-hour Traveler's Assistance hotline (800-626-2427; outside the U.S. call collect 713-267-2525) whose staff can provide help in medical, legal, and financial emergencies. ISTC also offers an **International Teacher Identity Card (ITIC)** with similar benefits. Many student travel offices issue ISICs and ITICs.

Most organizations that sell the ISIC also sell the **GO 25 Card**. The fee is $16 ($10 without travel insurance), CDN$15, or UK£5. For information about any of these cards, contact Council in the U.S. Like the ISIC, the GO 25 offers a range of discounts on transportation and admissions worldwide. Unlike the ISIC, the GO 25 can be obtained by anyone, including non-students, under the age of 26.

INTERNATIONAL DRIVER'S PERMIT

If you plan to drive here, consider obtaining an International Driver's Permit (IDP) from your national automobile association before leaving (you can't get one here). Though not required by law in the U.S., an IDP is a good idea for visitors from non-English-speaking countries, whose driver's licenses might be unfamiliar to American authorities. Make sure to have proper **insurance,** required by law in the U.S. You will need a green card, or International Insurance Certificate, to prove that you have liability insurance. The application forms are available at any AAA office or car rental agency.

If your home country signed the Geneva Road Traffic Convention, you can legally drive in the U.S. for one year. However, unless you are from Canada or Mexico, your personal cars must exhibit the International Distinguishing Sign, which must be obtained in your home country. Consult the resident sages at your national automobile association before you leave. Remember that the usual **minimum age** for car rental and auto transport services is 21, occasionally 25.

■■■ MONEY

CURRENCY AND EXCHANGE

CDN$1 = US$0.7399	**US$1 = CDN$1.3740**
UK£1 = US$1.599	**US$1 = UK£0.6254**
IR£1 = US$1.6407	**US$1 = IR£0.6095**
AUS$1 = US$0.7328	**US$1 = AUS$1.3646**
NZ$1 = US$0.6740	**US$1 = NZ$1.4837**

U.S. currency uses a decimal system based on the **dollar ($).** Paper money ("bills") comes in six denominations, all the same size, shape, and dull green color. The bills now issued are $1, $5, $10, $20, $50, and $100. You may occasionally see funny denominations of $2 and $500, which are no longer printed but are still acceptable as currency. Some restaurants and stores may be squeamish about accepting bills larger than $50. The dollar is divided into 100 cents (¢). Pick your favorite notation for values of less than a dollar: 35 cents can be represented as 35¢ or $0.35. U.S. currency uses these coins: the penny (1¢), nickel (5¢), dime (10¢), and quarter (25¢). Half-dollar (50¢) and one-dollar coins are rarely seen (but are both legal tender).

No matter how tight your budget or how short your trip, you won't be able to carry all your cash with you. Even if you think you can, don't; non-cash reserves are wise. Personal checks aren't readily accepted from abroad or out of state.

Before you arrive in the District, you might want to find out if your home bank is networked with any D.C. banks; **Cirrus** (800-424-7787) and **Plus** (800-843-7587) are both popular **Automatic Teller Machine (ATM)** networks. If you're here for a while, open a savings account at one of the local banks and get a local ATM card, which you can use 24 hours a day all over the city. Credit card holders should also ask their banks or credit card companies for four-digit PINs (Personal Identification Numbers) which will allow them to get cash at participating ATMs using their credit cards.

Banks in Washington are usually open from Monday to Friday 9am to 3pm; some extend their hours on Friday; some are open Saturdays from 9am to noon or 1pm. All banks are closed on legal holidays.

TRAVELER'S CHECKS

If you're only passing through the city or if you're on the road a lot, traveler's checks can eliminate the need for a bank account. Most tourist establishments accept them (though some might require a driver's license or major credit card), and almost all banks will cash them. Get your checks in your hometown bank, usually with a 1-2% surcharge; the surcharge may be waived if you have a large enough balance or a certain kind of account. Some travel organizations, such as the **American Automobile Association (AAA),** offer commission-free traveler's checks to their members, but you must go to one of their offices to purchase them.

Refunds on lost or stolen checks can be time-consuming. To accelerate the process and avoid red tape, hold onto the receipt from the purchase of your traveler's checks, a list of their serial numbers, and a record of which ones you've cashed. Keep these in a separate pocket or pouch from the checks themselves, since they contain the information you could need to replace the checks if they're stolen. It's also a good idea to leave a copy of the serial numbers at home.

American Express traveler's checks are perhaps the most widely recognized in the world and the easiest to replace if lost or stolen—just contact the nearest AmEx travel office or call the 800-number below. Other well-known banks market their own brands. Major traveler's check and credit card companies offer a variety of free services when you buy their checks or apply for their cards, including emergency cash advances; travel information hotlines; medical, legal, and interpreter referrals; emergency message relays; guaranteed hospital entry payments; assistance with lost documents and credit card cancellation; travel insurance; and help with travel arrangements.

American Express (800-221-7282). Traveler's checks may be purchased within the U.S. at AmEx Travel Services Offices, banks, and by phone. Visitors from abroad should contact their local AmEx office. There is a small fee for check purchases. (It is now also possible to purchase traveler's checks from automated American Express Dispensers (AEDs); call 800-CASH-NOW to inquire about this service.) AmEx offices cash their own checks commission-free and sell checks that can be signed by either of two people traveling together ("Check for Two"). American Automobile Association members can obtain AmEx traveler's checks commission-free at AAA offices. In D.C., American Express maintains **travel service offices** at 1150 Connecticut Ave. NW (457-1300, TDD 775-6990), 5300 Wisconsin Ave. NW (362-4000), and 1776 Pennsylvania Ave. (289-8800).

Barclay's Bank (800-221-2426). Barclay's sells Visa traveler's checks for a 1-3% commission, depending on the bank at which the checks are purchased. To report lost or stolen checks, in the U.S. call 800-227-6811; in the U.K. (0171) 937 8091; elsewhere call collect (212) 858-8500. Barclay's banks will cash Visa traveler's checks for free; unfortunately, there are no branches in Washington, D.C.

Citicorp sells both Citicorp and Citicorp Visa traveler's checks for a 1-2% commission, depending on the branch. To place orders and report lost or stolen checks, in the U.S. call 800-645-6556; in the U.K. (0171) 982 4040; elsewhere call collect (813) 623-1709. Citicorp's **Travel Assist Hotline** (800-523-1199) can connect check holders with an English-speaking doctor and lawyer, as well as provide traveler's check refund assistance. Numerous Citibank branches are located throughout D.C.; Citicorp's **World Courier Service** guarantees hand-delivery of traveler's checks anywhere in the world.

MasterCard International offers traveler's checks for a 1-2% commission; order through Thomas Cook for potentially lower commissions. To order, in the U.S. call (800) 223-9920; from abroad, call collect (609) 987-7300. To report lost or stolen checks from abroad, call collect 44 733 50 29 95. MasterCard traveler's checks are also available from participating banks displaying the MasterCard logo. **Thomas Cook** maintains two foreign exchange offices in D.C., at 1800 K St. NW (872-1233), and at Union Station, 50 Massachusetts Ave. NE (371-9219).

CREDIT CARDS

Even the best-budgeted trip can present unexpected expenses and emergencies; credit cards can save you. American Express is taken at most upper-level establishments; most places take both Visa and MasterCard.

American Express (800-528-4800) has a sizable annual fee ($55) but membership has its privileges. AmEx cardholders can cash personal checks at offices abroad (up to $1000, with Gold Card $5000) as well as withdraw money from their home bank checking accounts for free; offices can also help with reservations, lost travel documents, and the provision of temporary IDs. **Global Assist,** a 24-hour hotline available to cardholders, offers information and legal assistance in emergencies (800-554-2639 in the U.S. and Canada; from elsewhere call collect 202-783-7474). AmEx members can also have their mail held at one of the 1500-plus AmEx offices around the world. American Express features a free **Express Cash** service, which lets enrolled cardholders access cash from their accounts at any ATM with the AmEx trademark. Each transaction costs between $2.50 and $10, not including conversion fees and interest.

MasterCard (800-999-0454) and **VISA** (800-336-8472) credit cards are sold by individual banks, and each bank offers different credit card services. Both cards can be used at ATMs; to obtain a PIN (personal identification number), which is needed to access ATMs, contact the issuer of the card before you travel.

SENDING MONEY

If you run out of money on the road, you can have more mailed to you in the form of **traveler's checks** bought in your name or **certified checks;** another option is **postal money orders,** available at U.S. post offices (75¢ fee for orders under $25; $700 limit per order; cash only). Certified checks are redeemable at any bank, while postal money orders can be cashed at post offices upon display of two IDs (one of which must contain a photo). Keep receipts; money orders are refundable if lost.

American Express cardholders can cash personal checks at any full-service **American Express** office; if necessary, checks can be mailed to AmEx offices and held for recipients. The **American Express MoneyGram** service allows travelers (and the friends and families of travelers) to wire and receive money from over 70 countries. (Bear in mind, however, that some European and Australian AmEx offices can only *receive* MoneyGrams—which won't help you if you're stuck penniless in D.C.) Fees are commensurate with the amount of money being sent and the speed of the service being requested—10-minute, overnight, or 3-5 day delivery. Call (800) 543-4080 for information about rates and participating offices. For a list of American Express offices in Washington, see **Traveler's Checks,** p. 30.

To take advantage of a classic, time-honored, and expensive service, use **Western Union** (800-325-6000 in the U.S., Mexico, and Canada; in Europe, call the London office at 448 17 41 36 39 or 0 800 83 38 33). You or someone else can phone in a credit card number, or else someone can bring cash to a Western Union office. Fees depend not on how far the money's going, but on how much is being sent. Charges are $29 for $250, $40 for $500, and $50 for $1000. As always, you need ID to pick up your money. Funds will usually be available within 15 minutes. Western Union services are available at dozens of locations in D.C.

If time is of the essence, you can have money **wired** directly from one bank to another for about $30 (plus the commission charged by your home bank) for sums of less than $1000. Once you've found a bank that will accept a wire, write or telegram your home bank with your account number, the name and address of the bank to receive the wire, and a routing number. Also notify the bank of the form of ID that the second bank should accept before paying the money.

Bank drafts or **international money orders** are cheaper but slower. You pay a commission of $15-20 on the draft, plus the cost of sending it registered air mail. As a last resort for visitors from abroad, **embassies** may wire home for you and deduct the cost from the money you receive. Don't expect them to be happy about it.

TAXES AND TIPPING

The prices quoted throughout *Let's Go: Washington, D.C.* are the amounts before sales tax has been added. Sales tax in D.C. is 10%. Hotel tax is 13%, with an additional $1.50 occupancy tax per room per night.

Remember that service is never included on a D.C. tab. Tip cab drivers and waiters about 15%; especially good waiters—or those who work at especially good restaurants—are often tipped 20% of the tab. Tip hairdressers 10% and bellhops around $1 per bag. Bartenders usually expect between 50¢ and $1 per drink.

■■■ STAYIN' ALIVE

Emergency (police, fire, ambulance): 911, TDD 727-3323. **Police:** 727-1010. Use this for inquiries that are not urgent. 24 hrs.

SAFETY

In 1942, D.C. became the "Murder Capital of the U.S." according to *Newsweek*, with over twice New York City's murder rate. Exactly fifty years later, it happened again, thanks to widespread addiction to crack and the increasing availability of assault weapons. Although homicides have declined since 1992, and the nation's capital is no longer its leading supplier of corpses, Washington is still no city to be trifled with. The murder epidemic, while mostly an affair of drug dealers shooting one another, sometimes catches innocents in its crossfire. Most of the slaughters occur in places most visitors do not frequent, such as NE, SE, and east of 14th St. NW (although hold-ups and shootings, often in daylight, do take place in other, more tourist-populated parts of the city). If you enter these areas, try to do so in a car, and exercise extreme caution.

Use common sense. Protect yourself first, then your money. Avoid public parks after dark. Walk on busy, well-lit streets whenever possible. When you're walking alone, walk fast and look impatient to get where you're going—even if you don't know where you're going. Avoid dark alleys and doorways. Don't walk through parking lots at night. Whenever possible, *Let's Go* warns of unsafe neighborhoods, but only your eyes can tell you for sure if you've wandered into one; buildings in disrepair, vacant lots, and general desertedness are all signs.

Marginal areas such as Logan Circle and Chinatown now host community patrols consisting of civic-minded civilians in orange hats; these volunteers pound the pavement to scare away drug dealers and reassure the neighbors that the streets belong to everyone. Count on the orange hats for directions or other friendly assistance.

Both men and women may want to carry a small whistle to scare off attackers or to attract attention. You can call 911, for police or an ambulance, for free on any public phone. The Metro system itself is almost crime-free, but some areas it stops in are not. When deciding where to stay, think about where you'll be going late at night, and how you'll get back—especially in Adams-Morgan, a wonderful neighborhood with lousy Metro connections. After the Metro shuts down, around midnight, D.C.'s cheap zone fare system makes taxis a good choice for getting back home.

There is no sure-fire set of precautions that will protect you from all situations you might encounter when you travel. A good self-defense course will give you more concrete ways to react to different types of aggression, but it might cost you more money than your trip. **Model Mugging** (East Coast 617-232-7900; Midwest 312-338-4545; West Coast 415-592-7300), a national organization with offices in several major cities, teaches a comprehensive course on self-defense. (Course prices vary from $400 to $500. Women's and men's courses offered.) Community colleges frequently offer self-defense courses at more affordable prices.

SECURITY

Thieves prey on tourists for one good reason: they carry more money than the rest of the world. Your best bet is not to look like one, especially away from the Mall. The farther you go from the Smithsonian, the less you should stand out. Dress modestly. Leave the three cameras at home, and don't hang the one you did bring around your neck. Don't gawk at buildings or people, don't unfold maps on the sidewalk, and use discretion when asking for directions (when in doubt, try a storekeeper). Keep a sharp eye out for fast-fingered pick-pockets and slick con artists. Also, be alert in public telephone booths. If you must say your calling-card number, do so very quietly. And if somebody really insists on using the booth, give the phone up pronto—drug dealers often make transactions on public phones.

As for your property—don't carry your money in your back pocket; don't count it on the street; and don't leave it dangling from a bag or pouch that can be easily grabbed off your shoulder. Women should sling **purses** over the shoulder and under the opposite arm. Keep your important documents—ID, passport, traveler's check numbers and receipts—separate from the bulk of your belongings, along with a credit card. **Necklace pouches** that stay under your shirt are the best money carriers; they are not easily accessible, though, and large ones can be quite uncomfortable. **Money belts** can be worn around your waist and buried under one or all your layers of clothing—these are more convenient and nearly theft-proof. Try to memorize as many of your important numbers as possible in case your documentation disappears: passport, ID, driver's license, health-insurance policy, traveler's checks, and credit cards. Making **photocopies** of important documents will allow you to replace them with greater ease in case they are lost or stolen.

Wherever you stow your belongings, either for the day or for the evening, try to keep your valuables on your person. In the dorm-style rooms of some hostels, consider this rule ironclad. *Even a trip to the shower can cost you a wallet or camera.* At night, sleep with your valuables under your pillow, and put the straps of your backpack or bag around the leg of your bed. **Lockers** at bus and train stations are generally safe. **Safes** are fine in higher-quality hotels of international repute, but in guest houses, you may want to think twice before leaving your prized possessions with the owner.

Travel Assistance International, 1133 15th St. NW, Washington, D.C. (800-821-2828 or 331-1609; fax 331-1530), provides a 24-hr. hotline for emergencies and referrals.

ALCOHOL AND DRUGS

You must be 21 years old to purchase **alcoholic beverages** legally. Many bars and stores will want to see a photo ID (a driver's license or other valid government-issued document) before selling you alcohol. More popular drinking spots, as well as more upscale liquor stores, are likely to card—and ruthlessly, at that. Bars and clubs are allowed to serve alcohol until 3am. If you want to drink hard alcohol on Sundays, stock up on Saturday night—only beer and wine can be sold in D.C. on Sunday.

Possession of marijuana, cocaine, and most opiate derivatives (among many other chemicals) is punishable by stiff fines and imprisonment. Driving under the influence of alcohol or drugs is stupid. It is also punishable by law.

If you carry **prescription drugs,** have a copy of the prescriptions ready for U.S. Customs to inspect.

■■■ HEALTH

Before you leave, check whether your insurance policy covers medical costs incurred while traveling (see **Insurance,** p. 35). Always have proof of insurance as well as policy numbers with you. If you choose to risk traveling without insurance, you may have to rely on public health organizations and clinics that treat patients without demanding proof of solvency. Call the **local hotlines** or **crisis centers** listed on p. 35. Operators at these organizations have numbers for public-health organizations and clinics that treat patients without demanding proof of solvency. University teaching hospitals usually run inexpensive clinics as well. If you require **emergency treatment,** call **911** or go to the emergency room of the nearest hospital.

If you have a chronic medical condition that requires **medication** on a regular basis, be sure to consult your physician before you leave. Carry copies of your prescriptions and always distribute medication or syringes among all your carry-on and checked baggage in case any of your bags is lost. If you wear glasses or contact lenses, carry an extra prescription and a spare pair.

Any traveler with a medical condition that cannot be easily recognized (i.e., diabetes, epilepsy, heart conditions, allergies to antibiotics) may want to obtain a **Medic Alert Identification Tag.** The internationally recognized tag indicates the nature of the bearer's problem and provides the number for Medic Alert's 24-hour hotline. Attending medical personnel can call this number to obtain information about the member's medical history. Lifetime membership (tag, annually updated wallet card, and 24-hr. hotline access) begins at $35. Contact Medic Alert Foundation, P.O. Box 1009, Turlock, CA 95381-1009 (800-432-5378). The **American Diabetes Association,** 1660 Duke St., Alexandria, VA 22314 (800-232-3472), provides copies of the article "Travel and Diabetes" as well as diabetic ID cards, which show the carrier's diabetic status. Contact your local ADA office for information.

All travelers should be concerned about **HIV,** the virus that causes **Acquired Immune Deficiency Syndrome (AIDS),** the leading cause of death of Americans aged 25 to 44. D.C. has the fifth highest number of AIDS cases in the U.S. HIV is transmitted through blood, semen, vaginal secretions, and breast milk. To protect yourself and your partner, use a **latex condom.** Other types of condoms have larger pores than latex. While semen might not pass through these larger pores, HIV can. Only use **water based lubricant.** Oil based lubricants destroy the integrity of latex, rendering them ineffective as a barrier to infection. If you think you might have been exposed to HIV, you may want to consider getting an **HIV Antibody Test.** Once infection has occurred, there is a three to six month **window period** during which the body begins to produce antibodies, so you'll have to wait three to six months from the suspected incident to get tested. For more information on HIV/AIDS and testing, call The Center for Disease Control's **AIDS Hotline** (800-342-2437, TDD 800-243-7889. Spanish 800-344-7332. Spanish hotline operates daily 8am-2am Eastern Time. Other hotlines are 24 hrs.).

Other **sexually transmitted diseases (STDs)** are more common and easier to get than HIV. Condoms *may* protect you, but oral and even tactile contact with sores can lead to transmission. Most STDs are unpleasant but easily treated; others such as herpes (for which there is no cure) and Hepatitis B can cause problems for life. For more information contact the U.S. Center for Disease Control's **STDs Hotline** at 800-227-8922. (Open Mon.-Fri. 8am-11pm Eastern Time.)

Contraception is easily obtainable in D.C.; condoms can be found in any pharmacy, usually right on the shelves.

MEDICAL CARE

Children's National Medical Center, 111 Michigan Ave. NW (884-5000).
Georgetown University Medical Center, 3800 Reservoir Rd. NW (687-2000).

Howard University Hospital, 2041 Georgia Ave. NW (865-6100).
Sibley Memorial Hospital, 5255 Loughboro Rd. NW (537-4000).
George Washington Univ. Medical Center, 901 23rd St. NW (994-1000).

■■■ HELP LINES

Traveler's Aid Society: Main office at 512 C St. NE (546-3120). Helpful in emergencies. Open Mon.-Fri. 9am-5pm. Other desks at Union Station (546-3120, TDD 371-1937; open Mon.-Sat. 9:30am-5:30pm, Sun. 12:30-5:30pm), National Airport (703-419-3972, TDD 703-419-3977; open Mon.-Fri. 9am-9pm, Sat.-Sun. 9am-6pm), and Dulles International Airport (703-661-8636, TDD 703-260-0175; open Mon.-Fri. 10am-9pm, Sat.-Sun. 10am-6pm).
AIDS Information Line: 332-2437, Mon.-Sat. 10am-9pm, Sun. 10am-5pm.
Alcohol and Drug Hotline: 783-1300. 24 hrs.
Dept. of Human Services Crisis Line: 561-7000. 24 hrs.
Rape Crisis Center: 333-7273. 24 hrs.
National Organization for Victim Assistance: 232-6682. 24 hrs.
Gay and Lesbian Hotline: 833-3234. 7-11pm.
Medical Referral, at George Washington University Hospital: 994-4112.
Poison Center: 625-3333. 24 hrs.
Park Police: 619-7300. Emergencies in Rock Creek Park or on federal parklands.
Annoying Caller Service (yes, we mean prank phone calls): 508-7556. Mon.-Thurs. 8am-6pm, Fri. 9am-6pm.

■■■ INSURANCE

Beware of purchasing unnecessary coverage for a trip to D.C.—your current policies might well extend to many travel-related accidents. **Homeowners' insurance** (or your family's coverage) often covers theft during travel. Homeowners are generally covered against loss of travel documents (passports, plane tickets, railpasses, etc.) up to about $500. **Canadians** are protected by their home province's health insurance plan up to 90 days after leaving the country; check with your provincial Ministry of Health or the Health Plan Headquarters.

International Student or **Teacher ID Cards** provide $3000 worth of accident and illness insurance and $100 per day for up to 60 days of hospitalization while the card is valid, and give you access to a toll-free Traveler's Assistance hotline (800-626-2427; outside the U.S. call collect 713-267-2525) whose multilingual staff can provide help in medical, legal, and financial emergencies. **STA** offers a more expensive, more comprehensive plan. **American Express** cardholders receive automatic flight and car rental insurance on purchases made with the card.

Remember that insurance companies usually require a copy of the police reports for claims involving thefts. Evidence of having paid medical expenses (docto's statements and/or receipts) is necessary for medical claims to be honored. Don't ignore the time limits on filing for reimbursement that many companies impose, and always carry policy numbers and proof of insurance. Some of the plans listed below offer cash advances or guaranteed bills. If your coverage does not include on-the-spot payments or cash transferrals, budget extra for emergencies.

Access America, Inc., 6600 West Broad St., P.O. Box 11188, Richmond, VA 23230 (800-284-8300; fax (804) 673-1491). Covers trip cancellation/interruption, on-the-spot hospital admittance costs, and emergency medical evacuation. 24-hr. hotline.
Globalcare Travel Insurance, 220 Broadway, Lynnfield, MA 01940 (800-821-2488; fax 617-592-7720). Complete medical, legal, emergency, and travel-related services. On-the-spot payments and special student programs.
Travel Guard International, 1145 Clark St., Stevens Point, WI 54481 (800-826-1300 or 715-345-0505; fax 715-345-0525). "Travel Guard Gold" packages: Basic ($19), Deluxe ($39), and Comprehensive (9% of total trip cost) for medical

expenses, baggage and travel documents, travel delay, baggage delay, emergency assistance, and trip cancellation/interruption. 24-hr. emergency hotline.

■■■ INTERNS AND INTERNSHIPS

Sensible year-round Washington politicos escape in the summer from their sweltering city. Their ranks are fortified by an influx of collegiate go-getters from all over the country. To some, the pilgrimage to D.C. is the requisite first step toward the power and the glory. They are the **summer interns,** and for them, summertime Washington is *The Future.*

It's not really quite so glamorous as all that, however. The projects most interns spend their summer pursuing are so far from the heartbeat of American politics that they might as well be working as caddies. Interns are generally **glorified receptionist/gofers** who may, if they're lucky, get thrown a minor project to work on at the behest of a low-level staffer. Still, proximity to power is a decent substitute for real power; even if interns have nothing to do with the day's debates and scandals, they at least hear and chat about them constantly.

The main employer in the summer internship scheme is Congress; senators might hire anywhere from five to 15 interns, and the typical Representative's office has two or three. House interns usually hail from their boss's own district, whereas Senate internships are less bound by geography. Many interns work for a committee or a subcommittee, meaning *de facto* that they work for the committee chair (since the 1994 elections, invariably a Republican). Other prime intern-havens are think tanks, lobbying groups, and executive-branch departments or agencies like the State Department. If you're interested, start early; January is not too soon to be making inquiries. Connections help, of course—this *is* politics.

To begin the process, send many, many, many cover letters/resumes to congressional offices, the White House, government departments, the Smithsonian, and any other agency that interests you. The following is a list of potentially useful publications that may facilitate your internship search.

Peterson's Internships 1995 (Princeton, NJ; Perterson's, 1994).
The Complete Guide to Washington Internships, edited by Jeffrey Marc Parness (Brooklyn, NY; Washington Intern Services, 1988).
Student Access Guide to America's Top 100 Internships, by Mark Oldman (NY, NY; Villard Books, 1993).
Internships and Careers in International Affairs, by James P. Muldoon (NY, NY; United Nations, 1992).
The Technology and Society Internships Directory: A Comprehensive Guide to Washington, D.C. Internships 1985-86 (Student Pugwash Internship Clearinghouse, 1985). Still provides useful information; check it out at a library.
Directory of Washington Internships: A Guide to Current Internship Programs and Placements in the Nation's Capitol, by Debra L. Mann (National Society for Internships and Experiential Education).

The vast majority of the summer opportunities for college students are non-paying, and life in Washington is rarely cheap. Fortunately, there are ways to finagle some cash out of the deal. Some universities and foundations award **grants** to students to cover the summer expenses of working at an unpaid public-sector job. Here and there, a government branch might have some intern funds at its disposal; the House of Representatives, for instance, retains an endowment (the Lyndon Baines Johnson, or LBJ, fund) that gives each Member $2000 to split among any number of interns from his or her home district. In any case, interning in D.C. is rarely a profitable endeavor and usually requires a bit of savings or a magical source of disposable funds (or a well-placed extended family). Interning for half the summer is a viable and common option that allows time for some gainful employment; the wiliest get themselves out of Washington before the real dog days of August hit.

The intern social scene can be remarkably homogeneous; as a group, these upstart men and women are probably less diverse than the people that run our country (if that's possible). Most collegiate interns live in the dorms of George Washington, American, or Georgetown Universities (all of which are usually booked by April), in Georgetown townhouse sublets, or in apartments near Capitol Hill. Most of them also go to happy hours after work, hobnob in Georgetown or Hill bars at night, and play softball on weekends on the Mall for their college's D.C. summer squad. And *all* of them seem to take the oppressive #30/32/34/36 bus at 8:35am from the corner of Wisconsin and O St. NW. At all these locales—bus, bar, dorm—the unspoken main business of an ambitious Washington summer is going on: the schmoozing and smiling, the meeting and remembering, the shucking and jiving with peers that will someday pay off.

But for all the cynicism that a D.C. internship might inspire, it has the potential to be an unqualified winner. It is the most basic way of getting a foot in the door of national politics and the best way to start learning how Washington really works. For every internship that's reserved for someone's kid as a political favor, there are four that aren't. And despite the heat, summertime Washington has a mysterious ability to perpetually convince young people that it is definitely the place to be.

■■■ WOMEN TRAVELERS

Women exploring any area on their own inevitably face additional safety concerns. Forgo cheap accommodations in city outskirts—the risks outweigh any savings—and stick to our recommended youth hostels, university accommodations, bed and breakfasts, and organizations offering rooms to women only. A woman should *never* hitchhike alone; even in groups it can be dangerous.

If you find yourself the object of catcalls or unwelcome propositions, your best answer is no answer. Always look as if you know where you're going (even when you don't), and maintain an assertive, confident posture wherever you go. If you feel uncomfortable asking strangers for information or directions, it may be easier to approach other women or couples. Always carry enough change for a bus, taxi, or phone call. And in emergencies, don't hesitate to yell for help.

Know the emergency numbers for the area you're visiting; see **Stayin' Alive,** p. 32 and **Help Lines,** p. 35. More information and safety tips can be found in Maggie and Gemma Moss's *Handbook for Women Travelers,* available from Piatkus Books, 5 Windmill St., London W1P 1HF, England (11 44 0171 631 0710). The folks who produced *Gaia's Guide* (no longer available) are now publishing *Women Going Places* ($14), a women's travel and resource guide emphasizing women-owned and -operated enterprises. The guide is aimed at lesbians but useful to all women, and is available from INLAND Book Company, P.O. Box 120261, East Haven, CT 06512 (203-467-4257). The latest book on women's travel to hit the market, *A Journey of One's Own* by Thalia Zepatos, provides lots of good advice as well as a specific and manageable bibliography of books and resources. The book is published by Eighth Mountain Press and retails for $14.95.

■■■ GOLDEN GIRLS AND BOYS

Discounts abound in D.C. for travelers 60 and over. All you need is identification proving your age. Pick up the free *Golden Washingtonian Club Gold Mine* directory—which lists establishments offering 10-20% discounts to seniors on goods and services—at local hotel desks or at the **D.C. Office on Aging** (441 4th St. NW), or receive one through the mail by calling 724-5626 (ask for the directory by name). The D.C. Office on Aging also offers an information and referral service to residents and visitors 60 and over, and distributes a Senior Yellow Pages which lists caregivers and professionals of interest to senior citizens. You can obtain information over the phone on a range of topics affecting seniors, including nutrition, housing, transportation, Medicare, legal aid, and recreation (724-5626; open Mon.-Fri. 8:15am-4:45pm). The following are other organizations of interest to older travelers:

American Association of Retired Persons (AARP), 601 E St. NW, Washington, D.C. 20049 (434-2277). Membership open to U.S. residents aged 50 and over. Members can take advantage of benefits and services including the **AARP Travel Experience** from American Express (800-927-0111), the **AARP Motoring Plan** from Amoco (800-334-3300), and discounts on lodging, car rental, and sight-seeing. Membership $8 per couple. Office open Mon.-Fri. 9am-5pm.

National Council of Senior Citizens, 1331 F St. NW, Washington, D.C. 20004 (347-8800). Membership ($12/yr., $30 for 3 yrs., or $150 for a lifetime) provides an individual or couple with access to hotel and auto rental discounts, a senior citizen newspaper, a discount travel agency, and supplemental Medicare insurance (if you're over 65).

Gateway Books, 2023 Clemens Rd., Oakland, CA 94602 (510-530-0299; fax 510-530-0497). Publishes *Get Up and Go: A Guide for the Mature Traveler* ($10.95) and *Adventures Abroad* ($12.95) which offer recommendations and general hints for the budget-conscious senior. Call 800-669-0773 for credit card orders.

■■■ GAY & LESBIAN TRAVELERS

Washington has large openly gay and lesbian populations, but outlying communities in the region can be intolerant. In the District, pick up the free weekly *Washington Blade,* D.C.'s indispensable but dull gay newspaper covering restaurants, bars, services, meetings, and events. You'll find it in stores and restaurants across the District. *The Gay and Lesbian Services Guide* ($4) lists businesses and organizations in the metro area that serve the gay community; you can pick it up at the bookstore **Lambda Rising,** 1625 Connecticut Ave. NW (462-6969), near R St. In Baltimore, the *Baltimore Alternative* and the *Fun Map* cover bars, restaurants, and hotels for gays and lesbians. For more information about services for the gay and lesbian community, as well as current, up-to-date bar and club listings, see **Bisexual, Gay, and Lesbian D.C.,** p. 236.

Spartacus International Gay Guide: $29.95. Guide for gay men, listing bars, restaurants, hotels, bookstores, and hotlines across the globe. Available in the U.S. from Lambda Rising. Published by Bruno Gmünder, Postfach 301345, D-1000 Berlin 30, Germany (tel. 49 (30) 25 49 82 00).

The Damron Address Book: $14 plus $4 shipping. Over 8000 listings of bars, restaurants, guest houses, and services catering to gay males. Published by Damron.

Ferrari's Places of Interest ($16), **Ferrari's Places for Men** ($15), and **Ferrari's Places for Women** ($13). Available in bookstores, or by mail order (postage $3.50 for the first item, 50¢ for each additional item). Ferrari Publications, P.O. Box 37887, Phoenix, AZ 85069 (602-863-2408).

The Women's Traveler: $10 plus $4 shipping. A travel guide for lesbians. Maps of 50 major U.S. cities; 6000 listings of bars, restaurants, accommodations, book stores, and services. Published by Damron.

■■■ TRAVELERS WITH DISABILITIES

With a little research and planning ahead, the disabled traveler can gain access to all but the most awkwardly built establishments. Parts of Washington, especially the federally owned parts, do their best to accommodate those with disabilities. Call ahead to inquire about restrictions on motorized wheelchairs.

The **Information, Protection, and Advocacy Center for Handicapped Individuals** (966-8081, TDD 966-2500) can help in any sort of emergency, large or small. Contact the center for a copy of their book *Access Washington: A Guide to Metropolitan Washington for the Physically Disabled* ($4), which lists the best-equipped accommodations, restaurants, and sights. Visually impaired persons should write to **Washington Ear, Inc.,** 35 University Blvd. E., Silver Spring, MD 20901 (301-681-6636), which sells large-print and tactile atlases of the Washington area. **Columbia Lighthouse for the Blind,** 1421 P Street NW, Washington, D.C. 20005 (462-2900) distributes free tactile maps of the Metro system, as well as two free pamphlets: *Guide to Washington, D.C. for Visually Impaired People* and *Washington Highlights: Tour Information for People with Disabilities.*

You can also root around in a number of more general books helpful to travelers with disabilities. One good resource is *Access to the World,* by Louise Weiss ($16.95). Check local bookstores, or contact **Facts on File, Inc.,** 460 Park Ave., New York, NY 10016 (800-829-0500, 212-683-2244 from AK and HI). **Twin Peaks Press** publishes three books: *Directory for Travel Agencies for the Disabled* ($19.95), *Travel for the Disabled* ($19.95), and *Wheelchair Vagabond* ($14.95), which discusses camping and travel in cars, vans, and RVs. Order from Twin Peaks Press, P.O. Box 129, Vancouver, WA 98666-0129 (order desk 800-637-2256; fax 206-696-3210)

If you are planning to visit a national park or attraction run by the National Park Service, you should obtain a free **Golden Access Passport,** which is available at all park entrances and from federal offices whose functions relate to land, forests, or wildlife. The Golden Access Passport entitles disabled travelers and their families to enter parks for free and provides a 50% reduction on all campsite and parking fees.

Arrange transportation well in advance to ensure a smooth trip. If you give sufficient notice, some major car rental agencies offer hand-controlled vehicles at select locations. Both **Amtrak** and the airlines will accommodate disabled passengers if notified at least 72 hours in advance. Hearing-impaired travelers may contact Amtrak (800-872-7245, in PA 800-322-9537) using teletype printers. **Greyhound** buses will also provide free travel for a companion; if you are without a fellow traveler, call Greyhound (800-752-4841) at least 48 hours before you plan to leave and it will make arrangements to assist you. For information on transportation availability in D.C., contact the **American Public Transit Association,** 1201 New York Ave. NW, Suite 400, Washington, D.C. 20005 (202-898-4000).

The following organizations offer services and information which may be of interest to travelers with physical disabilities:

Moss Rehabilitation Hospital Travel Information Service, 1200 W. Tabor Rd., Philadelphia, PA 19141 (215-456-9603). A telephone resource center and an excellent source of information on tourist sights, accommodations, and transportation for the disabled. Refers callers if they cannot provide information.

Society for the Advancement of Travel for the Handicapped, 347 Fifth Ave., Suite 610, New York, NY 10016 (212-447-7284; fax 212-725-8253). Publishes quarterly travel newsletter, *SATH News,* and several information booklets (free for members, $3 for nonmembers). Membership is $45 per year, $25 for senior citizens and students.

American Foundation for the Blind, 11 Penn Plaza, New York, NY 10011 (212-502-7600). Open Mon.-Fri. 8:30am-4:30pm. For a catalog of products, contact **Lighthouse Low-Vision Products** (800-829-0500).

The following organizations arrange tours or trips for disabled travelers:

Directions Unlimited, 720 N. Bedford Rd., Bedford Hills, NY 10507 (800-533-5343; in NY 914-241-1700; fax 914-241-0243). Specializes in arranging individual and group vacations, tours, and cruises for the physically disabled.

Flying Wheels Travel Service, 143 W. Bridge St., Owatonne, MN 55060 (800-535-6790; fax 507-451-1685). Arranges trips for groups and individuals in wheelchairs or with other sorts of limited mobility.

The Guided Tour, Elkins Park House, Suite 114B, 7900 Old York Road, Elkins Park, PA 19117-2339 (800-738-5841 or 215-635-2637). Organizes year-round travel programs, domestic and international, for persons with developmental and physical challenges (including those requiring renal dialysis). Call or write for a free brochure.

■■■ TRAVELING WITH CHILDREN

Family vacations are recipes for disaster—unless you slow your pace and plan ahead a bit. Washington overflows with great opportunities for kids; some are obvious (the National Zoo), others are less so (the Folklife Festival). When deciding where to stay, remember the special needs of young children; if you pick a B&B, call and make sure it's child-friendly. If you rent a car, make sure the rental company provides a car seat for younger children.

Let's Go lists many sights of particular interest to children. The most comprehensive lists of kid-friendly events, however, appear every Friday in the *Washington Post's* Weekend section. Smithsonian Kite Day in April and the Navy Band Lollipop Concert in August are always popular. The following books can help you avoid the constant complaints of boredom: *Going Places with Children in Washington, D.C.* ($9.95; taxes may apply), published by the staff of Green Acres School, 11701 Danville Drive, Rockville, MD 20852, and *Washington! Adventure for Kids* ($6.95), published by Vandamere.

Also consult *Travel with Children* by Maureen Wheeler ($10.95 plus $1.50 shipping), available from Lonely Planet Publications, Embarcadero West, 155 Philbert St., Suite 251, Oakland, CA 94607 (800-275-8555 or 510-893-8555; fax 510-893-8563). Written *for* children, the *Kidding Around* series includes a book on D.C. ($10 per book, $2.75 shipping for 1st book, 50¢ for each additional). Write John Muir Publications, P.O. Box 613, Santa Fe, NM 87504 (800-285-4078).

■■■ VEGETARIAN AND KOSHER

Vegetarians won't have any problem eating well and cheap in D.C. *Let's Go* lists the best vegetarian places we could find. For more, contact the **North American Vegetarian Society,** P.O. Box 72, Dolgeville, NY 13329 (518-568-7970) for vegetarian eateries in D.C. and other travel-related publications.

Travelers who keep **kosher** should call the **Kesher Israel info line** (located in Georgetown) at 338-4808 or the **Jewish Information Line** at 301-770-4848 for information about kosher restaurants. *The Jewish Travel Guide* ($12 plus $1.75 shipping), from **Ballantine-Mitchell Press,** Newbery House 890-900, Eastern Ave., Newbury Park, Ilford, Essex, IG2 7HH ((181) 599 38 66; fax 599 09 84), lists Jewish institutions, synagogues, and kosher restaurants in over 80 countries.

■■■ NUTS & BOLTS

MEASUREMENTS

Although the metric system has made considerable inroads into American business and science, the British system of weights and measures continues to prevail in the U.S. The following is a list of U.S. units and their metric equivalents:

1 inch (in.) =25.4 millimeters (mm)
1 foot (ft.) = 0.30 meter (m)
1 yard (yd.) = 0.91 meter (m)
1 mile (mi.) = 1.61 kilometers (km)
1 ounce (oz.; mass) = 28.35 grams (g)
1 fluid ounce (fl. oz.; volume) = 29.59 milliliters (mL)
1 pound (lb.) = 0.45 kilogram (kg)
1 liquid quart (qt.) = 0.95 liter (L)
1 gallon (gal.) = 3.78 liter (L)

Electric outlets throughout the U.S., Canada, and Mexico provide current at 117 volts, 60 cycles (Hertz), and American plugs usually have two rectangular prongs; plugs for larger appliances often have a third prong for the purpose of grounding. Appliances designed for the European electrical system (220 volts) will not operate without a transformer and a plug adapter (this includes electric systems for disinfecting contact lenses). Transformers are sold to convert specific wattages (e.g., 0-50 watt transformers for razors and radios, larger watt transformers for hair dryers and other appliances). The U.S. uses the Fahrenheit **temperature scale** rather than the Centigrade (Celsius) scale. To convert Fahrenheit to Centigrade temperatures, subtract 32, then multiply by 5/9. 32°F is the freezing point of water, 212° its boiling point, and room temperature hovers around 70°.

TIME

U.S. residents tell time on the 12-hour, not 24-hour, clock. Hours after noon are *post meridiem* or pm (e.g. 2pm); hours before noon are *ante meridiem* or am (e.g. 2am). Noon is sometimes referred to as 12pm and midnight as 12am; *Let's Go* uses "noon" and "midnight." The Continental U.S. is divided into four **time zones:** Eastern, Central, Mountain, and Pacific. Hawaii and Alaska claim their own time zones as well. When it's noon Eastern time, it's 11am Central, 10am Mountain, 9am Pacific, 8am Alaskan, and 7am Hawaiian-Aleutian. D.C. follows Eastern Standard Time (EST) and, like most states, advances its clocks by one hour for **daylight saving time.** In 1996, daylight saving time will begin on Sunday, April 7, at 2am. It will end on Sunday, October 27, at 2am; set your clocks back one hour to 1am then.

GETTING THERE

BUDGET TRAVEL ORGANIZATIONS

AYH/HI Travel Center, 1108 K St. NW (783-4943), below Asian Kabab House! Metro: Metro Center or Mt. Vernon Sq. Travel guides, backpacks, and other equipment to go with your new *Let's Go* books. Discounts on airfares, Eurail passes, and binders full of information on different countries. AYH/HI cards and discounts on merchandise. Open Mon.-Fri. 10am-6pm, Sat. 10am-5pm.

Campus Travel, 52 Grosvenor Gardens, London SW1W 0AG. 37 branches nationwide in the UK. Puts out booklets including travel suggestions, average prices, dates of local holidays, and other general information for British travelers in Europe and North America. Also offers a bookings service via telephone: from Europe (0171) 730 34 02, from North America (0171) 730 21 01, worldwide (0171) 730 81 11.

Council Travel sells charter flight tickets, guidebooks, ISIC, ITIC, and GO 25 cards, hostelling cards, and travel gear. Their **Washington, D.C.** branch is located at 3300 M St. NW(337-6464) at the corner of 33rd St. in Georgetown. Forty other U.S. offices, including: 729 Boylston St., Suite 201, **Boston,** MA 02116 (617-266-1926); 1093 Broxton Ave., Suite 220, **Los Angeles,** CA 90024 (310-208-3551); 205 East 42nd St., **New York,** NY 10017 (212-661-1450); 530 Bush St., Ground Floor, **San Francisco,** CA 94108 (415-421-3473); Council Travel also has offices in Europe, including: 28A Poland St. (Oxford Circus), **London** WIV 3DB, England (011 171 437 7767).

Educational Travel Center (ETC), 438 North Frances St., Madison, WI 53703 (800-747-5551; fax 608-256-2042). Flight information and AYH/HI cards. Write for their free pamphlet *Taking Off.*

International Student Exchange Flights (ISE), 5010 East Shea Blvd., #A104, Scottsdale, AZ 85254 (602-951-1177). Budget student flights, ISE identity cards, and travel guides, including the *Let's Go* series. Free catalog.

Let's Go Travel, Harvard Student Agencies, Inc., 53-A Church St., Cambridge, MA 02138 (800-5-LETS-GO or 617-495-9649). The world's largest student-run travel

agency, Let's Go offers railpasses, AYH/HI memberships, ISIC cards, guidebooks *(Let's Go)*, maps, bargain flights, and a complete line of budget travel gear.

STA Travel, 5900 Wilshire Blvd., Ste. 2110, Los Angeles, CA 90036 (800-777-0112 nationwide). A student and youth travel organization with over 100 offices around the world offering discount airfares (for travelers under 26 and full-time students under 32), railpasses, accommodations, tours, insurance, and ISICs. In **Washington, D.C.,** it's located at 2401 Pennsylvania Ave. NW (887-0912, zip code 20037); enter on the 24th St. side of the building. Ten other U.S. offices, including: 297 Newbury St., **Boston,** MA 02116 (617-266-6014); 48 E. 11th St., **New York,** NY 10003 (212-477-7166); and 51 Grant Ave., **San Francisco,** CA 94108 (415-391-8407). In the **UK:** Priory House, 6 Wrights Lane, London W8 6TA (0171-938-4711). In **New Zealand:** 10 High St., Auckland (09-309-9723). In **Australia:** 224 Faraday St., Melbourne VIC 3053 (03-347-6911).

Travel CUTS, 187 College St., Toronto, Ontario M5T 1P7 (416-798-CUTS; fax 416-979-8167). Canada's national student travel bureau and equivalent of Council, with 40 offices across Canada. Also in the **UK:** 295-A Regent St., London W1R 7YA (0171- 637-3161). Discounted domestic and international airfares available to all; special student fares to all destinations with valid ISIC. Issuing authority for ISIC, FIYTO, and HI hostel cards. Offers free *Student Traveller* magazine, as well as info on Student Work Abroad Program (SWAP).

■■■ FROM NORTH AMERICA

■ BY PLANE

When dealing with any commercial airline, buying in advance is almost always the best bet. The commercial carriers' lowest regular offer is the **APEX** (Advanced Purchase Excursion Fare); specials advertised in newspapers may be cheaper, but have correspondingly more restrictions and fewer available seats. APEX fares provide you with confirmed reservations and often allow **"open-jaw"** tickets (landing and returning from different cities). APEX tickets must usually be purchased two to three weeks ahead of the departure date. Since it's impossible to predict exactly how far in advance a given ticket will need to be purchased, it's best to call for information as soon as you have even a rough idea of when you'll be traveling. Be sure to inquire about any restrictions on length of stay.

To obtain the **cheapest fare,** buy a round-trip ticket, stay over at least one Saturday, and limit your trip to less than 30 days if possible; traveling on off-peak days (Mon.-Thurs. morning) is usually $30-40 cheaper than traveling on the weekends. You will need to pay for the ticket within 24 hours of booking the flight, and tickets are entirely non-refundable. Any change in plans incurs a fee of between $25 (for some domestic flights) and $150 (for many international flights), even if only to change the date of departure or return. Since travel peaks between June and August and around holidays, reserve a seat several months in advance for these times. When inquiring about fares, get advance purchase as well as length of stay requirements, or else you may not be able to buy your ticket in time, or be forced to return home sooner than expected. Be aware that in the last few years, the major U.S. carriers have taken to waging **price wars** (sometimes including two-for-one specials) in the spring and early summer months. Because there is no way to tell when (if at all) such sales will occur, advance purchase may not always guarantee the lowest fare. It will guarantee a seat, though, which has its advantages.

The chances of receiving discount fares increase on **competitive routes;** flying smaller airlines instead of the national giants can also save money. Most airlines allow children under two to fly for free on the lap of an adult, but discounts for older children and seniors are more rare. Consider the **discount travel agencies** and **student-oriented agencies** listed on p. 41. Almost without exception, 21 day advance fares are cheaper than all other fares. In the summer of 1995, **Council Travel** offered the following regular (non-student) round-trip fares to Washington, D.C. The first price is the 7 day advance, the second price is the 21 day advance: **Los**

Angeles $508/$468; **Chicago** $98/$98; **Houston** $384/$369; **Miami** $158/$138; **New York** $110/$110; **Boston** $138/$98; **Seattle** $528/$488. Last-minute travelers should also ask about **"red-eye"** (all-night) flights, which are common on popular business routes.

Whenever and however you fly, call the airline the day before your departure to **reconfirm** your flight reservation. Get to the airport early to ensure that you have a seat; airlines often overbook. (On the other hand, being **"bumped"** from a flight does not spell doom if your travel plans are flexible—you will probably leave on the next flight and receive either a free ticket or a cash bonus. You might even want to bump yourself when the airline asks for volunteers.)

COMMERCIAL AIRLINES

Southwest Airlines (800-435-9792) offers quite a few outrageously low fares, but only flies to BWI. The slight inconvenience is probably worth it for the tremendous discounts. In Summer 1995, **Houston-BWI** was $99 off peak (after 7pm weekdays and all day weekends) and $122 on peak (21 day advance fare). **Chicago-BWI** was $59 off peak, $69 on peak with 21 day advance, $79 with 14 day advance. Southwest also offers occasional dirt cheap **24 hour advance** fares, and always offers student and senior discounts. **"Friends Fly Free"** allows you to take along someone for free when you purchase a regular round-trip fare.

Valujet Airlines (800-825-8538) offers cheap fares to Dulles Airport from selected major cities. The first price listed is the less than 7 days advance, the second the 7 day advances, and the last is a 21 day advance. As of late summer of 1995, Boston-Dulles was $91/$79/$52 and Chicago-Dulles was $99/$79/$59.

From New York's **La Guardia Airport,** the **Delta Shuttle** (800-221-1212) and the **USAir Shuttle** (800-428-4322) provide competing hourly flights to National Airport seven days a week (flights depart between 6:30am and 9pm on weekdays, 7:30am-9pm on weekends). While the shuttles were designed for businessfolk—with prices to match ($150 each flight on weekdays)—student and senior fares, available for anyone over 65 (on Delta 62) or under 24, stick to around $75 at all times. And on weekends (all day Saturday and until 3pm on Sunday), fares drop to $75 for everybody. Buy shuttle tickets at the gate in New York or D.C.

If you qualify for student or senior fares, expect to traverse the New York-D.C. route frequently, and have the cash on hand, you might consider buying the Delta or USAir **Flight Pack** (4 tickets $229, 8 tickets $419). Discount tickets can be used only on weekends and 10:30am-2pm and 7:30-9:30pm weekdays. Purchase Flight Packs at the airport; ID required. Both airlines also offer discounts (available to all travelers) to those who reserve early; call 7 days in advance for round-trip flights around $160, or 14 days in advance for rates around $140.

Travelers arriving from elsewhere in the U.S. may find it cheaper to fly into New York and catch a commuter shuttle than to fly directly to Washington. Call to see if this applies to your route.

CHARTER, COURIER, AND CONSOLIDATOR FLIGHTS

Charter flights can save you a lot of money if you can afford to be flexible. Many charters book passengers up to the last minute—some will not even sell tickets more than 30 days in advance. You must choose your departure and return dates when you book, and you will lose all or most of your money if you cancel your ticket. Charter companies themselves reserve the right to change the dates of your flight or even cancel the flight a mere 48 hours in advance. Delays are not uncommon. To be safe, get your ticket as early as possible, and arrive at the airport several hours before departure time (the earlier the better, since ticket agents seat passengers in the order that they've checked them in). Prices and destinations can change (sometimes markedly) from season to season; contact as many organizations as possible in order to get the best deal. Contact **Council Travel** or **Travel CUTS** for more information (see **Budget Travel Organizations,** p. 41).

Traveling as a **courier** is a little-known option. It works like this: you are a traveler seeking a cheap flight to a particular location; the courier service is a company seeking to transport merchandise to a particular location. If it happens that your destinations and schedules coincide, the courier service will sell you a cheap seat in exchange for the use of the checked luggage space which accompanies it. Courier services can offer some great deals, but their schedules may inhibit your flexibility, and their luggage restrictions limit you to carry-on items. Consult Kelly Monaghan's *Insider's Guide to Air Courier Bargains* ($15 plus $2.50 shipping), from Upper Access Publishing (UAP), P.O. Box 457, Hinesburg, VT 05461 (800-356-9315).

Ticket consolidators, also known as "bucket shops," sell unsold tickets on commercial and charter airlines. Look for their tiny ads in weekend papers (in the U.S., the Sunday *New York Times* is best), and start calling them all. Consult Kelly Monaghan's *Consolidators: Air Travel's Bargain Basement* ($5 plus $3.50 shipping), from the Intrepid Traveler, P.O. Box 438, New York, NY 10034, for more information and a list of consolidators. The following companies offer all three services:

1-800-FLY-ASAP, 1001 28th St. SW, Fargo, ND 58103 (800-FLY-ASAP; fax 701-280-5210). Friendly service and some great prices. In summer of 1995, **Chicago-D.C.** $98 roundtrip; **Boston-D.C.** $120 roundtrip; **Miami-D.C.** $140 roundtrip.

Air Tech, 584 Broadway #1007, New York, NY 10012 (212-219-7000). International flights to and from D.C. **London** or **Dublin** $179 each way. Let's Go has received multiple complaints about delays, inaccurate information, and poor service associated with AirTech. Delays of up to several days have been reported—if you are delayed, you could incur costs that outweigh initial savings.

Airhitch, 2641 Broadway, Third Floor, New York, NY 10025 (800-326-2009 or 212-864-2000 on East Coast; 800-397-1098 or 310-394-0550 on West Coast), works through more cities and to more destinations than most charter flights companies. Ask about "USAhitch" fares. Availability of flights varies *tremendously*. For a flight to D.C., call often to see if one has opened up. The Better Business Bureau of NY and Let's Go have received complaints about Airhitch; the company has recently changed ownership, but consumers should make careful inquiries. Delays of up to several days have been reported—if you are delayed, you could incur costs that outweigh initial savings.

■ BY TRAIN

The train is still one of the cheapest and most comfortable ways to travel in the U.S. **Amtrak,** 60 Massachusetts Ave. NE, Washington, D.C. 20002 (800-872-7245), offers a discount **All-Aboard America** fare that divides the continental U.S. into three regions—Eastern, Central, and Western—with three stopovers permitted and a maximum trip duration of 45 days. During the summer, rates are $198 if you travel in one region, $278 to travel in two regions, and $338 for all three (late Aug.-mid Dec. and early Jan.-mid June, rates are $178, $238, and $278). Your itinerary, including cities and dates, must be set at the time the passes are purchased; the route may not be changed once travel has begun, although times and dates may be changed at no cost.

Another discount option, available only to those who aren't citizens of North America, is the **USA Rail Pass,** which allows unlimited travel and unlimited stops over a period of either 15 or 30 days. As with the All-Aboard America program, the cost of the pass depends on the number of regions in which you wish to travel. The pass allowing 30 days of travel nationwide sells for $425 during the peak season and for $339 off-season; the 15-day nationwide pass sells for $340 during the peak season and for $229 off-season. Another discount option on Amtrak is the **Air-Rail Travel Plan,** offered in conjunction with United Airlines, which allows you to travel in one direction by train and then fly home, or vice-versa. The transcontinental plan, which allows coast-to-coast travel originating on either coast, sells for $605 peak-season and $516 off-season. The East Coast plan, which allows travel roughly as far west as Atlanta, is $417 during peak season, $373 off-peak.

Amtrak offers several **discounts** off its full fares: children ages two to 15 accompanied by a parent (½-fare); children under age two (free on the lap of an adult); senior citizens (15% off); travelers with disabilities (25% off); and current members of the U.S. Armed Forces and active-duty veterans and their dependents (20% off). Circle trips and special holiday packages can save you money as well. Keep in mind that discounted air travel, particularly for longer distances, may be cheaper than train travel. For up-to-date information and reservations, contact your local Amtrak office or call **800-USA-RAIL** from a touch-tone phone. Amtrak charges the same rate for both one-way and round-trip travel.

Amtrak's trains connect Washington to most other parts of the country through **Union Station,** 50 Massachusetts Ave. NE (484-7540). For most routes you can choose to take either a Metroliner or a regular train; Metroliners (800-523-8720) are speedier, more expensive, and usually not worth the money. Regular trains are efficient and quite pleasant.

Amtrak may be the speediest route to D.C. from **New York City,** although the USAir and Delta shuttles give it a run for its money. On weekdays, Metroliners (3 hrs.) leave approximately hourly between 6am and 8pm from Manhattan's Penn Station for Union Station; unreserved fares are $96 each way. Regular trains (3½ hrs.) leave at 3:45am, and about once an hour between 6am and 9:40pm; unreserved fares are $51. Amtrak also leaves for D.C. from **Baltimore** (Metroliner: $17, 30 min., regular: 45 min., $12), **Philadelphia** (Metroliner: 1hr. 38 min., $68; regular: 120 min., $28), and **Boston** (9 hrs., $55). Additional routes to Washington start in Richmond ($18-23); Williamsburg ($26-31); and Virginia Beach ($36-45).

Maryland's commuter trains, **MARC** (800-325-7245), also depart from Union Station. These offer weekday commuter service to **Baltimore** (5:30am-8am and 3:50-6:45pm; $5.25, roundtrip $9.50) and **Harpers Ferry, WV** ($6.75).

■ BY BUS

Getting in and out of D.C. can be done less expensively and more scenically by bus or train than by plane. Especially if you're coming from rural America or have a seriously tight budget, buses may be your best bet. **Greyhound** (800-231-2222) operates the largest number of lines, departing for D.C. daily from **Philadelphia** ($16, roundtrip $27), **New York City** ($25, roundtrip $48), **Baltimore** ($7, roundtrip $13), and **Richmond** ($17, roundtrip $32). Washington's modern **Greyhound** station, 1005 1st St. NE (800-231-2222) at L St., rises over a rather decrepit neighborhood.

A number of **discounts** are available on Greyhound's standard-fare tickets (restrictions apply): senior citizens ride for 15% off, children under 11 ride for 50% off, and children under 2 ride for free in the lap of an adult. Travelers with disabilities receive a 25% discount. Greyhound also offers **Ameripass,** deals for **unlimited travel** for 7 to 30 days ($259-559). Call for details.

East Coast Explorer, an alternative bus service connecting the cities of Boston, New York, and Washington, travels on back roads, stopping at sites of historic interest—a good bargain for those trying to tour the East Coast for cheap. Trips from New York to Washington leave Thursday mornings and visit the Amish countryside of Lancaster, Pennsylvania. Trips from Washington to New York leave Friday mornings, stopping at Newcastle, DE, and Independence National Park in Philadelphia. The bus (air-conditioned) makes pick-ups and drop-offs at most hostels and budget hotels; call between one month and one day in advance for reservations (718-694-9667 or 800-610-2680, between 8 and 11pm). Trips between New York and Washington cost $32. Buses traveling between New York and Boston leave on Mondays (northbound) and Tuesdays (southbound); $29 each way. Costs for all trips include tolls and tour guide.

■ BY CAR

The **speed limit** in and around D.C. is 55 miles per hour. D.C. is ringed by the **Capital Beltway,** or **I-495** (except where it's part of I-95); the Beltway is bisected by **U.S. 1,** which incorporates several local thoroughfares, and is intruded upon via Virginia by **I-395. I-95** shoots up from Florida, links Richmond, VA to Washington and Baltimore, then rockets up the East Coast past Boston. The high-speed **Baltimore-Washington Parkway** also connects D.C. and Baltimore. **I-270** runs northwest through Montgomery County to link up with the east-west freeway **I-70** in western Maryland. **I-595** trickles off the Capital Beltway and runs scenically east to Annapolis. **I-66** heads west through Virginia.

Most visitors who drive arrive from the north or south, on or parallel to I-95. **To go downtown from the Baltimore-Washington Pkwy.,** follow signs for **New York Ave**. From I-95, get onto the **Capital Beltway** and then choose your exit. Three of the easiest and most useful are Wisconsin Ave. (to upper NW and Georgetown), Connecticut Ave. (Chevy Chase, Upper NW, Adams-Morgan, Dupont Circle, and downtown), and New Hampshire Ave. (through Takoma to downtown). From the south, take I-95 to I-395 directly to the 14th St. Bridge or Memorial Bridge (both of which lead downtown). From the west, take I-66 east over the Roosevelt Bridge and follow signs for Constitution Ave. I-66 is simpler and faster than I-495. Vehicles on I-66 East (Mon.-Fri. 7-9am) and I-66 West (Mon.-Fri. 4-6pm) must carry at least three people (due to the "HOV-3" rule) or pay a hefty ticket. During the day, Maryland's major highways are sometimes congested; Virginia's usually are. Try to reach D.C. outside rush hour, especially if you're coming from Virginia.

■■■ FROM ABROAD

AIR PASSES

Many major U.S. airlines offer special **Visit USA** air passes and fares to international travelers. You must purchase these passes in Europe, paying one price for a certain number of flight vouchers. Each voucher is good for one flight segment on an airline's domestic system within a certain time period; typically, all travel must be completed within 30-60 days. The point of departure and the destination must be specified for each coupon at the time of purchase, and once in the U.S., any change in route will incur a fee of between $50 and $75. Dates of travel may be changed once travel has begun, usually at no extra charge. **USAir** offers voucher packages for the East coast (from $349) and all 48 states (from around $400). **United, Continental, Delta,** and **TWA** also offer programs.

■ FROM EUROPE

Travelers from Europe will experience the least competition for inexpensive seats during the off-season. Fares are least expensive around Feb.-Mar. Rates generally go up in May, and then go up again in mid-June. The highest priced fares last until around mid-Sept. Remember that discount travel agencies offer more reasonable rates even during the peak season and students receive discounts during all seasons.

If you decide to fly with a commercial airline rather than through a charter agency or ticket consolidator, you'll be purchasing greater reliability, security, and flexibility. Many major airlines offer reduced-fare options, such as three-day advance-purchase fares: these tickets can be purchased only within 72 hours of the time of the departure, and are restricted to youths under a certain age (often 24). Check with a travel agent for availability. **TWA** (800-892-4141) and **British Airways** (800-247-9297) both offer these fares on a variety of international flights. Seat availability is known only a few days before the flight, although airlines will sometimes issue predictions. The worst crunch leaving Europe takes place from mid-June to early July, while August is uniformly tight for returning flights; at no time can you count on getting a seat right away. In Summer 1995, average fares were $369 each way Mon.-

Thu. and $394 Fri.-Sun. Smaller, budget airlines often undercut major carriers by offering bargain fares on scheduled flights. Competition for seats on these smaller carriers during peak season is fierce—book early.

■ FROM AUSTRALIA AND NEW ZEALAND

Try one of the budget-travel agencies listed. STA Travel is the largest international agency you'll find, with offices in Sydney, Melbourne, and Auckland. For more information on STA, see **Budget Travel Organizations,** p. 41.

Qantas, Air New Zealand, United, and **Northwest** fly between Australia or New Zealand and the United States. Prices are roughly equivalent among the four (American carriers tend to be a bit less), but the cities they serve differ. Advance purchase fares from Australia have extremely tough restrictions. If you are uncertain about your plans, pay extra for an advance purchase ticket that has only a 50% penalty for cancellation. Many travelers from Australia and New Zealand reportedly take Singapore Air or other Far East-based carriers during the initial leg of their trips; check with STA or another budget agency for more comprehensive information.

■■■ WASHINGTON'S AIRPORTS

From within the U.S., it's most convienent to fly into **National Airport** (703-419-8000). Doing so will save you money and headaches, since National is on the Metro and close to Washington by car. Driving from downtown is easy (take I-395 south to the George Washington Pkwy. southbound; follow signs for the airport). In theory the ride from downtown to the terminal should take about 15 minutes; in traffic, it can take much longer. Metrorail's blue and yellow lines serve National Airport; the terminals are a short walk (and a shorter shuttle ride) away from the Metro. Cabs are obviously the most convenient way to get to and from the airport, but convenience carries a price ($10-15 from downtown); for all but the most luggage-laden, there's little reason not to take the Metro. **From National to downtown,** the **Washington Flyer Express** (703-685-1400) bus runs between National and the city every 30 minutes on weekdays 6:25am to 9:25pm; on weekends they leave hourly from 6:25am to 12:25pm and every 30 minutes from 12:55pm to 9:25pm ($8, roundtrip $14). Allow about 20 to 30 minutes travel time between downtown and National. $2-4 discount on all Flyer buses for International Student ID Card holders.

Though National is more convenient, **Dulles International Airport** (703-419-8000) is Washington's major international airport; a number of domestic flights also touch down here. Driving from downtown Washington will take you about 40 minutes—but more during rush hour. (To reach the airport, take the Capital Beltway (I-495) or I-66 through Arlington to the Dulles Access Rd.) Taxis to Dulles from downtown cost over $40. **From Dulles to downtown D.C.,** the **Washington Flyer Dulles Express Bus** hits the West Falls Church Metro every 20-30 minutes. (Mon.-Fri. 6am-10:30pm, Sat-Sun. 7:30am-10:30pm; last bus from Metro 11pm. One-way trip $8.) Non-express buses to the city center leave every 30 minutes from 5:20am to 10:20pm on weekdays; on weekends they leave hourly from 5:20am to 12:20pm and every 30 minutes from 12:50pm to 10:20pm. (45-60 min., $16, roundtrip $26.)

Less convienent but generally cheaper flights jet into **Baltimore-Washington International (BWI) Airport** (301-261-1000), which lies 10 miles south of Baltimore's center. From D.C., take I-95 north to exit 47A. Then follow airport signs. From Baltimore, take I-695 to exit 22A (the Baltimore-Washington Pkwy.) and then follow signs for the airport. Driving time is about 50 minutes from Washington and 30 minutes from Baltimore; but as always, allow for mega-traffic. **From BWI to downtown D.C.,** the **MARC** offers the least expensive option ($4.50, roundtrip $8). **Amtrak** also provides train service (40 min., $10-11) and the **SuperShuttle** (202-562-1234) runs buses every hour at 10 past the hour, daily 6:10am to 11:10pm (50 min., $19, $26 roundtrip.)

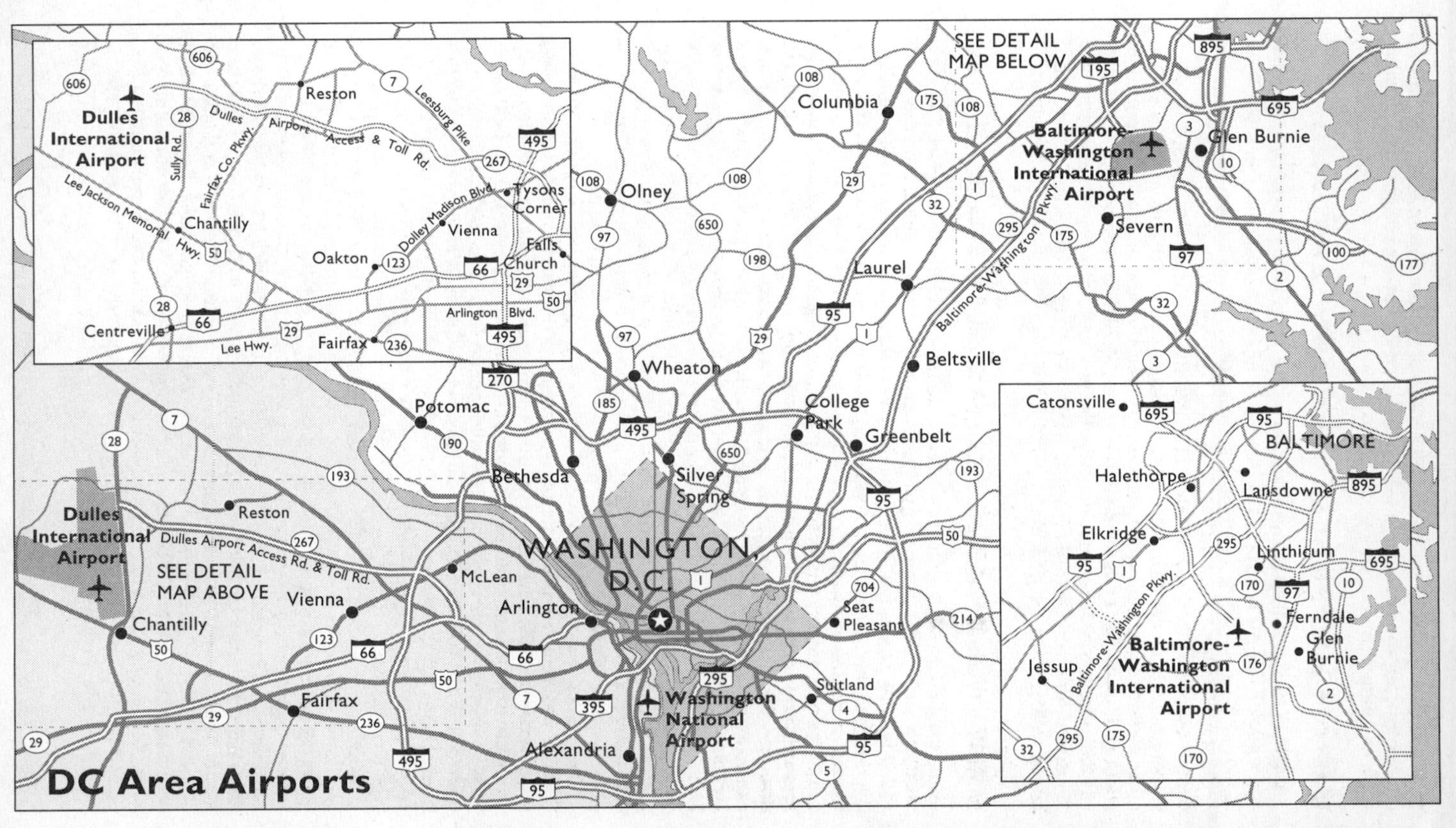
WASHINGTON'S AIRPORTS
DC Area Airports
Dulles International Airport
Reston
Leesburg Pike
Dulles Airport Access & Toll Rd.
Sully Rd.
Fairfax Co. Pkwy.
Lee Jackson Memorial Hwy.
Chantilly
Tysons Corner
Dolley Madison Blvd.
Vienna
Oakton
Falls Church
Arlington Blvd.
Centreville
Lee Hwy.
Fairfax
Olney
Columbia
Laurel
Beltsville
Wheaton
College Park
Greenbelt
Potomac
Bethesda
Silver Spring
SEE DETAIL MAP BELOW
Baltimore-Washington International Airport
Glen Burnie
Severn
Baltimore-Washington Pkwy.
SEE DETAIL MAP ABOVE
Dulles Airport Access Rd. & Toll Rd.
McLean
WASHINGTON, D.C.
Arlington
Seat Pleasant
Suitland
Washington National Airport
Alexandria
Catonsville
BALTIMORE
Halethorpe
Lansdowne
Elkridge
Linthicum
Ferndale
Jessup

ONCE THERE

■■■ TOURIST INFORMATION

TOURISM BUREAUS

Don't hesitate to contact the tourism bureaus in Washington no matter how long your stay. They're useful; some will even make reservations for you.

Washington, D.C. Convention and Visitors Association (WCVA), 1212 New York Ave., Ste. 600 NW (789-7000). Does not expect walk-ins. Write or call for copies of *The D.C. Visitor's Guide and Visitor Map* and a calendar of events.

White House Visitor Information Center, 1450 Pennsylvannia Ave. NW (208-1631). Metro: Metro Center. Opened in Spring of 1995. Distributes maps to all sights run by the National Parks Service as well as other major D.C. sights.

D.C. Committee to Promote Washington, 1212 New York Ave. NW, Ste. 200 (724-4091). Affiliated with the WCVA. Call or write for a tourist package containing information on events, festivals, and lots of other free materials.

Meridian International Center, 1630 Crescent Pl. NW (667-6800). Near Adams-Morgan. Call or write for brochures in a variety of languages. Office open Mon.-Fri. 9am-5pm.

The following offices may also be helpful: **Montgomery County Tourist Bureau,** 12900 Middlebrook Rd., Ste. 1400, Germantown, MD 20874 (800-925-0880, 301-588-8687); **Prince Georges County Visitors Bureau,** 9475 Lottsford Rd., Ste. 130, Landover, MD 20785 (301-925-8300); **Delaware Tourism Office,** 99 King's Highway, Dover, DE 19903 (800-441-8846, 302-739-4271); **Maryland Division of Tourism,** 217 E. Redwood St., 9th Floor, Baltimore, MD 21202 (800-542-1036, 410-333-6611); **Virginia Department of Tourism,** 901 E. Byrd St., Richmond, VA 23219 (804-786-4484); D.C. Branch, 1629 K St. NW 20006 (202-659-5523); and the **West Virginia Travel Office,** 2101 Washington St. East, Charleston, WV 25305-0312 (304-558-2766, 800-225-5982).

INFORMATION LINES

Time: 844-1212.

Weather: 936-1212.

News (a free service of the *Washington Post*): 334-9000. Ext. 5000 for AP news, 5100 for abridged news, 3000 for financial news, 2000 for stock market information, 4100 for sports scores. Anything else you could possibly want to know is accessible via other extension numbers.

Consumer Information: 703-ADS-1001 (237-1001). Phone numbers, addresses, and information on sales or special promotions at local businesses.

Dial-a-Hike: 547-2326. Sierra Club outings; updated weekly.

Dial-a-Museum: 357-2020. Smithsonian happenings; updated daily.

Dial-a-Park: 619-PARK. Happenings in park areas; updated daily.

■■■ FOREIGN EMBASSIES

Canada, 501 Pennsylvania Ave. NW (682-1740); **Great Britain,** 3100 Massachusetts Ave. NW (462-1340); **Ireland,** 2234 Massachusetts Ave. NW (462-3939); **Australia,** 1601 Massachusetts Ave. NW (797-3000); **New Zealand,** 37 Observatory Circle NW (328-4800); **South Africa,** 351 Massachusetts Ave. NW (232-4400). For a full listing, consult the local Yellow Pages under Embassies & Legations.

ORIENTATION

Make no little plans, for they have no power to stir men's minds.
—Daniel Burnham (designer of Union Station), 1899

When Pierre L'Enfant laid out D.C.'s streets, he had two things in mind: magnificent vistas and simple logic. Downtown Washington achieves both. The city is roughly diamond-shaped, with the four tips of the diamond pointed in the four cardinal directions. The irregular southwestern border is the Potomac River, flowing between D.C. and runaway Arlington, VA, which split off from the District in 1846. The other three borders are straight lines separating D.C. from Maryland. Washington's street names and addresses split up into four quadrants: NW, NE, SE, and SW, defined by their relation to the U.S. Capitol. NW is the largest; SW is tiny. The names of the four quadrants distinguish otherwise identical addresses: there are four intersections of 7th St. and G St., and consequently four addresses marked 700 G St., one falling in each of the four quadrants.

The basic street plan is a rectilinear grid. Streets that run from east to west run north and south from the Capitol alphabetically, from two A Streets two blocks apart (nearest the Capitol) out to two W Streets dozens of blocks apart. There is no A or B St. in NW and SW. Since the street plan was devised from the Roman alphabet, in which "I" and "J" are the same letter, there is also no J St. anywhere. After W St., east-west streets take on two-syllable names, then three-syllable names, then (at the north end of NW) names of trees and flowers. These names run in alphabetical order, but sometimes repeat or skip a letter and the number and frequency of discrepancies increase as you get farther away from downtown. The Mt. Pleasant neighborhood, for example, contains the following streets, in order: Belmont, Clifton, Chapin, Euclid. Streets running north-south are numbered (1st St., 2nd St., etc.) all the way out to 52nd St. NW and 63rd St. NE (both one block long). Numbered and lettered streets sometimes stop existing for a block, then keep going as if nothing happened. Addresses on lettered streets indicate the numbered cross street (1100 D St. SE is on the corner of D and 11th). The same trick works with addresses on some avenues (Pennsylvania but not Massachusetts or Wisconsin). The farther you get from the central city, the more these streets get interrupted or replaced by others not part of the alphanumeric system.

Downtown, the interruptions have a logic of their own. L'Enfant's plan included a sheaf of state avenues radiating outward from the U.S. Capitol (Pennsylvania, New Jersey, Delaware, Maryland) and the White House (New York, Connecticut, Vermont) and otherwise crossing downtown (Massachusetts, New Hampshire, Virginia). Massachusetts Ave. runs NW-SE parallel to, but north of, Pennsylvania Ave. Rhode Island Ave. does the same for New York Ave., both running SW-NE. This network of avenues is superimposed over the grid pattern, and the business traffic on these major thoroughfares overwhelms otherwise quiet areas with its constant motion. As the nation added states, the city added streets, and the Last Colony thus contains avenues named for all fifty. (Well, almost. California has a "Street" instead.) Besides the Capitol and the White House, downtown avenues meet at circles and squares: some important ones are Dupont Circle (Connecticut, Massachusetts, and New Hampshire Ave.); Washington Circle (New Hampshire and Pennsylvania); Scott Circle (Massachusetts and Rhode Island Ave. and 16th St.); and Mt. Vernon Square (Massachusetts and New York Ave.).

A separate group of streets runs in compass directions from the Capitol: North Capitol St., East Capitol St., and South Capitol St. separate the quadrants. There is no "West Capitol St."; instead, the Mall (a huge green lawn flanked on either side by the Smithsonian museums) extends west of the Capitol. An imaginary line down the middle of the Mall, from the Capitol to the Potomac River, divides NW from SW. Independence Ave. runs east-west south of the Mall (where B St. SW should be); Constitution Ave. runs east-west north of the Mall (where B St. NW should be).

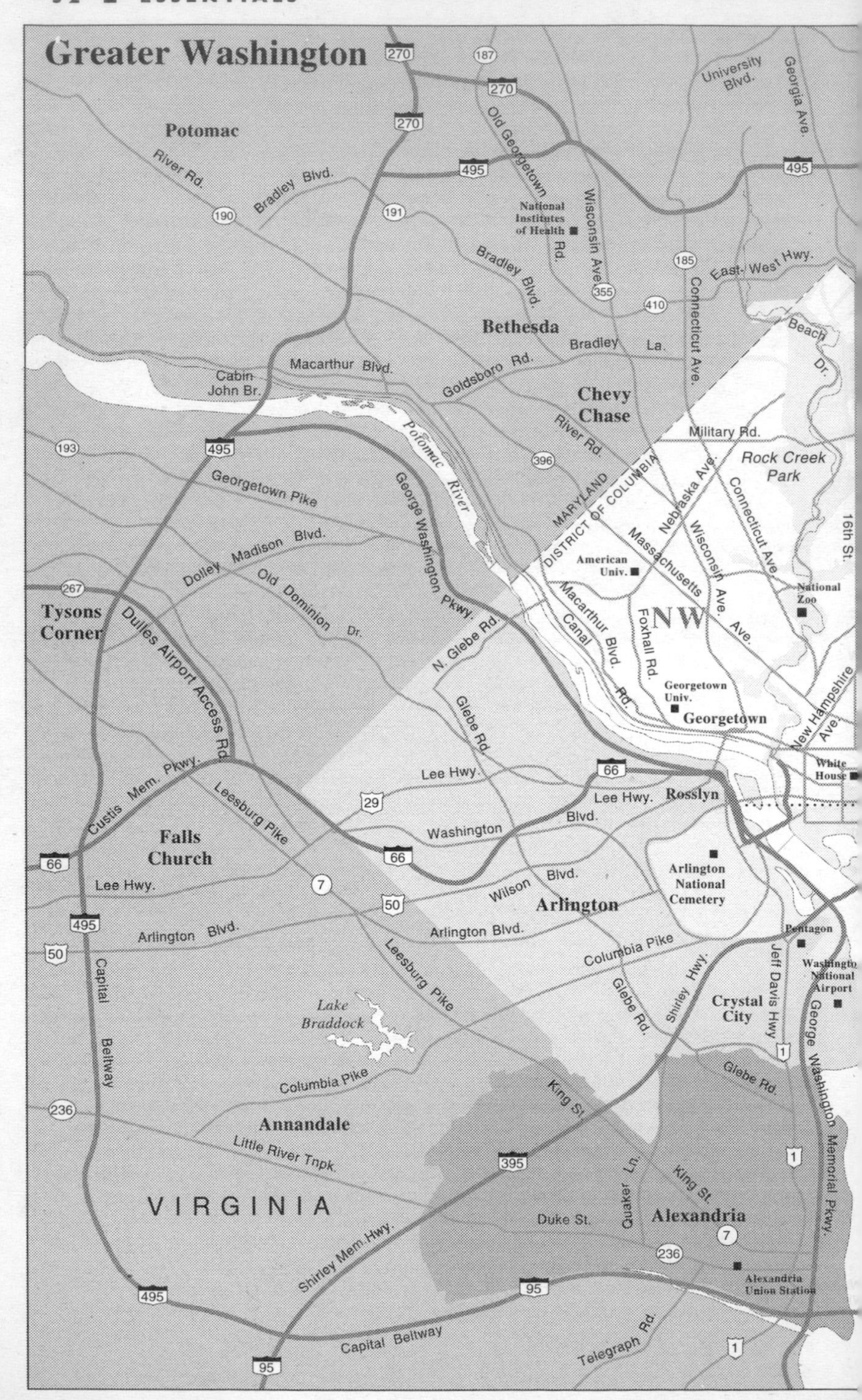
Greater Washington
Potomac
River Rd.
Bradley Blvd.
Old Georgetown Rd.
National Institutes of Health
Wisconsin Ave.
University Blvd.
Georgia Ave.
East-West Hwy.
Connecticut Ave.
Bethesda
Bradley La.
Macarthur Blvd.
Goldsboro Rd.
Cabin John Br.
Chevy Chase
River Rd.
Potomac River
Beach Dr.
Military Rd.
Rock Creek Park
Georgetown Pike
George Washington Pkwy.
MARYLAND
DISTRICT OF COLUMBIA
Nebraska Ave.
Connecticut Ave.
16th St.
Dolley Madison Blvd.
Old Dominion Dr.
American Univ.
Massachusetts Ave.
Wisconsin Ave.
National Zoo
Tysons Corner
Dulles Airport Access Rd.
N. Glebe Rd.
Macarthur Blvd.
Canal Rd.
Foxhall Rd.
NW
Georgetown Univ.
Georgetown
New Hampshire Ave.
Glebe Rd.
White House
Custis Mem. Pkwy.
Leesburg Pike
Lee Hwy.
Rosslyn
Falls Church
Washington Blvd.
Arlington National Cemetery
Lee Hwy.
Wilson Blvd.
Arlington
Arlington Blvd.
Arlington Blvd.
Pentagon
Columbia Pike
Capital Beltway
Leesburg Pike
Glebe Rd.
Shirley Hwy.
Jeff Davis Hwy
Washington National Airport
Crystal City
Lake Braddock
George Washington Memorial Pkwy.
Glebe Rd.
Columbia Pike
King St.
Annandale
Little River Tnpk.
Quaker Ln.
King St.
VIRGINIA
Duke St.
Alexandria
Shirley Mem. Hwy.
Alexandria Union Station
Capital Beltway
Telegraph Rd.
270
187
495
190
191
185
355
410
193
396
267
66
29
7
50
236
395
95
1

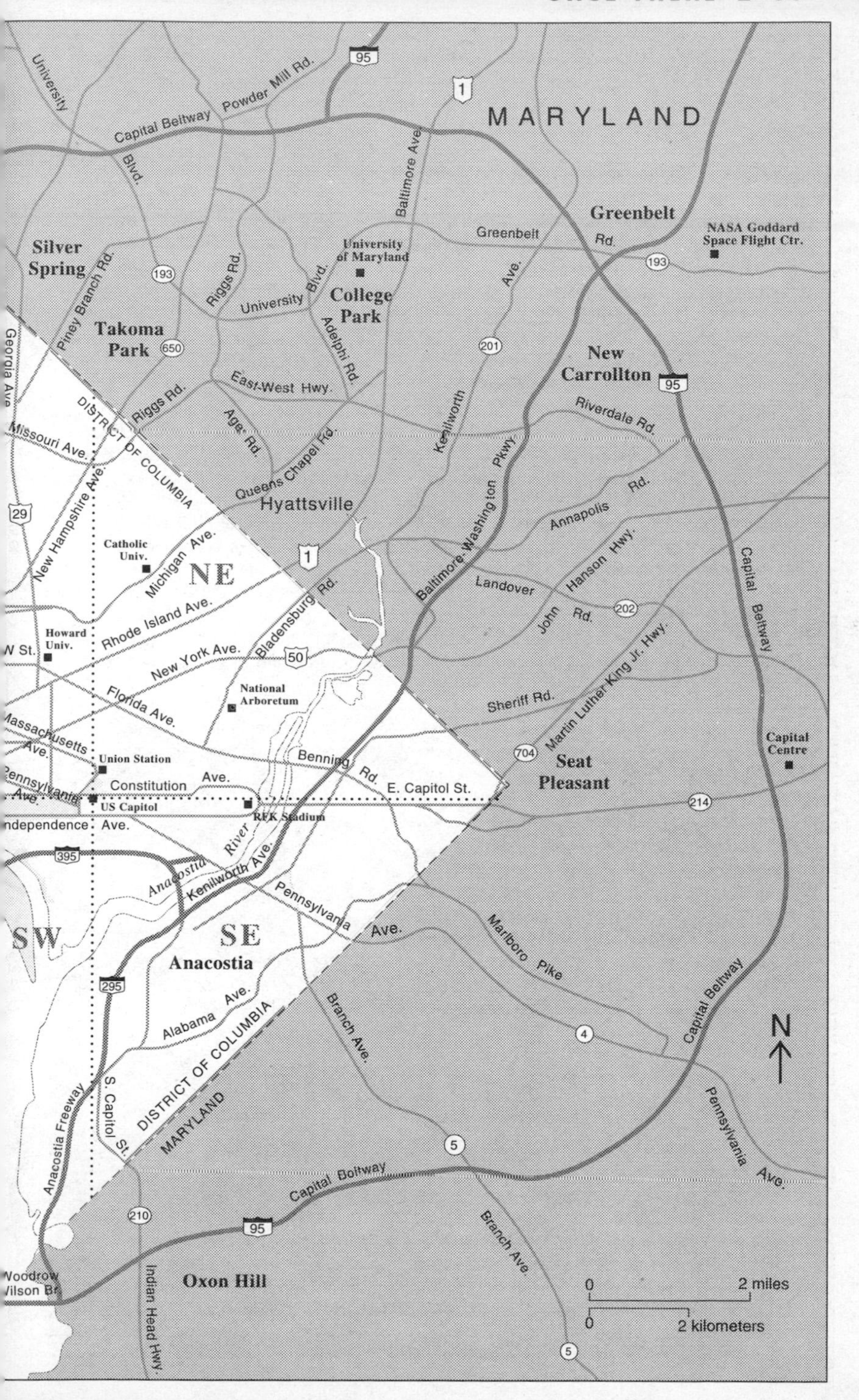
MARYLAND
Greenbelt
NASA Goddard Space Flight Ctr.
Silver Spring
University of Maryland
College Park
Takoma Park
New Carrollton
Hyattsville
NE
Catholic Univ.
Howard Univ.
National Arboretum
Union Station
US Capitol
RFK Stadium
Seat Pleasant
Capital Centre
SW
SE
Anacostia
Oxon Hill
DISTRICT OF COLUMBIA
MARYLAND
University
Capital Beltway
Powder Mill Rd.
Blvd.
Baltimore Ave.
Greenbelt Rd.
Riggs Rd.
University Blvd.
Piney Branch Rd.
Adelphi Rd.
Ave.
East-West Hwy.
Georgia Ave.
Riggs Rd.
Kenilworth
Riverdale Rd.
Missouri Ave.
Age. Rd.
Queens Chapel Rd.
Baltimore-Washington Pkwy
Annapolis Rd.
New Hampshire Ave.
Michigan Ave.
John Hanson Hwy.
Landover Rd.
Rhode Island Ave.
Bladensburg Rd.
W St.
New York Ave.
Martin Luther King Jr. Hwy.
Florida Ave.
Sheriff Rd.
Massachusetts Ave.
Benning Rd.
Pennsylvania Ave.
Constitution Ave.
E. Capitol St.
Independence Ave.
Anacostia River
Kenilworth Ave.
Pennsylvania Ave.
Marlboro Pike
Alabama Ave.
Branch Ave.
S. Capitol St.
Anacostia Freeway
Pennsylvania Ave.
Branch Ave.
Woodrow Wilson Br.
Indian Head Hwy.
95
1
193
650
201
29
50
202
704
214
395
295
4
5
210
0
2 miles
2 kilometers
N

Some parts of the city have their own ideas of order. Crowded, eternally fashionable Georgetown runs west of 28th St. between K and (approximately) R St. NW. (Many visitors wrongly think it's far from downtown.) Though Georgetown's streets predate L'Enfant's plan, the older grid harmonized with his, and many of Georgetown's streets have numbers and letters; many, however, retain older names (Thomas Jefferson St., Potomac St.). Wisconsin Ave. NW is Georgetown's north-south artery and main drag. Rock Creek Park beckons from below to drivers high-tailing it along Pennsylvannia Ave. between Georgetown and downtown (Penn becomes M as it hits 28th). Along the Creek, Rock Creek Parkway offers sheltered, scenic backdoor access to the Mall. And blighted Anacostia must have been slighted by D.C.'s original planners as well: its street plan is the most confusing in the city.

Some **major roads** in the city are **Pennsylvania Ave.,** which runs SE-NE from Anacostia to Capitol Hill to the Capitol, through downtown, past the White House, and ends finally in Georgetown; **Connecticut Ave.,** which runs north-northwest from the White House through Dupont Circle, past the Zoo, and out into the suburbs of Chevy Chase, MD; **Wisconsin Ave.,** north from Georgetown past the Cathedral to Bethesda; **16th St. NW,** which zooms from the White House north through hotels, offices, townhouses, Adams-Morgan, and Mt. Pleasant (in that order) and then forms Rock Creek Park's eastern border until it continues into Maryland; **K St. NW,** a major artery downtown; **Constitution and Independence Ave.,** just north and south of the Mall; **Massachusetts Ave.,** from American University past the Cathedral, then through Dupont and Old Downtown to Capitol Hill; **New York Ave.,** whose principal arm runs from the White House through NE; **Rock Creek Pkwy.,** north-south through Rock Creek Park; and high-speed **North Capitol St.**

NEIGHBORHOODS

Tourists who see the Smithsonian and the government halls, but don't escape the Mall and see the neighborhoods, haven't really seen Washington at all. Nearly

600,000 residents inhabit the federal city; rich and poor, black, white, Asian, and Latino are all well-represented.

Capitol Hill extends east from the Capitol; its townhouses and bars mix white- and blue-collar locals with legislation-minded pols. **The Mall** isn't a neighborhood but a long grassy stretch west of the Capitol where the Smithsonian museums are situated. West of the Mall proper, the grass grows around famous monuments like the Lincoln Memorial. The **Southwest** quadrant of the city, south of the Mall, begins as federal offices, then passes under I-395 and becomes a low-income neighborhood (to the east) and the waterfront area (to the west). North of the Mall, **Old Downtown** plays host to private business and government bureaucracy accompanied by **Foggy Bottom** (sometimes called the "West End") on the other side of the White House and **Farragut,** the area around K St. west of 15th St. NW.

Georgetown draws crowds and sucks away bucks nightly from its center at Wisconsin Ave. and M St. NW. This townhouse neighborhood harbors students and a few millionaires. Business and pleasure, embassies and streetlife, straight and gay converge around **Dupont Circle;** east of 16th St. the Dupont Circle character changes to struggling **Logan Circle,** to rundown **Shaw,** and finally to Howard University and **LeDroit Park,** an early residence for Washington's African-American elite. A strong Hispanic community rather peacefully coexists with black, white, and cool in **Adams-Morgan,** north of Dupont and east of Rock Creek Park; farther north in the equally multi-racial **Mount Pleasant** area, residents lead a more uneasy coexistence.

West of the park and north of Georgetown, spacious **upper Northwest** plays host to several smaller, mostly white neighborhoods, the National Zoo, and the Cathedral. American University and the affluent, landscaped Foxhall Road hover around the city's northwestern edges. 16th Street zooms due north past the Walter Reed Army Medical Center to Silver Spring, MD. Nearby suburb **Takoma Park** hangs out its batiks along the District's northeast edge. The NE quadrant itself, east of North Capitol St., includes the middle-class **Brookland** area, home of Catholic University, along with poorer neighborhoods and the expansive Arboretum. Across the Anacostia River, the rest of **Southeast** (including **Anacostia**), has been seriously damaged and further isolated by poverty, drugs, and guns.

■■■ GETTING AROUND

METRO

Metrorail

Metrorail (637-7000, TDD 638-3780), the Washington subway system, is a sight in its own right. (Its friends call it the "**Metro**.") The **main office,** 600 5th St. NW, is open Mon.-Fri., 6am to 10:30pm, Sat.-Sun. 8am-10:30pm. The Wheaton station has the world's longest escalator—230 ft. from street to mezzanine level. The sterile, monumental stations, with their high, curved ceilings and relentlessly brown-and-beige color scheme, zap first-time riders with their uniformity, efficiency, and artlessness; even the rows of parallel ceiling lozenges, meant to depress echoes, suggest the honeycomb decor of a beehive. And the mindless regularity with which D.C.'s working sector goes about its daily business seems only to confirm the Metro as a haven for drones and busybees. While the subway system has made tourists' lives infinitely easier since the first segment opened in 1976, designer Harry Weese's monotonous, futuristic plan has a lot to do with many visitors' mistaken impression of Washington as lifeless, efficient, and mostly governmental. Metro stations look alike—you'll feel at ease in all of them or in none.

Trains themselves are clean, quiet, carpeted, and air-conditioned. Between the profusion of brown-capped Metro cops and the stations themselves, which give hoods no place to hide, the system so far has remained **nearly crime-free.** Stations in troubled Anacostia opened in 1991. Other stations in progress will open between 1998 and 2001.

The Metro operates on a computerized **fare-card** system. Before you pass through the turnstiles, purchase a card from the machines in the station—you may choose to put any amount from $1.10 to $45 on it. You must pass it through an electronic reader in a turnstile both when you enter and when you leave the subway. The system calculates how far you've traveled and charges you appropriately. If there's still money on the card, you get it back; otherwise, the turnstile gobbles it up. If you don't have enough money on the card to cover the trip, insert the card into an exit fare machine and deposit whatever amount you're short. If you plan to connect with a bus after your ride, get a transfer pass from machines on the platform before boarding the train (transfers are not valid within four blocks of the station where they are issued). Metrobus rides are 25¢ with a valid transfer. If you plan to ride the subway several times, buy a $5 **One Day Pass.** This is definitely the most **economical** choice for a day's sightseeing. You get unlimited Metro usage from 9:30am to closing. **Flash Passes** (with unlimited usage of Metrobus and/or Metrorail for two weeks or a month) are also available. Passes are available at Metro Center, some banks and Safeway and Giant grocery stores. You will get a 10% bonus on farecards of $20 or more (max. farecard value is $45). Senior citizens and disabled persons are entitled to discount fares but need a special Metro ID. Elevators help with wheelchairs and strollers. **Trains run** Mon.-Fri., 5:30am to midnight and Sat.-Sun. 8am-midnight. Metro fares rose slightly in June 1995. Peak-hour (5:30am-9:30am and 3pm-8pm) **fares** now range from $1.10 to $3.25, depending on the distance traveled. At all other times, fares range from $1.10 to $2.10.

Metrorail Quick Glance Chart

Sight	Metro Station	Sight	Metro Station
American University	RED: Tenleytown-AU	Martin Luther King, Jr. Memorial Library	GREEN/YELLOW/RED: Gallery Pl./Chinatown
Arlington Cemetery	BLUE: Arlington Cemetery	National Academy of Sciences	ORANGE/BLUE: Foggy Bottom/GWU
Botanical Gardens	ORANGE/BLUE: Federal Cntr SW	National Aquarium	ORANGE/BLUE: Federal Triangle
Capitol Building	ORANGE/BLUE: Capitol South	National Geographic Society	RED: Farragut North
Capitol Children's Museum	RED: Union Station	National Theater	ORANGE/BLUE/RED: Metro Center
Chinatown	GREEN/YELLOW/RED: Gallery Pl./Chinatown	National Zoo	RED: Woodley Park-Zoo
Constitution Hall	ORANGE/BLUE: Farragut West	Old Post Office	ORANGE/BLUE: Federal Triangle
D.C. Armory/Starplex	ORANGE/BLUE: Stadium-Armory	Old Town Alexandria	YELLOW/BLUE: Braddock Rd.
Federal Bureau of Investigation (FBI)	ORANGE/BLUE/RED: Metro Center	Pentagon	YELLOW/BLUE: Pentagon
Folger Shakespeare Library	ORANGE/BLUE: Capitol South	Phillips Gallery	RED: Dupont Circle
Gay District	RED: Dupont Circle	Renwick Gallery	ORANGE/BLUE: Farragut West
George Washington University	ORANGE/BLUE: Foggy Bottom/GWU	RFK Stadium	ORANGE/BLUE: Stadium-Armory
Hirshhorn Museum & Sculpture Garden	GREEN/YELLOW/ ORANGE/BLUE: L'Enfant Plaza	Shakespeare Theater	GREEN/YELLOW: Archives-Navy Memorial
Howard University	GREEN: Shaw	Smithsonian Museums	ORANGE/BLUE: Smithsonian
Iwo Jima Memorial	ORANGE/BLUE: Rosslyn	Supreme Court	ORANGE/BLUE: Capitol South
Kennedy Center	ORANGE/BLUE: Foggy Bottom/GWU	Washington Monument	ORANGE/BLUE: Smithsonian
Library of Congress	ORANGE/BLUE: Capitol South	White House	ORANGE/BLUE: McPherson Sq.
Lincoln Memorial	ORANGE/BLUE: L'Enfant Plaza	Woolly Mammoth Theatre	GREEN: U St.-Cardozo

Metrobus

The extensive, complicated Metrobus (same address, phone, and hours as Metrorail) system reliably serves Georgetown, downtown, and the suburbs. Downtown, the bus stops every few blocks. Regular fare in the District is $1.10 (exact change required); fares may vary in Maryland. Seniors, disabled persons, and children ages four and under are entitled to discounts. Schedules and route maps for buses operating near Metrorail stations are available in those stations. A comprehensive bus map is available from the main Metro office; call or write for availability and price (ZIP code 20001). Metro information (637-7000) can describe the alchemical mix of buses and trains needed to reach any destination.

Bus routes with a letter followed by a number (e.g., D4, S2) or with a two digit number make stops in D.C. and Maryland, sometimes (like the "J" buses) only in Maryland, and sometimes (like the 30-something buses) only in D.C. If the number precedes the letter (18L, 5D), the route runs in Virginia. (Most Virginia routes connect to the Pentagon Metro stop.) 30-something buses run from downtown to some stretch of Wisconsin Ave. NW #30, 32, 34 and 36 buses take Pennsylvania Ave. NW to Georgetown, then drive up Wisconsin. The immensely useful D2, D4, D6, and D8 lines zip from far NW to Glover Park, Q St. in Georgetown, Dupont Circle, New Downtown, and Metro Center before ending up in far NE. Metro L2 and L4 buses run from downtown up Connecticut Ave. NW. Alexandria (DASH) and Montgomery County (Ride-On) also have their own, smaller bus systems.

TAXIS

Washington cab fares are lower but weirder than in other American cities; fares are based not on a meter but on a map that splits the city into 8 zones and a dizzying number of subzones. Roundabout routes designed to push up fares by crossing as many zones as possible should be a thing of the past since your fare is now based only on the zones where your ride starts and ends. Zone prices are fixed, so your driver can—but probably won't—ask you for the fare at the beginning of your trip. Prices between the confusing subzones within the zones vary only slightly. It's the major zone prices that really matter. A zone map and corresponding fare chart are posted in every legal cab. Be sure your destination is in the District before you hail a cab, though; cab trips to, from, and within Maryland and Virginia are priced by distance rather than zones and are exorbitant rather than affordable.

Within the sub-zones that surround the Capitol building, your fare will be around $3. **Fares** between other zones run $3.20 to $10.80, the maximum fare for any ride within D.C. During rush hours (Mon.-Fri. 4-6:30pm), there is a $1 surcharge. Fares are doubled during official snow emergencies. Groups riding to the same destination are sometimes charged $1.25 for each extra person. Travel into Maryland or Virginia will cost you $2 for the first half-mile and 70¢ for each additional half-mile or part thereof, which quickly gets ridiculous. The Metro system obviates daytime taxi-riding; but cabs are quite useful after dark in subwayless Georgetown or Adams-Morgan, to get home from bars and clubs, or wherever you feel unsafe walking around. A cab ride from the heart of the club district in Adams-Morgan or Dupont Circle to the accommodations-saturated Metro Center area runs about $4-5.

Hail any cab downtown, but farther out, call **Yellow Cab** (544-1212). Be ready to give some directions or to send the first few cabs away. Dispatched taxis cost $1.50 extra. Get a zone map and an informational brochure from the not-so-helpful **D.C. Taxicab Commission,** Rm. 200, 2041 Martin Luther King, Jr. Ave. SE, Washington, D.C. 20020 (767-8380). And remember, if you feel you're being ripped off, get the receipt, write down the cab number, and call either the D.C. Commission or the very helpful **Mayor's Office** (727-2980).

DRIVING

Drivers from rapid cabbie-infested cities like New York City or Boston often think Washington drivers are wimps. They're right. D.C. drivers are fairly polite, but that doesn't mean you can sleep all the way down North Capitol Street. **Rush-hour commuter traffic** can leave you in gridlock for hours. Going downtown (especially from Virginia) from 7am to 9:30am and leaving the city from 4pm to 6:30pm, your car will idle for so long you could probably get where you're going faster by walking. Lunchtime can also pose traffic problems, and Friday afternoons bring the worst nightmares. Most of the sights downtown are more easily accessible by Metro or by bus. In upper NW and in NE, a car won't hurt; traveling to some outlying attractions, you'd be nowhere without one.

Expect to pay about $7 to 10 for **garage parking.** Finding **on-street parking** during the day is almost impossible, especially near the Smithsonian. Afternoon rush hour (Mon.-Fri. 4-6:30pm) turns most downtown spaces temporarily illegal. Read the signs; cops tow. Traffic tickets will hit you for $15 for an expired meter. Nighttime parking is tough only in Georgetown and Adams-Morgan—the places you're most likely to drive to, since the Metro doesn't serve them.

All those numbers and letters are meant to make D.C. streets comprehensible. While the city makes sense to pedestrians, its seeming order can turn to chaos behind the steering wheel. If a one-way street isn't going your way, the next one up probably will be. Some streets, like Connecticut Ave., have "reversible lanes" whose directions depend on the time of day; a few turn one-way during rush hour. Watch for street signs indicating this. Certain intersections on the edge of Washington tend to plunge drivers into Virginia unawares. These are K St. NW west of 24th St., where the Whitehurst Freeway splits off above it; 8th St. SW south of D St., which sends drivers to Arlington or Anacostia—only; and the one-way spaghetti around the Lincoln Memorial. D.C. roads are in famously bad shape.

Some parts of Washington have their very own logic, which is often incomprehensible to outsiders. Congress is one. **Rock Creek Park** is another. Over the creek and through the woods is often the quickest way from one part of the city to another, since there are almost no traffic lights in the Park. But the park follows neither the grid nor the radial-avenue plan; instead, a few roads traverse the wooded areas and the major artery, Rock Creek Parkway, follows the Creek itself from Maryland through D.C. to the Potomac. Check a map before you race through the park. Most of Rock Creek Parkway turns one-way in rush hour (south in the morning, north in the afternoon). Beach Drive is closed to cars from Friday at 7pm until Sunday at 7pm. After a snowstorm, go through Rock Creek Park, where the Park Service promptly plows the roads.

Into, out of, or around the suburbs, you're bound to meet the behemoth known as the **Capital Beltway,** whose signs leave tourists panicked while cars race past exits at over 60 mph. A few hints: **I-495** and **I-95** both refer to the Beltway, which makes a huge circle around the city; **I-95** continues north and south to other states, though it also completes the loop of the beltway. For local traffic, the two numbers are interchangeable. The inner loop of the Beltway travels clockwise and the outer loop goes counterclockwise. Signs at entrance ramps often ask you to choose between Richmond or Baltimore when you want no part of either; read "south" for Richmond and "north" for Baltimore. If you screw up, just take the next exit and then reverse course; local signs usually give good return-to-Beltway directions.

The 14th St. Bridge, which downed an Air Florida plane in 1983, serves the more helpful and prosaic function of linking downtown D.C. and the Mall to Arlington, the George Washington Pkwy., and, through the parkway, Alexandria and the Beltway. (It's technically two bridges, the George Mason and the Arland Williams, running north and south respectively.) Arlington Memorial Bridge, universally called "Memorial Bridge," zips from Arlington Cemetery to the Lincoln Memorial at the

Mall's western end. The Theodore Roosevelt Bridge, a.k.a. I-66, runs from the George Washington Pkwy. to Constitution Ave. NW. Key Bridge, also on the G.W. Pkwy., links austere Rosslyn, VA, to happening Georgetown.

To pay a **D.C. traffic ticket,** go to the Bureau of (Traffic) Adjudication at 65 K St. NE (727-5000; open Mon.-Fri. 8:30am-7pm; Metro: Union Station). Pay with cash or credit card (MasterCard or Visa). Otherwise, make a check or money order payable to the D.C. Treasurer and send it to the Bureau of Adjudication, Washington, D.C. 20002. If your car is **towed,** go to the Bureau of Adjudication to pay for your towing fee and get directions to the Brentwood Impoundment lot in far-off NE. Towing costs $75 plus a $10 daily storage fee beginning 24 hrs. after towing.

Dangerous are the diplomats, foreign functionaries, and anyone with red-white-and-blue license plates beginning with "D" or "S." These drivers have diplomatic immunity, which means 13-year-old Sven may be racing down Wisconsin Ave. in the ambassadorial family car. Give them a wide berth.

CAR RENTAL

Although the cost of renting a car for days at a time can be prohibitively expensive, renting for local trips is often reasonable, especially if several people share the cost. When dealing with any car-rental company, make certain the price includes insurance against theft and collision. American Express automatically insures any car rented with the card. Although rental charges run $25-55 per day for a compact car, plus 30-40¢ per mile, most companies have special deals (especially on weekends). If you have a major credit card, you might avoid having to leave a large cash deposit and you'll have a better chance of not being spurned by minimum-age requirements. Some major companies are:

Alamo (800-327-9633). Ages 21-24 with a major credit card can rent for a $20/day additional fee.

Avis (800-331-1212). Min. age 25, unless the renter has a corporate account.
Budget (800-527-0700). Most branches rent to 25 and over only. Some branches rent to ages 21-24 for a $5-15/day surcharge.
Dollar (800-800-4000). At most branches, ages 21-24 may rent with a credit card for an additional daily fee of $15/day.
Enterprise Rent-a-Car, 927 N. Kansas St., (703-243-5404, 800-325-8007), in Arlington. $32 per day, $180 per week for a compact (but expect rates to differ from branch to branch). Unlimited mileage. Must be 21 or older with major credit card or cash deposit. Ages 21-24 pay $8/day surcharge. Open Mon.-Fri. 7:30am-6pm, Sat. 8am-noon.
Hertz (800-654-3131). Min. age 25, or 21-24 with a corporate account.
National (800-227-7368). Min. age 25 with credit card, or 21-24 with a corporate account.
Rent-A-Wreck (800-421-7253). All branches are independently owned and specialize in supplying vehicles that are past their prime. Cars may have dents and purely decorative radios, but they run and they're cheap. May rent to 21-24 with a credit card for $5/day surcharge.
Thrifty (800-367-2277). Ages 21-24 may be able to rent at some locations for an additional fee of $15/day.

Local companies often charge less than major companies, although you'll generally have to return to your point of origin to return the car. Car rentals are cheapest in Arlington, VA. The following are the addresses and phone numbers of local rental agencies.

Easi Car Rentals, 2485 S. Glebe Rd. (703-521-0188), in Arlington. Rates differ depending on season and make. Daily rates from $15, plus 10¢ per mile. Weekly rates from $105, with 200 free miles. Special weekend rates available. Must be 21. Reservations advised. Open Mon.-Fri. 9am-7pm, Sat. 9am-2pm.
Bargain Buggies Rent-a-Car, 912 N. Lincoln St. (703-841-0000), in Arlington. $20 per day and 10¢ per mile; $110 per week (local rental) with 200 free miles. Rates may differ from branch to branch. Must be 18 or older with major credit card or cash deposit of $250. Those under 21 need full insurance coverage of their own. Rates may alter depending on rental length and make of car. Open Mon.-Fri. 8am-7pm, Sat.-Sun. 9am-3pm.

BICYCLING

When cars leave the District each night, the emptied avenues here are a cyclist's dream. Biking during the day can be more harried, as you dodge crazed, spandex-clad bike messengers, taxis, and tourmobiles. Helmetlessness is illegal in Maryland, though not in D.C. and VA. If you must leave your bike unattended, use a strong "U" lock. Thieves laugh at (then cut through) weaker chain locks. For information on bike rental companies and prices, as well as cycling in and around D.C., see **Sports and Recreation,** p. 225.

■■■ KEEPING IN TOUCH

MAIL

Individual offices of the U.S. Postal Service are usually open Monday to Friday from 9am to 5pm and sometimes on Saturday. All are closed on national holidays. **Postcards** mailed within the U.S. cost 20¢ and **letters** cost 32¢ for the first ounce and 23¢ for each additional ounce. Within the U.S., up to 2 pounds of material can be sent **Priority Mail** (2-3 days to domestic locations) for $3. To Canada and Mexico, it costs 30¢ to mail a postcard. Postcards mailed overseas cost 40¢, and letters are 50¢ for a half-ounce, 95¢ for an ounce, and 39¢ for each additional half-ounce up to 64 ounces. **Aerogrammes,** printed sheets that fold into envelopes ready to be airmailed, are sold at post offices for 45¢. Most U.S. post offices offer an **International**

Express Mail service, which is the fastest way to send an item overseas. (A package under 8 ounces can be sent to most foreign destinations in 2 or 3 days for $10.75.)

The U.S. is divided into postal zones, each with a five- or nine-digit **ZIP code** particular to a region, city, or part of a city. Writing this code on letters is essential for timely delivery. Dial 202-526-3920 for the 24-hr. automated **Postal Answer Line (PAL),** which provides information on a variety of postal services and rates.

Receiving Mail

If you want to receive mail while on the road, it can be sent to you c/o **General Delivery.** Picking up mail sent to General Delivery in D.C. is more difficult than catching a bobcat with a titwillow; rather than going to a post office downtown, it goes to the main national sorting facility on Brentwood Rd. NE, miles from everywhere and not served by Metrorail (the closest is Rhode Island Ave.). Worse still, you can't send General Delivery mail to another D.C. post office, even if you know the ZIP—it all ends up at Brentwood. The envelope should also say "Please hold until (...)" the blank filled in with a date a couple of weeks after your correspondent expects you to pick up the letter (letters are normally held for around 30 days). When you claim your mail, you'll have to present ID; if you don't claim a letter within two to four weeks, it will be returned to its sender. Almost any morsel of D.C.-related postal information can be retrieved through the computer that answers the phone at the Postal Answer Line (see above).

American Express offices throughout the U.S. will act as a mail service for cardholders if you contact them in advance. Under this free "Client Letter Service," they will hold mail for 30 days, forward upon request, and accept telegrams. The last name of the person to whom the mail is addressed should be capitalized and underlined, and "Client Letter Service" should be written on the front of the envelope. For a complete list of offices and instructions on how to use the service, call 800-528-4800.

Post Office Branches

Call 682-9595 to find the post office nearest you. Some branches are:

Main office: indescribably inconvenient at 900 Brentwood Rd. NE (682-9595). ZIP code: 20090. Mail sent "General Delivery" always comes here—a good reason not to have anything sent General Delivery. Open Mon.-Fri. 8am-8pm, Sat. 10am-6pm. Sun. noon-6pm.

North Capitol Station: 2 Massachusetts Ave. NE (523-2628), near Farragut North and West Metro stations. Open Mon.-Fri. 7am-midnight, Sat.-Sun. 7am-8pm.

Farragut Station: 1145 19th St. NW (523-2506), in Farragut. Open Mon.-Fri. 8am-6pm.

Temple Heights Station: 1921 Florida Ave. NW (232-7613), near Connecticut Ave. between Dupont Circle and Adams-Morgan. Open Mon.-Fri. 8:30am-5pm.

Martin Luther King Jr. Station: 1400 L St. NW (523-2000). Open Mon.-Fri. 8am-7pm and Sat. 10am-2pm.

Columbia Heights Station: 1423 Irving St. NW (523-2397). Open Mon. 8am-7pm, Tues.-Fri. 8am-5:30pm., Sat. 8:30am-3pm.

Georgetown: 1215 31st St. NW (523-2405). Open Mon.-Fri. 8am-5:30pm, Sat. 8:30am-2pm.

TELEPHONES

Area Code: D.C. 202; Baltimore/Annapolis 410; rest of Maryland 301; Virginia 703; Delaware 302; West Virginia 304. To call between points in the D.C. metropolitan area that have different area codes (e.g., D.C. and Arlington), you must dial the area code, even though it's a local call. Unless otherwise noted, all telephone numbers in this book have a 202 area code.

Most of the information you will need about telephone usage—including area codes for the U.S., foreign country codes, and rates—is in the front of the local **white**

pages telephone directory. Use the **yellow pages,** published at the end of the white pages or in a separate book, to look up the phone numbers of businesses and other services. Federal, state, and local **government listings** are provided in the blue pages at the back of the directory. To obtain local phone numbers or area codes of other cities, call **directory assistance** at 411. Calling "0" will get you the **operator,** who can assist you in reaching a phone number and provide you with general information. For long-distance directory assistance, dial 1-(area code)-555-1212. The operator will help you with rates or other information and give assistance in an emergency. Directory assistance or the operator is free from any pay phone.

Telephone numbers in the U.S. consist of a three-digit area code, a three-digit exchange, and a four-digit number, written as 123-456-7890. Only the last seven digits are used in a **local call. Non-local calls within the area code** from which you are dialing require a "1" before the last seven digits, while **long-distance calls outside the area code** from which you are dialing require a "1" and the area code. For example, to call Trio Restaurant in Dupont Circle from outside D.C., you'd dial 1-202-232-6305. Generally, discount rates apply after 5pm on weekdays and Sunday and economy rates every day between 11pm and 8am; on Saturday and on Sunday until 5pm, economy rates are also in effect. Numbers beginning with area code 800 are **toll-free calls** requiring no coin deposit. Numbers beginning with 900 are **toll calls** and charge you (often exorbitantly) for whatever "service" they provide.

Pay phones are plentiful; put your coins (25¢ for a local call) into the slot and listen for a dial tone before dialing. To make a **long-distance direct call,** dial the number. An operator will tell you the cost for the first three minutes; the operator will cut in when you must deposit more money.

If you are at a telephone and don't have barrels of change, you may want to make a **collect call** (i.e., charge the call to the recipient). First dial "0" and then the area code and number you wish to reach. An operator will cut in and ask to help you. Tell him or her that you wish to place a collect call and give your name; anyone who answers may accept or refuse the call. If you tell the operator you are placing a **person-to-person collect call** (more expensive than a regular, **station-to-station collect call),** you must give both your name and the receiving person's name; the benefit is that a charge appears only if the person with whom you wish to speak is there (and accepts the charges, of course). The cheapest method of reversing the charges is MCI's **1-800-COLLECT** service: just dial 1-800-COLLECT, tell the operator what number you want to call, and receive a 20% to 44% discount (discounts are greatest when the rates are already cheapest). Finally, if you'd like to call someone who is as poor as you, simply **bill to a third party** by dialing "0," the area code, and then the number; the operator will call the third party for approval.

In addition to coin-operated pay phones, AT&T and its competitors operate a **coinless** version. Not only can collect and third-party calls be made on this kind of phone, but you can also use a **telephone calling card;** begin dialing all these kinds of calls with "0." Generally, these phones are operated by passing the card through a slot before dialing, although you can always just punch in your calling-card number on the keypad (a desirable alternative if you happen to be traveling in an area where carrying around credit cards is unwise). The cheapest way to call long-distance from a pay phone is by using a calling card or credit card.

You can place **international calls** from any telephone. To call direct, dial the universal international access code (011) followed by the country code (see below), the city/area code, and the local number. Country codes and city codes may sometimes be listed with a zero in front (e.g., 033), but when dialing 011 first, drop succeeding zeros (e.g., 011-33). In some areas you will have to give the operator the number and he or she will place the call.

The **country code** is 1 for the U.S. and Canada; 44 for the U.K.; 353 for the Republic of Ireland; 61 for Australia; 64 for New Zealand; and 972 for Israel.

TELEGRAM

Sometimes **cabling** may be the only way to contact someone quickly (usually within 1-3 days). Within the U.S., the minimum cost for a same day, hand-delivered telegram is $30.90 for 15 words. A "Mailgram" is a telegram that arrives on the next mail-day and costs $18.95 for 50 words. For foreign telegrams, **Western Union** (800-325-6000) charges a base fee for the first seven words *plus $9 delivery;* after seven words, an additional per-word charge is assessed. To Canada, the rate is $12.85 plus 55¢ per additional word; to Great Britain and Ireland, $13.27/61¢; and to Australia and New Zealand, $13.62/66¢, and $14.32/76¢ to Israel. In Washington, call 624-0100 to locate the Western Union office nearest you.

Accommodations

D.C.'s accommodations crunch isn't new. B&Bs, hotels, and temporary lodgings have been scarce since the Jackson administration (1829), when 15,000 Americans deluged the Capitol for Old Hickory's inauguration. One witness to the democratic exuberance wrote of the tumult, "lodgings could not be obtained, and the newcomers had to go to Georgetown, which soon overflowed and others had to go to Alexandria." The situation hasn't improved much in the last 167 years. Business travelers desert D.C. during the summer months, leaving business hotels to discount deeply and swell with tourists on summer weekends; discounts from June to August can run anywhere from $10 to 50% off the usual weekday rates (which hover around $100-120 in the summer). No less busy during the summer touring season are the hostels, guest houses, and university dormitories that round out the selection of D.C.'s temporary residences. For longer stays, the transiency of the D.C. population means that apartments for sublet or rent abound at all times of year (though the supply is greatest at the beginning and end of the summer, and when a new administration comes to Washington). Unfortunately, the demand for housing at these times equals the supply, so you'll have to be both aggressive and early to secure the place you want.

FOR A VISIT

If you plan to stay in D.C. for less than a month, you might consider the time-honored institution of budget travel: the **hostel.** Students, Australians, and other down-market *Let's Go* types fill up D.C.'s amiable AYH/HI hostel. Some hostel-like accommodations favor international travelers over Americans; most give cheap weekly rates along with a chance to meet other visitors; and almost all want guests to call in advance. If you're lucky enough to hit the District without a car and you don't want to stay in a hostel, the **guest houses** around Dupont Circle and Adams-Morgan should be your first try. These establishments are smaller, friendlier, and usually better-looking than any budget hotel.

Downtown **hotels** range from moderately to crazily expensive, but if you stay on a weekend in the off-season (read "sweltering summer"), you can live like a corporate executive for half the regular price or less. Check the *New York Times* Sunday Travel section for the latest deals before you go, and then bargain for a room as you would for a used car. It's important to note that D.C. adds an automatic **13% occupancy surcharge** and another **$1.50 per room per night** to your bill. If you're traveling in a group, keep in mind that hotels around here usually charge per room, not per guest. Even a $100 room becomes reasonable when you split it four ways. Many places will give your third or fifth occupant a cot for no extra charge. Suite hotels offer an especially good deal for groups of three or more (free breakfast and unlimited afternoon cocktails are often included).

With garage parking in the District a whopping $10 per day, the automobile-encumbered might find it easier to stay in a hotel in Arlington, VA, or Bethesda, MD, where there's no central-city real-estate crunch to preclude parking lots (and many hotels offer free parking). Alexandria, VA, 20 minutes by car from D.C., offers more **motel**-type options. Some upscale hotels do provide parking. If yours does not, it's a good idea to leave the wheels at home. Unless you know someone in the area, obtaining a parking permit (which allows on-street parking in one of the District's "zones") will be difficult.

Bed & Breakfast Accommodations, Ltd., P.O. Box 12011 (328-3510; fax 332-3885), Washington, D.C. 20005. Reserves a wide range of accommodations, from budget to luxury, as well as apartments for families or guests requiring longer stays. Rates in private home B&Bs start at $45 for singles, $55 for doubles in summer; rates are high in-season. $15 extra per additional person. Some historic properties and an interesting array of hosts and hostesses. Open Mon.-Fri. 10am-5pm, Sat. 10am-1pm.

The Bed and Breakfast League, P.O. Box 9490 (363-7767), Washington, D.C. 20016. Reserves rooms in private homes, from Capitol Hill townhouses to Cleveland Park inn-style mansions. All are accessible by public transportation. Room prices vary. Singles $40-110, with private bath $50-115. Doubles $55-95, with private bath $65-130. Booking fee $10; non-refundable room deposit $25. Call for reservations Mon.-Thurs. 9am-5pm, Fri. 9am-1pm.

■ FOR THE SUMMER

Interns and similar summer guests tend to stay in **university dorms,** where rates are cheap and students abound. Most university housing programs don't want, or even permit, non-student tourists. And even collegians who crave university summer housing should come up with a job or an official excuse to visit D.C. and then write or call several months in advance. Some colleges, at least in the United States, sponsor "summer in Washington" programs, which can put students in touch with D.C.-based alums who need **housesitting** or desire guests; if you're in school, see if yours has one before you visit the city.

Subletting an apartment or townhouse for the summer from local students provides a more homey and potentially cheaper alternative to dorms. **Newspaper listings** often include apartments for rent and for sublet, as well as requests for roommates and housesitters. Check *The Washington Post* (especially Fri.-Sun.) and *City Paper.* Also try the roommate assistance companies listed below.

■ FOR A YEAR

Bulletin boards and **newsletters** can help you find rentals and sublets; some are for everybody, others are special-interest. **Georgetown University's** off-campus housing office at Leavey Center 308 (687-8467) publishes listings for D.C., MD, and VA, with a separate listing for summer sublets. Stop by and pick them up for $1.50 each; there is also a daily supplement available for a minimal charge. Office open Mon.-Wed. 10am-1pm, Thurs.-Fri. 1-4pm. (Other university housing offices just might provide similar help.) The **Food for Thought** restaurant in Dupont Circle (see **Food,** p. 96) fills its bulletin board with all sorts of neighborhood requests, including those for apartments, tenants, and roommates. Gay and lesbian travelers especially should check the resource centers at **Lammas** and **Lambda Rising** bookstores, also in Dupont Circle (see **Bisexual, Gay, and Lesbian D.C.,** p. 239). Apartments for rent are listed in **local newspapers,** including the *Post* and *City Paper.*

Roommates Preferred, 2262 Hall Pl. NW, Suite 202 (965-4004). Metro: Tenleytown. Matches people who want roommates with those seeking rooms. The personable director will meet and talk with you, then suggest people with whom you might want to live. If you decide to use the service after the conversation, the fee is $50. They have hundreds of people on file. Drop by Mon.-Fri. 10am-7pm, Sat. 11am-3pm.

Capital Reservations, 1730 Rhode Island Ave. NW, Suite. 506 (1-800-847-4832; fax 452-0537). An efficient telephone service that offers discounted rates on hotels around Washington. They claim to screen all hotels for security. Room rates vary with the season but usually start at about $59. Credit card required. Open Mon.-Fri. 8:30am-6:30pm, Sat. 9am-1pm.

Home Exchange, PO Box 567, Northhampton, MA 01061, offers a registry service, linking homeowners all over the US and UK. Subscribers (US $50 fee) list their homes in a directory that is sent to all subscribers for the purpose of free exchange or rental.

■■■ UNIVERSITY DORMS

Georgetown University Summer Housing is available only for summer educational (i.e., non-profit) pursuits; they gladly take college-aged interns and members of summer programs but cannot house self-declared tourists. Housing is single-sex. 3-week min. stay. Singles $18, with A/C $19. Rooms available early June to early Aug. Apartments with kitchens also available, but must be rented for 5 weeks ($532) or 10 weeks ($1197). Newly renovated rooms have a strong college-dormitory mood. Bring your own linens and pillows! Requires mail application (or fax them at 687-4590) and 20% non-refundable deposit. Balance must be paid in full by the time of occupancy. Call or write G.U. Office of Housing and Conferences Services, Washington, D.C. 20057 (687-4560) or visit them on campus at 100 Harbin Hall. The on-campus housing office at 208 Leavey Center, G.U. (687-1457, open Mon.-Fri. 9am-5pm) lists on-campus sublets in a weekly listing. Drop by and pick one up for $1 when on campus (they won't mail them to non-Georgetown affiliates).

American University Summer Housing: Write to Summer Housing Office, 4400 Massachusetts Ave. NW, Washington, D.C. 20016 (885-2669) for info. and an application. Metro: Tenleytown-AU. Provides simple dorm rooms with A/C for students and interns from mid-May to mid-Aug. Double rooms ($105 per week per person) and triple rooms ($84 per week per person) available with hall bathrooms; come with a friend or they will find one for you. Required 4-week min. stay. A valid university ID (from any university) and full payment for stay must be presented at check-in. Reserve early for check-in dates in June; after mid-July you can call 24 hrs. before you want to stay, and reservations will be accepted if the dorms aren't full. Most interns stay on the Tenley campus, which is just steps from the Metro. $300 deposit required.

George Washington University Housing: Write to 2121 I St. NW, Suite 402, Washington, D.C. 20052 (994-6688). Metro: Foggy Bottom. For interns or students in academic programs only. Average dorm rooms, with hardwood floors and clean bathrooms. Apartments available. Suites may consist of 1 large room or 2 smaller ones. Laundry in dorms; restaurants close by. All rooms have A/C. Singles with kitchen $30. Doubles with kitchen $44-50. Suites with microwave $22-25 per person. A 30-night minimum stay is required and a $600 deposit must be submitted with the application. Rooms are available from late May through the middle of August.

Catholic University Housing: Write to Office of Conferences and Summer Programs, 104 St. Bonaventure Hall, Catholic U., Washington, D.C. 20064 (319-5277). Metro: Brookland-CUA. Close to the Metro but far from almost everything else; try other college housing first. Available from early May to mid-August, the rooms in the new Centennial Village complex are spacious with huge bay windows, large closets, and private baths. Without A/C, singles $22 ($17 for stays of over 2 weeks), doubles $17 per person. With A/C, singles $28.50 (more than 2 weeks $21), doubles $22.50 per person (more than 2 weeks $19). Stays of 30-74 days discounted 5%; stays over 75 days are discounted 10%. 20% deposit required in advance. Call ahead to request an application, which must be received at least 3 business days before expected arrival. Wheelchair access.

Howard University Housing is available for interns and students in the D.C. area for the summer. Metro: Shaw-Howard U. Not a great neighborhood. Affordable hostel-like rates in your choice of air-conditioned or non-air-conditioned singles, doubles, and suites in the university dorms. Single rooms $14, with A/C $18. Payment required in full upon arrival. Variable meal plans are available through university dining services (806-7400). Linen service $5 per week. Requests for applications should be directed to Rev. James Coleman at the Office of Student Development: Residential Life (806-5661 or 806-5653). Rooms available June 1-July 31.

Gallaudet University Summer Housing: Write to Summer Conferences and Intern Housing, Gallaudet University, P.O. Box 2302, 800 Florida Ave. NE, Washington, D.C., 20002 (651-5551; fax 651-5595). A tightly-patrolled campus in a decaying and dangerous neighborhood; offers free rush-hour shuttle buses to

Union Station and Eastern Market Metro stations. Standard collegiate dorm rooms with shared bathrooms. Two-week min. stay. Call or write ahead to reserve and send $250 deposit. Singles $21, doubles $15.50 per person.

■■■ HOSTELS

Washington International Hostel (AYH/HI), 1009 11 St. NW 20001 (737-2333). Metro: Metro Center; take the 11th St. exit, then walk 3 blocks north (away from the Mall). Not only a cheapo place to stay, the AYH/HI hostel is one of the friendliest; international travelers from everywhere appreciate the college-aged staff, bright spacious atmosphere, bulletin boards, kitchen, and common rooms. Clean, air-conditioned rooms hold 4-12 beds (usually 10-14 beds, but some rooms are broken up into 2-bed cubicles), accessible by elevator. Shared bathrooms are clean. Lockers and laundry room available, as well as game room. Quiet downstairs lounge. No alcohol or drugs; smoking room in basement. Staff organizes free activities every day, including concerts, plays, and walking tours. Fairly safe neighborhood, but not so safe northeast of here. Open 24 hrs. Bed $18; $3 membership charge per night for non-AYH/HI-members. (After 6 nights' stay, foreigners automatically become AYH members.) Telephone reservations recommended, written reservations must be received weeks in advance. MC and Visa accepted. Wheelchair access.

Simpkins' Bed & Breakfast, 1601 19th St. NW (387-1328), at the corner of Q in the heart of Dupont Circle. Metro: Dupont Circle. Washington's newest hostel, run by a friendly, frizzy-haired environmental lawyer, offers guests single and double beds in clean and spacious rooms. No frills, but you get a bed-and-breakfast atmosphere and unbeatable location at hostel prices. For travelers carrying passports (U.S. or foreign) or public-interest professionals, shared-room rates are $15 for a single bed, $20 for single occupancy of a double bed, or $25 total for double occupancy of a double bed; private single $40, private double $50. No breakfast included with this discount rate, and a pre-paid reservation is required. Without passport or public-interest affiliation, rates are $80 for a single and $100 for a double. Bring a passport! Linen $5, or bring your own. Very limited kitchen facilities. No min. or max. stay. No curfew or lockout. Call 2 or 3 weeks ahead to reserve.

■■■ GUEST HOUSES AND HOTELS

Kalorama Guest House at Kalorama Park, 1854 Mintwood Place NW (667-6369; fax 319-1262), off Columbia Rd. in Adams-Morgan. Metro: Woodley Park-Zoo (a long walk). Well-run, impeccably decorated, immaculate guest rooms in four Victorian townhouses in the upscale western slice of Adams-Morgan near Rock Creek Park. Enjoy evening sherry or lemonade among the oriental rugs—either by the fire in winter or on the patio in summer. All rooms have A/C and a clock radio. Refrigerator space, washing machines, and a guest phone for local calls. Free continental breakfast. Rooms with shared bath $40-65 for one, $45-75 for two. Rooms with private baths $55-85 for one, $60-95 for two. Two-room suite with private bath (3-6 people) $80-$115. 10% discount with International Student ID Card. Reservations with full prepayment or credit card required (try to call 1 to 2 weeks in advance); desk hrs. Mon.-Fri. 8am-8pm, Sat.-Sun. 8:30am-7pm.

Kalorama Guest House at Woodley Park, 2700 Cathedral Ave. NW (328-0860). Metro: Woodley Park-Zoo. By the people who brought you the Kalorama Guest House at Kalorama Park. This place meets the same high standards of quality, cleanliness, value, and Victorian charm as its older sibling— complete with the complimentary sherry. Free continental breakfast. Laundry facilities. Reservations with full prepayment or credit card required; cancel for full refund up to 2 weeks ahead. Free continental breakfast. Rooms with shared bath $45-75 for one, $45-80 for two. Rooms with private baths $55-95 for one, $60-105 for two. $5 per additional person. Seniors, AAA members, International Student ID Card holders 10% off. Call and reserve 1-2 weeks in advance; desk hrs. Mon.-Fri. 8am-8pm, Sat.-Sun. 8:30am-7pm.

Hereford House, 604 South Carolina Ave. SE (543-0102). Metro: Eastern Market. If you're facing the Metro escalator, South Carolina Ave. is at 10 o'clock; Hereford House is less than a block down. A British-style bed and breakfast in a Capitol Hill townhouse, this enchanting accommodation couples downtown convenience with quiet B&B charm. Friendly English hostess rents four rooms, each named for a county in the U.K. Singles $40-50, doubles $55-60. Two shared baths, laundry facilities, A/C, refrigerator, living room, garden patio, and dog ("Jip") make this place feel like home. Continental breakfast served 7:30-9:30am; cooled breakfast 8 and 8:30am. Senior discount 10% for stays longer than a week, $5 per day. Reservations advised.

Hotel Anthony, 1823 L St. NW (223-4320, 800-424-2970; fax 223-8546), near 18th St. Metro: Farragut North. Singles and doubles go for $99 summer weekends, $109-119 during the week. The rest of the year, rates range from $109 to $134, based on availability. Complimentary passes to nearby Bally's Holiday Spa. 10% discount for seniors. The earlier you make your reservations, the better; this friendly place fills up quickly.

Adams Inn, 1744 Lanier Place NW (745-3600 or 800-578-6807), near Ontario Rd. behind the Columbia Rd. Safeway supermarket, 2 blocks from the center of Adams-Morgan. Metro: Woodley Park-Zoo, then a 12 min. walk; or #42 bus to Columbia Rd. from Dupont Circle. Elaborate and elegant Victorian townhouses smothered in Persian rugs. Rooms have A/C. All shared-bath rooms have private sinks. Outdoor patio, coin laundry facilities, pay phones, and eating facilities. TV in common room. Office hrs. Mon.-Sat. 8am-9pm, Sun. 1-9pm. Singles with shared bath $45, with private bath $60. Doubles with shared bath $55, with private bath $70. Breakfast included. Reservations require deposit. Limited parking $7 per night. Prices include taxes. 10% discount with International Student ID Card.

Tabard Inn, 1739 N St. NW (785-1277; fax 785-6173), at 17th St. Metro: Dupont Circle. Romantic inn offers complimentary breakfast in a maze of darkened lounges, narrow stairwells, and big, heavy chairs. The wood-floored rooms vary tremendously in size—some lilliputian, some gargantuan—but all well-kept and stocked with antique furnishings. Dining outdoors in the courtyard. Singles $59-79, with private bath $99-135. $12 for each additional person.

Savoy Hotel, 2505 Wisconsin Ave. NW (337-9700, 800-964-5377; fax 337-3644), near Calvert St. north of Georgetown. Metro: Tenleytown, Foggy Bottom, or Friendship Heights—#30, 32, 34, or 36 bus from those stops, or from Georgetown, to Davis St. Also provides free shuttle service to and from Woodley Park-Zoo Metro stop. Well-maintained, spacious hotel-quality rooms, excellent for families on a budget. Kitchenettes and jacuzzis in some rooms, and all have either one king- or two queen-size beds. For rooms without kitchenettes, free microwave and refrigerator available on request. Don't hesitate to ask for a room with a jacuzzi and a view; when available, these beauties go at no extra cost. Call as far ahead as you can—on weekends with big events like Georgetown's graduation or on major holidays, they're sold out months in advance. Singles $69-119, depending on how full the hotel is. Doubles $79-129. Under 18 stays free with parents.

Quality Hotel Downtown, 1315 16th St. NW (232-8000, 800-228-5151; fax 667-9827). Metro: Farragut North, at Scott Circle. Huge, amenity-filled rooms, most with 2 double beds, some with a sofabed and kitchenette as well. No pool, but ask for a free pass to the National Health Club at 17th St. NW and Rhode Island Ave. Weekend rates: from $105 summer, $69 fall, $85 winter for 1-2 people; $15 per additional adult. Ask for promotional weekday rates (subject to availability, of course). Kids under 18 stay free; senior discount 30%, AAA discount 10%.

Days Inn Downtown, 1201 K St. NW (371-1473 or 800-562-3350; fax 289-0336). Metro: Metro Center. Comfortable, standard quality rooms with TV, A/C, and coffeemakers. Kitchenettes in some rooms. Bar/lounge and rooftop pool. Parking in the hotel garage $11 per day. Singles and doubles $79-89. Weekend rate $75 (subject to availability). Free use of hotel fitness room. Courtesy bus tours of the city at 7:55am, 1:30pm, 7:20pm.

Holiday Inn Central, 1501 Rhode Island Ave. NW (483-2000, 800-248-0016; fax 797-1078). Metro: McPherson Square, one block from Scott Circle. Cable TV, fitness center, rooftop swimming pool. Coffee makers, blowdryers, and "info phones" in every room; ask for a sofabed at no extra charge. In summer, singles and doubles $69 on weekends, $109 weekdays, subject to availability. Seniors, AARP/AAA members should ask for a 10% discount.

Connecticut Woodley Guest House, 2647 Woodley Rd. NW (667-0218). Metro: Woodley Park-Zoo. Modest furnishings in threadbare yet tidy rooms. Singles with shared bath $39-43, with private bath $49-56. Doubles with shared bath $45-48, with private bath $54-61. Group, family, and long-term rates available. Max. stay 4 weeks. No wheelchair access. A/C and free parking. Office open daily 7:30am-midnight.

Holiday Inn, 1155 14th St. NW (737-1200, reservations 800-465-4329; fax 783-5733), at Thomas Circle. Metro: McPherson Square. Rooftop pool. Pleasant singles and doubles $119 in summer and $79-89 the rest of the year, subject to availability; ask for "Great Rates" to get a 10% room discount for seniors; AAA discounts as well ($107). Call ahead for information. Parking $10 a day.

Davis House, 1822 R St. NW (232-3196; fax 232-3197), near 19th St. Metro: Dupont Circle. Charming and spacious wood-floored building equipped with common living room, sun room, patio, fridge, and microwave. Accepts international visitors, staff of Quaker organizations, and "representatives of other organizations working on peace and justice concerns." Other visitors occasionally accepted on a same-day, space-available basis. No smoking or alcohol. Max. stay 2 weeks. Open daily 8am-10pm. Singles in a shared room $30, private singles $35, doubles $60 (with hall bath). One night's deposit required. Reserve as early as possible. No credit cards accepted.

Brickskeller Inn, 1523 22nd St. NW (293-1885), between P and Q St. Metro: Dupont Circle. Small, clean, recently renovated rooms, usually with private sinks and shared hall bathrooms. Some rooms come with private bath, A/C, and TV. Singles $35-65, doubles $45-65 (taxes included). Weekly rates: singles from $150, doubles from $225.

HoJo Inn, 600 New York Ave. NE (546-9200; fax 546-6348). Metro: Union Station. A ½-hr. walk from the Metro; take N. Capitol St., then turn right on New York Ave. A cab or car is safer than walking. Clean, carpeted rooms with A/C and TV. Electronic key card system for your safety and the security of your valuables. Outdoor pool and free continental breakfast. Shuttle buses to the Mall, monuments, and Metro provided, but you'll have to be up at the crack of dawn to catch one: they run at 7:30, 8:30, and 9:30am daily ($4 for one person, $2 for each additional person in party). Singles and doubles range $47-95; doubles and triples $69-95. 10% discount for seniors and military types.

The Governor's House, 1615 Rhode Island Ave. NW (296-2100, 800-821-4367; fax 331-0227), at 17th St. Metro: Farragut North at Scott Circle. Oversized rooms come with all the amenities; some have kitchenettes and sofa beds as well. If the hotel's swimming pool doesn't meet your needs, use the free pass to the YMCA next door. July-Aug., $89 on weekdays, $69 on weekends subject to availability. $110 the rest of the year. 10% discount for seniors.

Swiss Inn, 1204 Massachusetts Ave. NW (371-1816, 800-955-7947). Metro: Metro Center. Four blocks from Metro Center; close to downtown. 7 clean, quiet studio apartments with refrigerator, private bath, high ceilings, kitchenettes, and air-conditioning. Free local phone calls and laundry. International crowd welcomed by French- and German-speaking managers. Singles and doubles $98 ($78 in summer), with 20% discount for travel-club members (including AYH/HI), *Let's Go* readers, and seniors 60 and over. Weekly rates: singles and doubles $78 per night. Park in the neighboring lot for $5 per day weekdays (free weekends), or call the managers from the bus stop, Metro station, or downtown airport terminal and they'll come pick you up.

Windsor Park Hotel, 2116 Kalorama Rd. NW (483-7700, fax 332-4547). Metro: Woodley Park-Zoo. A 5-min. walk across the Calvert St. Bridge, then a right on Kalorama. Small, cozy rooms at reasonable rates. Cable, phone, refrigerator, private bath. Complimentary continental breakfast. Singles $78, doubles $88. Weekends $64. 10% discount for International Student ID Card holders and seniors.

Allen Lee Hotel, 2224 F St. NW (331-1224, 800-462-0186), near 23rd St. and George Washington University. Metro: Foggy Bottom-GWU. Large, aging, blue hallways. Rooms vary widely in size, furnishings, and state of repair, so look at several before accepting one. Bedrooms and bathrooms, aging but clean, have air conditioning. Collection of delivery menus behind the desk for those who don't want to brave D.C. at night. Singles $28, with private bath $35. Doubles $35, with private bath $45. Twins $37, with private bath $49. Reserve a few days in advance in summer.

Harrington Hotel, 11th and E St. NW (628-8140 or 800-424-8532; fax 347-3924). Metro: Metro Center. The business-like center of Old Downtown; 3 blocks from the Smithsonian and closer to other major sights. International visitors abound. Elevators and hallways are unattractive and aging, but the 264 rooms are generally large and clean with TV, A/C, and great views. June-Aug. singles and doubles $79, weekends $69, student singles $49, student doubles $54. Sept.-May singles $75, weekends $69, students $49, doubles $54. Weekend rate all week for adults over 60. 10% off with International Student ID Card.

Super 8 Motel, 501 New York Ave. NE (543-7400), on the New York Ave. motel strip. Metro: Union Station. A 25-min. walk from the station on N. Capitol St., then a right on New York Ave. Do not walk here at night; take a taxi or drive. Standard, clean motel rooms with TV, A/C, and private bath. Outdoor pool. Shuttle bus from motel to Metro and Mall attractions every day at 7:35, 8:35, and 9:35am ($4 per person, $2 each additional person in your party). Singles $50. Doubles $59. 10% discount for military and seniors.

Travelodge Center City Hotel, 1201 13th St. NW (682-5300; fax 371-9624). Metro: McPherson Square. Two blocks from Thomas Circle. Clean, tastefully furnished rooms with TV, A/C, and coffeemakers. Complimentary continental breakfast and free use of hotel fitness center. Singles $75, doubles $85. $10 each additional person. Parking $10 per day. Seniors, students, and AAA members 10% discount. International Student ID Card rates: singles $50, doubles $59.

Holiday Inn, 2101 Wisconsin Ave. NW (338-4600; fax 333-6113), in northern Georgetown. Metro: Foggy Bottom, Tenleytown or Friendship Heights—take the #30, 32, 34, or 36 bus from those stops or from Georgetown to the front of the hotel. Outdoor swimming pool and cheap adjoining restaurant; nearby Safeway. Attractive, newly renovated rooms. Singles $134, doubles $144; students $92; seniors 10% discount. Ask for "Great Rates," which can go as low as $69 in the summer. Rollaway beds $10. Free use of hotel fitness center. Wheelchair accessible. Kids 19 or under traveling with parents sleep for free, 12 and under eat for free.

Best Western Downtown-Capitol Hill, 724 3rd Street, NW (842-4466, 800-242-4831; fax 842-4831). A small (58 rooms), elegant hotel in a convenient but less-than-safe location. Singles $91, doubles $99-105. TV and A/C in every room. Lower rates depend on availability. Weekend rate $91 for all rooms. Complimentary continental breakfast (7-9am) served in the basement cafeteria.

Holiday Inn on the Hill, 415 New Jersey Ave. NW (638-1616, 800-638-1116; fax 346-1813), across from the Hyatt Regency. Metro: Union Station. Walk 3 blocks northwest on New Jersey Ave. from the Capitol. Standard, well-maintained rooms, 24-hr. reception, and friendly front desk. Swimming pool on the top floor. Rates vary daily based on season and occupancy. Singles and doubles $79-$149, depending on availability.

WEEKEND RATES AND SPECIALS

One Washington Circle Hotel, One Washington Circle NW, between 23rd and New Hampshire (872-1680, reservations 800-424-9671; fax 887-4989). Metro: Foggy Bottom-GWU. The dark blue hallways and plush carpets lead to well-appointed suites, each with a full kitchen and lots of closet space. Interesting selection of carpets, wall paintings, and lobby furniture. First-class service; complimentary *Post* delivered each morning except Sun. Laundry and dry cleaning available. Variable summer weekend rates available for as low as $89 for a double.

The Windsor Inn, 1842 16th St. NW (667-0300, 800-423-9111; fax 234-3309), between Swann and T St. Metro: Dupont Circle. Clean guest house in a 1920s Art Deco townhouse. Atmosphere somewhere between traditional B&B and big hotel. 24-hr. reception desk. Continental breakfast and evening sherry served. Free daily newspaper. All rooms with private baths. Singles $69-99, doubles $79-

110, suites $105-150. Summer weekends all non-suites $55, subject to availability. Highest rates negotiable during the off-season (July-Aug., Nov.-Jan.). Seniors and AAA 10% discount.

Embassy Inn, 1627 16th St. NW (234-7800, 800-423-9111; fax 234-3309), near R St. Metro: Dupont Circle. Same management as Windsor Inn rents small, pastel rooms with a free nightly glass of sherry, daily newspaper, and continental breakfast. Library in living room. All with private bath and A/C. Singles $69-99, doubles $79-105. Summer weekends $55, subject to availability. Seniors 10% discount.

St. James Hotel, 950 24th St. NW (457-0500, 800-852-8512; fax 659-4492), near K St. Metro: Foggy Bottom-GWU. Chic European-style hotel just off Pennsylvania Ave. Small but sleek lobby belies almost 200 spacious rooms that come complete with kitchens. Compact swimming pool in back with Roman mural. Coin laundry. Wheelchair access. Complimentary breakfast Mon.-Fri. 7-9am, Sat.-Sun. 8-10am. $125-165, $89-119 on weekends. Special off-season rates of $69 and $79.

Carlyle Suites Hotel, 1731 New Hampshire Ave. NW (234-3200, 800-964-5377; fax 387-0085), between R and S St. Metro: Dupont Circle. Sparkles in renovated Art Deco charm. The "Official Art Deco Hotel" in D.C. Efficiency suites with kitchenettes. Singles $79-119, doubles $89-129. Weekend rate $69 (Fri.-Sun. or Sat.-Mon.) on availability. Rates are negotiable for large groups, especially during slow summer months. Laundry facilities and same-day dry cleaning available. 10% seniors and AAA discount. Did we mention the Art Deco?

New Hampshire Suites Hotel, 1121 New Hampshire Ave. NW (457-0565, 800-762-3777; fax 331-9421). Metro: Foggy Bottom (then 10-min. walk along 22nd St. and through Washington Circle). Fair-sized rooms with TVs, small refrigerators, small coffeemakers, and even smaller microwaves; irons, ironing boards, and hairdryers. Singles with queen-sized bed $129, doubles with pull-out sofa $149. Breakfast included. Ask about special packages. Health club passes $5. Parking $14.50 for valet, $11 otherwise. Call in advance for reservations.

Normandy Inn, 2118 Wyoming Ave. NW (483-1350, 800-424-3729; fax 387-8241), near Connecticut Ave. Metro: Dupont Circle or Woodley Park-Zoo (a hike from either). Quiet, old-world-style inn renting standard, comfortable rooms equipped with private baths, fridges, and coffee-makers. Singles $97. Doubles $107. $10 each additional person. Weekends all rooms $79, subject to availability.

Comfort Inn, 500 H St. NW (289-5959; fax 682-9152). Metro: Gallery Place-Chinatown. 2 blocks to Metro. This standard upper mid-range hotel dominates Chinatown. Friendly service and comfortable rooms. Prices vary by season and availability. 24-hr. check-in. In the summer, singles $109, doubles $119, weekend rates $79 and $89. Call to find out if their "Summer Sizzler" deal is available (800-234-6423): singles $69 (includes breakfast buffet and one-day Metro pass), doubles $79 (includes breakfast and 2 passes).

Hotel Lombardy, 2019 I St. NW (828-2600, 800-424-5486; fax 872-0503), near 21st St. Metro: Farragut West, three blocks from the Metro. An elegant hotel with all the amenities. Rooms are comfortable bordering on luxurious; most come with kitchenettes. In the summer, singles and doubles can go as low as $59 on weekends, $99 weekdays. The rest of the year, prices $99-145.

■■■ LONG-TERM LODGINGS

International Student House, 1825 R St. NW (387-6445; fax 387-4115), near 18th St. Metro: Dupont Circle. Welcomes primarily long-term international and some domestic students grandly and warmly in a romantic Tudor townhouse with a mammoth dining hall, important-looking library, large patio, and garden. The modern, dormitory-like rooms are fully furnished and single-sex and have A/C. Doubles, triples, and quads $600-760 per person per month; singles $805 per month. Additional fee for stays under 4 months. Daily breakfast and dinner included. Parking $50 per month if available. Must be at least 20 years old. Write to them (ZIP 20009) for an application or more information. Open Mon.-Tues. and Thurs.-Fri. 9am-5pm, Wed. 9am-8pm, Sat. 11am-1pm. Reserve early.

Thompson-Markward Hall, 235 2nd St. NE (546-3255), just 3 blocks from Union Station near C St., across from the Hart Senate office building. Metro: Union Station. For women ages 18-34 only. On the upper floors, 112 dorm-like single rooms and three double rooms line old but well-cleaned hallways. Small bedrooms (about 15 ft. by 10 ft.) have air-conditioning and phones; communal bathrooms are large and well kept. Large, airy laundry room. Maid service provided but bring your own sheets. Two cafeteria-style meals per day in a pleasant dining hall. Piano. Popular with Hill interns and graduate students. Men aren't allowed beyond the first floor, but may visit with women in the lavish lobby and adjoining lounge and library. Two-week min. stay, two-year max. stay. Call by early March to book a room for summer. $134 per week.

■■■ BETHESDA, MD

Manor Inn Bethesda, 7740 Wisconsin Ave. (301-656-2100, reservations 800-874-0050; fax 986-0375). Metro: Bethesda, then walk 2 blocks. Comfortable clone motel. Big, carpeted rooms with TVs and A/C. Free continental breakfast. Coin-operated laundry. Free shuttle to NIH—great for conventions. Check-out by noon. Singles $72, doubles $80. Off-season rates slightly lower.

American Inn of Bethesda, 8130 Wisconsin Ave. (301-656-9300, 800-323-7081; fax 656-2907). Clean, generic inn with A/C, free cable TV, complimentary continental breakfast, microwave use, and outdoor pool. All rooms have been recently renovated. Children under 18 stay free with parents. Singles $90, doubles $100. Awesome weekend and student rates: singles $58, doubles $68.

The Bethesda Ramada, 8400 Wisconsin Ave. (301-654-1000, 800-228-2828; fax 654-0751). Metro: Medical Center, then walk 3 blocks along Wisconsin toward Bethesda (if Wisconsin suddenly turns into Rockville Pike, you're going in the wrong direction). Clean, air-conditioned rooms with TVs, and decor a bit nicer than the usual. Courtyard pool. All rooms include either 2 doubles or 1 king-size bed. Guests are charged by room, so 4 can stay for the price of 2. Singles or doubles $110. Sweet weekend rates: Fri.-Sat. singles and doubles $79-89.

■■■ ARLINGTON, VA

Quality Hotel, 1200 North Courthouse Rd. (703-524-4000; fax 522-6814). Steep 10-min. walk from Courthouse Metro. Actually a complex of buildings; each building has a specific type of room at a specific price range. Rooms begin at $79 weeknights, $65 weekends. Ask about extended stay rates. Amenities like kitchenettes come with the pricier rooms; all rooms ample and tidy. Pool and fitness facilities. AAA/AARP 10% discount; wheelchair access.

Quality Inn Iwo Jima, 1501 Arlington Blvd. (703-524-5000, reservations 800-221-2222; fax 522-5484), on Rte. 50. Metro: Rosslyn. 10-min. walk from Metro stop. Dependable hotel with smallish, newish rooms, swimming pool, washers and dryers, hairdryers, HBO, and free parking. Convenient to Georgetown, but a long walk. Summer singles $83, doubles $88. Fall and winter singles $87, doubles $92. Weekend rates: summer $65, fall/winter $60. Ages under 18 free. AAA and AARP 10% discount. Wheelchair access.

Holiday Inn Westpark Hotel, 1900 North Fort Myer Dr. (703-807-2000). Metro: Rosslyn. Just across the street from the Metro. More amenities than the neighboring Rosslyn Key Bridge Hotel, listed below. All rooms have a balcony; ask for one with a view. Pool, sauna, and weight room. Complimentary parking. Look for the special weekend rates: $77 for a room with 2 double beds. Wheelchair access.

Highlander Motor Inn, 3336 Wilson Blvd. (703-524-4300, 800-786-4301). Metro: Clarendon. Two double beds in each room. Clean, spacious, aging motel rooms. Refrigerators on request. Free coffee & donuts go out around 6am. Singles $55, in winter $50. Doubles $60, in winter $55. Flash a copy of *Let's Go* for a $5 discount.

Rosslyn Key Bridge Hotel, 1850 North Fort Myer Dr. (703-522-0400; fax 524-5275). Across from Rosslyn Metro. Friendlier than most, with a helpful staff. Ideal for large families, since kids under 19 stay for free and kids under 12 eat for free in summer. Comfortable bedrooms. Pool, game room, and free parking. Depending on the season and latest deals, rooms from $108. Weekend rates from $69. Weekdays, the AAA/AARP rate is $95.

■■■ ALEXANDRIA, VA

The area from the Braddock Metro stop to Washington St. is not a great place to walk. At night, take a cab to your hotel.

Best Western Old Colony Inn, 625 1st St. (703-739-2222, 800-528-1234; fax 549-2568), near N. Washington St. Lobby at St. Asaph St. Metro: Braddock. Stay in the courtyard for reasonably priced, clean rooms; the main lobby leads to rooms that are more upscale. Near a convenience store; boasts indoor and outdoor pools, sauna, fitness center, and cable TV. Area is relitively safe. Complimentary shuttle to National Airport and Metro. Standard rate of $89. Weekend rate $74 for up to 5 people. Each person after 5, $10 each. AAA rate $59.

Ramada Hotel, 901 N. Fairfax St. (703-683-6000; fax 683-7597), at Montgomery St. A 15-min. walk from Braddock Rd. Metro station. Pool and restaurant on the premises. Free shuttle to National Airport. Nice rooms, some with a view of the river. $94 weekdays, $84 for seniors. $74 weekends. $10 each additional person after 3. 5 people max. per room. Kids under 18 with a parent stay for free.

EconoLodge, 702 N. Washington St. (703-836-5100; fax 519-7015), at Wythe St. Neat standard motel rooms with cable TV, A/C, and no-frills service. Convenient to bus stop and Braddock Metro; close to restaurants and other hotels. Complimentary shuttle to National Airport. Singles $50, seniors $45. Doubles $60. $5 per extra person. $10 key deposit required.

Towne Motel, 808 N. Washington St. (703-548-3500), near Madison. Metro: Braddock. No-frills hotel (except for the working telephones, HBO, and A/C); rooms are clean but could use a paint job. ID required to check in. Singles $38, doubles $45. Up to 4 people per room ($3 per additional person). $5 key deposit, $10 phone deposit.

■■■ SUBURBAN MARYLAND

Comfort Inn, 16216 Frederick Rd. (301-330-0023, reservations 800-228-5150; fax 258-1950), at Shady Grove Rd. in Gaithersburg. Metro: Shady Grove. By car: take I-270 to exit 8 onto Shady Grove Rd., turn right onto Frederick Rd. (Rte. 355). Comfortable rooms decorated in pastels, some with desks and couches. Large bathrooms. Free shuttle service to the Metro, ½mi. away. Free continental breakfast. Singles $65, doubles $72; occasional weekend rate: singles $49, doubles $55. Each additional person $6. Wheelchair access.

Colonial Manor Inn, 11410 Rockville Pike (301-881-5200, 800-752-3800; fax 231-7668), across from White Flint Mall. Metro: White Flint. Recently renovated. Outdoor pool (in the parking lot), and video game room. 10-min. walk to hotel from Metro or take the free shuttle to White Flint Mall, across from the hotel. Coin-op laundry. Rooms start at an amazing $49 and range up to $99. (With kitchenette, $69-125.)

Quality Hotel, 8727 Colesville Rd. (301-589-5200 or 800-221-2222; fax 301-588-1841), at Spring St. in Silver Spring. Metro: Silver Spring. Some aesthetic elements show signs of aging, but rooms are clean and comfy. Indoor pool, fitness center, sauna, cable TV, and breakfast included. Suites $59-100. Special $70 double weekend rate. Kids 18 and under stay free; AAA and senior citizen discounts.

■■■ CAMPING

Cherry Hill Park, 9800 Cherry Hill Rd. (301-937-7116; fax 595-7181). By car: from D.C. take route I-95 towards Baltimore, then take exit 29B onto Rte. 212. Follow 212 for a mile, then turn onto Cherry Hill Rd. From Baltimore and elsewhere take exit 25B off I-95 or I-495; make the first right onto Cherry Hill Rd. Once on Cherry Hill Rd., follow signs to the park. The closest campground to Washington, with

400 sites and modern amenities; most sites are for RVs. Metrobus stop located on the grounds takes you to the Greenbelt Metro stop (every 15min. during rush hour, otherwise every 30min.). Cable hookup available; coin-operated laundry; heated swimming pool with whirlpool and sauna. Pets allowed. 2-person tent site $25; RV site with electricity, water, and sewer $33. Extra person $2. $25 deposit required. Reservations recommended (call during the summer 7am-10pm; 7am-7pm otherwise). Seniors, AAA, military, and KOA members 10% discount.

Capitol KOA, 768 Cecil Ave. (410-923-2771, 987-7477; fax 923-3709), near Millersville. Full facilities for tents, RVs, and cabins. Free pool, movies. From D.C., take John Hanson Hwy. (Rte. 50) to Robert Crain Hwy. (Rte. 3 North), and bear right after 10mi. onto Veterans Hwy. (Rte. 197). Go a short distance to the bottom of the hill, then turn left under highway. Follow blue signs to campground. 18 mi. from Baltimore Beltway, 25mi. from D.C., 10mi. from Annapolis. Free weekday shuttle to D.C./Baltimore trains; commuter train (MARC) $6.75 round-trip to Union Station, ½-price for children. Weekend shuttle to New Carroll Metro. Tent site for two $22. RV site $29.75 with complete hookup. Each additional adult $4. Off-season prices: $18 for tent site, $26.75 for full hookup. Open April-Nov.

Greenbelt Park, 6565 Greenbelt Rd. (301-344-3948). By car: take I-95 South to exit 23 onto Kenilworth Ave. (Rte. 201), then head south toward Bladensburg and follow the signs. You can also take the Baltimore-Washington Pkwy. (I-295), exit onto Greenbelt Rd. (Rte. 193 East), and follow the signs. 174 sites available for tents, trailers, and campers at this park 12mi. from D.C. Showers are down Greenbelt Rd. at the Greenbelt Recreation Center and Pool (free). Camping limited to 7 days from Memorial Day to Labor Day and to 14 days the remainder of the year. Long drive to the tenting area. Admission $10, 50% discount for seniors with Golden Age Pass. If no ranger is present, the campground operates under a self-registration system.

Food

D.C. makes up for its days as a "sleepy Southern town" with a kaleidoscope of international restaurants. Haughty European dining rooms strive to impress the expense-account crowd, while bargains from Africa, Southeast Asia, and the Americas feed a melange of immigrants (and wise locals) from all over. Smithsonian-goers should plan to eat dinner far away from the triceratops and the biplanes: visitors to the Mall get stuffed at (and stuffed into) mediocre cafeterias, only blocks from the respectable food on Capitol Hill. You can eat for $4 or eat well for $7 at many places in D.C.; while Adams-Morgan is famous for budget restaurants, Dupont Circle and the Hill are worth the Metro rides as well.

It's an open secret among interns that **happy hours** provide the cheapest dinners in Washington. Bars desperate to attract early-evening drinkers set up plates, platters, and tables of free appetizers; the trick is to drop by and munch lots but drink little. The best seem to concentrate, along with the interns, on Capitol Hill or south of Dupont. The occasional public reception in a small museum or office lobby can also offer the courageous a free snack (especially those dressed for it). A week of nonstop nachos and mushrooms for dinner could make anyone (except an intern) sick; still, a dinner of happy-hour appetizers has salvaged many a knowing student from virtual starvation. (See **Bars,** p. 206.)

If you feel like getting away from eating elbow-to-elbow with the crowd (and saving a few pennies in the process), try picnicking with supplies from a local supermarket or specialty store. Prime picnic spots include Rock Creek Park, the Tidal Basin, and the Mall. Most large supermarkets have an excellent selection of prepared foods (including lasagne, salads, and even roasted chicken) and fresh breads, cheeses, and fruits. Try a smaller ethnic market for more unusual offerings.

If you prefer to dine in, many D.C. and suburban restaurants deliver— for free or for a small surcharge; there is often a minimum order as well. **Takeout Taxi** has three locations: D.C. (986-0111), Bethesda (301-571-0111), and Arlington (342-0700 from D.C.). **À La Carte Express** (546-8646) delivers to Dupont Circle and Capitol Hill.

We have prefaced the restaurant listings, which are organized by neighborhood, with a full list of D.C.-area restaurants, cross-referenced by type of food and by features. The "Splurge" category consists of restaurants where a typical dinner entree costs $10-15. Restaurants in the **Let's Go Pick** (denoted by a star) category combine exceptional cuisine with reasonable prices; the only picks whose prices are somewhat higher are so good they're worth saving up for. Every restaurant listed in these sections is followed by an abbreviated neighborhood label, which directs you to the section within the *By Neighborhood* list where you'll find the restaurant's write-up. The abbreviations used are as follows:

CH	Capitol Hill	*SH*	Shaw
SE	Southeast	*AM*	Adams-Morgan
WF	Waterfront	*UN*	Upper Northwest
OD	Old Downtown	*NE*	Northeast
CHT	Chinatown	*B*	Bethesda, MD
FB	White House Area and Foggy Bottom	*TP*	Takoma Park, MD
		AR	Arlington, VA
G	Georgetown	*AL*	Alexandria, VA
F	Farragut	★	*Let's Go* pick
DP	Dupont Circle		

BY TYPE OF FOOD

African

Café Bukom *AM*
Dahlak *AM*
★ Meskerem *AM*
★ Red Sea *AM*
★Zed's Ethiopian Cuisine *G*

Standard American

American Café CH, OD, G, UN
The Art Gallery Grill F
Belview Seafood AL
★Ben's Chili Bowl *SH*
Blue Castle Deli *SE*
★Booeymonger *G*
Booeymonger *UN*
Capital City Subs *SE*
Chadwick's *UN*
Cone E. Island *FB*
Don Arturo AR
Dupont Down Under DP
Dutch Mill Deli Restaurant *OD*
El Pollo Primo *AM*
★Florida Ave. Grill *SH*
The Gangplank *WF*
Hamburger Hamlet *G*
Hard Times Café *AR, AL*
Hawk 'n Dove *CH*
Heart & Soul Café CH
Houston's *G*
Jan Drake's Garden Café *OD*
Johnathan's Gourmet Deli/Market *FB*
Lindy's Bon Apétit *FB*
★The Market Lunch *CH*
Mr. Henry's *CH*
Omaha Coffee Shop *DP*
Outlaw's Kitchen *SH*
Philadelphia Mike's *OD, B*
Polly's Café *SH*
Recessions *F*
Royal Restaurant *AL*
The Scoop Grill and Homemade Ice Cream *AL*
Sholl's Colonial Cafeteria *F*
Tiffany's Deli *OD*
Tune Inn *CH*
Upper Deck *OD*
2 Quail *CH*

Bagels

Chesapeake Bagel Bakery *F, AL*
Georgetown Bagelry *G*
Whatsa Bagel *F*

Bakery

Le Palais du Chocolat *F*
Palais du Chocolat *UN, TP*
The Uptown Bakers *UN*

Bar and Grill

Colonel Brooks Tavern *NE*
Millie and Al's *AM*
Takoma Station Tavern *TP*

Barbecue and Ribs

★Head's *CH*
Kenny's Smoke House *CH*
King Street Blues *AL*
Red Hot and Blue *AR*
★Rocklands *UN*
Wingmaster's Grilled Chicken and Ribs *UN*

Café

Afterwords Café *DP*
a.k.a. Frisco's *UN*
Bread and Chocolate *CH*
Café Amadeus, *OD*
Caffè Northwest *G*
Cup'A Cup'A *F*
Everyday Gourmet *TP*
Food & Co. Gourmet Café *FB*
Java House *DP*
Jolt 'N Bolt *DP*
★Le Bon Café *CH*
Le Café Complet *CH*
New World Café *OD*
Old Town Sandwich Shop *AL*
Peacock Café and Market *G*
★The Pop Stop *DP*
Reeve's *OD*
Roasters on the Hill *CH*
★Soho Tea & Coffee *DP*
West Side Café *B*

Cambodian, Thai, Burmese, and Vietnamese

Burma Restaurant *CHT*
Busara *G*
Café Dalat *AR*
★Café Saigon *AR*
The Cambodian Restaurant *AR*
Little Viet Garden *AR*
Pad Thai *G*
Pho 75 *AR*
★Queen Bee *AR*
Saigon Gourmet Restaurant *UN*
Saigon Inn *G*

Saigonnais *AM*
Sala Thai *DP*
★Star of Siam *F*
Star of Siam *AM*
Thai Kingdom *F*
Thai Taste *UN*
Vietnam-Georgetown Restaurant *G*

Central and Eastern European

★Misha's Deli *CH*

Chinese & Mongolian

Chinacafé *FB*
Chinatown Express *CHT*
Chinese Express *B*
★City Lights of China *DP*
Dante's *DP*
Go Lo's *CHT*
Ho Wah Restaurant *CHT*
Hsiang Foon *AR*
Hunan Chinatown *CHT*
Hunan Dynasty *CH*
Hunan Number 1 *AR*
Mrs. Chang's Kitchen F
Szechuan Gallery *CHT*
Tony Cheng's Mongolian Restaurant *CHT*
Yenching Palace *UN*

Cookies

Holly's Cookie Company *FB*

Creole, Cajun, and Caribbean

Bardia's *AM*
Crescent City *AL*
Hibiscus Café *G*
★The Islander *AM*
Louisiana Express *B*
Montego Café *AM*
Negril *B*
Negrilia's Jamaican Bakery *WF*
Tom Sarris' Orleans House *AR*

Deli

Bob Rubin's New York Deli *AL*
Ebbitt Express *F*
German Deli *OD*
GW Deli *FB*
Irene's Deli *WF*
La Prima Market Café *F*
★Misha's Deli *CH*
Neil's Outrageous Deli *CH*
New York Gourmet Deli *F*
The Parkway Deli *UN*
Prego's *CH*
Provisions *CH*
Salad Bar Express *DP*
So's Your Mom *AM*
Toojay's *UN*
World Gourmet *FB*

Diner

The Georgetown Dinette *G*
International House of Pancakes *AR*
Jimmy T's *CH*
Murry and Paul's Restaurant *NE*
Stoupsy's Café *G*
Tastee Diner *B*
Trio Restaurant *DP*

Fast Food

A.J.'s Sub *CH*
Chun King Gourmet Inn *OD*
Vie de France *F*
Wings to Go *NE*

French

Au Croissant Chaud *G*
Café La Ruche *G*
Le Gaulois *AL*
Vie de France *F*

German

German Deli *OD*

Greek and Middle Eastern

Bacchus Restaurant *F*
★Bamiyan *AL*
Café Neek *G*
Calvert Café *AM*
Eye St. Café *F*
Fettoosh *G*
Food Factory *AR*
Gibran *F*
Kabul Caravan *AR*
The Lebanese Taverna *UN*
Mediterranean Deli *UN*
Olympic Carry-Out *G*
Paradise Restaurant *B*
Persepolis Restaurant *B*
Quick Pita *G*
★Skewers *DP*
Taverna the Greek Islands *CH*
Yanni's *UN*
★Zorba's Café *DP*

Health Food/Organic

Balajee Vegetarian Restaurant *F*
★Food for Thought *DP*
Health Zone *OD*
Health's A-Poppin! *CH*

Ice Cream

Bob's Famous Homemade Ice Cream *CH, B*
Ice in Paradise *CH*
Max's Best Ice Cream *UN*
The Scoop Grill and Homemade Ice Cream *AL*
Thomas Sweet *G*
U.S. Famous Homemade Ice Cream UN

Indian and Nepalese

★Aditi *G*
Balajee Vegetarian Restaurant *F*
Deli Dhaba *AR*
Katmandu *DP*
Paru's Indian Vegetarian Restaurant *DP*
Rajaji *UN*
Tandoor *G*
A Taste of India *UN*

Italian

A.V. Ristorante *OD*
Café Luna *DP*
Café Petitto *DP*
Caffè Sorrento *G*
Dupont Italian Kitchen *DP*
Ecco Café *AL*
Eye St. Café *F*
★Faccia Luna *UN*
Faccia Luna *AR*
Julio's *AM*
Mama Marie and Enzio's *G*
Milo's *FB*
★Paolo's *G*
Pasta Mia Trattoria *AM*
Pasta Nostra *AR*
Piccolo *G*
Positano and Aldo Café *B*
Stromboli Family Restaurant *B*
Taliano's *TP*
Treviso *FB*

Japanese and Korean

Atami *AR*
★Sushi-Ko *G*
★Tako Grill *B*
★Tokyo Terrace *F*
Yosaku *UN*

Kitsch

Gadsby's Tavern *AL*

Latin American and Spanish

The Argentine Grill *AM*
Casa Blanca *F*
El Caribe *G*
El Pollo Rico *AR*
El Tamarindo *AM, UN*
El Tazumal *AM*
Jaleo *OD*
Julia's Empanadas *AM*
Las Pampas *G*
Las Rocas *AM*
Terramar *B*

Mexican/Tex-Mex

★Austin Grill *UN*
Burrito Brothers *CH, G, DP*
★Cactus Cantina *UN*
Casa Juanita's *OD*
Enriqueta's *G*
Lauriol Plaza *DP*
★Mixtec *AM*
Rio Grand Café *AR*
★Rio Grande Café *B*
South Austin Grille, *AL*
Tortilla Coast *CH*

Microbrew

Capitol City Brewing Company *OD*
★Faccia Luna *UN*
★Hard Times Café *AR*

Multi-Ethnic

Atami *AR*
DJ's *FB*
Ivy's Place *UN*
Mark's Kitchen *TP*
Pan-Asian *F*
Pan Asian Noodles and Grill *DP*
Perry's *AM*

Pizza

Armand's Chicago Pizzeria *CH, UN, AL*
DC Café *DP*
Ecco Café *AL*
Enzo Trattorio *DP*
★Faccia Luna *UN*
Faccia Luna *AR*
Generous George's Positive Pizza and Pasta Place *AL*
Geppeto's *G*
Maggie's *UN*
★Pizzeria Paradiso *DP*
Taliano's *TP*
Trio Pizza *DP*
Volare Pizza *DP*

Seafood

★Aux Fruits de Mer *G*

Belview Seafood AL
★Bethesda Crab House *B*
Chesapeake Seafood Crab House *AR*
The Dancing Crab *UN*
The Fish Market *AL*
Hogate's *WF*
Steamer's *B*

Soul Food

Adelis *SH*
Dixie Grill *OD*
★Florida Avenue Grill *SH*
Hogs on the Hill *SH*
★Rocklands *UN*

South Asian

★Sarinah *G*

BY FEATURES

Delivery

Armand's Chicago Pizzeria *AL*
Burrito Brothers *G*
Café Neek *G*
Chun King Gourmet Inn *OD*
DC Café *DP*
Dupont Italian Kitchen *DP*
Gepetto's *G*
Hard Times Café *AL*
Hunan Dynasty *CH*
Louisiana Express *B*
Milo's *FB*
Pad Thai *G*
Pasta Nostra *AR*
Peacock Café and Market *G*
Persepolis Restaurant *B*
Quick Pita *G*
Saigonnais *AM*
Star of Siam *AM*
Stromboli Family Restaurant *B*
Trio Pizza *DP*
Trio Restaurant *DP*

Open Late

Afterwords Café *DP*
The Art Gallery Grille *FB*
★Ben's Chili Bowl *SH*
Booeymonger *UN*
Café Bukom *AM*
Chadwick's *G, UN*
Colonel Brooks Tavern *NE*
DC Café *DP*
Dahlak *AM*
Dante's *DP*
El Tamarindo *AM, UN*
Enzo Trattorio *DP*
Fettoosh *G*
The Fish Market *AL*
★Food for Thought *DP*
Go-Lo *CHT*
Hawk 'n Dove *CH*
Ho Wah Restaurant *CHT*
Hunan Number 1 *AR*
International House of Pancakes *AR*
Julio's *AM*
Las Rocas *AM*
Maggie's *UN*
Millie and Al's *AM*
Montego Café *AM*
★Paolo's *G*
Perry's *AM*
Polly's Café *SH*
★The Pop Stop *DP*
Quick Pita *G*
Steamers *B*
Stoupsy's Café *G*
Takoma Station Tavern *TP*
Tastee Diner *B*
Trio Pizza *DP*

Let's Go Picks

★Aditi *G*
★Austin Grill *UN*
★Aux Fruits de Mer *G*
★Bamiyan *AL*
★Ben's Chili Bowl *SH*
★Bethesda Crab House *B*
★Booeymonger *G*
★Cactus Cantina *UN*
★Café Saigon *AR*
★City Lights of China *DP*
★Faccia Luna *UN*
★Florida Avenue Grill *SH*
★Food for Thought *DP*
★Head's *CH*
★The Islander *AM*
★Le Bon Café *CH*
★Market Lunch *CH*
★Meskerem *AM*
★Misha's *CH*
★Mixtec *AM*
★Paolo's *G*
★Pizzeria Paradiso *DP*
★The Pop Stop *DP*
★Queen Bee *AR*
★Rio Grande Café *B*
★Rocklands *UN*

★Sarinah *G*
★Skewers *DP*
★Soho Tea & Coffee *DP*
★Sushi-Ko *G*
★Star of Siam *F*
★Tako Grill *B*
★Tokyo Terrace *F*
★Zed's Ethiopian Cuisine *G*
★Zorba's *DP*

Splurge

A.V. Ristorante *OD*
The Argentine Grill *AM*
★Bethesda Crab House *B*
Café Petitto *DP*
Capital City Brewing Company *OD*
Chesapeake Seafood Crab House *AR*
★City Lights of China *DP*
The Dancing Crab *UN*
The Fish Market *AL*
The Gangplank *WF*
Hibiscus Café *G*
Houston's *G*
Kabul Caravan *AR*
Katmandu *DP*
Las Pampas *G*
The Lebanese Taverna *UN*
Mama Marie and Enzio's *G*
Pad Thai *G*
★Paolo's *G*
Paradise Restaurant *B*
Perry's *AM*
Piccolo *G*
Rio Grand Café *AR*
★Rio Grande Café *B*
Saigon Inn *G*
Star of Siam *AM*
Steamers *B*
Stoupsy's Café *G*
A Taste of India *UN*
Taverna the Greek Islands *CH*
Terramar *B*
Yosaku *UN*

BY NEIGHBORHOOD

■■■ CAPITOL HILL

The secret to fine dining on "the Hill" is that the farther away from the white halls of power you stray, the more likely you are to find reasonably priced establishments free from congressional big wigs and government flunkies. Pennsylvania Ave. dominates the restaurant scene, but Mass. Ave. NE offers some more attractive (and expensive) alternatives. At night, use extra caution northeast of Union Station or southeast of Lincoln Park. Over 50 eateries inhabit **Union Station** (Metro: Union Station). The station's interior resembles a big, glitzy suburban mall; in the **food court** on the lower level, cheap takeout counters ring the walls with grub for under $5.

Government workers tend to lunch in **government cafeterias,** whose cheap, acceptable sandwiches and salads occupy many a building's basement around North Capitol St. One such place is the **Capitol Forum Bar and Grill** (Metro: Union Station) in the sunken plaza of the building at 941 North Capitol St. (682-0060). Somewhat above average for a cafeteria, this place serves burgers ($2.10) and fries (95¢). (Open Mon.-Fri. 6am-5pm.)

Do-it-yourselfers should brave the bustle of block-long **Eastern Market,** on 7th St. SE between Pennsylvania and Independence. Inside, butchers, bakers, and even the occasional candlestick-makers hawk their wares all week long. On weekends, they are joined by local farmers and growers who line the walk outside with fresh flowers and produce—even in December. Saturday is the best day for produce; Sunday tends to be more of a flea market. From the Eastern Market Metro, walk less than half a block northwest along Pennsylvania Ave., then turn right on 7th St. (Open Mon.-Sat. 7am-6pm, Sun. 9am-4pm.)

A.J.'s Sub, 229 Pennsylvania Ave. SE (543-5235). Metro: Capitol South. A formica and vinyl kind of place, with quick-witted service and laughably low prices—everything is under $5. Burger $1.65, subs $3.65-4.35, deli sandwiches $1.65-3.65. Open Mon.-Fri. 9:30am-9pm, Sat.-Sun. 10am-7pm.

American Café, 227 Massachusetts Ave. NE (547-8500). Metro: Union Station. A fairly upscale spot with substantial outdoor seating, this café boasts a healthy selection of non-fried American basics with Italian and Thai accents. Signature Sandwiches run $5.25-8 and entrees range from $7 to $14 (Tender Baby Back Ribs). Takeout available from market entrance. Sun. brunch served 10:30am-2:30pm (all entrees $7). Open Mon.-Thurs. 11am-11pm, Fri.-Sat. 11am-midnight, Sun. 10:30am-10pm.

Bob's Famous Homemade Ice Cream, 236 Massachusetts Ave. NE (546-3860). Metro: Union Station. Big-shot lawyer Bob quit the Firm to start the Store in the early 80s; this is one of three tasty offshoots. Oddball flavors include Mozambique Spice, Double Dutch, and Honey Graham. Cones $1.60-2.75. Try a delicious milkshake with your favorite ice cream flavor mixed in ($2.30-3). Open Mon.-Thurs. 7:30am-9:30pm, Fri. 7:30am-10pm, Sat. 10am-10pm, Sun. noon-9:30pm.

Bread and Chocolate, 666 Pennsylvania Ave. SE (547-2875). Metro: Eastern Market. An upscale café, bakery, and gourmet food-mart all in one. Sit and sip while nibbling on an omelette ($6), a sandwich ($6-7), or a generous entree salad ($6-9). Or pick up fresh strawberries ($4). Select from an attractive display of cakes and pastries. Open Mon.-Sat. 7am-7:30pm, Sun. 8am-6:30pm.

Burrito Brothers, 205 Pennsylvania Ave. SE (543-6835). Metro: Capitol South. Tacos and burritos to go, though you can also stand and eat at the counter. Behold the standard Burrito Brothers wall mural and shuffle to merengue or salsa as you order alongside government drones during weekday lunch (noon-3pm). The beef taco ($2.95), served very hot, bursts with beef, salsa, and beans. Tacos $2.75-2.95; burritos $3.25-5. Open Mon.-Sat. 11am-8pm.

Hawk 'n Dove, 329 Pennsylvania Ave. SE (543-3300). Metro: Capitol South. A popular "neighborhood meeting place and watering hole" with serviceable bar food, which interns, regulars, and powerful politicians eagerly consume. Restored to recreate its historic "turn-of-the-century" atmosphere, the Hawk 'n Dove cheerfully serves up sandwiches $4-6.50. 14 kinds of bottled beer and 11 drafts ($1.75 and up). Midnight breakfast served Mon.-Thurs. 11pm-1am, Fri.-Sat. 11pm-2am ($7, with steak $9). Open Sun.-Thurs. 10am-2am, Fri.-Sat. 10am-3am.

★ **Head's,** 400 1st St. SE (546-4545). On the corner of D St., right across from the Capitol South Metro stop. Washingtonian magazine thinks proprietor Nelson Head prepares the best barbecue in the District, and the bustling crowds at lunch and dinner seem to agree. This place is so popular with Congressfolk and their staffs that it keeps a few TVs tuned to C-SPAN at all times. If you see diners rush out mid-bite, you know a vote has been called in the House or Senate. Barbecued pork, beef, or chicken sandwiches $6, platters $7. Open Mon.-Sat. 11:30am-1am (kitchen closes at 10:30pm). Closed Sun. during the summer.

Health's A' Poppin, 209½ Pennsylvania Ave. SE (544-3049). Metro: Capitol South. Deli-style establishment with an appetizing salad bar and a wide array of munchable delights for $4 per lb. Also serves up ready-made salads ($3-5) and made-to-order sandwiches ($3-4.25). Open Mon.-Fri. 7am-6:30pm, Sat. 11am-5:30pm.

Heart & Soul Café, 424 8th Street SE (547-1892), off Pennsylvania Ave. Metro: Eastern Market. Sit back amidst the spacious, unpretentiously elegant surroundings and prepare yourself for "an experience in fine Southern cuisine." Sandwiches $4.50-5, entrees $9-13. Enjoy a buffet brunch Saturdays 10am-2pm and Sundays 11:30am-4pm for $9. 10% discount for *Let's Go* travelers. Open Mon.-Thurs. 11:30am-10pm, Fri. 11:30am-11pm, Sat. 10am-11pm, Sun. 11:30am-10pm.

Hunan Dynasty, 215 Pennsylvania Ave. SE (546-6161, 546-6262). Metro: Capitol South. Located upstairs; ultra-modern pale pink surroundings include goldfish and Hill staff on power-lunch breaks. Weekday lunch specials ($5.95, until 3pm). Entrees range from $5 to $12. Generous portions and reasonably good fare. Open Mon.-Thurs. 11:30am-2:30pm, 5:30-10pm; Fri. 11:30am-2:30pm, 5:30-11pm; Sat. 5:30-11pm; Sun. 5:30-10pm. Carryout available.

Ice in Paradise, 615 Pennsylvania Ave. SE (547-1554). Metro: Eastern Market. Named for the Middle Eastern dessert *yakh-dar-behesht* ("ice in paradise"). Counters take up most of the space, but five small tables seat two people apiece. Large selection of Hershey's ice cream (single scoop $1.35) as well as vegetarian and meat-filled sandwiches ($3-4). Open Mon.-Sat. 9am-7pm.

Jimmy T's, 501 East Capitol St. (546-3646). Metro: Eastern Market. At the corner of East Capitol and 5th St. under the brick octagonal turret. The paint's chipped and the red vinyl benches look old, but they tell us it's all part of the classic family-run, old-time diner charm. Workers from Capitol Hill, political big-wigs, and neighborhood regulars alike come for the friendly service and the fresh, no-nonsense fare. Nothing over $6. Sandwiches $1.50-3.55, dinner entrees $5. Come on by, relax and enjoy, but don't ask anybody for an autograph. Open Tues.-Fri. 6:30am-9pm, Sat. 8am-9pm, Sun. 8am-3pm. (Hours may vary so call ahead.)

Kenny's Smoke House, 732 Maryland Ave. NE (547-4561). Metro: Union Station. A bit of a hike from the Capitol, but those in the know make the pilgrimage regularly for Kenny's delicious barbecued ribs and chicken. Pigs decorate the pleasant polished wood and brick interior, and there is abundant outdoor seating. Lunchtime platters of ribs ($6.50) or chicken ($6) come with cornbread and a choice of side order. Dinner sandwiches $6-8, entrees $8-16. Carryout available around the corner on the 8th St. side of the building. Open daily 11am-10pm.

★ **Le Bon Café,** 210 2nd St. SE (547-7200). Metro: Capitol South. Bring your own newspaper or pick one up from the café's neat stack of abandoned ones and find out what's going on in the buildings all around you. A stone's throw from the Capitol and even closer to the Supreme Court, this café serves exquisite food made from scratch with all-natural ingredients. Espresso $1; café au lait $1.45. Buy 10 espressos, get 1 free (and shake like a leaf on a tree). Breakfast pastries 95¢-$1.35 (until 11am). Sandwiches (served after 11am) $4-6. Elegant salads $3-6. Open Mon.-Fri. 7:30am-7:30pm, Sat.-Sun. 8am-4pm.

★ **The Market Lunch,** 225 7th St. SE (547-8444), in the Eastern Market complex. Metro: Eastern Market. Hailed by newspapers around D.C. as one of the best deals in town. Strong smells of fish and fresh meat waft over a dozen stools. Crab cakes ($6-9) are the local specialty, but the Blue Bucks (buckwheat blueberry pancakes $3), have people lined up around the corner on Sat. mornings. Open Tues.-Sat. 7:30am-2:30pm.

★ **Misha's Deli,** 210 7th St. SE (547-5858), north of Pennsylvania Ave. on 7th St., across from the Eastern Market building. Metro: Eastern Market. Inexpensive, authentic Russian and Eastern European food. Practice your Russian on the friendly immigrant owner, and admire the posters of past and present Soviet leaders (the scorecard: Gorbachev 2, Yeltsin 1, Lenin 1). Ah, the Republic. Tasty knishes just $2, blintzes $1.75. Plenty of meats, cheeses, and breads to buy for your very own sandwich. Borscht $2-2.50; wide array of sweets and desserts. Open Mon.-Fri. 8am-7:30pm, Sat. 7am-6pm, Sun. 9am-5pm.

Mr. Henry's Victorian Pub, 601 Pennsylvania Ave. SE (546-8412). Metro: Eastern Market. Hardwood paneling, checkered tablecloths, and tasty nudes provide the backdrop for cheap, hearty burgers and sandwiches ($3.25-7), and entrees ($6-8). Its proximity to the Capitol attracts tourists; the tavern draws a mostly gay and lesbian crowd. Open daily 11:30am-1:30am.

Neil's Outrageous Deli, 208 Massachusetts Ave. NE (546-6970). Metro: Union Station. Deli/liquor store offers creative sandwiches to go and wines stacked up to the ceiling. Eat your sandwich in the grassy knoll enclosed by Massachusetts Ave. and 2nd and D St. NE. (Don't worry; this isn't Dallas.) Try the "Crazy Louie," sourdough rye topped with Dijon mustard, pastrami, turkey, and Thousand Island dressing ($4.30). A bristling array of sandwiches (24) ranges in price from $3 to $4.30. Open Mon.-Tues. 9am-7:30pm, Wed.-Sat. 9am-9pm.

Prego, 210 7th St. SE (547-8686). Metro: Eastern Market, next to Misha's Deli. Prego's deli boasts Italian takeout and delicious bread shipped in fresh daily ($1-2 per loaf). Also sells olives, olive oil, and Italian wines. No seating inside, but outdoor seating in front. Sandwiches $3.25-4.25. Try the "Prego Special," a sandwich bursting at the seams with Italian cold cuts, tomatoes, lettuce, and cheese ($3.25). Open Mon.-Sat. 9am-7:30pm, Sun. 11am-6pm.

Provisions, 218 7th St. SE (543-0694), across from the Eastern Market. Metro: Eastern Market. Sells everything from teapots and jam to salads and sandwiches. A handful of tables crouch in a two-story red brick alcove with a wall-to-wall skylight. Gourmet sandwiches $3.50-6. Try the ever-popular "218" sandwich, a sumptuous concoction of smoked ham and lingonberry jam ($5.50). Daily coffee specials. Open Mon.-Fri. 10am-7pm, Sat. 7am-6pm, Sun. 8:30am-4:30pm.

Roasters on the Hill, 666 Pennsylvania Ave. SE (543-8355). Metro: Eastern Market. Actually hides around the corner on the 7th St. side of the building. Watch the exhausted workers roast and grind coffee from a lovely cushioned stool at the counter or just sip the end product at a table outside. Friendly, energetic service in a colorfully decorated interior. Iced coffee 95¢, espresso from $1.15. A variety of quirky espresso drinks ($1-2). Open Mon.-Fri. 7am-6:30pm, Sat. 7am-6pm, Sun. 8am-5:30pm.

Taverna the Greek Islands, 307 Pennsylvania Ave. SE (547-8360). Metro: Capitol South. Requisite white stucco walls carry the requisite Greek Tourist Bureau posters. Frequent Kennedy sightings. Try some moussaka alla Greek islands for $7 or sample a Greek sandwich ($5.50), or entree ($6-11). Order the *Saganaki alla Paros* (melted cheese, $5) to see 8-ft. flames shoot from your plate. Open Mon.-Sat. 11am-midnight.

Tune Inn, 331½ Pennsylvania Ave. SE (543-2725). Metro: Capitol South. A popular bar stuffed with animal heads, vinyl booths, and the overpowering smell of stale beer. It's also known for good, cheap burgers. ($3-4.50). Sandwiches under $5. Open Sun.-Thurs. 8am-2am, Fri.-Sat. 8am-3am.

2 Quail, 320 Massachusetts Ave. NE (543-8030). Metro: Union Station. Three restored Victorian townhouses get cutely sumptuous with flowered curtains, flowered wallpaper, and wicker room dividers; tables set with cozy armchairs and plush, fluffy pillows. Uncategorizable and consistently excellent cuisine changes every season. Early-bird *prix fixe* (seated by 6:30pm) includes soup or salad, choice of entree, glass of wine or dessert, and coffee or tea ($18). Open Mon.-Thurs. 11:30am-2:30pm and 5-10:30pm, Fri. 11:30am-2:30pm and 5:30-11:15pm, Sat. 5:30-11:15pm, Sun. 5-10pm.

■■■ SOUTHEAST

Not the neighborhood in which to stroll around looking for the best culinary deal. Recreational diners should head north, but if you're in the neighborhood:

Blue Castle Deli, 770 M St. SE (544-0443), opposite the Navy Yard, in the big blue castle at the end of 8th St. Metro: Navy Yard. King-sized portions at knavely prices. Full breakfast menu (served until 11am), most items under $2. Lunch sandwiches $1.35-3.35. Hot dogs and half-smokes $1.50. Open daily 6:30-11am and 11:30am-2:30pm.

Capital City Subs, 751 8th St. SE (546-7827), opposite the main entrance to the Marine Barracks. Metro: Eastern Market. The most expensive nine-incher is the shrimp salad ($4.45). (They're free at the Barracks.) All others under $4. All sorts of subs plus salads ($1.50-3.50), and sandwiches ($1.50-4). Open Mon.-Fri. 8am-6pm, Sat. 9am-6pm.

■■■ WATERFRONT

Next door to the wharf markets on Water St. lie the Waterfront restaurants, mammoth seafood restaurant/monuments with the grand air of an Atlantic City boardwalk. Most, if not all, are exclusively for high rollers.

The Gangplank, 600 Water St. SW (554-5000). Metro: Waterfront. Even here, the most reasonable of the Waterfront restaurants, entrees hover in the $17 range. Eschew the Upper Deck restaurant in favor of the less expensive **Gangplank Patio Cafe** (burgers and sandwiches $3-8.50, entrees $11-13). Karaoke machine provides amateur entertainment Thurs., with a DJ and live shows rounding out Wed. and Fri.-Sat. All entertainment 7-11pm. Upper deck open Mon.-Thurs. 11:30am-1:30pm and 5:30-9:30pm; café open daily 4-11pm.

Hogate's, 800 Water St. (484-6300), at Maine Ave. and 9th St. Metro: L'Enfant Plaza. If nothing else will do but a true waterfront meal, try the lower-priced stuff here: fried seafood ($8-11), seafood sandwiches $7.25-9.25. It may be worth it just to see the endless (and endlessly tacky) interior of this place. Open Mon.-Fri. 11am-10pm, Sat. noon-11pm, Sun. 10:30am-10pm.

Irene's Deli, 300 7th St. SW (488-5555), between C and D St. in the Reporter's Building. Metro: L'Enfant Plaza. Relaxed outdoor lunch spot offers a needed respite from the overly businesslike L'Enfant Plaza. Standard breakfast items $0.50-2, lunch sandwiches $2-3.50 or $2.75-4 if served as a sub. Lunch served after 10:30am. No indoor seating. Open Mon.-Fri. 6:30am-4pm.

Negrilia Jamaican Bakery, 401 M St. SW (488-3636), in the Waterside Mall. Metro: Waterfront. Regulars line up for chicken loaves, a cross between a calzone and a pot pie, $1.75; vegetable patties (same principle), $1.60. No place to sit. Open Mon.-Fri. 6:30am-7pm, Sat. 9am-5pm.

■■■ OLD DOWNTOWN

Except for Chinatown (below), D.C.'s Old Downtown offers few quality restaurants. The hype-heavy **Pavilion** at the **Old Post Office,** at Pennsylvania Ave. and 12th St. NW (289-4224), stuffs its concourse with ethnic-food stalls and their many patrons, most from out of town. (Open Mon.-Sat. 10am-9pm, Sun. noon-8pm. Metro: Federal Triangle.) Somewhat less tourist-infested is the **Shops at National Place & Press,** 1331 Pennsylvania Ave. NW (783-9090), a three-level mall with the usual endless array of eateries. (Open Mon.-Sat. 10am-7pm, Sun. noon-5pm. Metro: Metro Center.) Ubiquitous hot-dog stands dot downtown streets, posing to hungry pedestrians an age-old dilemma: half-smoke or Super-Dog?

American Café, 1331 Pennsylvania Ave. NW (626-0770) in the Shops at National Place; enter at the corner of 13th and F St. NW. Metro: Metro Center. Choose your genre: café/market, bar, or restaurant. Restaurant menu features all-American fare from burgers ($5.45-6.45) to pastas ($7.95-13.95). Try the chicken Caesar salad pizza ($8.25) or the 100mph chili ($2.95 cup; $3.95 bowl). Restaurant open Tues.-Sat. 11am-11pm, Sun.-Mon. 11:30am-10pm. Café/market opens Mon.-Fri. 7am, Sat.-Sun. 8am and always closes 1 hr. before the restaurant.)

A.V. Ristorante, 607 New York Ave. NW (737-0550). Metro: Gallery Place-Chinatown. Three blocks away from the hubbub of commercial Old Downtown, though still frequented by suits on lunch break. Nighttime draws a hipper crowd and the occasional punk posse on break from the club scene. Chianti bottles top-heavy with melted wax, lamps turned so low they flicker on and off; red wine served in paper cups create the ambience; back room features a marble expanse of a bar and a large replica of the leaning tower of Pisa. Huge plates of pasta ($6-10), and pizza (starting at $8 for a regular small pie and $15 for white pizza). Open Mon.-Thurs. 11:30am-11pm, Fri. 11:30am-midnight, Sat. 5pm-midnight. Free parking for patrons.

Capitol City Brewing Company, mailing address: 1100 New York Ave. NW (628-2222), entrance on the corner of 11th and H. St. Metro: Metro Center. The first brewery in the District of Columbia since Prohibition, which means poor Washingtonians are sadly late on the microbrew scene. This stylized version of an industrial warehouse is known for its home-brewed beer, but don't hesitate to try hearty grub like the Vienna country sausage sandwich ($9) and the grilled sausage salad ($8.75). Open Mon.-Thurs. 11am-11pm, Fri.-Sat. 11am-midnight, Sun. 11am-11pm. For brewery hours, see **Entertainment & Nightlife,** p. 208.

Casa Juanita's, 908 11th St. NW (737-2520), near I St. Metro: Metro Center. Authentic Mexican and Salvadoran cuisine comes in huge portions heaping with beans and rice. Free chips and salsa. Try the Santa Ana—3 chicken enchiladas topped with cheese and a tangy sauce, served with refried beans and rice ($7.75). Decor consists of a few piñatas hanging from the ceiling and sombreros lining the walls. Open Sun.-Thurs. 11am-10:30pm, Fri.-Sat. 11am-11pm.

Dixie Grill, 518 10th St. NW (628-4800), next to the Petersen House, "the house that Lincoln died in." Metro: Metro Center. Dixie's Southern roots shine through in its menu and its down-home atmosphere. First-floor restaurant operates off a chalkboard menu, with dishes and prices changing every meal. House specialty is the chicken fried steak ($11); red beans and rice available at any meal ($4). Upstairs is a "roadhouse" bar complete with pool tables, barrels of peanuts, and racecar memorabilia. Stop by Wed. for local rockabilly bands and be reminded that D.C. was once a sleepy Southern town. Restaurant open Mon.-Thurs. 11:30am-2:30pm for lunch and 6-10pm for dinner; Sat.-Sun. 11:30am-2:30pm lunch and 6-11pm dinner, Sun. brunch buffet 11:30am-2:30pm. Downstairs bar open Mon.-Thurs. 11:30am-1:30am, and Fri.-Sat. 11:30am-2:30am. Upstairs bar open Tues.-Sat. 6pm-close.

Ebbitt Express, 675 15th St. NW (347-8881), in the Metropolitan Square plaza. Metro: Metro Center. Across 15th St. from the Treasury Building. The **Old Ebbitt Grill,** father of Ebbitt Express, lounges next door, reminiscing about the days when its clientele included presidents McKinley, Cleveland, Harding, Grant, Johnson (A.), and Roosevelt (T.). The snob appeal is undeniable, and prices reflect it. So stop into Ebbitt Express next door and pick up the daily pasta special (always $6), a stuffed baked potato ($2), or a yogurt fruit shake ($2.75), and scarf it down in the air-conditioned Metropolitan Square as you gaze at the stuffy patrons of the Grill eating their steaks and lobsters. Then go home and tell your friends that you lunched at Ebbitt's. Ebbitt's Express open Mon.-Thurs. 7:30am-8pm, Fri. 7:30am-6pm.

German Deli, 1331 H St. NW (347-5732), The front of a space that also contains the pricey Café Mozart, near the National Museum for Women in the Arts. Metro: Metro Center. Gourmet deli proffers specialty crackers, coffees, hors-d'oeuvres, and tricky-to-pronounce delicacies like *schnitze* (chicken or turkey $5.25), *sauerbrauten* (regular $4.95, large $7.45), and *spaetzle*. Cramped storefront conceals a roomy interior. Sandwiches ($1-7) and pastries ($3-4) are superb. Open Mon.-Fri. 7:30am-10pm, Sat. 9am-10pm, Sun. 11am-10pm.

Jaleo, 480 7th St. NW (628-7949). Metro: Gallery Place - Chinatown. Walk 2 blocks down 7th St. to the corner of 7th and E St. Your source for *tapas:* over 40 different kinds to choose from. Mixes the latest trend in yuppie dining with Spanish authenticity. Larger-than-life murals of flamenco dancers adorn the walls and supervise your meal. The entrees are pricey at dinnertime ($10.50-14.50), but you can make a meal out of hot and spicy Spanish tomato soup ($3.25) and one *tapas* ($2.75-6.25) plus unlimited bread refills. Open for lunch Mon.-Sat. 11:30am-2:30pm. For dinner, Mon. 5:30-10pm, Tues.-Thurs. 5:30-10:30pm, Fri.-Sat. 5:30-11pm, Sun. 5:30-10pm. For late-night tapas, Tues.-Thurs. 10:30-11:30pm, Fri.-Sat. 11pm-midnight, Sun. brunch 11:30am-3pm.

Jan Drake's Garden Café, 401 7th St. NW (393-1150), located on Gallery Row. Metro: Gallery Place-Chinatown. Sandwiches made to order and served hot or cold. Homey atmosphere is a relief from intimidating downtown office buildings. Deli sandwiches $3.30-5.25, regular-sized salads (vegetable, tuna, and chicken) $4-5. $3 breakfast special includes scrambled eggs, meat, home fries or grits, and toast, English muffin, or bagel (available Mon.-Fri. 7-10:30am, Sat. 8-10:30am). Open Mon.-Fri. 6:30am-7pm, Sat. 8am-5pm, Sun. 11am-5pm.

New World Café, 720 I St. NW (842-0045), across the street from the Greater New Hope Baptist Church. Metro: Gallery Place - Chinatown, one block up and one to the left of the 7th and H St. exit. Espresso, cappuccino $1.15-1.80, salad bar $3.90 per lb., sandwiches $4-4.60. Open Mon.-Fri. 6am-4pm.

Reeves, 1306 G St. NW (628-6350). Metro: Metro Center. This bakery/café is an Old Downtown institution; it's been around in some shape or form since 1886. Today it's best known for its breakfasts. Pancakes or french toast $3-4.40; all-you-can-eat fruit and breakfast bar $5-6 for adults, $3.50-4 for children (prices vary depending on day of the week). Slices of their "world-famous" pies $2-2.15. Open Mon.-Sat. 7am-6pm.

Tiffany's Deli, 415 12th St. NW (628-5751). Metro: Metro Center. A slightly cramped restaurant for a reason: the Chinese buffet table/salad bar (including fresh fruit) dominates the middle of the room (buffet $3.90 per lb.). Hot subs & sandwiches $4-5.35. Large drink selection. Open Mon.-Fri. 6am-5pm.

The Upper Deck, upstairs at 605 12th St. NW (624-0033). Metro: Metro Center. A sports bar/hoagie heaven, the Upper Deck specializes in cheesesteaks (6-inch $5,

9-inch $6) and equally sizable hoagie specialties. On Tuesdays, burgers are half price (from their original $5.50-5.75 range). Stop by for daily drink specials Mon.-Fri. 5-9pm. Carryout available. Open daily 11am-2am.

CHINATOWN

You don't have to dig a hole to China to find authentic Chinese food and groceries; Some of D.C.'s best Chinese food restaurants cling to tiny H St. NW. Don't be turned off by a decrepit-seeming exterior (or interior, even). A restaurant's appearance has little relation to its quality; apparent dives often serve wonderful food. Metro: Gallery Place-Chinatown, for all of the following.

Burma Restaurant, upstairs at 740 6th St. NW (638-1280). If you can't choose among the repetitive menus at Chinatown's restaurants, opt for something a little different. The owner, a retired Burmese diplomat and former U.N. delegate, loves to talk about Burma's rare cuisine, which replaces soy sauce with pickles, mild curries, and unique spices. Make it your mission at Burma to try the *Kauswe Thoke,* rice noodles with ground shrimp, fried onion, cilantro, hot pepper, garlic, and fresh lemon juice ($7.50), or anything served in the *Kotang* sauce, made from sesame, soya, cilantro, ginger, garlic, onions, and lemon juice. Most entrees go for $7.95, and all the noodle dishes are $7.50. Open for lunch Mon.-Fri. 11am-3pm, dinner daily 6pm-10:30pm.

Chinatown Express, 744-746 6th St. NW (638-0424/5). Choose your lunch special ($3.95) from 26 dishes offered; order an additional dish for just $1 extra (includes rice; served daily 10am-5pm). Dinner can range from $4.25 to $12, or find 3 friends and pay $30 for a "family dinner." Open daily 10am-11pm.

Go-Lo's, 604 H St. NW (347-4656). Two large dragons will greet you from above as you enter the restaurant—go low. Their Home-Style Cooking entrees, such as baby clams in black bean sauce ($9.50), are worth a try. Lunch specials ($5-6) vary according to the day of the week. What the menu doesn't tell you—although a plaque outside does—is that Go-Lo's used to be the Surrat Boardinghouse, where conspirators plotted the abduction of President Lincoln. Open Sun.-Thurs. 11am-midnight, Fri.-Sat. 11am-4am.

Ho Wah Restaurant, 611 H. St. NW (408-8115). For the bargain-hunter —$3.75 for lunch (Mon.-Fri. 10:30am-3:30pm) and dinner's not much more. (8 dinner special options for $4.25). Six tables in a small downstairs room. Open Sun.-Thurs. 10:30am-3am, Fri.-Sat. 10:30am-4am.

Hunan Chinatown, 624 H St. NW (783-5858). A haven for spicy-food lovers. Dinner can be pricey, so fire-eaters should munch on the Hot Spicy Eggplant ($6.50), the Kung Pao chicken ($6.75), or the hot and sour soup ($1.75) from the "Light Menu," the restaurant's new nutritional venture (all food on the menu gets less than 30% of its calories from fat; it's also cheaper than the regular menu). Open for lunch 7 days a week 11am-3pm. Dinner hours are Sun.-Thurs. 3-11pm, Fri.-Sat. 3pm-midnight.

Szechuan Gallery, 617 H St. NW (898-1180/1). Recognize this place? Schwarzenaegger-extravaganza *True Lies* was filmed here—the scene where Jamie Lee Curtis rendezvouses with her would-be lover—and they've got an autographed picture of Arnold himself and one of Jamie Lee with staff members to prove it. Stunning Taiwanese (mostly seafood) dishes, once hidden from English-speaking diners, have surfaced on the menu as Chef's Recommendations. Fragrant Crab (smelly whole crabs in spicy egg batter) around $10. Open Sun.-Thurs. 11am-11pm, Fri.-Sat. 11am-1am.

Tony Cheng's Mongolian Restaurant, 619 H St. NW (842-8669). Load your bowl with beef, leeks, mushrooms, sprouts, and such, then watch the cooks make it sizzle and shrink (1 serving $8.50, all-you-can-eat $14) at lunch. Originating with the armies of Genghis Khan, this style of sizzling meats on metal over glowing coal is known as "Mongolian barbecue." It's both dining and entertainment, as the cooks perform the ritual in the center of the room. Two or more can stir up their own feast in charcoal hotpots provided by the restaurant for $5 per person; more meat extra. Open Sun.-Thurs. 11am-11pm, Fri.-Sat. 11am-midnight.

■■■ WHITE HOUSE AREA AND FOGGY BOTTOM

Cheap, friendly restaurants congregate around the hungry youth of George Washington University. The best area for good budget dining lies north of F St. and especially along Pennsylvania Ave. Closer to the White House, the chow becomes more varied, but also more expensive.

Chinacafe, chain of five fast-food Chinese restaurants throughout NW. At 1018 Vermont Ave. NW (628-1350), 1411 K St. (393-6277), 2009 K St. (463-2129), 1723 Conn. Ave. (234-4053), and 1990 M St. The McDonald's of Chinese food. Drab gray furnishings and Hunan/Peking-style food are the dominant motifs. Each restaurant offers a choice of over 30 entrees, including *kung pao* chicken, *lo mein*, and sweet-and-sour chicken (each $4). No entrees exceed $4.25. Appetizers (about $1) differ by location. Open Mon.-Fri. 11am-9pm, Sat.-Sun. noon-9pm.

Cone E. Island, in the mall at 2000 Pennsylvania Ave. (822-8460). Metro: Foggy Bottom-GWU. No old-fashioned soda fountain here, this small, decidedly modern parlor features 2 arcade game tables and mini ionic columns ringed in neon lights. Try the tasty no-fat frozen yogurt or indulge yourself with a variety of fat-filled ice cream flavors. Cone $1.60-2.60 plus 40¢ for homemade cones. Open noon-midnight 7 days a week.

DJ's, 2145 G St. NW (429-0230), near 22nd St. Metro: Foggy Bottom-GWU. A smorgasbord of ethnic foods. Korean chef tosses out Italian, Chinese, American, and Middle Eastern fare at record speed. A cluttered, unsophisticated cafeteria-style diner, packed with collegians throughout the year. Most entrees under $5 (good veggie options). Open Mon.-Thurs. 7:15am-8:30pm, Fri. 7:15am-5:30pm, Sat. 10am-2:30pm.

Food & Co. Gourmet Café, 1200 New Hampshire Ave. NW (223-8070), at M St. Metro: Dupont Circle, Foggy Bottom-GWU, or Farragut North. Handwrapped jars, brown paper packages of biscotti tied up with strings, gourmet cheeses, pasta salads, and anything else the gustatory snob might require. Goat cheese and sun-dried tomato on crusty bread, $4. Twenty different salads and sandwiches every day, entrees $6-8.50. Open Mon.-Fri. 8am-9pm, Sat. 9am-7pm, Sun. 10am-5pm.

Holly's Cookie Company, 1800 G St. NW (289-6899), at 18th St. Metro: Farragut West. Around the corner from the Old Executive Office, this small sandwich shop offers mammoth cookies ($6 per lb.) in seven flavors, from traditional oatmeal-and-raisin to chocolate Heath bar. Open Mon.-Fri. 6am-4pm.

Jonathan's Gourmet Deli/Market, 2142 L St. NW (331-8458). Metro: Foggy Bottom-GWU. Don't be intimidated by the gold-plated exterior. Inside, Jonathan's boasts a salad bar and a hot Chinese food bar which conspire to attract middle-aged business types looking for a quickie (lunch). Deli sandwiches made to order $2.50-4.60. Gyro $4, burger $3.60. Open Mon.-Fri. 7am-8pm, Sat. 8am-3:30pm.

Leo's GW Deli, 2133 G St. NW (331-9391), near 22nd St. Metro: Foggy Bottom-GWU. Sandwiches ($1.50-4) and fresh salads make this deli popular with students. Sandwiches are deli-variety—ham, turkey, roast beef, etc. Breakfast sandwiches ($1-3), pre-packaged snacks, drinks, and some grocery items too. Open Mon.-Fri. 6:30am-8:30pm, Sat. 8am-4pm.

Lindy's Bon Apétit, 2040 I St. NW (452-0055), near Pennsylvania Ave. and Tower Records. Metro: Foggy Bottom-GWU. Ronald Reagan once said that life at George Washington University was not complete without a bone burger from this carry-out deli. Try a bacon cheeseburger ($3.35, $5.30 for a double), a Monterey sandwich with refried beans, raw onions, and American cheese ($2.95, $5.05 for a double), or a 6-in. sub ($2.85-3.90). Breakfast sandwiches under $2. Open Mon.-Fri. 8am-8pm, Sat.-Sun. 11am-4pm.

Milo's, 2142 Pennsylvania Ave. NW (338-3000). GW students as well as locals enjoy Euro-chic decor and Italian food. Let the Mediterranean pictures and Italian pop music take you away. All-you-can-eat lunch (pasta, pizza, and salad) for $7 and dinner (soup, salad, pasta, pizza, and stromboli) for $8. Or pick up some *gelato*! Open Mon.-Fri. 11:30am-2:30pm and 5-9pm, Sat. 5-10pm, Sun. 4-9pm. Free delivery with $10 minimum purchase.

Treviso, 2138½ Pennsylvania Ave. NW (338-5760). Metro: Foggy Bottom-GWU. Affordable, quality Italian food at a cozy spot with friendly owners. *Pollo, pesce,* and *paste* $7.25-14. Look for specials, and try to explain the squiggly design on the ceiling: it throws a crowbar into Treviso's otherwise traditional intimacy. Open Mon.-Thurs. 11:30am-2:30pm and 5:30-10pm, Fri. and Sat. 5:30-10:30pm.

World Gourmet, 1917 F St. NW (371-9048), near 19th St. A well-stocked deli caters to young white-collars who flock here at lunchtime for a selection of almost 20 tempting sandwiches ($3.69-4.29). Amusing sandwich names include "World Bank" ($4) and "Guilt" ($4.49). Outdoor seating is hard to secure; be "Aggressive." Open Mon.-Fri. 7:30am-7pm, Sat. 11:30am-5:30pm.

■■■ GEORGETOWN

The majority of Georgetown's dining options line the central thoroughfares of M St. and Wisconsin Ave., where they vie for the attention and patronage of wary tourists, power-lunching execs, and snacking suburban teeny-boppers. The eclectic array of eateries ranges from the pretention and expense of flashy dark wood and polished brass establishments to the much more affordable mixture of small Indian, Ethiopian, Thai, and Vietnamese.

Bustling during the day, Georgetown at night becomes a huge fête, a kaleidoscope of cruising scenesters. Walk M St. or Wisconsin Ave. on a summer Saturday night for that peculiar brand of skin-tight Georgetown glamour which owes more to Miami Beach than to Washington.

★ **Aditi,** 3299 M St. NW (625-6825), at 33rd St. The Sanskrit name translates as "creative power" or "abundance;" here it means great food. Try the $14 Aditi dinner for an Indian feast that will challenge any appetite, or eat light with a vegetarian entree, $5-8. Meat dishes $8-14. Open Mon.-Thurs. 11:30am-2:30pm and 5:30-10pm, Fri.-Sat. 11:30am-2:30pm and 5:30-10:30pm, Sun. noon-2:30pm and 5:30-10pm.

Au Croissant Chaud/Maison des Crepes/Au Pied du Cochon, 1329, 13333, and 1335 Wisconsin Ave. NW (333-2333, 333-5440), at Dumbarton St. Two sister restaurants with a petite patisserie between them. Au Pied serves up casual French fare (salads $3-6.50, crepes $7-10) in a cavernous dark wood panelled space with miniature wild pigs on display. Open Sun.-Wed. 11am-12am, Thurs.-Sat. 11am-5am.

★ **Booeymonger,** 3265 Prospect St. NW (333-4810), at Potomac St. Georgetown students and residents stop by for breakfast ($3 for the special) or a quick'n' tasty, giant sandwich (like the Pita Pan and Tuna Turner) for under $5. The $6 dinner special includes a specialty sandwich, soda, and choice of salad or soup. Free coffee refills (until 11am) to jump-start your weekday morning. Open daily 8am-midnight.

Burrito Brothers, 3273 M St. NW (965-3963), at Potomac St. Value menu features 80¢ taco and $1 tostada. Crisp, fresh ingredients (no lard!). Plenty of vegetarian fare. Delivery (546-TOGO). Open Sun.-Wed. 11am-midnight, Thurs.-Sat. 11am-3am.

Busara, 2340 Wisconsin Ave. NW (337-2340), below Calvert St. Busara means "blue topaz" and the sleek, neon-metallic and black modern decor justifies the appelation. This upscale Thai restaurant boasts indoor and garden seating as well as an extensive bar. Lunch $6-8, dinner $9-15. Veggie entrees $8. Open daily 11:30am-3:30pm and 5-11pm, Fr.-Sat. until 12am.

Café La Ruche, 1039 31st St. NW (965-2684), near M St. Spacious and pleasant French café with lovely wooden tables, lovely embedded tiles, and lovely street signs on the walls. Try the delicious gazpacho ($3.75) or choose from an array of quiches ($6-7). French entrees $5-7. Lovely desserts ($4). Lovely outdoor seating available. For carry out, call 965-2591. Open Sun.-Thurs. 11:30am-11:30pm, Fri.-Sat. 10am-midnight.

Caffè Northwest, 3251 Prospect St. NW (342-9002), near Potomac St. A mellow, artsy café specializing in espresso, Italian sodas, iced drinks, and light fare. Drinks

$1-3, sandwiches $3-4. Sip a drink, play some chess, stare at funky art in the spacious carpeted gallery, or hang out in the outdoor seating area. Open Mon.-Thurs. 7am-12am, Fri. until 1am, Sat. 8am-1am, Sun. 8am-midnight.

Caffè Sorrento, 1522 Wisconsin Ave. NW (338-2314). Small, family-owned Italian cafe is an oasis away from Georgetown's hubbub, with elegantly presented food and chessboard decor. Antipasti $1.25-6, sandwiches $4-6, Italian sodas $2, truly delicious desserts $1-3. Open Sun.-Thurs. 9:30am-10pm, Fri.-Sat. 9:30am-midnight, Sun. 11am-11pm.

Dean and Deluca Café, 3276 M St. NW (342-2500), near 32nd St. A pleasant and well-shaded outdoor café (glass-enclosed in the winter) situated between the namesake gourmet market and Georgetown Park and tucked away from the bustle of M St. Light fare, including salads and pastries. Espresso $1.35, cappuccino $1.80, beer $4. Live jazz Fri. 6-10pm. Open Sun.-Thurs. 8am-8pm, Fri. 8am-11pm, Sat. 9am-11pm.

El Caribe, 3288 M St. NW (338-3121). Treasured by Cubans and Cuba-philes throughout D.C. Your neighbor's elbow may be in your lap, but you're still happy to be in the only Washington restaurant to feature the cuisine of America's favorite Communist country. Tapas $5-7. Entrees $9-19. Open Mon.-Thurs. 11:30am-11pm, Fri.-Sat. 11:30am-11:30pm, Sun. noon-10pm.

Enriqueta's, 2811 M St. NW (338-7772), at Pennsylvania Ave. near 28th St. Famous for its lightly spiced, authentic Mexican cuisine. Friendly service in a bright festive environment of multicolored chairs and tablecloths. Try the *mole,* Mexico's national dish ($13). Entrees $11-14. Look for lunch specials for around $5. You'll find them. Authentic desserts for under $3. Open Mon.-Thurs. 11:30am-2:30pm and 5-10pm, Fri.-Sat. 5-10pm.

Fettoosh, 3277 M St. NW (342-1199), at Potomac St. Tree branches, lanterns, and black-and-yellow tiles adorn this fine Middle Eastern restaurant. Hummus $3. Falafel $4.75. Entrees $7-15. Free delivery. Some nights feature live entertainment. **Fettoosh Express,** a fast-food version of Fettoosh and the least greasy of Georgetown's cheap Middle Eastern spots, stands 2 doors away, convenient for Georgetown students on their way home from bar-hopping. Dining room open Sun.-Thurs. 11am-11pm, Fri.-Sat. 11am-5am, Sun. 11am-1am. Fettoosh Express open Sun.-Thurs. 11am-3am, Fri.-Sat. 11am-5am.

Georgetown Bagelry, 3245 M St. NW (965-1011), between Wisconsin Ave. and 33rd St. New York style bagel is a steal at 50¢. Bagel burger $3.25. Slice of pizza $1.75. Open Mon.-Sat. 6am-9pm, Sun. 7am-6pm.

Georgetown Café, 1623 Wisconsin Ave. NW (333-0215), near Q St. Don't let the name fool you. Cheap and greasy food. Sandwiches $3-6. Open 24 hrs.

The Georgetown Dinette, 3206 O St. (337-3649), near Wisconsin Ave. Small diner run by a husband-and-wife team (really) serving fast food and deli hot dogs and burgers ($1-5). Open Mon.-Sat. 11am-8pm.

Gepetto, 2917 M St. NW (333-2602), near 29th St. Small Italian eatery specializing in thin crust pizza. $11 will serve 2-3 people. Free pizza at the bar Mon.-Fri. 5pm-7pm. Carryout and free delivery (333-4315). Open Sun.-Thurs. noon-11pm, Fri.-Sat. noon-12:30am.

Hamburger Hamlet, 3125 M St. NW (965-6970), near Wisconsin Ave. Named for Rex Harrison, the Emperor Henry IV is piled so high with cheese, ham, tomato, bacon strips, and Thousand Island dressing, you'll need to crane your neck to see your dinner partner. Burgers $5.50-6. Salads, sandwiches, and seafood $6-11.50. Draw on the paper tablecloths while you wait (crayons provided). Open Sun.-Thurs. 11am-midnight, Fri.-Sat. 11am-1am. Bar stays open until 2:30am on weekends.

Hibiscus Café, 3401 K St. NW (965-0408), under the Key Bridge. Worth the walk from M St. just to view the modern neon decor. This former warehouse has become almost impossibly hip, but mere mortals may still partake of pizza ($8.50-$12) and beer ($4-5) while experiencing the chic, the sculptural, and the surreal. Open Tues.-Thurs. 11am-2:30pm and 6-11pm, Fri.-Sat. 11am-2:30pm and 6pm-midnight, Sun. 11am-2:30pm and 6-11pm.

Houston's, 1065 Wisconsin Ave. NW (338-7760), near M St. Perfect for meat-and-potatoes lovers. The hickory-grilled hamburgers are served with a slew of shoestring fries ($7). Don't try to eat light here. You may need to bring even salads home in a doggie bag ($6.25-7.75). Lines are long and reservations aren't taken, so walk around Georgetown while you wait or crowd into the bar. Open Sun.-Thurs. 11:15am-1am, Fri.-Sat. 11:15am-1am.

Las Pampas, 3219 M St. NW (333-5151). This elegant little joint earns high praise for its Argentinian renderings of beef—arguably the best steak in town—but prices reflect the quality ($13-22). More budget-oriented travelers should opt for the early (before 5pm) and late bird specials with a choice of appetizer, main course, and dessert for $10. Open Sun.-Thurs. noon-11pm, Fri.-Sat. 11am-1am.

Mama Maria and Enzio's, 2313 Wisconsin Ave. NW (965-1337), below Calvert St. Blue Mediterranean paintings surround you as you enjoy a $3 calzone, lunch pasta entree ($3-6), or dinner pasta ($6-8). Open daily 11am-3pm and 5-11pm. No credit cards accepted.

Olympic Carry Out, 3207 O St. NW (338-2478 or 337-1997), a block from Wisconsin Ave. Strictly delivery ($10 minimum) and carry-out, serving homemade Greek and Mediterranean specialties as well as subs. Big portions, rapid service. Gyros and steak-and-cheese subs $3.50, 8" subs $3-$4, homemade yogurt $2. Open Mon.-Thurs. 11am-10:30pm, Fri.-Sat. 11am-2:30am, Sun. noon-9:30pm.

Pad Thai, 1639 Wisconsin Ave. NW (342-3394), near Q St. Pad Thai $7 at lunch, $8 at dinner. Vegetarian dishes $7.25-8. Lunch specials with soup $6.25-7.25; dinner entrees $7.25-13. Delivery within 3-mi. radius ($12 minimum). Carry out available. Open Mon.-Thurs. 11:30am-10:30pm, Fri. 11:30am-11pm, Sat.11:30am-11pm, Sun. 4:30-10pm.

★ **Paolo's,** 1303 Wisconsin Ave. NW (333-7353), near N St. Huge, elegant Italian dishes well worth the price (pasta $10-17, pizza $7-10, other entrees $13-17). Try the *bresada*, dried beef served with baby lettuce, shaved Romano, and extra virgin olive oil, as an appetizer. Get a center seat to watch the chef bake your calzone in the wood-burning pizza oven or whip out your fettucine smoked salmon ($11). In the summer, sit by the open front and watch the world go by. Open Sun.-Thurs. 11:30am-1am, Fri.-Sat. 11:30am-2am.

Peacock Cafè and Market, 3203 Prospect St. NW (625-2740), at Wisconsin Ave. A quiet café/deli with small marble tables and a juice bar. Specialty sandwiches named after old Hollywood greats like Charlie Chaplin and Ginger Rogers, immortalized with fresh deli meats and cheeses ($3.75-5.50). Salads $2.50-6.25. Mel Brooks bagel sandwich $4. open Mon.-Sat. 8am-10pm, Sun. 10am-10pm.

Piccolo, 1068 31st St. NW (342-7414). Just off M St., this 2-story building with brown and white shutters is easily identifiable by the heaving flowers cascading down the side. Homemade pasta and other elegant entrees $9-14. Catch the early bird special: choice of entree and a glass of wine $9. Early bird special Mon.-Fri. 5-7:30pm ($9). Open daily11:30am-2:30pm and 5-11pm.

Quick Pita, 1210 Potomac St. NW (338-PITA), near M St. Good, cheap Middle Eastern fare, perfect for a Quick Snack or takeout. All sandwiches under $4. Falafel $3.25, miniature pies $1.25. Free delivery in the Georgetown area after 6pm ($12 min. order). Open Sun.-Wed. 11:30am-3:30am, Thurs.-Sat. 11:30am-4:30am.

Saigon Inn, 2928 M St. NW (337-5588), at 30th St. Slightly cheaper and more intimate than Vietnam-Georgetown, its ancient rival. Go for the lunch special: 4 dishes for $4. Dinner $7-15; try the triple delight platter for $8. The Saigon pancake is their specialty ($8). Open Mon.-Sat. 11am-11pm, Sun. noon-11pm.

★ **Sarinah,** 1338 Wisconsin Ave. NW (337-2955), near O St. (Also accessible through 3202 O St. around the corner.) Charge through the inauspicious doorway and you'll find yourself downstairs in a tropical jungle: broad-leaved potted plants, pulpy wooden fruits, and colorful statuettes. Delicious Indonesian food includes *satays*, grilled and skewered lamb, beef, chicken, or shrimp with spicy sauces ($9-10), and vegetarian entrees ($7-8). Long list of exotic desserts ($3.25-4.25). Open Tues.-Sat. noon-3pm and 6-10:30pm, Sun. 6-10:30pm.

Stoupsy's Café, 1301 Wisconsin Ave. NW (337-FOOD/337-3663). It's tough to miss this pink Gingerbread house on the corner of Wisconsin and N. Greek specialties ($8-13), salads ($3-$9). Diner-style food in a café atmosphere. Indoor and outdoor seating. $3 min. per person at dinner. Carry-out available. Open Mon.-Fri. 11am-11pm, Sat.-Sun. 8am-11:30pm.

★ **Sushi-Ko,** 2309 Wisconsin Ave. NW (333-4187), below Calvert St. Authentic, no-frills Japanese food prepared before your eyes. Try the affordable *Maki-sushi Nigiri* or *Temaki-sushi*, under $5. Fish offerings include the customary trout, salmon, and tuna, as well as the more exotic *Uzara* (fish eggs with quail eggs). Order of sushi (2 rolls per serving) $2-4.75. Open Mon. 6-10:30pm, Tues.-Fri. noon-2:30pm and 6-10:30pm, Sat. 5-10:30pm, Sun. 5-10pm.

Tandoor, 3316 M St. (333-3376), near 33rd St. Authentic, spicy northern Indian cuisine. $5 lunch specials. Dinner $11-15; vegetarian entrees $7-9. Beware your taste buds: even items not marked with a red pepper may fry your tender tongue. Open daily 11:30am-2:30pm, 5:30-10:30pm.

Thomas Sweet, 3214 P St. NW (337-0616), at Wisconsin Ave. Ice cream, frozen yogurt, gourmet sandwiches, muffins, and bagels made daily in the store. The best ice cream in D.C. by a light-year. Single-scoop $1.95. Hefty helpings of yogurt or ice cream mixed with fruit or candy $3.75. Open June-Aug. Mon.-Thurs. 9:30am-11pm, Fri.-Sat. 9:30am-midnight, Sun. 11am-11pm.

Vietnam-Georgetown Restaurant, 2934 M St. NW (337-4536), at 30th St. Relax in this unassumingly handsome spot with some *cha giú,* crispy Vietnamese spring rolls ($6.25), or grilled chicken or beef on skewers ($7.75).When it's warm, dine under a canopy of trees in an extensive outdoor seating area. Entrees $6-9. Open Mon.-Thurs. 11am-11pm, Fri.-Sat. 11am-midnight, Sun. noon-11pm.

★ **Zed's Ethiopian Cuisine,** 3318 M St. NW (333-4710), near 33rd St. Award-winning cuisine. Eat with your hands free from embarrassment in the company of youthful, savvy local clientele. Ask for a basket-weave table for a more authentic dining experience. Appetizers $4. Entrees $6-12. $5 weekday lunch specials. On a level with the Ethiopian fare in Adams-Morgan. Open daily 11am-11pm.

■■■ FARRAGUT

Restaurants in Farragut cater almost exclusively to the businesspeople who work in the area. Quick meals reign supreme. Delis proliferate, while small take-out restaurants and fast-food joints also make strong showings during lunchtime. Health-conscious yuppies have sparked an explosion of low-fat dining options: establishments hawking frozen yogurt, salads, and espresso (for that mid-afternoon caffeine high) compete for attention with bars offering free buffets during happy hour. Beware the occasional wallet-breakers, the scenes of power lunches and business dinners. Sightseeing and dining in Farragut is best accomplished during the week; you'll find that places shut down on weekends when all the lawyers and interns have gone away.

The Art Gallery Grille, 1712 I St. NW (298-6658), near 17th St. Metro: Farragut West. Art Deco interior, original Erté serigraphs, professional clientele. Breakfasts are traditional and inviting—Belgian waffles or creative granola, and various omelettes ($4.25). Van Gogh burger $8, dinner omelettes $6.25-8. Happy hour 5-7:30pm: drink specials and free food vary daily. DJ Wed.-Fri. 7pm-closing. Open Mon.-Wed. 6:30am-10pm, Thurs.-Fri. 6:30am-2am, Sat. 6:30am-11pm.

Balajee Vegetarian Restaurant, 917 18th St. NW (682-9090). Metro: Farragut West. Combines traditional Indian cuisine and fast-food techniques to forge an all-you-can-eat lunch buffet ($5; served Mon.-Fri. 11:30am-2pm). Or, order a regular dish like the *Masala Dosai,* a lentil and rice flour pancake stuffed with potato curry, served with lentil soup and coconut chutney ($4). Open Mon.-Fri. 11am-8pm.

Café Amadeus, 1300 I St. NW (962-8686). Metro: McPherson Square. Modern German café run by owners of Café Mozart (Café Wolfgang must be next). Sit-down entrees $6-17. Carry out a ¼-lb. burger with french fries ($2.50). Or try the house specialty Hunter Style Tikka dishes made with "low fat, low sodium" lamb, chicken, turkey, beef, or shrimp grilled their secret way and served with rice or potatoes ($8-10). Happy hour (Mon.-Fri. 4pm-8pm) offers free appetizers with any drink. These snacks change daily but can include fried veggies, meat balls, chicken wings, and sausage. Open Mon.-Fri. 7am-9pm.

Casa Blanca, 1014 Vermont Ave. NW (393-4430), near K St. Metro: McPherson Square. Modest, casual place serving Spanish, Mexican, Salvadoran, and Peruvian specialties. Two tacos ($3.50), pork or chicken tamales ($3.25), or *empanadas de carne* (meat pie) for $1.95. Aspiring Fujimoris can go for Peruvian *pollo a la braza,* ¼ roast chicken with salad and fried potatoes or rice and beans ($5.50). Open Mon.-Sat. 10am-10pm, Sun. 11am-8pm.

Chesapeake Bagel Bakery, 818 18th St. NW (775-4690). Metro: Farragut West. This branch of a local chain is frequented mostly for its 45¢ bagels and partially for its $4 per lb. pasta/sushi/noodle/salad bar. A bulletin board covers the wall with the announcements of CBB's patrons. Look here first if you need to buy or sell *anything.* Open Mon.-Fri. 6:30am-4:30pm, Sat. 8am-3pm.

Cup'A Cup'A, 1911 K St. NW (466-2872). Metro: Farragut North. Its name is dopey, but its espresso drinks ($0.95-2.65) are Washington's favorites. Lotsa lotsa little cookies and biscottis, too (cookies $1.20-1.60, undipped biscottis 75¢). But come for the coffee—everyone else in Farragut does. Open Mon.-Fri. 7am-6pm, Sat. 9am-3pm.

Eye St. Café, 1915 I St. NW (457-0773). Metro: Farragut West. Middle Eastern/Italian. High-quality, restaurant setting and food at café prices. Try the pepper salad ($6) or the *zaatar* pizza (wood-burning oven-baked, with thyme paste, roasted sesame, onion, feta, and tomato, $9); for dessert choose between baklava ($3) and tiramisu ($5). Open Mon.-Thurs. 11am-3pm and 5:30-9pm, Fri. 11am-3pm and 5:30-10pm.

Gibran, 1120 20th St. NW (887-0570), near L St. beside the mall. Metro: Farragut West or Farragut North. Delectable Lebanese dishes presented to you in a bright and friendly atmosphere. Don't be intimidated by some of the higher prices on the menu. Instead, go for the "light fare" meals ($6.25-8), like the mezza platter ($8), which offers a little of everything. Or make a meal out of Middle Eastern appetizers ($3.25-4.25). Of course, the real deal is happy hour, or "renewal hour" as translated from the Lebanese (Mon.-Fri. 5-7pm), with free appetizers. Open Mon.-Fri. 11:30am-3pm and 5-9:30pm, Sat. 5-9:30pm.

Health Zone, 1445 K St. NW (371-2900). Metro: McPherson Sq. Mmm...steamed veggies and rice ($4.60). If that doesn't sound appealing, the Health Zone burger (veggie, $3.70) is actually tasty, and the veggie pizza ($4.50) deserves a try. Large FroYo only $1.60. New age music and health-oriented quotations displayed on burlap banners complete the motif. Open Mon.-Fri. 7am-4pm.

La Prima Market Caffè, 950 14th St. NW (898-1140), near K St. Metro: McPherson Square. Create your own sandwich by filling out a "sand-wish card" ($4.30). Hot Italian dishes ($2-4.60) and ready-to-eat salads ($2-4.30) receive equal attention from patrons. Open Mon.-Fri. 7am-5pm.

Mrs. Chang's Kitchen, 1010 15th St. NW (347-2098). Metro: McPherson Sq. Generous portions of decent Chinese fast-food dirt cheap. No dish on the menu costs more than $7. Look for the sign outside that advertises the day's special, (only $2.99, served 11am-3pm), or try the rice-bowl special for a measly $1.50.

New York Gourmet Deli, 2000 L St. NW (296-8113). Metro: Farragut North. The size and selection make this place king of the deli/cafés. Jam-packed during lunch due to its indoor and outdoor seating and hot and cold lunch bars (each $4 per lb.). Fill up on the breakfast bar for only $3.30 per lb. All this serve-yourself action leaves the guys behind the sandwich counter bored to death. Open Mon.-Fri. 6:30am-4pm.

Palais du Chocolat, 1200 19th St. NW (659-4244), at M St. Metro: Farragut North or Farragut West. If you're the type who likes breakfast food all day long, avoid the local bars and try this sweet tooth's happy hour instead: 2 scones for the price of 1, or 3 tarts or cake slices for the price of 2. (Happy hour Mon.-Fri. 4-6:30pm.) Come for lunch and have a *croque monsieur* (grilled cheese sandwich, $4) while drooling over the white chocolate replicas of the Capitol dome. Open Mon.-Fri. 8am-6:30pm.

Pan Asian, upstairs at 1018 Vermont Ave. NW (783-8899). Metro: McPherson Sq. This quiet, two-floor establishment offers Far Eastern cuisine from Japan to the Philippines. Try the hot-and-spicy drunken noodles, noodles with minced chicken and a spicy basil sauce, the Pud-Thai, or the Singapore Curry Vermicelli (all dishes $6 lunch, $7 dinner). Open Mon.-Fri. 11:30am-8:30pm.

Recessions, 1700 K St. NW (296-6686), ironically located in the basement of the Commerce building. Metro: Farragut North. Claiming to serve "too much for your money," this tick-tacky café sports old advertisements on its walls from the days when a brand-new Buick was $1000. Prepare to line up at lunchtime. Hot entrees are never more than $7 (and that includes the ½ lb. steak), and 10-oz. burgers with all sorts of toppings go for $6 or less. Open Mon.-Fri. 11am-9pm.

Sholl's Colonial Cafeteria, 1990 K St. NW (296-3065), in the Esplanade Mall (enter by way of 20th St.). Metro: Farragut West. The last of its kind, Sholl's serves up good cooking at exceptionally low prices, cafeteria-style: breast of lamb or plain roast beef $2.25. These guys have been around forever; so have dozens of their patrons. Try the homemade pies for dessert ($1-1.50 per slice). Open Mon.-Sat. 7am-2:30pm and 4-8pm, Sun. 8:30am-6pm.

★ **The Star of Siam,** 1136 19th St. NW (785-2839), between L and M St. Metro: Farragut West or Farragut North. This critically-acclaimed restaurant is a favorite of both business folk and true connoisseurs. Try the *Gang Keo-Wan,* or green curry with chicken or beef, coconut milk, bamboo shoots, eggplant, and green beans ($7.50 lunch, $8.50 dinner), and raise the temperature of the roof of your mouth to a whole new level. Open Mon.-Sat. 11:30am-11pm, Sun. 5-10pm.

Thai Kingdom, 2021 K St. NW (835-1700), near 21st St. Metro: Farragut West or Foggy Bottom-GWU. Ornate and overflowing with gilt decorations and photos of famous Thais, Thai Kingdom prides itself on its Gai Yarng Kingdom dish—grilled chicken served with rice and several sauces ($6.50). Open Mon.-Thurs. 11:30am-2:30pm and 5-10:30pm, Fri. 11:30am-2:30pm and 5-11pm, Sat. noon-2:30pm and 5-11pm, Sun. noon-2:30pm and 5-10pm.

★ **Tokyo Terrace,** 1025 Vermont Ave. NW (628-7304), near K St. Metro: McPherson Square. Join every other sushi-lover in Farragut for an inexpensive Japanese lunch fast-food-style. The "Sushi Deluxe" (6 California rolls, 2 *futomaki*, and 2 *inari*) is only $5.25. Just $9.75, or $5 for children will buy you all-you-can-eat sushi rolls plus salad, vegetable roll, and miso soup on Fri. 6-9pm and Sat. noon-9pm. Open Mon.-Thurs. 9am-7:30pm, Fri. 9am-9pm, Sat. noon-9pm.

Vie de France, 1615 M St. NW (659-0992). Metro: Farragut North. French-inspired fast food here includes pizza on a croissant crust ($3) and *Pain Bagnat,* a French take on the tuna sandwich ($5.50). Espresso drinks $1.25-2.50, cookies 90¢. Look for daily specials and the funny hats the waitstaff must wear. Open Mon-Fri. 7:30am-5pm, but café/deli closes at 4pm.

Whatsa Bagel, 1216 18th St. NW (293-8990), enter on Jefferson Pl. Metro: Farragut North. 50¢ bagels come in wacky daily varieties like sundried tomato, cheese, banana nut, granola, "everything," and rotating specialty flavors like chocolate chip, carrot, and piña colada. "Overstuffed" bagel sandwiches can also be offbeat: chopped liver for $2.90 or 1 scrambled egg for $1.50. Pizza $1.25-1.50 per slice. Staffed by youths. Open Mon.-Thurs. 7am-7pm, Fri. 7am-6pm, Sat. 7:30am-5pm, Sun. 8am-4:30pm.

■■■ DUPONT CIRCLE

Dupont Circle's food is more expensive but more varied than that of the funkier Adams-Morgan to the north. Cheap coffee shops, one-of-a-kind American restaurants, and a pricey *patisserie* or two complement the ethnic assortment.

Afterwords Café, 1517 Connecticut Ave. NW (387-3825), near Q St. Late-night sweets behind a bookshop. Some expensive *nouvelle* entrees, but Washington's best cakes, pies, and mousses ($3.25-6.25) are rich rewards for living the literary life. Cappuccino freaks should head here too. Live music Wed. at 8pm, Thurs. at 9pm, Fri.-Sat. 10pm. Open Sun.-Thurs. 7am-1am, Fri.-Sat. 24 hrs.

Bacchus Restaurant, 1827 Jefferson Place NW (785-0734), near 19th St. Metro: Dupont Circle. While entrees tend to hover around the $13 level, don't give up on this Lebanese den named after the god of good times. It offers pages and pages worth of tantalizing appetizers, ranging in price from $4 to $5.75 and ranging in ingredients from okra to eggplant to pomegranate to lamb. Open Mon.-Fri. noon-2:30pm and 6-10pm, Sat. 6-10pm.

Bua, 1635 P St. NW (265-0828, delivery 232-8646), near 17th St. Thai cuisine in a cool, spacious dining room or on the patio. Dinner entrees $8-13, with most meals hovering around $8; lunch entrees $6-7.50. Happy hour Mon.-Fri. 5-7pm serves up margaritas, rails, and selected beers for $2. Open Mon.-Thurs. 11:30am-2:30pm and 5-10:30pm, Fri. 11:30am-2:30pm and 5-11pm, Sat. noon-4pm and 5-11pm, Sun. noon-4pm and 5-10:30pm.

Burrito Bros., 1524 Connecticut Ave. NW (332-2308), near Q St. Made-to-order, over-the-counter, fast-and-fresh California-style (hyphen-heavy!) fare. Tacos $2.75-3. Open Mon.-Sat. 11am-11pm, Sun. 11am-8pm.

Café Luna, 1633 P St. NW (387-4005), near 17th St. Health-and-self conscious locals flock here for extensive menu of veggie and fat-free dishes and artsy atmosphere. Pasta $5.50-8. Sandwiches $3.75-5. Breakfast ($2-4.25) served all day. A la carte brunch served Sat.-Sun. 10am-3pm ($5-6). Open Mon.-Thurs. 8am-11:30pm, Fri. 8am-2am, Sat. 10am-2am, Sun. 10am-11:30pm.

Café Petitto, 1724 Connecticut Ave. NW (462-8771), between R and S St. Excellent and popular Italian regional cooking in an understated atmosphere. Start with the delicious pizza-like *focaccia* ($4.75). Sample all of their delicious antipasti for free at Capo's next door. Open Mon.-Thurs. 11:30am-11pm, Fri.-Sat. 11:30am-1am, Sun. 11:30am-10:30pm.

★ **City Lights of China,** 1731 Connecticut Ave. NW (265-6688), between R and S St. Probably the District's best Chinese restaurant, City Lights serves carefully prepared Szechuan-Hunan standards ($9-22, most at the low end) and widely acclaimed house specialities, like the crispy fried shredded beef ($13). Try the steamed dumplings with chives and pork to start ($4.50). Open Mon.-Thurs. 11:30am-10:30pm, Fri. 11:30am-11pm, Sat. noon-11pm, Sun. noon-10:30pm.

Dante's, 1522 14th St. NW (667-7260). A 10-min. walk east on P St., left on 14th. Not to be missed after midnight, when punk rockers, actors, and their friends jam the place with hipness and hair. Dim lights and diabolical decor contrast with heavenly pita sandwiches ($5-6.50). House specialty drinks like the Fallen Angel (a peppermint cocktail with gin and lime, $3.50) complete the infernal motif. Don't come around here alone at night. Open Sun.-Thurs. 5pm-3am, Fri.-Sat. 5pm-4am.

DC Café, 2035 P St. NW (887-5819), near 21st St. Excellent pizza ($6 for a plain 10-in. pie that feeds two). Indoor and outdoor dining areas conveniently located near several of the Circle's well-known clubs and bars. Free delivery within 4-block radius ($5 minimum). Cool and cheap. Open 24 hrs.

Dupont Italian Kitchen, 1637-41 17th St. NW (328-3222), at R St. Delicious, no-frills Italian food at excellent prices. Pasta $4.50-7, hot sandwiches $3-4, small pizza with cheese $4.50. Indoor seating plus a sidewalk café. Free delivery in the Dupont Circle area. Open Mon.-Sat. noon-11:30pm, Sun. 11am-10:30pm.

Dupont Down Under, entrance at Mass. Ave. and 19th. Underground pedestrian bypass offers an alternative way to cross the Circle via a multiethnic food court. Open Sun.-Thurs. 10am-9pm, Fri.-Sat. 10am-10pm.

★ **Food for Thought,** 1738 Connecticut Ave. NW (797-1095), three blocks north of the circle. Casual coffeehouse atmosphere attracts alternative youth, and veggie dishes satisfy the healthiest appetites. Evening sets by local acoustic musicians add a Bohemian touch; open mike every Mon. 9-11:30pm. Bulletin boards announce everything from rallies to beach parties to rides to LA. Pool table upstairs. Great chunky gazpacho ($2.95 a cup). Lunch combos with soup or salad $4.75-6.75 (Mon.-Fri. until 4:30pm), dinner $6-10. Open Mon. 11:30am-3pm and 5pm-12:30am; Tues.-Thurs. 11:30am-12:30am, Fri. 11:30am-2am, Sat. noon-2am, Sun. 4pm-12:30am.

Java House, 1645 Q St. NW (387-6622), near 17th St. Come here for good coffee; go elsewhere for good ambience. Espresso ($1.50), cappuccino ($2). Open Sun.-Thurs. 7am-midnight, Fri.-Sat. 7am-1am.

Jolt 'N Bolt, 1918 18th St. NW (232-0077), near S St. Espresso $1.05, cappuccino $1.75, coffee $1. In summer, they'll ice just about anything (even Grandma). Open Mon.-Thurs. 7am-11pm, Fri. 7am-midnight, Sat. 8am-midnight.

Lauriol Plaza, 1801 18th St. NW (387-0035), near S St. Authentic Mexican food—no greasy chimichangas here—served on a charming patio by gracious waiters. Fried *bananas* side dish $2.50. Or try one of the many entrees served with rice and *frijoles* ($7-16). Free parking for patrons (a plus in this dense neighborhood). Open Sun.-Thurs. 11:30am-11pm, Fri.-Sat. 11:30am-midnight.

Omaha Coffee Shop, 1666 Connecticut Ave. NW (462-5300), near R St., hidden in an office building. No atmosphere and bland cuisine but dirt-cheap: grilled cheese $1, hamburger $1.70. Open Mon.-Fri. 7am-3pm.

Pan Asian Noodles & Grill, 2020 P St. NW (872-8889), near 20th St. Oodles of noodles in every soup, sauce, and style. Vegetarian dishes on request. Lunch $6-9, dinner $7-10. Open Mon.-Thurs. 11:30am-2:30pm and 5-10pm, Fri. 11:30am-2:30pm and 5-11pm, Sat. noon-2:30pm and 5:30-11pm, Sun. 5-10pm.

Paru's Indian Vegetarian Restaurant, 2010 S. St. NW (483-5133), near Connecticut Ave. Vegetarian fast food served southern-Indian-style in a quiet diner atmosphere. Rice platters served with vegetable *pilav, raitha, paratha, papoid,* and lemon pickle ($8). Open Mon.-Sat. 11:30am-8:45pm.

★ **Pizzeria Paradiso,** 2029 P St. NW (223-1245), near 21st St. The lines are permanently long most nights, but wouldn't you expect them to be for the best pizza in the city? The toppings are tasty and traditional—basil, prosciutto, capers—but the crispy crust is the real star around here. Sides include the tangy *panzanella* (Tuscan bread and vegetable salad) and elegant salads. All meals come with a small bowl of black and green olives. Open Mon.-Thurs. 11am-11pm, Fri.-Sat. 11am-midnight, Sun. noon-10pm.

★ **The Pop Stop,** 1513 17th St. NW (328-0880), near P St. The price of a cup of coffee buys you several hours in the easy chairs upstairs at this hippest of D.C. cafés. Of course, you could also stake out a table downstairs within easy reach of the well-stocked magazine rack. Or why not settle in for some serious people-watching on the streetside patio? The structural diversity attracts a diverse crowd, though it's weighted toward the local, gay, and young; many stop by on their way to or from bars and clubs. The café serves a wide range of coffee drinks ($1-3) and a handful of sandwiches (with chips $4). Open Sun.-Thurs. 7:30am-2am, Fri.-Sat. 7:30am-4am.

Sala Thai, 2016 P St. NW (872-1144), at 21st St. Light spicy Thai fare draws locals to this modern downstairs dining room. Delicious crispy fish is affordable for lunch at $8. Most other lunch entrees $6. Dinner entrees $7-13. Critics rave about the soft-shelled crabs ($13). Open Mon.-Thurs. 11:30am-2:30pm and 5-10:30pm, Fri. 11:30am-2:30pm and 5-11pm, Sat. noon-11pm, Sun. noon-10:30pm.

★ **Skewers,** 1633 P St. NW (387-7400, delivery 546-8646), near 17th St. Defies the neighborhood tendency towards multiethnic menus and sticks exclusively to Middle Eastern fare; coupled with its tapestry-hung, pottery-filled interior, the result is authenticity. Chicken kabob and 2 side dishes, $7. Open Sun.-Thurs. 11am-11pm, Fri.-Sat. 11am-midnight.

★ **Soho Tea & Coffee,** 2150 P St. NW (463-7646). Directly en route to any of the bars or clubs near P St. west of the Circle. This hip new coffeehouse benefits from its strategic location drawing crowds of bar-and-club-hoppers in the wee hours of the morning, serving a steady stream of patrons, gay and straight, all day long. Try a veggie bowl ($4.25) or a sandwich ($5.25). Espresso $1.25-3.50. Admire the artwork on the walls or watch passers-by. Open daily 6am-4am.

Trio Restaurant, 1537 17th St. NW (232-6305), at Q St. The 1963 March on Washington planners met in this diner, nowadays popular with the gay community. Those who prefer good grub to fine dining will appreciate this sturdy diner and its hearty American meals. Sandwiches $1.75-5.75. Open daily 7:30am-midnight.

Volare Pizza, 2011 S St. NW (234-9150), just off Connecticut, 3 blocks north of the Circle. Cheap food in large portions. Full-meal daily specials $6, subs and enormous gyros $3.50-6, whole pizzas (plain $5-11), and greasy breakfasts ($1.45-3; served until 11am). Open Mon.-Sat. 7am-11pm, Sun. 8am-10pm.

★ **Zorba's Café,** 1612 20th St. NW (387-8555), near Connecticut Ave., by the Q St. entrance to the Dupont Circle Metro. Mediterranean folk music played for the indoor and outdoor customers enjoying popular Greek food. The restaurant is self-service; place your order with the cashier inside. Try the *yero* plate, which comes with Zorba's excellent french fries and a small salad ($5.40). Open Mon.-Wed. 11am-11:30pm, Thurs.-Sat. 11am-2:30am, Sun. noon-10:30pm.

■■■ SHAW / U DISTRICT

The immediate vicinity of 14th and U St. NW, on the area's edge near the U St.-Cardozo Metro stop, is a safe source for supreme soul food, a uniquely African-American cuisine. Come during the day. The Shaw area Metro stops (at 13th and U and at 7th and U) opened in the summer of 1991; the hoped-for commercial revitalization is slowly but surely taking place. A new mall-in-the-making rises in the lot across from the Metro. Its glossy walls have improved the area cosmetically, but have yet to interfere with the neighborhood's authenticity. The U is still the best place for a taste of home cookin'. Metro: U St.-Cardozo, for all of the following.

★ **Ben's Chili Bowl,** 1213 U St. NW (667-0909), at 13th St. The self-declared "Home of the Famous Chili Dog," this venerable (30-year-old) neighborhood hangout got a facelift a few years ago, with a jukebox, smooth counters, and a molded ceiling to prove it. More exciting than photos of Bill Cosby's visit here are the multiple shots of Denzel Washington, taken on the day a scene from *The Pelican Brief* was filmed here. Spicy homemade chili—on a chili dog (served with onion, mustard, and potato chips, $2), on a half-smoke ($2.75), or on a ¼-lb. burger ($2.25). Die-hards eat it plain: small bowl $1.90, large bowl $2.55. Open Mon.-Thurs. 6am-2am, Fri.-Sat. 6am-3am, Sun. noon-8pm.

★ **Florida Avenue Grill,** 1100 Florida Ave. NW (265-1586), at 11th St. From the U St.-Cardozo Metro stop, walk east on U to 11th St., then walk north up 11th St. to Florida Ave. or take the Metrobus that runs up 11th St. Small, enduring (since 1944) diner once fed Black leaders and famous entertainers. Now their framed faces beam down at the hordes of locals who frequent the place. Don't miss the article in the first booth about a 32-year veteran Grill server: "I'd love to serve [President Reagan] chitlins," she says. "It might straighten his head out." Awesome Southern-style food: breakfast with salmon cakes or spicy half-smoked sausage, grits, apples, or southern biscuits ($2-6). Lunch and dinner dishes served with choice of 2 vegetables ($6.50-9). Also various dishes featuring pig's foot. Open Tues.-Sat. 6am-9pm.

Hogs on the Hill, 2001 14th St. NW (332-4647), at U St. Fast-food joint decor offsets enticing smells from the kitchen. You'll get big portions, too. Half chickens $4, whole chickens $7. Platters, served with corn bread and 2 side orders, are $3.50-8. Choices include pork ribs, chopped BBQ beef, or chicken. Sides include collard greens, potato salad, cole slaw, red beans and rice, and fries (all $1.15). Open Tues.-Thurs. 11am-10pm, Fri.-Sat. 11am-11pm, Sun. noon-10pm.

Julio's, 1604 U St. (483-8500), near 16th St. Metro: U St.-Cardozo. An upscale restaurant/bar with 2 floors of dining, including a popular rooftop, as well as a bar and a pool room. All-you-can-eat lunch buffet $7 (Mon.-Fri. 11:30am-3pm). Sandwiches $6-7.25. All-you-can-eat Sun. brunch $13 (10am-3pm). Happy hour Mon.-Fri. 5-7pm features $2 rails and drafts as well as free pizza Mon.-Thurs.; $1 pizza slices Fri. Open daily 11:30am-10:30pm.

★ **Outlaw's,** 917 U St. NW (387-3978), between Vermont Ave. and 9th St. Should be the in-laws'. Family-run takeout establishment crowds in local regulars for real, meat-laden "home-cooking." Cramped downstairs quarters open onto the kitchen, where daily specials like liver and onions (Mon.), meat loaf (Tues.), and Salisbury steak (Thurs.) are cooked up. Food is cheap, too: cornbread 50¢, dinners served with 2 vegetables $5.30-7.65, sandwiches $3.25-4.85. Upstairs the Family Bar and Lounge turns out jazz tunes Tues.-Wed. Open Mon.-Fri. 11am-6pm.

Polly's Café, 1342 U St. NW (265-8385), near 14th St. Sardine-can packed neighborhood restaurant/bar caters to a mixed crowd of professionals, students, and area residents. A cozy, dark wood interior and a varied menu with reasonable prices draw many for Sunday brunch featuring hearty American fare (i.e. meat, potatoes, and eggs, $6.50-7.50) and including a choice of beverages like Screw Drivers, Bloody Marys, and Mimosas. Cultivated palates will go for the Portabello mushroom steak with bean salad ($8), while swillers, swiggers, and guzzlers will be attracted to the mixed drink pitchers ($13-17). Happy hour Mon.-Thurs. 11pm-2am knocks $1 off rails and drafts. Open Mon.-Thurs. 5pm-midnight, Fri. 5pm-2am, Sat. 10am-3pm and 5pm-2am, Sun. 10am-3pm and 5pm-midnight.

■■■ ADAMS-MORGAN

Adams-Morgan's jambalaya of cultures can satisfy all sorts of unusual tastes, from Latin American to Ethiopian to Caribbean—all for around $10. Adams-Morgan has justifiably become D.C.'s preferred locale for budget dining, but it has recently become interspersed with a slew of decidedly overpriced spots. Don't be taken in; good food at a good price is literally around the corner. The action radiates from 18th, Columbia, and Calvert St. NW uphill along Columbia or down 18th.

The Argentine Grill, 2433 18th St. NW (234-1818), near Columbia Rd. Chic brick, art pix, a cured cow's skin, blue fans, and a mural. The cook's as artful as the decorators, even on the low end of the menu. Lunch sandwiches are a manageable $5-7. Dinner entrees $11-19. Open Sun.-Thurs. 11am-3pm and 5-11pm, Fri.-Sat. 11am-3pm and 5-11:30pm.

Bukom Café, 2442 18th St. NW (265-4600), near Columbia Rd. A mellow, funky West African restaurant and bar serving up stews, sugar cane, and other specialty dishes (entrees $8-10). Two-time "Taste of Adams-Morgan" contest winner. Live entertainment: jazz Tues. at 8pm, West African music Wed.-Thurs. and Sun. starting at 9pm, Fri.-Sat. at 10pm. Open Tues.-Thurs. 4pm-2am, Fri.-Sat. 2pm-3am, Sun. 3pm-2am.

Calvert Café, 1967 Calvert St. NW (232-5431), between Connecticut and Columbia Ave. right at the foot of the Duke Ellington Bridge. Metro: Woodley Park-Zoo, then hoof it down Calvert for 10 mins. Look for the brown and gold tiles; though it looks boarded-up, this landmark has lasted nearly 40 years. Huge, unadorned platters of Middle Eastern food. Dinner entrees $6-8.50. Try the combo platter for $10.50 or eat light with falafel or tabouli for $3.50. Open daily 11:30am-11pm.

Dahlak, 1769 U St. NW (332-6435), near 18th St. Not as fancy as many of its Ethiopian competitors, but the food is just as good. Choose from any of the individual entrees ($4.50-7.25) and you can't go wrong. Better yet, try the a combo platter for $6.50-7.50. The combo platters are served with salad and, of course, *injera,* Ethiopian sour pancake bread. Lunch specials $5. Open daily 11am-midnight. Live entertainment Fri.-Sat. 10pm-2am.

El Pollo Primo, 2471 18th St. NW (588-9551), near Columbia Rd. By their awning shall ye know them. Produces moist, flavorful, tender, greaseless, cheap chicken on a big smoky grill behind the counter. 2-piece chicken dinner with tortillas, salsa, and 2 side orders $3.30, 3-piece dinner $4.19. Side orders include beans and rice ($2 each à la carte). Open daily 9:30am-10pm.

El Tamarindo, 1785 Florida Ave. NW (328-3660), just east of the corner of Florida and 18th St. Be cautious after dark in this area. Superb and cheap Salvadoran and Mexican food served into the early morning. House combination plate of appetizers presents cheese quesadillas, nachos, chicken wings, a *taquito,* and guacamole and sour cream ($6.25). Entrees run $5.50-11, with nearly all under $10. Open Mon.-Thurs. 11am-2am, Fri.-Sat. 11am-5am, Sun. 10am-5am.

El Tazumal, 2467 18th St. NW (332-6931), near Columbia Rd. Ample portions of good Salvadoran and Mexican food. Large and clean interior boasts a cute bar dressed up as a small cottage with a Spanish-tile roof. Try one of the lunch specials (meat dish, corn chips, hot sauce, rice, and beans $5), or the *tacos al carbon* ($6). Appetizers $3-7, entrees $6-13. Open daily 11am-11pm.

★ **The Islander,** 1762 Columbia Rd. NW (234-4955), easy to miss above a jewelry store. Some of the best food in D.C. Small Trinidadian and Caribbean restaurant has been winning regulars for over 15 years with its exotic but unpretentious cuisine. Consider curried goat or Calypso chicken (each $8.50). 9 kinds of *roti* (thin pancakes stuffed with vegetables/meat) are a bargain for $3.50-7. Appetizers

$1.50-3. Wash it all down with sweet ginger beer ($1.50). Open Mon. 5-10pm, Tues.-Thurs. noon-10pm, Fri.-Sat. noon-11pm. Closed Mon. in summer.

Julia's Empanadas, 2452 18th St. NW (328-6232), near Columbia St. Julia's tasty meat- and veggie-filled pastries are "made by hand, baked with love" according to the carryout menu, but rest assured—she uses an oven, too. Baked empanadas $2.59-2.73, fried $1.89. One's a snack, two's a meal. Don't overlook the delicious dessert empanadas, $2. Open Sun.-Thurs. 11am-10pm, Fri.-Sat. 11am-midnight.

Las Rocas, 2450 18th St. NW (483-4851, takeout 232-3273). Serious barrio atmosphere. Downstairs diners speak Spanish in a dark, cramped, sparsely decorated neighborhood bar and dining room. The fare is unexceptional but cheap: entrees $6-9. Wide assortment of Mexican beers $2.25-3. Open daily 11am-3am.

★ **Meskerem,** 2434 18th St. NW (462-4100), near Columbia Rd. Fine Ethiopian cuisine in a beautiful setting. Cheery yellow 3-level interior incorporates an upstairs dining gallery with Ethiopian woven tables and a view of the diners below. Lunch entrees $7.25-11, dinner $9-12. Open daily noon-midnight.

Millie and Al's, 2440 18th St. NW (387-8131), near Columbia Rd. Old-time local bar and grill makes darkness its theme. The crowd includes locals and students, but you can barely see them. Sandwiches $2.50-3.50, dinners $4.75-5.50. Drafts $1.50, pitchers $5.75. Happy hour, with reduced drink prices, Mon.-Fri. 4-7pm. Open Mon.-Thurs. 4pm-2am, Fri.-Sat. noon-3am, Sun. noon-2am.

★ **Mixtec,** 1792 Columbia Rd. NW (332-1011), near 18th St. A cheap, friendly, and refreshing bastion of authentic Mexican food. 2 bright rooms wear neat paper lanterns and wooden Mexican chairs, while a neon window-sign flashes the specialty, *tacos al carbon.* The $3 version consists of 2 small tortillas filled with beef and served with 3 kinds of garnish. Mixtec makes a mind-bending chicken *mole,* too ($9). Entrees $7-8. Open Sun.-Thurs. 10am-10pm, Fri.-Sat. 10am-1am.

Montego Café, 2437 18th St. (745-1002), near Columbia Rd. Rollicking restaurant/bar serving American-style Caribbean food late into the night. Seafood entrees $9-11, chicken entrees $6.50-8, sandwiches $4.50-5.75. A la carte brunch ($4.50-9) served daily until 3pm. Open Sun.-Thurs. 10am-3am, Fri.-Sat. 10am-6am.

Pasta Mia Trattoria, 1790 Columbia Rd. NW (328-9114), near 18th St. Practice makes perfect, and Pasta Mia has had plenty of practice with pasta—other than a few traditional appetizers and desserts, there's nothing but noodles on the menu. Airy rooms and big pasta portions ($7-9). Open Mon.-Sat. 6-10:30pm.

Perry's, 1811 Columbia Rd. (234-6218), near 18th St. A funky modern dining room provides the backdrop for nouvelle Mediterranean/Japanese cuisine. Or, enjoy entrees ($12-16) and sushi ($1.50-2.50 a piece) on one of Washington's most popular rooftops, where the owners grow orange and lemon trees. Open Mon.-Sat. 6pm-1am, Sun. 5pm-1am. Kitchen closes Sun.-Thurs. at 10:30pm, Fri.-Sat. 11:30pm.

★ **Red Sea,** 2463 18th St. NW (483-5000), near Columbia Rd. The first of Adams-Morgan's famous Ethiopian restaurants and still among the best. The red-painted exterior is weather-beaten but enticing. Use the traditional pancake bread, *injera,* to scoop up spicy lamb, beef, chicken, and vegetable *wats*. Entrees $7-9. Open Sun.-Thurs. 11:45am-11pm, Fri.-Sat. 11:45am-midnight.

Saigonnais, 2307 18th St. (232-5300), near Kalorama Rd. An elegant and intimate dining room crowded with white-linen draped tables serves tasty, reasonably priced Vietnamese food. Lunch specials $5.50-7, dinner entrees $7.25-11.75. Delivery available. Open daily 11:30am-3pm and 5-11pm.

So's Your Mom, 1831 Columbia Rd. NW (462-3666). Deli with mock-New York sensibility (get it?!). Meats are shipped from the Big Apple itself; baked goods fresh daily from Baltimore?! No seating available?! Sandwiches $3-5. Open Mon.-Fri. 7am-8pm, Sat. 8am-7pm, Sun. 8am-3pm.

Star of Siam, 2446 18th St. (986-4133), near Columbia Rd. Acclaimed Thai cuisine served in an attractive second-floor dining room or on a rooftop deck. Entrees $6.25-10 at lunch, $8-13 at dinner. Delivery available daily 5-10:30pm. Open Mon.-Thurs. 5-11pm, Fri. 5pm-midnight, Sat. noon-midnight, Sun. noon-11pm.

■■■ UPPER NORTHWEST

WOODLEY PARK

A diverse group of popular eateries, some dirt-cheap, some wallet-smashing, gather on a single block of Connecticut Ave. around the Woodley Park-Zoo Metro, north of Dupont Circle, and just a Calvert St. bridge away from Adams-Morgan. Metro: Woodley Park-Zoo, for all of the following.

The Lebanese Taverna, 2641 Connecticut Ave. NW (265-8681). Relatively generous appetizers, many of them vegetarian ($3.50-7), and costlier entrees served in a casual outdoor or fancier indoor setting. Come here for the sandwiches ($5.50-6) served only at lunch; dinner entrees may be a little expensive ($8.75-14.50). Free parking underground on Woodley Rd. behind the restaurant. Open Mon.-Thurs. 11:30am-2:30pm and 5:30-10:30pm, Fri.-Sat. 11:30am-2:30pm and 5:30-10:30pm, Sat. 11:30am-3pm and 5:30-11pm, Sun. 5-10pm.

Rajaji, 2603 Connecticut Ave. NW (265-7344). Near-total darkness complements spicy vegetarian curries ($5-6 at lunch, $6-7.50 at dindin). Spicy vegetarian curries. Very, very spicy. Wide selection of Indian breads $1.25-2. Open daily 11:30am-2:30pm and 5:30-11pm.

Saigon Gourmet Restaurant, 2635 Connecticut Ave. NW (265-1360). Standard, traditional Vietnamese comfort. Reasonable prices. Try the *hâ iò*, Vietnam's spring roll-like appetizer ($3.25-4). Entrees like *bò xào xâ* (lemon grass beef) $6-10. Open Mon.-Sat. 11:30am-3pm and 5-10:30pm, Sun. 11am-3pm and 4:30-10pm.

A Taste of India, 2623 Connecticut Ave. NW (483-1115), a few doors down from Rajaji. Tandoor-oven and curried entrees (lunch $6-10, dinner $6-11) with tasty appetizers ($1-5). More mainstream than Rajaji, i.e. for Westerners who can't take the heat. Open daily 11am-3pm and 5-11pm.

Thai Taste, 2606 Connecticut Ave. NW (387-8876). D.C.'s voyeuristic black-and-neon magnet for Thai-food lovers. Mirrors at every table so you can watch yourself eat the spicy house noodle specialty ($8), then the Thai iced coffee ($2). Rama, rama. Dinner from $6.50. Open daily 11:30am-10:30pm.

GLOVER PARK

A ten-minute walk up Wisconsin Ave. from Georgetown proper, this area between Calvert and R St. seems to hog more than its fair share of D.C.'s top budget eateries.

★ **Austin Grill,** 2404 Wisconsin Ave. NW (337-8080). The Austin Grill sets the standard for Tex-Mex in Washington, relying on a foundation of brilliantly prepared standards and a range of more inventive dishes featuring fresh and unusual meats topped with exquisite house sauces. Try the carnitas ($9), which are melt-in-your-mouth braised pork fajitas, or the Austin special ($8), a pair of enchiladas striped with a trio of house sauces. The place is small and hip, so lines are long. While you wait, enjoy the Stars and Bars, a powerful margarita worth the $4.75 price. Open Mon. 11:30am-10:30pm, Tues.-Thurs. 11:30am-11pm, Fri. 11:30am-midnight, Sat. 11am-midnight, Sun. 11am-10:30pm.

★ **Faccia Luna,** 2400 Wisconsin Ave. NW (337-3132). Pizza-crust connoisseurs, this is your Mecca, your Delhi, your Jerusalem. Forget pepperoni and top it with eggplant, spinach, or pesto. Don't even think about asking for tuna. Basic 10-in. pie $6.05, 12-in. $8.30, 14-in. $9.95, and 16-in. $11.50. Toppings extra. Open Sun.-Thurs. 11:30am-11pm, Fri.-Sat. 11:30am-midnight.

Max's Best Ice Cream, 2416 Wisconsin Ave. NW (333-3111), near Calvert St. Max's Best is pretty darn good. An old-fashioned ice-cream parlor featuring cones at modern prices ($1.65). A variety of subs and sandwiches as well ($1.65-5.60), including good old peanut butter and jelly ($1.65). Open Sun.-Thurs. 11am-11pm, Fri.-Sat. 11am-midnight; in winter open daily 9am-9pm.

★ **Rocklands,** 2418 Wisconsin Ave. NW (333-2558). South Carolina/Florida-style tangy grilled barbecue. Quarter-rack of pork ribs $4.50, BBQ pork sandwich $4. Eat at the mahogany counter or take it on the road. If you eat in, you can raid owner John Snedden's shelf of some 100 different hot sauces; have just one or sample as extensively as your deviously promiscuous little mouth will permit. Open Mon.-Sat. 11:30am-10pm, Sun. 11am-10pm.

CLEVELAND PARK AND TENLEY CIRCLE

No one would place Cleveland Park or Tenley Circle on the cutting edge of anything. Still, these areas have the best of both worlds: back streets almost as quiet as the suburbs and two avenues where good food hides from the masses.

Cleveland Park

Budget ethnicity dominates the food in otherwise white Cleveland Park, on Connecticut Ave. Metro: Cleveland Park, for all of the following.

Ivy's Place, 3520 Connecticut Ave. NW (363-7802). A mixture of Indonesian and Thai fare, though not so much a collision of cuisines as a coexistence—the menu has separate Indonesian and Thai listings, none over $9. The lunch special ($6), early bird dinner special (4:30-6:30pm; $7), dinner special ($11) include soup, appetizers, and a choice of entree. A good choice for vegetarians. Open Sun.-Thurs. 4:30-10:30pm, Fri.-Sat. 11:30am-11:30pm.

Palais du Chocolat, 3309 Connecticut Ave. NW (363-2462). If death by chocolate is the way to go, this is the place to do it. The two principal cake categories are "Chocolate Chocolate Chocolate" and "Chocolate Chocolate," the difference being the number of incarnations of chocolate featured. Individual pastries $2.75, croissants 95¢. Open Sun.-Thurs. 8am-10pm, Fri.-Sat. 8am-midnight.

The Uptown Bakers, 3313 Connecticut Ave. NW (362-6262), near Macomb St. Absolutely amazing breads and pastries baked on the premises. Loaves in flavors like raisin pecan and Irish sodabread $1.50-5.50. Open daily 7am-9pm.

U.S. Famous Homemade Ice Cream, 3510 Connecticut Ave. NW (244-4465). Modest and unoriginal carry-out ice cream. $1.25 for a single, $1.70 for a double. Open Sun.-Thurs. 9am-11pm, Fri.-Sat. 9am-11:30pm.

Wingmaster's Grilled Chicken and Ribs, 3514 Connecticut Ave. NW (244-1111). Tasty and cheap side orders (60¢-90¢) complement the grilled chicken and ribs. Try the sweet and springy corn bread (60¢). Lunch and dinner samplers ($5.30 and $7.30, respectively) bring you varying combinations of grilled breasts, ribs, wings, and side orders. Open Sun.-Thurs. 11am-10pm, Fri.-Sat. 11am-11pm.

Yanni's, 3500 Connecticut Ave. NW (362-8871). A bright and airy neighborhood favorite serving some of the finest Greek food in town. Start with the *tzatziki,* a cool yogurt and cucumber dip ($3.50), or move straight into one of the heaping souvlaki platters ($8), which come with *tzatziki* as well as french fries and a Greek salad. Open daily 11:30am-11pm.

Yenching Palace, 3524 Connecticut Ave. NW (362-8200). The 1961 Cuban Missile Crisis came to an end here, when emissaries from Khrushchev and Kennedy finalized the Soviet missile removal over a Chinese banquet. Today, the handsome semicircular booths host less nail-biting diplomacy and more finger-licking feasting; the food remains great and reasonably priced. Dinner entrees $6.25-$9.50. Free parking. Open Mon.-Thurs. 11:30am-11pm, Fri.-Sat. 11:30am-11:30pm.

Tenley Circle

Mostly shoppers, American University students, and local professionals eat at these places. Metro: Tenleytown, for all of the following.

a.k.a. Frisco's, 4115 Wisconsin Ave. NW (244-7847). Charming deli/café with a stupid name copies San Francisco prototypes: bright, airy and decked out in the whitest of whites. Generous sandwiches test combinations—try the Berkeley ($3.85): diced turkey, extra virgin olive oil, tarragon vinegar, capers, onions, lemon pepper, tomato, and sprouts in a pita. Sandwiches substitute gourmet mustards, lemon, vinegars, relishes, and other spices for mayonnaise and salt. Sandwiches $3.50-4.05. Salads $2.85-4.05. HUGE baked potatoes ($1.25-3.25) make a meal. Huge lines. Open Mon.-Fri. 11am-4pm, Sat. 11am-3pm.

Armand's, 4231 Wisconsin Ave. NW (686-9450). Chicago-style deep-dish pizza invades Washington. Part of a chain. Small pizza (triple cheese) $6.35, medium $9, large $10.35. Also boasts thin-crust New York-style pizza and Armand's gourmet California-style pizza with exotic toppings like Thai chicken (marinated chicken breast and a peanut ginger sauce with scallions, shredded carrots, red pepper, and bean sprouts). All-you-can-eat pizza and salad bar buffet, $5 (Sun.-Thurs. 11am-2:30pm and 9-11pm, Sat.-Sun. 10am-1pm and 9-11pm). Open Sun.-Thurs. 11am-11pm, Fri.-Sat. 11am-1am. Go down the street to **Armand's take-out-only window** at 5000 Wisconsin Ave. NW (363-5500) for cheaper slices. Open Sun.-Thurs. 11am-10pm, Fri.-Sat. 11am-midnight.

★ **Cactus Cantina,** 3300 Wisconsin Ave. NW (686-7222), at Macomb St. near the Cathedral. Metro: Tenleytown, then Metrobus #30, 32, 34, or 36 towards Georgetown. How fresh is the food here? The kitchen doesn't even own a can opener and the salsa is no more than 30 min. old when it arrives at your table. A total local hangout with great food. Try the exceptional Tex-Mex standards, like the enchiladas ($7.50 for 3), or order something from the mesquite-fired grill ($9.50-20). Open Sun.-Thurs. 11:30am-11pm, Fri.-Sat. 11:30am-midnight.

The Dancing Crab, 4611 Wisconsin Ave. NW (244-1882), at 41st St. Locals dive in for fresh seafood, especially crabmeat sandwiches ($7) and Maryland-style crabcakes ($15). Climb upstairs to the Malt Shop (see **Nightlife & Entertainment,** p. 213) for a cold brew. Open Mon.-Thurs. 11am-10:30pm, Fri. 11am-11pm, Sat. noon-11pm, Sun. 3-10:30pm.

Maggie's, 4237 Wisconsin Ave. NW (363-1447). Families pick Armand's next door; students come here. NY-style thin-crust pizzas, Italian pasta, and sub staples in a pub atmosphere. Happy hour (Mon.-Fri. 3-7pm), the bar serves a very young crowd free pizza along with $1.25 domestic drafts and $8.25 pitchers. Small pizza $10, large $11.50. Daily salad and pizza bar $4 with beverage purchase (11am-3pm). Open Sun.-Thurs. 11am-2am, Fri.-Sat. 11am-3am.

Mediterranean Deli, 4629 41st St. NW (362-1006), at Wisconsin Ave. This small, nondescript eatery dishes out some of the best and cheapest Mediterranean food in town. Vegetarian fare includes vine leaves—grape leaves stuffed with rice, onion, lemon, and parsley ($3.25). Sandwiches like *baba ghanoush* (an eggplant concoction, $4), and falafel ($3). Open Mon.-Sat. 11:30am-10pm, Sun. noon-8pm.

Toojay's, 4620 Wisconsin Ave. NW (686-1989). Popular deli that imports many of its fine ingredients from more deli-dependent cities like New York. Smoked fish ($9-14), matzo ball soup ($3.50), and pastrami ($6.50) all have a place on Toojay's menu. Order one of the $14 nightly dinner specials, including soup or salad, beverage, main course, and dessert. Open daily 8am-10pm.

FRIENDSHIP HEIGHTS

Restaurants get pricier as you approach Western Ave., more reasonable as Maryland grows more distant. Metro: Friendship Heights, for all of the following.

American Café, 5252 Wisconsin Ave. NW (363-5400), above Booeymonger's at Jenifer St. An old standby. Light salads and sandwiches ($5.25-8). Desserts to die for like the Messiest Sundae which will put you up to your elbows in ice cream and chocolate chip cookies ($3.45). Open Mon.-Thurs. 11am-11pm, Fri.-Sat. 11am-1am, Sun. 10:30am-11pm.

Booeymonger, 5252 Wisconsin Ave. NW (686-5805), at Jenifer St. A blood relation of the one in Georgetown. Elaborate sandwiches, all under $5. Try to fit your jaw around the Patty Hearst: turkey, bacon, melted provolone, and Russian dressing on an English muffin ($4.50). The puns are obscure (the English muffin and Russian dressing represent Hearst's Anglo-Saxon stock and conversion to Communism, respectively) but delicious. Salads $4-5.25. Decent but unexciting breakfast served too, all under $4. Open Sun.-Thurs. 7:30am-1am, Fri.-Sat. 7:30am-2am.

Chadwick's, 5247 Wisconsin Ave. NW (362-8040). Walk downstairs into the shade, but ask to sit in the greenhouse area out front. Sandwiches and burgers $5-8, salads $6-8. For a real treat, share a chunk of mud pie ($4) or chug a thick mocha milkshake ($3). Happy hour Mon.-Fri. 4-7pm: margaritas $2, domestic bottles or glass of house wine $1.50. Open Mon.-Thurs. 11:30am-2am, Fri.-Sat. 11:30am-3am, Sun. 10am-2am.

El Tamarindo, 4910 Wisconsin Ave. NW (244-8888), near Fessenden St. Yeah, they do great Mexican staples like enchiladas ($6.50-7.25) and chimichangas ($7.25-9), but try the Salvadoran cuisine for a change, like *pollo encebollado* (chicken sautéed with garlic butter, onion, pepper, tomato, and vinegar, $7.25). Go before 3pm and get the same dish for $6. Open Mon.-Thurs. 11am-1am, Fri.-Sat. 11am-3am, Sun. 11am-2am.

Pleasant Peasant, in the Mazza Gallerie, an intolerable shopping mall at 5300 Wisconsin Ave. NW (364-2500). Black-and-white glossy decor and the piano player's salary push the entrees upstairs out of the *Let's Go* price range, but each dessert can feed two with a flourish. Lose your balance over the chocolate intemperance cake ($6). Open Sun.-Thurs. 11:30am-10pm, Fri.-Sat. 11:30am-midnight.

Yosaku, 4712 Wisconsin Ave. NW (363-4453). You like sushi? Lunchtime sushi or sashimi $6.75. Dinnertime sushi or sashimi $12.50. Grab some lame friends for karaoke (50¢ a song). Open Mon.-Thurs. 11:30am-2:30pm and 5:30-10:30pm, Fri. 11:30am-2:30pm and 5:30-11pm, Sat. 5:30-11pm, Sun. 5:30-10pm.

WORTH DRIVING TO

Parkway Deli, 8317 Grubb Rd. (301-587-1427), just over the District line in Maryland. Obscure shopping center hides Washington's best deli from all but true connoisseurs, who often wait up to an hour for weekend breakfasts. Try any sandwich ($3.20-9) or a bagel with Nova lox ($6.15); the pickle bar (free after 4pm) makes national treasures of vinegar and peppercorns. Take 16th St. NW all the way north to East-West Hwy., turn left on East-West, then left onto Grubb. For blank stares, tell 'em *Let's Go* sent you. Open Mon. 8am-9:30pm, Tues.-Fri. 8am-9:30pm, Sat. 7am-10pm, Sun. 7am-9:30pm.

■■■ NORTHEAST

An area not known for its fine cuisine, Northeast offers a few budget options clustering near Catholic University. Metro: Brookland-CUA, for all of the following:

Colonel Brooks Tavern, 901 Monroe St. NE (529-4002). Pick up Monroe St. at its intersection with Michigan Ave. in front of the University Center building, at the south end of Catholic U.'s campus, on 9th and Monroe St. Half-restaurant, half-bar is the casual hangout for Catholic U. students and staff alike. The entrees ($9-13) are tasty, but the pub grub is cheaper and just as good. Try the Colonel's favorite sandwiches, a three-story tower of pastrami, turkey, swiss cheese, slaw, and dressing ($7). Wash it down with a mug of a microbrew like Pete's Wicked Ale or Wild Goose Porter ($2.75) or go traditional with a premium (mug $2.25), a domestic (mug $2), a domestic (mug $2), or one of the brews of the month (mug $2.50). Free parking. Open Sun.-Thurs. 11am-2am, Fri. 11am-3am, Sat. 11:30am-3am.

Murry and Paul's Restaurant, 3513 12th St. NE (529-4078). Standard greasy diner, with a linoleum counter facing a sizzling grill and orange vinyl booths held together with duct tape. $5 lunch special includes choice of entree, two vegetables, and bread. Modest selection of subs and sandwiches ($1.45-5.75). Open Mon.-Sat. 6am-4pm, Sun. 8am-2pm.

Wings to Go, 3502 12th St. NE (529-7619), near the corner of Monroe St. Metro: Brookland-CUA. Wings, wings, wings, and more wings, for takeout in quantities of 10. They'll charge you $4 for 10, but only $35 for 100. Corn dog deal (2 dogs, fries, and a soda) $3. "Lunch break" consists of 10 pieces, fries, and a soda ($4.75) Both specials served Mon.-Fri. 11am-3pm. No seating. Open Mon.-Thurs. 11am-10pm, Fri.-Sat. 11am-3am, Sun. noon-8pm.

■■■ BETHESDA, MD

All those white-collar suburbanites must have exceptional taste buds, because Bethesda's concrete renaissance maintains many of the D.C. area's best restaurants. Bethesda boasts about 150 restaurants; because there are so many so close together, downtown Bethesda almost demands a pre-dinner stroll to check out menus and compare ambiences. Wander the area bounded roughly by Wisconsin Ave. on the east, Bethesda Ave. on the south, Rugby Ave. on the north, and Arlington Rd. and Old Georgetown Rd. on the west. Since Bethesda is in Maryland, all its phone numbers claim the **301 area code.** Metro: Bethesda, for all of the following.

★**Bethesda Crab House,** 4958 Bethesda Ave. (652-3382), near Arlington St. This extraordinary restaurant is a little like the crabs it serves: not much to look at, but boy is it good. Camp-style tables and benches—covered in newspaper—crowd a small room and patio, but succulent all-you-can-eat crabs crowd the plates (served daily for $18, including coleslaw and corn). Also serves shrimp, lobster, and other hard-shell crawlies. One of Bethesda's great institutions, with 33 years of experience to back it. Reservations recommended. Open Mon.-Sat. 9am-midnight, Sun. 11am-midnight.

Bob's Famous Homemade Ice Cream, 4706 Bethesda Ave. (657-2963). One of Washington's most popular local scoopers, with branches here, in Cleveland Park, and on the Hill. Small, clean, and cool, with a counter and tables. Ice cream from $2.70-3.50, brownie sundaes $4.30, and frozen yogurt $1.55-2.45. Also has bakery and deli selections, with sandwiches $3.50-4.20. Open Mon.-Thurs. 7:30am-10:30pm, Fri. 7:30am-midnight, Sat. 11am-midnight, Sun. noon-10:30pm; call for winter hours.

Chinese Express, 7613 Wisconsin Ave. (656-6111). Red and yellow awning, murals of dragons, and black-and-white TV characterize this suburban Chinese place. $4.50 lunch special is a real bargain (Mon.-Fri. 11am-3pm). Free delivery ($10 min. purchase). Open daily 11am-10pm.

Louisiana Express, 4921 Bethesda Ave. (652-6945), near Arlington St. White lattice and the smell of Cajun cuisine beckon. Try the chicken jambalaya, a rice dish with a symphony of chicken, tomatoes, vegetables, and spices ($4.95). Critically acclaimed crawfish bisque $3. Half-chicken with Cajun spices, vegetable jambalaya, and biscuits soft as grandma's belly $5.50. On Sun. budgeteers can feast on a concoction of scrambled eggs with ham, bacon, and sausage on french bread with melted cheese. Delivery available ($15 min. order). Open Sun.-Thurs. 7:30am-10pm, Fri.-Sat. 7:30am-11pm.

Paradise Restaurant, 7141 Wisconsin Ave. (907-7500, delivery 571-0111), near Bethesda Ave. "Kebab Cuisine" from a wood-burning grill. Lose yourself in the charm of a black, pink, and green dining room among tempting flowers and mirrors, then gain weight at the $7 all-you-can-eat luncheon buffet consisting of soup, 6 entrees, salad, and fruit (served daily noon-3pm). Or bite into a *sambosa,* a deep-fried pastry filled with spiced beef (4 for $3). Cold appetizers $3-5, hot appetizers $4-5, entrees $7-12. Baklava $2.50. Open daily noon-10pm.

Persepolis Restaurant, 7130 Wisconsin Ave. (656-9339, delivery 571-0111), near Bethesda Ave. "Exquisite Persian cuisine" locked in Manichaean struggle with Paradise Restaurant across the street; everybody wins. Friendly service delivers kebab and other Middle Eastern food. All-you-can-eat lunch buffet $7 (served daily noon-3pm). Hummus and pita $4; *chelo kabob-e kubideh* (ground sirloin of beef with onions, saffron, and seasonings) $8. Open Sun.-Thurs. noon-10pm, Fri.-Sat. noon-10:30pm.

Philadelphia Mike's, 7732 Wisconsin Ave. (656-0103/4/5, delivery 571-0111 with $12 minimum), near Middleton Ave. That broken bell may be the only reason to visit Philadelphia now, because Mike's has mastered the Philly cheesesteak. Read the dead-on rave reviews on the wall as you wait for your green-bedecked table. Superb cheesesteaks $3.64-7. Burgers $3-4, breakfast subs under $2.50. Open Mon.-Fri. 8am-10pm, Sat. 9am-10pm, Sun. 9am-9pm.

Positano and Aldo Café, 4940-8 Fairmont Ave. (Positano 654-1717, Aldo Café 986-0042/3), near Old Georgetown Rd. Aldo's sordid past (as a garage) is revealed by ads for Walker mufflers and Pelco batteries; the garage has since been transformed into a quaint, open-air restaurant. Pasta $5.50-7.50, pizza $2-4. The adjoining Positano with its Mediterranean arches and grand palazzo style is fancier and more expensive, although they share a kitchen. Pasta dishes run $6-10 at lunch, $8-13 at dinner. Positano open Mon.-Thurs. 11:30am-2:30pm and 5:30-10pm, Fri.-Sat. 11:30am-2:30pm and 5:30-10:30pm, Sun noon-midnight. Also open Mon.-Thurs. noon-2:30pm and 5-10pm, Fri.-Sat. noon-11pm, Sun. noon-9pm.

★ **Rio Grande Café,** 4919 Fairmont Ave. (656-2981), near Old Georgetown Rd. Louder than Texas and more crowded than Mexico City—with reason. Diego Rivera-style murals depict Mexican beer, lit by Christmas lights over the bar. Appetizers $3.25-10. $3 buys a huge, tasty taco, $7 buys 3. Tacos *al carbon* $12, quesadillas $5.50-9. Open Mon.-Thurs. 11am-10:30pm, Fri. 11am-11:30pm, Sat. 11:30am-11:30pm, Sun. 11:30am-10:30pm.

Steamers, 4820 Auburn Ave. (718-0661), near Norfolk Ave. Seating both indoors and on the outdoor patio. Serves fresh fish, lobster, crab cakes, shrimp, steamers, mussels, ribs, and steak. Entrees usually about $15. Medium crabs $22 per dozen. Happy hour (Mon.-Fri. 4-7pm, Sat.-Sun. noon-5pm) features drafts for $1.25, mixed drinks for $1.50. Kitchen closes Sun.-Thurs. at 11am, Fri.-Sat. at midnight. Open Mon.-Fri. 4pm-12:30am, Sat.-Sun. noon-1:30am.

Stromboli Family Restaurant, 7023 Wisconsin Ave. (986-1980), near Leland St. Italian standards in a Stromboli family atmosphere. Spaghetti with tomato sauce and garlic bread $4 for lunch, $6 for dinner; subs $4.70-6. Highly touted calzone $5. "Award-winning" small cheese pizza $4. Delivery $1.50 extra. Open Mon.-Thurs. 10am-10pm, Fri.-Sat. 10am-11pm, Sun. noon-9:30pm.

★ **Tako Grill,** 7756 Wisconsin Ave. (652-7030). A dangling red lantern lures customers to this modern Japanese grill, slick with glazed wood and track lighting. Young professionals struggle with chopsticks or devour excellent sushi, unfazed by mournful stares from the prominent aquarium. Unbelievable $6 lunch special stuns customers with miso soup, a sprout salad, 6 pieces of sushi roll, a bowl of rice, and an entree—it's one of the best bargains in the city (Mon.-Fri. 11:30am-2pm). Also worthwhile are the *Donburi,* large steaming bowls of rice topped with noodles, vegetables, and grilled meat (with miso soup and a sprout salad, $5.95). Open Mon.-Thurs. 11:30am-2pm and 5:30-9:45pm, Fri. 11:30am-2pm and 5:30-10:15pm, Sat. 5:30-10:15pm.

Tastee Diner, 7731 Woodmont Ave. (652-3970), at Cheltenhem Dr. A classic diner survival from the 50s, the Tastee puts its remodeled, glitzy imitators to shame. Veteran service, wooden booths, a long counter, and jukeboxes at tables, all gloriously and anachronistically intact. Breakfast all day and all night: grits $1.15, hot cakes with syrup $2.65. Entrees range from $3 to $6 but cluster around the $5 mark. Hamburgers $2-3.45. Daily dinner specials available Mon.-Sat. 11am-10pm, Sun. noon-10pm. Open 24 hrs. except on Dec. 25.

Terramar, 7800 Wisconsin Ave. (654-0888). Superb and pricey Nicaraguan cuisine a little out of budget range (entrees around $20), but worth the stretch. The inside has the feel of a Latin American plaza without the summer heat; stucco columns divide the expansive chamber. Live Latin music Fri.-Sat. nights. Reservations recommended. Open Mon.-Thurs. 5-10pm, Fri.-Sat. 5-11pm, Sun. 5-9pm.

■■■ TAKOMA PARK, MD

No one should come to Takoma for the food—there are few restaurants and fewer good ones on these quiet streets. But when hunger does strike, while window shopping or people watching, you won't have to reach far into your wallet—it's hard to find a meal over $10 in Takoma. Since Takoma Park is in Maryland, use the **301 area code** unless otherwise noted. Metro: Takoma, for all of the following restaurants.

Everyday Gourmet, 6923 Laurel Ave. (270-2270). Do it yourself or let them do it for you. Off-the-rack gourmet supplies fill one side of this clean, airy café; a counter serving coffee, baked goods, and inventive sandwiches fills the other.

Sandwiches $4-5, soup $2.55, muffins $1. Open Mon.-Fri. 8am-8pm, Sat. 9am-5pm, Sun. 10am-3pm.

Mark's Kitchen, 7006 Carroll Ave. (270-1884). Looks like an all-American diner—long counter, sizzling grill, checkered tablecloths—but the smells are distinctly Korean. The menu, dominated by unspectacular American fare, is dotted with more worthwhile Korean delights, such as seaweed soup ($2.25) and Korean steak ($5.50). Try the spinach salad with chicken teriyaki ($5.50), the dumplings ($2), or the curried vegetables ($5.50). Open Mon.-Sat. 8am-9pm, Sun. 8am-8pm.

Palais du Chocolat, 6925 Willow St. (723-4280). As you approach the center of Takoma from the Metro, Willow St. will appear mere feet before the Maryland border; head south of Eastern Ave. This industrial-looking pastry shop in an industrial-looking building supplies its more genteel sisters downtown and in Woodley Park with all things sweet. It can supply you too. Cookies $1.25. No seating available, so make a picnic of its daily lunch special, which includes a sandwich, a tart, and a drink for $4.50. Open Mon.-Sat. 9am-6pm.

Takoma Station Tavern, 6914 4th St. NW. (829-1999). Just steps west of the Metro (away from central Takoma), this popular jazz club has recently started playing a new tune: lunch. Most sandwiches are $7, including the house specialty crab-cake sandwich. For finger-lickin' fun, try the $7 chicken wing basket. Happy hour (Mon.-Fri. 6-9pm) brings $1 off drinks and free buffet. Open Mon.-Fri. 11:30am-2am, Sat.-Sun. 4pm-2am.

Taliano's, 7001B Carroll Ave. (270-5515). The only bar on Takoma's main drag serves up standard Italian specialties such as pasta ($5.25-7.25), calzones ($5.50), and pizza amidst checkerboard classic diner decor. A 12-inch Taliano's special, piled high with 8 toppings, goes for $14. After 5pm on Mon. it's half-price pizza night, and on Fri.-Sat. the place mellows out to live folk, blues, and rock. Bar open Mon.-Thurs. 11:30am-midnight, Fri.-Sat. 11:30am-1am, Sun. noon-midnight. Kitchen closes 1-2 hrs. earlier.

■■■ ARLINGTON, VA

If you think you've exhausted Adams-Morgan's ethnic eateries, Arlington may be the way to go. The hodgepodge of ethnic foods from Rosslyn to Ballston defies glib classification. The Clarendon area, nicknamed Little Saigon, holds not only Vietnamese but also worthwhile Japanese, Chinese, and Thai food. But even the name "Little Asia" would slight the nearby all-American establishments dishing out chili and ribs.

Many Arlington restaurants are accessible by Metro; drivers should beware of one-way streets. From Rosslyn to Clarendon, Wilson Blvd. runs one way from Washington into Arlington; Clarendon Blvd. runs parallel to it in the other direction. Some restaurants provide parking, notably in Ballston, but street parking is usually easy enough. All phone numbers in Arlington have the **703 area code.**

Atami, 3155 Wilson Blvd. (522-4787, delivery 527-9000). Metro: Clarendon. Sample both *nigiri* sushi (fish seasoned with *wasabi* horseradish on rice) and *maki* sushi (rice, fish, and vegetables rolled in seaweed). Sushi platters served with miso soup, salad, and rice (lunch $6.25, dinner $10.25). Vietnamese fare also available. Open daily 11am-2:30pm and 4:30-10pm.

Café Dalat, 3143 Wilson Blvd. (276-0935). Metro: Clarendon. Yet another award-winning Vietnamese restaurant in Little Saigon. This family-run establishment offers a variety of Vietnamese dishes, all for $7-9. Large vegetarian menu. Open Sun.-Thurs. 11am-9:30pm, Fri.-Sat. 11am-10:30pm.

★**Café Saigon,** 1135 N. Highland St. (243-6522 or 276-7110, delivery 527-9000), across from Clarendon Metro. "French" decor. Popular dishes are the grilled pork and crispy rolls (*cha gio*) on "funny" rice noodles ($8). Cow-eaters will enjoy the beef wrapped in beans, vermicelli noodles, wine, mushrooms, and chopped onion ($8). Open Sun.-Thurs. 10am-10pm, Fri.-Sat. 10am-11pm.

The Cambodian Restaurant, 1727 Wilson Blvd. (522-3832), near Quinn St. Metro: Court House. Less expensive than its Vietnamese counterparts up the road. Lunch entrees $5.50-7.25; dinner entrees $6.25-9. Open Mon.-Fri. 11:30am-2:30pm and 5:30-10:30pm, Sat.-Sun. 5:30-11pm.

Chesapeake Seafood Crab House, 3607 Wilson Blvd. (528-8888/8896). Metro: Clarendon. A real "seaside" crabhouse with cheery outdoor seating, brown paper tablecloths, and hammers to break open the crab shells. Most people come here for the steamed and spiced crabs, but this "Vietnamese, Chinese, French, and American" restaurant also offers standards like fried chicken and hush puppies, and crazy stuff like *Ech Xaao Lan,* curry frogs legs ($10). Vegetarians get a whole page of appetizers, soups, and entrees. Don't confuse this place with the similarly named chain. Open daily 11am-10pm.

Delhi Dhaba, 2424 Wilson Blvd. (524-0008), not visible from the street. Access through the parking lot (it's behind a deli/convenience store). Metro: Clarendon or Courthouse. Order your Indian dishes at the counter, deli (and Delhi) style, then carry them back to a table. Dishes are $6 at most; most vegetarian dishes are $4.50. Hard-core budget travelers will just fill up on Indian breads ($1-2.50 for generous servings). Open Sun.-Thurs. 11am-10pm, Fri.-Sat. 11am-11pm.

Don Arturo, 2716 N. Washington Blvd. (276-1050). 15-min. walk southeast of Clarendon Metro. Colorful rugs adorn the tables in this South American bistro. Lunch specials Mon.-Fri. $6.50. Sanwiches $3.50. Dinner entrees $6-8.25. Salvadorian beer $2.75. Open Mon.-Thurs. noon-10pm, Fri.-Sun. 10am-2am.

El Pollo Rico, 2915-2917 N. Washington Blvd. (522-3220/3282, delivery 527-9000), 2 blocks from Wilson Blvd. at Fillmore St. Metro: Clarendon. Charcoal-broiled rotisserie chicken Peruvian-style ($3.10-9.55). Eat inside on laminated butcher-block tables, or take it with you. Open daily 11am-10pm.

Faccia Luna, 2909 Wilson Blvd. (276-3099). Metro: Clarendon. This small local chain is revered by Washingtonians for its classy pizzas. A basic pizza (red or white) comes in 4 sizes ranging in price from $6-11.50 (although it's hard not to spend more when there are 25 toppings to choose from). Calzones $5.65. Try to explain the ManRay photos that decorate the walls as you sip a microbrew. Open Mon.-Thurs. 11:30am-11pm, Fri.-Sat. 11:30am-midnight, Sun. 4-11pm.

Food Factory, 4221 N. Fairfax Dr. (527-2279, delivery 527-9000), across from Ballston Metro; entrance in back. Ignore the name and devour the Pakistani char-broiled kebabs, which put American "shish kabobs" to shame. Tear off a piece of *nan* (tandoori bread) and wrap it around chicken, beef, or lamb on skewers ($4.70-6). Above the kebabs in the display case, note the rows and rows of *samosas,* pastries filled with peas and potatoes ($1). All meats are *halal* (prepared according to Islamic law); the clientele is almost 100% Middle Eastern. Look for daily specials. To find the Factory, look for its sign across from the Ballston Metro; then walk through the parking lot and behind the dumpsters until you see the Foodsters. Open Mon.-Thurs. 11am-10pm, Fri. 11am-10pm, Sat.-Sun. noon-10pm.

Hard Times Café, 3028 Wilson Blvd. (528-2233, delivery 908-0700), across from Clarendon Metro. Used to be a rough neighborhood joint in Rockville that served great chili in huge, heartburn-inducing portions; now it's renowned, upscaled, and no longer the best bargain in town, but still a good deal. Famed for Cincinnati chili with hot and sweet spices (like cinnamon), Texas chili, and vegetarian chili. Crumbly cornbread with each order. Chili $4-6.40; microbrews $3-3.25. Open Mon.-Thurs. 11:30am-10:30pm, Fri.-Sat. 11:30am-11pm, Sun. noon-10pm.

Hsiang Foon, 2919 N. Washington Blvd. (522-6677/1121, delivery 578-3663), at Fillmore St. Metro: Clarendon. Standard Chinese dishes for those who aren't quite ready yet to try Vietnamese, but want to tell their friends they dined in Little Saigon. Lunch is never more than $7. Open Sun.-Thurs. 11am-9:30pm, Fri.-Sat. 11am-10:30pm.

Hunan Number 1, 3033 Wilson Blvd. (528-1177/8, delivery 578-3663) about 1½ blocks from the Clarendon Metro. Entrance on Garfield St., but you can't miss the huge bronze(like) Fu dogs perched on either side of the front doorway. Try their *dim sum,* an immense and ongoing affair served daily 11am-3pm: 27 different varieties, $2-3 each. Check for special lunch deals. Open daily 11am-2am.

International House of Pancakes, 935 N. Stafford St. (522-3118), corner of N. Fairfax Dr. Metro: Ballston. A chain, but it's open 24 hrs.

Kabul Caravan, 1725 Wilson Blvd. (522-8394). Metro: Court House. The surroundings feel like a museum, thanks to the owners' fine collection of Afghan weapons, costumes, and other objects, all of which hang gracefully from the walls (and predate the Russian invasion). Entrees $8-16. Open Mon.-Fri. 11:30am-2:30pm and 5:30-11:30pm, Sat.-Sun. 5:30-11:30pm.

Little Viet Garden, 3012 Wilson Blvd. (522-9686), 1 block from the Clarendon Metro stop. Inexpensive Vietnamese food (surprise, surprise!). What sets it apart from its neighbors is its snazzy interior featuring sleek black chairs, a padded bar, and live palm trees. Or maybe it's the outdoor seating. At any rate, the food is good; there are three $10-11 dishes on the menu; everything else is under $9. Open Mon.-Fri. 11am-2:30pm and 5-10pm, Sat.-Sun. 11am-10pm.

Pasta Nostra, 1721 Wilson Blvd. (527-5515). Metro: Clarendon. This award-winning Italian restaurant serves up delicious pasta ($6.25-14), pizza (a basic 16-incher is just $7), and canoli ($3). Take-out and free delivery. Open Mon.-Fri. 11am-11pm, Sat. 4-11:30pm, Sun. 3-10pm.

Pho 75, 1711 Wilson Blvd. (525-7355), near Quinn St. Metro: Court House. Full of Vietnamese people slurping *pho*, a noodle soup filling enough for a meal. Regular bowl $4.25, large $5. Salty plum soda $1.50. Open daily 9am-8pm.

★ **Queen Bee,** 3181 Wilson Blvd. (527-3444). Metro: Clarendon. When you see how long the line is some nights, you'll think people are waiting for concert tickets instead of Vietnamese food. Most people say you can't order wrong here, even though everyone orders the same spring rolls (*cha gio*) for appetizers ($2.50). Entrees $5.50-9. Open daily 11:15am-10pm.

Red Hot and Blue, 1600 Wilson Blvd. (276-RIBS or 276-7427, delivery 578-3663), under an office building near Pierce St. Metro: Court House. Pit barbecue direct from Memphis, with logo to match—two pigs with shades, guitars, and Elvis pompadours. The late Republican media mogul Lee Atwater, among others, licked his lips over the down-home pork BBQ ribs. Regular order $9.45, full rack $16.45 (feeds two). Try them wet (basted with sauce) or dry (rubbed with traditional Memphis spices). Some opt for a pulled-pig sandwich ($4.50). Expect a wait some weekend nights. Open Sun.-Thurs. 11am-11pm, Fri.-Sat. 11am-midnight.

Red Hot and Blue Express, 3014 Wilson Blvd. (243-1510), at the Clarendon Metro. Same food faster with the same hours.

Rio Grande Café, 4301 N. Fairfax Dr. (528-3131). Metro: Ballston. Painted cactuses and sombreros adorn the stucco walls, along with bags of rice and cases of beer. Combo plates of enchiladas, tacos, *chile rellenos*, and tamales $7.25-12; or start your day with a jolt from a breakfast taco or Mexican egg dish (breakfast $6.75-7.50). Spacious, with popular outdoor seating. Open Mon.-Thurs. 11am-10:30pm, Fri. 11am-11:30pm, Sat. 11:30am-11:30pm, Sun. 11:30am-10:30pm.

Tom Sarris' Orleans House, 1213 Wilson Blvd. (524-2929). Metro: Rosslyn. Steak and fish are the specialties in this fantastical cross between a medieval castle and a New Orleans dining room. The stained glass, the thrones in the waiting area, and the suit of armor make for a strange aura when combined with curly-Q wrought iron and strings of Christmas lights. Lunch has the best deals: try the famed prime rib ($7, $8 at dinner) or the superlative crab cakes ($5). Fresh fried catfish $8. Lunch entrees cluster around $5-6. Most dinners around $8-12. Open Mon.-Fri. 11am-11pm, Sat. 4-11pm, Sun. 4-10pm.

■■■ ALEXANDRIA, VA

Old Town's food scene resembles Georgetown's—but in a more quaint and less crowded kind of way. The city has reeled in and kept cheap barbecue and expensive seafood as its specialities. Remember that all numbers in Alexandria have the **703 area code.** Metro: King St., for all of the following (except Royal Restaurant):

Armand's Chicago Pizzeria, 111 King St. (683-0313). Spacious, wooden restaurant caters to families. All-you-can-eat pizza buffet and salad bar (Mon.-Fri. 11:30am-2:30pm, Sat.-Sun. 11:30am-3:30pm) and midnight munch buffet (Fri.-Sat. 10:30pm-1am) are steals at $5; children 6-11 get them at half-price, under 6 free. Deep-dish pizzas come topped with everything from pineapple to sausage (small

$6.50 10, medium $9-13.50, large $10.75-15.25). All sandwich platters (steak, for example) under $5. Open Sun.-Thurs. 11:30am-11pm, Fri.-Sat. 11:30am-1am

Belview Seafood, 1018 King St. (660-6085). Ki Choi, former executive chef of the ritzy Watergate Restaurant, owns this jewel disguised by a modest façade. Prides itself on its inexpensive and fresh selection of seafood entrees. Different types of fish every day, but you can't go wrong with the constant charbroiled salmon steak ($9). Also serves a limited menu of non-seafood items like chicken kabobs ($7.95). Open Mon.-Thurs. 11am-9:30pm, Fri.-Sat. 11am-10:30pm, Sun. 11am-8:30pm.

Bob Rubin's New York Deli, 222 N. Lee St. (684-0372), at Queen St. If you can squeeze into this tiny place and onto a high chair, order up a hearty breakfast ($1.75-7.50) or a deli sandwich ($4.50-7). Breakfast served Mon.-Fri. until 11am, Sat. until 11:30am, and Sun. all day. Open Mon. 6am-3pm, Sat.-Sun. 8am-3pm, Sun. 9am-4pm.

Chesapeake Bagel Bakery, 601 King St. (684-3777), at St. Asaph St. In a laid-back setting—complete with small tables, a huge gumball machine, and a community bulletin board—this café serves up bagels (45¢), freshly blended cream cheeses, bagel sandwiches, hot sandwiches, salads, and soups. Oh yes: and mouth-watering baked sweets. Open Mon.-Sat. 6:30am-6:30pm, Sun. 7am-5pm.

Crescent City, 1120 King St. (684-9505). Part of a successful conglomerate of restaurants including Red Hot and Blue and Fleetwoods (owned by members of Fleetwood Mac), Crescent City blasts early jazz and bluegrass hits onto the street as it serves up Cajun cookin' inside. Whoo-ee!: the Sampler with shrimp, crawfish, eggplant, and real alligator meat ($10) or the Po Boy Andouille ($8) just might make you do a Zydeco dance. Open Mon.-Thurs. 11am-10pm, Fri.-Sat. 11am-11pm, Sun. noon-9pm.

Ecco Café, 220 N. Lee St. (684-0321), at Queen St. A wax Charlie Chaplin greets patrons of this jazzy place—which would like to think of itself as new and original. Eat pizzas jammed with toppings ($7.50-9) and homemade luncheon pastas ($8-10) while gawking at neon-lit portraits of the famous. Open Mon.-Thurs. 11am-11pm, Fri.-Sat. 11am-midnight, Sun. 11:30am-10pm.

The Fish Market, 105 King St. (836-5676), near Union St. This rollicking seafood restaurant seats 785 and features live ragtime piano, Broadway tunes, jazz, and acoustic guitar with enthusiastic audience participation (Thurs. 7pm, Fri.-Sat. 8pm). Six bars and a small balcony make this baby-blue building a happening twentysomething hangout. Creaky floors and exposed rafters for reminiscent types. Clam chowder $2, seafood sandwiches $4-7.50. Kitchen always closes at midnight. Open Mon.-Sat. 11:15am-2am, Sun. 11:15am-midnight.

Gadsby's Tavern, 134 N. Royal St. (548-1288), near King St. Tour the museum, and then stop by to eat off your own pewter; waiters in 18th-century dress deliver generous (but pricey) helpings of 18th-century cooking (dinner stews, colonial pies, and the like $10-20). Surprisingly good traditional tea bread, and English trifle for dessert ($5). Delivery ($10 min.). Nightly "colonial" entertainment. Open daily 11:30am-3pm and 5:30-10:30pm. Tours Tues.-Sat. 10am-4pm, Sun. 1-5pm.

Generous George's Positive Pizza and Pasta Place, 3006 Duke St. (370-4303). House specialty is an invention of overindulgence—pasta-topped pizza ($12). Toppings galore. Kids love this place. Open Sun.-Thurs. 11am-11pm, Fri.-Sat. 11am-midnight.

Hard Times Café, 1404 King St. (683-5340), near West St. Cincinnati, Texas, and vegetarian chili (all $5, $4 for kids) make the HTC deservedly popular. Cincinnati (the most delectable) is finely ground beef in a tomato sauce with cinnamon; Texas is coarsely ground chuck without tomatoes, mildly seasoned. A chili-spaghetti plate with beans, cheese, onions, and homemade cornbread ($5.70) would stuff anyone. Top a burger or pasta with some chili. Homemade beer-batter onion rings too. Delivery available. Open Mon.-Thurs. 11am-10pm, Fri.-Sat. 11am-11pm, Sun. noon-10pm.

King Street Blues, 112 N. St. Asaph St. (836-8800), near King St. A tribute to the South, with its slow-smoked ribs, pork and turkey BBQ, fresh salads, and po' boy sandwiches. To counteract all that lard, the menu has many low-calorie, low-fat offerings as well. Blue plate special ($5) changes daily: Wed. features Virginia beef stew, Thurs. fried chicken. Pub-like dining room with bar downstairs; decor includes paper-maché figures, murals, and painted *faux* shuttered windows and flower boxes. Open Mon.-Thurs. 11:30am-10pm, Fri.-Sat. 11:30am-midnight, Sun. 11:30am-10pm. Bar stays open until 1:45am.

Le Gaulois, 1106 King St. (739-9494), near N. Henry St. Moved here from downtown D.C., and brought its older crowd with it. Flavorful French entrees $6-19, although daily special tends to be pricier. Low-calorie entrees available ($7.25-10). Dinner prices are steep; try to come here at lunch. Open Mon.-Thurs. 11:30am-5pm and 5:30-10:30pm, Fri.-Sat. 11:30am-5pm and 5:30-11pm.

Old Town Sandwich Shop, 127 S. Peyton St. (684-6775), between King and Prince St. Bagels with cream cheese $1.10, danish and breakfasts $0.80-3.20, sandwiches $2-3.80. Perfect for a quick bite to eat and a newspaper in the morning. Fresh food and quick service. Open Mon.-Fri. 7am-4pm.

Royal Restaurant, 734 N. Asaph St. (548-1616). Metro: Braddock. Alexandria's oldest and least pretentious restaurant dishes out home-style meals and 50s jukebox hits. Sandwiches $2-7; omelettes $3.30-5 for breakfast, $5.50-5.75 for lunch or dinner; entrees $5.50-12. "Alexandria's Best Breakfast" menu $2.50-8 ($8 buys 2 eggs with steak). Those who don't want to bop to "Splish Splash" and "Under the Boardwalk" should sit on the left. You *must* try the rice pudding ($1.95). All-you-can-eat Sun. brunch buffet ($5.95, excludes beverages). Karaoke Fri. 7:30pm. Open Mon.-Thurs. and Sat. 6am-9:30pm, Fri. 6am-midnight, Sun. 7am-2:30pm.

The Scoop Grill and Homemade Ice Cream, 110 King St. (549-4527). Funky flavors (like bittersweet, Jack Daniels, and Adam's Apple) make this ice cream store a cut above the rest. Filled with families during the day and students at night. Burgers $3. Ice cream: small $2, medium $2.45, large $3. Be warned: the hours can vary tremendously according to the owner's whims. Open Mon.-Thurs. 8am-11pm, Fri.-Sat. 8am-midnight, Sun. 9am-11pm.

South Austin Grille, 801 King St. (684-8969), at Columbus St. Moderately priced Tex-Mex in this cheery pastel hangout, complete with the AG signature hot pepper lights. Fajitas ($9-14), tacos ($6-7), and burritos ($6-7). The hot Texas chili ($5-6) is very popular. Too popular, perhaps: sometimes the line gets so long that they give you a beeper to carry around while you wait. Brunch ($5-9) served Sat.-Sun. 11:30am-3pm. Also a popular place to drink. Domestic bottled beers $2.75, imports $3.25. Kitchen closes one hour earlier than the bar. Open Sun.-Mon. 11:30am-11pm, Tues.-Thurs. 11:30am-midnight, Fri.-Sat. 11:30am-1am.

Sights

Beneath a thicket of museums and monuments lies the real Washington. The ethnically diverse neighborhoods of Adams-Morgan and Shaw beckon with exotic foods and a thriving club scene that could compete with even the likes of New York. Dupont Circle is *the* place to sit and schmooze over coffee, to hang with the eternally hip, or to discover D.C.'s large and active gay community. In Anacostia, a struggling African-American community tries to rebuild its troubled neighborhood. In Capitol Hill pubs, politicians make deals, trade gossip, and leak stories to the press. In Georgetown, preppy students and ambitious interns crowd the shops and bars, oblivious of tourists. And in Northeast and the Upper Northwest, a number of spread out residential communities beckon with their suburban charm. Before or after the inevitable Smithsonian odyssey, the rest of Washington deserves your time; away from the major attractions, *real* Washingtonians go about their business in art galleries and ethnic communities and at parks and embassies. There are plays worth seeing, music worth listening to, and streets to delight and educate the attentive pedestrian. These areas can reveal the difference (and the hidden links) between D.C.-as-government-town and D.C.'s various homegrown cultures.

■■■ SIGHTSEEING TOURS

Tens of thousands of out-of-towners leave D.C. yearly without having set foot in anything but museums and monuments. If they only knew what they were missing. Guided tours cost substantially more than Metro fares, confine visitors to the central section of the city, and isolate them from actual Washingtonians. If you read this book, don't mind long walks, and can orient yourself to a new city without too much difficulty, there's no reason to take a tour.

If you're short on time or like riding around in unusual vehicles, however, try **D.C. Ducks,** 1323 Pennsylvania Ave. NW (966-DUCK). Providing an entertaining land and water tour of the monuments and the sights on the Mall, D.C. Ducks does it all on a van that transforms into a boat. Kids love it. (Adults $16, seniors $14, children $8.) For a more traditional tour, try **open-air buses** and **trolleys.** They operate on all-day tickets, so you can get off at any stop, then get back on when another coach comes by. The most popular tour company is **Tourmobile Sight-seeing,** 1000 Ohio Dr. SW (recorded messages 554-7950 and 554-5100), near the Washington Monument. Tours (in blue and white buses) run between 9am and 6:30pm from mid-April to mid-September, otherwise between 9:30am and 4:30pm. For the standard 18-sight loop, get on at any stop and buy tickets from the driver. (Adults $10, children 3-11 $5.) Special routes travel to the Frederick Douglass home (a 2½-hr. loop; adults $5, children $2.50) and to Mount Vernon (daily 10am, noon, and 2pm; adults $17, children $8.25; price includes admission). For these routes, purchase tickets up to an hour prior to departure from booth. Combination specials available. The orange-and-green coaches of **Old Town Trolley** (301-985-3021) follow a 2-hr. narrated circle with stops in downtown Washington, Georgetown, the National Cathedral, and Arlington Cemetery. Not all stops sell tickets, but passengers may board at any stop and pay at the next ticket-vending location. (Trolleys run Mon.-Fri. 9am-5pm, until 5:30pm Sat.-Sun. Tours $16, children 5-12 $8.)

Other companies avoid the more obvious sights with specialized tours of thematically linked D.C. sights. **Scandal Tours** (783-7212), a comedy show on wheels, hires actors to impersonate disgraced politicians as they steer tourists from one place of infamy to the next. In good weather, the 75-minute tour whizzes past Gary Hart's townhouse, Watergate, and the Vista Hotel, where Mayor Barry was caught with his pants down ($27). Tours depart from the Old Post Office April-Sept., Sat. 1pm. Reservations required. Capitol Entertainment Services (636-9203) runs standard tours of major sights, but specializes in a three-hour **Black History Tour** through Lincoln Park, Anacostia, and the Frederick Douglass home. (Tours begin from area hotels. $22, children 3-11 $12.)

For guided strolls around Adams-Morgan or Lafayette Square, try nationally recognized Anthony S. Pitch's walking tours (301-294-9514). The 1-hr. Lafayette Square tour is Sat. at 10 and 11:30am ($6) and the 2-hr Adams-Morgan tour is Sun. at 11am ($5). Call for details.

■■■ THE U.S. CAPITOL

It is natural enough to suppose that the center and heart of America is the Capitol, and certainly, in its outward aspect, the world has not many statelier or more beautiful edifices.

—Nathaniel Hawthorne, 1862

While the U.S. Capitol (dial 224-3121 for operator) may no longer be America's, or even Washington's, most beautiful building, its scale and style still evoke the power of the republic. (Metro: Capitol South or Union Station.) The Capitol's symmetries suggest the republic's checks and balances (or maybe a tug-of-war between the House and the Senate). There are two wings, two fronts, and no back (since all D.C. street coordinates begin from the compass stone in the crypt). The three-tiered **East Front** faces the Supreme Court. From Jackson (1829) to Carter (1977), most Presidents were inaugurated here; for Reagan's 1981 inauguration, Congress moved the ceremony to the newly fixed-up **West Front,** which overlooks the Mall, a fountain and pool, a grassy plaza, and steps and steps and steps. If there's a U.S. flag over the House wing (to your left as you face the East Front), the House of Representatives is in session; a flag over the Senate wing (to your right) says that the Senate is.

Amateur architect William Thornton won a design-the-Capitol competition in 1793; feisty expert designer Benjamin Latrobe assessed and reassembled the interior after Congress arrived here in 1800. The British burned down the whole shebang in 1814. The mellower Charles Bullfinch replaced Latrobe in 1818, finishing the Capitol's central section. When Congress ran out of office space around 1850, President Fillmore tapped Thomas U. Walter to expand the edifice and *erect* the rotunda. Since then, the office of the architect of the Capitol has grown in some ways (the current architect approves anything built within a few blocks) and shrunk in others.

Bulfinch built the first Capitol Dome of copper-plated wood. He built big, but not big enough for the expanded House and Senate sections; Walter, assisted by Montgomery Meigs, executed the current cast-iron hemisphere in the 1860s. If there's light in the dome by night, Congress is still meeting. Atop the whole edifice stands Thomas Crawford's statue "Freedom," which actually stood in the parking lot for cleaning between May and October 1993. Hoisting her not-so-svelte seven-and-a-half tons off the dome required a high-powered helicopter named "Bubba."

Outside the West Front of the Capitol at 1st St. NW, the 1922 **Grant Memorial** stands encircled and out-maneuvered by driveways and barricades. General Ulysses S. Grant, whose willingness to sustain huge losses led the Union Army to victory, contemplates war morosely in his battered uniform. Seven horsemen charge to the north, while three horses strain and tug a cannon through mud to the south. Henry Shared took 21 years to design the 252-ft.-long memorial, praised today—by those who notice it—as a realistic monument to the arduous and terrible aspects of battle.

THE INTERIOR

The **public entrance** is through the East Front. Lines are shortest in winter—in February, you can basically walk right in—and longest in spring when roving bands of middle schoolers in matching t-shirts terrorize the city; between mid-March and mid-June, expect to wait as long as three hours. In summer, the wait averages about 90 minutes. In general, Sundays and Mondays see shorter lines, as do the lunch hours (about 11:30am-1:30pm) every day.

As you wait outside, look up to see the female trio of America, Hope, and Justice (President John Quincy Adams wouldn't let Hercules, a heathen, join them). Through the East Portico, scrutinize Randolph Rogers's huge, bronze **Columbus Doors.** The doors mimic Ghiberti's *Gates of Paradise* doors in Florence but (in uncharacteristic sepraration of Church and State) substitute Columbus's biography for the Bible.

Inside the doors, the 180-ft.-high, 96-ft.-wide **rotunda** stretches and yawns. The *grisaille* (brown-and-white) frieze around the dome is mostly by Constantino Brumidi, who died three months after falling off his scaffold in 1877; in the overhead *Apotheosis of George Washington,* George takes his place at the center of a giant allegory, as Liberty, Victory, the 13 states, and countless virtues attend. Eight big paintings hang below the fresco, four of them by John Trumbull including *The Declaration of Independence,* which graced the ill-fated $2 bill. Busts and statues of luminaries ranging from Washington himself to Martin Luther King, Jr. stare up at the art. Statesmen from Lincoln to JFK have lain in state in the Capitol's center; recently, in his much-publicized "Living Will," late President Richard Nixon opted to forgo this highest of national honors.

The Capitol sees over 10,000 visitors a day. Most get lost. The 19th-century design yields little logic and less help for disoriented tourists, so be an oriented one instead: pick up a map from the tour desk in the rotunda. The desk is also the place to sign up for a **tour:** free guided tours begin here daily every 20 minutes or so from 9am to 3:45pm if Congress is in session, and every 10 minutes or so if not. If you set off on your own and can't find your way, try asking one of the 1200 Capitol police; they may not be tour guides, but they know their way around.

Just south of the rotunda, still on the second level, is **Statuary Hall,** the first meeting place of the House of Representatives. The House changed rooms when embarrassed Members realized their chamber was also an echo chamber: stand at one edge, and you can hear anything whispered at the opposite edge. (American folk mythology maintains that John Quincy Adams figured this out early—the old weasel used to "sleep" at his desk while listening to his enemies converse.)

North of the rotunda, visitors can find The **Old Senate Chamber,** just off to the right. The comparatively modest old room might remind you of a time when oratory from the Senate floor actually mattered—Daniel Webster, John C. Calhoun, and Henry Clay all held forth in this chamber. It was restored in 1976 for the American Bicentennial celebration to look as it did when it was last occupied in 1859. As on the house side, the current senate chamber lies farther north of here, but must be accessed by way of the crypt (first) level.

Stairs lead down to the crypt level from landings on both the north and south sides of the rotunda. The **crypt** itself was built to house George Washington's body; the state of Virginia blocked the exhumation and the tomb has been empty since. In the central area of this level, a display on the Capitol's history competes with a souvenir counter for visitors' attention. A statue of Lincoln, formerly in the rotunda, keeps an eye on the chaos. His head has **no left ear**—the sculptor claimed to be representing Lincoln's unfinished life.

The **Old Supreme Court Chamber,** where the Supremes met until they got their own building across the street, is also on the crypt level. It's another beautiful, well-fixed-up old room (last restored in 1976), this time with a more sinister history: in 1806, the ceiling handed down its opinion on architect Latrobe's assistant, crushing him when he tried to move blocks before the masonry had dried.

CONGRESSIONAL CHAMBERS

Once you've had your fill of marble and granite, there are two basic ways to see Congress in action. For a spectacle, but little insight, climb to the **House and Senate visitors galleries.** Americans should request a gallery pass (valid for the whole 2-year session of Congress) from the office of their representative, delegate, or senator. Show up at his or her office or write in advance. Foreign nationals may get passes valid for a single day by presenting a passport, driver's licence, or birth certificate (or photocopies thereof). For a House pass, they should go to the desk immediately outside the House visitors gallery. For a Senate pass, foreigners should *not* go to the Senate visitors gallery, but to the "Appointments desk" located at the extreme North End (i.e., Senate side) of the main hallway of the crypt level of the building. The desk is large, on the right, and (naturally) unlabeled.

In the ceremony-laden House and Senate chambers (in separate wings of the Capitol), expect a few bored-looking elected officials failing to listen to the person on the podium who might be speaking for the exclusive benefit of home-district cable TV viewers. Former House Speaker Tip O'Neill once ordered a cameraman to pan the empty chamber while an especially obnoxious congressman was speaking, thus showing TV-land that the man was orating into the void. Snazzy desks and lecterns at the center of each semicircular chamber are reserved for the chamber's leadership. The Vice President technically presides over the Senate, though he rarely shows up. The Speaker of the House, called "Mr. Speaker," presides over the House. In the Senate chamber, notice the elementary-school look of the Senators' desks. The bigger, more ornate House chamber packs in all of official Washington every January for the President's annual televised State of the Union Address.

Congress has grown too big, and its issues too complex, for floor debates to accomplish much. The real business of Congress is conducted in **committee hearings** all over the Capitol and the additional House and Senate office buildings. Most hearings are open to the public. Look for the *Washington Post's* "Today in Congress" box in the paper's A-section. Then go to the assigned rooms of the hearings that look interesting. Unlike in their grand chambers, here Congresspeople sit at tables across from you—not two stories below you; rather than conduct pompous ceremonies, they debate, inquire, and consider facts and laws. Keep in mind that especially interesting hearings can get crowded, that most hearing rooms don't have many seats, and that most of these are reserved for lobbyists and other hangers-on. Show up early and keep your fingers crossed.

A third way to find out what Congress does is to wander around the Capitol's office space. You'll see a few real Congresspeople and plenty of important-looking imitations. Look at which offices are busy or see what you can overhear. American citizens will surely be well-received at the office of their Representative or Senator, though your chances of seeing the Member him- or herself are slight. A majority of Members have public offices in House or Senate office buildings, which lie outside the Capitol itself. To get there, you may ride the **Capitol subway,** which shunts Congressfolk, staffers, and tourists between the Capitol and the office buildings. If you hear a buzzer or see a red light flash, watch the Members rush to the floor for an imminent vote. Subways to the House offices leave from the sub-basement of the House side of the Capitol; the elevator is best reached near the far southern end of the crypt level's central hallway. Subways to the Senate office buildings leave from the basement of the Senate side of the Capitol; that elevator is best reached near the far northern end of the crypt level's central hallway.

Basement perks and shops in the Capitol and the House and Senate offices are generally open only to Members, who guard their privacy well. One favorite Congressional perk is the Members-only gym, where Democrats and Republicans alike try to get former pro-basketball standouts Tom McMillan (D-MD) and Bill Bradley (D-NJ) to play on their team. The basement of the Capitol itself once held a blacksmith shop, a water reservoir, and an 800-ton coal vault to keep the Members warm.

Some unmarked rooms on the Senate side of the Capitol are used by Senators as private **"hideaways."** The Senate Rules Committee doles out by seniority these secret second offices. Some are just oversized closets, but the best are roomy, furnished offices where esteemed legislators can spend plenty of time working incommunicado. Only janitors and senators know where the hideaways are—any unmarked door could have a Senator inside. They're used to being interrupted for directions, which doesn't mean you should wander around opening doors in search of hideaways (unless you just love the Capitol Police). While most legislators use their hideaways as a second office, legends remain that these lairs have often been put to **less forthright uses.**

The Capitol is open daily from 9am to 4:30pm (Memorial Day-Labor Day daily 8am-8pm). Tours and special assistance for **visitors with disabilities** are available from the Special Services Office in the central first floor crypt area (or call 224-4048, TDD 224-4049). Tours visit the rotunda, the downstairs crypt area, and sometimes Statuary Hall.

■■■ CAPITOL HILL

Metro: Capitol South; Eastern Market; Federal Center; Union Station.
With the National Tourist Mecca, Congress, and the President to the west, and the city's worst slums to the south, Capitol Hill seems incongruously friendly; its townhouse-filled center (around East Capitol St. between 2nd St. and 11th St. NE/SE) gracefully accommodates blue-collar, white-collar, Black, Hispanic, Asian, and White people. Restored townhouses abut buildings in various states of decay, and Jaguars mix freely with humbler autos. Close to the Capitol building, most pedestrians are Congressional and government workers whose silk power ties connote self-importance. East of 2nd St., corner drugstores, grocery stores, and a diner (Jimmy T's) relax with the residents amid trees and lawns. You may even spot a few Congresspeople driving home, though their aides are more likely to live here than the Members themselves.

Safety in the neighborhood is indeed something of a concern; here as nowhere else, blocks can change character abruptly. Be aware of your surroundings, human and architectural. Avoid the areas east of Lincoln Park or south of Pennsylvania Ave. SE (except along 8th St.). After events at RFK Stadium, raging hordes of concert-goers proceed westward down East Capitol St.; don't be afraid to join them.

Capitol Hill's approximate boundaries are North and South Capitol streets on the west, H St. NE on the north, Lincoln Park on the east, and the Southeast-Southwest Freeway on the south. Close to the Capitol building itself cluster major sights, including the Library of Congress, the Folger Shakespeare Library, and the Supreme Court. At dusk, head for the bars and restaurants that line Pennsylvania Ave. between 2nd St. and 7th St. SE.

THE SUPREME COURT

While they're not publicly accountable—they're not elected, after all—the nine justices of the nation's highest court graciously open their courtroom to the touristic masses who stream daily from the Capitol across the street into the imposing Supreme Court Building, 1 1st St. NE (479-3000). (Metro: Capitol South or Union Station.) When the court is in session, early risers may have a chance to see the justices in action, by staking out one of the public seats at an oral-argument session. And when the court is not in session, lectures in the courtroom introduce visitors to the history and workings of the court.

The Supreme Court wasn't always so hospitable to visitors, though, for it is only relatively recently that the court has been housed in a building of its own. From 1800 to 1935, the justices met in the Capitol, first in any empty office they could find and later in the room now known as Old Supreme Court Chamber. This chamber was so poorly illuminated that when some justices complained that a newly arrived statue of Justice depicted her without the traditional blindfold, Chief Justice John Marshall replied that it was fine—she couldn't possibly see anything in that room anyhow. In 1935, the court decided it was time to take the nation's separation of powers literally, and it moved out of the Capitol—and across the street—into the faux-Greek temple designed for it by architect Cass Gilbert.

Visitors should enter through the main entrance on 1st St., climbing the stairs flanked by James Earle Fraser's sculptures *Contemplation of Justice* (on the left) and *Authority of Law* (on the right). Nine important-looking figures posture in the pediment. Three are former Chief Justices. Three are classical Greek virtues. One is a former Senator. The other two are Cass Gilbert, the building's architect, and Robert Aitken, the pediment's sculptor. The atrium is a columned chamber sporting busts of former chief justices. Straight ahead, literally behind the red curtain, is the Supreme Court Chamber, where the court meets to hear cases.

When the court is in session (Oct.-June), it hears oral arguments Monday to Wednesday from 10am to 3pm for two weeks each month. Attorneys get only half an hour each to make arguments and field questions from the Nine—liberal Justice Ruth Bader Ginsburg supposedly asks the most (annoying) questions. There is no jury: the Supreme Court, like any appeals court, doesn't decide facts; it just interprets the laws and the Constitution. **Arguments** are open to the public on a first-come, first-served basis. Seating begins at 9:30am; a line usually begins to form at 8:30am. If you show up too late to be seated, walk through the standing gallery to hear five minutes of the argument. The *Washington Post*'s A-section can tell you if the court is sitting and what case it plans to hear. Be forewarned: the May and June sessions are reserved almost exclusively for reading decisions.

Any time the court is not sitting, visitors can hoof through the courtroom. On these days, brief **courtroom lectures,** every hour on the half hour between 9:30am and 3:30pm, cover the history, operations, duties, and architecture of the court and its building.

The excitement continues below the court, where a larger-than-life statue of John Marshall, known as the "Great Chief Justice" around these parts, presides over an exhibit on the history of the court and its building. Around the corner from the exhibit hall, a small theater screens a 22-minute adaptation of the PBS series *This Honorable Court,* which serves up an intelligent summary of U.S. legal history as

well as interviews with real live justices. The levels above the courtroom are closed to the public. In addition to offices, they contain a third-floor gymnasium where justices and their staffs ply their basketball skills above the highest court in the land. (Open Mon.-Fri. 9am-4:30pm. Free.) For more about the political role of the Supreme Court, see **U.S. Government and Politics,** p. 10.

LIBRARY OF CONGRESS

The Library of Congress, 1st St. SE (707-5000, recorded events schedule 707-8000), between East Capitol and Independence Ave., has surpassed its original mission—to be Congress's library—as well as its second mission—to be the nation's library. (Metro: Capitol South.) Its current aspirations are global: it wants to be the world's library, a great repository for humankind's accumulated knowledge, with "all answers stored in a single place." The library is already the world's largest, with 26 million books and over 80 million other holdings, including Stradivarius violins, a Gutenberg Bible, newsreels, periodicals, and phonograph records. Less than a quarter of the 26 million books are in English; most aren't even in the Roman alphabet, but in Arabic, Chinese, Japanese, and other scripts.

The original library was founded in 1800, when Congress began to assemble mostly law and history books for members' personal use. The British torched them all in 1814, so Congress bought Thomas Jefferson's personal collection (6487 volumes) and started all over. An 1870 copyright law guaranteed the library a free copy of every book the United States registered, and the L of C took off. The library occupies three buildings: the 1897 Beaux Arts Jefferson Building, which hogs the display space; the 1939 Art Deco Adams Building across 2nd St.; and the 1980 Madison Building, a marble slab across Independence Ave. that is the largest office building in Washington, with 48 acres of floor space (doubling the library's space).

The **Jefferson Building,** whose green copper dome seals a spectacular octagonal reading room, is one of the most beautiful in Washington. Infrequent **library tours** leave from the Visitors Orientation Theater, just past the information desk in the lobby of the Madison Building. The theater screens an informational 22-minute video introduction to the library every half hour beginning at 9am. Currently, tours of the Jefferson Building leave at 10:30am, 11:30am, 1:30pm, and 3:30pm.

On the tours, guides scuttle quickly through tunnels to the Jefferson. Corrugated metal in the tunnels conceals a conveyor belt that runs books between the buildings. In the Jefferson Building, the Great Hall expands among grand staircases and ceiling frescoes. The octagonal Main Reading Room, with 236 desks, spreads out under a spectacular dome. Statues march in rows around the room, painted winged figures around the cupola illustrate the "Stages of Human Knowledge," and a syncretic statue grafts Lincoln's head and wings onto the body of Rodin's Thinker. After about an hour, the tour returns to the Madison Building. If the guide doesn't lead you to the **Gutenberg Bible** display, seek out the Good Book for yourself. It's next to the statue of James Madison, in the main display room immediately to the left as you enter from Independence Ave.

For those with sincere scholarly interests, perhaps the best way to see the library is to do some research there. All of the vast collection, including rare items, is open to anyone of college age or older with a legitimate research purpose. Even the Main Reading Room in the Jefferson Building is open to scholars. It's a closed-stack library, so they'll bring the books to you. It's also a non-circulating library, so you must do your reading there. (Most reading rooms open Mon.-Fri. 8:30am-9:30pm, Sat. 8:30am-6pm, call 707-5000 for further information.)

Near the Library of Congress

The **Fountain of Neptune** splishes and splashes in the front plaza of the Library of Congress Jefferson Building, on 1st St. between Independence Ave. and East Capitol St. You can see the 1897 fountain only from a very narrow swath of sidewalk, but it's well worth the trouble to stop and look. Wildly twisting horses flank the central figure of Neptune, turtles spit water at Nereids (high-class mermaids), Tritons (mer-men) recline half-hidden in water, and twisting snakes spit water at *you* in this homage to Rome's famous Trevi Fountain.

Next to the Library of Congress Adams Building, the **Folger Shakespeare Library,** 201 East Capitol St. SE (544-4600), houses the world's largest collection of Shakespeareana. That's over 275,000 books and manuscripts. Unless you've got a Ph.D. and research to do, you can't see them. You can go inside the building, though, and see the Great Hall exhibition gallery, a re-created Tudor gallery with dark oak panels and carved Elizabethan doorways. The **Shakespeare Theater** at the Folger is no longer at the Folger; the company, which puts on Shakespeare's plays almost exclusively, has moved downtown to 450 7th St. NW (393-2700; see **Nightlife & Entertainment: Theater,** p. 222). During the day, tourists can peek at the theater itself, which imitates the Elizabethan Inns of Court indoor theaters, like the Blackfriars, where Shakespeare's company performed. The Folger also sponsors high-quality readings, lectures, and concerts; call for details. Recurring highlights are the **PEN/Faulkner poetry and fiction readings** and the **Folger Consort,** a chamber music group that specializes in Renaissance works and songs. Outside on the 3rd St. side of the building, tourists can stop for a rest or a quiet read in the authentic Elizabethan **"knot" garden,** so named because the different plants—all popular in Shakespeare's day—are arranged in intertwining patterns. (Exhibits open Mon.-Sat. 10am-4pm; library open Mon.-Fri. 8:45am-4:45pm.)

Flanking the Library of Congress and the Capitol grounds on Constitution Ave. between Delaware Ave. and 2nd St. NE, and on Independence Ave. between 1st St. SW and 2nd St. SE, are the **House and Senate Office Buildings.** (Metro: Capitol South. Open Mon.-Fri. 8am-7pm and whenever their respective houses of Congress are in session.)

These office buildings are hardly designed for tourists—they're needed partly because so much space in the Capitol *is* designed for tourists. Nevertheless, energetic patriots could learn a lot about how Congress works by walking through one of the buildings. American citizens can find the offices of their Congresspersons without much trouble; consult the **directories** posted near all entrances and elevators. Once there, show proof of residence in your state and district and obtain passes to the House and Senate galleries and free information on some Washington sights. You can always ride the underground subway to the Capitol, but if you're hearing bells, save some seats for the Senators and Representatives who are being called to the Capitol for a vote.

Twentieth-century sculptor Alexander Calder's last work, *Mountains and Clouds,* takes up nine stories of the Hart Senate Office Building's atrium (on Constitution Ave. NE between 1st and 2nd St.). Calder died in 1976 on the night after he met with architects in D.C. to work out the sculpture's details; the $650,000 sculpture was not completed until 1986. You can view the sculpture in its natural light from the ground floor or from the various open balconies in the building. The stable black "mountains," sculpted from sheet metal, weigh 39 tons; the mobile "clouds," made from aircraft aluminum, weigh 4300 lbs. A computer controls the mobile's rotation.

Nestled up beside the Hart building is the **Sewall-Belmont House,** 144 Constitution Ave. NE (546-3989). (Metro: Union Station.) One of the oldest houses in Washington is now the headquarters of the National Woman's Party. Today the floors upstairs constitute a museum of the women's movement (see **Museums & Galleries,** p. 196).

NEAR UNION STATION

Moving northwest from the Capitol, the **Taft Memorial** stands on the triangular park between Constitution Ave., New Jersey Ave., and Louisiana Ave. NW. The 1958 statue of former Ohio senator Robert A. Taft (son of President William Howard Taft) assiduously defends a large, fluted concrete obelisk. Call Taft by his nickname, "Mr. Republican." Twenty-seven bells set into the obelisk ring like church chimes every 15 minutes.

Two blocks north of the Capitol grounds, **Union Station,** 50 Massachusetts Ave. NE (general information 371-9441) draws nearly three times as many visitors each day—50,000—as the Capitol itself. Most are there to use the Metro or hop an Amtrak train, but many come to admire Daniel Burnham's monumental Beaux Arts design, which took $25 million to erect from 1905 to 1908 and $160 million to renovate in 1988. The site of the shoot-out in *The Untouchables,* the station now welcomes visitors with 120 chic shops and a glitzy food court rather than crossfire. To reach the station, walk northeast down Delaware Ave. from the Capitol or take the Metro to the Union Station. Outside, Christopher Columbus sails toward the Capitol in the large and striking sculpture that anchors the plaza. Inside, colonnades, archways, and huge domed ceilings equate Burnham's Washington with imperial Rome and the then-dominant train network with Roman roads. The station's wall tracings in the East Hall even copy examples from Pompeii. Downstairs, the train concourse is so expansive, it could hold the Washington monument horizontally. It also houses the National Map Gallery, the cavernous American Multi-Cinema, and lots of eateries. (Retail shops open Mon.-Sat. 10am-9pm, Sun. noon-6pm; call 842-3757 for cinema information.) For train information, see **Getting to Washington, D.C.,** p. 45.

Directly west of Union Station across 1st St. is the **City Post Office** (842-3812), another of Burnham's Beaux Arts buildings, completed in 1914. Officials lobbied for the post office to be constructed next to Union Station in order to expedite the collection and distribution of mail. Italian marble and granite constitute the exterior, which now houses the new **National Postal Museum** (see **Museums & Galleries,** p. 197). The post office still operates; enter on North Capitol St. (Open Mon.-Fri. 7am-midnight, Sat.-Sun. 7am-8pm.)

Farther up on North Capitol is the **Government Printing Office** (512-0132), a large building in finely worked dark red brick. The G.P.O. contracts out most of the government's printing needs but still prints thousands of federal documents yearly, in addition to postcards, passports, and civil-service exams. Plant tours ended in the 60s, when someone realized that the electric forklifts, hot molten lead, and six-foot pneumatic knives could hurt someone. To visit the bookstore, enter on the North Capitol St. side of the building. The G.P.O. stocks what the government prints; there are Washington guidebooks, studies of U.S. history, and entertaining tomes only the U.S. Government could produce (e.g. *Design of Small Dams, Perspectives on John Philip Sousa,* and the *Amateur-Built Aircraft Flight Testing Handbook).* You may find the government *Advisory Circulars,* the foreign-country guides, or the military *Back Yard Mechanics* books actually useful. Across the hall, the **Congressional Sales Office** sells things Congress prints; the *Congressional Record* sold out in one day when a conservative Senator, debating a bill to ban pornographic 900 numbers, inserted the text of some steamy recordings into his speech. (Both stores open Mon.-Fri. 8am-4pm.)

Northeast of Union Station is the **Capital Children's Museum,** 800 3rd St. NE (675-4127), a large red-brick building that looks like a city school. (Metro: Union Station.) Enter on 3rd St. between H and I St. NE (See **Museums & Galleries,** p. 198).

EAST OF 3RD STREET

Three blocks southeast of Union Station, down Massachusetts Ave. NE, **Stanton Park** offers benches, lots of shade, and a playground with a black rubber floor. An eclectic mix of white-collar lunchers, homeless loungers, and children playing on the playground will give you an instant sense of Capitol Hill's diversity. The park's visual anchor is a skillful equestrian statue of Nathaniel Greene, Esq., a Revolutionary War Major General. Greene rides along in Continental uniform, complete with tri-cornered hat and fringed shoulder epaulets. A 1930 windstorm toppled horse and rider off the pedestal and onto their heads in the middle of the park.

When he first moved to Washington after the Civil War, the famous African-American abolitionist, orator, autobiographer, and statesman Frederick Douglass lived at 316-318 A St. NE, two blocks east of the Supreme Court. Once the site of the Smithsonian Museum of African Art, the three-story gray house now houses the **Caring Institute,** which honors benevolent Americans. (Open Mon., Wed., Fri. 2-4pm. $3.).

From the Capitol Building, stroll east on East Capitol St. to see neighborhood life in an upscale part of Capitol Hill. A 10-block walk from the Capitol will bring you straight to **Lincoln Park,** a good people-watching spot during the day. (As with all parks downtown, however, it becomes dangerous after dark.) One statue remembers Abraham Lincoln as the Great Emancipator; the monument was supposedly constructed solely through contributions from former slaves. Another memorial, the only statue of a black woman in D.C., depicts Mary McLeod Bethune, who founded the National Council of Negro Women.

■■■ SOUTHEAST

Metro: Eastern Market; Navy Yard; Anacostia.

Southeast isn't so much a neighborhood as a geographical fact, a perfect right triangle bounded by East Capitol St., South Capitol St., and the District line. The two notable neighborhoods that crouch within Southeast's confines, Capitol Hill and Anacostia, lead a paradoxical coexistence: the Hill's famous law-absorbed offices seem like an odd companion for Anacostia's notorious crime-filled streets. But by no means should Southeast be ignored: a handful of captivating sights, including a pair of museums in Anacostia and the Washington Naval Yard, as well as some great clubs (most notably *Tracks*) reward street-smart walkers and confident drivers.

BARRACKS ROW

To get a taste of Southeast Washington, try walking down 8th St. SE from the Eastern Market Metro stop to the **Navy Yard,** a stretch sometimes known as "Barracks Row." Although technically a part of Capitol Hill, the area has more in common—in look and feel—with the Southeast part of the District than with the Capitol and its environs. Barracks Row is usually safe during the day (Marines keep watch over some of the blocks), but don't walk alone at night.

The **Marine Barracks,** 8th and I St. SE (433-2258), house what are nicknamed the "Eighth and Eye Marines." The head of the Marine Corps dwells at one end of the parade ground in a house built in 1806 (the British spared it when they torched D.C. in 1814). The barracks also house "The President's Own," the Marine Corps marching band that John Philip Sousa led from 1880 until 1892. The band now totes its Sousaphones on international tours. The infantry, though they served in the Gulf, are mostly here for ceremony; they march at Arlington Cemetery, stand around at White House ceremonies, and guard Camp David, the President's retreat. Visitors may not tour the grounds unaccompanied, and no official tour program exists. You may, however, be able to finagle a personal tour; ask the Marine at the guardhouse. The only sure way to see the grounds is to attend one of the **Friday evening parades,** at 8:30pm every Friday, May-Aug.

NAVY YARD

Three museums and a destroyer stay ship-shape among the booms at the Washington Navy Yard. (Metro: Navy Yard.) Enter from the gate at 9th and M St. SE and ask for directions or look at the maps posted just inside. Follow the main road (9th St. SE) one and a half blocks to the big white stucco Building 58, the **Marine Corps Historical Center and Museum** (433-3534). An immediate right past the museum and then a left will put you on the road that travels past the diminutive **Navy Art Gallery** (433-3815), with its biannually changing depictions of naval activity, and down to the waters of the Anacostia River. Here, the **Navy Museum** (433-4882) in Building 76 should buoy anyone let down by the admire-but-don't-touch Air & Space Museum on the Mall; here you can climb on or in many of the display pieces.

The **USS Barry,** a decommissioned destroyer docked a few steps from the Navy Museum, offers a glimpse of maritime life. Climb aboard and a snappily dressed seaman will lead you through berths, control rooms, the bridge, the captain's quarters,

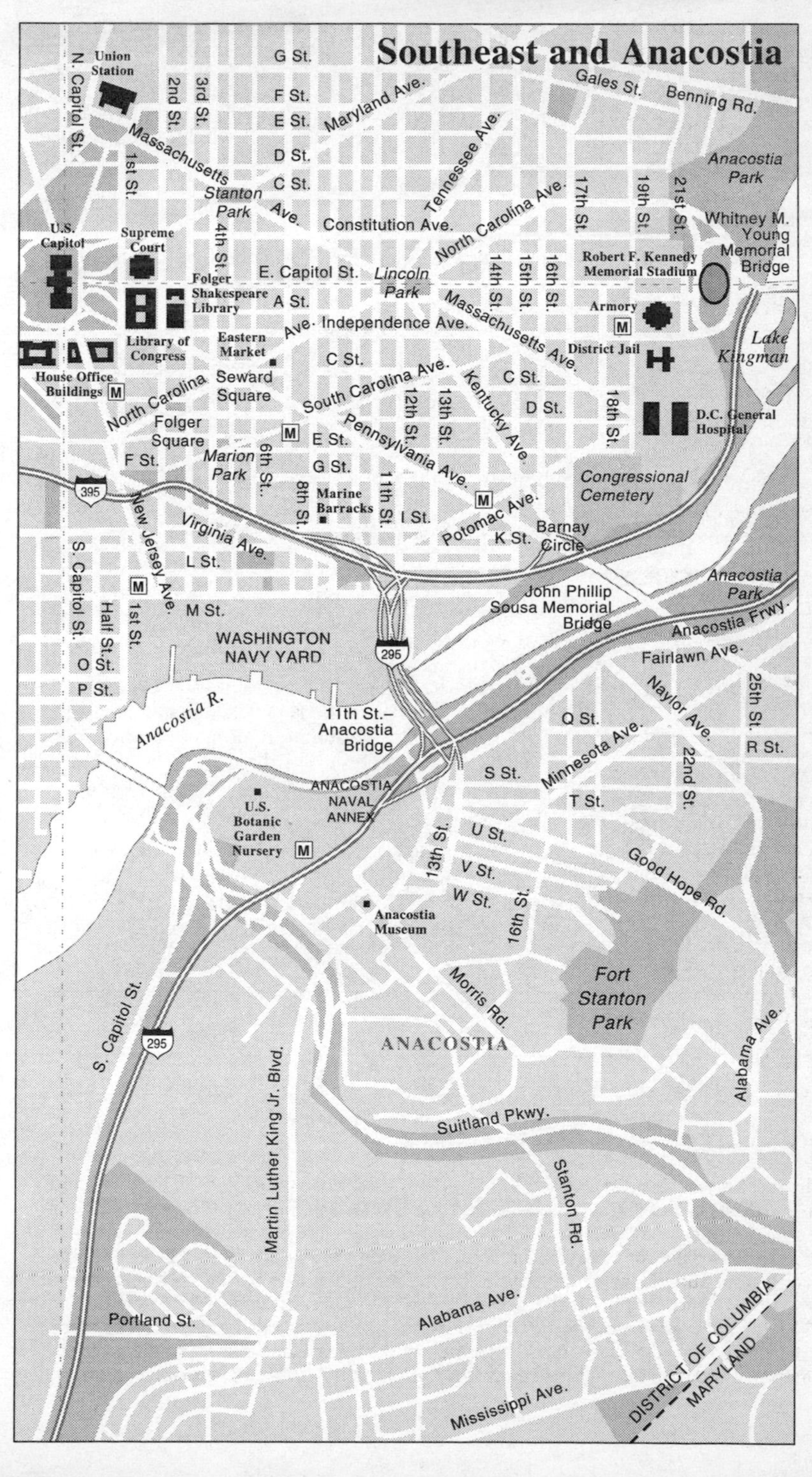
Southeast and Anacostia
Union Station
N. Capitol St.
2nd St.
3rd St.
G St.
F St.
E St.
D St.
C St.
Maryland Ave.
Gales St.
Benning Rd.
Tennessee Ave.
Massachusetts Ave.
Stanton Park
1st St.
4th St.
Constitution Ave.
North Carolina Ave.
17th St.
19th St.
21st St.
Anacostia Park
Whitney M. Young Memorial Bridge
U.S. Capitol
Supreme Court
Folger Shakespeare Library
E. Capitol St.
Lincoln Park
14th St.
15th St.
16th St.
Robert F. Kennedy Memorial Stadium
A St.
Massachusetts Ave.
Armory
Independence Ave.
Library of Congress
Eastern Market
District Jail
Lake Kingman
House Office Buildings
C St.
Seward Square
North Carolina
South Carolina Ave.
12th St.
13th St.
Kentucky Ave.
C St.
D St.
18th St.
D.C. General Hospital
Folger Square
E St.
Pennsylvania Ave.
F St.
Marion Park
6th St.
G St.
Congressional Cemetery
395
New Jersey Ave.
8th St.
Marine Barracks
11th St.
I St.
Potomac Ave.
Barnay Circle
K St.
Virginia Ave.
L St.
S. Capitol St.
1st St.
Half St.
M St.
O St.
P St.
WASHINGTON NAVY YARD
John Phillip Sousa Memorial Bridge
Anacostia Park
Anacostia Frwy.
295
Fairlawn Ave.
Naylor Ave.
25th St.
Anacostia R.
11th St.–Anacostia Bridge
Q St.
Minnesota Ave.
22nd St.
R St.
S St.
T St.
ANACOSTIA NAVAL ANNEX
U.S. Botanic Garden Nursery
13th St.
U St.
V St.
W St.
Good Hope Rd.
Anacostia Museum
16th St.
Fort Stanton Park
Morris Rd.
S. Capitol St.
295
ANACOSTIA
Alabama Ave.
Martin Luther King Jr. Blvd.
Suitland Pkwy.
Stanton Rd.
Portland St.
Alabama Ave.
DISTRICT OF COLUMBIA
MARYLAND
Mississippi Ave.

and the combat center. The small mess room, the largest open area in the ship, will give you boundless sympathy for the men (and, recently, women) who have to live cooped up in one of these machines for months at a time. Also dig the decoy used during anti-submarine operations—it's a large motor that sailors threw overboard and dragged behind the ship so that noise-homing torpedoes would strike it instead of the ship's hull. Tours every 15 min. Open April-Sept. Tues.-Sun. 10am-5pm, Oct.-March 10am-4pm. Free.

ANACOSTIA

Anacostia began, ironically enough, as Washington's first suburb: white developers in the 1850s founded "Uniontown" on farmland across the river for settlers disturbed by the growing working-class presence on Capitol Hill. After the Civil War, one-acre plots ($200-300) sold by the Freedmen's Bureau drew freed slaves, who founded the Barry's Farm community. Blue-collar African-Americans would cross the 11th St. bridge to work by day in the city and then return at night to build their houses by firelight. Isolation from the rest of the city built a strong community but also made Anacostia easy to ignore. And as the Black population increased in the 1950s, this neglect worsened—plumbing and electricity were inadequate and the housing, education, and employment opportunities grew few and far between.

Despite the opening of the Anacostia Metro station (on the green line), the neglected neighborhood remains largely unattractive to tourists. While community residents struggle to overcome drug-related violence, progress is slow and costly. **If you prefer exploring on foot, do so here only during the day and with a friend or two.** A drive down Martin Luther King, Jr. Ave. SE is much safer, though, and equally rewarding. You can see the shards of a once-strong community for yourself; people still congregate to socialize along this central artery, enriching the neighborhood with a sense of urgent vitality lacking in calmer areas like Bethesda.

Look north from the parking lot of **Our Lady of Perpetual Help Church,** 1600 Morris Rd. SE (678-4999), across the street from the Lucy Ellen Molten Elementary School, for a good view of downtown, the Washington Monument, the Lincoln Memorial, and the Capitol building. But watch out for the drug dealers; although *Washingtonian* called this lot the best vantage point for gazing at the monuments, and the *Post* recommends it as one of the best spots for viewing the Fourth of July fireworks, they didn't mean for anyone to roam this area on foot.

Anacostia is also home to the **Anacostia Museum,** 1901 Fort Place SE (357-2700), which focuses generally on African-American history and culture (see **Museums & Galleries,** p. 199). Nearby, at 1411 W St. SE, the **Frederick Douglass Home** (426-5960) pays tribute to the great Abolitionist and statesman. Also known as Cedar Hill, the house was Douglass's final residence. Douglass escaped from slavery in 1838, published the *North Star* newspaper in the 1840s, and served in the 1880s as a D.C. official and as the U.S. Ambassador to Haiti. He broke a Whites-only covenant when he bought the Old Anacostia house in 1877. Cedar Hill remains as Douglass furnished it, including a cane belonging to Abraham Lincoln given to Douglass by Mrs. Lincoln after the assassination. Take the Mt. Ranier B-2 bus from Howard Rd. near the Anacostia Metro station to the home. House tours (every ½ hr. from 9am to 4pm) begin with a movie and continue with a walk through the house. (Open daily Nov.-April 9am-5pm; Oct.-March 9am-4pm. Free.)

■■■ THE WATERFRONT

Yes, Virginia. D.C. has a waterfront too, a whole mile of it stretching south of G St. SW, along Maine Ave. and the parallel, smaller Water St. SW. Yachts congregate here at the **Washington Marina,** under the noses of high-priced seafood restaurants and hordes of joggers. In the summer, fairs reel in hundreds of Washingtonians, kids in tow, to check out the t-shirts and food and to ogle the boats. Theater-lovers park here for the **Arena Stage** (see **Nightlife & Entertainment,** p. 222).

The outstanding attraction is the **Wharf Seafood Market,** between 9th and 11th St. SW and Maine Ave. NW (next to the Memorial Bridge). Take the Metro to Waterfront, or from the L'Enfant Plaza stop walk two blocks to 9th St. SW from the exit at 7th and D St. SW and then down 9th St. (away from the Mall) to Maine Ave. No matter the season, no matter the day (except Christmas and perhaps New Year's), the vendors stand in their markets, floating platforms tied to the dock, and sell seafood galore. It's the oldest open-air seafood market in the U.S., beating out even New York's famous Fulton Fish Market; sellers have been at it here since 1794, and nothing's going to stop them now. During low tide you'll find yourself looking down at mounds of ice cubes, coral lobsters, and crawling crabs, as well as at rows of their aproned caretakers. Almost all the fishermen sell at the wharf from about 8am to 9pm. The seafood, most from the Chesapeake Bay, couldn't be fresher. Be warned, however: none of the markets furnishes seating, and the fishy smell packs a wallop.

At the opposite side of Water St. from the wharf, two **touring ships** sail the harbor; the *Spirit of Washington* and the *Potomac Spirit* depart from Pier 4, at 6th and Water St. (554-8000). See **Sports & Recreation,** p. 227, for details.

■■■ THE MALL AND ENVIRONS

Metro: Smithsonian; L'Enfant Plaza; Archives.

The Mall, the U.S.'s taxpayer-supported national backyard, was until this century D.C.'s central cipher, a vacant lot in the middle of everything. Today, it's grassy and green. On any sunny day, hundreds of natives and out-of-towners sunbathe and lounge, play frisbee or football, knock down their little brothers, or go fly a kite. The Mall serves as the hub of much of this city's activity, both governmental and touristic: adjacent to its green swaths are many of the **Smithsonian Museums** (p. 186), the **U.S. Capitol,** and the **White House** (connected via the Ellipse); within its boundaries are such landmarks as the **Washington Monument,** the **Lincoln Memorial,** and the **Vietnam War Memorial** (the **Jefferson Memorial** is just across the Tidal Basin). Nearby, the **Bureau of Engraving and Printing** and the **U.S. Holocaust Memorial Museum** butt heads with lesser-known attractions like the **U.S. Botanical Gardens.**

Just east of the Smithsonian Castle on the south side of the Mall, a musical **merry-go-round** delights all creatures great and small for only $1 a go. Thousands of people with trucks full of musical instruments and traditional cuisines congregate on the Mall early July for the **Festival of American Folklife;** don't miss it, especially the evening dancing, if you're around. Other occasional celebrations, like the **Fourth of July,** swamp the Mall with tents and blankets. See **Appendix** (p. 293).

Exotic foliage from all continents and climates vegetates inside and outside the **U.S. Botanical Garden,** 1st St. and Maryland Ave. SW (225-7099) in front of the Capitol. (Metro: Federal Center SW.) Look for the amusing sausage tree near the entrance, and enjoy the burbling fountains, glass-covered atriums, and orchids. Don't miss the display of dinosaur-era plants; temporary exhibits can also be interesting. Forty-minute guided tours begin at 10am and 2pm (call ahead; open 9am-5pm).

WASHINGTON MONUMENT

D.C.'s quintessential tiny, crowded, overheated elevator leads to equally tiny windows with nauseating views. The Washington Monument inspires never-ending crowds of tourists to sacrifice their sweat, time, and patience ascending, descending, and photographing it. A vertical altar to America's first president, the marble-faced monument weighs 81,120 tons, stands on a foundation 126½ sq. ft. and 37 ft. deep, and could withstand a super-tornado blowing at 145 miles per hour (at least that's what the experts say). Two-foot blocks of marble, along with rubble masonry, make up the base exterior; the interior support switches to New England granite about 450 ft. up, then gives way to solid marble capped by a 9-in. aluminum pyramid. In 1986, D.C. cops left bullet holes at eye level on the monument when they gunned down a man who parked his van here, claimed it was full of dynamite, and threatened to blow up the famous structure.

For an obelisk, the monument took plenty of time and energy to build. Robert Mills's 1845 design called for a one-story, 30-column temple around the base. After Congress agreed to Mills's plan, construction began on July 4, 1848, but soon ran out of money; Alabama, which couldn't afford to send cash, contributed a stone instead, starting a trend that saved the monument. France, the Cherokee Nation, the American residents of Fu-Chow Fu, China, and over 100 other nations, states, towns, and people sent stones. When the Vatican sent a block of Italian marble in 1854, the Know-Nothings—an anti-Catholic and anti-immigrant political party—raided the grounds and stole "the Pope's stone;" afterwards, contributions dried up.

During the Civil War the half-finished obelisk was nicknamed the "Beef Depot Monument" in honor of the cattle that Army quartermasters herded on the grounds. The monument's stone changes hue 150 ft. up: when construction began again after the Civil War and the builders returned to their favorite Maryland quarry, the layer of stones of the original color had already been used up. George Marsh, the U.S. Ambassador to Italy and an obelisk fan, nixed Mills's Doric temple in 1880 and the structure opened four years later.

The first men to ascend the monument could choose between the steam elevator and the stairs; women and children had to climb the 698 steps, since Mr. Otis's invention was considered dangerous. The stairs up the monument were a famous (and strenuous) tourist exercise until the Park Service closed them after heart attacks (on the way up) and vandalism (on the way down). The line for the elevators isn't as slow as it looks; it takes 45 minutes to circle the monument. Up at the top, tiny windows offer lookout points. From 500 ft. up, you can look down on all of D.C.'s major sights. The view from the top of the **Old Post Office** (see p. 87), however, is even better; in fact, the monument is almost more attractive when viewed from afar. Busy tourists may find their time better spent elsewhere.

The monument ascends Constitution Ave. and 16th St. NW, west of the Mall proper and east of the Lincoln Memorial (Metro: Smithsonian). A wheelchair is available for any visitor who needs it; people with disabilities may bypass the long lines. (Open April-Aug. daily 8am-midnight; Sept.-March daily 9am-5pm. Free.)

Near Washington Monument

The **Reflecting Pool,** between the Washington and Lincoln memorials, reflects Washington's obelisk in seven million gallons of lit-up water 24 hours a day. If you lean far enough over, it might reflect you too. Based on pools at Versailles and the Taj Mahal, the Reflecting Pool's design minimizes wind ripples while maximizing poetic effect. A demonstration big enough to surround the 2,000-ft. long pool with people—such as the 1994 Gay Rights march—makes an impressive sight indeed.

Constitution Gardens stretches out north of the Reflecting Pool. The gardens are actually landfill—everything west of the Washington Monument and south of Constitution Ave. was once a swamp. On a weeping willow-dominated island in the park's lake, a granite and gold plate lists the signers of the Declaration of Independence. Feathered types hang out at the gardens; the prevailing greeting is "quack."

VIETNAM VETERANS MEMORIAL

Maya Ying Lin, who designed the memorial, called it "a rift in the earth—a long, polished black stone wall, emerging from and receding into the earth." "The memorial is a moving composition," she explained, "to be understood as one moves into and out of it; the passage itself is gradual, the descent to the origin slow, but it is at the origin that the meaning of the memorial is to be fully understood." While still an undergraduate at Yale, Lin beat 1400 contestants with her design. This subtlest of D.C.'s memorials changes its sheen and mood between day and night. Its granite reflects the Washington and Lincoln memorials at equal sizes.

Each of the 58,132 Americas who died in Vietnam has his name chiseled onto the stark black edifice. (Those Americans who are still missing in action have yet to be acknowledged.) Books at both ends of the structure serve as indexes to the memorial's numbered panels. Families and veterans come here to ponder and to mourn; many make rubbings of their loved ones' names from the walls. Other visitors leave letters, flowers, or more unusual objects; these items are collected by the Park Service. The National Museum of American History's "Personal Legacy" exhibit displays a sampling of some of these offerings. See **Museums** (p. 187).

Some soldiers (and congresspeople) objected to the memorial's nonmilitary appearance, so the government commissioned Frederick Hart to sculpt realistic-looking (i.e., exhausted) bronze troopers emerging from an unknown battlefield. The statues seem to stare straight at the memorial's central corner, as if to apologize for breaking the silence Lin's design commands.

Three bronze figures at the east end of the memorial balance the three troopers to the west—they are the **Vietnam Women's Memorial.** Each woman, sculpted by Glenna Goodacre in 1993, strikes a different pose; one aids a wounded soldier, another mourns a lost one, staring into his helmet. The third looks out into the sky and clutches her friend's arm as danger approaches.

The Vietnam Veterans Memorial descends into the earth northeast of the Lincoln Memorial, north of the Reflecting Pool, and south of Constitution Ave. at 22nd St. NW. (Metro: Foggy Bottom or Smithsonian.) It's entirely outdoors, so the memorial stays "open" 24 hrs.; park rangers leave at midnight. Call 634-1568 for information.

LINCOLN MEMORIAL

Though consensus demanded some memorial to Lincoln almost immediately after his assassination in 1865, the present marble temple wasn't built until 50 years later. The current marble Parthenon-like superstructure stands 80 ft. high, with simple Doric columns climbing 44 ft. to the frieze, where an inscription holds the names of the 36 states in existence during Lincoln's presidency. A massive layer of stone atop the columns lends the building the watchful solemnity of a crypt. The names of the lower 48 states wrap around the memorial's roof; a plaque at the bottom of the 130-ft.-wide stairway footnotes Alaska and Hawaii. The memorial's steps have hosted many famous gatherings; African-American soprano Marian Anderson sang from the steps here after she was barred from segregated Constitution Hall in 1939. Martin Luther King, Jr., gave his "I Have a Dream" speech to the 1963 March on Washington crowd from these stairs. Today the base of the memorial most notably hosts vet-related vendors who find it easier to park their carts on the Lincoln Memorial's flat concrete than the grass of the Vietnam Memorial.

Daniel Chester French's seated Lincoln presides over the memorial from the inside, keeping watch over the Reflecting Pool, protest marchers, and Fourth of July fireworks. The stonecutting firm Picirilli Bros. couldn't find a block of marble big enough for Honest Abe; instead, they joined 28 blocks so tightly that you can barely see the seams. In American Sign Language, Lincoln's hands spell "A" and "L"—French's reminder that it was Lincoln who signed Gallaudet College (the only college in the country for deaf students) into existence. The arms of the marble seat bear Roman *fasces,* symbols of imperial power—an unfortunate choice, given Mussolini's concurrent ascension to power in Italy.

Lincoln's stirring **Gettysburg Address** graces the wall to the left of the statue. Also note his (longer) 2nd inaugural address, given 63 days prior to his assassination, and the un-subtly corrected "engravo" where "euture" has been changed to "future." Looming above Lincoln's famous words are Jules Gurin's allegorical gold-detailed canvas murals. To the south, the Angel of Truth frees slaves, flanked by Justice and Immortality; to the north, the Angel of Truth brings the North and the South together after the Civil War, with help from Fraternity and Charity.

The memorial's interior looks best early in the morning, when the rising sun shines through the marble roof; builders soaked it in paraffin to improve its translucency. At night, Lincoln glows in electric lights; memorial-goers can watch the Washington Monument's image shimmer in the Reflecting Pool and meditate from the steps. The memorial anchors the west end of the Mall across the Reflecting Pool from the Washington Monument; from Foggy Bottom, just walk south along 23rd St. NW. (Metro: Smithsonian or Foggy Bottom; it's a long walk.) Since it has no doors, the Memorial is open 24 hrs.; a ranger hangs around daily from 8am until midnight.

Korean War Memorial

On June 25, 1950, North Korea launched a surprise attack on South Korea. Twenty-one countries sent troops to help defend South Korea; China sent troops to bolster North Korea's effort. The "conflict" (it was never officially called a "war") ended with the signing of an armistice that solidified the separation of the two countries on July 27, 1953.

The three-year conflict resulted in more than 628,000 UN troops lost; over 54,000 Americans lost their lives. (For perspective, 57,000 Americans died in Vietnam over the 10 years of U.S. involvement in that conflict.)

Forty-two years after the armistice was signed, on July 27, 1995, The Korean War Memorial was dedicated. The $18 million tribute got 60% of its funding from American Korean War veterans, and made use of no federal money. Located at the west end of the Mall near the Lincoln Memorial, 19 colossal polished steel statues (14 Army men, 3 Marines, a Navy medic, and an Air Force officer) trudge up a hill, rifles in hand, an eternal expression of weariness mixed with fear frozen upon their faces. A black granite wall with over 2000 sandblasted photographic images from the war stands nearby. One edge of the wall extends into a shallow pool of water, a symbol of the Korean peninsula.

While the war has finally been commemorated, there are still over 8000 Americans missing from that often-forgotten war.

JEFFERSON MEMORIAL

I think this is the most extraordinary collection of talent, of human knowledge, that has ever been gathered together at the White House, with the possible exception of when Thomas Jefferson dined alone.
—JFK, addressing a gathering of Nobel Prize winners in 1962

The third member of D.C.'s white-marble triumvirate, finished in 1942, holds court due south and across the Tidal Basin from the Washington Monument. A 19-ft. hollow bronze Thomas Jefferson stands enshrined in a domed, open-air rotunda surrounded by massive Ionic columns. The memorial's graceful design, by John Russel Pope, pays homage to Jefferson's Charlottesville home, Monticello. The cherry trees (which bloom in the spring) were a gift from Tokyo to Washington in 1912.

Franklin Roosevelt had all the trees between the memorial and the White House razed so he could watch the construction. High-society ladies tried to protect the 33 cherry trees standing in the monument's way by chaining themselves to the trunks; the bureaucrat in charge of construction served them coffee and tea until their bladders protested, then bulldozed the trees while they were in the powder room. A path of grass is still clearly visible today, allowing visitors to the memorial a view of the White House.

Jefferson himself designed a number of neoclassical buildings during his life, including the Virginia state capitol and the quadrangle and library at the University of Virginia. Corn and tobacco, Virginia's cash crops, are visible under his coat, the tobacco forming a sort of column as a reminder of Jefferson's architectural bent. The interior walls quote from Jefferson's writings: the *Declaration of Independence,* the *Virginia Statute of Religious Freedom,* his *Notes on Virginia,* and an 1815 letter. The Declaration of Independence extract contains 11 discrepancies with the original; several of these were committed to shorten the quote so it would fit on the wall. The carved squares get smaller near the top of the dome, so the ceiling looks higher than its short 30 ft.

Today, Jefferson's pocket of peacefulness is disturbed by the restoration of cracked columns—the sorry result of time, automobile exhaust, and acid rain. The memorial remains open 24 hrs., with the lights always on. Park rangers answer questions from 8am until midnight, except on Christmas (426-6822 or 425-6821). The memorial overlooks the Tidal Basin along D.C.'s southwestern edge; walk to it along the Basin's rim from Independence Ave. or 14th St. SW. (Metro: L'Enfant Plaza or Smithsonian.) To drive here, take 14th St. SW (don't try it during the day).

TIDAL BASIN AREA

The Jefferson Memorial overlooks Washington's most popular man-made lake, the **Tidal Basin,** where **paddleboats** ripple in and out of Thomas Jefferson's shadow. Visitors finishing their tours of the Mint get dumped out here. The lake is small enough for the whole thing to be visible at once, but big enough to sustain plenty of boaters. For paddleboat rentals, see **Sports and Recreation** (p. 227).

Too famous for their own good, the Japanese **cherry trees** surround themselves with a protective ring of botanically minded tourists during the two weeks in late March or early April when most of them are in bloom along the Tidal Basin's rim. The original batch of trees, sent in 1909 from Japan as a symbol of trans-Pacific friendship, arrived bearing insects and fungi and were promptly obliterated by the Department of Agriculture. The current bloomin' wonders, received in 1912, were Japan's second try. After Japanese bombers attacked Pearl Harbor in 1941, irate Washingtonians took buzzsaws to several of the trees.

Mellow **West Potomac Park** and **East Potomac Park,** replete with trees, lawns, and sculptures, park themselves on either side of the Tidal Basin along Ohio Dr. SW. The former is more popular, but the latter is bigger. West Potomac Park holds summer polo games at 3pm on Sundays.

It's hard to spend more than 10 minutes south of the Lincoln Memorial without hearing military helicopters motoring away over the Potomac: if you see one heading due north, toward the White House, it might well contain the President.

SOUTH OF THE MALL

Millions of listeners on every continent but this one tune into the **Voice of America,** 330 Independence Ave. SW (619-3919; Metro: Federal Center SW), the U.S. government's overseas radio and TV organ. Tours start at the C St. entrance between 3rd and 4th St.; watch radio announcers at home in the studio, speaking anything from English to Dari to Uzbek. (Public tours lasting 45 min. begin Tues.-Thurs. at 10:40am, 1:40pm, and 2:40pm, except holidays.)

Bureaucrats shop till they drop in the low-ceilinged, light-bulby **L'Enfant Plaza,** named for Pierre L'Enfant, D.C.'s ubiquitous original urban planner. The plaza itself is an immense underground structure that takes up an entire block between 9th and 10th St. at D St. SW. The plaza's construction threatened to topple the saw-tooth-based **Department of Housing and Urban Development,** an unhealthy-looking X-shaped building on D St. SW between 7th and 9th. A long-standing HUD rumor holds that the building was designed to resemble a particularly admired Paris post office. Unfortunately, the HUD building was twice the size of the one in Paris; the square-cube law, which says that anything of given proportions gets weaker as it gets bigger, made the outsized HUD structure unsound from the outset.

The Mint, or the **Bureau of Engraving and Printing** (622-2000), 14th St. and C St. SW, just southeast of the Washington Monument (Metro: Smithsonian), offers unguided tours (along claustrophobic tunnels smelling of ink) of the presses that annually print over $20 billion worth of money and stamps. Look for the bins of shredded bills. Crowd-herders fondly refer to the place as "the money factory;" and signs affixed to the presses announce "the buck starts here," taunt visitors with "Have you ever been so close and yet so far away?" and poke fun at employees: "Think how I feel: I printed my lifetime salary in a few minutes!" Skip breakfast, or expect to grow old in line. Thankfully, the wait is relieved by lots of stamps, discontinued bills, TV screens, and other displays along the way. Free muzak, too. (Open Mon.-Fri. 9am-2pm; free.)

Just north of the mint, at 100 Raoul Wallenberg Place SW, the **U.S. Holocaust Memorial Museum** (488-0400; Metro: Smithsonian) reminds huge crowds of the atrocities visited upon European Jews by the Nazis. See **Museums** (p. 194).

■■■ OLD DOWNTOWN

Metro: Metro Center; Gallery Place-Chinatown; Judiciary Sq.; Archives-Navy Memorial; Federal Triangle.

"Old Downtown" is an arbitrary label for the area north of the Mall bounded by Constitution Ave., 2nd St., New York Ave., and 15th St. NW. Federal business centers on Old Downtown, where many U.S. agencies and departments do their regulating thing. But Old Downtown also harbors a thriving commercial culture, with plenty of street vendors, luncheon spots, and pricey hotels to rival the few block-long department stores around Metro Center. This schizoid tendency reflects the area's history: before government moved in, 7th St. NW was D.C.'s main commercial center. During the 1800s, it boasted the largest outdoor market (the no-longer-extant Center Market, opened in 1801) and the monumental Patent Office building. Old Downtown's split personality is evident from its pedestrians, as well: subnetworks of tourists, professionals, bureaucrats, and the city's homeless throng the streets on weekdays. At night they find their respective havens—hotels, bars, 'burbs, and benches. Each group has its own hubs and hotspots, but none claims the neighborhood for its own. If you find the area a little overwhelming, it's probably because you can't figure out how all the pieces (and the people) fit together. The answer is they don't.

Pennsylvania Avenue between the White House and the Capitol (now closed to commercial vehicles), and especially between 6th and 15th St. NW, is probably the most discussed street in Washington. New Presidents traverse it quadrennially in the Inaugural Parade, which earns it the logical nickname "Street of Presidents;" most new Chief Executives ride in limos, but Jimmy Carter showed his energy-consciousness in 1976 by walking the 16 blocks to the White House. Before and during the Civil War era, the avenue, which runs all the way from Northwest to Anacostia via the John Philip Sousa Bridge, was D.C.'s most important thoroughfare. At night, the street became "Hooker's Division," named for the hard-living Union General Joseph Hooker. Shady bars and prostitution flourished here. But anyone who says the term "hooker" (for a prostitute) came from General Hooker's name is probably just a proud native Washingtonian: the word, older than the general, most likely derives from Brooklyn (NY)'s old Red Hook district.

An array of old-time Greco-Roman Revival federal buildings includes the **Federal Trade Commission** at 6th St., which is blessed with a profusion of outdoor sculptures. (The half-naked man wrestling a horse near the eastern doorway represents the Commission's controlling monopolies.) Other neoclassical structures along the avenue are the **National Archives** (between 7th and 9th), the **Justice Department** (between 9th and 10th), the taxing **Internal Revenue Service** (between 10th and 12th), and the **Interstate Commerce Commission** (between 12th and 14th). These buildings, along with the District Building and the Dept. of Commerce, form the **Federal Triangle complex,** once the site of the notorious slum Murder Bay. The looming **FBI,** the enchantingly anachronistic **Old Post Office,** and the elegant **Willard Hotel** make their contrasting marks on the avenue's wide vistas, as does the **District Building** at 14th and D St. NW. Congress invented the Pennsylvania Ave. Development Corporation in 1972 to encourage private enterprise along the government-dominated street; the result has been a string of offices, so a walk up the avenue on a weekday lets you survey Washington architecture and Washington office-people all at once. Small parks and plazas along the length of the street offer calm resting places for exhausted walkers.

NEAR JUDICIARY SQUARE

Leaving the Judiciary Square Metro at the 4th and D St. exit, turn right onto D St. and walk one block to the **D.C. Courthouse** (879-1010) at Indiana Ave., 5th St. and D St. NW (mailing address 500 Indiana Ave. NW). This modern building can show you how the legal system really operates. Suspects, lawyers, cops, and taxi drivers compete for sidewalk space outside, while lawyers rush up and down three levels of escalators inside, scampering to file their briefs in time. The D.C. Superior Court and the D.C. Court of Appeals share the building; confusingly, the Superior Court is the *inferior* of the two. They say Justice is blind; here, she's just oblivious to tourists. Pick up an info pamphlet at the Public Information Desk (to your left as you walk in) and ask which criminal cases you can sit in on. Alternatively, you can eat in the cafeteria on the "C" level or just ride the escalators. Whee. (Courthouse open Mon.-Fri. 8:30am-5pm; free.)

Toward the Mall, across C St. NW, the **U.S. Courthouse** (535-3555), at 333 Constitution Ave., squats in conservative austerity on the east side of John Marshall Park (Metro: Judiciary Square). At the Constitution Ave. entrance, examine the monument to Civil War general George Meade, who led Union forces at Gettysburg and now stands guard over the courthouse building flanked by an ecletic brigade of nymphs, Roman warriors, and a medieval knight figure in a bizarre mixing of artistic and historical topes. Or, enter on 3rd St. and catch a glimpse of the **Department of Labor.** The federal court building claims to be open to the public (past a metal detector), but even though it's legal, you may still feel like an intruder. Better-dressed lawyers and Constitutional issues stalk these marbled halls, which contain the Court of Appeals for the D.C. Circuit. Both civil and criminal cases are generally open to the public, depending on availability of space. Check the trial schedule in Room 1825 for interesting cases. (U.S. Courthouse open Mon.-Fri. 9am-4:30pm; free.) In **John Marshall Park,** workaholics and alcoholics compete for a lunch bench alongside a lifelike statue of two chess players. Take a closer look. One player looks smug, the other dismayed; that's because the game is over and one player is in checkmate. Watch the pigeons perch on of the oversized statue of Marshall, the fourth and most important chief justice of the Supreme Court (who here resembles a haggard Anthony Hopkins). Across the street, facing the East Wing of the National Gallery of Art, the small bit of parkland once held the boardinghouse where poet Walt Whitman lived in 1864.

The **Canadian Embassy** (682-1740), at 501 Pennsylvania Ave. NW behind the D.C. Courthouse, deserves more than a glance (Metro: Judiciary Square or Archives-Navy Memorial). The east front, bordering Marshall Park, is a spacious court surrounded by six 50-foot columns of smooth, pale, unpolished aluminum that hold three of the embassy's six modern floors high above. The Rotunda of the Provinces, on the southeast corner of the court, creates a shady platform and caps a cascading pool of water. At the embassy's Marshall Park entrance, check out Bill Reid's black bronze 11,000-lb. sculpture, *The Spirit of Haida Gwaii.* The Haida are a Native-American tribe indigenous to Canada's Queen Charlotte Islands; this striking piece, perched in a pool of water, depicts a number of Haida mythical figures crammed into a canoe and paddling for their lives. A gallery in the embassy's basement displays rotating exhibitions of other modern Canadian art. Open Mon.-Fri. 10am-5pm. Free.

National Law Enforcement Officers Memorial

The National Law Enforcement Officers Memorial (Metro: Judiciary Sq.), is situated, appropriately, in Judiciary Sq. between E and F St. and 4th and 5th St. NW in front of the **National Building Museum** and directly above the Metro station. (See **Museums & Galleries,** p. 199.) Dedicated by President Bush in October 1991, the memorial's three acres recognize the service of all officers and honor the more than 13,000 federal, state, and local officers who have died in the line of duty. In the creation of his composition, architect Davis Buckley drew from Michelangelo's Piazza del Campidoglio in Rome as well as Maya Ying Lin's Vietnam Veterans Memorial just blocks away. Buckley utilized Michelangelo's geometric solution for presenting an off-center base as centered in the semi-elliptical walkway around the edge of the memorial. And in transforming the walkways into "pathways of remembrance" (with the names of fallen officers engraved in the gray marble bordering the paths), Buckley nods to Lin's design for the Vietnam memorial. A bronze lion or lioness guards each of the four entrances along the pathways while watching over slumbering cubs, conveying the responsibility, strength, and courage of those who enforce the nations's laws.

With the monument's dual role as both memorial and public park, pedestrians and casual visitors share the space with the families and friends of slain officials. As at the Vietnam memorial, rubbing-pads for etching names are available onsite and at the National Building Museum. The **Visitors Center,** two blocks west at 605 E St. NW, details the history of the memorial. (Memorial open 24 hrs. Visitors Center open Mon.-Fri. 9am-5pm, Sat.-Sun. noon-5pm; free.)

NATIONAL ARCHIVES

The United States' founding documents can still be found at the National Archives, between 7th and 9th St., and Constitution Ave. NW (general information 501-5000, TDD 501-5404, guided tours 501-5205, library and research 501-5400; Metro: Archives-Navy Memorial). Visitors line up outside to view the original *Declaration of Independence, U.S. Constitution,* and *Bill of Rights* (often, unfortunately, ignoring the rotating exhibits that flank them). Humidity-controlled, helium-filled glass cases preserve and exhibit all three documents in the central rotunda. Every night these cases sink into the floor; the documents' nightly repose in a basement vault makes them harder to steal, slower to deteriorate, and safe from nuclear attack. Look for the dent in the metal of the casing, a reminder that, in 1986, someone tried to shatter the glass with a hammer and destroy the Bill of Rights. Also largely ignored by tourists is the 13th-century *Magna Carta,* King John of England's famous guarantee of rights to his angry barons. Today it's on indefinite loan to the Archives from its owner, full-time billionaire and part-time political pest H. Ross Perot. Don't it figure. The document on display is one of four existing copies of the 1297 version, endorsed by Edward I. The *Magna Carta* was originally approved by King John in 1215, and guaranteed such fundamental rights as the right to trial by jury, equality before the law, and freedom from arbitrary arrest. Long tiered steps, stone friezes, fluted columns, and mammoth bronze doors (1 ft. thick and 40 ft. high) remind you that neoclassicist John Russell Pope, of National Gallery of Art fame, also designed the Archives. (Main exhibit area open daily April-Aug. 10am-9pm, Sept.-March 10am-5:30pm. Free.) The Archives will even play Nixon's infamous Watergate tapes for the public, though at a safe distance from the White House. The tapes are stored, along with increasing amounts of Archives material, in a new facility, Archives II, located in College Park, MD. Most research materials are now at Archives II. (Open Mon. and Wed. 8:45am-4:45pm, Tues. and Thurs.-Fri. 8:45am-9pm, and Sat. 8:45am-4:45pm. Call 301-713-6400 for information.)

The Archives preserves over four billion papers and paraphernalia from American history. Its files hold about 2% of the paper the federal government generates, including maps, patents, photographs, police journals, and census forms. A very small percentage of the Archives' possessions can be displayed at one time. The Archives owns but does not display the *Emancipation Proclamation,* President Lincoln's slave-freeing document of 1862. Unusual items stored here include a portrait of Richard Nixon painted on a grain of rice; a 7-ft. roll of names on paper tape (part of an 1893 petition); a red wig worn by Watergate villain Howard Hunt; and a file of Topps baseball cards taken as evidence in a 1960s lawsuit.

The **Microfilm Room** on the building's fifth floor lets visitors check military records, census records, and Confederate and Revolutionary papers. Genealogy buffs tending family trees find plenty of historical fertilizer here; professional writers, like Alex Haley *(Roots)*, come here to research upcoming best sellers. At the Central Research Library, librarians will track the information you need from the

Archives' reams of data. (Research facilities open Mon. and Wed. 8:45am-5pm, Tues. and Thurs.-Fri. 8:45am-9pm, Sat. 8:45am-4:45pm; enter at Pennsylvania Ave. and 8th St.)

The **tour** of the Archives can show you more, like the vault into which the Declaration, Constitution, et al. are lowered each night, and the patents for an "escape coffin." (Call in advance to arrange tours.) Also on display are the Reagan family census; the arrest record for John Wilkes Booth; a photo of Helen Keller with President Eisenhower (that she never saw); and President Nixon's 1974 letter of resignation. (Call 501-5205 in advance to make reservations for a tour; U.S. citizens may call their congresspeople instead. Tours daily at 10:15am and 1:15pm. Free. Tour-takers enter at Pennsylvania Ave. and 8th St.) Exhibits for 1996 include a changing display entitled "American Originals," which will present some of the Archives' hidden treasures and as-yet-undisplayed crucial documents like the Louisiana Purchase Treaty and President Reagan's 1987 speech at the Berlin Wall.

UNITED STATES NAVY MEMORIAL

The United States Navy Memorial (737-2300) on Pennsylvania Ave. at 8th St. NW, across Pennsylvania Ave. from the National Archives (Metro: Archives-Navy Memorial), is a popular rest and lunch spot for tourists and local workers alike. The circular memorial harbors weekly **concerts** by the Navy Band (Tues. at 8pm in the summer months). Petrophiles will love the largest-ever **stone map** of the world, which is set into the ground; compass-heads will note that the map's north is exactly aligned to the true north. Figure out the pictographs along the walls, hum the Naval Hymn carved into the steps, or stand next to Stanley Bleifeld's statue *The Lone Sailor* and contemplate the ocean (aaah, the ocean). Enter the Visitors Center at the back right of the memorial and head downstairs. The descent is accompanied by the "Wave Wall," which holds glass panels into which ships are etched. The waves lead into the Gallery Deck, another nautical room that leads into the Presidents' Room. The room honors presidents who have served in or led the Navy—both Roosevelts (who served as assistant secretaries of the Navy), Kennedy, Johnson, Nixon, Ford, Carter, and Bush. As you enter the Gallery Deck, look behind you to your left for the entrance to the Theater, where the movie *At Sea* flaunts its high-tech graphics. Memorial open 24 hrs. Visitors Center open Mon.-Sat. 9:30am-5pm, Sun. noon-5pm.

THE FBI

The block-long J. Edgar Hoover FBI building, 10th St. NW at Pennsylvania Ave. (324-3000), represents the nadir of Washington modernism, one block west from the Navy Memorial. Waiting in line for a glimpse of the interior, you may get to know it well. Once inside, serious-minded agents will guide you through the popular FBI tour, casting light on some of the organization's tricks (and none of its scandals). Tour lines form on the building's outdoor plaza; tour entrance at E St. NW (Metro: Federal Triangle or Archives-Navy Memorial).

The end of the go-go, right-wing 80s hasn't fazed the Federal Bureau of Investigation. Today's FBI still hunts Commies, druggies, homosexuals, and interstate felons with a vigor little diminished since J. Edgar Hoover's 25-year stint as its chief. Hoover earned himself, and the Bureau, a reputation by nabbing the nation's notorious criminals of the 30s and 40s, then driving the FBI through over a decade of political espionage, homophobic innuendo, and hounding of left-wing figures. He fired all of the Bureau's female agents upon taking the helm, proclaiming that a woman would serve the FBI "over his dead body." Until Hoover's death in May 1971, the FBI's female employees could only be found filing and photocopying. July 1971 saw the appointment of the Bureau's first female agent since the 30s.

Tourists can't wander around the high-security interior—you must wait for the tours, which occur as often as the guides can give them and open with a corny movie. Real FBI agents sport walkie-talkies (and a strange resemblance to flight attendants) as they speed you through gangster paraphernalia and photos, relics of crime bosses, confiscated marijuana and cocaine, a display of 5000 illicit guns (including a gun disguised as a cane), old cryptographic devices, and mugshots of the nation's 10 most wanted criminals. Tourists have identified felons from their mugshots on two separate occasions; each led to an arrest. In the wake of all this excitement, your tour-agent will probably burst your bubble by announcing that 25% of all Federal agents are accountants assigned to unglamorous white-color crimes.

The FBI's crack team of scientists will ignore you as you watch them analyze hair, blood, and DNA samples from behind plexiglass. At the tour's end, a marksman picks up an FBI-standard revolver and a German HNK-MP5 fully automatic submachine gun and blasts away at cardboard evildoers. Tellingly, the mostly American audience always applauds when the shooting ends.

In theory, you can park on 9th St. near the Bureau. In practice, you'd do better to take the Metro or to walk here from the Mall. In June and July, crowds sometimes wait up to four hours for a tour; come early in the morning, during lunch hour, or at the end of the day to shorten the wait. Tours Mon.-Fri 8:45am-4:15pm; free.

Near the FBI

"Sic semper tyrannis!" shouted Abraham Lincoln's killer John Wilkes Booth as he jumped to the stage just seconds after shooting the President during a performance at **Ford's Theatre** (426-6924, TDD 426-1749), 511 10th St. NW, one block north of the FBI (Metro: Metro Center, 11th St. exit). An actor, Booth had no trouble sneaking into the theater. Lincoln's April 14, 1865 appearance at *Our American Cousin* was his first time in public since the Civil War had ended. At 10:15pm, while the audience was laughing, Booth entered the President's box, shot Lincoln, then injured his leg jumping onstage. The Maryland doctor who set the broken bone was exiled to Dry Tortuga for his pains. The museum below the theater runneth over with placards and portraits of Lincoln. At night, Ford's Theatre becomes a contemporary playhouse (see **Nightlife & Entertainment: Theater,** p. 223). *"Sic semper tyrannis,"* by the way, means "Thus always to tyrants"—it's the motto of the state of Virginia, usually printed under a picture of Virginia mercilessly quashing a tyrant (presumably) with her foot. The theater is under the jurisdiction of the National Parks Service. See if you can goad one of the rangers into narrating the events of the assassination for you. (Open daily 9am-5pm; free.)

The next morning, President Lincoln passed away across the street at the **Petersen House** (426-6830), 526 10th St. NW. He slept, and later died, diagonally, in the small bed. The tiny room where he died now looks as it did then, and the intimacy of the room—its dotted white curtains, low walnut bed and bureau, and simple tumblers and pitchers—makes visitors seem like strangers at a wake. The bloodstained pillows, recently treated and restored, may make it feel like a crime scene. The crowds rotating through the house create the nagging impression that their presence, and yours, constitutes some form of sacrilege. (Open daily 9am-5pm.)

The **Old Post Office,** at Pennsylvania Ave. and 12th St. NW (606-8691, TDD 606-8694), sheathes a shopping mall in architectural wonder (Metro: Federal Triangle). Its arched windows, conical turrets, and 315-ft. clock tower are a standing rebuke to its sleeker contemporary neighbors. Completed in 1899, the Post Office Building was criticized by the *New York Times* for looking "like a cross between a cathedral and a cotton mill." The building has also been referred to as a tooth in need of extraction. Today, the wayward edifice, having avoided demolition in the 1950s, houses a one-room post office, some federal office space, a multi-ethnic food court, shops, and a stage. Offices rise on all four sides of a 12-story space in which tourists and businesspeople enjoy cheap but tasty meals and incessant musical performances. For information on the shops—collectively known as the Pavilion—call 289-4224. The National Park Service can show you around the **clock tower** (tour info 606-8691). The 15-min. tour meets every 5 min. at the glass elevators in the patio area, where food tables cluster. The view from the top may be D.C.'s best, especially since the archways are open-air (wired for safety), not glassed-in or minuscule (like the Washington Monument's). The Washington Ringing Society makes the tower chime for hours on end on Thursdays (for practice), and on federal holidays. (Tower open mid-April to mid-Sept. 8am-10:45pm; otherwise 10am-6pm. Shops open Mon.-Sat. 10am-8pm, Sun. noon-6pm.)

CHINATOWN

This five-square-block community shares enough with its larger namesakes to make it worth exploring (Metro: Gallery Place-Chinatown). Start at 7th and H St. NW; you'll know where you are by the bilingual street signs and by the dragon-covered multicolored gilded archway. Mainland Chinese money paid for the arch in the mid-80s, sparking protests by local leaders on anti-Communist grounds. Chinatown's history resembles that of Chinese districts across the nation. After the Chinese Exclusion Act of 1882 had restricted immigration, barred Chinese aliens from most jobs, and banned Chinese women and children from the United States, the persecuted immigrants lived and worked near 4th St. and Pennsylvania Ave. NW. Two rival *tongs* (merchants' associations) formed to offer protection to Chinese-owned businesses. When government buildings displaced the old Chinatown, the *tongs* led the move to today's neighborhood.

Technically bounded by 5th, 8th, F, and I St. NW, Chinatown is slowly shrinking under the pressure of crime and rising rents, but the remaining shops and restaurants serve many first-generation Chinese immigrants. While Chinatown streets are safe during the day, exercise extra caution at night and bring a friend or two, especially on weekends. (For how and where to eat in Chinatown, see **Food,** p. 89.)

FROM GALLERY PLACE TO METRO CENTER

The **National Museum of American Art** and the **National Portrait Gallery** (357-2700, TDD 357-1729) share the **Old Patent Office Building,** a Neoclassical edifice two blocks long (American Art entrance at 8th and G St., Portrait Gallery entrance at 8th and F; Metro: Gallery Place-Chinatown). The NMAA houses the largest collection of American art in the world, while the NPG is a surprisingly engrossing museum devoted exclusively to portraiture. (See **Museums & Galleries,** p. 201.)

At 901 G St. NW, across 9th St. from the National Gallery of American Art, is the **Martin Luther King, Jr. Memorial Library** (727-1111), the flagship of D.C.'s library system. The brick and black glass rectangular building is the only one in Washington designed by Bauhaus celeb Ludwig Mies van der Rohe. Inside, see Don Miller's mural of Rev. King, one of the United States' most important civil rights leaders, who led the nonviolent protests that helped end legal segregation. Local history aficionados will find their heaven in the Washingtoniana Room. (Open during the summer Mon. and Thurs. 9am-9pm, Tues.-Wed. and Fri.-Sat. 9am-5:30pm; open the rest of the year Mon.-Thurs. 9am-9pm, Fri.-Sat. 9am-5:30pm, Sun. 1-5pm. Free.)

The church-like building on 8th St. between H and I St. NW used to be a synagogue; now it's the **Greater New Hope Baptist Church.** Founded in 1852, Washington Hebrew (now far away on Massachusetts Ave. NW) was the first Jewish congregation in D.C. The charmingly eclectic building, erected in 1898, attracts a healthy stream of architecture buffs for its hodgepodge of styles: the combination of the twin-tower stone facade, two shades of brick, and the high silver dome reflects the diversity of faiths that have worshipped here. Although the church does not have any specific tourist program, don't hesitate to knock on the front door. Whoever is around will probably be happy to take you upstairs for a better view of the stained-glass Star of David and the high dome.

Two blocks west of the MLK library, the **National Museum of Women in the Arts,** 1250 New York Ave. NW (783-5000; Metro: Metro Center) exhibits the work of women artists in a former Masonic Temple. (See **Museums & Galleries,** p. 201.)

Just west of the NMWA, **New York Ave. Presbyterian Church,** at New York Ave., H St., and 13th St. NW (393-3700), displays relics of Abraham Lincoln's history (Metro: Metro Center). In a meeting room one floor below the sanctuary, Lincoln's failed proposal to compensate states that freed their slaves hangs above the settee where he drafted it. A room next door holds letters from Mary Lincoln to the church's then-Rev. Gurley. Seventeen Presidents have worshipped here. Modern Presidents who attended services here, like Carter and occasionally Reagan, have preferred to sit where Lincoln did. (Tours given Tues.-Sun. 9am-5pm)

ALONG 14TH AND 15TH ST.

Washington's branch of the **National Aquarium,** the nation's first, cowers in the basement of the Commerce Department building, at 14th St. and Constitution Ave. NW (482-2825; Metro: Federal Triangle; enter on 14th St.). Kids will stare yearningly at the 60-odd small tanks of exotic sea creatures and delight in the "touch tanks." The saltwater fishes' vibrant colors and wild shapes (some flat as pancakes, others round as marbles) will keep you watching. Look for the obese catfish, the four lumbering sharks (non-vegetarian, man-eating variety), and the disappointingly petite American alligators. Models and placards make the aquarium easy to understand. This National Aquarium is less sophisticated, and less spectacular than the one in Baltimore; many tanks are empty and the fish often look bored. On the other hand, the air-conditioned basement provides shelter from Washington's summer weather. (Open daily 9am-5pm. Popular feedings at 2pm daily: sharks Mon., Wed., Sat.; piranhas Tues., Thurs., Sun. Admission $2, children/seniors 75¢.)

The renovated **Willard Hotel** (628-9100) spreads its silvery finery over 1401 Pennsylvania Ave. NW like an engraved announcement of its century-old marriage to the rich and influential. President Grant hung out in the hotel's carpeted, chandeliered lobby, where office- and favor-seekers came to plead their cases. Ever since then, the Washington representatives of companies and causes have been called **"lobbyists."** (Now you know.) Peek inside today and listen to the rumble: it's the sound of the suited people making deals in the lobby. Some things never change.

Next to Freedom Plaza, **Pershing Park** provides the corner of Pennsylvania Ave. and 15th St. NW with a refreshing fountain and pool. A statue of General John "Black Jack" Pershing, leader of U.S. forces in World War I, stands triumphant among marble slabs whose blue and pink tracings map his battles. Today the General's battle sights are a haven for youths on skateboards.

Old Downtown ends at 15th St. NW with the **Treasury Building,** a Greek Revival monolith with all the **charm of an iceberg.** Adding insult to injury, its north wing breaks the long arm of Pennsylvania Ave. and blocks the White House from view. The stone-faced statue of Alexander Hamilton (America's first Secretary of the Treasury) offers no consolation. (To reach the President's residence, walk north along 15th St. one block until Pennsylvania Ave. reappears.) The building's imposing presence in the corporate end of Old Downtown is a constant reminder to big business that no matter how much money they make, the government will always have more.

■■■ WHITE HOUSE AREA AND FOGGY BOTTOM

Metro: Foggy Bottom/GWU.

Before the Civil War, when most of Washington remained undeveloped, the White House anchored its own neighborhood: socialite circles and Cabinet secretaries liked to live around Lafayette Square, across from the President's House, or slightly farther up 16th St. NW. Since World War II, development on all sides has turned the White House from a center into a boundary: the blocks it occupies separate the lawyer-heavy Farragut to the north, the government-heavy Old Downtown to the east, Foggy Bottom to the west, and the Mall south of the Ellipse.

Though unscrupulous writers claim all of D.C. was "built on a swamp," only Foggy Bottom can truthfully carry that banner. The misty, low-lying swamp air gave the neighborhood its name before it was absorbed by heavy industry (and its fog-resembling pollutants) in the early 20th century. During World War II, while industrial contraction and government expansion swept manufacturing out of Northwest, the State Department took up quarters here at 23rd and C St. NW. Just as "the Pentagon" means the Defense Department, "Foggy Bottom" has become journalese for State; the neighborhood's old name now suggests the intellectual fog and diplomatic doublespeak in which the State Department indulges. Today's Foggy Bottom rolls from 15th St. NW to the Potomac River, and from I St. to Constitution Ave. New Hampshire Ave., Pennsylvania Ave., K St. NW, and 23rd St. NW all meet at **Washington Circle,** where ol' George is situated on his horse. Near the Mall, government departments butt headquarters with old, respectable organizations in an unbroken sprawl of gardens, columns, and statuary. Above F St., George Washington University competes for breathing room with cheap hotels and moderately priced townhouses. Farther east, the low-rise office buildings of Farragut edge closer and closer to their target in the White House.

THE WHITE HOUSE

The White House, at 1600 Pennsylvania Ave. NW (456-7041, TDD 456-6213), isn't Versailles; the President's house, with its simple columns and expansive lawns, seems a compromise between patrician lavishness and democratic simplicity. In 1792 Thomas Jefferson suggested a contest to design the President's residence. But Jefferson's own diagrams lost out to James Hoban's more regal plan when then-President George Washington judged the competition. John Adams was the first chief executive to actually live in Hoban's structure, and Jefferson himself became the first to build additions. All this work was ruined when the British burned down the house, and much of Washington, in 1814; First Lady Dolly Madison interrupted her dinner to flee the flames, taking with her one of Gilbert Stuart's famous portraits of Washington. The White House has boasted wheelchair access since at least 1933, when FDR, who needed it, took office. (He also installed a swimming pool.) Martin Van Buren, who fenced off the lawns, started keeping the White House gardens spic-and-span; 120 years later, Jacqueline Kennedy made the Rose Garden famous, spurring later journalists to call Gerald Ford's stay-at-home reelection effort the "Rose Garden Campaign" in 1976. (Voters, who never promised him a Rose Garden, replaced Ford with Jimmy Carter.)

Despite remodelings in 1902 and 1948, the central third of the Executive Mansion looks more or less as Hoban planned it (he didn't design the East and West Wings). The White House is home to press conferences, state receptions, busloads of security guards, and even the occasional Presidential nap. When the President is in town, an American flag flies over his house. The President's personal staff works on his speeches and schedules and such in the West Wing, while the First Lady's cohort occupies the East Wing. The President does his own paperwork (and sometimes makes televised speeches) in the famous Oval Office. Helicopters land on the White House lawn to spirit him away to conferences and vacations. One façade stays floodlit all night for the benefit of TV news reporters. Big lawns, fences, long driveways, and closed gates discourage terrorists; if you wait long enough, though, you can sometimes glimpse Clinton himself through the bushes.

You may **tour** certain rooms at the White House after obtaining a free ticket at the ticket booth at the northeast corner of the **Ellipse,** the park south of the White House on Constitution Ave. between 15th and 18th St. NW. To be sure of obtaining a ticket during the peak tourist season, arrive at the Ellipse by 7:30am. (Disabled visitors can go straight to the Pennsylvania Ave. entrance without an admission ticket.) After you get a ticket, you'll wait about 2½ hours for the tour. (Tours Tues.-Sat. 10am-noon; tickets distributed starting at 8am). American citizens can arrange a more comprehensive and intimate tour of the White House through their Congresspeople; write to or call your Congressperson several months in advance.

The regular (non-Congressional) tour is guarded, but unguided; you might try posing your questions to the Secret Service guards. You'll start on the ground floor of the East Wing; the **lobby** here contains a portrait of the late Jacqueline Kennedy

Onassis with roses and a sign saying "In Memoriam." The **China Room** betrays the changes in American taste and style through a display of the long succession of presidential china. The **Diplomatic Reception Room** is notable for its wallpaper: Jackie Kennedy, well-known for her preservational instincts, practically ran out in front of the wrecking ball to salvage it from a derelict mansion. Upstairs, the **East Room** has been used for the wakes of those presidents who died in office. It also served as a suitable spot for Abigail Adams's clothesline, Susan Ford's senior prom, and Teddy Roosevelt's favorite boxing and wrestling matches. Look for the portrait of Washington that Dolly Madison so heroically saved. The **Blue Room,** said to be the White House's most beautiful, frequently receives ambassadors paying their first formal visits to the president. The furniture set, purchased by President Monroe, is not complete; a later President thought it was ugly and sold it off. Furniture-savior Jackie Kennedy found the sofa in a garage in Georgetown. The **Red Room** is red; it also displays a painting of Philadelphia's Independence Hall that was lost at one point, then recovered (not, this time, by Jackie Kennedy) in Bombay, India, where it sold for $7. The **State Dining Room** entertains large groups of guests, such as the Queen of England and her entourage. Its gold and white elegance served hunter Theodore Roosevelt when he mounted his trophies there. An obsolete bomb shelter under the Treasury building, built during World War II, connects to the White House by a tunnel under the East Lawn; aides in-the-know use the tunnel as a quick exit to 15th St. NW. You probably won't see the President, but you can find out where he is; call 456-2343 for his daily schedule. You can get to the White House from anywhere downtown by walking towards 16th St. NW along Pennsylvania Ave. (Metro: McPherson Square, Vermont Ave. exit.)

Near the White House

Due south of the White House, the empty grass of the **Ellipse** sometimes fills up with political demonstrators or congregating tour groups. A small granite shaft in the Ellipse bears the names of the 18 landowners who gave up their plantations so D.C. could be built. Directly in front of the White House, where the green grass meets E St. NW, Washington's Zero Milestone provides tangible evidence of early surveyors.

Sometimes it's hard to tell the homeless, the political demonstrators, and the statues apart in **Lafayette Park,** across Pennsylvania Ave., north of the White House. All three are more-or-less permanent presences, with the "Peace Park" denizens on the one-square-block park's southeast edge promising to stay there (in their sleeping bags) until the U.S. gives up nukes—not soon. Clark Mills's stone-faced Andrew Jackson stands in the center of the park. All of Jackson's companion statues represent Revolutionary War heroes, reminders that the U.S. could not have won its independence without help from foreign lands. The Marquis de Lafayette joined Jackson in 1891, on the southeast (15th and Pennsylvania) corner of the park. A half-dressed woman (France?) hands him his sword. (An old joke has the lady saying, "Give me back my clothes, and I'll give you back your sword.") At the southwest corner of the park, notice Lady Liberty brandishing her sword and—oops!—nearly stabbing the American Eagle to death. Although the eagle jumps back with a screech and a squawk, Lafayette's compatriot Rochambeau doesn't notice: he's too busy pointing to the southwest. Polish Brigadier Thaddeus Kosciuszko, who fortified West Point and Saratoga for the Continental Army, defends the northeast corner, and Baron Von Steuben, who trained American troops at Valley Forge, drills pedestrians from the northwest corner (and looks like a cross between John Wayne and Elvis).

St. John's Church, at 16th and H St. NW (347-8766), at the north end of Lafayette Park, is known as the Church of Presidents; each one since Madison has dropped in at least once. The ubiquitous Benjamin Latrobe designed it for free; look for his half-moon windows. President Clinton sometimes attends the 8:30am service. (Open daily 9am-3pm. Tour after Sun. service.)

Though Benjamin Latrobe (of U.S. Capitol fame) designed it, **Decatur House,** 748 Jackson Place NW at the west end of Lafayette Park (842-0920; enter on H St.)

retains mostly historical interest. (Metro: Farragut West or Farragut North.) Naval hero Stephen Decatur, the navy's youngest captain ever, defeated the Barbary Pirates and captured the top British frigate during the war of 1812 before he moved in; after only one year in his new house, Decatur died in a duel with a former military mentor. During the 1830s and 40s, hotelier John Gadsby entertained Washington's elite in the ballrooms while he kept slaves chained behind the house. In 1871 the house was purchased by Edward Beale, best remembered for having carried official news of the Gold Rush to Washington in a frontiersman disguise. The Beales were responsible for most of the later improvements to the house, including the elegant inlaid floors and "Romantic eclectic" furnishing (in evidence in the upper drawing room). The first floor, decorated in the Federal style, displays Decatur's furnishings, carefully selected to impress. The salon has big windows and a tiny fireplace, but it was well heated in the winter during cocktail hour, called "crush or squeeze" back then. Walk-in tours, provided immediately, last about 40 minutes. (Open Tues.-Fri. 10am-3pm, Sat.-Sun. noon-4pm. Admission $3, seniors, students, and children $1.50. Large gift shop (842-1856) open Mon.-Fri. 10am-5pm, Sat.-Sun. noon-4pm.)

Blair House, 1651-53 Pennsylvania Ave. NW, near the southwest corner of Lafayette Park, hosts foreign dignitaries who visit Washington; see if there's a guest by looking for Secret Service agents and diplomatic limousines. Harry Truman lived here during White House renovations; a plaque on the wrought-iron gates remembers a guard who saved him from a would-be assassin by "taking a bullet." The house is not open to the public.

On the same block, the **Renwick Gallery,** at 17th St. and Pennsylvania Ave. NW, devotes itself to "American craft," an amazingly broad artistic category which includes all manner of original, off-beat objects. (See **Museums & Galleries,** p. 201.)

The **Old Executive Office Building,** at 17th St. and Pennsylvania Ave. NW, amazes pedestrians with its gingerbread complexity; President Truman called it "the greatest monstrosity in America." Cascades of small plain columns, tall chimneys, an endless array of mini-colonnades, pediments, and porches give the Second Empire-styled building its Baroque distinction. Cannons flank the entrance steps. On weekdays, you'll have to stand outside and stare. Since the building continues to house White House staff, tours only happen on Saturdays. Tour-takers will gasp at the Indian treaty room's marble wall panels, 800-pound bronze lamps, and gold ornamentation. Gilded domes and frilly balustrades grace much of the interior. The ornate front side is currently obscured by scaffolding, as extensive roof renovation is underway (to be completed in 1997). To schedule a free tour, call 395-5895 a few weeks in advance.

A Capital Paradox

Sign-toting demonstrators used to congregate on the White House side of Pennsylvania Ave. until the Secret Service punted them across the street. But during 1995, a number of bizarre breaches in security (one man crashed a plane into the White House; one fired a gun at the President's home; several people hopped the fence and made it onto the White House lawn before being restrained by Secret Servicemen) led to tighter security measures. Pennsylvania Ave. is now closed to commercial traffic. The plan was to reroute the masses away from the White House, but paradoxically the masses have inched even closer. Protesters and tourists now crowd in the street up to the gates of the White House—exactly the opposite of what was intended.

WEST OF THE ELLIPSE

The **Organization of American States,** at 17th St. and Constitution Ave. NW, across the street from the southwest corner of the Ellipse (information 458-3000, museum/gallery 458-6016), is a Latin American extravaganza: dappled sunlight engulfs its air-conditioned center, where a fountain gurgles over greenery. The patio's tiles copy traditional pre-Colombian designs. During parades, the OAS locks up so that would-be snipers have no opportunity to take advantage of its strategic rooftop position. (Metro: Farragut West.)

The OAS's main-floor art gallery is small but fresh, displaying 20th-century art from Central and South America. Upstairs are the OAS **meeting rooms,** which hold formal sessions. The meetings, held largely in Spanish, welcome curious tourists; Spanish-less visitors can hook up to translation machines. (Call to ask when they're in session.) Peek into as many rooms as are open and admire grand Tiffany chandeliers and ornately reliefed ceilings. Or wander through the **Hall of the Americas** (more of a pleasant open-air atrium than a hall), which is decorated by the flags of the OAS member nations and busts of their founders. The flags hang in alphabetical order according to their nations' Spanish names. Downstairs and outside, the God of Flowers, Xochipilli, whom the Aztecs honored with hallucinogenic feasts and sacrificial frenzies, reclines in the **Aztec Garden.** The garden path leads to the Museum of the Americas, a collection of art from Mexico, Peru, Brazil, and other member states. The two-story building houses a permanent collection of modern art, as well as several temporary exhibits each year. (OAS open Mon.-Fri. 10am-5pm. Free.)

If you can find the entrance at 1776 D St. NW, the **Daughters of the American Revolution Museum** (628-1776) will open historical doors for you—more than 33, in fact. (Metro: Farragut West, then walk south on 17th St.) The building complex is the largest block of buildings in the world entirely owned, operated, and payed for by women. Follow a docent around the Beaux-Arts Memorial Centennial Hall to see 33 period rooms, each room conceived, designed, and furnished by the DARs of a different state to illuminate early American lifestyles. New Jersey's room, for instance, is furnished with the remains of a sunken ship, downed in the Battle of Red Bank. Even the anchor and chain were used; their iron has been transformed into a gargantuan lighting fixture. California's tri-cultural room incorporates Chinese vases, Mexican serapes, and American horsehair furniture. Check out the cavernous library: now a home for books on genealogy, it once hosted the first meeting ever on the subject of arms limitation (after World War I). The DAR insignia (hanging over the obligatory portrait of George Washington) was made from a cannonball from the Battle of Saratoga. Call the DAR's Education Office for a guided tour. (Museum open Mon.-Fri. 8:30am-4pm, Sun. 1-5pm. Tours Mon.-Fri. 10am-2:30pm, Sun. 1-4:30pm. Free. Library open Mon.-Fri. 9am-4pm. Entrance for the disabled at 1775 C St.)

Adjoining the building is **Constitution Hall,** located on 18th St. between C and D St. NW (638-2661). This 4000-seat auditorium holds concerts and ceremonies, and is also where the DAR's President General presides over her Continental Congress. Draped from the box sections of the U-shaped amphitheater are the buff and blue of the DAR State seals. Tapestries of Revolutionary moments, like the Boston Tea Party and George Washington's inauguration, dangle over the stage. It's been used for patriotic purposes and civic occasions, though it's most famous for an unpatriotic one: in 1939 the DAR wouldn't let African-American soprano Marian Anderson sing here, so she sang from the steps of the Lincoln Memorial.

The **American Red Cross** at 17th and E St. NW (737-8300) looks out of Tiffany stained-glass windows that deserve a look. Inside the east building's bronze doors, a receptionist will point you first to a video on CPR, then up the marble staircase, where Hiram Powers's busts of Faith, Hope, and Charity abide. In the second-floor assembly room, Louis Tiffany's stained glass portrays figures from Spenser's *Faerie Queene:* Filomena, virtuous Una, and of course, Redcrosse the knight. (Open Mon.-Fri. 9am-4pm. Free.)

Once housed in the Renwick's mansion, the **Corcoran Gallery of Art,** Washington's oldest art museum, now displays works by the likes of Thomas Cole and Roy Lichtenstein in much larger, Neoclassical quarters on 17th St. between E St. and New York Ave. NW, just north of the Red Cross building. (Metro: Farragut West. See **Museums & Galleries,** p. 202.)

Completely surrounded by the American Institute of Architects (AIA), **The Octagon,** 1799 New York Ave. NW at 18th St. (638-3105), continues the Foggy Bottom tradition of hiding historic houses among office buildings. (Metro: Farragut West; walk down 18th St.) Arrive at the right moment, and an expert will guide you around the house; grab an "Exterior Walking Tour" pamphlet as well, and you'll feel like an architectural expert yourself before the hour is through. The Madisons fled here when British troops torched the White House in 1814; they spared the Octagon, probably because the French ambassador flew his nation's flag over the house. Despite its name, the house is hexagonal; a tower in one corner interrupts its geometry. The table on which the Treaty of Ghent was signed is here; it's a curious furnishing, with 12 ivory-inlaid drawers marked "receipts," "bills paid," and "letters." Dolly Madison, a suicidal slave girl, and Colonel Taylor's daughter are some of the ghosts said to roam the Octagon. The house just underwent a massive renovation project. On display in the cellar is a collection of artifacts uncovered by recent excavations, from old fibers and china to more recent plastic cups. (Open Tues.-Sun. 10am-4pm. Admission $3, seniors and children $2.) Exhibits continue in the modern AIA building behind The Octagon, and the **AIA Bookstore** is worth a visit. Open Mon.-Wed. and Fri. 8:30am-5pm, Thurs. 8:30am-6:30pm.

The **Department of the Interior** (208-4743) covers a square area on C St. NW between 18th and 19th and extends to D St. Franklin Roosevelt laid the cornerstone for the building in 1936, using the same trowel George Washington employed to lay the Capitol's cornerstone in 1793. The National Park Service desk spews helpful brochures about forests and outfitters. Sign in and present ID to a guard at the main entrance on 18th and C St. and walk down the hallway. To the right is the park office; to the left is the Interior Department's museum. Enter here to learn how to make a topographic map, look at fossils, and follow dioramas portraying the "opening" of the American West. Museum open Mon.-Fri. 8am-5pm.

The **Federal Reserve** counts its change in a heavy-set, clean-lined building on Constitution Ave. between 20th and 21st St. NW. The Federal Reserve Board and its head, Alan Greenspan, control the nation's money supply; they decide how much dough there should be and what interest rates major banks should pay when they borrow it. The actual greenbacks sleep in regional banks in Boston, New York, Cleveland, Dallas, and San Francisco (among other cities); this building is just where the Board meets and has its offices, and where some economic research takes place. Paul Cret's skimpy temple to Mammon has the settled, staid look of established wealth. An eagle on the lintel oversees hundreds of square feet of flatness (and hundreds of rollerbladers) in front.

The **National Academy of Sciences,** at 21st and C St. NW, one block from the Fed (enter on Constitution Ave.; 334-2000), holds lots of really smart people. It also holds space for art exhibits, and a fantastic heliocentric gold-tiled dome decorated with ancient Greek philosophical types. Dangling from its center is a bizarre pendulum swinging over an Egyptian-inspired pedestal. When all of this starts to lose its goofy novelty, ask the guard at the front desk to slide aside the massive bronze doors to reveal eight panels, each of which depicts an important scientific personality, from Aristotle to Einstein. Then head out to the corner of 22nd St. NW and Constitution Ave., where the beloved physicist sits above a star map: the 28-ft. field of emerald pearl granite holds metal studs that represent the planets, sun, moon, and stars. Einstein's aphorisms are carved on the back of his bench. (Notice that the man who formulated the Theory of Relativity seems to be wearing Tevas.) Open Mon.-Fri. 8:30am-5pm.

Few collections of American furniture and art compare with that of the **State Department,** 21st and C St. (647-3241), whose cement HQ extends to 23rd St. (Metro: Foggy Bottom-GWU.) You must reserve a space on the 45-minute guided tour to see the inside of the State Department. The free tours fill up very quickly; call at least a month in advance. The original walls of the reception rooms were avocado-green, with floor-to-ceiling windows, wall-to-wall carpeting, and exposed steel beams. The undiplomatic decor prompted 1960s Secretary of State Dean Rusk to launch Project Americana, in which the State accumulated Boston highboys and lowboys, Chippendale chairs, paintings of Washington, and other cute items made between 1750 and 1825. There's a portrait of Thomas Jefferson in a toga; a highboy capped by a bust of political thinker John Locke; and the desk where Thomas Jefferson wrote the Declaration of Independence and Nixon signed Constitutional Amendment #26, giving 18-year-olds the vote. The Benjamin Franklin dining room makes a spectacle of itself in mauve and gold; the French carpet took a whole weekend to lay. (Tours of diplomatic reception rooms Mon.-Fri. 9:30am, 10:30am, and 2:45pm; call for reservations. Strollers not permitted. "Tour not recommended for children under 12.")

Foggy Bottom north of F St. is the province of **George Washington University** (994-GWGW or 994-4949). The Visitor Center desk in the Academic Center, at 801 22nd St. NW (enter at H St.), gives away brochures, newspapers, and *The Big To Do*, an entertainment calendar.

Across G St. NW from the Kennedy Center, at the western end of Virginia Ave., the looming black-and-white half-cylinders of the **Watergate** buildings (offices, apartments, and a luxury hotel) seem to bend away from the White House, toward the Potomac River. The Watergate scandal took its name from these buildings—the office space housed the Democratic National Committee's headquarters when Nixon ordered them burgled in 1972. Find the statue of Mexican hero and former president **Benito Juarez** across Virginia Ave. near G St. Enter the Watergate complex just behind Benito, between the North and South lobbies. There you'll find a pleasant lowered courtyard of fountains and shops. The boring building at 25th and F St. NW is the **Embassy of Saudi Arabia.** Clothed in white marble with black panels, the embassy is T-shaped, and that's about it.

THE KENNEDY CENTER

Above Rock Creek Parkway, the white rectilinear **John F. Kennedy Center for the Performing Arts** (Tickets and information 467-4600, TDD 416-8524) rises and glows like a marble sarcophagus. (Metro: Foggy Bottom-GWU, then walk away from downtown on H St. and turn left, or south, onto New Hampshire Ave.; pedestrian entrance off 25th St. at the end of New Hampshire Ave. NW.) Built in the late 1960s, the center boasts four major stages and a film theater; its sumptuous interior rolls out wall-to-wall red carpets under mirrors, bronze busts, and crystal chandeliers. Many nations have donated rooms, free-standing art, and other materials in memory of JFK. Student tickets, sometimes well-discounted, make taking in a show here possible on most budgets. Before entering the Kennedy Center, stop at the parking lot to marvel at A. Teno's 1976 contorted statue of Don Quixote. Stop again to view Jurgen Weber's bronze reliefs, located outside the east ends of the Hall of Nations and Hall of States, respectively (see below).

Almost everything in the Kennedy Center has a self-explanatory name. State flags hang in the **Hall of States** in the order in which they joined the Union. Stop at the **Information Desk** as you enter, and make a mental note of the **American Film Institute Theater** on your right (for more on the Theater, see Entertainment & Nightlife: Movies). Continue on to the west end of the Hall to borrow equipment for the hearing impaired (free). In the **Hall of Nations,** the flags of all nations with which the U.S. has diplomatic relations hang in alphabetical order. Look for an empty pole next to Ireland's and Israel's banners to see if the Iraqi flag has been put back up (watch out for neck strain). Both grand halls lead to the **Grand Foyer,** which could swallow the Washington Monument with room to spare. A rather unsavory 7-ft. bronze bust of JFK stares up at 18 ponderous Swedish chandeliers.

In the **Concert Hall,** an audience of 2750 can hear up to 200 classical musicians. The President's box includes a reception room and a banner with his seal, which hangs from the balcony when he deigns to attend. The impressive organ has over 4144 pipes. The stage was a gift from over 692 high school, college, and community organizations from the U.S., Canada, Britain, and Japan. The National Symphony Orchestra calls the KenCen Concert Hall home. Kick back in the **Israeli Lounge** on the Box Tier of the Concert Hall (that means just outside it and up the stairs). The lounge's vivid turquoise, red, yellow, and olive ceiling depicts musical instruments. Admire the Hebrew message inlaid (in 24-carat gold) in the wooden wall mosaic; intricate sepia sketches adorn the other walls. Carved from a 700-year-old tree, 12-ft.-high, intricate Nigerian doors lead into the **African Room.** Tapestries, ornate bowls, print cloth, and reliefs show off the continent's traditions.

If no rehearsals are in progress, you can visit the opulent, all-red **Opera House.** Snowflake-shaped chandeliers, gifts from Austria, cover a 70-ft.-diameter circular space and require 1735 electric light bulbs. Japan's more sensible gift, the red silk curtain, adds to the grandeur. A Waterford crystal chandelier, with 4000 perfectly matched prisms, hangs from 22-carat gold-leaf ceiling panels in the **South Opera Lounge.** This lounge also holds two hand-woven Spanish tapestries, copies of paintings by Goya. When red turns to purple on the roof level, you're near the Terrace Theater, an acoustic marvel and home to an excellent chamber-music series. Art scattered about the Center's levels ranges from blast-damaged sheet metal polished to a glow to tapestries depicting the seven days of creation. Greece donated a bronze casting of a statue discovered beneath the Aegean Sea. Henri Matisse designed France's gift, a set of blue and white tapestries.

The **Eisenhower Theatre** is the smallest of the main-floor theaters, seating only 1100 people. The steep angle of the seats, which are made of East Indian laurel wood, to the stage can be slightly unnerving. Comic operas, Classical Greek plays, and small productions are performed here.

The Roof Terrace Restaurant would bankrupt almost anyone, but you can walk along the outdoor **roof terrace** itself for free. Acrophiles will especially enjoy the view of the Watergate complex, the spires of Georgetown, and Roosevelt Island. The terrace becomes unbeatable around 10pm for an hour of nighttime skyline-watching. You can bring food up here, too.

Excellent disabled access includes provisions for sight- and hearing-impaired audience members; all theaters are wheelchair-accessible. (Center open daily 10am-midnight. Free tours 10am-1pm, every 15min.) Parking in the commercial basement lot is available for short- and long-term visits.

■■■ GEORGETOWN

The heights in this neighborhood, above the Potomac River, are very picturesque and are free, I should conceive, from some of the insalubrities of Washington.

—Charles Dickens, American Notes *(1842)*

Metroless: closest stations are Foggy Bottom/GWU or Dupont Circle (both 15 min. walk).

At once residential and commercial, bustling Georgetown offers a much-needed respite to those wearied by the gleaming white halls of power and colossal museums that are Washington's tourist industry staples. Petite restaurants and overpriced shops, rowdy saloons, and a smattering of nightclubs crowd together along Wisconsin Avenue and M Street NW, anxious for the patronage of tourists, students, and Georgetown's upscale locals alike. To the west, Georgetown University students quaff kegs and study a mere bus ride away from the residence of their alma mater's most famous alumnus, Bill Clinton (class of '68). Georgetown serves well its eponymous university, obliging students with all-night food and late-night record stores, international newspapers and magazines, and easy access to the halls of power just over the Pennsylvania Ave. bridge. Residential Georgetown, a genteel neighborhood whose small scale and steep brick-lined streets lend it a decidedly European flavor, provides the glue that holds the commericial and academic together. Behind the tidy windows of its resplendent old townhouses, the capital's ossified A-list Establishment carries on its salon life as it has since the city's early days. Only the dullest figures of the Clinton administration, led by the numbing Secretary of State

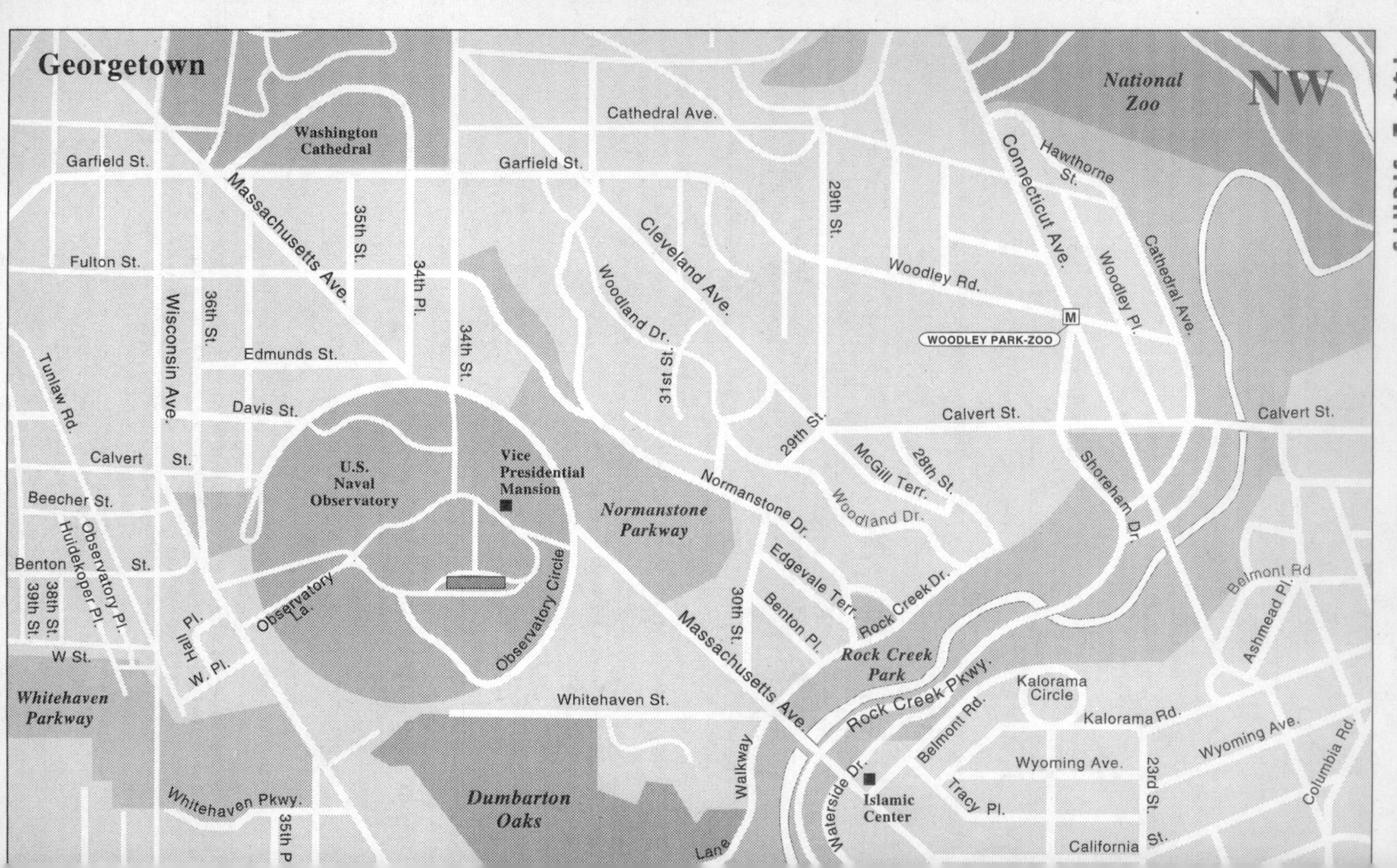
Georgetown
National Zoo
NW
Cathedral Ave.
Washington Cathedral
Garfield St.
Garfield St.
Massachusetts Ave.
35th St.
34th Pl.
34th St.
Fulton St.
Wisconsin Ave.
36th St.
Edmunds St.
Tunlaw Rd.
Davis St.
Calvert St.
Beecher St.
Huidekoper Pl.
Observatory Pl.
Benton St.
38th St.
39th St.
W St.
Hall Pl.
W. Pl.
Whitehaven Parkway
U.S. Naval Observatory
Vice Presidential Mansion
Observatory La.
Observatory Circle
Normanstone Parkway
Whitehaven St.
Whitehaven Pkwy.
35th P
Dumbarton Oaks
Lane
Walkway
Cleveland Ave.
Woodland Dr.
31st St.
29th St.
29th St.
Woodley Rd.
M
WOODLEY PARK-ZOO
Connecticut Ave.
Hawthorne St.
Woodley Pl.
Cathedral Ave.
Calvert St.
Calvert St.
McGill Terr.
28th St.
Woodland Dr.
Normanstone Dr.
Shoreham Dr.
Edgevale Terr.
Rock Creek Dr.
Benton Pl.
30th St.
Massachusetts Ave.
Rock Creek Park
Rock Creek Pkwy.
Belmont Rd.
Ashmead Pl.
Kalorama Circle
Kalorama Rd.
Belmont Rd.
Wyoming Ave.
Wyoming Ave.
Columbia Rd.
23rd St.
Tracy Pl.
Waterside Dr.
Islamic Center
California St.

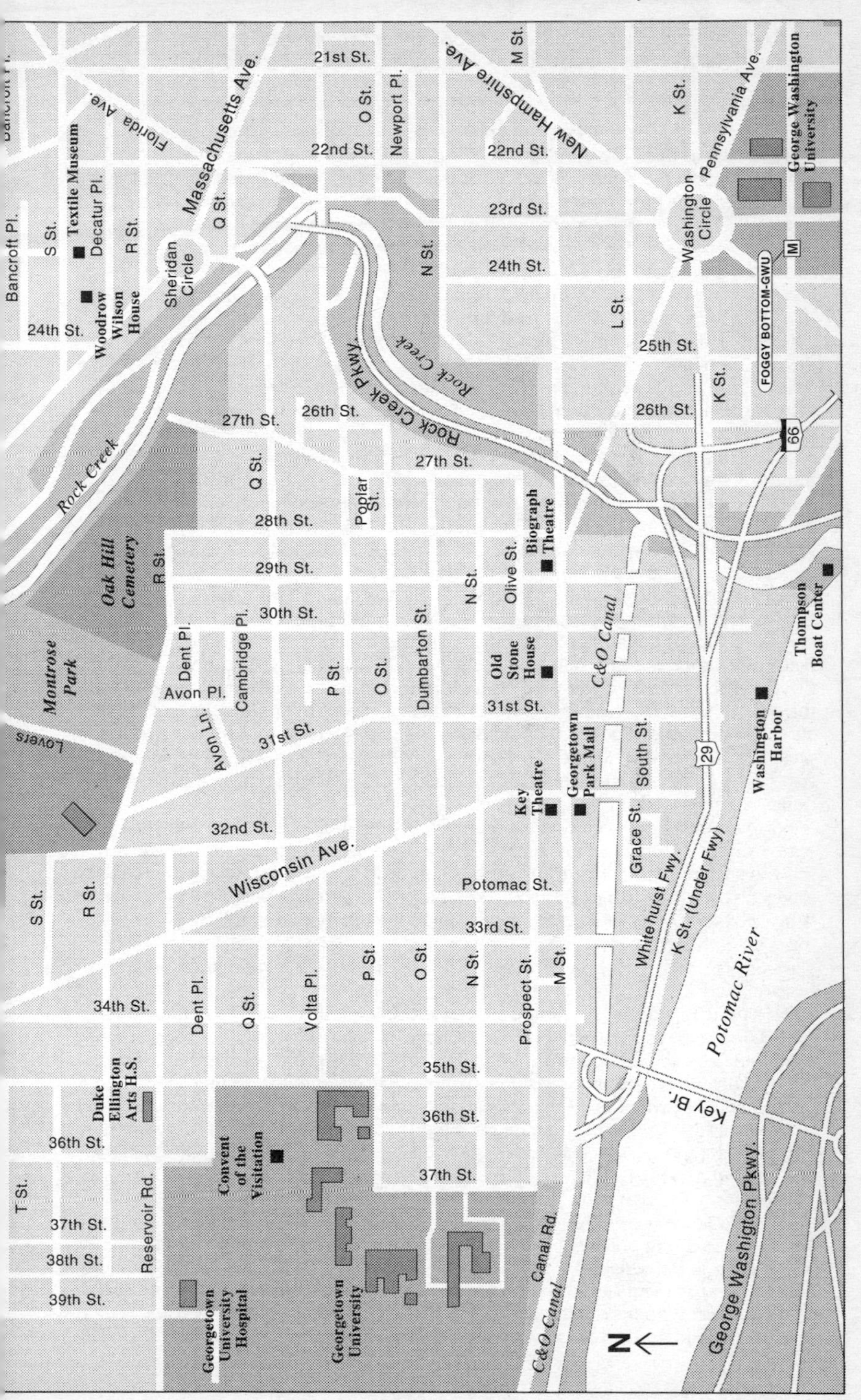
21st St.
M St.
New Hampshire Ave.
Massachusetts Ave.
O St.
Newport Pl.
Florida Ave.
Textile Museum
22nd St.
22nd St.
K St.
Pennsylvania Ave.
George Washington University
Bancroft Pl.
S St.
Decatur Pl.
R St.
Q St.
23rd St.
Washington Circle
Sheridan Circle
N St.
24th St.
Woodrow Wilson House
24th St.
FOGGY BOTTOM-GWU
L St.
Rock Creek
Rock Creek Pkwy.
25th St.
K St.
26th St.
26th St.
27th St.
27th St.
66
Rock Creek
Q St.
Poplar St.
Biograph Theatre
28th St.
Oak Hill Cemetery
R St.
29th St.
N St.
Olive St.
30th St.
C&O Canal
Thompson Boat Center
Montrose Park
Dent Pl.
Cambridge Pl.
Dumbarton St.
Old Stone House
Avon Pl.
P St.
O St.
31st St.
Lovers
Avon Ln.
31st St.
Georgetown Park Mall
South St.
29
Washington Harbor
Key Theatre
32nd St.
Grace St.
Wisconsin Ave.
Whitehurst Fwy.
K St. (Under Fwy)
S St.
R St.
Potomac St.
33rd St.
P St.
O St.
N St.
M St.
Prospect St.
Potomac River
34th St.
Dent Pl.
Q St.
Volta Pl.
35th St.
Duke Ellington Arts H.S.
Key Br.
36th St.
36th St.
Convent of the Visitation
37th St.
T St.
37th St.
Reservoir Rd.
38th St.
Canal Rd.
39th St.
Georgetown University Hospital
Georgetown University
C&O Canal
N
George Washington Pkwy.

Warren Christopher, have moved here. All the hipsters have long since drifted to Adams-Morgan or Kalorama, but old Georgetown does not care.

HISTORY

In 1702 Queen Anne of England granted the "Rock of Dunbarton," a huge blob of land, to Ninian Beall. By the 1730s the Beall family was complaining to the colonial government about "squatters" on its land at the edge of the Potomac. The "squatters"—Scottish merchants—founded the town of George, after George II of England. The town was incorporated in 1789, the same year of the inauguration of Georgetown University. The port brought the new town commerce and people; as the farthest point up the Potomac to which a ship could travel, Georgetown proved ideal for the sorting and shipping of tobacco from Virginia and Maryland. Not until the 1800s were the Bealls fully paid for their land.

Georgetown has been referred to as the 'parent of the Federal City' since Suter's Tavern, a no-longer-extant local watering hole, was thought to have hosted George Washington and his cohorts as they negotiated the establishment of a Capital City. (The same pub was later used by Pierre L'Enfant and Andrew Elicott when the two were laying out plans for the Capital.)

As the only existing town within the District's limits, Georgetown was the logical hangout for Washington's first bigwigs—while much of central Washington remained unbuilt, Georgetown prospered. Most of its Federal-style buildings were erected between 1780 and 1830, when the port was thriving. You can still distinguish the smaller townhouses below Dumbarton St., built for the workers, from the larger houses of upper Georgetown (around R and S St.).

Georgetown's incarnation as a harbor town was colorful but short-lived. In 1828 President John Quincy Adams turned the first shovelful of dirt for the Chesapeake and Ohio (C&O) Canal. The same day that Adams opened the canal dig, workers in Baltimore drove the first spike for the Baltimore and Ohio Railroad, whose steam-driven efficiency KO'd the C&O as a commercial route. Although the canal still thrived in the 1870s, steamships of the next decade couldn't fit into the harbor; after an 1889 flood, ports such as those in Baltimore and Norfolk—not to mention Southwest Washington—rendered Georgetown's harbor obsolete. The canal survives as part of the national park system; long-winded bicyclists have replaced barge-pulling mules along its towpaths.

Washington's free Black population nearly doubled between 1830 and 1861, and many African-Americans moved here: D.C.'s first Black congregation, the still-active Mt. Zion United Methodist Church, was also an Underground Railroad station for slaves on their way to a free Canada. Yet, despite its proximity to the Union capital, White Georgetown was a determinedly Confederate city during the Civil War, buzzing with Southern spies.

As Georgetown's economy faltered, working-class black families took quarters in historic mansions subdivided into apartments. Employed as domestics, cooks, and stable attendants to the remaining estates, more than 1000 families occupied "Herring Hill" (south of P St. between Rock Creek Park and 29th St.), so called because residents subsisted on fish from the harbor. In the early 20th century Georgetown was racially integrated and unfashionable; the first Washington zoning act labeled it "industrial." But when FDR's New Deal (masterminded by his "Brain Trust" at 3238 R Street) and World War II nearly doubled the number of federal jobs, the new white-collar (and white) civil servants invaded Georgetown. Black families sold their homes, and African-American culture moved downtown.

Today only the rich can afford the inflated real estate, and only the chic feel the need to do so. Trace the history of those who have resided in Georgetown to get a feel for the shifting political winds. John F. Kennedy lived here as a U.S. Senator (at 3260 N St.), as did Senator John Warner and his wife Liz Taylor. A smattering of rent-controlled apartments around Georgetown are inhabited largely by the unmonied; some of the townhouses between M St. and R St. have been subdivided and rented out to Georgetown University students and gaggles of interns, though others nearby may hide lovely inner courtyards and Warhols in every bathroom. Hollywood has found the area's geography mildly interesting, if not irresistible: movies set partly in Georgetown include *The Exorcist* and *St. Elmo's Fire.*

ORIENTATION

Wisconsin Ave. and **M St.** are the main thoroughfares, and their intersection (Washington's oldest) centers the neighborhood. Address numbers on Wisconsin Ave. start below M St. and go up as the avenue goes north (in this area, uphill). Numbered streets run parallel to Wisconsin and perpendicular to M, increasing east to west. For most of its Georgetown length, K St. is directly under the Whitehurst Freeway and thus hard to find on maps. (At twilight, enjoy the *Blade Runner* style view of the looming Whitehurst.) East of Georgetown is the K St. Business District and, north of that, the Dupont Circle neighborhood; Rock Creek Park provides a clear boundary. M St., Pennsylvania Ave., P St., and Q St. are the only ways to Georgetown for pedestrians coming from downtown or Dupont Circle. West of Key Bridge, M St. becomes Canal Road (leading to Bethesda, MD), and neon and brick abruptly give way to the trees and vines of Glover Archibold Park.

GETTING THERE

If you try to **park** your car in Georgetown, you just may send your brain into gridlock—weekends are particularly infamous. Try 35th St. near the university (particularly promising in summer) or Georgetown's eastern edge on the other side of Wisconsin Ave., around 28th St. Garages are wallet-draining (and are frequently full) but are conveniently located near the center of town. On weekend nights, choose a block and drive around in circles, scrounging for a place—raucous teens will miraculously arrive and drive their Mercedes off to the suburbs.

The nearest **Metro** stop, Foggy Bottom-GWU, is about eight long blocks from the center of Georgetown. When you exit the station, you'll find yourself facing 23rd St. NW. Turn left down 23rd and walk counterclockwise around Washington Circle against traffic until you reach Pennsylvania Ave.; then trudge down Pennsylvania over the bridge and to M St. From Dupont Circle, just follow P St. east, past Rock Creek Park, or, alternatively, walk southeast on New Hampshire Ave. and take a right onto M St. **Metrobuses** #30, 32, 34, 36, and T2 run from M St. up Wisconsin past Dumbarton Oaks and up to the Friendship Heights Metro and the Maryland border. Metrobuses tagged D go from Union Station to Georgetown via Dupont Circle. From Adams-Morgan, take the #42 bus (at Columbia Ave.) to Dupont Circle, then switch to the #G2 bus (at 20th and P St.) to Georgetown.

No Way Down

When Kevin Costner, in the movie *No Way Out,* escaped Pentagon nasties by racing deep into the bowels of the "Georgetown Metro," D.C. audiences laughed out loud. Persistent rumors claim that the Georgetown Citizens' Association vetoed a Georgetown Metro stop, illogically voting to clog their streets with other people's autos just to keep away carless proletarians. In fact, a Georgetown subway would have posed a prohibitive engineering problem—a 90-degree turn in an underground tunnel just at the water's edge.

HISTORIC GEORGETOWN

Away from Wisconsin Ave. and M St., genteel Georgetown just oozes old townhouses and historic properties. Many of these locations open themselves up to the curious public; others, like their reclusive residents, reveal no more than their aristocratic façades. The **Dumbarton Oaks** estate, at 1703 32nd St. NW between R and S St. (recorded info. 338-8278, tour info. 342-3212), includes two must-see sights: the mansion-museum, which displays Byzantine and pre-Columbian art, and the magnificent terraced gardens. (See **Museums & Galleries,** p. 202.)

George Washington's granddaughter slept at **Tudor Place,** 1644 31st St. (965-0400), south on 31st St. from Dumbarton Oaks between Q and R. Martha Custis Peter used the $7000 her grandfather willed her to purchase the property at 1644 31st St. and build this Neoclassical house, completed in 1816 and designed by William Thornton, an amateur architect whose previous credits included work on the U.S. Capitol. Mrs. Peter and a friend watched the British torch Washington in 1814 from what is now the dining room. The property passed through six successive generations until the last owner, Armistead Peter III, formed a foundation so that the house could be open to the public after his death (which was in 1984). The required tour lasts about an hour, but you can hang out in the gardens for longer. (Open by reservation only; tours Tues.-Fri. 10am, 11:30am, 1pm, 2:30pm. Sat. every hour, 10am-3pm. $5, $2.50 for students; gardens open Mon.-Sat. 10am-4pm).

The Federal-style **Dumbarton House,** 2715 Q St. (337-2288), displays 18th- and 19th-century furniture and decorative arts, and serves as headquarters for the National Society of the Colonial Dames of America. Relax in the garden free of charge, or let a genteel "dame" guide you around the immaculate house. (Guided tours Tues.-Sat. 10am-12:15pm; $3 admission, or $2.50 each for groups of 10 or more; students free.)

2803 P St. seems like every other house on the block. The fence seems like every other fence. But every stake of the **Gunbarrel Fence** is really a 1767 Charlevoix rifle barrel, with the rifle stocks buried in the retaining wall. Reuben Dawes, a stonecutter, built three houses (numbers 2803 to 2811) on this block of P St. in 1843 and used surplus Mexican War rifles to build his cheap fence. Some of the fence stakes have a small notch near the top—the rifle sight.

Mount Zion Methodist Church, 1334 29th St. (234-0148), was founded in 1816 by about 125 African-Americans. The church was a stop on the Underground Railroad; passengers sometimes hid in a vault on the Old Methodist Burying Ground (later to become the Mount Zion/Female Union Band Cemetery) a few blocks away. Today Mount Zion's congregation remains full and active, and its interior is just as it was in 1800. Behind the church at 2906 O St., the **Community House,** erected in 1810-11, holds old records, manuscripts, and photographs of past congregants, including Leontine Kelly, the first black woman to become a bishop. To see the Community House and Church, call ahead to make an appointment. The **Mount Zion Cemetery** and **Female Union Band Cemetery,** both at 27th St. NW and Mill Road NW, behind Q St., remain open to the public. In 1842 the Female Union Band, a benevolent association of women, purchased this plot for the burial of free blacks, thus establishing the first African-American cemetery in D.C. The Mt. Zion Methodist Church later rented (and renamed) the Old Methodist Burying Ground next to it "for the sum of one dollar in hand." The two cemeteries cannot be told apart today; both are sadly decayed and overgrown. You can still read some of the gravestones, some haunting or sad, others marked by sweet and gentle charm.

Unfortunately, Georgetown's only synagogue, the **Kesher Israel** at 2801 N St. NW, is not open for tours. Built in 1911 by local merchants, it does, however, offer services every morning and evening as well as a useful information line. Call 333-4808 for the latest on local **Kosher restaurants** and special hotel discounts (available to Kesher Israel congregants). The office administrator (333-2337) is another helpful source of information.

The only surviving pre-Revolutionary building still standing in Washington, the **Old Stone House** at 3051 M St. (426-6851) has been restored and refurbished with reproductions and relics of pre-Revolutionary Georgetown. Low doorways and lumpy beds provide an accurate indication of the colonists' height, as well as a sense of the rough "comfort" of colonial living. Rumors that Pierre L'Enfant lived here while designing the city helped convince Congress in 1950 to protect the house. The National Park Service demonstrates 18th-century cooking, bread-baking, candle-making, and fabric-spinning every so often (house open Wed.-Sun. 9am-5pm; tiny garden open April-Sept.; free).

Flag-lovers may be disappointed by the **Star-Spangled Banner Monument** at **Francis Scott Key Park** (at the southwestern corner of 34th and M St.); it's merely a circular trellis-like structure. The park marks the former site of Francis Scott Key's house with some benches and wild roses. But the namesake bridge over the **C&O Canal** affords a picturesque view of the sandy towpath.

GEORGETOWN UNIVERSITY

When Archbishop John Carroll learned where the new capital would be built, he rushed to found Georgetown University (main entrance at 37th and O St.), which opened in 1789 as the United States' first Catholic institution for higher learning. Reacting against the religious persecution which forced him to seek his own education in Europe, Carroll was anxious to welcome students of varied backgrounds, and even early Georgetown University classes boasted a religious mixture that would have turned many modern universities green with envy. (In spite of this religious tolerance and diversity, women were only admitted as recently as 1969.) Father Patrick Healy, who became President of Georgetown in 1873, was the first Black American to hold a Ph.D. He reorganized the college and graduate schools and began construction of the central Healy building (the one with the clock tower). Though today approximately 50% of the 6000 undergraduates are Catholic and a Jesuit brother resides in every dorm, students of many creeds and nations attend. Georgetown's undergraduate programs are rather pre-professional. Students enroll in one of five different schools: Business, Foreign Service, Language and Linguistics, Nursing, or the College of Arts and Sciences. The distinctions are purely academic, however: students of the several schools live, study, and party together. In addition to the five undergraduate schools, the University contains three graduate schools—Law, Medicine, and the Graduate School of Arts and Science. All facilities are located on the main Georgetown campus with the exception of the Law School (which makes its home in the midst of the nation's law-making bodies). With several dormitories as well as newly renovated apartment "villages" surrounding the U., Georgetown students have a substantial array of living options to choose from. On-campus living is required for the first two undergraduate years; guaranteed for three years; and possible for all four. Many students prefer to live off campus in the many townhouses that line the narrow, brick-paved streets which surround the U.

Georgetown's student body encompasses the usual array of 'types'—jocks, pre-professional grinds, intellectuals, and foreign politicos—but its proximity to the nation's political heart means a preponderance of the politically fixed. No financial aid for international students makes for a wealthy, chi-chi crowd; and the campus has a decidedly preppy, conservative tilt.

The vast selection of bars and clubs in the neighborhood lures many students to popular haunts such as Winston's, Champions, and the Tombs. Drinking, and partying, like at most colleges, are favorite Georgetown pastimes.

What's a Hoya?

Georgetown **teams** are called Hoyas, which supposedly derives from the old, half-Greek, half-Latin cheer *hoya saxta,* "what rocks," developed back when students were forced to study both languages. Tour leaders on campus further test the gullibility of prospective students by explaining that the correct answer to the question: "What's a *Hoya*?" is "Yes." Famous Hoyas have included pro basketball player Patrick Ewing, New York prelate John Cardinal O'Connor, Supreme Court Justice Antonin Scalia, and Senate Majority Leader George Mitchell (D-Maine). The basketball team, perennial contender for the national college title (they won in 1984), plays at the Capital Centre in Landover, MD, since crowds are far too large for a college gym. (Call 301-350-3400 for information.) Purchase tickets through Ticketmaster (432-7328) or through the campus Ticket Office (687-4692) or Athletic Department (687-2449).

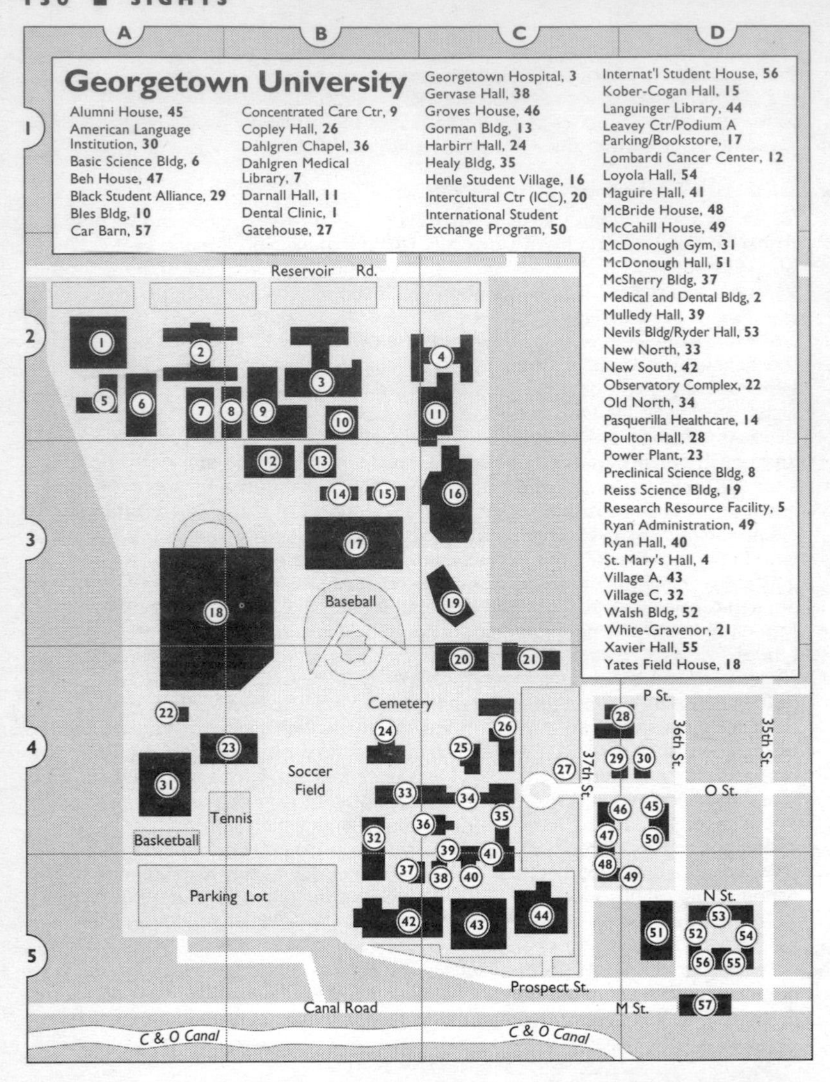

With a strong focus on undergrad teaching, classes are quite small (around 50 people on average). Mild winters give way to the oppressive heat and humidity of the D.C. summers during which the campus fills with power-hungry, ambitious young interns who watch and discuss CNN and C-Span religiously, as well as high school debaters.

The Campus

With the exception of a relatively small number of old buildings which owe their design to Flemish Renaissance and English Gothic, most campus architecture—largely constructed in the last two decades—is firmly rooted in the post-modern aesthetic. The recent and largely red-brick structures make a concerted effort to blend in with their setting, but this admirable endeavor meets with variable success. Enter through the **main gate** (located on 37th St., across from its intersection with O St.) and get maps and directions from the student in the **information booth** to your left.

THUMBS UP FROM LET'S GO

With pen and notebook in hand, a change of underwear in our backpacks, and a budget as tight as your own, we spent the summer roaming the globe in search of travel bargains.

We've put the best of our discoveries into the book you're now holding. Our researchers hit the road for seven weeks of exploration, from Anchorage to Ankara, Estonia to El Salvador, Iceland to Indonesia. Editors work from spring to fall, massaging copy written on Himalayan bus rides into witty yet informative prose. A brand-new edition of each guide hits the shelves every year, only months after it is researched, so you know you're getting the most reliable, up-to-date, and comprehensive information available.

We're an indispensable companion, but the best discoveries are often those you make yourself. When you find something worth sharing, drop us a line. We're Let's Go Publications, One Story Street, Cambridge, MA 02138, USA (e-mail: LetsGo@delphi.com). Good luck, and happy travels!

Photo: R. Olken

The Gothic splendor of **Healy Hall** lies straight ahead, as does the statue of Archbishop John Carroll in the center of **Healy Circle.** Healy and Copley Lawns lie to your left and right respectively. During warm weather, these lawns are a major social gathering ground. They formerly held the university football field and students used to sit along the old stone wall which helps to enclose the quadrangle to cheer (*"Hoya saxta!"* of course). Almost every Georgetown student takes a photo seated in John Carroll's lap at some point during their undergrad tenure. To the left is the **Lawinger Library;** built in memory of an alum who perished in Vietnam, it was erected as a modern counterpart to Healy. With 2.2 million volumes, it's the main repository of the university's library materials. Lowinger's reading room is open daily until 2am and 24 hours during exam periods. To the right of the lawns lies the Gothic **White Gravenor,** named for two of America's first Jesuits, houses the **Office of Undergraduate Admissions** (667-3600 in rm. 108). Campus tours begin here; call to reserve a spot. Go look for the hands on the **Healy Hall clock,** if they're there. Each year seniors (try to) steal them and ship them to someone famous.

Through Healy lies the smaller and quieter **Dahlgren Square.** A fountain and the **Dahlgren Chapel** lend a more meditative atmosphere to this secondary campus quadrangle. Facing the chapel, to the right a small white balcony from Lincoln addressed troops during the Civil War.

Turn right at Healy Hall and walk past Copley Hall (on your left) until you reach the new **Intercultural Center (ICC),** a ziggurat-like, modern red-brick building which overlooks a small cemetery on campus—a peculiarly touching juxtaposition. Past the ICC, cross the bridge to your left to reach **Leavey Center,** the infinitely helpful student union. The building houses an **Information Center** (687-1457), and. bulletin boards in the hall leading towards the **bookshop** (687-7750) advertise apartments for rent, job openings at the University, and furniture sales. The bookshop is your source for Hoya paraphernalia (open Mon.-Fri. 9am-8pm, Sat.-Sun. 11am-5pm). There's a **bank** inside as well, and some **fast food joints**. At night the center fails as the student hangout it was envisioned as; the place can be more deserted than the library.

Outside of Leavy, in front of Henley Village is the **Georgetown U. Transportation Service (GUTS)** shuttle bus stop. The shuttle runs about every 15 minutes during the academic year to nearby **Metro stops** in Rossyln and Dupont Circle.

SOUTHERN GEORGETOWN

Pretend to shop for other people's art in **Spectrum Gallery,** 1132 29th St. NW (333-0954), an artists' cooperative owned and run by 29 local artists. Pick up a *Galleries* guide at any local gallery and look for an opening at the Spectrum—they're open to the public. Postcards and posters are also for sale. (Open Tues.-Sat. 11am-6pm, Sun. noon-5pm. Free.) The **Alif Gallery,** upstairs at 1204 31st St. (337-9670), displays Arabian art and sponsors cultural events, including readings, lectures, movies, concerts, and plays. Ring the doorbell—your curiosity will be well rewarded. (Open Mon.-Fri. 10am-6pm, Sat. noon-6pm. Free.)

Retired from commercial use since the 1800s, the **Chesapeake & Ohio Canal** (301-299-3613) extends 185 mi. from Georgetown to Cumberland, MD. Nature abounds along the **C&O Canal towpath** (below and parallel to M St.), the dirt road along which trusty mules once pulled barges on the canal. The benches under the trees around 30th St. make a prime city lunch spot. After Georgetown, the C&O changes from a polluted relic suitable for romantic strolls to a clean waterway whose towpath accommodates gamboling families and mountain-bikers. Kayakers often practice on the water; fishermen used to walk the trails in search of trout or bass. The towpath, a flat and wide sandy path, grows monotonous after a few miles of running, walking, or biking, though the uniformity is broken by long bridges, small waterfalls man-made and natural, and historical spots. To reach the canal's relatively unspoiled bits without straying too far from public transportation, take the

D4 bus out along Macarthur Blvd., then turn left and walk through the subdivisions until you reach the canal.

Too tired to walk along the canal? *The Georgetown,* a **C&O Canal boat** (653-5190), may be your ticket. Huge mules pull the passenger-filled boat down the canal; National Park Service guides wear 19th-century costumes, guide the boat through a lock, and explain the history of the canal. Board (and pay) for the 90-minute ride at the canal's **Visitor Center,** south of M St. at 1057 Thomas Jefferson St. NW. (Boats leave April to mid-Sept. Wed.-Sun. 10:30am, 1pm, 3pm; mid-Sept. to Oct. Wed.-Fri. 1pm, 3pm, Sat. 10:30am, 1pm, 3pm, 5pm, Sun. 10:30am, 1pm, and 3pm. Rides $5, seniors and children $3.50.) The Visitor Center also provides information on horseback riding, fishing, and camping.

For info on renting a bike or boat, see **Sports and Recreation,** p. 226. For information on dining, see **Food,** p. 91. For information on activities and sights specific to the evening and nighttime, see **Nightlife & Entertainment,** beginning on p. 208. For cool stores in Georgetown, see **Shopping & Services,** beginning on p. 229.

■■■ FARRAGUT

Metro: Farragut North; Farragut South; McPherson Square.
Dupont Circle and Foggy Bottom melt imperceptibly into this glass-walled business district, bounded roughly by N, I, and 15th St. NW on the north, south, and east, and by 21st St. on the west. With government just a few Metro stops to the east wrapped up in its own affairs, lawyers, lobbyists, and other professionals labor on behalf of every interest group around. The 13-story height limit prevents New York-style claustrophobia from plaguing the District, but white-collar joggers, honking taxicabs, and street vendors hawking everything from $1 hot dogs to $3 silk ties to $100 wool rugs all signal that this place means business. Connecticut Avenue, K Street, New Hampshire Avenue, and 17th Street boast most of the retail and hotel hubbub, while several sights hover around M Street and Rhode Island Avenue. The business of Washington is best observed on a walk down Connecticut Avenue between N and K streets; E.J. Applewhite called it "a monotonous uniformity of office buildings poured out like ice cubes."

For a kaleidoscopic glimpse of Washington, old and new, take the Vermont Ave. exit from the McPherson Square Metro and walk northeast (toward N St. NW) on Vermont Ave. On the way, stop at **Thomas Circle** to see General Thomas sticking his chin out indignantly as his horse sneezes. The two have been frozen in this uncomfortable position since 1879. Continue to a quiet residential neighborhood where two museums fight a war of ideas: The **Bethune Museum and Archives,** 1318 Vermont Ave. NW (332-1233; Metro: McPherson Square), chronicles the life of leader and civil rights activist Mary McLeod Bethune (see **Museums and Galleries,** p. 203), while two doors down the **Confederate Memorial Hall** commemorates the Southern cause during the Civil War. The Romanesque hall, at 1322 Vermont Ave. NW, once housed Confederate veterans. The impassioned docents speak dolefully of "those Yankees" and lament the statues of Union Generals Thomas and Logan taunting the Hall from nearby traffic circles. (Open by appointment; call 483-5700 for information. Free.)

If you simply *must* see another Civil War general frozen in time, seemingly longing to direct traffic, head west on Mass Ave. to **Scott Circle.**

At 1601 Massachusetts Ave. NW, the **Australian Embassy** (797-3000) welcomes visitors to exhibits that change every month or so. See what an embassy looks like inside; play with the **neato electric doors**, and enjoy the Australian accents. (Open Mon.-Fri. 9am-4:30pm. Free.)

As Rhode Island Ave. heads west to M St., Farragut takes a break from business to wrestle with more existential questions. The pensive **B'nai B'rith Klutznick National Jewish Museum** holds forth at 1640 Rhode Island Ave. NW (857-6583; Metro: Farragut North). (See **Museums and Galleries,** p. 203.) Switch religious gears at **St. Matthew's Cathedral,** 1725 Rhode Island Ave. NW (347-3215), one block away. The vibrant, vaulted ceiling frescoes and candle-filled chapels embrace worshippers for Sunday Mass, in Latin (10am) and Spanish (1pm). (Guided tour Sun. 2:30-4:30pm. Free.)

On the corner of M St. and 17th St. NW, the **National Geographic Society Explorer's Hall** conquers the first floor of its pin-striped building. (857-7588, group tours 857-7689, N.G. Society 857-7000; Metro: Farragut North.) The museum proffers interactive films, a live parrot, a miniature tornado that you can touch, a huge globe, and fascinating changing exhibits, often by *National Geographic* magazine's best photographers. For $3, get a *National Geographic* cover made with your face on it. (Open Mon.-Sat. 9am-5pm, Sun. 10am-5pm. Wheelchair access. Free.)

From M St., head east and make a right onto 15th St. to tour the **Washington Post** in its domineering tan building at 1150 15th St. NW (334-7969; Metro: Farragut North). Spin controllers, press secretaries, leakers, and flacks in this media-conscious town make the well-respected *Post* their #1 target. Watch the next day's edition come to life on a guided tour; you'll see the hectic news room, enormous presses, and the mock-brick-floored mailroom. (One-hour tours Mon. 10am, 11am, 1pm, 2pm, and 3pm. Reservations necessary. Free. No kids under 11.) See graybox below.

L and M streets lead toward the shops and office buildings of Connecticut Avenue. Take the shortcut from 17th to Connecticut Ave. and Desales St. through the long, elegant, marble lobby of the **Mayflower Hotel,** 1127 Connecticut Ave. NW (347-3000; Metro: Farragut North). Warren & Wetmore, who built Grand Central Station in New York City, also designed this High Society gem, nicknamed the "grand dame" of Washington hotels. Peek into the grand ballroom (site of every inaugural ball from Presidents Coolidge to Reagan) as you pass. Gleaming gold-colored fixtures recall the Roaring Twenties, when this hotel was the largest in the United States.

"I got my job through the Washington Post"

In the room where top editors decide which news will lead *The Post* everyday is a steel plate covered with ink, baked on two decades ago. Nixon Resigns. The biggest headline ever printed in "the president's newspaper."

The Post made it happen and they know it. And, be you a visitor or staffer, they won't let you forget it. Older editors wandering the fifth floor newsroom of the downtown headquarters have been overheard breaking out into verbatim renditions of the Senate Watergate hearings. Young reporters offer up reverent inquiries as semi-retired former Executive Editor Ben Bradlees works the room.

Some say the *Post* hasn't moved on much from its glory days when they felled a president. Still, most industry observers consider it the best metropolitan daily in the country. It's the most widely read paper (in terms of readers who live within its intended geographic region), putting it well ahead of the *NY Times* in "penetration." It helps that the paper only costs 25¢ to buy on the street, a price well below what it takes in ink and paper to produce the product.

Call ahead and ask the public relations office (334-7969) for a tour, which they'll gladly conduct for you and your friends. Make sure to stop on the fifth floor, where reporters reign. Recent renovations have changed the newsroom a bit from its '70s look as immortalized in "All the President's Men," but it's still a thrill for the byline-junkie.

And, if it's not 2 or 6pm when important decisions are being debated by 20 or so top editors, wander into the conference room—you'll be greeted by not only the Nixon plate and a library of books penned by Post reporters and editors, but with a Watergate memento that reveals the depth of recognition upon which the *Post's* continuing obsession is based. On the right wall as you enter the room, framed along with an inlaid signed photo, is a graphic of the slogan for a major 1970s classified-ad sales campaign. The slogan: "I got my job through the *Washington Post.*" The signature: Jerry Ford.

Picnic to the (occasional) summer sounds of flute duets and jazz sax players in **Farragut Square,** three blocks south of Connecticut Ave. on 17th St. between I and K St. NW. The statue, staring off into the distance, spyglass in hand, is Admiral David Farragut, the guy who said: "Damn the torpedoes—full speed ahead!" (He said it in the Battle of Mobile Bay (Alabama) in 1864, when "torpedoes" meant floating mines.)

Washington's golden age of outdoor statues lasted for 50 years after the Civil War; you can learn more than you wanted to know about the War Between the States by looking at D.C.'s public sculpture. **McPherson Square,** where Vermont Ave. meets I, K, and 15th St. NW, promotes the memory of Gen. James McPherson, who commanded an army during Sherman's scorched-earth march through Georgia.

One block away between 13th, 14th, K and I St. NW, **Franklin Square's** shady benches invite you to contemplate the protruding belly of Revolutionary War Commodore of the Navy John Barry; his coat is unbuttoned to afford a prime view

■■■ DUPONT CIRCLE

Metro: Dupont Circle.

Dupont Circle used to be called Washington's most diverse neighborhood; then it turned expensive and Adams-Morgan turned cool. Nevertheless, the Circle and its environs remain a haven for Washington's artsy, international, and gay communities. The neighborhood's mix of businesses and wayward pleasures makes for aesthetic delight but a zoning commission's headache; artists, ambassadors, antique dealers, beggars, bike messengers, booksellers, and committees all congregate within a few blocks north of N St. As the night moves in, the street crowds shift from lunching lawyers to café-hopping couples. Along Connecticut Ave. north of the Circle, hot-shot staffers of the *New Republic* stroll nervously past buzz-cut gay activists from ACT UP and OUT! (D.C.'s equivalent of Queer Nation). Sidewalks scream timely social messages stenciled with spray-paint. West of Connecticut and along Massachusetts Ave., embassies from flap their flags, while lobbyists flap their mouths in nearby townhouse offices. Those tired of the fast lane can relax with new art in the many galleries or ogle Old Masters in the Phillips Collection.

In its residential and commericial development, Dupont Circle was a late bloomer. No one lived on its streets until after the Civil War. When the growth spurt hit, however, change came quickly. Big-spending, fast-acting Boss Shepherd took *de facto* charge of the city in 1871, then poured money into the area around his Dupont Circle home. The circle itself became a federal park (it still is), Connecticut Avenue got paved, and railroad tracks ran up it from downtown. When the British built their new legation at Connecticut and N in 1874, the millionaires' race to Dupont Circle began. The area kept its social prestige until the 1940s, by which time segregated Washington's Black elite had built a parallel neighborhood of its own, "Striver's Row" along U St. near 17th. As the rich fled the city, hippies moved in and made Dupont their own during the 60s and 70s, until rising real estate prices and gentrification drove them out.

The Dupont Circle neighborhood presses eagerly against its boundaries at 16th, 24th, N and S St. NW. Its only Metro stop, helpfully named Dupont Circle, can get you within walking distance of everything in the area. The **D2, D4, D6, and D8 buses** pass 20th and P St. on their way to Georgetown, while the **L2** and **L4** buses head up Connecticut Ave. and the **S2 and S4** speed down 16th St. Parking at night is nearly impossible except along Massachusetts Ave.; if you must drive around during the day, try the neighborhood's eastern edge (near 16th St.) and pray. Massachusetts Ave. runs through the circle northwest-southeast, linking Old Downtown with the placid National Cathedral area. New Hampshire Ave. zooms through on its way from the Kennedy Center to NE and Takoma Park. Connecticut Ave. runs almost, but not quite, north-south to (and under) the circle, between downtown and the Zoo; Florida Ave. branches off from Connecticut Ave. at S St. and heads for neighborhoods with more dangerous reputations. Columbia Rd. splits up with Connecticut just afterwards and steers itself towards Adams-Morgan and Mt. Pleasant. Pedestrians leaving the Dupont Circle Metro can head up Connecticut for shopping and dining, up Massachusetts Ave. for embassies, northwest (between the two) for art, east to the earnest, slightly run-down 14th St. theater district, or south to the bustling charmlessness of Farragut.

The heart of the neighborhood throbs in **Dupont Circle** itself, a grassy hub for the incoming spokes of six avenues and streets. Admiral DuPont's millionaire descendants moved his statue to Delaware; a fountain adorned by semi-nude goddesses now hosts the chess players, lunching office workers, drug dealers, and herds of spandexed bike messengers who populate the island.

At the **Christian Heurich Mansion,** 1307 New Hampshire Ave. NW (785-2068), the Historical Society of Washington, D.C. leads visitors through the German-American beer baron's "castle on the Rhine." Exquisite woodwork renders the Romanesque mansion worth a scan. Tours of the house permit a glimpse of the decorative arts, architecture, and domestic life of Washington at the turn of the century. (House may be visited only by tour Wed.-Sat. noon, 1pm, 2pm, and 3pm. Historical Society research library, with over 100,000 items, open Wed. and Fri.-Sat. 10am-4pm. Washingtonia Bookstore and a changing exhibit area open Tues.-Sat. 10am-4pm. Admission $3, students and seniors $1.50, under 18 free.)

The eastward leg of Mass. Ave. is flanked by embassies as it heads towards Farragut. The prestigious **Brookings Institute** at 1775 Massachusetts Ave. NW acts as a liberal stronghold and an appropriate buffer between the Circle's alternative activism and the business buffs to the east. Richard Nixon once contemplated blowing up the files at Brookings, whose influence has declined since its Kennedy-era glory

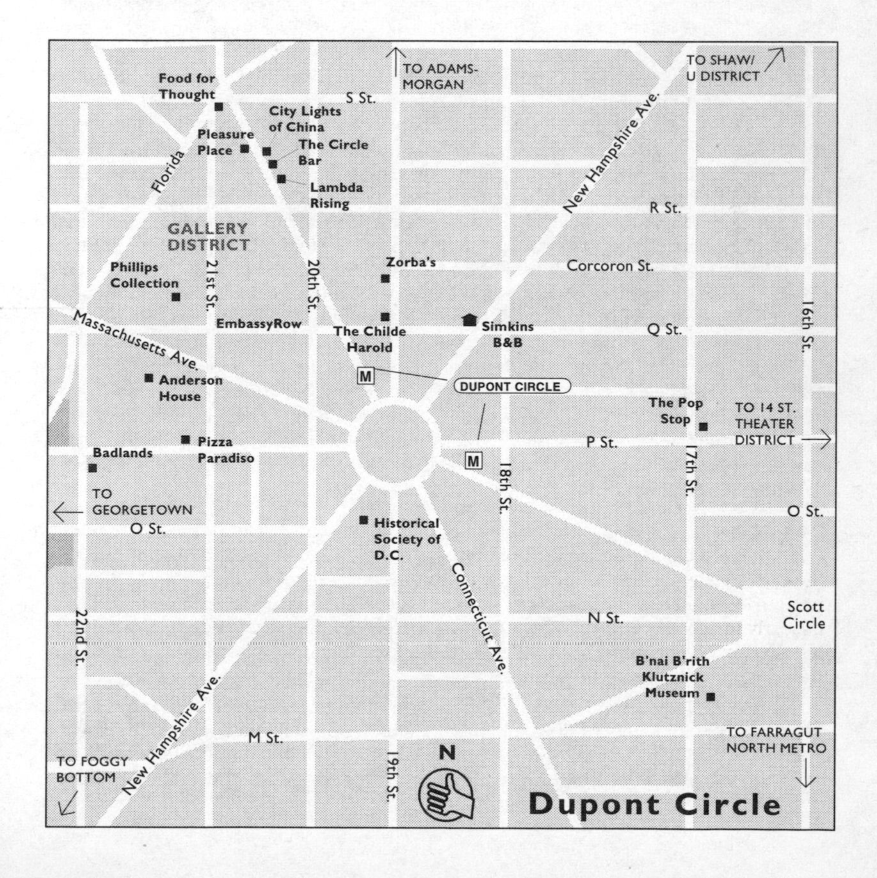

days. You can check out your favorite resident academic at the interactive computer in the lobby.

EMBASSY ROW

Massachusetts Ave. between Dupont Circle and Observatory Circle is also called **Embassy Row.** Before the 1930s, Washington socialites lined the avenue with their extravagant edifices; status-conscious diplomats found the mansions perfect for their purposes, and embassies and chanceries moved in by the dozen. Major industrialized nations have designed their own compounds (Great Britain and Japan) or moved away from downtown for more room (France and Germany); smaller or poorer countries occupy the still-grand townhouses. Identify an embassy by the national coat-of-arms or flag out front; identify an international scandal by reporters on the sidewalk. The ornate **Indonesian Embassy,** 2020 Massachusetts Ave. (293-1745), once belonged to the McLean family, the last private owners of the infamous Hope Diamond (now housed at the National Museum of Natural History).

Turn right from Massachusetts Ave. onto 21st St. for the **Phillips Collection,** 1600 21st St. at Q St. NW (387-2151), the first museum of modern art in the U.S. and the classiest non-Smithsonian showplace in town (see **Museums**, p. 203).

A little further along Massachusetts, pass through the grand arched and gravel-paved entrance of **Anderson House,** 2118 Massachusetts Ave. NW (785-2040) next to the Ritz-Carlton Hotel, to see the **Museum of the Society of the Cincinnati.** Look for the pervasive egg-and-dart design along the outside moldings. The house retains the robber-baron decadence of U.S. ambassador Larz Anderson, who built it in 1902-5, as well as his original furnishings. (Open Tues.-Sat. 1-4pm; free.)

Past still more embassies, Massachusetts eventually circumnavigates **Sheridan Circle** at 23rd St. NW. General Philip Sheridan looks dashing and equestrian in the circle's arboreal center. A small raised plaque on the sidewalk of the Q St. side of the circle commemorates ex-Chilean ambassador Orlando Letelier, who was killed in 1973 by a car bomb along with Ronni K. Moffitt. Letelier represented the Marxist government of Salvador Allende, which dictator Pinochet overthrew with CIA help in the same year. After the assassination was featured on the TV show *America's Most Wanted* four years ago, the culprit was apprehended. From the circle, the **Dumbarton Bridge** leads 23rd St. pedestrians over Rock Creek Park to Georgetown via a pair of powerful but dejected-looking bronze buffaloes.

Several embassies later, Massachusetts makes one last stop before crossing Rock Creek Park into Upper Northwest, at the **Islamic Center,** 2551 Massachusetts Ave. NW (332-8343). Flags line the entrance to this brilliant white building whose stunning designs stretch to the tips of its spired ceilings. Ambassadors of several Islamic nations (Egypt, Iran, Turkey, and Afghanistan) founded the mosque after World War II. Visitors may enter the mosque, but note that shorts are not allowed and women must cover their heads and wear sleeved clothing (no short dresses allowed). (Open daily 10:30am-5pm. Donation requested. Prayers held 5 times daily.)

On the other side of Rock Creek Park, Massachusetts Ave. links some particularly striking embassies, including those of Brazil, Norway, and Britain, before it reaches the Vice President's mansion and the Naval Observatory.

GALLERY AREA

From the Q St. exit of the Dupont Circle Metro, walk one block north on Connecticut Ave. to R St. to reach many of Dupont Circle's 25 art galleries, which cluster between 21st and 22nd St. See **Art Galleries** on p. 204.

Turn right from R St. onto 22nd St.; then walk up the hill past Decatur Pl. to the tiny fountain and spreading **Spanish steps.** Take the steps to S St., turn left, pass the embassies of Laos, Ireland, and Myanmar (formerly Burma), and enter the **Textile Museum,** 2320 S St. NW (667-0441), the world's largest repository of rare and valuable textiles, with some 14,000 holdings, of which only a few are shown at a time. Open Mon.-Sat. 10am-5pm, Sun. 1-5pm. Admission by contribution. A few doors away, the **Woodrow Wilson House,** 2340 S St. NW (387-4062), preserves the memory of former president Woodrow Wilson with a detailed and informative tour of his house and belongings enlivened by snippets of personal history. The aging and embittered Wilson spent his last years here after the Democrats lost the White House in 1920. Today, a 20-min. film and a 1-hr. tour introduce visitors to the nation's last great intellectual president and the only one to have taken up residence in Washington after leaving office. (Open Tues.-Sun. 10am-4pm. Admission $4, students and seniors $2.50, under 7 free. Wheelchair access.)

East of Fondo del Sol on R St., the **National Museum of American Jewish Military History,** 1811 R St. NW (265-6280), offers surprisingly rich displays on a seemingly thin subject. Upcoming exhibits include "Women in the Military: A Jewish Perspective" (in 1997). Open Mon.-Fri. 9am-5pm, Sun. 1-5pm. Free. Continue east on R St. to discover the **House of the Temple,** 1733 16th St. NW (232-3579). Flanked by 33-ft. columns, guarded by turbaned sphinxes, utilized by Scottish Rite Masons, and designed by John Russell Pope, the ancient-looking temple struts imposingly among the apartments and offices of lower 16th St. Pope's design copies the Mausoleum at Halicarnassus, one of the Seven Wonders of the Ancient world. The lengthy tour (90 min. or more) is a fascinating look at the quasi-religious aspects of this secretive selective society. (Open Mon.-Fri. 8am-4pm. Last tour at 2pm. Free.)

■■■ SHAW / U DISTRICT

Metro: Shaw-Howard University; U St.-Cardozo.

Shaw was once the address of choice for important African-American senators (Reconstruction-era Sen. Blanche K. Bruce), poets (Jean Toomer and Langston Hughes), musicians (Duke Ellington), journalists, and lawyers. These American legends and their cohorts developed the "Striver's Section," along U St. between 7th and 15th St. NW; businesses on 7th St. boomed. Music lovers of every color and creed crowded into the Howard Theater and the Lincoln Theater was the first theater in the area to show movies to an integrated audience. Fashion flourished in Shaw in the 30s and 40s when stepping out meant dressing up. Desegregation in the 1950s played taps for the theaters—as other parts of the city were opened up to the black middle class, Shaw's population and importance were reduced. The final blow came in 1968, when news of the assassination of Martin Luther King, Jr. touched off three days of looting, smashing, and burning along 14th St., 7th St., and H St. NW—the former arteries of Black D.C.

Shaw today is best viewed along its edges, in the Logan Circle neighborhood along 13th St. NW above M St. (Greater Shaw runs roughly between 14th and North Capitol and between M St. and Florida Ave. NW.) U St. has become a major east-west artery, originating at the intersection of Florida Ave. and 18th St. NW (the no-man's land between Adams-Morgan and Dupont Circle) and extending to the Howard University campus. Some blocks remain leveled from the '68 riots. Run-down tenements, boarded-up and abandoned buildings, and crumbling storefronts abound. Constant violence, usually drug-related, threatens even the residents hanging out on their stoops. Shaw can become deserted away from its business center. Areas around housing projects are especially dangerous. Exercise caution and travel in groups.

But don't give up on Shaw. In fact, give it your attention at mealtime or in the evenings, when safe areas offer spectacular dining and entertainment options. The Howard Theater remains a half-demolished marquee, but the Lincoln was bought and restored by the city and reopened in February of 1994. Venerable neighborhood institutions like Ben's Chili Bowl and the Florida Avenue Grill have, like their customers, weathered the troubles for decades. Meanwhile, the long-delayed Shaw Metro stations have finally opened. U St. itself, once a haven for prostitution in the '70s and '80s, has become a destination for the ever-roaming hip. Youthful types head west on U St. to boogie, read poetry, or fatten up on Sunday brunch. Some of the city's best clubs and bars are in the U. Go and party, then take a cheap taxi ride home. (For up-to-the-minute coverage of the U scene, see **Nightlife & Entertain-**

ment, beginning on p. 211.) Rush to the soul food restaurants, which serve Southern-derived, pork-and-greens-heavy cuisine unique to African-American culture.

Howard University (806-6100), whose roughly 20-block campus slopes northeast from 7th and W St. NW, is America's most historically important black university (Metro: Shaw-Howard Univ.). From the Metro, walk north on 7th St., which changes into Georgia Ave. (a 20-min. walk). The 89-acre campus stretches to the east along 7th and Georgia. (Be very careful walking here at night, and do not walk alone.) Founded in 1867 to help newly freed slaves, the private research university now has 12,000 students, most of them African-American. Late Supreme Court Justice Thurgood Marshall, ex-New York City Mayor David Dinkins, and novelist Toni Morrison are only a few of Howard's zillions of famous alums. The campus has one of D.C.'s highest elevations—be sure to take in the view of downtown while you're here. Two-hour campus tours (including a videotape presentation and question-and-answer session) are available from Monday to Friday between 10am and 3pm by appointment only (call 806-2900 for scheduling). The university library at 500 Howard Pl. (on the Howard campus; 806-7250) is open to the public; its **Moorland-Springarn Research Center** keeps the largest collection of black literature in the United States (open Mon.-Thurs. 8am-midnight, Fri. 8am-5pm, Sat. 9am-6pm, Sun. 12:30-9pm; limited hours during summer months).

Urban Renewal

From the turn of the century until the 1960s, the U St., 14th St., and 7th St. corridors were the center of Washington's black commercial and entertainment community. Area residents pooled academic and economic resources to create not just a "city-within-a-city", but a society and a culture: from its restaurants to its theaters to its dance halls, the community was tight-knit, vibrant, and profitable. Theatres like the Howard, Lincoln, and Dunbar developed national reputations while dance halls like the Lincoln Colonnade gathered entertainers like Duke Ellington, Hollywood favorites like Jimmy Stewart, and even President Franklin Roosevelt for Big Band dances.

The 1954 Supreme Court ruling outlawing segregation sent the Shaw-U District into decline. New residential possibilities and economic opportunities meant movement out of old communities. The violent rioting following the assassination of Martin Luther King, Jr. and 20 years of drugs and decay seemed to seal the neighborhood's fate as a victim of crime and urban plight.

Beginning in the early 1980's, however, renewed interest and investment in the area brought hope of restoration. Today's Shaw streets are busier and safer than they've been in 30 years. U St. in particular is fast becoming an entertainment haven for neighborhood residents, D.C. yuppies, alternative youth, and the city's gay community. Located strategically at the intersection of Shaw, Dupont Circle, and Adams-Morgan, the U District benefits from the diverse popularity of all three neighborhoods. A small-scale mall, located next to the U St.-Cardozo Metro houses two restaurants and a cafe, and U St. businesses eagerly await the new look and new patrons it will bring to the area. Revitalization should make Shaw as safe and stylish as it once was, placing its nightlife scene on par with that of its hip neighbors to the west.

■■■ ADAMS-MORGAN

Metroless: closest stations are Woodley-Park Zoo (15-min. walk) and Dupont Circle (20-min. walk).

Though Dupont Circle remains the artsiest of Washington's neighborhoods, sometime in the late '80s the mantle of multicultural hipness passed to Adams-Morgan. Cool kids and the cool at heart, mostly white, arrived alongside immigrants from Mexico, El Salvador, and Ethiopia bringing great diversity to Adams-Morgan (which had already been defined by its mix of ethnic backgrounds). Slick dance, world

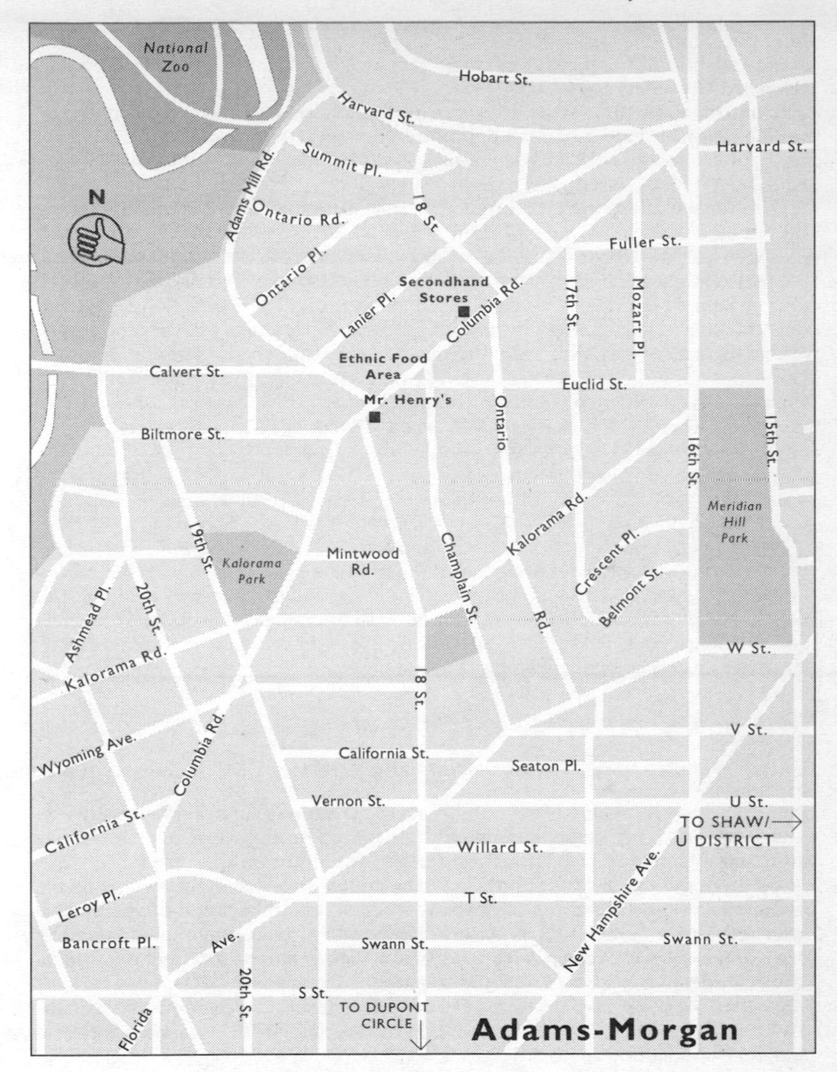

beat, and rickety do-it-yourself punk venues start, change names, and fold each year around here; even older squares have long ago discovered that a wreath of awesome **ethnic food** circles 18th, Columbia, and Calvert St. NW. A wealth of street carts and **secondhand stores** lines Columbia Rd. east of 18th St. Stroll around here in the daytime to shop or simply to browse.

Poorly served by public transportation, Adams-Morgan is also a tough place to park, especially at night, when the streets tend to jam. From the Woodley Park-Zoo Metro, walk to Calvert St., turn left, and hoof east. The Duke Ellington Bridge lifts walkers stories above Rock Creek Park's treetops—take a look, then walk three blocks and fall in love with Adams-Morgan's center, the five-pronged meeting place of Columbia and 18th. Florida Avenue NW divides Dupont from Adams-Morgan on the south; Connecticut Ave. lines its western side. Church-clogged 16th St., the wide east edge, leaves Adams-Morgan behind for streets more rough; a vague north boundary, Harvard St., bears Adams-Morgan into Mount Pleasant, where a similar, but poorer mix of migrants and young white-collar types survives. As long as you stay west of 16th St. (and, at night, walk with a friend), this area is relatively trouble-free.

Kalorama Park, nicknamed "dog-walk park," is a grassy triangle between Columbia Rd., 19th St., and Kalorama Rd. It houses benches, trees, a small park shelter, a playground, and basketball and tennis courts that local kids often use as soccer fields. Kids rollerskate down the hill to 19th St.

Columbia Road between 16th and 18th St. is packed with **street vendors** during the summer, selling African and Latin American wares as well as fresh fruit. Salsa music blares from stands whose proprietors hawk cassettes of Latin music.

Three churches defend the broad intersection of Harvard, 16th, and Columbia Rd. NW. Watchful pedestrians can see the round tower of the **National Baptist Memorial Church** all the way from 18th St.—look for the cylindrical pilasters and pillars. Across the street is the **Unitarian All Souls Church,** since the mid-80s an important venue for all-ages hard-core shows. The 1921 church copies closely the 1721 Church of St.-Martin-in-the-Fields in London, a model for Anglican parishes all over the world. The severely vertical **Unification Church** (a former Mormon Temple) reads its *Washington Times* across 16th St. from All Souls.

Grocery stores abound in Adams-Morgan, as the Hispanic residents support small corner bodegas with Latin American staples. The selection of items is a sight in itself. Make a point of visiting at least one of these places (see **Shopping,** p. 232).

Meridian Hill Park lies off 16th Street between W and Euclid St. NW. High retaining walls run the two-block length of the park, which encloses a high hill carved into a rectangular, 900-ft. esplanade complete with a long, impressive waterfall. The park, for all its impressive landscaping, is rather sinister; high walls and the hill block any escape except to W or Euclid St., making the lawns a mugger's paradise. Check it out in a group during the day; stay away at night.

■■■ UPPER NORTHWEST

Metro: Woodley Park-Zoo; Cleveland Park; Van Ness-UDC; Tenleytown-AU; Friendship Heights.

Immense Upper Northwest (the portion of D.C.'s northwest quadrant west of Rock Creek Park and north of Georgetown) is home to a gaggle of suburbish (and largely indistinguishable) residential communities. There are no discrete boundaries between these neighborhoods, though Fessenden St. NW may be said to divide **Tenleytown** from **Friendship Heights,** Quebec St. to cut between the **Cathedral area** and **Glover Park,** and R St. to separate the latter from Georgetown. Connecticut Ave. parallels Wisconsin Ave., but it has a slightly more urban feel. City politicians call upper Northwest "west of the park;" the moderately well-to-do residents choose to live in the twilight zone between city and suburb. These neighborhoods lead Washington, D.C. in trees, parks, and private schools. The **National Cathedral** and the **National Zoo** are the outstanding sights.

GETTING THERE & GETTING AROUND

The L2 and L4 **Metrobuses** shuttle up and down Connecticut Ave, linking Chevy Chase, MD with Dupont Circle and Farragut; the Van Ness-UDC, Cleveland Park, and Woodley Park-Zoo Metro stations are all stops along the bus route. The #30, 32, 34, or 36 buses can shuttle you all the way up Wisconsin Ave. from Georgetown; at the District line in Friendship Heights, a central Metrobus terminal lets you change buses to go into Maryland. **Metro stations** are located at Woodley Park, Cleveland Park, Van Ness (on Connecticut Ave.), Tenley Circle (Tenleytown), and Friendship Heights. Once there, these neighborhoods are easy to get around in. Most of the cross streets fit into D.C.'s alphabetical-order scheme: letters, then two-syllable names, then three-syllable names.

Connecticut Ave. connects Dupont Circle to Woodley Park, the Zoo, Cleveland Park, and finally the District line at Chevy Chase Circle. Wisconsin Ave. NW runs

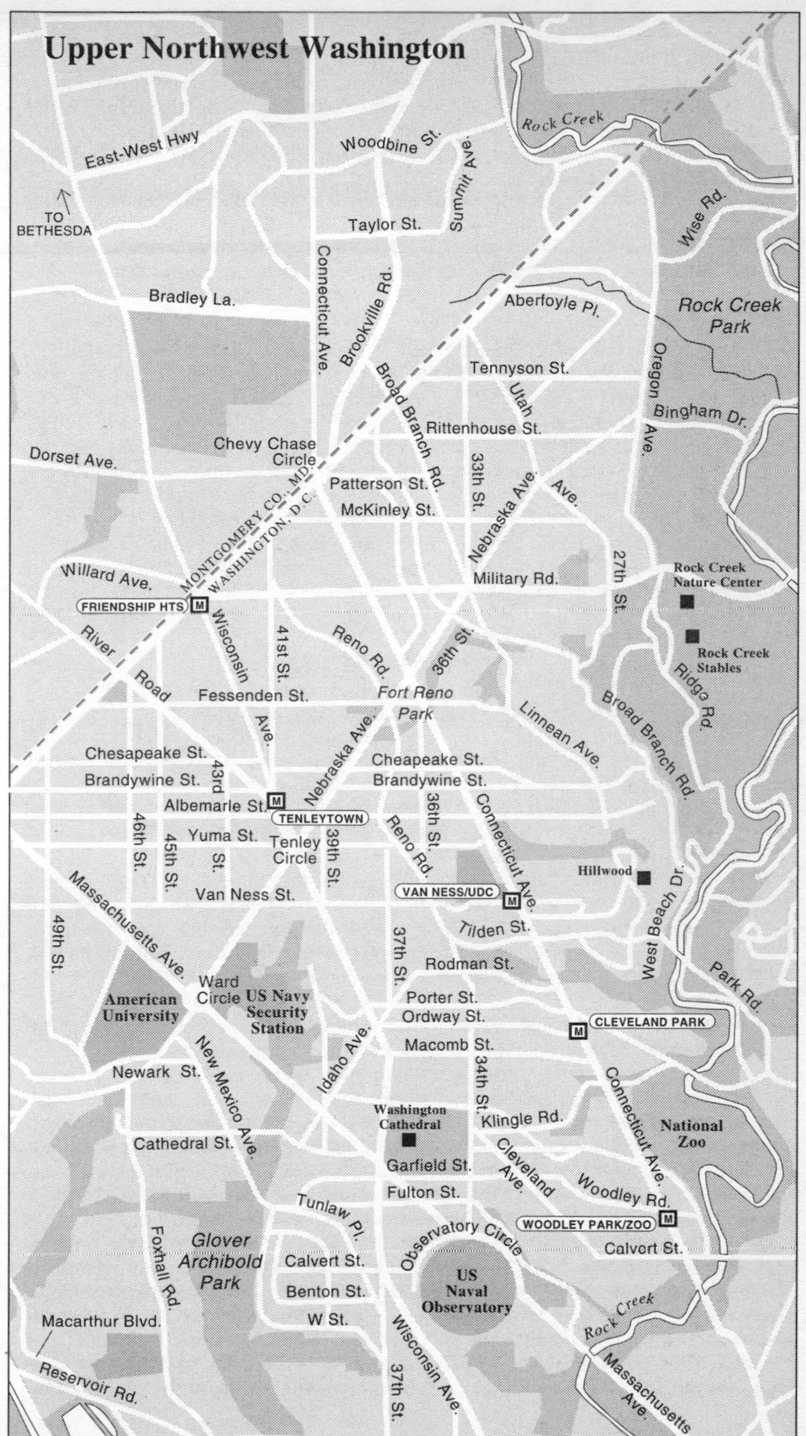
Upper Northwest Washington
East-West Hwy
TO BETHESDA
Woodbine St.
Summit Ave.
Rock Creek
Taylor St.
Wise Rd.
Connecticut Ave.
Brookville Rd.
Bradley La.
Aberfoyle Pl.
Rock Creek Park
Tennyson St.
Broad Branch Rd.
Utah Ave.
Oregon Ave.
Bingham Dr.
Rittenhouse St.
Chevy Chase Circle
Dorset Ave.
33th St.
Patterson St.
McKinley St.
Nebraska Ave.
MONTGOMERY CO., MD.
WASHINGTON, D.C.
27th St.
Willard Ave.
Military Rd.
Rock Creek Nature Center
FRIENDSHIP HTS
M
Wisconsin Ave.
River Road
41st St.
Reno Rd.
36th St.
Rock Creek Stables
Ridge Rd.
Fessenden St.
Fort Reno Park
Linnean Ave.
Broad Branch Rd.
Chesapeake St.
Cheapeake St.
Brandywine St.
43rd St.
Albemarle St.
TENLEYTOWN
Yuma St.
Tenley Circle
39th St.
46th St.
45th St.
Van Ness St.
VAN NESS/UDC
Hillwood
West Beach Dr.
Massachusetts Ave.
49th St.
Tilden St.
37th St.
Rodman St.
Park Rd.
Ward Circle
American University
US Navy Security Station
Porter St.
Ordway St.
CLEVELAND PARK
Idaho Ave.
Macomb St.
New Mexico Ave.
Newark St.
34th St.
Washington Cathedral
Klingle Rd.
National Zoo
Cathedral St.
Garfield St.
Cleveland Ave.
Woodley Rd.
Fulton St.
Tunlaw Pl.
Observatory Circle
WOODLEY PARK/ZOO
Glover Archibald Park
Foxhall Rd.
Calvert St.
Calvort St.
Benton St.
US Naval Observatory
Macarthur Blvd.
W St.
Wisconsin Ave.
Rock Creek
Massachusetts Ave.
Reservoir Rd.
37th St.

north from Georgetown past the Cathedral, through Tenley Circle and the Friendship Heights area, and on into Bethesda, Maryland.

Massachusetts Ave. runs northwest from downtown and Dupont Circle to the Cathedral (at Wisconsin Ave.), past American University, and north to the District line at Westmoreland Circle. Nebraska Ave. connects residential areas, running southwest-northeast from American University to Wisconsin Ave., Connecticut Ave., and finally Rock Creek Park.

Western Ave., the District's northwest border, meets Wisconsin in Friendship Heights at what was once measured as the city's most polluted intersection. Military Road marches east from Wisconsin and Western to Connecticut, through Rock Creek Park, and on to 16th St. NW.

NATIONAL ZOO

The first giant pandas left China for Washington's National Zoological Park (673-4800) as a gift from Mao to Nixon. But after years of tragically unsuccessful attempts to birth a baby panda in captivity, Ling-Ling recently died (see graybox below). Her mate Hsing-Hsing remains alone (and reportedly depressed) in the Panda House, which is now covered with condolence cards and well wishes from around the world. Tourists still flock in droves to see Hsing-Hsing, then open their wallets for panda t-shirts, backpacks, and fridge magnets at the gift shop next door.

But Hsing-Hsing is hardly the only reason to visit the National Zoo; after the obligatory pilgrimage to the Panda House, visitors can watch the fish and monkeys in the cageless **"Amazonia"** exhibit, wander through the **rainforest** exhibit, or play St. Francis by strolling through the skyscraper-sized bird cage. The zoo tries to enshrine its captives in environments they enjoy; some exhibits are even complete with their own wooded islands.

The Zoo spreads out east from Connecticut Ave. a few blocks uphill from Calvert St. NW and the Woodley Park-Zoo Metro; follow the crowds to the entrance at 3000 Connecticut Ave. NW. For a flatter but longer walk, go down Connecticut from the Cleveland Park Metro. In good (i.e., not sweltering) weather, pedestrians might enjoy walking up Connecticut Ave. from Dupont Circle (about 16 blocks). Drivers can park their worldly vehicles inside the Connecticut Ave. entrance.

The zoo occupies a swath of land liberated from Rock Creek Park and is criss-crossed with paths. All the paths are parts of either the blue **Valley Trail** (marked with bird tracks) or the red **Olmsted Walk** (marked with elephant feet). The more level Olmsted Walk links land-animal houses, while the hilly Valley Trail connects the bird and sealife exhibits. To see all of the exhibits, just traipse along one trail from the entrance to the far end of the zoo, near the lion-tiger hill, where you can pick up the other trail and return to the entrance. The non-linear layout and its lack of sightlines make a **map** invaluable; pick one up at the **information office** near the entrance. Open May-Sept. 9am-6pm, Oct.-April 9am-5pm. It is possible to see all of the exhibits in a long morning or afternoon, and it is certainly more satisfying to linger a little than to rush through in search of the major attractions.

Valley Trail runs on down to the great **flight cage,** where eagles (and many other birds) spread their wings, past the tranquil **artificial wetlands**—where cranes, mallards, and herons shine—and into the indoor **Bird House.** The bongo that ranges on the hill beside the flight cage looks like a balding old lady wearing high heels and bunched pantyhose. Children adore the spooky **bat cave** and the playful **sea lions,** visible above ground or (through a window) under water. **Invertebrates** (starfish and sea urchins and such) get their own house, the only one of its kind.

Along Olmsted Walk, rhinos, giraffes, and obscure pachyderms stretch out and stress out in a concrete barn. The boxed-in **elephants** stand around in unhealthy-looking tiny spaces, usually indoors. Visitors flock with open mouths and pointing fingers to the **Great Ape and Monkey Houses,** where they are either tactfully ignored or obligingly entertained by the cosmopolitan primates on the other side of the glass. The Great Ape House, with its statues of animals on the roof, was once the main zoo building, back when vacationing circus animals made the zoo's winter population bulge. The split-level **Panda House** shows evidence of serious overattention; crowd in at **feeding times** (11am and 3pm) for your best glimpse of Hsing-Hsing.

The zoo has made recent efforts to bring its scientific operations into the public eye; in Sept. 1995, it opened a new research facility for primates next to the Reptile House. **Think Tank** enables visitors to watch zoo biologists study animal behavior. The monkeys are free to climb along the wire back and forth between Think Tank and the Ape House, and scientists plan to chart their movements to study their social behavior. Almost any large animal that can stand the climate will be found outdoors; the polar bears are probably sweating worse than you are. Bizarre herd animals like the okapi frequent the fenced-off hillsides. Small animals, like lizards, still live indoors. The overdue shift from bare concrete and black iron to natural settings tends to hide the residents from the visitors; the free-ranging tamarins at the zoo swing freely (and often invisibly) from limb to limb.

Some of the houses contain kid-centered learning laboratories; the bird house has the **BirdLab.** (Open Fri. 10am-1pm and Sat.-Sun. 10am-2pm.) **Summer Serenade concerts** by the U.S. Navy Band take place on certain evenings; call the zoo for information. Both trails claim wheelchair access, though it's easier to wheel down Olmsted Walk. The zoo is accessible by bike from the Rock Creek bike path; you must lock up your wheels once you get there, though. (Auto parking $4 for 1st 3 hrs., $2 per hr. thereafter, $10 max. Free handicapped parking in lots B and D. Zoo grounds open daily 8am-8pm, Oct.-April 8am-6pm; buildings open daily 9am-6pm, Sept.-March 9am-4:30pm. Free. Scheduled feedings listed at information desk.)

Pandemonium

During the inevitable Panda visit at the Zoo, pay attention to the panels next to the exhibit that no one ever reads. They detail the **surreal mating rituals of Hsing-Hsing and Ling-Ling.** Shortly after acquiring the pandas, the braintrust at the Zoo decided that they'd like to get them to mate. They waited for the animals to reach breeding age and then began putting them in the same pen when Ling-Ling was in heat. Time after time, Hsing-Hsing mounted Ling-Ling in strange and uncomfortable positions. (The photos that accompany these panels are too outrageous to miss.) While Hsing-Hsing seems to be enjoying himself he "fails to align himself in an effective breeding posture" and Ling-Ling looks bored. Researchers speculate that perhaps the Pandas hadn't been given enough time to socialize before Ling-Ling went into heat. Starting in 1982, the Pandas were coupled long before mating season. In 1983, Hsing-Hsing finally figured out where to "align" himself. "Dr. Debra Kleinman, kneeling, cheers the pandas on." The snapshot that accompanies this success is particularly entertaining, with a hoarde of press in the background watching the couple mate. The look on Ling-Ling's face is pure ecstasy. The rest of the story is unfortunate. The cubs produced from this encounter and all subsequent encounters didn't survive long. And with the death of Ling-Ling, Hsing-Hsing is left alone with fond memories of his headline-making misadventures.

Near the Zoo

Next door to the zoo at 3133 Connecticut Ave. NW, the **Kennedy-Warren Apartments** spent the 1930s as one of Washington's fanciest addresses. The Egyptian-themed roof adornments and exterior panels on this three-section, block-long building merit some serious stares, as does the garden out front.

Up Connecticut Ave., at 3400 International Drive NW, the **Intelsat headquarters** (944-6800) gleam like a science-fictional ant colony. (Metro: Van Ness-UDC.) Intelsat is a cooperative satellite producer supported by 121 countries; a high-tech tour orbits the ground floor. Pass under the prototypes and models of the Intelsat satellites, take the hokey introductory film with a grain of salt—the end contains awesome special effects—and analyze this company, which wouldn't look out of place in *Star Trek*. Fascinating. (One-hour tours by appointment only.)

Hillwood, 4155 Linnaean Ave. NW (686-5807), once the mansion of General Foods heiress Marjorie Meriweather Post, now displays her jewels—not just pretty earrings and necklaces but a wing of Russian decorative arts, coins, and Fabergé eggs said to be the largest outside Russia. You may have to sell your own jewels to see it, though—a two-hour tour of the newly remodeled collection costs $10. Outside, 25 acres of gardens replicate England, Japan, and imperial Russia in begonian glory. (Garden is included in the tour price, or $2 without tour. Tours Tues.-Sat. 9am, 10:30am, noon, 1:30pm, and 3pm. Garden open Tues.-Sat. 11am-3pm.)

WASHINGTON NATIONAL CATHEDRAL

The Cathedral Church of Saint Peter and Saint Paul, also called the **Washington National Cathedral,** at Massachusetts and Wisconsin Ave. NW (537-6200; recording 364-6616), took a long time getting off the ground: more than a century passed between 1791, when George Washington proposed (in a move characteristic of the separation between Church and State) "a great church for national purposes," and 1893, when Congress empowered a foundation to build the thing. Where to put the cathedral, and what style to build it in, occasioned more church-state conflict: some called the chosen site, 57 acres on Mount St. Albans (D.C.'s highest point), too far from government buildings. Others complained that the planned Gothic style would clash with downtown's neo-Athenian architecture. In any event, the well-kept grounds keep the business world (if not the Wisconsin Ave. traffic) at a distance.

Building the cathedral (the world's sixth largest) took over 80 years, from 1907 until 1990, though the interior spaces have been in use for decades. As Gothic architecture dictates, the cathedral has the shape of a cross, with the nave in the main body of the church, the apse at the altar, and the transepts forming the cross-piece. Indiana limestone is the only structural material here; all details were carved from the walls by hand.

The cathedral has always endeared itself to official Washington. At the cornerstone-laying ceremony in 1907, President Theodore Roosevelt showed up to speak, and every U.S. president since has dropped by. Even in this political city, however, the cathedral has risen majestically to its religious functions. Rev. Martin Luther King, Jr. preached his last Sunday sermon from the Canterbury pulpit; more recently, another Nobel Peace Prize winner, the Dalai Lama, spoke here. Writers, as well as speakers, have taken note of the cathedral: Margaret Truman's *Murder in the Cathedral* was set in Bethlehem Chapel. Christmas and Easter services attract plenty of tourists and quite a few dignitaries. Anyone can come to the regular Episcopal services (Mon.-Sat. 7:30am, noon, and 4pm; Sun. 8, 9, 11am, and 4 and 6:30pm; also Sept.-June and special occasions Sun. 10am. Only the Sun. 11am service takes place in the main upper church).

Explore the cathedral with the aid of a **map,** available at the northwest entrance. (The **wheelchair ramp** and **restrooms** are also near this entrance.) Don't forget to descend to the crypt level and ascend to the Observation Gallery. Take the free 45-minute guided **tour,** led by purple-clad docents. (Tours available Mon.-Sat. 10am-3:15pm every 15 min., Sun. 12:30-2:45pm, except on holidays like Thanksgiving, Christmas, Palm Sunday, and Easter.) Suggested donation $2 adults, $1 children.

President Woodrow Wilson's tomb juts from the south aisle (under the window commemorating him). Look immediately to Wilson's right for the cathedral's most unusual stained-glass window, a blue and red **spacescape** donated by a former NASA director; an actual moon rock is embedded in the center of the window. Others buried here include blind and deaf education pioneer Helen Keller; her companion and teacher Anne Sullivan Macy; Larz Anderson, capitalist, diplomat, and builder of Anderson House; and Cordell Hull, secretary of state during World War II. Stone carvings and statues depict, not surprisingly, biblical figures. One of the best, the

Statue of Christian Majesty surrounded by all the angels and archangels, sits behind the High Altar.

Downstairs, on the **crypt level,** burrow into the Bethlehem Chapel, the Chapel of St. Joseph of Arimathea, and the Resurrection Chapel. The Chapel of the Good Shepherd awaits flocks on this level as well and stays open until 10pm. (Enter from the west end of the cathedral at night.) Be warned, though: the stairs to the crypt level are hardly user-friendly to handicapped persons and may exhaust or distress those with mobility problems.

Ride the elevator (located near the main doors of the west entrance) to the **Pilgrim Observation Gallery;** get out on the top floor and turn right. You won't see pilgrims, but you will see Washington—from the highest vantage point in the city. Check out the cathedral's **museum** to the left of the elevator. One display explains cathedral vocabulary, like the difference between a grotesque and a gargoyle.

The **Bishop's Garden** near the South Transept resembles a medieval walled garden. Herbs and roses grow in this sanctuary (open daily until dusk). Though the garden is technically closed at night, young Washingtonians have taken midnight strolls here for years. The lights illuminating the fountain cast flowing shadows against the cathedral—the perfect romantic hideaway. Education returns to the Middle Ages at the well-connected **National Cathedral School** for Girls (NCS), established in 1899, and **St. Alban's School** for Boys, founded in 1905; both educate on the Cathedral grounds. NCS's Hearst Hall relaxes in a softer Italian Renaissance style; St. Alban's Gothic excess matches the cathedral (and the school environment) more closely. According to ex-headmaster Canon Charles Martin, "St. Alban's exists to help boys not into the Kingdom of Harvard but into the Kingdom of Heaven."

Children and families "build" parts of their own cathedrals at the **Medieval Workshop** (537-2930). Carve stone, see how a stained-glass window is created, mold a gargoyle out of clay. (Open Mon.-Fri. July-Sept. 1-4:30pm, and year round Sat. 11am-2pm.) June and July host an irregular schedule of **outdoor classical music.** In late September or early October an **Open Hours day** resounds with organ music, choral recitals, and the only chance all year to climb the tower and see the carillon.

Public transportation can take you to the cathedral—with some hassle. (Metro: Tenleytown, then take the #30, 32, 34 or 36 bus toward Georgetown; or walk up Cathedral Ave. from the equidistant Woodley Park-Zoo Metro.) Driving from downtown, take Massachusetts Ave. north and turn right on Wisconsin Ave.; the cathedral is on your immediate right. Parking is free but limited to the parking lot between the northwest and North Transept entrances and on the streets on or near the grounds. (Cathedral proper open May-Aug. Mon.-Fri. 10am-9pm, Sat. 10am-4:30pm, Sun. 12:30-4pm; Sept.-April Mon.-Sat. 10am-4:30pm, Sun. 12:30-4pm. Call about disabled and hearing-impaired access.)

GLOVER PARK

Busy with physicists and astronomers during the day, the **U.S. Naval Observatory** (653-1507) opens up—sort of—for guided tours on Monday nights at 8:30pm (except federal holidays). Enter the South Gate on Observatory Circle across from the New Zealand embassy. **Parking** is available outside the gate on Observatory Circle. The gate opens at 8pm, but show up by 7:30pm—only the first 90 people are allowed in. Be prepared to show identification and to go through a metal detector as you enter. Don't plan on leaving until the 1½-hour **tour** is over: either from concerns about spying or fear of damage to the equipment, visitors can't leave the touring party. The tour has three parts: a ½-hour video, a visit to a 12-inch refracting telescope in order to view celestial objects, and a look at the super-accurate atomic clock. Take the tour only if the observatory's science and history intrigue you; your glimpse of the night sky will be all too fleeting. To experience the observatory's timekeeping functions, set your watch by its **atomic clock**—call 653-1800 for the official U.S. hour, minute, and second. The grounds of the observatory are closed to the public at all other times, in part for the security and privacy of the circle's other tenant: the Vice President. The looming, white **Vice Presidential Mansion** is best viewed from the intersection of Massachusetts Ave. and 34th St., though even here high fences and dense foliage conceal it pretty well.

Across the street from Al's place, Norwegian diplomats beat the heat in their ultramodern embassy, a green glass and copper edifice that looks like it was gift-wrapped in a chain-link fence. Along with the embassy of Cape Verde next door, the Norwegian embassy marks the end of the stretch of Mass. Ave. known as "Embassy Row" that begins southeast of Dupont Circle.

For the ultimate diplomatic snub, circle back around Observatory Circle to Calvert St., head west, and then hang a right on Wisconsin. Soon you'll see the **Russian embassy** compound on the left, behind high stone walls and higher fences, most definitely off-limits to all comers. The embassy's location, on top-dollar property near the summit of Mount St. Albans, incensed Cold Warriors when construction began in the early '80s. Smile for the security cameras as you walk by.

TENLEY CIRCLE

You can recognize **Sidwell Friends School,** at Wisconsin Ave. and Rodman St. NW, by the tennis courts visible from the street. The school, reaffirming its history of educating offspring of the D.C. powerful (past parents include Bob Woodward, Tim Wirth, David Brinkley, and Bill Bradley), became the talk of the town with the arrival of First Daughter Chelsea Clinton. Farther up at Wisconsin and Davenport, rival **Georgetown Day School** studies and plays in a tile-faced building that seems to have a bad case of measles. Both schools lay claim to liberal philosophies and hefty tuitions. Across Wisconsin Ave., public **Woodrow Wilson High School** serves a diverse student body; see them hang out in **Fort Reno Park** across Chesapeake St. at 40th St. NW. Summer punk shows in the park include embarrassing amateurs and brilliant local talent alike, sometimes on the same evening.

Few of these high school students stay in the neighborhood after graduation, but college could be as close as just down the street at **American University,** which fans out behind Ward Circle at Massachusetts and Nebraska Ave. NW. Among AU's few attractions are its cheap performing-arts events. The movies shown during the school year (for film classes) are free to visitors; some are landmarks in the history of cinema. (See **Nightlife & Entertainment,** p. 224.) Theater, dance, and musical events at AU proliferate, but their quality varies; contemporary-classical composers-in-residence may give several cheap performances (non-students $6). Call 885-2787 for more information on performing arts at AU.

South of American University, hills and forests hide opulent homes along prestigious **Foxhall Road.** Glover Archibald and Battery Kemble parks rise only blocks away. A few houses, like philanthropist David Lloyd Kreeger's, hide their custom architecture behind concrete fences up to a city-block long. Few tourists come this far west of Georgetown, but the neighborhood's relative isolation and botanical proliferation make it perfect for an afternoon stroll.

An afternoon stroll is out of the question at the **Israeli Embassy,** 3514 International Dr. NW at Reno Rd., several blocks east of Tenley Circle (Metro: Van Ness/UDC). You'll recognize it by what's not there: lacking the ornate coat-of-arms, the statuary, and the refurbished-mansion look that normally signal an embassy, the Israeli delegation works securely inside a blocky concrete building whose heavy construction and difficulty of approach represent the last word in anti-terrorist architecture. During the Gulf War, the embassy received an extra round of security from circling Secret Service cars.

FRIENDSHIP HEIGHTS

The words "Friendship Heights" conjure up the secret addiction of many Washingtonians—ritzy stores and fabulous buys. Exit signs inside the Metro station point you in the direction of different stores. If you haven't decided exactly where to go, exit at Western Ave. and Military Rd., which puts you on street level and lets you ponder your choices. Like the neighborhood itself, the shopping areas are a mix of suburbia and downtown, blocks of street-level boutiques with malls nearby.

Beside this shopping mecca, the quaint **Washington Dolls' House & Toy Museum** cavorts at 5236 44th St. NW (244-0024), one block west of Wisconsin Ave. next to the Jenifer Mall. Six rooms inside showcase a carefully researched collection of antique dolls, dolls' houses, toys, and games. The collection captures the social history of America (some international pieces are also displayed) and attracts more adults than children. (Admission $3, seniors $2, children under 14 $1. Open Tues.-Sat. 10am-5pm, Sun. noon-5pm.) At night after the stores close, their **parking lots** stay open, so you can park here and walk down Wisconsin Ave. for dinner.

■■■ BETHESDA, MD

Metro: Bethesda.
Bethesda lets out a relaxed and self-satisfied yawn as it stretches itself along Wisconsin Ave. from D.C.'s Maryland border to the National Institutes of Health. Born of a boondocky crossroads in the early, agrarian days of Montgomery County, a wave of suburban housing shook the sleepy, rattletrap cowtown out of its past and set it down again on the edge of this century. Soon enough, immigrants were boring wells here and calling this soil their own. In no time, various and exquisite cuisines and a healthy crop of new cultural offerings had made Bethesda an important social center. In the last decade, however, corporate real estate has beanstalked the happy town with uniform, concrete, and tiny-windowed office towers. But some of Bethesda's mid-century charm does remain, however hidden: it will take some sniffing to uncover the stubbornly rundown diners and silvery Art Deco shopfronts.

Visitors stop in Bethesda to shop, explore the neighborhood, think about urban planning, or, most of all, to eat well and cheap; the lack of major sights hardly precludes a visit here. Walk through a collection of outdoor modern sculpture. Bill Wainwright's *Rainbow Forest,* an aluminum-disc sculpture, sways securely above the Bethesda Metro's top escalator. Hover around it until you see the incorporated holograms. The bright yellow aluminum sculpture on the plaza itself is Mary Ann Mears's *Beacon.* Crowds of up to 500 dance each Friday night between May and September from 6pm to 9pm in the open plaza just outside the Metro. Dancing fashions range from business suits to zebra prints to unfortunate spandex outfits. From Thanksgiving to February, outdoor ice-skaters zoom across the plaza.

A short block south of the Metro station the old, stoney-faced **Bethesda Post Office,** 7400 Wisconsin Ave., glowers at the encroaching mass of steel and glass (30-441-2664; open Mon.-Fri. 8am-6pm, Sat. 8:30am-1pm). Directly north of the post office is the *Madonna of the Trail,* a 1929 stone memorial to the mothers of covered-wagon days. A detour west off Wisconsin Ave. will bring you to **Hampden Square,** an attractive condo and office complex at 4801 Hampden Lane. Around the base of the building, a shady courtyard gives the illusion of a bit of seclusion. The columns around it suggest a Mediterranean grotto, while Tom Supensky's blue ceramic *The Wave* simply suggests the Mediterranean. Raymond Kaskey's *Neptune,* a concrete rendering of the god's face, entrances children from a nearby wall.

Farther south at 7155 Wisconsin Ave., near Bethesda Ave., is the **Montgomery Farm Women's Cooperative Market** (301-652-2291). On Wednesdays and Saturdays (beginning in the early morning and running thorugh the middle of the afternoon) the low white building can barely hold its bustling farmer's market. The cooperative, begun in 1932, is still run entirely by farmers; the first man joined its governing board in 1968. For information on other special events in Bethesda, call the **Bethesda Urban District's Special Events Line** recording at 301-652-8798; for their local calendar, write to Bethesda Urban District, 7815 Woodmont Ave., Bethesda, MD, 20814.

NATIONAL INSTITUTES OF HEALTH

Like rats in a maze, some 3500 researchers in white coats scurry among NIH's 45 buildings and 316 acres. Their quest: cures for cancer, AIDS, and their ilk—and maybe a Nobel Prize or two along the way. Most of the action takes place in labs that are closed to the public, but the biologically curious can still wander around the expansive grounds, located between Wisconsin Ave. (Rte. 355) and Old Georgetown Rd. just inside the Beltway in Bethesda (Metro: Medical Center). For a more directional stroll, pick up a free, 90-minute tour cassette and player from the **Visitor Information Center,** building 10, room B1C-218, under a three-story atrium in the building's center (301-496-1776). **Building 10** is the largest on the campus. A glass and brick behemoth atop a hill that you can reach on foot from the Metro, or by hopping an NIH "campus shuttle" bus from the station, the Visitors Center also experiments with a slide show, videotaped exhibits, a working lab, and guided **tours.** (Visitors Center open Mon.-Fri. 8:30am-5pm. Tours Mon., Wed., and Fri. at 11am.) The **Foundation Bookstore,** also on the lower level of building 10 in room BIL-101, sells medical sketch books and notebooks, anatomical charts, stethoscopes, and blood-pressure cuffs (open Mon.-Fri. 8:30am-4pm). Many people come to the Visitors Center for literature on specific areas of disease research; more information can also be found in the **National Library of Medicine,** the world's largest library devoted to a single subject (301-496-6095). (Free tours Mon.-Fri. 1pm; meet in the lobby of building 38A. Library open Mon.-Fri. 8:30am-5pm, Sat. 8:30am-12:30pm; Sept.-May Mon.-Thurs. 8:30am-9pm, Fri.-Sat. 8:30am-5pm.)

A Different Kind of Museum

For a change of pace, take the kids to the **National Museum of Health and Medicine,** Building 54, 6825 16th St. NW (782-2200), near Rock Creek Park. The guys at this place jovially study assassinations, birth defects, military doctors, and other medical unusualments (take an S2 or S4 bus up 16th St. from downtown, or a 52 or 54 bus from the Takoma Metro Station). Presidents Lincoln and Garfield, both shot while in office, get their own displays. The **actual bullet that ended Lincoln's life** is on display as well as a **skull fragment** and a lock of his hair. The museum's high points are its pathology displays, which are accompanied by case histories of the unfortunate subjects. A **grisly skeleton** whose fused bones keep the adult owner frozen in a seated position is just one of the creepy items in the Walter Reed closets. (Open daily 10am-5:30pm. Free.)

■■■ ROCK CREEK PARK

City-weary voices crying out for wilderness can rejoice in the 15 miles of hiking trails and bridle paths in Rock Creek Park. More like a managed forest than a landscaped city park, the 2100-acre green is a leafy home for joggers, park rangers, and bustling wildlife. (Supposedly, Charles de Gaulle once mistook it for the French Embassy's new backyard.) This opiate for nature addicts takes the shape of a bent syringe, with the needle pointing at the Kennedy Center and the plunger west of 16th St. NW, at the District's northern tip. **Rock Creek Parkway,** which becomes Beach Drive north of Klingle Rd. NW, winds through the park from north to south alongside its watery namesake. Some of the forest trails run near the parkway—which offers a noisy reminder of nearby city traffic—but the tiny bridges and sporadic creeks keep wilder sections of the park to themselves.

Thanks to plentiful shady trees, it's about 10 degrees cooler inside the park than outside. Along Rock Creek Pkwy., starting at Calvert St. and Connecticut Ave., is a 1½-mi. "Parcourse" **exercise trail,** complete with 18 **workout stations** where you can push-up, pull-up, and sit-up to your heart's content (and benefit). A 4-mi. run starts where Rock Creek Pkwy. crosses under Connecticut Ave.; run north toward Pierce Mill and then retrace your route. In upper Rock Creek Park, there's a standard 11-mi. run from Beach Dr. to Tilden St. to East-West Hwy. in Chevy Chase. Cyclists will find plenty of **bicycle trails** crisscrossing the park and plenty of signs pointing them out. These same cyclists compete with rollerbladers for control of Beach Dr. from 7am on Saturdays until 7pm on Sundays, when the park closes its gates to motorized vehicles for most its length north of Broad Branch Rd. Parking is

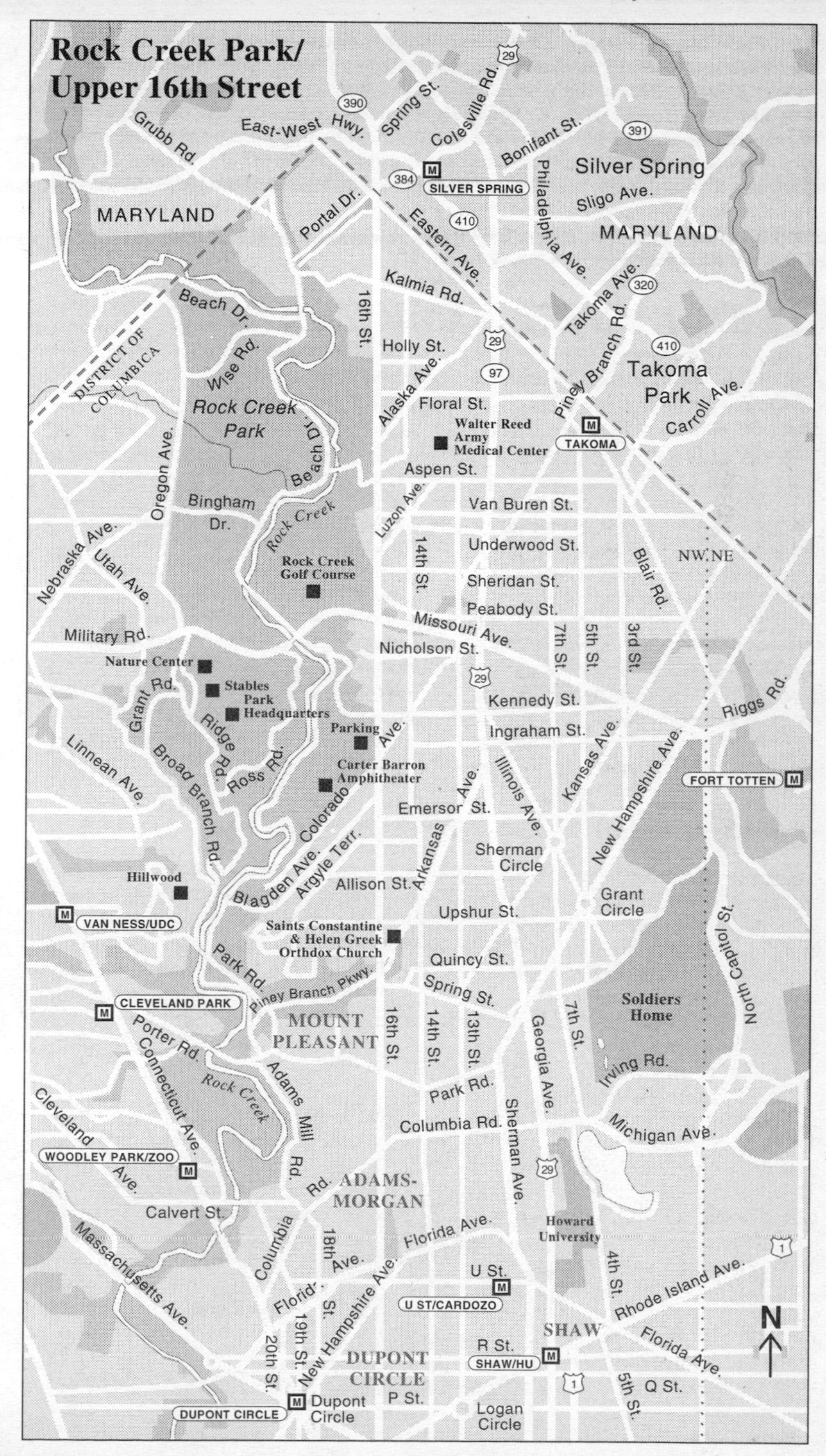
Rock Creek Park/
Upper 16th Street
MARYLAND
Silver Spring
MARYLAND
Takoma
Park
DISTRICT OF
COLUMBIA
Rock Creek
Park
Grubb Rd.
East-West Hwy.
Spring St.
Colesville Rd.
Bonifant St.
Sligo Ave.
Portal Dr.
Eastern Ave.
Philadelphia Ave.
Kalmia Rd.
Takoma Ave.
Piney Branch Rd.
Beach Dr.
Wise Rd.
16th St.
Holly St.
Alaska Ave.
Floral St.
Carroll Ave.
Walter Reed
Army
Medical Center
SILVER SPRING
TAKOMA
Oregon Ave.
Aspen St.
Bingham
Dr.
Rock Creek
Luzon Ave.
Van Buren St.
Underwood St.
Sheridan St.
Peabody St.
Nebraska Ave.
Utah Ave.
Rock Creek
Golf Course
14th St.
Blair Rd.
NW NE
Military Rd.
Missouri Ave.
Nicholson St.
7th St.
5th St.
3rd St.
Nature Center
Stables
Park
Headquarters
Grant Rd.
Ridge Rd.
Kennedy St.
Ingraham St.
Riggs Rd.
Parking
Ave.
Linnean Ave.
Broad Branch Rd.
Ross Rd.
Carter Barron
Amphitheater
Colorado
Illinois Ave.
Kansas Ave.
New Hampshire Ave.
FORT TOTTEN
Emerson St.
Arkansas Ave.
Sherman
Circle
Argyle Terr.
Blagden Ave.
Allison St.
Hillwood
VAN NESS/UDC
Grant
Circle
Upshur St.
Saints Constantine
& Helen Greek
Orthdox Church
Park Rd.
Quincy St.
North Capitol St.
Piney Branch Pkwy.
Spring St.
CLEVELAND PARK
Soldiers
Home
MOUNT
PLEASANT
13th St.
Georgia Ave.
Porter Rd.
Connecticut Ave.
Adams Mill Rd.
Irving Rd.
Park Rd.
Cleveland Ave.
Columbia Rd.
Sherman Ave.
Michigan Ave.
WOODLEY PARK/ZOO
ADAMS-
MORGAN
Calvert St.
Howard
University
Columbia Rd.
Massachusetts Ave.
18th St.
Florida Ave.
Rhode Island Ave.
U St.
U ST/CARDOZO
4th St.
New Hampshire Ave.
Florida Ave.
SHAW
R St.
SHAW/HU
DUPONT
CIRCLE
20th St.
19th St.
Dupont
Circle
P St.
Q St.
Logan
Circle
DUPONT CIRCLE
N

plentiful at lots throughout the park, and **sporadic grassy knolls** along Beach Drive are designated as daytime **picnic spots.** Camping in Rock Creek Park, however, is always illegal, probably dangerous, and mostly impossible anyway.

Park information can be had by mail, by phone, or in person from the park's **Nature Center,** at 5200 Glover Rd. NW (426-6828/9), which also screens films (Sat.-Sun. at 11am) and offers a planetarium show (Sat.-Sun. at 1 and 4pm, Wed. at 3:45pm). **Guided walks** are offered at 3pm on Saturday and Sunday. Call and ask about "Ranger's Choice" events. (Nature Center open daily 9am-5pm; September-May Wed.-Sun. 9am-5pm.) **Rock Creek Horse Center** (362-0117) rents horsies. See **Sports & Recreation,** p. 228, for details.

■■■ TAKOMA PARK, MD

Metro: Takoma.

Takoma Park straddles two lines. One is the D.C. line; half its own town, half a Washington neighborhood, Takoma Park aspires simultaneously to small-town coziness and subdued hip. The other line divides the '60s generation from their yuppie successors: neighbors divide evenly between tie-dyes and suit-and-ties, and most of them seem happy about the compromise. Colorful bungalows, trees, and roomy Victorian houses dominate the idyllic streetscape. Crystals, tiny Ozark harps, and South American cotton clutter the retail scene and fit the low-key, neo-Woodstock dress code. As any resident could tell you, the town declared itself a nuclear-free zone during the mid-80s height of Reaganism, joining Berkeley, CA, and Madison, WI. Recently, both Takoma types pulled together to push for environmental reform.

There aren't major sights this far from downtown, but Takoma Park still merits a stroll-through, not to mention **window-shopping** and browsing. For Takoma Park's commercial heart, head up Carroll Ave. from the Takoma Metro and into the town proper, where Carroll bends off to the left and Laurel Ave. picks up to the right. Talk to storekeepers, peek in corners, and shop to the point of spiritual fatigue. The shops are open all week, though the people-watching is certainly best on weekends. (See **Shopping,** p. 229, for stores in this area.)

■■■ NORTHEAST

> *As you move about the city you will see that outlying tracts of land, once the broad receptacles of dead animals and where no better scavengers appeared than the buzzards or the crows, have been reclaimed and added to the city and made to blossom like the rose.*
>
> —*Frederick Douglass,* Lecture on the National Capital (1877)

Metro: Rhode Island Ave., Brookland/CUA, Ft. Totten, Minnesota Ave., Deanwood.

Northeast Washington is too big to be a neighborhood. The triangle formed by North Capitol St., East Capitol St., and the District line encloses over a quarter of the District's land area, including parts of Capitol Hill (covered under that section), Takoma Park, and some lesser-known middle-class neighborhoods. Many parts of Northeast have been overwhelmed by the crack epidemic, especially near the Prince George's County line and east of the Anacostia River. On the other hand, **Catholic University** guards (and landscapes) its acres north of Michigan Ave. off North Capitol St., while the **National Arboretum** and **Kenilworth Gardens** landscape (and guard) even more space east of Capitol Hill.

North Capitol St. cruises from the Capitol to the northern tip of the D.C. diamond at startlingly high speeds for city driving. Four roads run roughly parallel through Northeast on a southwest-northeast diagonal: Maryland Ave., which shoots out from the Capitol, eventually becoming Bladensburg Rd.; New York Ave., home of the cheap-motel strip; Rhode Island Ave.; and meandering Michigan Ave., which leads to the Catholic U. area. Maryland Ave. is the southernmost of the quadruplets. 13th

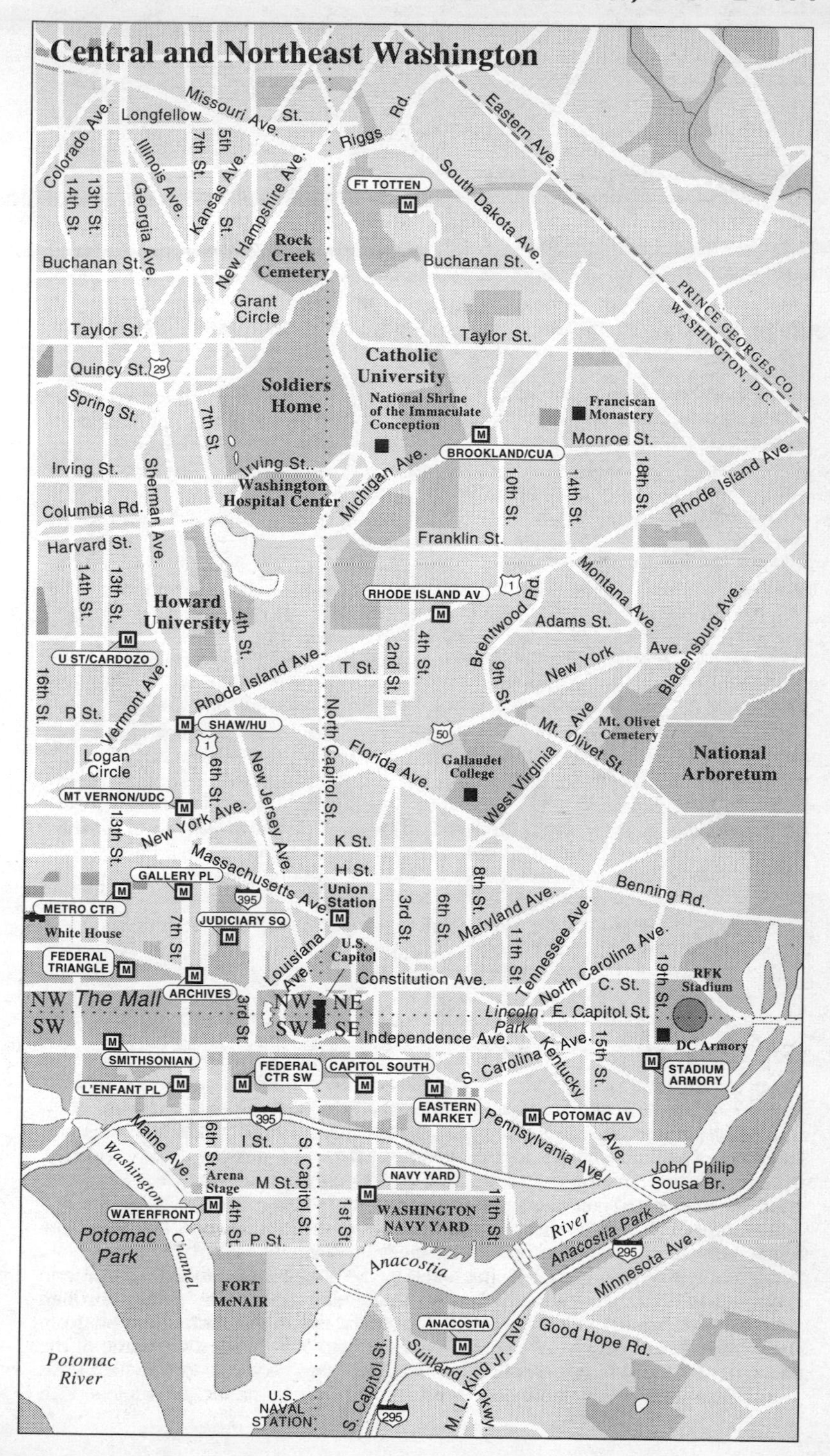
Central and Northeast Washington
Rock Creek Cemetery
Grant Circle
Soldiers Home
Washington Hospital Center
Catholic University
National Shrine of the Immaculate Conception
Franciscan Monastery
Howard University
Logan Circle
Gallaudet College
Mt. Olivet Cemetery
National Arboretum
Union Station
U.S. Capitol
White House
The Mall
RFK Stadium
DC Armory
WASHINGTON NAVY YARD
FORT McNAIR
Arena Stage
Potomac Park
Potomac River
Washington Channel
Anacostia River
John Philip Sousa Br.
U.S. NAVAL STATION
PRINCE GEORGES CO.
WASHINGTON, D.C.
FT TOTTEN
BROOKLAND/CUA
RHODE ISLAND AV
U ST/CARDOZO
SHAW/HU
MT VERNON/UDC
GALLERY PL
METRO CTR
JUDICIARY SQ
FEDERAL TRIANGLE
ARCHIVES
SMITHSONIAN
L'ENFANT PL
FEDERAL CTR SW
CAPITOL SOUTH
EASTERN MARKET
POTOMAC AV
STADIUM ARMORY
NAVY YARD
WATERFRONT
ANACOSTIA
NW NE SW SE
Missouri Ave.
Eastern Ave.
Riggs Rd.
South Dakota Ave.
New Hampshire Ave.
Rhode Island Ave.
Michigan Ave.
Florida Ave.
New York Ave.
Massachusetts Ave.
Maryland Ave.
Benning Rd.
Bladensburg Ave.
Montana Ave.
West Virginia Ave.
Mt. Olivet St.
Constitution Ave.
Independence Ave.
Pennsylvania Ave.
Kentucky Ave.
North Carolina Ave.
Tennessee Ave.
Maine Ave.
Minnesota Ave.
Good Hope Rd.
Suitland Pkwy.
M. L. King Jr. Ave.
Anacostia Park
North Capitol St.
S. Capitol St.
Lincoln Park
E. Capitol St.

St., which becomes Brentwood Rd. south of Rhode Island Ave., slices through the middle-class Brookland neighborhood. South Dakota Ave. parallels the District line, while off-again, on-again Eastern Ave. follows the line itself. What there is to see in Northeast spreads out all over the quadrant, so expect to spend some time driving or riding the Metro between the clumps of sights.

NATIONAL ARBORETUM

The National Arboretum, 3501 New York Ave. NE (245-2726), main entrance at 24th and R St. NE, is the United States's living library of trees and flowers. Nearly 10 miles of roads crisscross some 444 acres of land, which sprout flora ranging from crabapples to crapemyrtles. Every passing month in spring or summer sees flowers and blooms explode in a different corner of the arboretum. The May azaleas are particular favorites, as are the April cherries. Detailed information and brochures about seasonal highlights available from **Arbor House** (the visitors center).

A few attractions, such as the gargantuan **herb garden,** draw visitors year-round, but none more so than the arboretum's world-class stock of **bonsai** (dwarf trees) and **penjing** (potted plants landscaped with rocks, figurines, boats, and pagodas). Gardens, pavilions, and wooden tables show off more than 130 miniature flora, many of which are not only rare but also expensive (some bonsai cost over $10,000) and hard to keep alive.

From the bonsai collection, visitors will notice what seems to be an ancient Greek ruin sitting atop a hill at the center of the arboretum. The columns in question actually had a more local, though no less distinguished, origin—they once spanned the East Portico of the Capitol. Completed in 1826, the **Portico** was dismantled in 1958 to make room for an addition to the Capitol; the twenty-two columns were held in storage until 1984, when they were moved to the arboretum.

The arboretum is large enough to make a drive through it worthwhile, although a long, leisurely stroll is undoubtedly the best way to proceed. Bike riding is another option. Drive to the arboretum if at all possible, since the surrounding area is somewhat dangerous; **parking** is readily accessible inside the R St. entrance. The hopelessly carless can Metro themselves to Stadium-Armory, then board a B2, B4, or B5 bus. The buses take you to Bladensburg Rd. and R St. Just walk east on R. (Open daily 8am-5pm; July-March Mon.-Fri. 8am-5pm, Sat.-Sun. 10am-5pm. Bonsai collection open daily 10am-3:30pm. Free. **Arbor House** open daily 8am-4:30pm; July-March Mon.-Fri. 8am-4:30pm. Gift shop open daily March-Dec. 10am-3pm.)

Bonsai!!

Love of the bonsai has engendered an international network of fanciers, cultivators, and weirdos: in July 1991, a mysterious thief nabbed a $1000 bonsai from the Arboretum and then returned it three days later in improved condition—it had been pruned rather expertly. Go figure.

THE REST OF NORTHEAST

Across the Anacostia River from the National Arboretum, **Kenilworth Aquatic Gardens,** Anacostia Ave. and Douglas St. NE (426-6905), does for aquatic plants what the arboretum does for trees. (Metro: Deanwood.) Dozens of ponds sacrifice their surfaces to thousands of lilies, lotuses, and hyacinths. The gardens look best in July and Aug., when the tropical plants bloom, and unless you have a fondness for unadorned lily pads, come in the morning before the midday heat closes up the complex flowers. Plan to spend at least half an hour hoofing the paths amid the ponds, and leave an hour for the 1.5-mile **river trail,** which leads to the last natural marsh on the Anacostia river. The floating flora accompany a virtual army of turtles, frogs, waterfowl, muskrats, raccoons, and opossums. (A few blocks from the gardens, more dangerous virtual armies hold periodic turf wars. Watch your step.) A **Visitors Center** offers pamphlets and brochures, an exhibit on the history of the gardens, and an aquarium exhibit. From the Deanwood Metro, tramp over a green-cage bridge, walk straight down Douglas St., and cross the parking lot. The entrance is at Anacostia Ave. and Douglas St. By car, take New York Ave. NE out of the city, hang a right on Kenilworth Ave. just after crossing the District line, and follow the signs. (Open daily 6:30am-dusk in summer, 7am-4pm in winter; Visitors Center open daily 8am-4pm. Tours Sat.-Sun. and holidays at 9am, 11am, and 1pm.)

Catholic University, Michigan Ave. and 4th St. NE (319-5200), is an urban anomaly, a campus in the city but not of the city. (Metro: Brookland-CUA.) Don't be misled by the suburban grade-school architecture that greets you at the edge of campus nearest the Metro. Not far beyond lie the sort of Gothic buildings, creeping foliage, and spacious quadrangles that you might expect of a small-town college. The school doesn't offer guided tours, but feel free to wander on your own. Periodically posted campus maps will keep you oriented, or you can pick one up at the information desk on the first floor of University Center East, at the southern end of campus. **Information Center** open Mon.-Thurs. 8:30am-10pm, Fri. 8:30am-9pm, Sat. 3-9pm, Sun. 1-9pm. Buildings like the Marian Scholasticate and Salve Regina Hall will remind you that you're at a school where 80% of the students, and most of the professors, are Catholic. CUA's Hartke Theatre puts on arias for a professional-quality Summer Opera series. See **Nightlife & Entertainment** (p. 220) for more info.

Pedestrians won't miss the **Basilica of the National Shrine of the Immaculate Conception** (526-8300), located on the edge of the Catholic U. campus at Michigan Ave. and 4th St. NE. (Metro: Brookland-CUA.) After all, it's the eighth largest church in the world, and the largest Catholic Church in the Western Hemisphere (take that, St. Patrick's). The shrine's striking, boundary-crossing architecture catches eyes too, as Romanesque arches support stark, Byzantine-flavored façades and a blue-and-gold onion dome that seems straight from Kiev. The bell tower beside the main entrance is cleverly disguised as an Islamic minaret. The interior continues the architectural mix 'n' match, as some 59 kneeling chapels dedicated to the Virgin Mary line the walls of the main Church and crypt level. Many of them are decorated with stained-glass windows and colorful, intricate mosaics—part Byzantine, part Romanesque, and part neither. Funded partially by children who mailed in pennies, the National Shrine hosts weekly masses, which most CUA students attend. Reach the Basilica by walking straight across the CUA campus from the Metro; the main entrance is at street level on the front side of the shrine, to the right of the stairs leading up to the Upper Church. (Basilica open April-Oct. daily 7am-7pm, Nov.-March 7am-6pm; **tours** Mon.-Sat. every hour on the hour 9am-3pm; Sun. every hour on the half hour 1:30-4pm. Free. Upper Church masses held Sat. 5:15pm; Sun. 9am, 10:30am, noon, and 4:30pm. Crypt Church masses held Sun. 7:30am; Latin mass 1:30pm. Weekday masses held 7am, 7:30am, 8am, 8:30am, 12:10pm, and 5:15pm in the Crypt Church. Call about holiday services.) Free parking.

The peaceful **Franciscan Monastery,** 1400 Quincy St. NE (526-6800), brings a little bit of the Holy Land to America. (Metro: Brookland-CUA.) Some 700 years ago, the Roman Catholic Church entrusted the Franciscans with the guardianship of the Holy Land's most precious tombs and temples, and the monastery commemorates that duty with replicas of these holy shrines spread throughout the church and the surrounding grounds. Enter through the main arches at the corner of Quincy and 14th St., and proceed straight ahead to the main entrance while admiring the stately Byzantine architecture rising above. Fight through the maze of glass display cases to the waiting area, adorned with gilded copes and chasubles, where you can wait for a tour led by a Franciscan monk. You may set out into the main church on your own, though, and see the first of the many religious replicas—a model of Jesus' Sepulcher, including the rolling rock he pushed away in the Resurrection. Red lights lead to **murals** depicting Christ and the Apostles, as well as to a three-dimensional mural of the crucifixion. The advantage of taking the tour is that it also leads visitors downstairs to the replicas of the Roman **catacombs,** where holy relics and wall mosaics trace Bible stories. On deposit in the reliquaries are a collection of St. Benigus's bones wrapped in cotton; a statue of St. Cecilius, whom soldiers tried unsuccessfully to decapitate; and a statue of St. Sebastian—a popular subject of

Renaissance painters—who miraculously survived being shot full of arrows by Roman soldiers. Outside the monastery, you may wander the well-tended **gardens** or explore the replicas of a number of noted tombs and grottos. From the Brookland-CUA Metro, take an H2 bus or walk across the Michigan Ave. bridge, continue for about 2 blocks, and then turn right on Quincy St. (open Mon.-Sat. 9-11am and 1-4pm, Sun. 1-4pm. Free.; **tours,** led by Franciscan monks, leave every hour.) Free parking in two lots on 14th St. Wheelchair accessible.

Rock Creek Cemetery (829-0585) loads up on monuments and graves between New Hampshire Ave. NW and North Capitol St. (Metro: Fort Totten; enter at Rock Creek Church Rd. and Webster St. NW.) Section E of the cemetery contains Augustus Saint-Gaudens's **Adams Monument.** Henry Adams's wife Marian committed suicide by drinking photographic chemicals. Saint-Gaudens's bronze depicts her, but it's commonly called "Grief" instead: the hooded, cloaked, and seated figure seems to recall all human pain. (Open daily 7:30am-dusk.)

Gallaudet University, 800 Florida Ave. NE (651-5000, TDD 651-5000), established in 1864, is still the world's only university for the deaf. (Metro: Union Station.) Protesters shouting and signing "Deaf President Now" made national news in 1989; the students subsequently got a deaf president, Dr. I. King Jordan, and the deaf community got more nationwide media attention than ever before. An exhibit in the Visitors Center (651-5050) behind College Hall on the right shows several short films and videotapes and an array of photographs. (Open Mon.-Fri. 9am-5pm. Free.)

■■■ ARLINGTON, VA

Metro: Crystal City, National Airport, Braddock Rd., King St.

Washington abandoned Arlington in 1846 when Virginia snatched back its contribution to the Federal City. Nevertheless, Arlington's inclinations remain Washingtonian. With four bridges to downtown D.C. as its above-ground umbilical cords, Arlington continues as the Last Colony's first colony. While buildings in Washington can't rise higher than the Capitol dome, corporate high-flyers take power trips in Rosslyn's skyscrapers, which lie just across the Potomac from Georgetown. Arlington's suburban status also means more land for the taking: Arlington Cemetery, National Airport, and the Pentagon would be unthinkable in the capital on account of their sheer size. South or west of these behemoths of business and government, thousands of commuters find Arlington's modest houses convenient. Several Asian and Hispanic communities call Arlington County home.

ORIENTATION

The Arlington Vistors Center, 735 18th St. (358-5720 or 800-677-6267) will answer your questions and give you armloads of brochures (Metro: Crystal City; open Mon.-Sat. 9am-6pm, Sun. 9am-6pm). If you try to drive in Arlington for any space of time, you'll probably get lost. The original, D.C.-style street plan featured two- and three-syllable streets in alphabetical order (Upton, Vermont, Wakefield, Woodstock, Abingdon, Buchanan) running roughly north-south and crossed by east-west numbered streets. While these streets exist, they are often only a few blocks long; some end and pick up again miles from where they began. Add the network of non-parallel numbered routes, highways, and boulevards—designed to move commuters from downtown D.C. to their Fairfax bungalows—and you have non-linear, mind-bending insanity. These disorienting major roads include I-395 and the Columbia Pike (Rte. 244) in South Arlington, Arlington Blvd. (Rte. 50), Wilson Blvd., and Washington Blvd. (Rte. 237). I-66 can take you *through* Arlington, but not *to* much of it.

Fortunately, the Metro and Metrobus can take you where you want to go. Buses cruise down Columbia Pike, Arlington Blvd., and Wilson Blvd. Check with the Metro (637-7000) before you make the trip. The Metro's orange line can shuttle you out to most of Arlington's hotspots for ethnic cuisine. The major sights, Arlington Cemetery and the Pentagon, are just across the river at the Metro stops named for

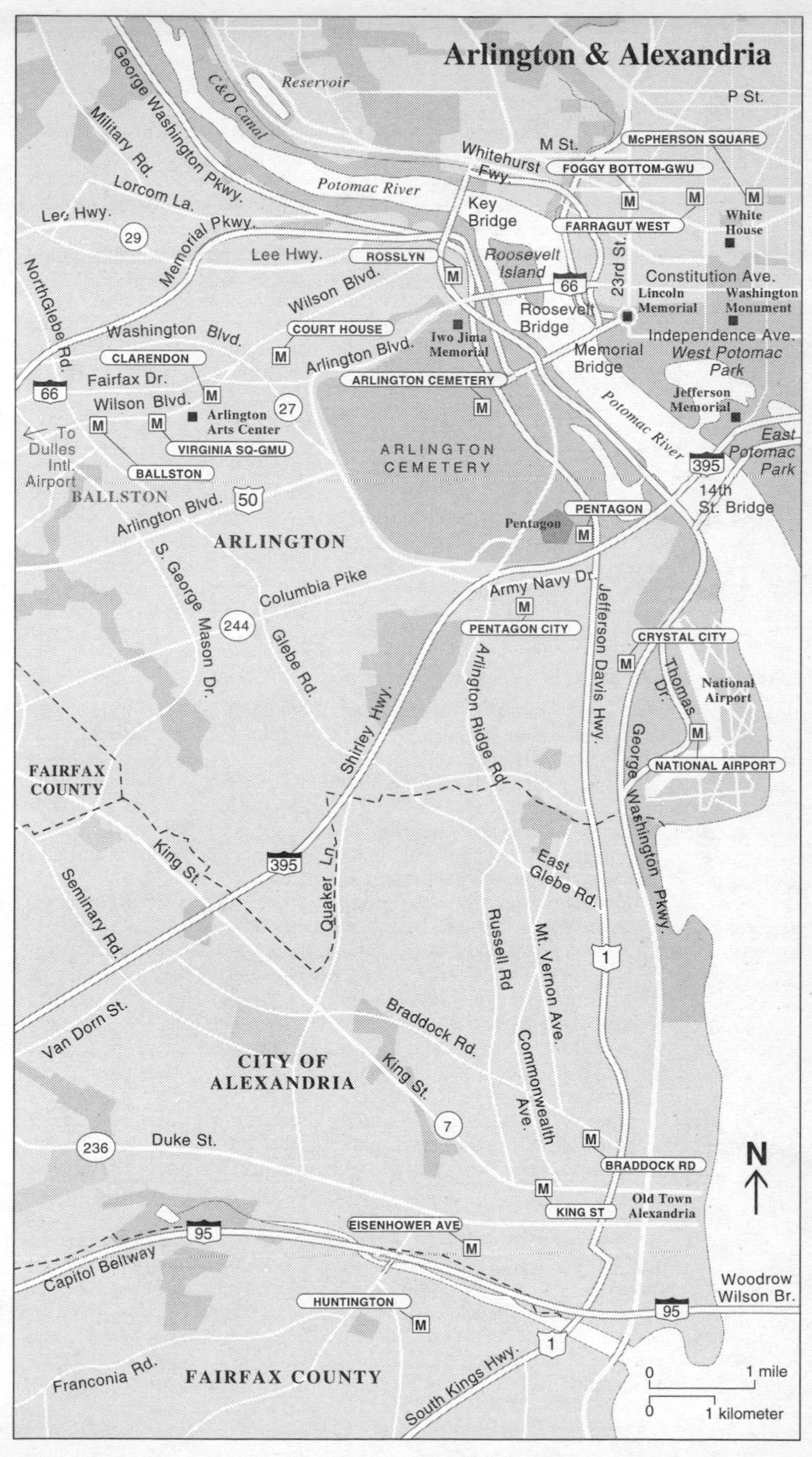
Arlington & Alexandria
Reservoir
C&O Canal
George Washington Pkwy.
Military Rd.
Lorcom La.
Lee Hwy.
Memorial Pkwy.
Potomac River
Whitehurst Fwy.
M St.
P St.
McPHERSON SQUARE
FOGGY BOTTOM-GWU
FARRAGUT WEST
Key Bridge
White House
Lee Hwy.
ROSSLYN
Roosevelt Island
23rd St.
Constitution Ave.
Lincoln Memorial
Washington Monument
Wilson Blvd.
Roosevelt Bridge
NorthGlebe Rd.
Washington Blvd.
COURT HOUSE
Iwo Jima Memorial
Independence Ave.
CLARENDON
Arlington Blvd.
Memorial Bridge
West Potomac Park
Fairfax Dr.
ARLINGTON CEMETERY
Wilson Blvd.
Arlington Arts Center
Jefferson Memorial
To Dulles Intl. Airport
VIRGINIA SQ-GMU
Potomac River
East Potomac Park
BALLSTON
ARLINGTON CEMETERY
14th St. Bridge
BALLSTON
Arlington Blvd.
PENTAGON
Pentagon
ARLINGTON
S. George Mason Dr.
Army Navy Dr.
Columbia Pike
Jefferson Davis Hwy.
Glebe Rd.
PENTAGON CITY
CRYSTAL CITY
Arlington Ridge Rd.
Thomas Dr.
National Airport
Shirley Hwy.
George Washington Pkwy.
NATIONAL AIRPORT
FAIRFAX COUNTY
King St.
Quaker Ln.
East Glebe Rd.
Seminary Rd.
Russell Rd
Mt. Vernon Ave.
Van Dorn St.
Braddock Rd.
CITY OF ALEXANDRIA
King St.
Commonwealth Ave.
Duke St.
BRADDOCK RD
N
KING ST
Old Town Alexandria
EISENHOWER AVE
Capitol Beltway
Woodrow Wilson Br.
HUNTINGTON
Franconia Rd.
FAIRFAX COUNTY
South Kings Hwy.
0
1 mile
0
1 kilometer

them. If you get really lost, check streets signs for "N" (north of Rte. 50, or Arlington Blvd.) or "S" (south of it). Remember that the area code in Arlington is **703.**

SIGHTS

Rosslyn is just what D.C.'s planners were trying to avoid. It's not worth a detour, but look around on your way into Georgetown or out of D.C. toward Little Saigon. In this mess of skyscrapers, the Gannett/*USA Today* building looms so large that it is routinely blamed for the navigation mistakes of airplanes landing at National Airport.

Crystal City, another concrete community of offices and condos, reclines (like real crystal) half-underground. Its miles of underground tunnels connect block upon block of buildings, and the Metro will bring you straight to a massive underground shopping mall, **Crystal Underground.** Three air-conditioned, underground blocks away from the Metro in Building 3 of Crystal Plaza (follow the signs to "Plaza 3"), the **Patent and Trademark Office** (on the third floor) has all the country's millions of patents on file. On the lobby level is the dinky **National Inventor's Hall of Fame,** which honors Alexander Graham Bell, Charles Goodyear, Louis Pasteur, Samuel Morse, and others. Check out G.M. Pratt's 1877 sewing machine. Special events take place on National Inventors Day, which falls on or near February 11 (Thomas Edison's birthday) during a weekend. (Open Mon.-Fri. 8am-8pm. Free.)

Luckily, the Smithsonian museums don't have a patent on displaying exciting art. The four galleries at the **Arlington Arts Center,** 3550 Wilson Blvd. (524-1494), near the Virginia Square Metro, contain paintings, drawings, sculptures, and mixed-media pieces, most of which are for sale. Classes are available in life drawing, painting, and other media. Call about fall programs like Thursday evening seminars and discussion groups, as well as the periodic poetry readings, most of which require some sort of fee. (Open Tues.-Fri. 11am-5pm, Sat.-Sun. 1-5pm. Free.)

ARLINGTON NATIONAL CEMETERY

The silence of Arlington National Cemetery honors those who sacrificed their lives in war. The 612 acres of rolling hills and tree-lined avenues hold the bodies of U.S. military veterans—from five-star generals to unknown soldiers. As the largest military cemetery in the U.S., Arlington National Cemetery holds 200,000 veterans and their dependents. The hundreds who visit each day aren't exactly tourists—a walk through the cemetery's endless rows of white headstones is too solemn an experience to be confused with sight-seeing. Still, marble monuments to nurses and military groups often cross the line, sliding into memorial kitsch.

Robert E. Lee once owned an estate covering most of the cemetery grounds, but the general abandoned his land when he moved to Richmond with his family to serve the Confederacy. Since the Lee family couldn't show their faces to pay property taxes on the land (because they would have been arrested), the Union government seized the property. Major General Montgomery Meigs, who hated the Lees for joining the South, began to bury Union troops in places like Mrs. Lee's rose garden so that the family could never reclaim their estate. Since then, many prominent soldiers have come to rest in peace in Arlington. Pierre L'Enfant, who laid out Washington, was reinterred here along with soldiers from the Revolutionary War and the War of 1812. His grave on the hillside in front of Arlington House overlooks the city he designed. General Philip Sheridan, who fought for the Union in the Civil War, lies near Confederate General Lee's former home; the Arlington Memorial Bridge symbolizes the reunification of the country by connecting the Lincoln Memorial with Arlington House.

Among the plain headstones of World War I soldiers lies General of the Armies John J. Pershing, commander of U.S. forces during World War I, who asked to be buried among his men. Second World War heroes include Generals George C. Marshall and Omar Bradley. Gen. Daniel "Chappie" James, who flew 78 missions in the Vietnam War, was the highest-ranking African-American officer ever, a four-star general in the Air Force. Arlington also holds Joe Louis, the longest-lasting world heavyweight boxing champion in history, and Abner Doubleday, the supposed inventor

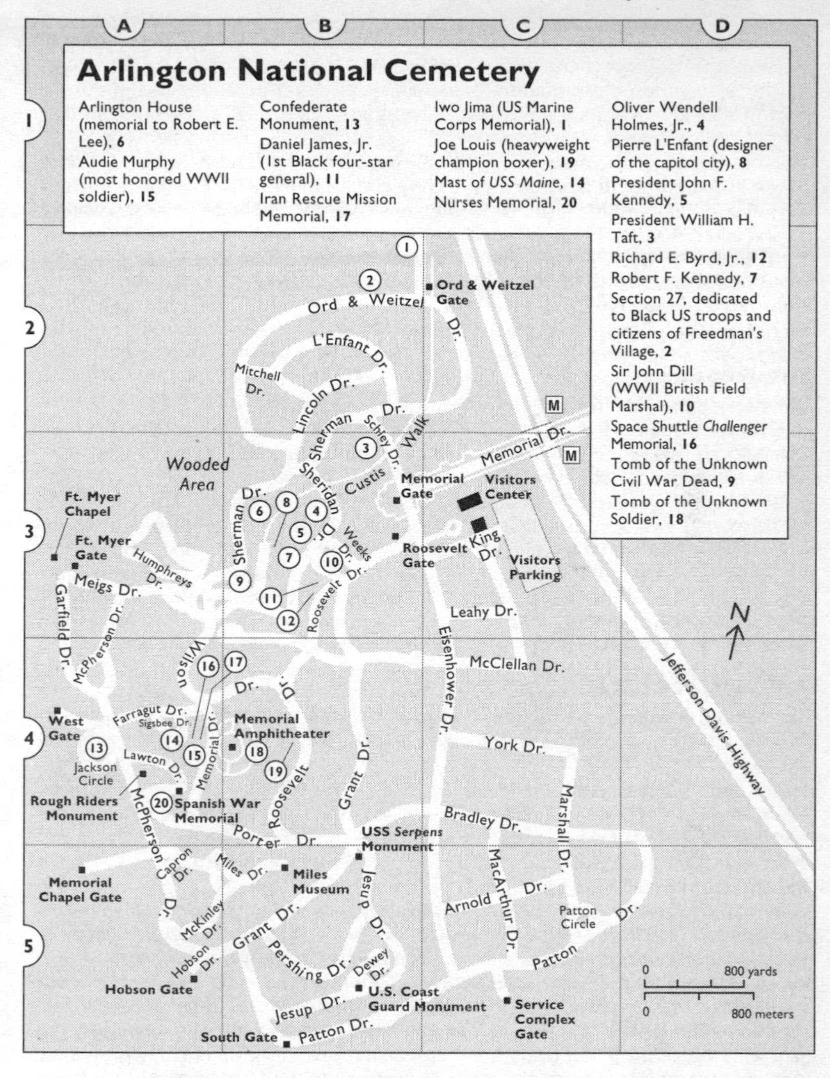

of baseball, at whom the first shot in the Civil War was fired. Arctic explorers Robert E. Peary and Richard Byrd lie on the same hallowed ground as Supreme Court Justices Earl Warren and Oliver Wendell Holmes. Presidents Taft and Kennedy round out the cemetery's list of honored tombs.

Tombstones note the war in which the soldier fought. A sunken shield represents service in either the Civil War or the Spanish-American War. Pointed headstones signify Confederate soldiers and can be found around the Confederate Memorial in section I-23. Each day, an average of 15 burials take place; during each ceremony, the flag at Arlington House stands at half mast. For some high-ranking officers, a caisson carrying the casket leads the funeral procession.

The Cemetery is **free. Hours** are Apr.-Sept. 8am-7pm, Oct.-May 8am-5pm. **Parking** costs $1.25 per hour for the first three hours and $2 for each additional hour.
Take the **Metro** to Arlington Cemetery. **To drive** from downtown Washington, take Independence or Constitution Ave. and turn left onto 23rd St. to cross the Arlington

Memorial Bridge. Visitors from Virginia and Maryland have a variety of options, but the easiest is probably the Beltway (I-495) to the Virginia side of the George Washington Pkwy., then the Arlington Memorial Bridge. **Cyclists** coming from the Mt. Vernon Trail should look for a turnoff just south of the Arlington Memorial Bridge; follow it to the cemetery.

Before you enter the main gate, go to the **Visitors Center** near the parking area. The information booth at the center of the building (692-0931) dispenses explanatory, gridded maps of the grounds. Winding paths are intended to provoke contemplation and reflection, but may induce fatigue as well; the short-winded should take the Tourmobile (tour $3, children 3-11 $1.50). Those wishing to find the grave of a loved one should visit the **Arlington Information Center.** Temporary passes to drive into the cemetery can also be obtained here. They will look up the location on microfiche and give you instructions on how to get there.

The Grounds

The **Kennedy Gravesites** hold President John F. Kennedy and his brother, Senator and Attorney General Robert F. Kennedy. John Kennedy's wife, Jacqueline Kennedy Onassis, and two of their children who died shortly after birth are also buried here. JFK supposedly once stood near Arlington House, and, seeing the spectacular view of Washington, declared, "I could stay here forever." The Purple Heart he won in World War II won him just that privilege. Look for the Eternal Flame, lit by his widow at his funeral, which flickers above his simple memorial stone. Famous sentences from his inaugural speech are inscribed on a low wall near the site, reminding all who pass of the soaring eloquence of speechwriter Ted Sorensen. RFK's famous words are similarly inscribed near his more modest grave: the statesman wished for nothing more than a wooden cross to mark his final resting place.

The **Tomb of the Unknowns** honors all servicemen who died fighting for the United States. Unidentified soldiers from World Wars I and II, the Korean War, and the Vietnam War lie under the white marble sarcophagus overlooking the city. The famous inscription reads, "Here rests in honored glory an American soldier known but to God."

The tomb is guarded 24 hours daily by delegations from the Army's Third Infantry, who sport woolen dress blues, white gloves, and bayonets. You can watch the ritualized **changing of the guard** every hour on the hour from October to March and every half hour from April until September. The towering sentinels take 21 steps and then turn to face the tomb for 21 seconds to symbolize the 21-gun salute, the highest military honor. **Memorial Amphitheater** is closed for repairs, but will eventually resume its Easter Sunrise, Memorial Day, and Veterans Day services. Memorials near the amphitheater include the **Space Shuttle Challenger Memorial,** the **Iran Rescue Mission Memorial,** the **War Correspondents Memorial,** and the **Canadian Cross of Sacrifice,** remembering U.S. citizens in the Canadian Armed Forces.

"A rose is a rose is a rose," wrote Gertrude Stein; in the same vein, what seems to be a ship's mast rising out of the ground is a **ship's mast rising out of the ground.** The mast belonged to the *U.S.S. Maine,* which exploded in the harbor of Havana, Cuba, in 1898. The rallying cry "Remember the Maine!" helped start the Spanish-American War, though no one knows whether the Spanish caused the explosion. Polish statesman and musician Ignace Jan Paderewski was interred in the memorial until Poland became "free." He was returned to his homeland in June 1992.

The **Confederate Memorial** was commissioned in 1900 when a goodwill gesture set aside an area for the burial of Confederate troops. The memorial itself shows the female representation of Peace facing south and holding a plow and a pruning hook. Inscribed around the base is the passage from Isaiah, "They shall beat their swords into plowshares, and their spears into pruning hooks." A bronze frieze surrounding the base depicts Confederate soldiers leaving home, and then returning in defeat. A **Civil War Memorial** lies along Crook Walk near Arlington House; more American soldiers died in this war than in any other. The bones of 2111 soldiers who fell in the Battle of Bull Run and along the route to Rappahanock lie beneath the stone sarcophagus; the remains were never identified, but the soldiers' names and deaths were recorded in the Archives.

Restored **Arlington House,** built in 1802 by George Washington Parke Custis, Robert E. Lee's father-in-law and distant relative, overlooks the cemetery with the poise appropriate to a Lee possession. Enter the pastel-peach mansion at the front door and pick up a sheet with a self-guided tour from one of the women in antebellum costume. The parlor connects through a series of arched doorways to the Family Dining Room. Up the narrow staircase, the girls' dressing room, playroom, and bedrooms contain antique dolls and clothing. Colonel Robert E. Lee penned his resignation from the United States Army in his bedchambers. Downstairs, you can see the White Parlor and the Morning Room, where paintings of George Custis lean against an easel. The storeroom, conservatory, and Lee's office close the tour. (You won't find Lee's grave in Arlington Cemetery: he chose to be buried at the southern college he helped to found, Washington & Lee, in Lexington, Virginia.)

Near the Cemetery

If you continue down Custis Walk in front of Arlington House and leave the cemetery through Weitzel Gate, you can walk to the **Iwo Jima Memorial.** On the way lies President William Howard Taft's grave, to the left of the path in section 30. The walk from Weitzel Gate to the memorial takes 20 minutes, so you may prefer to drive to the junction, located between Arlington Blvd. and Ridge Rd., especially on hot days. Or, take the Metro to Rosslyn and walk for 5 minutes east on Ft. Myer Dr. until you reach Arlington Blvd.; the memorial will be on you left. Its design is based on Joe Rosenthal's Pulitzer Prize-winning photograph of six Marines straining to raise the U.S. flag on Iwo Jima's Mount Suribachi. The island saw 6321 U.S. soldiers die in battle in February 1945, including three of the men the memorial depicts. Admiral Nimitz's comment on the battle, "Uncommon valor was a common virtue," adorns the statue's base. The U.S. flag is real, but the "flagpole" is a lead pipe—just as in the photo. The memorial became a gay cruise area in the 70s; today, the Marine Marathon begins here each year, and military concerts and parades take place in the summer on Tuesdays from 7pm until 8:30pm. (For information on the memorial, call 202-619-7222.)

Near the Iwo Jima Memorial (just walk in the direction that the marines are leaning) rises a rectangular 127-ft.-high tower that houses the **Netherlands Carillon** (285-2598), a set of 49 bells made in Dutch foundries in order to commemorate Holland's liberation from the Nazis on May 5, 1945. The carillon is played from June to August on Saturdays between 6pm and 8pm, as well as on national holidays; in April, May, and September it rings on Saturdays from 2pm to 4pm and on national holidays. If the bells are ringing, you can climb the towers and enjoy the view or watch the *Carillomeurs* do their stuff. A park ranger briefs the crowd on carillons ½-hour before performances. Two bronze panthers guard the bells, and the grounds bloom with more than 15,000 tulips each spring.

THE PENTAGON

If the Washington Monument's smooth obelisk symbolizes the vigor of the American nation and the Capitol's Classical dome represents the dignity of democratic government, the Pentagon's mass of concrete shows just how huge a military bureaucracy can get. On July 17, 1941, the War Department gave its planners one weekend to design a building that would hold all the capital's military offices. On Monday morning, the architects returned with the familiar five-sided behemoth, which was designed to fit between two highways; objections to the original site within Arlington Cemetery forced a move to Hell's Bottom, swampy government-owned land next to the Potomac. A work force of 13,000 toiled 24 hours a day for 16 months to create the steel-reinforced concrete edifice. Thanks to FDR's stipulation that no marble be used in the thing's construction, the resulting polygon cost "only" $50 million to build, a savings to taxpayers who were paying that much in rent every eight years for the military's old offices.

When the military moved in May 1942, the building's one completed wing was too small. Today, many of the Pentagon's offices and corridors are still empty—there's more room than they'll ever need (we hope). As chief avatar of the military-industrial complex, the Pentagon was the natural target of the mammoth anti-Vietnam War march of 1968, which inspired poems by Robert Lowell and Norman Mailer's famous book *The Armies of the Night.* Some marchers tried to exorcise the "war demon" supposedly kept in check by the building's mystical shape. TV coverage of the marchers, who joined hands to form a huge ring around all five sides, exhibited to the rest of the country the extent of anti-war feeling.

Today the world's largest office building boasts the world's largest parking lot and a bus terminal longer than most trains. The Pentagon has five sides, five stories, five concentric hallways, a five-acre courtyard in the center, ten radial hallways, four zip codes of its own, and $400 toilet seats. 2½ Washington Monuments would fit across it lengthwise. Twenty-six thousand civilians, soldiers, and sailors sprawl over 6.5 million sq. ft. They take the Metro or park 8770 cars in 16 parking lots. They climb 131 stairways and ride 19 escalators to walk through 17½ mi. of corridors. Yet it takes no more than seven minutes to walk between any two points in the building, if you know how to read the address: 2E651, for example, is on the second floor, ring E, near corridor 6, and room 51.

You'll never have the chance to get lost on the **guided tour,** though. The public had free run of the place until 1972, when somebody bombed a bathroom. Now all visitors must sign in, walk through a metal detector, get X-rayed, show proper identification, and stick to the tour. The tour guide walks backwards to keep an eye on the visitors and keeps the pace so brisk that the tour is like a military music video: lots of pictures whizzing by, but very little information. Many tour-takers are veterans and servicepeople. Attentive tour-takers can nonetheless learn a lot with their eyes. Between the memorials and exhibits, the myriad uniforms, the private shopping mall, and the motorized mini-mail carts, you'll discover the achievements, attitudes, structure, and sheer size of the United States defense establishment.

A corny film will show you the **War Room**—whose large screens light up with maps and data during national emergencies—and the **National Command Center,** but you'll never get to these basement chambers yourself. If you've seen *Dr. Strangelove* or *War Games*, though, you can already guess what they look like.

The **Commander-in-Chiefs' Corridor** depicts each U.S. president beside a montage of drawings and newspaper headlines. Another display models famous aircraft. Its most recent addition is a model of the **Stealth bomber,** whose low-altitude flight eludes radar while its high price ($500 million per plane) provokes disgust. Used in the U.S. invasion of Panama and in the Persian Gulf, the Stealth is one of several technically secret projects the tour guide will discuss. Look for the **Delta Force** patch on display; the government won't even acknowledge the existence of this secret anti-terrorist team, but the Pentagon exhibits its insignia anyway.

Endless corridors commemorate exceptional soldiers. Hallways celebrate military topics including General George Marshall, women in the military, and Vietnam POWs. An array of flags and a memorial to valiant dogs ends your tour. Look out the window at the **hot dog stand** in the middle of the courtyard; it's called **"ground zero"** because during the cold war the Soviets thought it was a strategic nuclear weapons control room and planned to bomb it first if war should have erupted.

Tours are **free** and given every half hour on weekdays between 9:30am and 3:30pm, except on federal holidays; from October to May, the 10:30am, 1:30pm, and 3pm tours are eliminated. Be ready to go 10 min. early; there is a mandatory briefing. No reservations are necessary, but large groups and those with special needs may reserve tours by calling 695-1776. All persons must present a photo ID. Acceptable photo IDS are passports, drivers licences, college IDs, and International Student ID Cards. Try coming early in the morning to avoid the lines and to fit in the 90-minute tour before lunch. No facilities for meals are available, *nor are restrooms open to the public during the tour.* The Pentagon has its own Metro stop; one of the Metro escalators leads directly to the tour office. The Pentagon hankers down inside a triangle formed by three highways—Rte. 110 and 27 and I-395; those who must drive here should take the 14th St. Bridge from D.C. to I-395 and find the Pentagon exit about 15 seconds into Virginia. Visitor parking is available but limited, and the walk from the lot takes a few minutes; enter through Corridor One at the South Parking Entrance.

ROOSEVELT ISLAND

The Theodore Roosevelt Memorial Association felt their boy deserved better than the standard statue-and-pedestal memorial package. To commemorate the popular hunter, conservationist, and President, they purchased an entire 88-acre island which, with Congress's consent, became Roosevelt Island in 1932. Now a wilderness preserve, the island squats in the Potomac River just west of Foggy Bottom, a mere 15 minutes from downtown. To transform the place from "swamp" to "memorial," Congress erected an impressive statue of Roosevelt and a parking lot, but not much else. The island's natural ruggedness is itself a fitting memorial to the man famous for starting the Panama Canal, leading the charge up San Juan Hill during the Spanish-American War, negotiating an end to the Russo-Japanese War, and expressing his great love for the outdoors by regularly disappearing into the forest, seeking solitude and things to shoot at.

Add to Roosevelt's list of accomplishments the establishment of the U.S. Forest Service and the creation of America's first national park. The island which bears his name today contains swamp, marsh, and forest habitats which host such critters as turtles, muskrats, cottontails, and foxes (also look for Redwing Blackbirds, whose calls contrast strangely with the noise of cars rushing over Roosevelt Bridge). Woody climbers and epiphytes hang from the trees, jungle-style. The island's three miles of **trails** take about an hour to hike through; wide, flat paths make the long walks relaxing. More adventurous walkers may follow smaller subsidiary trails, literally off the beaten path. Rocky **beaches** reward those who find them with views of the Kennedy Center, the Watergate complex, and the Gothic spires of Georgetown University. On weekends, local fisherfolk cast off from here, into the murky waters of the Potomac where swimming is most emphatically for fish only. (Explorers beware: the narrow footpaths leading to the beaches tend to be cob-webby and lined with nettles.) Even harder to find than the beaches are the **restrooms,** hidden in the delicately designated "comfort station," a brown lodge at the southwest corner of the island near Theodore Roosevelt Bridge.

The **memorial** lurks just west of the center of the island's northern half. The design by Eric Gugler includes a 17-foot bronze statue of Roosevelt (executed by Paul Manship) in front of a 30-foot slab of granite reminiscent of *2001: A Space Odyssey.* In front is an oval terrace surrounded by a moat spanned by a series of footbridges. Four 21-foot granite "tablets" are inscribed with juicy Roosevelt soundbites, among them: "There are no words that can tell the hidden spirit of the wilderness" and "Keep your eyes on the stars, but remember to keep your feet on the ground."

Rangers will give combined nature and historical **tours** if called 7 days in advance; call 703-285-2600 for arrangements. (No tours given in the winter season.) For a rundown of the ever-shifting hours and services, call 426-6922 or 703-285-2598.

From Washington, drive across the Roosevelt Bridge, take a right onto the George Washington Parkway's northbound lanes, and exit into the Roosevelt Island lot; if you see Key Bridge, you've missed it. Public transportation enthusiasts should take the Metro to Rosslyn, then walk down N. 19th St. and look for footbridges across the highway spaghetti on the Virginia shore; or, you could walk across Key Bridge from Georgetown and follow the Mt. Vernon Trail along the river. There is a footbridge at the parking lot which all visitors must cross to get to the island. Sadly, bikes are not allowed on the island, although there is a bike rack in the parking lot.

■■■ ALEXANDRIA, VA

Metro: Braddock Rd.; King St.

When Scottish tobacco merchants founded Alexandria in 1749, quaintness was not their aim; its location on the Potomac River seemed perfect for bundling up and shipping out the great weed from down south. Though included in the land grant that created D.C. in 1791, Alexandria stayed an independent-minded (and very Southern) shipping town; when Virginia removed it from the District of Columbia in 1846, one resident reported "great rejoicing and cannon firing." When Washington ballooned after World War II, the spreading wave of bedroom communities crashed over the town. It didn't become a sight until the 80s, when Old Town re-cobblestoned the streets, rebricked the sidewalks, installed gardens and patios, restored over 1000 old façades, and invited tall ships and contemporary shops to share the 1700s atmosphere. On weekends, half of northern Virginia joins a smattering of tourists to shop, stroll, and dine. Old-time sailors might enjoy some of the many pubs and clubs, but sophisticated jazzers, **angst-ridden teens**, and modern singles will all find some appropriate nightlife.

ORIENTATION

Old Town Alexandria lies in the square formed by Oronoco St. on the north, the Potomac River on the east, Gibbon St. on the south, and Alfred St. on the west. Restaurants, bars, small art galleries, and shops nestle here in a perpetual state of cuteness. Old Town's streets form a grid; north-south streets have random names, while east-west streets in central Old Town have royal names (King, Prince, Duke, Queen, etc.). Street layout in the rest of Alexandria has all the sense of a bowl of pasta; after all, it's northern Virginia. I-395 cuts Alexandria off from Arlington to the north, and the Beltway rushes along its southern border. King St. (Rte. 7) connects I-395 to Old Town, and the George Washington Parkway runs nearly along the river until Old Town, where it becomes Washington St. To find Old Town from the King St. Metro, start walking down King St. (to your left as you leave the Metro; walk away from the tracks, not under them). A DASH bus also runs from the Metro to Old Town at random intervals. **DASH** runs throughout the city (75¢) and to the Pentagon ($1). Call 370-DASH for more info. If you're driving, take the East King St. exit from the George Washington Pkwy.; Old Town is about 20 minutes from downtown D.C. Remember that the area code for Alexandria is **703.**

SIGHTS

King Street is the main thoroughfare through Old Town. It's the king of streets for eating seafood and visiting art galleries and shops. The galleries huddle closer to the Metro, while the restaurants, like lemmings, cluster closer and closer to the river. Each Saturday the town hosts a morning fair, complete with waterfront activities, riverboat rides, and a **Farmer's Market** at 301 King St. in Market Square (370-8723; market open 5-9am). Fresh baked goods, meats, produce, and handicrafts are sold in the brick arcades, replete with fountains, trees, and hanging baskets, on the south plaza of the city hall. Beware of visiting Alexandria on a spring or summer weekend; you may find yourself barred from many museums and houses by the hundreds of weddings that take over every picturesque place in town.

A newly renovated information center, the **Lyceum,** 201 S. Washington St. (838-4994), shows exhibitions and audio-visual presentations on historic Alexandria; it's for the visitor who wants in-depth historical background to many of the sites on the walking tour. The brick and stucco Greek Revival building has been a military hospital, a private home, and an office building. Its collection of period objects includes prized Alexandria silver. Free parking is available. Travelers with disabilities should call to take advantage of the Lyceum's resources. Tours are offered, some in Braille, but call in advance to make arrangements. (Open Mon.-Sat. 10am-5pm, Sun. 1-5pm.)

George Washington and Robert E. Lee prayed at **Christ Church,** 118 N. Washington St. (549-1450) at Cameron St., a red-brick Colonial building with a domed steeple. Its quiet, shady cemetery with well-tended gardens is an inviting rest stop for modern-day visitors to Alexandria. Practically as bright as the outdoors on a sunny day, the interior of the church has stark white walls and an unusual domed window behind the altar. You can also see original hand-lettered tablets containing the Apostle's Creed and the Lord's Prayer. Guided tours are available. (Open Mon.-Sat. 9am-4pm, Sun. 2-4:30pm. Free.)

The authentically Victorian **Lloyd House,** 220 N. Washington St. (838-4577), is primarily a genealogical library, but visitors might enjoy the drawing rooms and exhibits full of old models of clipper ships, paintings, and antique books. Historians and novelists study the house's reams of historical and genealogical data. (Tours available. Open Mon.Fri. 9am-6pm, Sat. 9am-5pm. Free.)

Restored to its 18th-century good looks, **Gadsby's Tavern,** 134 N. Royal St. (838-4242), allows you to see how budget travelers did it 200 years ago (when as many as 4 people would be assigned to a bed). Upstairs, large dancing rooms are still used

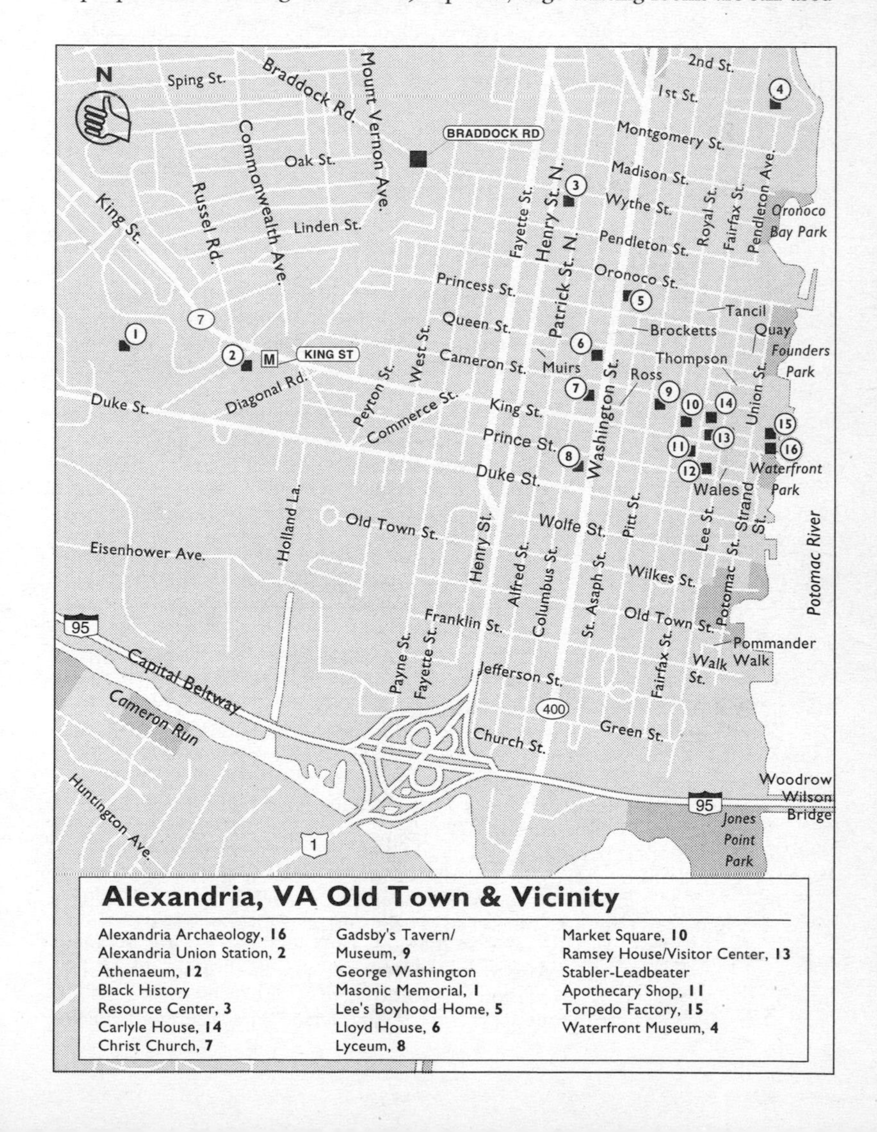

today for special functions. Note the vivid colors in the largest hall, and the stairless minstrels' gallery. (Open Oct.-March Tues.-Sat. 10am-4pm, Sun. 1-4pm. Admission $3, children 11-17 $1.)

The **Stabler-Leadbeater Apothecary Shop and Museum,** 105-107 South Fairfax St. (836-3713), the second-oldest in the country, still operates. Martha Washington's letter requesting castor oil hangs in a glass case. Old-time druggists used the shop's hundreds of colorful hand-blown bottles, mortars and pestles, powders, eyeglasses, weights, and scales (and probably appreciated the Gothic detailing on the shelves), as the high-pitched recording will attest. The museum has recently undertaken a massive project to sort through old order slips. Soon it will be known just who was sick—and from what. Senators Daniel Webster, Henry Clay, and John Calhoun supposedly had some "drug store" conversations here. And Robert E. Lee was hanging out here when he received the message to stop John Brown's insurrection at Harper's Ferry. The gift shop sells antique apothecary items. (Open Mon.-Sat. 10am-4pm, Sun. 1-5pm. Admission $2, students $1, under 11 free.)

Restored so faithfully that even its vivid colors are called authentic, the **Carlyle House,** 121 North Fairfax St. (549-2997), home of Scottish merchant John Carlyle, showcases Alexandria's favorite century. Carlyle patterned his home after those in 18th-century Scotland and northern England. Tours start in the basement, where the servants lived; the white-plaster, stable-like rooms look nothing like the ornate upstairs. The second-story floors show off *trompe l'oeuil* "marble," along with the requisite exquisite antique furniture. The last room has been left unrestored, with beams and wall exposed just as they were found. (Open Tues.-Sat. 10am-4:30pm, Sun. noon-4:30pm. Tours given every ½ hr. Admission $3, seniors and students $1, under 10 free.) The gazebo-ed garden in the back serves as a public park—a good choice for an intimate picnic.

Alexandria's oldest house, the **Athenaeum,** 201 Prince St. (548-0035), holds local and touring art shows as well as the Alexandria ballet (379-8997). The rose-colored building, with its large, round columns and dignified pediment, merits attention; notice how its Greek Renaissance flair differs from the surrounding Colonial architecture. (Open Wed.-Fri. 11am-4pm, Sat.-Sun. 1-4pm.)

Over 160 artists paint, draw, and sculpt in public on two floors of the **Torpedo Factory,** 105 N. Union St. (838-4565). With 83 studios, five galleries, an art school, and an archaeology lab, the art world has conquered the World War I-era munitions factory, leaving the former occupants only a small exhibit and an inert torpedo. Works from just about every mode of artistic creation await aesthetic completion or financial commodification in the myriad workshops, most of which are open to visitors. A quick walk across the wharf behind the Torpedo Factory will lead you to its **Food Pavilion.** High quality cheap eats are complemented by an understandably artsy interior. Open daily 8am-midnight. (Torpedo Factory open daily 10am-5pm. Suggested-donation box. Wheelchair access.)

On the third floor of the factory, **Alexandria Archaeology,** 105 N. Union St. (838-4399), the city's urban archaeology lab and museum, displays 18th- and 19th-century artifacts. (Open Tues.-Fri. 10am-3pm, Sat. 10am-5pm, Sun. 1-5pm.)

George Washington slept in the guest bedroom of **Robert E. Lee's Boyhood Home,** 607 Oronoco St. (548-8454) near Asaph St. The Revolutionary War hero, "Light Horse" Harry Lee, was the first to lease this home in 1812; Robert E. Lee went to the Quaker school next door as a young child. Not much of the Lee family's belongings are here—they're mostly at Washington and Lee University. But check out one of America's first indoor kitchens and a set of miniature furniture (one carpenter's method of advertising). United Mine Workers president John L. Lewis lived here from 1927 to 1969. Candlelight tours are offered in December. (Open Mon.-Sat. 10am-4pm, Sun. 1-4pm. Admission $3, $1 for students 10-17 yrs. old.)

No George Washington, but over 37 different Lees inhabited the **Lee-Fendall House** at 614 Oronoco St., across from Robert E. Lee's Boyhood Home. The suburby-looking white and black mansion was constructed by Philip Fendall in 1785 on land once owned by man-about-Alexandria "Light Horse" Harry Lee. Tours make public yet more Lee family knick-knacks and documents, for those who just can't get enough. (Open Tues.-Sat. 10am-4pm, Sun. noon-4pm. Last tour 3:45pm. Admission $3, students $2, under 12 free.)

The **Black History Resource Center,** 638 N. Alfred St. (838-4356; enter on Wythe St.), is housed in the Robert H. Robinson Library, originally for blacks only. Built in 1940 after local African-Americans staged the nation's first "sit in" to protest the segregation of the library system, the Center today showcases paintings, photographs, and other memorabilia that untangle black history in Alexandria. A printed walking tour lists historical sights, including several churches, the Franklin and Armfield Slave Market, and the house of George Seaton, a free black master carpenter who was elected to the city council and state legislature in the 1870s. (Open Tues.-Sat. 10am-4pm. Wheelchair access.)

The **George Washington Masonic National Memorial,** at 101 Callahan Drive (683-2007), at the top of King St., rises 400 ft. over Alexandria. The lofty Greek-temple-style portico supports a steep pyramid. Look for the careful blending of all five orders of Classical architecture: Doric, Ionic, and Corinthian on the three exterior levels of the tower, Composite in Memorial Hall, and Tuscan in Assembly Hall. Inside, the ninth floor claims to reproduce parts of King Solomon's Temple. Another five floors of museums celebrate George Washington and Masonry. Points of interest are the 17-ft. bronze statue of America's first president and murals of George Washington celebrating St. John's Day and laying the cornerstone of the Capitol. A 370-year-old Persian rug valued at $1 million is also on display. A 330-ft. observation deck provides a fair view of the city. To go above the second floor, you must take the (free) 70-minute tour. (Tours on the half-hour in the morning, and on the hour in the afternoon. Open daily 9am-5pm.)

Museums & Galleries

SMITHSONIAN MUSEUMS

The Smithsonian is the catalogued warehouse of American cultural memorabilia. Words that might describe this country—grand, hegemonic, diverse—easily fit this mammoth museum and research institution as well. The world's largest museum complex stretches out along Washington's longest lawn, the Mall. Other exhibits are displayed in Anacostia, up Connecticut Ave. at the National Zoo, and in New York City. The institution's scientists are similarly situated in a variety of outposts, classifying and investigating from Panama to Nepal to Arizona. Smithsonian curators manage over 139 million objects, most of which you'll never see. Scientists and historians worldwide take an interest in the millions of beetles, thousands of works of art, and hundreds of airplanes that make the Smithsonian Institution outstanding in science and the arts as well as in tourism. These collections also mean that the Smithsonian can assemble almost any exhibit it chooses: individual halls and chambers may be filled with gleaming minerals, orbital satellites, teenage fashions, or models by Rodin. Tourists throng the Mall to see the dinosaurs at Natural History, the Apollo XI capsule at Air & Space, and the luminous pyramids next to the East Wing building—many, in fact, don't budget enough time to see much else. The sensible visitor will take at least three days to roam the ten Smithsonian buildings and the U.S. Holocaust Museum on and near the Mall, then return to his or her favorite museum.

The Smithsonian began as the magnanimous idea of British scientist James Smithson. The chemist had never visited America, but his will left 105 bags of gold sovereigns to "found at Washington, under the name of the Smithsonian Institution, an establishment for the increase and diffusion of knowledge among men." (Had Smithson's nephew had children, they would have inherited the gold instead.) Congress voted to take the money, British though it was, in 1835. The red-brick, Victorian "Castle" was institutionalized in 1855 as the Smithsonian's first permanent home; bachelor scientists boarded there along with the growing collections. The Victorian-with-a-vengeance Arts and Industries Building, the second-oldest, initially opened its doors to President Garfield's inaugural ball in 1881; the rest of the Mall splits neatly into domed neoclassical sprawl (Natural History, National Gallery's West Wing, Freer) and smooth, geometric modernity (Air & Space, East Wing, American History, Hirshhorn). Since 1980, new museums have had to hide below ground, the casualties of space limitations. The Sackler Gallery and Museum of African Art crawl under stone entrance pavilions behind the Castle.

ORIENTATION AND PRACTICAL INFORMATION

Eleven Smithsonian buildings and the U.S. Holocaust Museum flank the Mall (see The Mall Area color insert map for a visual orientation). On the north side, to the left as you face the Capitol from the center of the Mall, are the National Gallery of Art's East Wing and West Wing, the National Museum of Natural History, and the National Museum of American History. Closest to the Capitol on the right is the National Air & Space Museum, then the Hirshhorn, and then the Arts & Industries Building. The red Smithsonian Castle hides the Sackler Gallery and the National Museum of African Art in its dainty backyard garden. Next is the Freer Gallery. Completing the lineup of museums on the west side of the Castle is the U.S. Holocaust Museum, nestled in the southwest corner of the Mall, farther up past the Dept. of Agriculture on Independence and 14th. Tour-bus-congested Jefferson and Madison Drives run east-west along the Mall. The Smithsonian Metro stop isn't always the best way to reach a given museum; L'Enfant Plaza is closer to Air & Space and the Hirshorn. Federal Triangle is closer to Natural History and American History, and Archives-Navy

Memorial is closer to the National Galleries of Art. Don't even think about parking in or north of the Smithsonian complex. You can probably find on-street spaces south of Independence Ave. SW, but *caveat conductor:* one wrong turn, and you may be irrevocably Virginia- or Anacostia-bound. If you see signs for the SE-SW Freeway, don't follow them.

All Smithsonian museums are **free** and **wheelchair-accessible;** many offer written guides in French, German, Spanish, Italian, and Japanese with some Chinese, Arabic, and Portuguese also available. Smithsonian museums are open daily from 10am to 5:30pm (except for the Anacostia Museum, which closes at 5pm), with extended summer hours for the more popular museums (Air & Space, Natural History, and American History don't shut their doors until 6:30pm); the National Gallery's East Wing stays open late on Friday evenings. Some museums close on winter weekends.

Choose the museums whose subjects interest you; too many visitors give up longed-for hours among the airplanes just to say they've seen the Abstract Expressionists (or vice versa). An hour in one museum is better spent than an hour dashing through three. Call 357-2700 (TDD 357-1729) to contact a Smithsonian operator for **information** on all the museums. For recorded information on tours, concerts, lectures, films, and performance art, call 357-2020. Information desks in the Castle and the museums distribute the **Smithsonian Guide for Disabled Visitors,** but be sure to get there between 10am and 4pm; the volunteer staff doesn't stick around all day. Most museums have two main entrances, one from the Mall and one from Constitution or Independence Ave.; the latter is often easier for wheelchairs to negotiate. Visitors with disabilities who call a specific museum a day before their visit can obtain more extensive literature and assistance. Sight- or hearing-impaired visitors should call 786-2942 to arrange for interpreted tours.

SMITHSONIAN CASTLE

The **Smithsonian Castle,** 1000 Jefferson Dr. SW (357-2700, Dial-a-Museum recording 357-2020, TDD 357-1729), holds no real exhibits, but it does have information desks and two small theaters that continuously play a 20-minute introductory movie. Come here for information on any Smithsonian museum except the National Galleries—they're a separate entity and have their own information centers. But have fun finding out about other museums with **touch-sensitive computer screens.** The Castle also contains a **crypt** that holds James Smithson's body (he finally got to America after all). The whole crypt was moved from Genoa, Italy in 1904. Near the crypt is the symbolic **Smithsonian mace** (a silver staff with a ball at the end of it), and a display about the varieties of zinc that Smithson identified and had named after him. The building itself, designed by James Renwick, Jr., is crowned by 11 towers, no two of which are the same. This intentional assymetry and integration of architectural styles conveys either the originality or the indecisiveness of the Castle's creator. The posh-looking, roped-off hallways lead to Smithsonian offices and services for "associates" (who pay annual dues to be "members" of the museum). (Open daily 9am-5:30pm, information desk open daily 9am-4pm.)

NATIONAL MUSEUM OF AMERICAN HISTORY

Henry Ford once said that "History is bunk." The National Museum of American History prefers to think that history is junk: several centuries' and thousands of artifacts' worth of machines, textiles, photographs, vehicles, harmonicas, guns, fiber-optic cable, hats, and uncategorizable American detritus reside here behind plexiglass and plaques. When the Smithsonian inherits a quirky artifact of popular history, like Dorothy's slippers from *The Wizard of Oz* or Archie Bunker's chair, it usually ends up here. The museum, opened in 1964, was renamed the National Museum of History and Technology until 1980, and a certain techno-focus remains evident in halls like "A Material World" or "Information Age." Recently, the museum has turned politically correct, with a spate of new exhibits on social and cultural history. The most famous displays are individual objects, like the **Star-Spangled Banner;** don't let the crowds around them distract you from the more informative halls of this national attic.

Enter the boring rectilinear building from the Mall or from 14th St. and Constitution Ave. NW. (Metro: Smithsonian or Federal Triangle.) Pick up a map from an information desk. As in the other major Smithsonian museums, you'll need to be picky about where you linger. Seeing all of the exhibits properly takes at least a full day, but three hours should suffice for a more selective tour.

If you come in from the Mall, on the second floor, you'll face the swinging **Foucault's pendulum.** Fixed in a single plane of perpendicular motion, it knocks over pegs set up in a circular pattern and thereby proves that the Earth rotates.

When Francis Scott Key, detained on a ship in Baltimore Harbor, saw an American flag fly over Fort McHenry at dawn on September 14, 1814, he knew British invaders had failed to take Baltimore; the elated Key sat down and wrote "The Star-Spangled Banner," the U.S.'s unsingable national anthem. The enormous flag that inspired the song now hangs behind the pendulum on the museum's second floor.

From the building's crowded center, visitors can turn left for 20th-century African-American history in "Field to Factory" or right for 18th-century European-American history in "After the Revolution." Also to the right, "First Ladies" traces the evolution of the role of Presidential wives from parlor socialites to political allies. Immediately to the left of the flag, "American Encounters" marks the quincentenary of Columbus's landmark visit to this continent by depicting cultural interactions in the American Southwest since 1539. Outside the "Field to Factory" exhibit entrance, seek out the famous "topless" statue of George Washington. Horatio Greenough, in Florence, carved the thing by request of Congress in 1832; the statue was so big the Capitol's doors had to be removed to drag George inside, and so heavy it threatened to collapse the Capitol's floor. The sculpture was reinstalled outdoors, where snow collected in his lap and on his bare chest. The Smithsonian finally acquired the boondoggle in 1908.

Specialized collections of musical instruments, coins, and military paraphernalia dominate the third floor. "A More Perfect Union" chronicles the World War II internment of Japanese-Americans in relentless, self-flagellating detail. The third floor also houses the stirring "Personal Legacy," a sampling of some of the 25,000 items that mourners have left at the Vietnam Memorial, including a decorated Christmas tree, a wedding ring, and a lonely teddy bear, worn with age. The collection is on indefinite loan from the National Parks Service.

The mechanically inclined will love the first floor, where entire galleries lavish their plexiglass on electricity, trains, cars, clocks, and power tools. "A Material World" takes over the central first floor, along with the museum bookstore. Electronics reign in "Information Age;" clunky early computers like EDSAC give way to microprocessors and high-definition TV. Get a copy of your fingerprint, try to trade currencies, or discover who lives in your home ZIP code at the interactive displays throughout the exhibit. The recently opened "Science in American Life" serves up a brief history of the nation's scientific progress and its cultural implications, from the tabletop science of the 19th century through the dinner-table science of genetic engineering and the futuristic quest for the perfect tomato.

The sprawling **bookstore** on the lower level sells quality Smithsonian jazz and folk records. An old-fashioned, functioning U.S. Post Office and a 1910-style **ice cream parlor** (located in the Palm Court resting area) also enliven the first floor. The museum hosts year-round special events, including dance, music, and lectures. Splendid silent (or sometimes just plain forgotten) **films** are screened in the Carmichael Auditorium, often for free. Grab a schedule at the information station near the first-floor exit. In the summer, the Carmichael Auditorium plays host to **free public concerts** by the Smithsonian Jazz Masterworks Orchestra; call for further details. (357-2700, TDD 357-1563; Museum open daily 10am-6:30pm; Sept.-May daily 10am-5:30pm. Volunteers staff the information desks from 10am to 4pm.)

NATIONAL MUSEUM OF NATURAL HISTORY

The golden-domed, Neoclassical Museum of Natural History, built in 1911 at 10th and Constitution Ave. (Metro: Smithsonian or Federal Triangle), considers the earth and its life in two and a half big, crowded floors of exhibits. As with the Museum of American History, several hours of gazing time are required to do the halls justice. Back when the museum was conceived, "natural history" meant geology and biology; the rarely seen tag "and National Museum of Man" licensed the curators to add anthropology exhibits (some displays have women in them, too). Corridors, cases, dioramas, and hanging specimens reflect the Victorian mania to kill, collect, catalogue, and display. Among the dusty specimens of birds and mammals and the endless dioramas of "native peoples," you'll find some real jewels: from actual minerals like the Hope Diamond to educational gems like scampering, iridescent arthropods in the recently remodeled Orkin Insect Zoo.

Inside the stone-floored entrance, the largest African elephant ever "captured" (i.e., killed) stands under dome-filtered sunshine amid the hubbub of running children and slack-jawed tourists. (Don't feed him—he's stuffed.) Look up and around for colored banners pointing out the various exhibits. Pick up armloads of brochures at the **information desk** to the right of the pachyderm as you walk in. Skip the $3 "self-guided audio tour," narrated by the lovely Meryl Streep. Children will appreciate this museum for its many low-to-the-ground view windows and displays, and signs begging visitors to "Please Touch!"

Begin at the beginning in the "History of Life" exhibit just to the right of the Mall entrance, behind the information desk. Huge dinosaur skeletons dwarf the nearby hallway, and an intriguing exhibit lets you pretend you're an archaeologist looking by remote camera at a partially uncovered fossil. Can you remember when dinosaurs were the coolest things in the world? If not, ecstatic kids in this hall will remind you. Next door, explore "Life in the Ancient Seas," where you'll find big fish with teeth and dinosaur-sized turtles.

Don't miss the Ice Age rooms, where the giant ground sloth, the saber-toothed tiger, and the woolly mammoth reside; waltz swiftly through "Fossil Plants," if only to see the surprisingly colorful petrified trees. The "Human Evolution" display offers the first of many disclaimers scattered throughout the museum (the staff has discovered that their exhibits are often inaccurate, sexist, and biased). You'll notice more of these disclaimers among the "Mammals" and "Birds" displays across the Rotunda, although you may find yourself bothered less by animal sexism than by the fact that all of these animals are dead and stuffed, and many are squashed flat against walls. The disclaimers are perhaps most necessary, however, in the exhibits on native cultures (Asian, African, Pacific, South American, and indigenous North American), where you'll see a Maori getting his butt tattooed and read about how the Shuar of eastern Ecuador shrunk their enemies' heads. The native cultures displays continue on the second floor, as do the dead animals; skip "Reptiles" and "Bones" and visit the zoo sometime instead. The **Insect Zoo** is worth a glance, however, if only for the fact that many of its exhibits are living, including giant cockroaches (a lively bunch), exotic millipedes, and walking sticks (invisibly still). Unfortunately, the second floor mineral wing is temporarily closed, due to reopen in Dec. 1996. The museum kept the celebrity of the collection on display, however; prepare to line up for a glimpse of the famously cursed **Hope Diamond.**

Those who enter the museum from the less-used Constitution Ave. side get in on the ground floor, where temporary exhibitions strut their stuff. An escalator hauls visitors up and down from the Rotunda.

Kids can touch nearly everything in the **Discovery Room** (357-2287), hidden beyond the Sea Life at the end of the Hall of North American Mammals. The room contains a human skeleton and various bones and stones to handle. Call the Education Center at 357-2747 to arrange a group visit. You need a ticket to enter the Discovery Room, so get one at the door 15 min. before the room opens; in the busy season, passes usually run out by early afternoon. (Open Mon.-Fri. noon-2:30pm, Sat.-Sun. 10:30am-3:30pm. Closed on major holidays.)

Docents give free guided **tours** of the museum daily at 10:30am and 1:30pm from September to June. (357-2700, TDD 357-1729; museum open daily 10am-6:30pm; Sept.-May daily 10am-5:30pm.)

NATIONAL GALLERY OF ART: WEST BUILDING

The National Gallery (737-4215, TDD 842-6176) houses and hangs its world-class jumble of pre-1900 art in a domed marble temple to Western Tradition designed by the Pope himself—John Russell Pope, whose more-reverent-than-thou columns and stairs also adorn the National Archives and Jefferson Memorial. The original, Ionic-style National Gallery building (now known as the West Wing) was conceived, proposed, financed, and named by financier Andrew Mellon, who realized that other collectors would be more likely to donate to a gallery if it didn't bear his name. The West Wing and the East Wing considered as a whole constitute North America's most popular art museum, with over six million visitors annually (next is the Metropolitan Museum of Art in New York, with four million). The West Building holds works by El Greco, Raphael, Rembrandt, Vermeer, and Monet.

Enter the West Wing building from the Mall or from 6th St. and Constitution Ave. NW. (Metro: Archives-Navy Memorial.) At the Constitution Ave. entrance, note the Zodiac symbols on the outdoor Mellon fountain. Whichever portal you choose, you'll wind up in the round central "court" under the dome, where black marble pillars and a fountain celebrate the god Mercury. Sculpture-clogged hallways lead east (left) to Italian, Dutch, Spanish, German, and Flemish work from medieval times onward, and west (right) to later French, British, and American painting.

This museum's contents are like an encyclopedia of Western art. You will recognize famous works in every room. It's all here, from the two-dimensional gold-leaf pre-portrait paintings of the Middle Ages to the rough strokes of Impressionism to bold American landscapes. The West Building hangs its canvases in lots of small rooms rather than a few big ones—if you speed from one end of the building to the other, you'll miss seeing most of the paintings. West and East Garden Courts relieve the potential monotony of the Old Masters with fountains, ferns, sunlight, and benches. Leonardo da Vinci's earliest surviving portrait (and the only painting by that artist in the U.S.), *Ginevra de' Benci,* stands in the center of Gallery 6, in the West Wing's startlingly fine collection of Italian Renaissance Art. Gallery 24 consists only of ceiling, upon which Titian's 1547 *John the Baptist* is painted. Auguste Renoir's *Girl with a Watering Can* and other well-known French Impressionist pieces hang in Galleries 85-93 across the rotunda from the Italians. The museum's prize rooms are a hall of knock-'em-dead Dutch masters with a few of the world's 30-odd Vermeers, and a special room just for Jan Van Eyck's *The Annunciation.* Early-twentieth-century American works begin in Gallery 70.

Look for throngs of youths admiring Salvador Dali's science-fictional *Last Supper* in the turn of the stairway between the underground concourse and the first floor of the West Wing, then head downstairs to the relatively low-key collections of sculpture (including a room full of Rodins), prints and drawings, and temporary exhibits.

Even the cheapest connoisseur can exult in the museum's guided tours, "gallery talks," free classical music concerts, and general profusion of special events, whose mercurial schedules are available at the information desk in the rotunda (as well as in the East Wing). Vocal, piano, and chamber music concerts most Sundays between October and June at 7pm in the West Garden Court (call 842-6941 for the schedule). (Open Mon.-Sat. 10am-5pm, Sun. 11am-6pm.)

NATIONAL GALLERY OF ART: EAST BUILDING

Completed amid much fanfare in 1978, the "East Wing" of the National Gallery of Art (737-4215) houses (and sometimes hides) much of the museum's plentiful 20th-century collection. I. M. Pei's celebrated design is a logical outcome of the idea that a building itself should be a work of art. The smooth marble four-story gallery outlines high, interlocking triangles, glass-topped to flood the atrium with sunlight. On one hand, the building is at once calming and innovative. The design accommodates large-scale works—by Alexander Calder, Anthony Caro, and others—created especially for the new structure. On the other hand, all those visitors admiring the empty atrium aren't seeing any paintings; the East Wing is utterly inefficient as an exhibit space. Whereas the West Building sacrificed beauty in an attempt to house large collections, Pei filled potential gallery space with air to make the design pleasingly bright and spacious; he succeeded, but not without a price.

Enter the East Wing from Constitution Ave., Pennsylvania Ave. at 4th St. NW, the Mall, or the gallery's West Building (via the underground moving walkway). (Metro: Archives-Navy Memorial.) The immense red and black Calder mobile hanging in the entrance hall is the gallery's trademark; it quietly recalls the knife-edge exterior of the building itself, one of the sharpest corners in modern architecture. Believe it or not, two galleries for temporary exhibits are tucked into the corners of the ground floor; see if you can find them. Other temporary-exhibit galleries lurk on the mezzanine and upper levels. A **directory** on the ground floor tells you what's where.

The East wing hangs its permanent collection in two places. A spacious gallery on the 4th St. side of the upper level currently holds most of the European works, including over a dozen Picassos representing most of his phases, and nearly that many Matisses. In the gallery's early rooms, Surrealists like Miró, Magritte, and Man Ray play with your mind while Fauves like Derain assault your retina with brash, colorful brushstrokes. To track the post-war shift of the art world's gravitational center from Europe to America, you'll have to shift as well, to the gallery downstairs on the Concourse level. Here you'll find Warhol's 32 Campbell's soup can paintings, a couple of Lichtenstein's comic-like Pop canvases, as well more recent works by lesser-known artists. The Concourse level is also home to Matisse's famous giant paper collages, which can be viewed only at certain hours to minimize light damage (Mon.-Sat. 10am-2pm, Sun. 11am-3pm). At the very tippy-top of the building, on the Tower level, you can admire a comprehensive assortment of sculptures by the technologically inspired American sculptor David Smith.

To see the East Wing properly takes at least an hour and a half. Outdoors, between the West and East Buildings, a scattering of glass pyramids (skylights for the underground restaurant) and a sleek fountain complement the spiffy architecture of the building itself. (Open Mon.-Sat. 10am-5pm, Sun. 11am-6pm.)

NATIONAL AIR & SPACE MUSEUM

The National Air and Space Museum, on the south side of the Mall between 4th and 7th St. SW, is just plain **big.** There's no better word to describe the **expanse** of its galleries, the **scope** of its ambitions, or the **sheer size** of its exhibits. Where other museums might try to win you over with a delicate piece of ceramic or a dainty cultural artifact, Air and Space dangles DC-3s over your head, balances 80-foot rockets in a pit that reaches from basement to skylight, and churns your stomach with life-like films projected on a five-story IMAX screen. Even the science exhibits deal with nothing smaller than a planet and pass gleefully to galactic scales and beyond.

Of course, the scale of the museum is commensurate with the scale of the achievements it commemorates. Before 1903, human beings had never left the surface of the planet by mechanical means—the Wright brothers did so that year in a rickety biplane which now hangs in the museum's entrance gallery. But by 1969—just 66 years later—humans had the know-how to leave the Earth's surface far behind, and on July 20, Neil Armstrong and Buzz Aldrin landed on the moon in a rickety lunar module, a duplicate of which is on display in the museum. These landmark episodes are the first and last chapters in the museum's story, with countless others filling in the details in between, and, to a lesser extent, before and since.

The scope of the history and the size of the exhibits have combined to make Air & Space the most popular museum in the world, drawing some 7.5 million visitors each year. Everyone is bound to be fascinated by at least something, and no one should try to see everything. Go to the information desk, get brochures and a map, and make choices before hitting the exhibits. Plan to see a movie in the middle of the day to rest your legs. A guide leads free **tours** of the museum at 10:15am and

1pm daily from the tour desk in the entrance gallery. Several shorter visits might be best, though the whole museum can be sampled in three hours if you race through.

Air and Space's best exhibits are, well, its biggest—the actual planes and crafts from all eras of flight. The **Wright brothers' biplane** in the entrance gallery looks intimidated by all its younger kin. Actual airplanes and rockets congregate in Galleries 100 (Entrance), 114 (Space Hall), and 102 (Air Transportation). Here are the walk-through **Skylab** space station, the **Apollo XI** command module, and the walk-through **DC-7.** Early jet planes park on the ground in Gallery 106 (Jet Aviation). The duplicate lunar lander has touched down outside the cafeteria. In the Vertical Flight gallery (Gallery 103), the Marine Sikorsky UH-34D whirlybird takes center stage, although a display about the first helicopter to circle the globe catches eyes because of the co-pilot's lineage: Ross Perot, Jr. helped fly that bird.

Sick of propellers? Soak up the science in Gallery 207 (Exploring the Planets), which shows what we know about the earth's eight orbital buddies, as well as how we know it. Gallery 211 shows how images of flight and space worm their way through all the arts, from Wagner's "Evening Star" (from the opera *Tannhauser)* to the rock group KISS's star-shaped makeup. Gallery 102 is your ticket to Commercial Air Transportation, with old airliners like the Douglass DC-3 and an exhibit about air-traffic control. The plastic mannequins can never go on strike.

Few exhibits are interactive; most are there to be stared at, period. One exception is Gallery 213 (Beyond the Limits), where you can use a computer program to design your own airplane; another is Gallery 203 (Sea-Air Operations) where (via computer) you can pilot a fighter, try to land it on a carrier, and, probably, crash or sink. With the aid of films, interactive displays, and a simulated Martian environment, an exhibit in the museum entitled "Where Next, Columbus?" (Gallery 209) brings an historical perspective to issues dealing with past and future space exploration, solar sails, and human contact with extraterrestrials.

Air and Space takes an understandable interest in mass-market science fiction. One gallery test-flies the **U.S.S. Enterprise** from Star Trek. Around such galleries, of course, genuine technology and detailed explanations show how real spacecraft get designed. The atmosphere is educational and at times militaristic, but various video displays, the IMAX films, and the Star Trek exhibit can be oodles of entertainment for those wearied by endless facts and figures.

IMAX movies give spectators vertigo in the Langley Theater, home of the 5-story movie screen. The perennially popular "To Fly," an aerial tour of America from balloons to spaceships, shows along with four other rotating films. Headsets translate some of the IMAX films into other languages. (Films run 9:30am-6:45pm. Tickets $3.25, children, students, seniors $2; available at the box office on the ground floor of the museum.)

The **Einstein Planetarium** will have you seeing stars on the 70-foot dome above. The standard show, "Universe of Illusions" will introduce you to some of the oddities that go blink in the night, from comets to planets to black holes. (Shows run every 40 min. 11am-5:40pm. Tickets $3.25, children, students, seniors $2; available at the box office on the second floor near the Spirit of St. Louis.)

Self-guided **cassette tours** are available in English and several other languages ($3.50, students and seniors $3). (357-2700, TDD 357-1505; museum open daily 10am-6:30pm; Sept.-June daily 10am-5:30pm. Metro: L'Enfant Plaza.)

HIRSHHORN MUSEUM & SCULPTURE GARDEN

If you're convinced that art ended with Picasso, stay away from the Hirshhorn Museum and Sculpture Garden, home to the modern, post-modern, and post-post-modern at 8th St. and Independence Ave. SW (357-2700, TDD 357-1729). The reinforced circular structure sits on four piers 14 ft. above the ground to create a plaza area for the display of sculpture. The four-story, squat concrete cylinder on stilts has outraged traditionalists since 1966. Each floor consists of two concentric circles: an outer ring of rooms and paintings, and an inner corridor of sculptures. From the inner circle, windows face the courtyard and its penny-collecting fountain. (The staff apparently finds this layout simple enough to absolve them of any obligation to provide a floor plan at the information desk.)

Built around immigrant philanthropist Joseph Hirshhorn's gifts, the museum still carries the flavor of personal preference rather than institutional design. Of the museum's architecture, S. Dillon Ripley, former secretary of the Smithsonian, once said, "If it were not controversial in almost every way it would hardly qualify as a place to house contemporary art. For it must somehow be symbolic of the material it is designed to encase." Whatever.

The Hirshhorn's best shows feature art since 1960; no other gallery or museum in Washington even pretends to keep up with the Hirshhorn's avant-garde paintings, mind-bending sculptures, and mixed-media installations. Hirshhorn halls hallow 20th-century artists from Calder to Kelly to de Kooning to Stella; even visitors who could supply the missing first names might fall in love with some unknown work. But innocents of modernism need not fear: the work of artists like Georgia O'Keefe, René Magritte, Max Ernst, Jackson Pollack, Edward Hopper, and Joan Miró is intermingled with the more intimidating stuff by lesser-known artists.

The museum claims the world's most comprehensive set of 19th- and 20th-century Western sculpture, including small works by Rodin and Giacometti. The collection also includes pieces by Renoir, Degas, Matisse, Gaugin, and Picasso. The second and third floors show changing parts of the museum's permanent collection. The lowest level gathers temporary exhibits, an auditorium, and a film on the appreciation of modern art (subtitled for the hearing impaired; comfy chairs for everybody).

Outdoor sculpture shines in the courtyard of the museum, with aluminum and steel and bronze and silver and red creations set up artfully along the stony pavement. Enter the museum from the revolving doors at Independence Ave. (Museum open daily 10am-5:30pm. Sculpture Garden open daily 7:30am-dusk. Tours of the museum Mon.-Sat. 10:30am, noon, and 1:30pm; Sun. 12:30pm. Sculpture tours for the blind and sign-language tours also available. Call 357-3235 for tour information.)

ARTS AND INDUSTRIES BUILDING

Between the Castle and the Hirshhorn, the recursive Arts and Industries Building is an exhibition of an exhibition, the 1876 Centennial Exhibition of American technology in Philadelphia. After the exhibition had ended, most of the foreign exhibitors donated their shows to the U.S. government to save themselves the cost of shipping them home. Congress ordered the Smithsonian to house the inherited objects (over the museum's objections) and paid for the Arts and Industries Building, America's first national museum. Before you go in, pause for the exterior: the polychromatic, multi-style chaos of gables, arches, rails, shingles, bricks, and windows, along with the nearby silly Smithsonian Castle and merry-go-round, makes tourists wonder what theme park they have stepped into.

The dust that has gathered on some of the old-fashioned glass cases is part of this museum's charm. Light fare, like furniture and candy-making equipment, congregates near the Mall entrance; further back, heavy machinery—like an old-fashioned elevator and generator—will delight advocates of steam power. The **Discovery Theater** presents plays especially for children, like *Winnie the Pooh* and *Binker*. An **experimental gallery,** facing Independence Ave. on the other side of the main fountain, showcases innovative (usually interactive) exhibits from individuals, museums, and non-profit organizations around the world. Exhibition space is available through an application process and serves as a testing ground from which exhibitors learn how to improve their shows before taking them on tour. (Museum open daily 10am-5:30pm. Discovery performances Tues.-Fri. 10 and 11:30am, Sat. 11:30am and 1pm. Admission $4, children 12 and under $3.50. Reserve by calling the box office at 357-1500 (voice and TDD) Mon.-Fri. 10am-4pm.)

NATIONAL MUSEUM OF AFRICAN ART AND ARTHUR M. SACKLER GALLERY

Built in 1987, the National Museum of African Art and the Sackler Gallery hide their non-Western treasures underground, behind the Castle and below the beautifully landscaped 4-acre **Enid A. Haupt Garden.** The Garden is as carefully crafted and meticulously sculpted as the art beneath it, whose main entrance faces Independence Ave. and 10th St. SW (garden opens at 7am, closing hours change with the seasons; Metro: Smithsonian). Both museums have two underground exhibit levels and connect to the International Gallery and the S. Dillon Ripley Center three stories underground. Connecting halls let you walk between the Sackler, the African, and the Freer (see below). The museums reach the outside world through paired post-modern pavilions in the Haupt Garden; if you face the Castle, the Sackler entrance will be on your left, the African entrance on your right.

The **National Museum of African Art,** 950 Independence Ave. SW (357-4600, TDD 357-4814), collects, catalogues, polishes, and shows off artifacts from Sub-Saharan Africa, offering insight into cultures where craftsmanship and artistic creativity go hand in hand, and where texture, color, form, and iconography are regularly incorporated into even the simplest of everyday objects. Entering the first-level central hall, you are greeted by a **slit-gong,** a drum in the shape of an unidentifiable animal. Permanent exhibits include a collection of bronzes from what is today Nigeria and assorted pottery. There are also pieces by contemporary African artists. The second floor houses temporary exhibits. (Open daily 10am-5:30pm. Hour-long tours Mon.-Fri. 10:30am, 1:30pm; Sat.-Sun. 11am, 1pm, 3pm.)

The small **International Gallery,** 1100 Jefferson Dr. SW (357-1300), inside the S. Dillon Ripley Center, continually offers new and thoughtful temporary exhibits. Recent exhibits have featured lithographs from a politically-transformed Eastern Europe, and "Talents of the Brush," featuring entrants in the Jill Sackler Chinese calligraphy competition.

The **Arthur M. Sackler Gallery,** 1050 Independence Ave. SW (357-2041, TDD 786-2374), showcases Sackler's extensive collection of art from China, South and Southeast Asia, and Persia. Illuminated manuscripts, Chinese and Japanese paintings from many centuries, carvings and friezes from Egypt, Phoenicia, and Sumeria, Hindu gods, jade miniatures, and other such works repose in low light and air-conditioned majesty. Permanent displays include "Monsters, Myths, and Minerals," and "Sculpture of South and Southeast Asia." Exhibits occasionally have excellent self-guided tour materials for children under 12. Call for tour information. The **Sackler Library** (357-2091), on the second level, is open to the public Mon.-Fri. 10am-5pm. (Museum open daily 10am-5:30pm.)

FREER GALLERY

The Freer Gallery of Art, on the Mall at Jefferson Dr. and 12th St. SW, is the small, delicate pearl on a Mall-encircling necklace of big, showy gems. A fraction of the size of most Smithsonian museums, the Freer quietly displays Asian as well as American art, much of which betrays Eastern influences (for instance, the paintings and designs of James McNeill Whistler; see his opulent "Peacock Room"). A sequence of connected galleries surround an elegant courtyard and lead you from the American art past Japanese, Korean, Chinese, Buddhist, South Asian, and finally Islamic works. Recently connected to the Sackler via a new shared exhibition gallery, the Freer collection (comprising over 26,000 objects) is as richly historical and fabulously opulent as its neighbor's—Chinese bronzes, precious manuscripts, jade carvings, and so forth reward hour upon hour of viewing and consideration. (Open daily 10am-5:30pm. Free daily highlights **tour** at 1:30pm.)

U.S. HOLOCAUST MUSEUM

Though not technically a Smithsonian, the museum's location at the Mall, its breadth of scope, and the skill with which exhibits are presented warrant its inclusion in this section. The U.S. Holocaust Memorial Museum, 100 Raoul Wallenberg

Place SW (488-0400; Metro: Smithsonian), opened in April 1993 after more than a decade of preparation. The project was the brainchild of Carter administration advisors, and in 1979, Carter himself asked Holocaust survivor and author Elie Wiesel to create a plan for the museum. The federal government threw in a piece of land, and the U.S. Holocaust Memorial Council began private fundraising efforts to pay for the building's construction ($168 million so far).

In a 1989 address to the Council, President George Bush declared that "this building will testify more powerfully than any words to the importance of protecting freedom and dignity for all people." The museum project has been hailed over the years by three more Presidents and thousands of government officials, clergymen, and lay leaders as a necessity for a country whose living memory of the Holocaust years is rapidly fading and becoming increasingly distorted. The museum's prominent and symbolic site—close to the Mall and within view of the Washington Monument and Lincoln Memorial—inevitably places the museum, and its subject matter, in the midst of America's storehouses and in the context of its history. Unlike Europe, where the history of the Holocaust is told in aging synagogue-museums or in the worn buildings of former concentration camps, the new U.S. museum is uniquely suited to its audience. Its displays move beyond mere historical narrative; visitors are *made* to experience events from a more personal perspective. Those entering the **permanent exhibition** are given a card with a photo and description of a real Holocaust victim. The card chronicles the changes in that individual's life over the course of the war. A "Tower of Photos" surrounds observers in another part of the Hall, inundating them with pre-Holocaust photos of an entire village. Invariably, it is the pictorial evidence, the photos of individual faces, which forces upon the potentially detached observer an emotional contact with the documented events. The museum rightly assumes ignorance on the part of its visitors and gives them the whole story, beginning on the fourth floor (accessible by elevator) with **"Nazi Assault, 1933-39,"** which chronicles not only the rise of Nazism, but also the events leading up to the war in Europe and the history of anti-semitism from the beginnings of Christianity onward. Through film footage, artifacts, and clearly written descriptions, the exhibit guides observers through the increasingly explicit persecution of German Jews in the years preceding the second world war. Vistors are made to experience the progression towards genocide and the exhibit's assertion that the passive acceptance of the German populace made it all possible. **"The Final Solution, 1940-44"** is less forgiving; a black-and-white film (behind walls too high for small children to peek over) shows barbaric medical experiments performed by Nazi doctors. Fully visible still photos and dioramas depict Jews and others being rounded up and sent to concentration camps, then exterminated in gas chambers or at gunpoint. One photo shows a sea of women's hair, shorn off prisoners to be sold and eventually used as a manufacturing fiber. Victims' personal items, on loan from Holocaust museums in Poland and Germany, are also displayed here. Finally, **"Aftermath—1945 to the Present"** brings it all together. Films show Soviet, British, and American troops entering the concentration camps, shocked by the mass graves and emaciated prisoners they encounter. A wall lists the names of those who heroically defied the Nazis to save Jewish lives, while more films and tapes bear the testimony of Holocaust survivors.

Throughout the permanent exhibition, instances of U.S. and world callousness to the plight of the Jews are justifiably condemned. One display discusses FDR's refusal to bomb the extermination facilities at Auschwitz, despite pleas from American Jews. At the end of the permanent exhibit is the entrance to the free-standing octagonal **Hall of Remembrance,** with its eternal flame symbolically placed within the museum to emphasize the central theme of the exhibits—to never forget.

James Ingo Freed used forms derived from the Holocaust itself to create a building that is as much about the Holocaust as the exhibits it contains. Set between the neoclassical Bureau of Engraving and Printing and the Victorian Auditor's Building, the museum brings together the materials of both neighboring buildings—limestone and red brick—with the forms of the concentration camp guard towers (in the four glass-topped "towers" that line the north side of the building) and the ovens in which prisoners died (as the arched brick portals in the Hall of Witness). The center beam of the steel-and-glass skylight ceiling of the Hall of Witness runs at a diagonal, giving the whole room a warped feeling.

The "Americanization" of the Holocaust embodied in this museum—both its presence in the capital and its conscious efforts to engage American crowds—has led critics to contend that the museum is just "one more American theme park," complete with interactive computer set-ups and video displays, films that play and replay atrocities for each new slew of visitors, and shiny, visually striking exhibits that entertain as much as they educate. Yet even detractors must give credit to the fine presentation of a vast amount of material in a coherent, sensitive, and ultimately effective exhibit. While most of the museum is inappropriate for the very young, children should be encouraged to explore the **"Remember the Children"** exhibit on the first floor (no ticket required). Here, the story of the fictitious Holocaust survivor Daniel is told through his diary entries and depictions of his homes before the war, in the ghetto, and in a concentration camp. Children can open Daniel's drawers, lift up his blankets, and open windows to see how Daniel lived both "before" and "after" the institution of anti-semitic laws.

The museum also houses a resource center for teachers and the **Wexner Learning Center,** where visitors conduct research on Holocaust topics through computers and interactive films.

Massive overcrowding has forced the museum to require all visitors to the permanent exhibition to have **tickets.** To acquire tickets on the same day as your visit, get in line before 9am at the 14th and C St. entrance. Otherwise, it's safer to buy tickets through Ticketmaster two weeks in advance (in D.C. call 432-7328; in MD 410-481-7328; in VA 703-573-7328; out of region 800-551-7328) and submit to the agency's $4 service charge (tickets are free for those who stand in line). Tickets are good for admission to the exhibition *at certain times only;* try to get an early time, if possible. You don't want to be rushed as you make your way through the exhibits, and crowds often necessitate a wait to get a good view of the more popular displays.

The museum sits on a parcel of land between 14th St. and Raoul Wallenberg Place SW (a portion of 15th Street renamed in honor of Raoul Wallenberg, the Swedish diplomat who saved thousands of Hungarian Jews from the Nazis), just south of Independence Ave. Don't try to see everything in one day; allow at least four hours for the briefest of breeze-throughs. (Museum open daily 10am-5:30pm.)

■■■ OUTSIDE THE MALL

CAPITOL HILL

Sewall-Belmont House

Just a few blocks from Washington's largest museums sits a small, intimate museum, quietly dedicated to the achievements of women. Nestled up beside the Hart Senate office building, Sewall-Belmont House, 144 Constitution Ave. NE (546-3989), holds a museum of the U.S. women's movement, as well as the offices of the National Woman's Party. (Metro: Union Station.) Travelers who have battled the Smithsonian crowds will appreciate the peace and attention they are granted here. When visitors arrive, the sole guide on duty greets them at the door, puts out a "Tour in Progress" sign, and whisks them off for a personal tour of the premises. Along the way, visitors can admire some of the oldest digs in Washington; the house was built in 1800 by Robert Sewall, incorporating parts of a house dating to 1680. Treasury Secretary Albert Gallatin was one of the first to reside in the house, and in 1803, he negotiated the Louisiana Purchase from one of the front rooms because he despised the 20-minute carriage ride to the Treasury Building. In 1814, American resistance troops fired upon camping British soldiers from the house's top floors. The annoyed and pyromaniacal British set fire to the house, as they did to most of official Washington, but a fortuitous rainstorm spared most of the building. Restorations returned the house to tip-top shape, and in 1929, the National Women's Party bought the house for its headquarters.

Most of the tour focuses on the NWP's fight for suffrage, as well as on the life of Alice Paul, who founded the party in 1913. The main hall, referred to as the "Hall of Fame," holds busts of noted suffragettes and feminists Susan B. Anthony, Lucretia Mott, and Elizabeth Cady Stanton, as well as a life-sized statue of Joan of Arc. Sybil Ludington is shown on the horse she rode on the night of April 26, 1777, to warn the militiamen in Danbury, CT of an impending attack by the British. Her ride was twice as long as Paul Revere's and, unlike Revere, she did not get caught by the British. At the end of the hall hangs the large yellow and purple banner used to picket the White House for suffrage in 1917. Other rooms contain art and photographs related to the women's movement as well as beautiful period furnishings, including the sort of rope bed whose fickle tension apparently gave rise to the expression "sleep tight." (House open Tues.-Fri. 11am-3pm, Sat.-Sun. noon-4pm. Free. For a tour, simply go up the front staircase and ring the bell.)

National Postal Museum

Established in 1993, the National Postal Museum (357-2700, TDD 357-1729), located on the lower level of the City Post Office at 1st St. and Massachusetts Ave. NE (Metro: Union Station), is the latest jewel in the Smithsonian Crown, and it has learned from the institution's previous mistakes. While other Smithsonian museums bombard visitors with an indigestible amount of information—often in painfully small fonts—the Postal Museum delivers an intelligent and accessible summary of the nation's postal and philatelic history. In under an hour, visitors can navigate a replica of the forest paths used by the nation's first mailmen, and create work for its current mailmen by addressing, stamping, and mailing their very own National Postal Museum postcards. An escalator leads down to the museum from the center of the cavernous lobby of the City Post Office. Look up as you ride down: three airmail planes hang far overhead in the 90-ft.-high atrium. The display at the foot of the escalator, "Moving the Mail," is dedicated (not surprisingly) to the vehicles used to transport mail. It shows off some of the museum's larger pieces, including the red, white, and blue "long-life vehicle" standard on streets today, and a more dated railway mail car where visitors can try their hand at sorting the mail. Also in this area, free postcards are available from "postcard kiosks," where visitors generate an addressed postcard, put it through one of the metering machines (the stamp will still cost you 20¢—the U.S.P.S. draws the line at free postage), and drop it through a slot to mail it off.

A number of passages radiate off this main hall, each containing a separate exhibit; the passage directly opposite the escalator is probably the best place to start. The exhibit there, "Binding the Nation," tells the early story of the postal system. As every mail aficionado can tell you, neither rain nor sleet nor dark of night can stay these couriers from their appointed rounds. But the rounds were much tougher going before the advent of motorized mail trucks and electronic ZIP code scanners, as this display makes eminently clear. The exhibit covers the history of the postal system from Colonial times to the Civil War. Not surprisingly, the Pony Express gets big play, but the gallery's entrance recreates the King's Best Highway, the roadless postal route that ran between New York and Boston in the 1670s (a path that has since become the motel-infested Route 1). At a computer video terminal inside the exhibit, visitors can attempt to choose the best mail route between various U.S. cities in the 1800s. The next gallery, "Customers and Communities," picks up where "Binding the Nation" left off. The Rural Free Delivery section displays the five winners of a contest to find the most unusual RFD mail boxes—the replica of the U.S. Capitol held at arm's length by Uncle Sam is a classic. The exhibit winds up with a section on postal oddities, including the charred remains of the Craig, Alaska Post Office, collected and stored in a jar and the letter-carrier uniform worn by Cliff Clavin, everyone's favorite oedipal oddity, in the late TV series *Cheers*.

Across the main hall from this exhibit, "The Art of Cards and Letters" displays examples of wartime correspondence from U.S. military conflicts, including the Persian Gulf War. Letter-writing stations are available for those so inspired. The "Stamps and Stories" gallery overflows with the museum's renowned collection of philatelic rarities (including the priceless "Inverted Jenny") as well as a smaller collection of overexcited philatelists.

The museum's **Discovery Center** is adjacent to the exhibition galleries and offers daily activities and projects for children and adults, from deciphering a bar code to solving a postal crime. The **Library Research Center,** with more than 40,000 volumes and manuscripts, is the world's largest postal-research facility. The Center houses a specimen study room, an audio-video viewing room, and a separate library of rare books. The library facilities are available to scholars and the interested public by appointment only (633-9370). The museum also houses a gift shop, a stamp store, and (surprise) a fully functional post office.

Stop at the **information desk** for a map and information. Special **tours** for groups may be arranged in advance by calling 357-2991 (Mon.-Fri. 10am-3pm). To arrange tours for persons with visual or hearing impairments, call 786-2942 (TDD 786-2414) one week in advance (Mon.-Fri. 10am-3pm). Sign language and oral interpreters for programs other than tours are available by calling the same number two weeks in advance. The museum is open daily 10am-5:30pm. Free.

Capital Children's Museum

Release your Smithsonian-induced tension by touching and feeling every exhibit in this huge interactive experiment of a museum, located at 800 3rd St. NE (675-4125) in a large red-brick building that looks like a city school (Metro: Union Station). Grind and brew your own hot chocolate while trying on ponchos in the two-story mock-up of a Mexican plaza. Try your hand at writing with a quill and ink or learn how a printing press works by printing a simple plate yourself. Walk through the life-sized cave or leave your mark on the wall in the shadow theater. A model town lets children play in a miniature community complete with a bus to drive, a manhole to descend, and a working telephone system. The museum also has a high-tech animation exhibit, which teaches the basic principles of cartoon-making and even lets kids be filmed against an animated background, à la Roger Rabbit. On weekends, the museum sponsors an acclaimed Holocaust education program for children, led by Holocaust survivors; call for details. If you're in a hurry, go first to the Mexico exhibit, the mock-up town, and the animation exhibit; otherwise plan to spend at least two hours poking and prodding everything in sight. Because the museum is independently funded, some equipment is in disrepair. A more irksome consequence is that you gotta pay to go inside. (Open daily 10am-5pm. Admission $6, children under 2 free. All children must be accompanied by an adult.)

SOUTHEAST

Navy Museum

You can play Popeye at this refreshingly hands-on paean to things naval, located in Building 76 at the Navy Yard (433-4882). Metro: Navy Yard. Climb inside the space capsule, man the huge ship guns (3-in., 50-caliber), jam yourself into a bathysphere used to explore the sea floor, or give orders on the bridge. Fondle the life-sized replicas of "Little Boy" and "Fat Man," the atomic bombs detonated over Japan at the close of WWII. While you play, don't forget to look up at the Alvin and Trieste undersea vehicles that hang from the ceiling next to Navy airplanes, or to look around at the countless model ships laid up in glassy drydocks—the American craft are up to 14 ft. long, and their anachronistic opponents include a 1916 Austro-Hungarian warship and a Greek trireme. Next door, technology steams on at the unpretentious **Museum Annex.** "Just" a small building full of old submarines, the Annex shows off the Intelligent Whale, a hand-propelled submarine the Navy bought in 1869. Run your hands along the Seehund, a well-designed mini-sub the Nazis used for coastal defense in the days of World War II. Museum open June-Aug.Mon.-Fri. 9am-5pm, Sat.-Sun. 10am-5pm; Sept.-May Mon.-Fri. 9am-4pm, Sat.-Sun. 10am-5pm.

Marine Corps Historical Museum and Navy Art Gallery

The **Marine Corps Historical Museum,** in Building 58 at the Navy Yard (433-3534; Metro: Navy Yard), marches through Marine Corps time from the American Revolution to the present. Twenty exhibit cases tout the actions, guns, uniforms, and swords of marines from the halls of Montezuma to the shores of Kuwait. Don't blink or you'll miss the 48-hr. invasion of Grenada. A temporary exhibit on the Marines in World War II, which will show through 1996 sometime, displays a miscellany of marine mementos such as the flag immortalized on Iwo Jima. Open June-Aug. Mon.-Thurs. and Sat. 10am-4pm, Fri. 10am-4pm and 6-8pm, Sun. noon-5pm; Sept.-May Mon.-Sat. 10am-4pm, Sun. noon-5pm. Nearby, in Building 67 (433-3815), the one-room **Navy Art Gallery** hangs paintings of naval action, all by talented sailors and "combat artists." These specialized artists sailed, ate canned rations, and braved gunfire with the sailors, all to record on canvas the action on board. Exhibits change every six months. Open Wed.-Fri. 9am-4pm, Sat.-Sun. 10am-4pm.

Anacostia Museum

1901 Fort Place SE (287-3369, Sat.-Sun. 357-2700). Metro: Anacostia. (Walking here from the Metro can be dangerous; take a cab.) Founded in 1967 in a former movie theater and later moved to modern quarters, this Smithsonian "neighborhood museum" holds temporary exhibits on African-American history and culture. From Oct. 1995 to March 1996, the exhibit "Southern City, National Ambition: Washington, D.C., 1800-1860" will be on display. At other times, call or pick up a flyer at the Smithsonian Castle (on the Mall) to see what's showing. A small museum store sells cards, posters, and books by and about African-Americans. To reach the museum by car, take MLK Ave. SE to Morris Rd., left on Morris (which becomes Erie St., then Fort Pl.); by bus, take the W-1 or W-2 on Howard Rd. near the Anacostia Metro station and ride to the museum's doorstep at Fort Place. Open daily 10am-5pm; free.

OLD DOWNTOWN

National Building Museum

It's only proper that an architectural marvel should house the National Building Museum (272-2448), which towers above F St. NW between 4th and 5th St. (Metro: Judiciary Square, directly across from the F St. exit). In 1881, Congress asked military engineer Montgomery Meigs to design a cheap brick building for the 1500 clerks of the Pension Bureau. The bureaucrats lucked out: Meigs's Italian-inspired edifice remains one of Washington's most beautiful. A terra-cotta frieze, 3 ft. high and 1200 ft. long, frames an endless parade of Union soldiers arriving to collect their pensions; look for doctors, wounded soldiers, and artillery pieces amid the crowds of infantry. Early photographer Eadweard (not Edward) Muybridge, who analyzed the motions of walking and running, inspired Caspar Buberl, sculptor of the frieze. Inside, the expansive **Great Hall** exhibits a sort of budget opulence. On one hand, its eight Corinthian columns are among the world's largest; life-sized busts peer down from 244 wall niches; and a terra-cotta fountain is 28 ft. in diameter. The Great Hall—big enough to hold a 15-story building—may even cause visitors sensitive to scale, spectacle, and splendor to make small gasping noises. But on the other hand, the columns are brick (their marble look took 4000 gallons of rose paint) and the roof, partly corrugated metal, rests on iron supports. Meigs wanted to fill the niches with busts of prominent Americans; to stay within his budget, however, he had to revise his plans and base the busts on Smithsonian life masks of Native Americans. In 1984 the busts "were discarded" and replaced with 244 replicas of eight models by artist Gretta Bader of "American Builders."

"Washington: Symbol and City," one of the N.B.M.'s first permanent exhibits, records D.C.'s dual history. Half the exhibit covers the planning of monuments and central Washington; the other half covers D.C.'s residential aspects. Other highlights include models of the rejected designs for the Washington Monument and the chance to design your own Capitol Hill rowhouse.

The museum also sponsors free lunchtime **concerts** (at 12:15pm) on selected Wed. and Thurs. afternoons in the Great Hall, generally by chamber and jazz ensembles or military bands. (Museum open Mon.-Sat. 10am-4pm, Sun. noon-4pm. Tours Mon.-Fri. 12:30pm, Sat.-Sun. 12:30pm, 1:30pm. Excellent wheelchair access, including exhibits for visually impaired visitors. Free.)

National Museum of American Art and National Portrait Gallery

The National Museum of American Art and the National Portrait Gallery (357-2700, TDD 357-1729) share the **Old Patent Office Building,** a Neoclassical edifice two blocks long (American Art entrance at 8th and G St., Portrait Gallery entrance at 8th and F; Metro: Gallery Place-Chinatown). Washington's ubiquitous Greek temple motif, complete with Doric columns, seems more appropriate to these museums—which moved here in 1968—than to the 19th-century bureaucrats the Patent Office once employed. Robert Mills, architect of the Washington Monument, designed the more delicate, less imposing south wing (now the Portrait Gallery). You'll know American Art by the glistening fiberglass cowboy (called *Vaquero)* in front and the Portrait Gallery by its hanging banners. A courtyard connects the Americans to the portraits and allows visitors to sit, eat, and tan in the sun.

National Museum Of American Art

Although this museum houses the largest collection of American art in the world, the curators haven't made up their minds about what their museum is for, and their loss might be your gain: the surprisingly deserted corridors contain a pleasantly diverse and disorganized collection of major 19th-century painters and folk and ethnic artists, as well as a scattering of contemporary innovators. Of course, the expected Gilbert Stuarts aren't lacking, either.

D.C. janitor James Hampton stayed up nights in an unheated garage for 15 years to assemble the *Throne of the Third Heaven of the Nations' Millennium General Assembly.* Now on permanent display down the corridor to the left of the main entrance, this array of sculptures may permanently alter your spiritual life. *Time* has called it "the finest work of visionary religious art produced by an American." The throne comprises 177 objects, including ruined furniture, electrical cables, and dead light bulbs sheathed in aluminum and gold foil. No one exhibited or knew of the work until years after Hampton's death in 1964. The *Throne*'s framework of religious symbolism and cryptic writing system has yet to be decoded; mere mortals will just stare, dumbfounded.

Other pieces on a similarly grandiose scale include Paul Feeley's six-foot -tall gold fiberglass *Jack,* and Thomas Moran's gargantuan canyon landscapes in the second-floor lobby. The museum's "Art of the American West" room (first floor) offers an abundance of 19th-century depictions of Native Americans, including important works by Native American artists. Selections from what the NMAA calls the finest collection of African-American art of any general museum are displayed on the second and third floors.

If you still think the museum deserves the sparse crowds it gets, head to the third floor for 20th-century work. The Lincoln Gallery was originally designed as the Patent Office exhibition room and served its country as a makeshift hospital during the Civil War. Today, it houses works by everyone from Franz Kline to Georgia O'Keefe to Roberta Rauschenberg. Exhibits rotate regularly.

If you don't trust your own artistic judgement, show up at noon Mon.-Fri. or 2pm on weekends for a **free tour** of the museum. Temporary exhibitions are given real weight at the NMAA, since they give the museum a chance to show off aspects of its immense collection normally forced into storage by lack of display space (the NMAA owns over 35,000 works). Wheelchair access at 9th and G; sign language tours available (786-2942, TDD 786-2414). Museum open daily 10am-5:30pm.

Directly above the Portrait Gallery and accessible via the NMAA's third floor modern art collection is the **Great Hall,** once the largest room in the United States. Its gilded American Victorian Renaissance walls were witness to Lincoln's second inaugural ball in 1865; now restored to its antebellum splendor, the hall fufills the building's original purpose by displaying patent models.

National Portrait Gallery

If a museum devoted exclusively to portraiture sounds monotonous, think again; the wide range of media, periods, styles, and people represented make these narrow halls more like a museum of the American character. Portraits in the gallery come in all shapes and sizes, from a miniature superimposition of P.T. Barnum's head on a beetle's body (thus rendering the curiosity king a "hum-bug") to a life-sized painting of opera star Marian Anderson in a long red gown. A caricature of Rachmaninoff shows the Russian composer pensively playing piano; nearby, depictions of Theodore Roosevelt proliferate wildly.

The gallery's temporary exhibits and unmarked rooms are more fun and offbeat than the staid permanent collections, which include a **Hall of Presidents** (2nd floor) and the **Meserve Collection** (3rd floor), which contains Matthew Brady's Civil War photos of Lincoln. The expected dryness of the **Galleries of Notable Americans** is relieved by portraits whose conservatism is so extreme, it's funny. A portrait of **Pocahontas** painted when she was living in England (circa 1595-1617) presents a stuffy maiden in velvet with a Protestant's lace cuff around her neck; Davey Crockett is also depicted in a surprisingly austere manner, looking more like a State Representative than a fur-trapper. The gallery also boasts a life-sized portrait of Samuel Clemens (Mark Twain), an image of Elizabeth Cady Stanton looking very clever, a bust of Geronimo, and a portrait of Mary Cassatt painted by Edgar Degas.

NPG museum **tours** on a walk-in basis or by request (357-2920). Museum open daily 10am-5:30pm. Wheelchair access near the garage at 9th and G St.

National Museum of Women in the Arts

The National Museum of Women in the Arts, 1250 New York Ave. NW (783-5000; Metro: Metro Center), suffers slightly from the architectural constraints of its home. The bottom two floors were once a Masonic Temple, and a hunt for the museum's permanent collection, which begins on the third floor, feels like an initiation rite. From outside, the NMWA resembles the neighboring office buildings; inside, sweeping staircases, pink marble, and celestial chandeliers are better suited to a mansion than a museum. The ground floor contains the museum shop and information desk. A second-floor balcony holds changing displays of consistent interest.

Avail yourself of the elevator, or climb the stairs, traverse the balcony, and ascend the spare, hidden staircase to the third floor. Women artists have come into their own in the last 100 years, and the permanent collection proves it with works by Mary Cassatt, Georgia O'Keeffe, Lilla Cabot Perry, and Alma Thomas. Helen Frankenthaler's expansive landscape-like canvas compels a visit. The comparatively young museum invites a flood of temporary exhibitions; check the museum listings in *City Paper* or the *Washington Post* Weekend section to find even more reasons why you should pay it a visit. (Open Mon.-Sat. 10am-5pm, Sun. noon-5pm. Suggested donation $3, seniors and students $2.)

FOGGY BOTTOM

Renwick Gallery

At 17th St. and Pennsylvania Ave. NW, the Renwick Gallery (357-1300, 357-2531) fills its Second Empire mansion with some of D.C.'s most interesting art. (Metro: Farragut West.) This Smithsonian-owned gallery says it displays "American craft," but its holdings aren't just for macrame buffs. The first floor's temporary exhibits often show fascinating mixed-media sculptures, tapestries, and constructions by important contemporary artists. Upstairs, the **Grand Salon** and the **Octagon Room** display epic 19th-early 20th-century works in grand style. These rooms, however, are not indicative of the museum's true bent; check out the second floor's displays of contemporary "craft." Although many pieces in the collection are rotated, look for two of the Renwick's most arresting works: Wendell Castle's 1985 *Ghost Clock* and Larry Fuente's 1988 *Game Fish*. The former, at first glance simply a grandfather clock with a sheet thrown over it, was actually carved from a single piece of mahogany; the latter is a huge sailfish trophy ingeniously plastered with children's toys (!). The displays on the first floor change every few months. (Open daily 10am-5:30pm. Weelchair access. Free.)

Corcoran Gallery of Art

Once housed in the Renwick's mansion, the Corcoran (638-3211, 638-1439, or 638-1070), Washington's oldest art museum, now exhibits in much larger, Neoclassical quarters on 17th St. between E St. and New York Ave. NW. (Metro: Farragut West.) Frank Lloyd Wright called it "the best-designed building in Washington." The Corcoran shows off American artists like portraitist John Singer Sargent, impressionist Mary Cassatt, and seascape-master Winslow Homer. An air of medieval romance is provided by Thomas Cole's 1841 *Return from the Tournament,* on display in the North Atrium, and Louis-Maurice Boutet de Monvel's gold-leafed series on Joan of Arc, which begins on Clark Landing. Montana Senator Clark donated many of the Corcoran's more interesting 19th-century pieces, as well as the wildly baroque **Salon Doré,** a gaudy gold-leaf room that the Senator had transported from its early 18th-century Parisian home to his equally flagrant New York palace.

The Corcoran also houses a fine selection of contemporary American art, displaying such greats as Willem de Kooning and Ellsworth Kelly. Look for Andy Warhol's 1973 *Mao* as well as a slew of Roy Lichtenstein pieces. Four major exhibitions, not necessarily modern, sweep the second floor yearly. In 1988 the Corcoran reneged on its promise to house a touring exhibit of photography by the late Robert Mapplethorpe; the ensuing uproar over homophobia, obscenity laws, and federal funding of the arts rendered the Corcoran notorious and made Mapplethorpe one of the best-known names in photography.

Free **tours** of the Corcoran take place daily at 12:30pm and on Thursdays at 7:30pm. Free **jazz concerts** take place in the Hammer Auditorium every Wednesday from 12:30pm to 1:30pm. The Corcoran also incorporates an art school. (Open Mon. and Wed. and Fri.-Sun. 10am-5pm, Thurs. 10am-9pm. Suggested donation $3, families $5, students and seniors $1, under 12 free.)

GEORGETOWN

Dumbarton Oaks

This 16-acre estate, at 1703 32nd St. NW between R and S St. (recorded info. 338-8278, tour info. 342-3212), is all that remains of the original Rock of Dumbarton property, out of which settlers carved the town of George. The mansion-museum's attractive displays showcase Byzantine and pre-Columbian art, and the terraced gardens are the best cheap date in town.

The mansion (not to be confused with the entirely separate Dumbarton *House*) switched names and styles frequently since its construction in 1801. Robert and Mildred Bliss renovated it to accommodate the library and collections, then donated the house and gardens to Harvard University in 1940. Don't fear the imposing gates or the solemn hush as you enter the Dumbarton Oaks building: the cold, scholarly atmosphere hides treasures. The **Garden Library** gathers rare books, reference materials, and illustrations related to landscape architecture, garden history, and botany. To the dismay of a flower-enthused public, only scholars are permitted inside. The **Byzantine Collection** contains floor mosaics, bronzes, ivories, ecclesiastical silver, and jewelry, mostly from the Byzantine Empire (AD326-1453). Philip Johnson's 1963 gallery holds Robert Bliss's **pre-Columbian art** collection; the eight circular glass pavilions, arranged like flower petals around a fountain, vie in beauty with the art they contain. Stand in the center of one of the round rooms and try talking—only you can hear the echoes. The gallery includes carvings and tools from the Aztec and Mayan civilizations, displayed in natural light against the backdrop of the woods outside. The **Music Room** displays El Greco's *The Visitation.* Igor Stravinsky's *Dumbarton Oaks* concerto premiered here for the Blisses' 30th wedding anniversary in 1934. Subscription concerts still take place in the room every winter (collections open Tues.-Sun. 2-5pm; "suggested contribution" $1, otherwise free).

Save at least an hour for the **Dumbarton Oaks Gardens,** at 31st and R St., inside the gates of the estate; once you go in, you're guaranteed to stay at least that long. The formal gardens only occupy 10 acres; 27 acres of Dumbarton Oaks Park, 10 acres of the Danish Embassy, and 6 acres of estate buildings and grounds insulate the garden from the fallen world outside. Even in winter, the "bones" of the garden are serene and lovely: some trees were chosen for their distinctive branches when bare. Energetic walkers should find the 2-mi. trail that leads through Rock Creek Park up to the National Zoo. (Zoo info. 673-4800. Gardens open daily April-Oct. 2-6pm, Nov.-March 2-5pm. Admission $3, seniors and children $2; Nov.-March free.)

FARRAGUT

The Bethune Museum and Archives

At 1318 Vermont Ave. NW (332-1233; Metro: McPherson Square), the Bethune Museum commemorates the life of educator, leader, and pioneer civil rights activist Mary McLeod Bethune with exhibits on the first and second floors and a ½-hour video. The townhouse that holds the museum once served as headquarters for the National Council of Negro Women, which Bethune founded. One of 17 children of former slaves, she grew up to be the founder of a college, FDR's head of the Division of Negro Affairs, and a leading member of the NAACP, among other things. The museum chronicles her achievements and emphasizes her determination throughout a career that spanned two decades and four presidential administrations. The house is also home to the extensive **Archives for Black Women's History.** (Open Mon.-Sat. 10am-4pm; Aug. 29-June 4 Mon.-Fri. 10am-4pm. Archives open by appointment. Free.)

B'nai B'rith Klutznick National Jewish Museum

This pensive museum, 1640 Rhode Island Ave. NW (857-6583; Metro: Farragut North), contains Jewish cultural and ritual objects, including George Washington's famous letter to a Newport, Rhode Island synagogue which contains the first statement enunciating America's commitment to religious and ethnic toleration. Look for the gripping drawings by Auschwitz survivor David Wainapel. A wall of archives is available, and the rotating exhibits are fascinating. The security guard and accompanying bulletproof glass aren't just evidence of paranoia: terrorists held over 100 people hostage in the B'nai B'rith building in 1977. (Open Sun.-Fri. 10am-4:30pm, except Jewish holidays. Suggested donation $2, seniors, students, and children $1.)

DUPONT CIRCLE

Phillips Collection

The Phillips Collection, at 1600 21st St. at Q St. NW (387-2151), houses the first and one of the finest modern art collections in the United States. Its founder, Duncan Phillips, was a graduate of Yale and heir to a family steel company with money to spend and impeccable taste in art. Opened in 1921 by Phillips in the family mansion, the museum is now home to some 2500 pieces of art, only a fraction of which can be shown at any time. The works on display are thus something of an ever-changing, collective work of art, harboring a larger structure and logic as curators attempt to mesh the works with each other and with whatever temporary exhibits occupy the galleries. Each individual gallery is hung with an internal logic as well; discerning the connections may require a Ph.D. in art history in some cases, but well-informed docents can help out.

Enter the museum through the new **annex** at 1612 Massachusetts Ave., added when the collection grew too large for Phillips' original Victorian mansion at 1600 Massachusetts Ave. Walk through the annex's three floors before crossing over to the original mansion and descending through three more. On the first floor as you enter is one of the few relatively permanent installations—the **Rothko room.** Other such rooms include a **Klee room** and, most famously, a **Renoir room** holding Renoir's masterpiece *Luncheon of the Boating Party.* The third floor of the annex is generally reserved for temporary exhibits. The stroll up the annex and down through the original mansion is a delightful parade of works by Delacroix, Matisse, Van Gogh, Mondrian, Dega, Miro, Gris, Kandinsky, Turner, Courbet, Daumier, Prendergast, O'Keefe, and Hopper—to name a few. "Artful Evenings" with live music and gallery talks during the summer every Thurs. 5-8:30pm; admission $5. Open Tues.-Sat. 10am-5pm, Sun. noon-7pm. Admission Sat.-Sun. $6.50, students and seniors $3.25, under 18 free (Tues.-Fri. admission by contribution). **Tours** Wed. and Sat. 2pm.

■■■ ART GALLERIES

Take a relaxing and rewarding stroll through Washington's art gallery district. Contained in an area northwest of **Dupont Circle,** the space is bounded by Connecticut Ave. on the east, Florida Ave. on the west, and Q St. to the south. The neighborhood houses around 25 galleries displaying everything from contemporary photographs to tribal crafts; most of the galleries reside in townhouses on otherwise residential streets. Twenty galleries have organized themselves into **"Galleries of Dupont Circle."** They publish a map of member galleries and hold a joint **open house** the first Fri. of each month (except Aug. and Sept.) from 6-8pm. Call 232-3610 for more information. These "First Fridays" are the best way to discover D.C.'s local art scene. You can also explore the contents of the galleries almost any afternoon of the week; a stroll down R St. will put nine of them directly in your path.

The gallery district is readily accessible from the Q St. exit of the Dupont Circle Metro station. As you head north from the circle on Connecticut Ave., stop by the **Kathleen Ewing Gallery,** upstairs at 1609 Connecticut Ave. (328-0955), for a glimpse of 19th-and-20th century American and European photography. The gallery favors striking juxtapositions of contemporary photos with earlier works. (Open Wed.-Sat. noon-5pm.)

Continuing north on Conn. Ave., turn left onto R St., the main drag of the gallery area. The R St. galleries cluster together on either side of 21st St., complementing one another's styles and exhibits. **Gallery K,** 2010 R St. (234-0339), boasts contemporary art in all media displayed in three rooms and two floors. (Open Tues.-Sat. 11am-6pm.) Downstairs from Gallery K is **Africa** (745-7272), whose traditional African tribal masks and pottery contrast sharply with the modern sculptures in the gallery above. (Open Tues. 2-6pm, Wed.-Sat. noon-6pm.) At the end of the block near 21st St., the **Robert Brown Gallery,** 2030 R St. (483-4383), covers its white walls with prints and paintings by contemporary international artists. Exhibits change every six weeks. (Open Tues.-Sat. noon-6pm.)

Across 21st St., the townhouse-cum-gallery trend continues with the **Washington Printmakers Gallery,** 2106 1/2 R St. (332-7757), the only D.C. gallery devoted exclusively to original prints. (Open Wed.-Sat. 11am-5pm, Sun. noon-5pm.) **The Studio** (232-8734) and **Anton** (328-0828) galleries share a home at 2108 R St. Both contain the works of local and international painters and sculptors; the Anton particularly prides itself on its emphasis on women artists. You'll know the building by the pseudo-sign in front bearing the word "Studio." (Studio open Wed.-Sat. 11am-5pm, Sun. 1-5pm. Anton open Wed.-Sun. noon-6pm.)

Perhaps the most popular R St. attraction, **Fondo del Sol Visual Arts Center,** 2112 R St. NW (483-2777), is a bilingual artist-run visual feast. Occupying the nebulous territory between gallery and museum, it showcases Latino and other minority art in a four-story townhouse. Often features works by Native American, Afro-American, and immigrant American artists in addition to the more frequent Hispanic art displays. Fondo del Sol presents daily video programs, as well as occasional special programs. (Open Wed.-Sun. 1-5:30pm or by appointment. Admission $2-4, students $1, children free.) Rounding out the R St. art spaces is the highly focused **Burdick Gallery,** 2114 R St. NW (986-5682), which houses a collection of Eskimo sculptures and graphics. (Open Tues.-Sat. 11am-5pm.)

Other galleries are scattered throughout the area, with none more than a 10-min. walk from the Dupont Circle Metro. Gallery-hopping can make an artful afternoon adventure, and since none of these places charges admission, the price is always right.

Nightlife & Entertainment

Just about everyone should be able to find a play, performance, concert, club, or flick to suit his or her taste. Major culture purveyors, especially the **Kennedy Center,** make up for high ticket prices with **student discounts** and frequent low-cost or free events. Smaller **theaters** do things differently, and often more cheaply, along 14th St. and elsewhere. **Chamber music** emanates from seasonal midday concert series, often at the same museums and churches you might visit as sights. And of course in Washington, like everywhere else, **drinking** is a favorite activity.

Washington teems with **annual events** (see the **Appendix,** p. 293); many of them involve theater, music, dance or movies, such as the American College Theater Festival, Filmfest D.C., various outdoor military band concerts, Adams-Morgan Day, Malcolm X Day, the Blues Festival, Gay Pride Day, and the Folklife Festival.

In the following listings, **Let's Go Picks** (the best of the best) are denoted by a star preceeding the entry.

BARS AND LIVE MUSIC

Most of the bars in Washington feature some type of live music. If you don't mind a young crowd, squeeze into a local pub for rock-and-roll, punk, reggae, R&B, and folk; the D.C. punk scene is, or at least was, one of the nation's finest. To see what's up with local bands, just look at *City Paper.* (Also see Music above under Washington, D.C.: An Introduction.) The **9:30 club** is the leading venue, and many of the best shows are cross generational (and fairly safe) gatherings in churches, rented halls, or at Fort Reno. Flyers advertise small theaters and rock-related events around Dupont Circle and Adams-Morgan—**Second Story Books,** 20th and P St. NW, is a good source for event announcements. (Metro: Dupont Circle.) Go-go music is best experienced at outdoor gatherings, but **Breeze's** in Northeast is a fine indoor venue.

Like any large city, Washington has arenas where devotees shell out over $20 to see acts they've seen on MTV. The biggest events hit sports arenas: **RFK Stadium** in the summer and the **USAir Arena**—formerly the Capital Centre—year-round (see Sports). The newest of D.C.'s live music venues, **Capitol Ballroom,** 1015 Half St. SE (703-549-7625; Metro: Navy Yard) is a colossal concert hall that seats 2000 and admits all ages. Opened in July 1995, the Ballroom boasts an impressive line-up of big-name alternative bands and small-name, big-draw local groups. Tickets $10-20, available from Ticketmaster (432-SEAT). Doors open at 7pm. Slightly less popular bands play **Meriweather Post Pavilion** (410-730-2424/2425/2426), at Rte. 29 Columbia Pike in Columbia, MD, under an hour from D.C. or Baltimore. Outdoor lawn tickets $15-25, seats inside $20-100. For tickets, call the Pavilion or Ticketmaster (432-SEAT).

George Washington University sponsors shows in **Lisner Auditorium,** 21st and H St. NW (202-994-1500). Lisner hosts plays and rock concerts by well-known "alternative" acts (like Billy Bragg); tickets are sometimes free and never cost more than $25. Call in advance for prices and purchase locations.

On summer Saturdays and Sundays, jazz and R&B shows occupy the outdoor, 4200-seat **Carter-Barron Amphitheater,** set into Rock Creek Park up 16th St. and Colorado Ave. NW (426-6837; tickets around $16). Most of the above venues also sell tickets conveniently but expensively through Ticketmaster (432-SEAT), whose outlets exact a several-dollar service charge.

From late June to late August, rock, punk, and metal preempt soccer-playing at **Fort Reno Park** (619-7225), at Chesapeake and Belt St. NW above Wisconsin Ave. (Metro: Tenleytown Circle.) Most concerts feature two or three groups; some are ragged amateurs, some are seasoned scenesters, and some play wonderful, crunchy rock and roll. Find out who's scheduled (look them up in *City Paper*), then play frisbee while you flex your head.

CAPITOL HILL

★**Hawk 'n Dove,** 329 Pennsylvania Ave. SE (543-3300). A Hill institution since 1967, when its several rooms separated pro- and anti-Vietnam War clients ("hawks" and "doves"). Wood-paneled walls hold antique signs, railroad lights, vintage neon signs, and even a brass bar. Interns hang out while the neighbors watch sports and singles watch each other; as in '67, different rooms serve different crowds (one room is for non-smokers). The three buildings, over 100 years old, have been a blacksmith shop, a salt-water taffy plant, and D.C.'s first gas station. Happy hour Mon.-Thurs. 4-7pm. Sandwiches $4-6.50. Beer $1.75 and up. 14 kinds of bottled beer and 11 drafts available. Midnight breakfast served Mon.-Thurs. 11pm-1am, Fri.-Sat. 11pm-2am ($7, with steak $9). DJ Sat. nights. Sat.-Sun. brunch (10am-3:30pm) offers Screwdrivers, Mimosas, or Bloody Marys for $2. Open Sun.-Thurs. 10am-2am, Fri.-Sat. 10am-3am.

Kelley's "The Irish Times," 14 F St. NW (543-5433). Metro: Union Station. Walk out of Union Station and take a right turn (west) down Mass. Ave.; F St. shoots off to your left at the intersection with North Capitol. Irish street signs, the *Irish Times,* and Joyce on the wall give the pub an authentic Irish feel, but the mood is quickly dashed by the hordes of noisy Georgetown law students. This is the site of the annual June marathon Ulysses reading (see p. 295). Live music Tues.-Sun. starting at 8:30pm. Happy hour Mon.-Thurs. 4-7pm. Drafts $2.50, bottled beers $3.50. Open Sun.-Thurs. 11am-2am, Fri.-Sat. 11am-3am.

Tune Inn, 331½ Pennsylvania Ave. SE (543-2725). Metro: Capitol South. Unpretentious fun has meant slumming at the Tune Inn since 1933; *Esquire* calls it one of America's 100 best bars. Clients range from Congressional staffers to construction workers to students. Walls hold mounted fish, game heads, and sports trophies. Sandwiches under $5. Beer $1.50 for draft, $2.25 for bottles. Open Sun.-Thurs. 8am-2am, Fri.-Sat. 8am-3am.

Taverna the Greek Islands, 307 Pennsylvania Ave. SE (547-8360). Metro: Capitol South. First-floor bar complements two floors of dining with comfortable service and a jovial young crowd. Look for fresh mint sprigs from the boss's garden in vases at the bar. Happy hour (Mon.-Fri. 3:30-8pm) brings $1.85 mixed drinks and $1 draft beer. Bar offers a sandwich special every night (except Sun.) after 7:30pm. Open Mon.-Sat. 11am-midnight, Sun. 2-11pm.

The Li'l Pub, 655 Pennsylvania Ave. SE (543-5526). Neighborhood pub distinguished by a friendly and diverse crowd (black and white, gay and straight), yellow stucco walls, and a large framed photo of a customer being accosted by a stripper. Pool tournament every Thurs. in the large back room; winners receive a Pub gift certificate. Drafts start at $1.50. Microbrews $3.50. 50¢ or more off drinks during happy hour (Mon.-Fri. 3-8pm). Open Mon.-Thurs.11am-2am, Fri.-Sat. 11am-3am, Sun. 1pm-2am.

Jenkins Hill Pub, 319 Pennsylvania Ave. SE (544-4066). Metro: Capitol South. Don't let the stained glass over the downstairs bar distract you from the ESPN-tuned TVs that hang at either end. Of course, serious sports fans head upstairs, where a large-screen TV competes with two pool tables and a dartboard for their attention. A third bar downstairs, the **Underground,** features live music Wed.-Sun. Drink prices vary among the bars: drafts start at $1.75, bottle beer at $2.50, mixed drinks at $3.25. Bars can't sell alcohol between 3 and 7am, so Jenkins serves tea, coffee, and breakfast. Open Sun.-Thurs. 11am-2am, Fri.-Sat. 24 hrs.

OLD DOWNTOWN

★**9:30 club,** 930 F St. NW (393-0930 or 638-2008). Metro: Metro Center. D.C.'s most established local and alternative rock venue since the legendary D.C. Space closed down. Occasionally $3 to see 3 local bands; $5-20 for nationally known acts, which often sell out weeks in advance. Crowd ages and styles vary according to concert line-up. Cash-only box office open Mon.-Thurs. 1-6pm, to 11pm if there's a show, Fri. 1-11:30pm, Sat. 9-11:30pm, Sun. 7:30-11pm. Door time Sun.-

Thurs. 7:30pm-midnight, Fri.-Sat. 9pm-2am. Tickets also available from Ticketmaster (432-7328). Under 21 admitted and hand-stamped

Atlantis, downstairs at 930 F St. NW (393-0930). Metro: Metro Center. The 9:30 club recently tucked this subterranean miniclub, its official sidestage, into its old coatroom, and the fit is a little snug. But while the sidestage is dimmer and danker than its big sibling, it's also usually cheaper ($5 cover or free). Admission is free if you pay the upstairs cover. Mostly local and sometimes lesser talent. Hours are the same as 9:30 club .

Capitol City Brewing Company, technically 1100 New York Ave. NW (628-2222); enter on the corner of 11th and H St. Metro: Metro Center. Get sloshed the yuppie way: drink microbrew. Hop on a stool, take a gander at the massive copper vats of brew, and see what's on tap. Half pints $2.80, pints $3.95. Open daily 11am-2am.

Stoney's Restaurant, 1307 L St. NW (347-9163), near 13th St. Metro: Farragut North. Everyone here is a regular—or gets treated like one. Half bar, half greasy spoon, Stoney's serves up half price steak and cheese on Mon., burgers on Tues., and pizza on Wed. during the lengthy happy hour (4pm-midnight). Despite the name, the place is a bustling bar. Open daily 9am-midnight.

Kilimanjaro, 1724 California St. NW (328-3839), between Florida Ave. and 18th St. Dimly lit, big-deal club for international music—African, Latin, and Caribbean groups; ju-ju, reggae, and salsa DJs (reggae on Sun.). Karaoke Tues. night, international music Wed.-Thurs. Caribbean food (restaurant open Tues.-Sun. 5-11pm). No sneakers, shorts, sweats, torn jeans, or tank tops on weekends. No cover Tues.-Thurs.; $5 Fri.-Sat. before 10pm, $10 after 10pm. Up to $20 for live bands. Happy hour Tues.-Fri. 5-8pm: 2-for-1 domestic beers and rail drinks. Open Tues.-Thurs. 5pm-2am, Fri. 5pm-4am, Sat. 8pm-4am.

WHITE HOUSE AREA AND FOGGY BOTTOM

Mr. Henry's Washington Circle, 2134 Pennsylvania Ave. NW (337-0222). Metro: Foggy Bottom-GWU. Plush red wallpaper and centuries-old *Sunday Telegraph* clippings—all in chronological order—grace this pseudo-Victorian saloon. Sit near the jukebox and control the music; Mon.-Sat. there's also an outdoor porch area for eating or sordid carousing. Happy hour (4-7pm) features $1 drafts and $1.50 rails. Open Mon.-Thurs. 11am-2am, Fri. 11am-3am, Sat. 5pm-3am.

Quigley's, 1825 I St. NW (331-0150), enter through the mall or the outside world. Metro: Farragut West. Relax upstairs or boogie down below. Business-types crowd into this large upscale spot. Drafts $2, bottled beers $3. Save about $1 during happy hour (Mon.-Fri. 5-7pm). Thurs.-Sat. brings occasional live music with a $5-15 cover. Open Mon. 11:30am-midnight, Tues.-Thurs. 11:30am-2am, Fri. 11:30am-3am, Sat. 9pm-3am, Sun. 10pm-1am.

Lulu's New Orleans Café, 1217 22nd St. NW (861-5858), at M St. Metro: Foggy Bottom-GWU or Dupont Circle. As schizophrenic as Flicks (see p. 209); its alternate personality is the **Deja Vu** dance club. The Fri. happy hour (4-8pm), featuring 22-oz. Bud, Bud Ice, and Bud Lite for $1.50 and free food (like blackened shrimp, chicken fingers, and Cajun catfish), makes Lulu's a favorite hangout of summer interns. Regular happy hour has only drink specials (Mon.-Thurs. 4-8pm). DJ plays progressive and rock for Deja Vu dancers, Sun.-Thurs. 8pm-2am and Fri.-Sat. 8pm-3am. Live jazz accompanies Sun. à la carte brunch (10am-4pm). Bar is open Mon.-Tues. 6pm-1:30am, Wed.-Thurs. 5pm-1:30am, Fri.-Sun. 4pm-2:30am.

GEORGETOWN

★**Old Glory,** 3139 M St. NW (337-3406). This open-front restaurant which features southern American cuisine by day becomes a hot spot at night for the young and young-at-heart. Drafts $2.50-3.25, bottled beer $3-6. Mixed drinks $3.50-4. Try a specialty "White Lightening" or "Old Glory Slush" drink. Live music Tues. nights. Open Mon.-Sat. 11:30am-2am, Sun. 11am-2am.

★**The Tombs,** 1226 36th St. NW (337-6668), at Prospect St.; entrance to the right of 1789 restaurant. Recognize the bar? Designers for the movie *St. Elmo's Fire* based a stage set on it. Georgetown students as well as some high profile clientele (Clinton, Beau Bridges, Chris O'Donnell) drop in for burgers and beer. $3 cover on

Tues. nights (live music) and Sun. nights (DJ and dancing). Mixed drinks $3.25 and up. Open Mon.-Thurs. 11:30am-2am, Fri 11:30am-3am, Sat. 11am-3am, Sun. 9:30am-2am.

★**The Bayou,** 3135 K St. NW (333-2897), under the Whitehurst Freeway in Georgetown; take any #30 Metrobus to M St. and walk 2 blocks down Wisconsin Ave. Bands on their way up and bands on their way down, with a rough 'n ready crowd that loves them all. Music varies from metal and rock to blues and jazz. Comedy at 6:30pm Sat. Most shows 18+; the rest all ages. Cover $3-20. Open Sun.-Thurs. 8pm-1:30am, Fri. 8pm-2:30am, Sat. 6:30pm-2:30am, but call ahead; no band means no Bayou.

The Saloun, 3239 M St. NW (965-4900), near Potomac St. Two of the best things in life: live jazz by local musicians every night and 75 different kinds of beer (18 on tap!). Draft $4, bottled beer $4.25. Appetizers $1.25-6. Attracts a late twenties and thirties crowd. Cover: Thurs $2, Fri-Sat. $3. Open Sun.-Thurs. 4:30pm-2am, Fri.-Sat. 4:30pm-3am.

Garrett's, 3003 M St. NW (333-1033), near 30th St. Up the street from Charing Cross; fluid movement between the two. G-town's most popular bar is a body-to-body, all-night frat party. If you can move or see, look for the "Hemingway" rhino, shot by one of Ernest's wives. No cover charge. Stuff your face with Gorganzola bread for $3. Beer and mixed drinks, $3. Happy hour Mon.-Fri. 5-7pm: ½-priced drinks, beer, house wine. Wed. nights ½-priced microbrews. Open Sun.-Thurs. 11:30am-2am, Fri. 11:30am-3am.

J. Paul's, 3218 M St. NW (333-3450), near Wisconsin Ave. King of the Georgetown restaurant/saloons—it even has its own award-winning brand of amber lager (pint $4.25). Open Sun.-Thurs. 11:30am-1:30am, Fri.-Sat. 11:30am-2:30am. Hours may vary slightly in the winter.

Charing Cross, 3027 M St. NW (338-2141), near 30th St. Collegians pound beers early in here, then head down the street to Garrett's. Clean-cut prep-school types are the norm, with interns filling in when the college regulars leave. During summer months, enjoy the open front—listen to drinkers make condescending remarks about passersby. Draft beer $2, bottled $2.50-3.50. Mixed drinks $3-4.25. Open Sun.-Thurs. 11:30am-2am, Fri.-Sat. 11:30am-3am, Sun. 5pm-1:30am.

Grog and Tankard, 2408 Wisconsin Ave. NW (333-3114), below Calvert St. in Glover Park, north of Georgetown proper. Sounds like a motorcycle joint, but attracts college kids from American University and Georgetown. Live music every night. Mon. is Grateful Dead night; Tues. is acoustic blues for an older crowd; Wed. is local progressive bands. Mon. 18+. Cover: Sun.-Wed. $3, Thurs-Sat. $5. Open Sun.-Thurs. 6pm-2am, Fri.-Sat. 6pm-3am.

Mr. Smith's, 3104 M St. NW (333-3104), near 31st St. A generally convivial atmosphere pervades this self proclaimed "friendliest saloon in town". Popular nightspot and active singles scene. Live bands Fri. and Sat. nights upstairs and a piano bar on the ground floor. $1 draft weekdays 4-7pm. Mixed drinks $3.25-6. Open Sun.-Thurs. 11am-2am, Fri.-Sat. 11am-3am.

Champions, 1206 Wisconsin Ave. NW (965-4005), at the end of an alley near M St. Strapping jocks abound. Signed photos of sports stars on the wall, Redskins (football) and Capitals (hockey) players stop by, and the "big game" is always on TV. Around 11pm young singles (mid-20s to mid-30s) replace aging armchair quarterbacks. Europeans come by to gawk, and can you blame them? Happy hour Fri. 8-10pm. Live music on Sun. and dancing on weekends. No cover, but a one drink minimum on weekends. Draft $2.60, bottled beer $4.10. Open Mon.-Thurs. 5pm-2am, Fri. 3pm-3am, Sat. 5pm-3am, Sun. 11:30am-2am.

FARRAGUT

★**15 Minutes,** 1030 15th St. NW (408-1855), between K and L St. Metro: McPherson Square or Farragut North. Parading a circus-inspired interior of bright banners and plastic trapeze artists dangling from the ceiling, this club gets its share of freaks and thrill-seekers. Patrons turn out for happy hour (Mon.-Fri. 5-8pm) and wait for night when the music gets louder and the crowd thickens. Mostly bar on weekdays becomes mostly dance club on weekends, with a schizophrenic assemblage of blues, jazz, and punk on different evenings. All nights officially 21+. Thurs.-Sat.

live bands, DJ and dancing the rest of the time. Sun. "Berserk" nights on 3-day weekends: open bar 9pm-1am. Open Mon.-Thurs. 4:30pm-2am, Fri. 4:30pm-3am, Sat. 8pm-3am. $6 cover on weekends, varies on weekdays. Tickets for some popular bands can be purchased through Ticketmaster (432-SEAT).

★**Crow Bar,** 1006 20th St. NW (223-2972). Metro: Farragut North or Farragut West. For everyone from bikers to business types. Stop by for the house brew, Crow Beer ($3.75, $3 during Happy hour), space-age dance room "Forbidden Planet" (open Thurs.-Sat. 9pm-close), or just for the off-beat decor, featuring a plaster-and-paper-maché Lady Liberty who leads you upstairs. Two floors; a game room featuring foosball, pool; a photo booth; outdoor seating. Happy hour 4-7:30 pm. Open Mon.-Thurs. 11:30am-1:45am, Fri. 11:30am-2:45am, Sat. noon-2:45am, Sun. noon-1:45am.

Acme, 1207 19th St. NW (833-2263). Metro: Farragut North. "Think globally, drink locally," says this friendly local hangout. Pool room upstairs is quieter and more removed from the hubbub of the bottom 2 floors. DJ and dancing Thurs.-Sat. nights. Happy hour (Mon.-Fri. 4-7pm) pleases patrons with $6 pitchers and half-price nachos on Wed. Tues. feature a live blues band with no cover. Open Sun.-Thurs. 11:30am-1:30am, Fri.-Sat. 11:30am-2:30am.

The Madhatter, 1831 M St. NW (833-1495), near 19th St. Metro: Farragut North or Farragut West. Packs 'em in every night of the week. Starts hopping during Happy hour (Mon.-Fri. 4-8pm) and stays happening until closing. DJ Tues.-Sun. beginning at 9pm. Open Mon.-Thurs. 11:30am-1:30am, Fri. 11:30am-2:30am, Sat. 10:30am-2:30am, Sun. 11:30am-1:30am.

Flicks, 1160 20th St. NW (296-8644). Metro: Farragut West, Farragut North, or Foggy Bottom-GWU. Flicks, a full-time saloon, moonlights on the weekends as a dance club. Covered from floor to ceiling with movie photos and photos, this joint caters to college crowds during the year and a more eclectic group in the summer. Cover: Thurs. during the academic year $8 with open bar, Fri. $5, Sat. $10. Happy hour 4:30-7:30pm. Open Mon.-Sat. 4pm-2am.

Ha' Penny Lion, 1101 17th St. NW (296-8075 or 296-8076). Pick up a schedule of drink specials. Free happy hour buffet, Mon.-Fri. 4-7pm. Happy hour Mon. and Fri. 4-11pm. Fri. Open Mon.-Fri. 10am-11pm, Fri. 11:30am-midnight.

DUPONT CIRCLE

★**Brickskeller,** 1523 22nd St. NW (293-1885), between P and Q St. Metro: Dupont Circle. *THE* place for beer. If you drank a different beer every day, it would still take you nearly two years to work your way through Brickskeller's list of over 600 brews—the world's largest beer selection. Six continents and some sixty countries contribute brews representing virtually every style of beer in existence, from common ales and lagers to smoked beers and oatmeal stouts. Go down under with a Van Diemens lager from Australia ($4.50), mate, or Middle Eastward with a bottle of Maccabbe from Israel ($2.95). Or try one of the saloon's original "beer-tails": mixed drinks made with beer, like the house classic Black Velvet (stout and champagne, $4.50) or the Ruddy Mary (with beer instead of vodka, $3.25). Attend one of the bi-monthly beer-tasting events and hear brewers plug their potables ($24 for the night; call ahead for schedule and reservations). Must be 21. Open Mon.-Thurs. 11:30am-2am, Fri. 11:30am-3am, Sat. 6pm-3am, Sun. 6pm-2am.

★**The Fox and Hounds,** 1537 17th St. NW (232-6307). Metro: Dupont Circle. Local residents claim it owns the best jukebox in D.C. Early-20s crowd races to the patio for strong drinks and shoulder-to-shoulder company, while a mellower, more diverse crowd makes conversation inside. Happy hour features $1.50 domestic beers, $1.50 rails, and free chips and salsa (Mon.-Fri. 4:30-6:30pm). Regular drink prices are good, too: most bottled beers are $2.50. Open Mon.-Thurs. 11am-2am, Fri. 11am-3am., Sat. 10am-3am, Sun. 10am-2am. Patio closes at midnight.

★**Planet Fred,** 1221 Connecticut Ave. NW (331-3733 or 466-2336). Between the eclecticism of the clientele and the craters, neon spacescape, and lava lamps decking the walls, a trip to Planet Fred may feel like an alien experience. Occasional live bands pack in wall-to-wall punks, while Wed. night's "Drag Freak Bingo" draws a zany bunch ($7 cover) and "Female Trouble" every other Sun. is an ever-popular lesbian dance party. Sun. is also rockabilly night; Mon. offers free salsa lessons (7-9pm) and $2.75 marguerltas; Thurs. is DJ dancing and $10 all-you-can-drink; Fri-Sat. cost $5 for DJ dancing. Daily happy hour (5-8pm) with varying specials blasts out of this world with 99¢ Rolling Rocks on Fri.. Open Sun.-Thurs. 11:30am-2am, Fri. 11:30am-3am, Sat. 8pm-3am.

The Big Hunt, 1345 Connecticut Ave. NW (785-2333). You won't have to hunt for long in this jungle-painted mega-bar to find the features that make it one of the hottest spots in town. Everything about this place is big: the beer list (27 on tap, mostly microbrews), and the crowd (everyone from yuppies to couriers). Pool, too. Don't miss the lively happy hours Mon.-Fri. 4:30-7:30pm, when Rolling Rock, Coors, and rail drinks are all $1.75. Open Mon.-Thurs. 11am-2am, Fri. 11am-3am, Sat. noon-3am, Sun. 4pm-2am.

Capo's, 1722 Connecticut Ave. (462-8771), between R and S St. Metro: Dupont Circle. An attractive new bar attached to Café Petitto draws on a top-notch kitchen to offer a top-notch happy hour: all-you-can-eat antipasto with a $4.50 min. drink purchase. If you don't believe it, check out the spread in the window. Drinks are cheap then, too, with domestic drafts going for $2 and rails and wine for $2.75. Happy hour Mon.-Fri. 5-7:30pm and daily 10:30pm-close (drinks only). Bar open Mon.-Thurs. 11:30am-1am, Fri.-Sat. 11:30am-1:30am, Sun. 11:30am-midnight.

The Childe Harold, 1610 20th St. NW (483-6700), near Connecticut Ave. Metro: Dupont Circle. One of the last real saloons in Washington has served up burgers and beer in shadowy red-brick splendor since 1967. Ignore the pricy restaurant with the same name upstairs and join the mixed bohemian and professional crowd downstairs, especially at happy hour (Mon.-Fri. 3-7pm), which discounts all rails ($2.25), Rolling Rocks ($1.75) and house wines ($1.95). Open Sun.-Thurs. 11:30am-2am, Fri.-Sat. 11:30am-3am.

El Bodegón, 1637 R St. NW (667-1710, delivery 546-8646), near 17th St. Metro: Dupont Circle. As close to Spain in America as you'll get. Cool stucco walls hung with pottery and tile. Garlic, peppers, and curing hams (complete with little cups to catch the drippings) dangle from wood beams. Live flamenco music and dancing every night at 7:30 and 9:30pm. Enjoy the show and the atmosphere—forget the entrees ($15-25) and nosh on *tapas* instead—little Spanish appetizers that go for $3.50-8. Smack your lips on the *empanadillas* (pastries stuffed with spiced ground beef, $3). Open daily 11:30am-2:30pm and 5-11pm.

The Front Page, 1333 New Hampshire Ave. NW (296-6500). Metro: Dupont Circle. Well-known among the intern crowd for its generous happy hours, which smile down on the starving waifs with free chicken wings (Mon.-Wed. and Fri. 4-7pm) or taco bar (Thurs. 4-7pm). Happy hours also bring $2 domestic beers, rails, and house wines. All-you-can-eat brunch Sat. ($9) and Sun. ($12). 10am-3pm. Open Sun.-Thurs. 11:30am-1:30am, Fri.-Sat. 11:30am-2:30am; bar closes earlier if business slows.

SHAW / U DISTRICT

★**The Grand Poobah,** 1399 U St. NW (588-5709), above Hogs on the Hill. Like many of its neighbors on the new and improved U, this casual yuppie-filled bar provides an unusual unpretentious trendiness. Considered by many patrons to be the best place to watch Melrose Place, the Poobah turns over its screen to an ever-eclectic stream of weird old movies on Tues. for "Pschychotronic Film Society" night. Don't miss Wed. Bad Beer night, with $1.50 cans of the worst stuff around. If it's good brews you want, wait until Thurs., when local microbrews take over for the evening. A DJ spins on Sun. Happy hour daily 5-8pm with special $2 drinks. Open Sun.-Thurs. 5pm-2am, Fri.-Sat. 5pm-3am.

★**Asylum in Exile,** 1210 U St. NW (319-9353; 232-9354 for info.). Metro: U St.-Cardozo. An alternative alternative to D.C.'s bigger and badder band clubs. Asylum's tendency to book lesser known live musicians has made it Washington's most-overlooked nightspot. Ignore the death-goth decor and instead enjoy the intimate setting, the DJ dance beats, and the outdoor patio. Bands Wed.-Fri. with acoustic music on Wed. and no cover. $3 cover on Thurs., $5 on Fri. When there's no band, there's still drinking and dancing. Nightly happy hour 8-11pm, with varying

$2 pints and $2 Rolling Rock pitchers on Tues. 18+. Open Sun.-Thurs. 8pm-2am, Fri.-Sat. 8pm-3am.

The Black Cat, 1831 14th St. NW (667-7960), between S and T St. Metro: U St.-Cardozo. One of Washington's best live music venues, brought to you by the people from Dante's, turns its stage over to a variety of alternative and folk bands. They also have pool, pinball, and 12 beers on tap in the Red Room (no cover in the Red Room even when there's a show in the main room next door). Happy hour Fri.-Sat. 6-7:30pm takes $1 off all drinks. Some shows free, most $5-10. Open Sun.-Thurs. 8pm-2am, Fri.-Sat. 6pm-3am.

Las Cruces, 1524 U St. NW (328-3153). The King lives on at this restaurant/bar/shrine to Elvis which celebrates authentic New Mexican cuisine. Regulars come here for made-to-order enchiladas ($5.75-6.50), 50¢ pints of Rolling Rock during the Elvis happy hour (daily 5:43-7:30pm), and the frozen margueritas ($5). You should come to ogle the altar to Elvis in the backroom.

ADAMS-MORGAN

Mr. Henry's, 1836 Columbia Rd. NW (797-8882), near 18th St. Dark bar with dark wood furniture; mixed gay and straight clientele. Mr. Henry discovered Roberta Flack here. Nightly live entertainment. Open mike Tues.-Wed. and $7 minimum; bands every other day, with $5 cover and comedy on Thurs. Sat. DJ after 11pm. Draft beer $2.25. Appetizers $3.75-4.25. Sandwiches $4.75-6. Happy hour Mon.-Sat. (4-8pm): 75¢ off drinks. Cover Fri.-Sat. $7.50. Open Mon.-Thurs. 4pm-2am, Fri. 4pm-3am, Sat. 10am-3am, Sun. 9am-2am.

Cities, 2424 18th St. NW (328-7194), between Belmont and Columbia Rd. Cities' packed restaurant 'n bar stays hip, or tries to, by changing decor and menu every year or so to mimic a different city. They'll be La Habana, Cuba until Feb. 1996; after that, who knows? The chef keeps her job through all the culinary mutations; the chic decor hints at out-of-budget-range entrees. Upstairs hosts a 12-piece Latin band Thurs. from 10pm with salsa dancing. $5 cover. DJ Fri.-Sat. after 10pm. Beer $4, mixed drinks $5. Open Sun.-Thurs. 5pm-1:30am, Fri.-Sat. 5pm-2:30am.

Café Bukom, 2442 18th St. NW (265-4600), near Columbia Rd. A mellow, funky West African restaurant and bar. Live entertainment by West African bands, usually starting at 10pm. Beer $3.50-4. Open Tues. 4pm-midnight, Wed.-Thurs. 4pm-2am, Fri. 4pm-3am, Sat. 2pm-3am, Sun. 4pm-2am.

Kala Kala, 2439 18th St. NW (232-5433), near Columbia Rd. In a fit of self-important painting frenzy, new-kid-in-town Kala Kala pronounces "one world, one bar" to all comers. The music—be it live or Memorex—is always African or reggae; call for the live events schedule. DJ Wed.-Sun. Try the mild malt liquor Ngoma from Togo. Happy hour, daily 5-9pm, features 2-for-1 drafts, rails. Open Sun.-Thurs. 5pm-2am, Fri.-Sat. 5pm-3am.

Chief Ikes Mambo Room, Chaos, and Pandemonium, 1725 Columbia Rd. (Chief Ikes 332-2211, Chaos 797-GODS, and Pandemonium 797-4637), near Ontario Rd., about 2½ blocks from 18th St. Downstairs at Chief Ikes, pub-style American food ($4.25-10, most under $5) accompanied by live R&B Mon.-Tues. and DJ Wed.-Sat. Up a long red staircase are Chaos and Pandemonium, 2 tumultuous rooms featuring alternative music and pseudo-Japanese decor. Pool table in Pandemonium. Usually no cover and $1 off all drinks during happy hour (daily 4-8pm). Beer $3; rails $3.50. Prices higher when a band plays. Must be 21. Chief Ikes open Mon.-Thurs. and Sun. 4pm-2am, Fri.-Sat. 4pm-3am. Chaos and Pandemonium open Mon.-Thurs. and Sun. 6pm-2am, Fri.-Sat. 6pm-3am.

UPPER NORTHWEST

★**Oxford Tavern "Zoo Bar",** 3000 Connecticut Ave. NW (232-4225), across the street from the zoo. Metro: Woodley Park-Zoo. Washington's oldest saloon with a cheery wildlife mural and a bright neon subtitle, but Steely Dan and Duke Ellington are still on the jukebox, so everything is allright. They say the first time you come in here is the last time you'll be a stranger, and it's true: tourists, locals, and regulars mix and mingle at happy hour (Mon.-Fri. 3-7pm) and chug $1.50 drafts, $2.50 rails, and $1.75 domestics. A DJ plays on Fri. nights, and live jazz, rock, and blues bands hold forth Tues.-Thurs. and Sat. At other times, the jukebox offers an unparalleled 7 plays for a dollar. Open Sun.-Thurs. 10:30am-2am, Fri.-Sat. 10:30am-3am.

Ireland's 4 Provinces, 3412 Connecticut Ave. NW (244-0860). Metro: Cleveland Park. Draws a family crowd to communal tables and small stage with nightly Irish and folk music; soloists on Sun.-Mon. croon traditional ballads, while groups Tues.-Sat. get the crowd's feet tapping and sometimes dancing. Mon. night football viewing draws area locals, too. Happy hour Mon.-Thurs. 5-8pm and Fri. 4-8pm discounts everything from domestics ($2.50) to imports ($3.25) to rail ($2.50), and of course Guinness ($2.50). Outdoor café-style seating too. Open Sun.-Thurs. 4pm-2am, Fri.-Sat. 4pm-3am. Cover varies.

Nanny O'Brien's, 3319 Connecticut Ave. NW (686-9189). Metro: Cleveland Park. The across-the-street neighbor and arch rival of the 4Ps, Nanny's reputedly serves the best Guinness in town. The crowd is a three-way mix of locals, AU students, and D.C.'s young Irish population. Cheap drinks and free buffet at happy hour (Mon.-Fri. 4-8pm): $1.50 domestic bottles and drafts, $2.50 import bottles and drafts, $1.75 mixed drinks and house wine. Nightly traditional Irish music; highlights include a Mon. open mike session and Wed. performances of Irish countryside dances. Open Sun.-Thurs. 4pm-2am, Fri.-Sat. 4pm-3am.

The Malt Shop, 4611 Wisconsin Ave. NW (244-9733), at 41st St. above the Dancing Crab. Metro: Tenleytown. Get yourself a brew and watch the game on TV with the regulars. In the good old days, the Redskins drank here after taping "Redskin Sideline" down the street at WUSA-TV. Because they didn't want to say they were going to a bar, they said they were going to a malt shop. Hence the name. Ogle pictures of famous 'Skins on the theme wall. Drafts $2.25, imported bottles $2.50, pitchers $6.50. During happy hour, Rosie serves up $2 drafts and $2.25 domestics and rails; she's almost as much of a Malt Shop institution as the 'Skins themselves once were. Open Mon.-Fri. 4pm-12:30am, Sat.-Sun. noon-1:30am.

Quigley's, 3201 New Mexico Ave. NW (966-0500), three blocks southeast of the American University campus. Metro: Tenleytown. American restaurant by day: burgers ($6.50), sandwiches ($5-8), and salads ($5.50-8); American U. hangout by night. Students come for ½-price burgers and chicken sandwiches on Sun. nights from 6 to 11pm. Last Mon. of each month brings ½-price food to the bar from 5 to 8pm. Happy hour (Mon.-Fri. 4-7pm) will have you smiling at $1.50 pints of Bud, $1.75 house wine, $2 rails, and discounted appetizers. Sat.-Sun. all day $2.50 varying specials. Live bands Tues.-Sun. Open Mon.-Thurs. 11:30am-2am, Fri. 11:30am-3am, Sat. 11am-3am, Sun. 11am-2am.

NORTHEAST

Breeze's Metro Club/Deno's, 2335 Bladensburg Rd., NE (526-8880) in Northeast. Go-go got going here, and it keeps the beat Wed.-Thurs. with local live bands (19+, cover $5-12). On Fri., Deno's films its own "oldie but goodie" cable TV show which gets broadcast on local stations (free admission). Sat.-Sun. are either cabaret nights or oldie-but-goodie tapings (cover $3-8). No alcohol served. Take a cab or a car; parking is provided. Open Wed.-Sun. 9pm-2am.

Kitty O'Shea, 3514 12th St. NE (832-3945). Metro: Brookland-CUA. A larger than life painted leprechaun by the door greets the locals who come here to shoot pool and guzzle mugs of the bar's 31 beers; multiple signs declare that "work is the curse of the drinking classes." Domestic pitchers $5 every day until 11pm. The fare is good and greasy: try one of the giant appetizers ($2.25-5), a basket of miniburgers ($4.25), or the self-proclaimed best cheesesteak in town ($5). Open daily 3pm-3am.

Colonel Brooks Tavern, 901 Monroe St. NE (529-4002). Metro: Brookland-CUA. Pick up Monroe St. at its intersection with Michigan in front of the University Center building, at the south end of Catholic U.'s campus. Fine food draws crowds by day, fine beer draws crowds by night. A handful of local microbrews tops the list (mug $2.75, pitcher $12.50), but they'll serve you the usual Bud if they have to (mug $2, pitcher $8.50). Open Sun.-Thurs. 11am-2am, Fri. 11am-3am, Sat. 11:30am-3am.

BETHESDA, MD

Tequila Sunrise Café, 7940 Wisconsin Ave. (907-6536). This outdoor cantina, bar, and patio wouldn't fail as a movie set. Things move inside when the mercury drops below 50. Happy hour (Mon.-Fri. 4-7pm) offers $1 off drinks and a buffet of free appetizers. Bottled beer $3.25. Mixed drinks $3.50-5. Open Sun.-Mon. 4:30pm-1am, Tues.-Thurs. 11:30am-1am, Fri.-Sat. 11:30am-2am.

Nantucket Landing, 4723 Elm St. (654-7979, delivery 571-0111 with $10 minimum), between Woodmont and Wisconsin Ave. Cool place for ceiling buffs. Fancy food by day, fancy bar by night, with molded ceiling and a stained-glass ceiling vault. Happy hour Mon.-Thurs. 3-7pm, Fri. 3-6pm. Drafts $2.75, $1 on Wed. (3-9pm). Mixed drinks from $3.50. Mon. half priced burgers with drink purchase. Tues. and Thurs. alternative bands; Wed., Fri.-Sat. DJ and dancing. Open Mon.-Thurs. 11:30am-1am, Fri. 11:30am-2am, Sat. 4pm-2am, Sun. 4pm-12:30am.

Parker's, 4824 Bethesda Ave. (654-6366, delivery 571-0111), near Woodmont Ave., 2 blocks from Wisconsin Ave. A family restaurant, local hang-out, and bar. Burgers and sandwiches $5.50-7. Daily specials on both food and drink. Happy hour (Mon.-Fri. 5-7pm) beams with half-priced appetizers. Drafts start at $3, mixed drinks at $3.25. Sat. live music. Open Mon.-Wed. 11:30am-midnight, Thurs. 11:30am-1am, Fri.-Sat. 11:30am-2am, Sun. 11am-midnight.

Bethesda Theater Café, 7719 Wisconsin Ave. (656-3337). Metro: Bethesda. 2 blocks north of the Metro. Crack open a cold one while Schwarzenegger cracks heads. Nibble on a tasty burger while T-Rex munches on a slimy lawyer. Beer, wine, and deli food are served while you watch older first-run movies from cushy chairs at low-lying tables. Sound like fun? It is. B.T.C. evokes the days when going to a movie was a great social event instead of a chance to watch glorified TV with 300 of your closest friends. Sun. and Tues. are no-smoking days. Admission Sun.-Thurs. $3.50, Fri.-Sat. $5. Matinees always $1.50. Beers from $1.90, wine from $3.75 per glass, 12-in. pizza $7. Amusingly named sandwiches, like One Flew Over the Turkey Breast, sell for $4.75-6. Popcorn $1.50. Must be 21 to get in. Call or consult local papers for movies and showtimes. Plan to arrive a ½-hr. early for tickets on Sun. and weeknights, 45 min. early Fri.-Sat.

TAKOMA PARK, MD

Taliano's, 7001B Carroll Ave. (270-5515). The only bar on Takoma's main drag. After 5pm on Mon. it's half-price pizza night, and Fri.-Sat. the place mellows out to live folk, blues, acoustic, and rock music. Bar open Mon.-Thurs. 11:30am-midnight, Fri.-Sat. 11:30am-1am, Sun. noon-midnight. Kitchen closes 1-2 hrs. earlier.

ARLINGTON, VA

★**Bardo,** 2000 Wilson Blvd. (527-9399). Metro: Court House. 1 block east (downhill) from the Metro. This is the bah where William Kennedy Smith got a beatin' from a bouncah. Hugely popular twentysomething haunt is the self-proclaimed "largest microbrewery on the continent." At least 11 types of Bardo microbrews on tap. Happy hour weekdays before 8pm and all day Sun. with $1.50 mugs and $2 pints of Bardo beer. Billiard room with 24 tables opens daily at 5pm. Free brewery tours, Thurs. 7pm. Free parking. Open Mon.-Fri. 11:30am-2am, Sat. 1pm-2am, Sun. 4:30pm-2am.

Galaxy Hut, 2711 Wilson Blvd. (525-8646). Metro: Clarendon. Limited liquor but exotic beers: over 50 to choose from. Local art decorates the walls, ceiling, and table tops. Entertainment is provided by a 100-CD jukebox. Live music and poetry readings on weekends. Open Mon.-Fri. 5pm-2am, Sat.-Sun. 7pm-2am.

Strangeways, 2830 Wilson Blvd. (243-5272). Metro: Clarendon. Huge cut-outs of famous faces in black and white look ghoulish on the lime-green walls. Black and white patterned tabletops will have you seeing cross-eyed. Or maybe you just drank too much. 22 beers on tap. Happy hour Mon.-Fri. 5-8pm: $1 drafts. Mon. is open mike. $3 appetizers Sun. 7-11pm. Open daily 5pm-2am.

Iota, 2832 Wilson Blvd. (522-8340). Metro: Clarendon. A destination mostly for its musical acts, performances of every style and genre. Sip a drink (microbrews $3.50-4.25, 31 bottled beers start at $2.80) and tap your toes almost every night from 9pm on. Happy hour Mon.-Fri. 4-7pm: $1.50 microbrews and $1 off rails and drafts. Wed. is open mike. Open Mon.-Sat. 11:30am-2am, Sun. 11am-2am.

ALEXANDRIA, VA

219 Basin St. Lounge, 219 King St. (549-1141). Metro: King St., a 20-min. walk. Local tavern sells $2.50 drafts and $3 rails. Live piano Tues.-Wed. at 8:30pm, jazz Thurs.-Sat. at 9pm. Open Mon. 11am-midnight, Tues.-Thurs. 11am-1:30am, Fri.-Sat. 11am-2am, Sun. 10am-midnight.

Ireland's Own, 132 North Royal St. (549-4535). High-spirited pub and restaurant whose nightly live Irish entertainment fills Old Town's largest patio. Even the owner sings along on weekends. A visit from Ronnie hasn't been forgotten: a sign reading "Reagan's corner" hangs on a beam near the bar, and souvenir postcards of the event are for sale. Happy hour Mon.-Fri. 4-7pm features $1.50 domestic drafts, free buffet, and other assorted discounts. Drink prices rise when the entertainment begins (Sun.-Thurs. at 8pm, Fri.-Sat. at 9pm). Don your green, take a look at the "Blarney Room," and clap along. Open Mon.-Sat. 11am-1:30am, Sun. 10:30am-1:30am.

Laughing Lizard Lounge, 1322 King St. (548-2582), upstairs from the Stage Door. Young crowd rocks loudly past 1am. Spontaneous dancing to rock or reggae in the back room. Order lizard legs (small $5, large $7). 4 pool tables, 2 dart boards, and 3 juke boxes decorate this bar that attracts a young crowd. Bud on tap $3, rails $3.75. Happy hour Mon.-Fri. 5:30-7pm. Tues. and Thurs. are open mike, Fri.-Sat. live jazz and blues. Downstairs deli feeds hungry masses of people daily until 1:30am. Open daily 5:30pm-2am.

Tiffany Tavern, 1116 King St. (836-8844), near S. Fayette St. Homey and laid-back with a mellow crowd. Mon. and Wed.-Thurs. nights are open-mike, usually featuring talented local folk singers. Bluegrass dominates. Heavy wood interior and big bar. Happy hour Mon.-Fri. 5-7:30pm. Sandwiches $5-7, catfish nuggets $5.50 (plus a crabmeat omelette for $6.25, and entrees $7-9 for lunch, $7-12 for dinner). Irish music Tues. nights, bluegrass/country Fri.-Sat. nights. Open Mon.-Thurs. 11:30am-2:30pm and 5pm-midnight, Fri. 11:30am-2:30pm and 5pm-2am, Sat. 5pm-2am.

■■■ JAZZ AND BLUES

Washington has a surprisingly large and thriving jazz and blues scene. With so many clubs to choose from (in most sections of the city), there's one for virtually everyone's budget. A free lunchtime summer jazz series takes place downtown at the **Corcoran Gallery,** 17th St. between E St. and New York Ave. NW (638-3211), in the Hammer Auditorium every Wednesday at 12:30pm. (Metro: Farragut West.) The **Kennedy Center** and the **Smithsonian Museums** also put on free jazz shows.

★**Madame's Organ,** 2003 18th St. NW, near Florida Ave. in Adams-Morgan. (667-5370). The neon sign above the door shouts "Sorry, we're open" and in flows an eclectic clientele that can only be described as fab. Pink walls, dark red lighting, and wolf skin greet patrons. This blues club features live music nearly every night, with Sat. reserved for "a DJ from outer space." Cover hovers around $3. Drafts $2.50, mixed drinks $3.50. Open Sun.-Thurs. 6pm-2am, Fri.-Sat. 6pm-3am.

★**Vegas Lounge,** 1415 P St. NW (483-3971), 4 blocks east of Dupont Circle. Metro: Dupont Circle. Tiny tables, dim red lights, and a devoted crowd of regular patrons and performers give this blues den its aura of authenticity. Professional jam sessions Tues.-Wed. (otherwise known as "open mike nights", but these guys play like pros) and bands Thurs.-Sat. (cover $5-9) churn out an assortment of styles the manager, "Dr. Blues", enthusiastically describes as Chicago-meets-New Orleans. Happy hour Tues.-Sat. offers $1 off beers. Be careful in this area at night. Open Tues.-Thurs. 7pm-2am, Fri.-Sat. 7pm-3am.

Blues Alley, 1073 Rear Wisconsin Ave. NW (337-4141), in an actual alley, below M St. in Georgetown. Cool jazz in an intimate supper club dedicated to the art. The club's music society sponsors a youth orchestra to nurture new talent. Past performers include Mary Wilson of the Supremes and Wynton Marsalis. Ticket prices are steep, ranging from $13 to 38. If you can't afford to pay, hang out in the alley and listen anyway. $7 food-or-drink minimum. Creole cuisine (entrees $14-19) served from 6pm. Beer $4, mixed drinks $5 and up. Upscale casual dress; some sport tuxes on big nights. Shows at 6pm and 10pm. Call for reservations and prices or pick up a 3-month schedule.

One Step Down, 2517 Pennsylvania Ave. NW (331-8863), near M St. More casual and less expensive than Blues Alley. Jukebox well-stocked with jazz. Local jazz Wed.-Mon.; out-of-town talent Fri.-Sat. Daily happy hour features 90¢ drafts 3pm-7pm. Cover $5 weeknights, $10-15 weekends. Open daily 10:30am-2am.

Bar Nun, 1326 U St. NW (332-0533). Metro: U St.-Cardozo. Opened in July 1995, this flamboyant new restaurant and lounge jazzes it up every night with live blues bands or DJ acid jazz amid purple walls and colossal sunflower ceiling ornament. The newest recruit to the U St. club scene, Bar Nun promises to do its part to restore the area's historically hip reputation. Happy hour Mon.-Fri. 4:30-7pm serves up $3.50 rails and $1 drafts. Weekend brunch from the Creole-style menu 11am-3pm. No cover.

Café Lautrec, 2431 18th St. NW in Adams-Morgan. (265-6436). Spot this chic establishment from a distance by the enlarged mural of a Lautrec print across the front of this converted townhouse. Live jazz every night. Tues. is Brazilian night! Fri.-Sat. features tap dancing on the bar (hehehe). $6 minimum per person once music starts. Beer $3.75-6. Open Sun.-Thurs. 5pm-2am, Fri.-Sat. 5pm-3am.

Takoma Station Tavern, 6914 4th St. NW (829-1999). Metro: Takoma. A largely African-American crowd appreciates quality jazz Mon.-Sat.; on Sun. night the sound system thumps with the rub-a-dub beat of reggae. Two large and tidy bars serve a generous, 4-shot Long Island Iced Tea that'll knock you off your stool. Happy hour (Mon.-Fri. 4-8pm) brings $1 off drinks and free buffet. No cover charge. Ever. Open Mon.-Fri. 11:30am-2am, Sat.-Sun. 4pm-2am.

City Blues, 2651 Connecticut Ave. NW (232-2300). Metro: Woodley Park-Zoo. Local blues and jazz musicians toot and strum daily in the bay window of this townhouse *cum* restaurant. The dinner entrees are a little pricey ($9-18), but you can come to just sway by the bar and nurse a drink. No cover for diners. $4 cover for bar patrons on Thurs., $5 cover on Fri. and Sat. nights after 9pm. Brunch Sun. 11am-3pm. The live music starts Sun.-Thurs. at 8:30pm, Fri.-Sat. at 9:30pm. Open Mon.-Thurs. 11am-4:30pm and 5pm-1am, Fri. 11am-4:30pm and 5pm-2am, Sat. noon-3pm and 5pm-1am.

Wharf, 119 King St. (703-836-2834) in Alexandria. Metro: King St. Jazz/blues bar. $2.75 drafts, $3.25 rails. Mon. and Fri.-Sat. live jazz, Tues.-Thurs. blues, Sun. folk or pop. Music starts at 8:30pm on Mon., 9pm Tues.-Thurs., and 9:30pm Fri.-Sat. Cover: Mon. and Fri.-Sat. $5, Tues.-Thurs. and Sun. $3. Open Mon.-Thurs. 7pm-1am, Fri.-Sat. 7pm-1:30am, Sun. 7pm-midnight.

Fleetwood's, 44 Canal Center Plaza (703-548-6425) in Alexandria. Metro: Braddock Rd., about 10 blocks east through a questionable neighborhood. Take a taxi from the station ($3-5). Live music every night. Mon. live piano, Tues.-Sat. blues, Sun. jazz. Music starts Mon.-Thurs. at 8pm , Fri.-Sat. at 9pm, Sun. at 7:30pm. No cover during the week, Fri.-Sat. $7-10. Drafts $3.25-3.50. Open Mon.-Thurs. 11:30am-midnight, Fri.-Sat. 11:30am-1am, Sun. 11:30am-10:30pm.

■■■ DANCE CLUBS

Let's Go has the most up-to-date club listings you'll find anywhere. These are *the* places to go. But, alas, dance clubs in D.C. have been known to fold as fast as honest congressfolk. So call ahead. And beware: some clubs move too fast to be caught in print. You might catch these transient gems in the pages of *City Paper;* more likely you'll just see a flyer posted somewhere in Georgetown or Dupont Circle.

SOUTHEAST

★**Tracks,** 1111 1st St. SE (448-3320). Metro: Navy Yard. The hottest dance club in D.C. Two dance floors, three bars, a patio, an outdoor volleyball court, and a set of bleachers overlooking the main dance floor (all packed into an old warehouse) ensure that there's something for every type of club goer to do. Thurs. is college night: alternative youth with baggy pants and small knapsacks pay the $5 cover and enjoy the open bar 9-10:30pm. Fri.'s music is deep house with no cover 8-9pm, $5-7 9-11pm, $8-10 after 11pm; bar serves $1 drinks and $4 pitchers until midnight in the summer. Sat. is gay (see p. 238 for more info.). Sun. brings 2 simultaneous tea dances, one country western, the other house. Both are free and run 4-8pm. At 8pm, the club opens for an evening of house beats with a $3 cover until 9pm, $3-5 9-11pm, and $5 after 11pm. All drinks $2.25. Women's night last Tues. of every month. Doors open at 8pm with no cover before 9pm, $3 after. Secured parking nearby. Open Thurs. 9pm, Fri.-Sat. 8pm, Sun. 4pm. No set closing time. Always 18+.

OLD DOWNTOWN

★**Fifth Colvmn,** 915 F St. NW (393-3632), near 9th St. Metro: Gallery Place-Chinatown. Euro-crowd brings serious soul into the trendy 90s. He-who-no-longer-wants-to-be-known-as-Prince has been spotted here. Art exhibits change periodically. Bright lights and bold colors make this bank-turned-nightclub more of a museum of cool culture than a hip hotspot—prepare to feel passé. The basement offers an alternative scene with a music selection to match. The week's line-up reads like a hip house-music menu. Mon. is "Pangaea" with techno upstairs and industrial downstairs, $7 before 10pm, $8 after, 18+ and open bar 9-10:30pm; Tues. is 21+ with no cover; Wed. "Fusion" is punk progressive upstairs, funk/new soul downstairs, $5 cover ($7 for under 21); Thurs. is "Pacha," 18+ international night with a dress code and $7 cover; Fri. is techno and underground house with $8 cover ($10 under 21); Sat. is 21+ with a dress code and $10 cover for hot hip house. Open Mon. 9pm-2am, Tues. and Thurs. 10pm-2am, Wed. 10pm-2:30am, Fri.-Sat. 10pm-3am.

★**The Insect Club,** 625 E St. NW (347-8884). Metro: Gallery Place-Chinatown. True to its name, the Insect Club crawls with plastic, painted, and paper maché bugs and swarms with barflies. Happy hour (Mon.-Fri. 5-8pm) draws interns and pool players for $1.50 domestic drafts, $2 rails, $1 off domestic bottles, and $3 32 oz. pitchers, on Fri. these specials last until 10pm. Tues. is "Passion," an international dance party; Wed. is "Valley of the Dolls" at 8:30pm featuring women DJs; Thurs. has a $10 cover for all-you-can-drink 9pm-1am with DJ dancing; Fri.-Sat. bring a $5 cover for DJ hip hop, reggae, rock, and retro. Open Mon.-Thurs. 5pm-2am, Fri.-Sat. 5pm-3am.

The Ritz, 919 E St. NW (638-2582), near 9th St. Metro: Gallery Place-Chinatown. Rumored to be the largest club on the East Coast, the Ritz boasts 5 clubs and music for every kind of crowd. The Gallery is strictly reggae; live jazz by candle light in a moody blues atmosphere in a room downstairs. Sun is 18 plus. college night. Wed. is reggae with $5 cover. Fri. is rave night. Fri.-Sat. no cover before 8:30pm, $10 cover after. Proper attire required. Dress on other nights is casual but fashionable—that means no sneakers. Open Wed. 9pm-4am, Fri. 5pm-4am, Sat. 9pm-4am, Sun. 10pm-4am.

Coco Loco, 810 7th St. NW (289-COCO), between H and I St. Metro: Gallery Place-Chinatown. Chic Brazilian restaurant lends its bright mosaic-tiled floor to DJ-driven salsa, merengue, and samba dancing every Thurs-Sat. beginning at 10pm. No food during nightclub hours: the kitchen has to close to make room for the Brazilian dance show (Fri.-Sat.) on the countertops. Cover: $10 for men, $5 for women. Thurs is 18+. Dress is casual, but you might want to look like you just left the office. Nightclub open Thurs.-Sat. 10pm-3am.

FOGGY BOTTOM

Deja Vu, 1217 22nd St. NW (861-5858), at M St. Metro: Foggy Bottom-GWU or Dupont Circle. DJ plays progressive and rock Sun.-Thurs. 8pm-2am and Fri.-Sat. 8pm-3am. Fri.-Sat. $3 cover. For info on Lulu's, see **Bars** (p. 208).

GEORGETOWN

★**The Tombs,** 1226 36th St. NW (337-6668), at Prospect St.; entrance to the right of 1789 restaurant. $3 cover Sunday nights for DJ and dancing, 10pm-2am. For more info., see **Bars** (p. 208).

★**Winston's,** 3295 M St. NW (333-3150), near 33rd St. So many men, so little hair. Marines and Navy soldiers come for R&R. Georgetown, American, and George Washington University guys crowd in too. A happenin' dance scene every night of the week. 18+. Mon. is ladies night. $4 cover and women drink free. $2 cover other weeknights, $5 weekends. Beer $1.50-3. Mixed drinks $3-4. No tank tops. Open Sun.-Thurs. 8pm-2am, Fri.-Sat. 8pm-3am.

Crazy Horse, 3259 M St. NW (333-0400). The college-military crowd shows up for pop music upstairs, hip-hop downstairs on Fri.-Sat. nights. Live music on Sun. Happy hour Fri.-Sat. 9-11pm. Beer, mixed drinks $3. 18+, $4-5 cover. Open Sun., Wed.-Thurs. 9pm-2am, Fri.-Sat. 9pm-3am.

Sports Fans, 3287 M St. NW (338-7027). A sports bar that doubles as a dance club; note the plastic football player bursting through the wall as you and your friends head down to boogie to top-40 hits. No cover Mon., $6 on Tues. with 10¢ drafts; $7 on Wed. with open bar on drafts; Thurs. is college night with $5 cover for women, $6 for men and open bar for all. Fri.-Sat. 2 for 1 on domestic beers 8pm-10pm and no cover before 9:30pm. Otherwise Fri.-Sun. $10, with women getting in free on Sun., and an open bar for all. Sun. night, $1 cover, $1 any drink. Open Sun.-Thurs. 9pm-2am, Fri.-Sat. 8pm-3am.

The Hennessy, 3263 M St. NW (342-0406), near Wisconsin Ave. Toward the Georgetown University end of M St. Newly expanded with more bar space and a large dance floor filled with sweaty collegiate bods humping to a mix of music from reggae to top 40. 2-for-1 happy hour weekdays 4-7pm. Cover for under 21. Open Sun.-Thurs. 4-11pm, Fri.-Sat. 5pm-12am. Hours are longer in the summer.

Champions, 1206 Wisconsin Ave. NW (965-4005), at the end of an alley near M St. Strapping jocks abound. Dancing Fri.-Sat.10pm-3am. No cover, but a one drink minimum on weekends. See **Bars** (p. 208) for more info.

FARRAGUT

★**Forbidden Planet,** 1006 20th St. NW (223-2972), at the **Crow Bar.** Metro: Farragut North or Farragut West. This space-age dance room of a hip bar is one of the most densely populated nightspots in the city. Open Thurs. 9pm-1:45am, Fri.-Sat. 9pm-2:45am.

★**Zei,** 1415 Zei Alley (842-2445), between H and I St. NW. Metro: McPherson Square. Attire is "funky to formal," and the students and yuppies who frolic here treat it like a fashion show. Mon. is "Groove," an 18+ house dance party with open bar 10-11pm and a $5-8 cover; "Wax" on Tues. churns out funk and acid jazz to an 18+ crowd for $3-7; Wed. is $5 for reggae with $2.50 drinks until 11pm, 21+; Thurs. is "Paradiso" with an open bar 10-11pm and international dance beats for an 18+ crowd and a cover of $6-8; Fri.-Sat. DJs spin Top 40 dance music for a 21+ crowd and $5 cover before 11pm, $10 after. Open Mon.-Thurs. 10pm-2am, Fri.-Sat. 10pm-3am.

Rumors, 1900 M St. NW (466-7378). Metro: Farragut North. Huge and well-frequented (hair gel all but required). Happy hour Mon.-Fri. 4-8pm, includes $2 domestic beers and rail drinks, and a free buffet. DJ dancing daily starting at 7pm. $2 cover Fri.-Sat. Open Sun.-Thurs. 11:30am-2am, Fri.-Sat. 11:30am-3am.

The Madhatter, 1831 M St. NW (833-1495), near 19th St. Metro: Farragut North or Farragut West. Packs 'em in every night of the week. DJ Tues.-Sun. beginning at 9pm. See **Bars** (p. 209) for more info. Open Mon.-Thurs. 11:30am-1:30am, Fri. 11:30am-2:30am, Sat. 10:30am-2:30am, Sun. 11:30am-1:30am.

Flicks, 1160 20th St. NW (296-8644). Metro: Farragut West, Farragut North, or Foggy Bottom-GWU. Flicks, a full-time saloon, moonlights on the weekends as a dance club, 10pm-2am. Cover: Fri. $5, Sat. $10. See **Bars** (p. 209) for more info.

DUPONT CIRCLE

★**Planet Fred,** 1221 Connecticut Ave. NW (331-3733 or 466-2336). Between the eclecticism of the clientele and the craters, neon spacescape, and lava lamps decking the walls, a trip to Planet Fred may feel like an alien experience. Thurs. is DJ dancing and $10 all-you-can-drink; Fri-Sat. cost $5 for DJ dancing. Daily happy hour (5-8pm) with varying specials blasts out of this world with 99¢ Rolling Rocks on Fri. Open Sun.-Thurs. 11:30am-2am, Fri. 11:30am-3am, Sat. 8pm-3am. For more information, see **Bars**, p. 210.

The Roxy, 1214 18th St. NW (296-9292/3), at Connecticut Ave. Metro: Dupont Circle. Reggae bands Thurs. and Sat., starting at 9pm 18+ and $6-12 cover. Wed. and Sat. it's a Roxy progressive dance party with ½ off rail drinks until 10:30pm. Look for $1-off-cover coupons that frequently appear in area book and record stores, and in *City Paper.* $2 on Wed. before 10pm for 21 and over, $3 for 18-21; after 10pm it's $5 for everybody. On Fri., $5 for 18 and over. Open Wed.-Sat. 9pm-3am.

SHAW / U DISTRICT

★**Bent,** upstairs at 1344 U St. NW (986-6364), near 13th St. Metro: U St.-Cardozo. This is the place with the big Dali clocks melting off the roof, about to slip onto the pavement below. More surrealism awaits you inside with a heterogeneous mix of gay and straight, black and white, male and female. The silver walls sweat with disco dancing in riotus retro fashion. Happy hour Thurs.-Fri. 6-9pm with free fondue and salsa, $2 rails, and $1.50 Rolling Rocks. Wed.-Sat. DJ 70s-90s disco grooves with a $2 cover after 11pm. Sun. 70s funk soul with no cover but $7 all-you-can-drink. Open Wed. 9pm-2am, Thurs. 6pm-2am, Fri. 6pm-3am, Sat. 9pm-3am, Sun. 9pm-2am.

★**The Grand Poobah,** 1399 U St. NW (588-5709), above Hogs on the Hill. A DJ spins on Sun. until 2am. See **Bars** (p. 211) for more info.

Utopia, 1418 U St. NW (483-7669), near 14th St. Metro: U St.-Cardozo. This Soho-style "bar and grill, art and eat" joint hosts free dancing in the back for a young and eclectic group of locals. The North African art in the front was painted by owner Jamal Sahri himself; the back room features a rotating exhibit (try not to knock the art off the walls). Lunch, brunch, dinner, and happy hour (Mon.-Fri. 4-8pm and Sun.-Thurs. 10pm-2am: draft $2-3, bottled beer $2, rail drinks $3). Thurs. is Brazilian live music and Sun. has live blues and jazz. Open Sun.-Thurs. 10:30am-2am, Fri.-Sat. 10:30am-3am.

State of the Union, 1357 U St. NW (588-8810), near 14th St. Metro: U St.-Cardozo. This restaurant/bar/dance club's name is a play on words: step inside and confront busts of Karl Marx and other Soviet regalia. Music of the jazzier genre: jazz, blues, salsa, acid jazz, and hip-hop reign. Happy hour Mon.-Fri. 5-8pm with $2 Rolling Rocks, $3 Sam Adams, $3.75 mixed drinks. Mon. is live jazz in the front room, Tues. is live acid jazz in the back, Wed. alternates between world beat and poetry readings, Thurs. jazz and reggae, Fri.-Sat. deep house. Sun. brunch 11:30am-3pm. The back room has a removable wall for some patio action in the summer. Usually no cover; when there is one, it's only after 10:45pm. 21+. Open Mon.-Thurs. 5pm-2am, Fri.-Sat. 5pm-3am, Sun. 11:30am-3pm and 5pm-2am.

Manute Bol's Spotlight, 1211 U St. NW (265-5833). Metro: U St.-Cardozo. Owned by and named for a former Washington Bullets' hoopster, this classy club draws dance fiends, jazz musicians, and b-ball fans alike to its African art-bedecked bar and lounge. Get warmed up during happy hour (Mon.-Fri. 4-9pm) with 2-for-1 domestic drafts and free appetizers from 5 to 7pm. Mon. is oldies, Tues is DJ dancing with a $5 cover, Wed. is open mike, Thurs. is live blues, Fri is live jazz, Sat is DJ house, and Sun is live jazz and blues. Usually no cover, sometimes $5 on DJ nights. Proper attire required on weekends. Open Sun.-Thurs. 11am-2am, Fri.-Sat. 11am-3am.

ADAMS-MORGAN

Though the nightlife isn't super-cheap budget, Adams-Morgan's multi-purpose nightspots are popular with twentysomething club-hoppers.

★**Club Heaven** and **Club Hell,** 2327 18th St. NW (667-4355), near Columbia Rd. Hell's downstairs, Heaven's upstairs, so the ground-floor Italian restaurant must be *purgatorio.* In Hell, smoke blurs the funky gold tables and loud music emanates from spooky, yellow-backlit masks. It's every high schooler's dream of a

New York café and bar. Heaven looks rather like an old townhouse: scuffed wood floor, comfy couches, a small bar, and 3 TVs, but the dance floor throbs to pounding beats and Heaven's back patio is crowded with timid souls who can't take the noise. 80's dance party in Heaven on Thurs. with $4 cover. No cover other nights. Domestic beer $3, imports $3.75; $1 off during happy hour (daily 6-8:30pm in Hell). Dancing starts about 10pm. Heaven open Sun.-Thurs. 10pm-2am, Fri.-Sat. 10pm-3am. Hell open Tues.-Thurs. 9pm-2am, Fri.-Sat. 6pm-3am.

Rancho Deluxe, 2218 18th St. NW (745-2478). Skulls, human and animal, and assorted Latin Americana come together at this popular club where DJs spin progressive dance tunes every night except Wed. Music starts at 10:30pm. Happy hour daily until 9pm: $1 off all drinks. Domestic beers $3, imported $4. Open daily 5:30pm-1:30am.

UPPER NORTHWEST

★**Oxford Tavern "Zoo Bar,"** 3000 Connecticut Ave. NW (232-4225), across the street from the zoo. Metro: Woodley Park-Zoo. A DJ plays on Fri. nights until 3am. No cover. See **Bars** (p. 212) for more info.

BETHESDA, MD

Nantucket Landing, 4723 Elm St. (654-7979, delivery 571-0111 with $10 minimum), between Woodmont and Wisconsin Ave. DJ and dancing Wed until 1am, Fri-Sat. until 2am. See **Bars** (p. 214) for more info.

■■■ CLASSICAL MUSIC

D.C. is home to the well-respected **National Symphony Orchestra.** They perform in the **Kennedy Center,** 25th St. and New Hampshire Ave. NW (416-8000), which is to say that their tickets are normally on the expensive side ($18-45). On the other hand, the whole Kennedy Center rigmarole about half-price tickets applies to NSO performances. The NSO also gives three free concerts a year in celebration of particular holidays: Memorial Day, the Fourth of July, and Labor Day. Many other free concerts enliven the summer; see **Special Events** (p. 293) for specifics. The **Washington Opera** (416-7890) also calls the Kennedy Center home. Chamber music in the Kennedy Center, though a smaller deal, is more often cheap or free, especially during December's furious round of events, which culminate in the pre-Christmas *Messiah* sing-along.

The **Library of Congress,** 1st St. SE (concert line 707-5502), sponsors concerts in the **Kennedy Center.** Concerts sometimes feature valuable instruments in the Library's collection, like a Stradivarius violin.

The **Summer Opera Theater Company** (526-1669, summer box office 319-4000), in Catholic University's **Hartke Theater,** runs a summer opera series better than anyone has a right to expect; operas run in June and July; call for exact dates. (Tickets $20-50, standing room $10; ushers and volunteers see the shows for free—call in advance.)

The **Washington National Cathedral's Summer Festival of Music** (537-6200) draws even atheists to free concerts (mostly chamber and choral music) in July and August. **The Phillips Collection,** 1600-1612 21st St. at Q St. NW (387-2151), provides an appropriate setting for chamber music and classical piano concerts—along with the occasional jazz show—each Sunday from September to May at 5pm (free with museum admission). Check the *Washington Post's* Weekend section for information. **The Society of the Cincinnati at Anderson House,** 2118 Massachusetts Ave. NW (785-2040), next to the Ritz-Carlton Hotel (Metro: Dupont Circle), also hosts free chamber music concerts, generally on the 2nd Saturday of every month (year-round), by various artists, and on the 2nd and 4th Wednesdays of every month (Oct.-May), by the Air Force Chamber Players. All concerts are at 1:30pm, and seating is on a first-come, first-served basis. From October to May, **Dumbarton Concert Series** sponsors chamber, choral, jazz, and Celtic concerts in an intimate, historic candlelit hall in **Dumbarton Church,** 3133 Dumbarton St. NW (965-2000), near

Wisconsin Ave. in Georgetown. Lack of A/C in the summer often makes the 300 person hall prohibitively hot. (Admission $22-28, student and senior discounts available; reserve at least 1 week in advance). The **Smithsonian museums** (357-2700) also host a smorgasbord of classical performances; try to grab a schedule at the Smithsonian Castle on the Mall.

■■■ COMEDY CLUBS

Comedy Café, 1520 K St. NW (638-5653), between 15th and 16th St. Metro: Farragut North or McPherson Square. Johnny Carson and David Letterman have entertained in this informal space, as have Merle Hobbs and Felicia Michaels. Long menu peaks with $7.50-9 entrees. Headliner shows (Fri. 8:30 and 10:30pm, Sat. 7, 9, and 11pm) run $10-18. Open mike Wed. 8:30pm and local pro night Thurs. 8:30pm have $5 cover.

Chelsea's, 1055 Thomas Jefferson St. NW (298-8222), in the Foundry Building below M St. in Georgetown. Home of the **Capitol Steps,** a renowned political-satire troupe composed of Congressional staffers, whose proximity to the absurd spectacle of national government inspires them to write and perform political parody. Has included such favorites as "Fools on the Hill" and "the Joy of Sax." Tickets $30 without dinner, $45 with dinner. Capitol Steps performs most Fri.-Sat. at 7:30pm; arrive early or call in advance. Open Sun.-Mon. and Wed.-Thurs. 9pm-2am, Fri.-Sat. 6pm-4am. Live bands: Sun. Persian, Mon. Ethiopian, Wed. Arabic, Thurs.-Sat. Latin. Cover $5 on Wed, $10 Fri-Sat., other nights free.

The Improv, 1140 Connecticut Ave. (296-7008) in New Downtown. Metro: Farragut North. Cheap, wacky comedy for a youthful crowd. Shows $8-12. Shows Sun.-Thurs. 8:30pm, Fri.-Sat. at 8:30 and 10:30pm.

■■■ POOL HALLS

As recently as three years ago, Washington had no pool halls to speak of. But the cult of the cue has begun to take root, prompted by the opening of chain pool halls in Dupont Circle, Adams-Morgan, and Cleveland Park.

Buffalo Billiards, 1330 19th St. NW (331-7665). Metro: Dupont Circle. Across from the 19th St. Metro exit. The mothership of the new chain lines up 33 tables (including D.C.'s only regulation snooker table) in a cleaner, classier version of an old-fashioned saloon. Regular rates $5 per hour for 1 person, $10 for 2, $12 for 3, $14 for 4. Lower rates during slow daytime hours, higher during peak weekend hours. Full bar and food service available. Open Mon.-Thurs. 11:30am-2am, Fri.-Sat. 11:30am-3am, Sun. 11:30am-1am.

Bedrock Billiards, 1841 Columbia Rd. (667-7665), in Adams-Morgan. Metro: Dupont Circle. During peak hours, regulars pack this cave-painted hall to enjoy good play in a prehistoric atmosphere. Just 8 tables, so expect longer waits than at Buffalo. Same rates as Buffalo. Limited bar service (beer $3-4.50); no food. Open Mon.-Thurs. 4pm-1am, Fri. 4pm-2am, Sat. noon-2am, Sun. noon-midnight.

Atomic Billiards, 3427 Connecticut Ave. (363-7665), in the heart of Cleveland Park. Metro: Cleveland Park. The funkiest of the places, with a Jetsonian space-age mural behind the bar, vintage furniture lining the walls, and plenty of board games to bide the wait for one of the 6 tables. Same rates as Buffalo. Limited bar service with beer and plenty of coffee drinks. Limited food service includes grilled-cheese sandwiches ($2.50) and potato chips. $2 longnecks until 8pm every day. Open Mon.-Thurs. 4pm-1am, Fri. 4pm-2am, Sat. noon-2am, Sun. noon-midnight.

Babe's Billiards Café, 4600 Wisconsin Ave. NW (966-0082), in Tenleytown. Metro: Tenleytown-AU. A bright, windowy pool hall/restaurant. Prime-time pool (7pm-last call) $11/hr. per table, otherwise $6.60/hr. per table. Happy hour Mon.-Fri. 4-7pm and Sat-Sun. noon-7pm means $1 Miller, Bud, and Rolling Rock, and ½-price appetizers. Open Sun.-Thurs. 10:30am-4am, Fri.-Sat. 10:30am-5am.

Georgetown Billiards, 3251 Prospect St. NW (965-7665), in Georgetown. This independent pool hall has been claimed by Georgetown U. students as their official hangout/snack bar. Bring friends if you play here; the price is fixed, so it's not worth it if you're alone, but a great deal if you're with some friends. $10/hr, $2 each person above 4. 19 tables. Thurs. are half price with college ID. Open Sun.-Thurs. noon-2am, Fri.-Sat. noon-3am.

■■■ THEATER

Arena Stage (488-3300), 6th St. and Maine Ave. SW, is often called the best regional (non-New York) theater company in America (Metro: Waterfront). The 45-year-old theater has its own acting company and three performance spaces. The Kreeger Theater and Fichandler Stage itself present high-quality new and used plays, and the Old Vat Theater holds smaller, more experimental performances. (Tickets $21-45; for the Fichandler and Kreeger, $12-18, seniors 15% off, students 35% off; half-price tickets usually available 90 min. before start of show.) Very wheelchair friendly. Visual and hearing aids available. Box office generally open Mon.-Sat. 10am-7pm, Sun. noon-7pm.

The prestigious **Shakespeare Theater,** at the Lansburgh, 450 7th St. NW (box office 393-2700; Metro: Archives-Navy Memorial), at Pennsylvania Ave., offers a Bard-heavy repertoire. The 1995-96 season (fall-spring) includes *Henry V, Macbeth, All's Well that Ends Well,* and *Volpone.* Call months in advance for reservations, ticket prices, performance times, and discounts for students and seniors. Standing-room tickets (currently $10) are available two hours before each performance. Disabled access (call at least 24 hrs. in advance).

At 25th St. and New Hampshire Ave., the **Kennedy Center's** (416-8000) zillions of performing-arts spaces include two theaters, the Terrace Theater and the Theater Lab. The highest grossing play in the history of the Center, *Shear Madness* still packs in the crowds and keeps 'em laughing. The Something New series takes the conservative Center over the edge into performance art. Though tickets get expensive (many range from $10 to 65), most Kennedy Center productions offer half-price tickets right before the start of an event and earlier on the day of performance to students, seniors, military personnel, handicapped persons, and those who can show they're poor; call 467-4600 about discount tix. Free events dot the Kennedy calendar like the American College Theater Festival, which showcases free performances of top college productions (see **Annual Events,** p. 294).

Thespians thrive in Washington's **14th St. theater district,** where tiny repertory companies explore and experiment with truly enjoyable results. *City Paper* provides very good coverage of this scene. If tickets are out of your price range, don't despair; **usher.** All of the regular companies need unpaid help in the aisles, and once the paying crowds are inside, ushers usually watch the play for free. Call the theaters as far in advance as you can. Woolly Mammoth, Studio, the Source, and the Church St. Theaters dwell in a potentially dangerous neighborhood east of Dupont Circle, near or on 14th St. NW between P and Q St.; not all the action is on stage, and not all the commerce goes on in ticket booths. Don't come here alone at night.

TICKETplace, 720 21st St. NW (842-5387), at George Washington University's Lisner Auditorium, 21st and H St. NW. Metro: Foggy Bottom-GWU. Sells half-price (plus 10% surcharge) day-of-show tickets for theater, music, dance, and special events on a walk-up basis. Cash only. (Also some full-price advance sales for cash or credit card.) Open Tues.-Fri. noon-6pm, Sat. 11am-5pm.

Woolly Mammoth, 1401 Church St. NW (393-3939). Metro: Dupont Circle. Take P St. east, away from the Circle, to 14th St. Make a left on 14th and another left on Church St. The theatre is the poorly marked building on your immediate right. Make the pilgrimage to see intense, daring productions by local playwrights performed by local artists. The theater encourages would-be playwrights to send in manuscripts for readings. Box office open Mon.-Fri. noon-6pm, Sat. 11:30am-6pm, Sun. 10am-2pm. All kinds of cheap seats, like "far side seats," and occasional pay-what-you-can shows; call to check. Tickets $16-32; $5 discount for students, seniors, and groups of 8 or more. Call for ushering info.

Studio Theater, 1333 P St. NW (332-3300). Metro: Dupont Circle. All kinds of drama and comedy on 2 stages (Mainstage Wed.-Sun. and Second Stage Wed.-Sat.). Tickets for Second Stage are $15 Wed.-Fri., $20 Sat.; for Mainstage $18-23.50 Wed.-Thurs. and Sun., $24.50-29.50 Fri.-Sat. Students with ID and seniors $5 off Mainstage shows; students can sometimes get half-price tickets ½-hr. before Mainstage shows. Call about ushering or group discounts. Box office open Mon.-Fri. 10am-6pm, Sat.-Sun. 10am-1pm, 2:15-5pm.

The Source Theater, 1835 14th St. NW (462-1073), between S and T St. The biggie; 14th St.'s oldest and most established "alternative" theater. Produces the Washington Theater Festival every summer at various Washington locations, in addition to its regular assortment of Off-Broadway shows. Shows Wed.-Sun.; tickets $20 Wed.-Thurs. and $25 Fri.-Sun. 2-for-1 specials on Wed. Students and seniors $2 off with advance purchase. Half-price student rush tickets available a half hour before curtain. Call for information on ushering programs; ushers watch for free. Box office open Mon.-Fri. noon-6pm, Sun. noon-3pm.

Church St. Theater, 1742 Church St. NW (265-3748). Metro: Dupont Circle. A variety of drama ranging from Shakespeare to experimental. Tickets $15-18, with student and senior discounts decided on a show-by-show basis. Performances Wed.-Sat. at 8pm and Sun. at 3pm. Box office open an hour before showtime.

National Theatre, 1321 Pennsylvania Ave. NW (628-6161). Metro: Metro Center or Federal Triangle. Big-name, big-budget theater often hosts visitors from Broadway, and the ticket prices reflect it ($35-65). But the fall-spring "Monday Night at the National" program puts on a variety show for free (recording 783-3372), while old movies occasionally pop up as part of the "Summer Cinema" program on Mon. "Saturday Morning at the National" is a separate, free series of kids' events. ½-priced tickets available for students, seniors (65 and over), military, and the disabled Tues.-Wed. (usually at 8pm) and Sun. matinees (2pm). Call in advance for help for sight-or hearing-impaired.

Lincoln Theater, 1215 U St. NW (328-6000), directly across from the U St.-Cardozo Metro. Built in 1920, the Lincoln hosted such acts as Pearl Bailey and Duke Ellington, and was the first theater in the area to show movies to an integrated audience. For its historical significance, the city bought the decaying theater and restored it; the Lincoln reopened in Feb. 1994. All kinds of musical and comedy acts play here. Part of the **D.C. Jazzfest** takes place here; plays and musicals also go up. Tickets range from $25 to 40. Box office open Mon.-Fri. 10am-6pm and on showdays until showtime, or buy through Ticketmaster (432-SEAT).

Warner Theatre, 1299 Pennsylvania Ave. NW (628-1818). Metro: Metro Center or Federal Triangle. A recently-refurbished ornate relic of its days as a vaudeville showhouse, the Warner now hosts high-priced concerts and plays ($20 and up). Tickets available in person at the box office (open Mon.-Fri. 10am-4pm, Sun. noon-3pm) or from Ticketmaster (432-SEAT). 1996 productions include *The Nutcracker* and *Ain't Misbehavin'*.

Ford's Theatre, 511 10th St. NW (347-4833). Metro: Metro Center, 11th St. exit. Where President Lincoln was assassinated, now has schedule of musicals and big-budget shows. Tickets $24-36 (Sat. is the most expensive). Rush tickets available at the box office for seniors (55 and over) and students 1 hr. before showtime ($15). Groups of 20 or more get 15-25% discounts (call 638-2367).

Stage Guild, at Carroll Hall, 924 G St. NW (529-2084). Horseshoe-shaped balcony, high stage, and unbolted floor seats in this former school auditorium give set designers a rare opportunity. 4 plays in the Sept.-May season. Weekdays and matinees $18, weekend nights $20. Call 48 hrs. in advance for group rates (10 or more qualify for half-price tickets).

GALA Hispanic Theatre, 1625 Park Rd. NW (234-7174), in rickety Mount Pleasant; walk northeast on Columbia to 16th, turn left and walk 3 blocks to Park Rd. Turn left; GALA is behind the Sacred Heart school. The national-award-garnering *Grupo de Actores Latino Americanos* presents 4 plays by modern or classical Latin American or Spanish authors each season (Sept.-June). Plays are in Spanish, with a simultaneous English translation provided via headset. Also hosts the

Poesía en Escena series, a program of poetry presented from the stage. Tickets $18, students and seniors $16, groups of 10 or more $12. Productions Thurs.-Sat. 8pm, Sun. 4pm. Reservations recommended; call Mon.-Fri. 10am-4pm.

■■■ MOVIES

D.C. is awash with movie theaters; *Let's Go* lists only theaters with unusual programming or discounts. Check the *Washington Post's* Style or Show sections for all the film that's fit to print.

The Smithsonian's **Hirshhorn Museum** (357-2700), on the Mall at Independence Ave. and 8th St. SW, runs three separate weekly (or so) free film series: foreign and independent films at night (usually at 8pm), documentaries about modern art, and animated matinees for kids. Grab a *Calendar* brochure when you visit the Hirshhorn; it should contain the film schedule. The Smithsonian's **Museum of American History** also hosts classic and art films, sometimes with a talk before the flick. The excellent **American Film Institute** (828-4000), at the Kennedy Center, shows classic American, foreign, and avant-garde films, usually two per night.

American University film classes show movies most nights on a varying schedule, free and open to the public; for a schedule, call 885-2040 (8:30am-5pm).

Biograph, 2819 M St. NW in Georgetown (333-2696). First-run independents, foreign films, and classics. Film festivals frequent; the eclectic is the norm. Animation festivals and Peter Greenaway (of *The Cook, the Thief, His Wife, and Her Lover* fame) films are highlights. Occasional daytime porn keeps the theater afloat. Movie posters are also for sale ($10-20). Admission $6, seniors and children $3. Handicapped access. System for the hearing impaired.

Key Theatre, 1222 Wisconsin Ave. NW in Georgetown (333-5100), near Prospect St. (1 block north of M St.). First-run art films every critic raves about. Subtitled films and exclusive showings offer plenty of chances to polish up your French. Admission $7, over 65 $4, children $3, 1st show of the day $3.50.

Bethesda Theater Café, 7719 Wisconsin Ave. (656-3337). Crack open a cold one while Schwarzenegger cracks heads. Nibble on a tasty burger while T-Rex munches on a slimy lawyer. Beer, wine, and deli food are served while you watch older first-run movies from cushy chairs at low-lying tables. Sound like fun? It is. B.T.C. evokes the days when going to a movie was a great social event instead of a chance to watch glorified TV with 300 of your closest friends. Sun. and Tues. are no-smoking days. Admission Sun. and Tues.-Thurs. $3.50, Mon. $1.50, Fri.-Sat. $5. Matinees (before 5pm weekdays, 1st show only weekends) always $1.50. Must be 21 to get in. Call or consult local papers for movies and showtimes. Plan to arrive a half hr. early for tickets on Sun. and weeknights, 45 min. early Fri.-Sat.

Outer Circle, 4849 Wisconsin Ave. NW (244-3116), across the street from Safeway. Metro: Tenleytown. First-run foreign films, some exclusive engagements. If the Key isn't showing it, this place is. Admission $7.25, seniors and children $4.25. All shows before 6pm $4.25.

■■■ DANCE PERFORMANCES

The Dance Place, 3225 8th St. NE (269-1600). Experimental studio and theater leaps with dance, performance art, and/or music nearly every weekend (Fri.-Sat. at 8pm and April-Oct. Sun. at 7pm, Oct.-March 4pm.) Controversial performers like Holly Hughes and hot, new modern-dance choreographers and companies make their D.C. debuts here. Native American, Japanese, and ethnic dance shows join the commotion. Each June the **Dance Africa D.C. Festival** explodes with hourly free traditional dance performances from all over Africa, accompanied by an outdoor food and crafts market. Regular performances $10, students and seniors $8, children under 18 $5. Ushers watch for free (call for info.) Free parking.

Sports & Recreation

When it comes to the wide world of sports, Washington adopts a characteristically self-conscious approach: it lauds and loves its successful teams while quietly ignoring its laurel-lacking losers. The city goes "Hog Wild" over the Redskins but neglects the lackluster Capitals, and elevates the victorious Georgetown Hoyas to pro-ball status by giving them equal court time at the USAir Arena to the oft-defeated Bullets. Recreational athletes take themselves as seriously as D.C. spectators do. Joggers, bikers, rollerbladers all throng the streets and footpaths; whether fitness freaks or fans, Washingtonians play as hard as they work.

■■■ SPECTATOR SPORTS

BASEBALL

While D.C. packs in the hard-hitters where national politics are concerned, it falls short when it comes to the national pastime. The city hasn't had a major league baseball team since 1970, when the Washington Senators left to become the Texas Rangers. For the last 25 years, Washington has been content to play godparent to the **Baltimore Orioles,** supplying thousands of fans to the brand new park at **Camden Yards**. See **Nightlife & Entertainment** in **Baltimore,** p. 261.

FOOTBALL

The **Washington Redskins** are a source of pride and joy for avid D.C. sports fans and seemingly disinterested residents alike. Three-time Superbowl champions ('82, '87, '92), the 'Skins draw crowds to **Robert F. Kennedy Stadium,** 2400 East Capitol St. SE, for season games Sept.-Dec. Regular season tickets are difficult to come by; they've sold out for each of the last 28 years. Preseason tickets are available from the **RFK ticket office** (546-2222) for $30-45.

BASKETBALL

When it comes to hoops, the NCAA has more to offer Washingtonians than the NBA. The **Washington Bullets,** the city's professional team, are a perennial disappointment on the court. Good teams come to play them, though, and you can catch the action between Nov. and Apr. at the **USAir Arena,** 1 Harry S. Truman Dr., Landover, MD between Landover Rd. and Central Ave. Take the Beltway to exits 15A or 17A and follow the signs. Tickets range from $11 to $33; call the **ticket office** at 301-622-3865. The real stars are the college teams, and the **Georgetown Hoyas** lead the pack by fielding a consistently good team every year. Call 301-350-3400.

HOCKEY

The **Washington Capitals** don't exactly dominate the high speed game of hockey, but faithful fans still turn up at the USAir Arena for games during the Oct.-Apr. season. Tickets ($12-39) are always available. To order, call 301-386-7000.

■■■ PARTICIPATORY SPORTS

Having heavily borrowed from the ancient Greeks in designing its monuments and crafting its republican forms of government, Washington has no qualms about filching their athletic ethic as well. A stroll down the jogger-infested Mall during a weekday lunch hour will confirm that D.C.'s policy wonks exercise more than just their influence. If you're unconvinced that the city takes recreation as seriously as legislation, call the **Department of Recreation and Parks** (673-7660 or 673-7671) for detailed proof.

SWIMMING

Beaches

The best D.C.-accessible beaches are at the **Delaware seashore,** a 3-hr drive from the city (see **Daytripping,** p. 288). If the sweltering heat is too much, do what most of the city does on summer weekends—leave. But if you haven't the money or mobility to make the exodus, there are plenty of public pools where you can beat the heat.

Pools

Pools can be found in nearly every neighborhood. The facilities themselves are generally clean and safe; many of the surrounding areas are not. When choosing a pool, stick to the same cautionary procedures you might use when choosing an accommodation: don't swim anywhere you wouldn't sleep. The following are several pools easily accessible by Metro. Call the **Aquatics Branch** of the Dept. of Recreation and Parks at 576-6436 for more complete listings.

Wilson, Nebraska Ave. and Chesapeake St. NW (282-2216). Metro: Tenleytown-AU. Open during the summer Mon.-Fri. 10-11am for laps and noon-1:15pm, 1:30-5:30pm, and 7-8pm to the general public. Free.

Capitol East Natatorium, 635 N. Carolina Ave. SE (724-4495). Metro: Eastern Market. Summer hours Mon.-Fri. 6:30-9am, 1-5pm, 6-7pm (until 9pm on Tues., Thurs., Fri.); Sat.-Sun. 10am-5pm. Free.

Georgetown, 34th St. and Volta Pl. NW (282-2366). Metro: Tenleytown or Friendship Heights, then take #32, 34, or 36 bus to Wisconsin in Georgetown. Open Tues.-Fri. noon-1pm for laps, 1-8pm otherwise; Sat.-Sun. noon-7pm. Free.

BICYCLING

Cycling enthusiasts will love Washington's street plan for its long blocks and wide avenues, but Washington won't love them back: the crazy antics of bike messengers have bred hatred in most city drivers. Stay off the streets and sidewalks during the day, but pick any of the numerous bike paths and you can't go wrong. One of the best options is the **Mount Vernon Trail,** an 18-mi. trail which starts on Theodore Roosevelt Island and follows the Potomac River and the George Washington Parkway to its namesake, George Washington's scenic mansion. Another is the **C & O Canal Towpath,** a 184-mi. stretch that links Georgetown to Cumberland, MD. For more cycling ideas, try useful publications like the ADC's **Washington Area Bike Map** or the longer distance **Greater Washington Area Bike Map,** available at local book and sporting stores.

Thompson Boat Center, 2900 Virginia Ave. NW (333-4861), at the intersection of Rock Creek Pkwy. and Virginia Ave. Metro: Foggy Bottom/GWU. 18-speed mountain bikes $6 per hr., $22 per day. Open May-Aug. Mon.-Fri. 6am-8pm, Sat.-Sun. 7am-7pm; Sept.-Oct. and Mar.-Apr. daily 6am-7pm.

Big Wheel Bikes, 315 7th St. SE (543-1600). Metro: Eastern Market. Mountain bikes for $5 per hr., $25 per business day; 3-hr. min. For an extra $5, you can keep the bike overnight, giving you a full 24 hrs. Major credit card, driver's license, or $150 cash per bike required for deposit. Open Tues.-Fri. 11am-7pm, Sat. 10am-6pm, Sun. 11am-5pm.

Better Bikes, (293-2080). Will deliver a bike anywhere in the D.C. area. 10-speeds $25 per day, $95 per week; mountain bikes $38 per day, $125 per week. Helmet, map, backpack, locks, and breakdown service included. $25 deposit; driver's licence, credit card, or passport required for collateral. Cash only. Open 24 hrs.

City Bikes, 2501 Champlain St. NW (265-1564), near the 18th St. and Columbia Rd. intersection in Adams-Morgan, next to Ben & Jerry's. Mostly mountain bikes and hybrids. Bikes $10 per hr., $25 per day, $90 per week. Tandems $10 per hr., $40 per day. Locks and helmets free. Children's seats and trailers. $400 credit-card deposit required, or cost of bike in cash. Open Mon.-Wed. and Fri.-Sat. 10am-7pm, Thurs. 10am-9pm, Sun. noon-5pm.

Fletcher's Boat House, 4940 Canal Rd., NW (244-0461). On the C & O towpath. *Bicycles can be used only on canal towpath.* $4 per hour (2-hr. min.), $12 per day. ID necessary as deposit. Open daily 7:30am-7:30pm. Hours vary seasonally and depend on weather.

JOGGING

Those who choose to traverse Washington on their own unaided feet will find the **C&O Canal Towpath** and **Rock Creek Park** jogger-friendly–at least before dusk. Near the **Tidal Basin,** on the **Mt. Vernon Trail,** and along the **Mall** are especially good areas to jog. Serious runners may want to enter the **Marine Corps Marathon** on Nov. 1, which commences at the Iwo Jima Memorial and goes through most of downtown D.C. ($21 entrance fee). If a marathon sounds daunting, check the *Washington Post* "Weekend" section for upcoming races.

BOWLING

Bowling lanes are scarce inside the District; you'll probably have to trek to the suburbs for a crack at the pins.

Bowl America, 8616 Cameron St. in Silverspring, MD (301-585-6990). The closest lanes to D.C. Mon.-Fri. $1.30 before 6pm, $2.70 after. Sat.-Sun. $1.50 before 6pm, $2.70 after. Shoes $1.75. Open Mon.-Fri. 8am-11:30pm, Sat.-Sun. 8am-2am.

Shirley Park Bowl, 2945 S. Glebe Rd. in Arlington (703-684-5800). Take 395 south and get off at exit 7. $1.50 before 4pm, $3 after. Shoes $1.85. Open Sun.-Wed. 9am-1am, Thurs.-Sat. 24 hrs.

GOLF

A favorite pastime for D.C.'s social and political elite, golf is mostly contained to the grassy greens and rolling hills of the city's exclusive country clubs. There are, however, a few public courses open to the masses at the **Robert F. Kennedy Stadium** (397-8638; Metro: Stadium-Armory), and in **Rock Creek Park** at 16th and Rillenhouse NW (882-7332). The **East Potomac Park Golf Course** on Ohio Dr. (863-9007) is another option. All charge $9 for 9 holes Mon.-Fri. and $10.50 for 9 holes Sat.-Sun. **Miniature golf** fans should head over to **Circus Mini Golf Putt-4-Fun** at Hains Point (488-8087). One round is $2.25 per person Mon.-Fri., and $2.75 Sat.-Sun. Open May-Sept. Sun.-Thurs. 11am-9pm and Fri.-Sat. 11am-10pm; call for winter hours.

BOATING

Boat Trips

Most **cruises** on the Potomac include meals and entertainment and are priced accordingly. The **Dandy Restaurant Cruise Ship,** 0 Prince St., Alexandria (703-683-6076) will take you out for lunch ($26-30 person) or dinner and dancing ($48-56 per person). The **Spirit of Washington,** 6th and Water (554-7447) offers lunch ($27-32), dinner ($46-55), and moonlight cruises ($23) leaving Tues.-Sun. from Pier 4. Metro: Waterfront. For less money, take a 90-min. **monument tour.** The **Potomac Riverboat Company** (703-684-0580) runs cruises from April through October, Tues.-Fri. and Sun. Tours depart from the city pier in Old Town Alexandria ($13 adults, $10 seniors, $6 children).

Boat Rentals

If cruises are too expensive, stuffy, or sedate for your blood, grab an oar, rent a boat, and take to the waters yourself.

Fletcher's Boathouse, 4940 Canal Rd. NW (244-0461). Canoes $17 per day, rowboats $15 per day. Open daily 9am-7pm.

Jack's Boats, 3500 K St. NW in Georgetown below Key Bridge. (337-9642). Boats $5 per hour, $25 per day. Open Mon.-Fri. 10am-8pm and Sat.-Sun. 8am-8pm.

Thompson Boat Center, Rock Creek Prkwy. and Virginia Ave. NW (333-4861). Canoes $6 per hour, $20 per day. Sea kayaks $7 per hour, $24 per day. Sailboats $12 per hour. Open Mon.-Fri. 6am-8pm, Sat.-Sun. 7am-7pm.

Tidal Basin Boat House, 1501 Maine Ave. SW (484-0206). Will send you **paddle-boating** across D.C.'s cherry tree lined man-made lake. $7 per hour for a 2-seater or $14 per hour for a 4-seater. Open daily 10am-8pm.

ROLLERBLADING

To see D.C. on wheels but without a car, try the latest funky fad in fun and fitness. If you want some company, meet the **Washington Area Rollerskaters** in the parking lot off Beach Dr. in Rock Creek Park Sat. at noon for a social skate through the park, or at 9th and Constitution Ave. (by the ice rink) Sun. at 12:30pm and Wed. at 6:30pm for a city skate. Call 466-5005 for details.

City Bikes, 2501 Champlain St. NW (265-1564). $10 per hour, $25 per day. Helmet and pads included. Open Mon.-Wed. 10am-7pm, Thurs. 10am-9pm, Fri.-Sat. 10am-7pm, Sun. noon-5pm.

Ski Center, Mass. Ave. and 49th St. NW (966-4474). $5 per hour, $15 per day, $40 per week. Open Mon.-Wed. 11am-6pm, Thurs. 11am-9pm, Sat. 10am-5:30pm, Sun. noon-5pm.

ICE SKATING

When winter hits hard, there's **free ice skating** on the Reflecting Pool in front of the Lincoln Memorial and on the C&O Canal. If these options aren't available, try the **National Sculpture Garden Rink,** 9th and Constitution Ave. NW (371-5342; Metro: Smithsonian). Admission $4.50, rental $2.50.

TENNIS

Aspiring Grafs and Lendyls practice their serves at D.C.'s **public tennis courts** in **Rock Creek Park** at 16th and Kennedy NW (722-5949) and at **East Potomac Park,** 1090 Ohio Dr. SW (554-5962). Hard, clay and indoor courts. Summer rates range from $3.25 to $8 for hard/clay courts and $11-15 for indoor courts. Open Mon.-Thurs. 6am-11pm, Fri. 6am-10pm, Sat.-Sun. 6am-8pm. Call for winter hours.

HORSEBACK RIDING

Those with romantic hopes of galloping across woodlands at breakneck speeds will find their hopes dashed at the **Rock Creek Park Horse Centre,** 5110 Glover Rd. NW (362-0117). Guided 1-hr. trail rides are walk-only, so you'll probably find yourself astride a mild mare instead of a swift stallion. $20 per person. Tues.-Thurs. at 3pm, Sat. at noon and 1:30pm, Sun. at noon and 3pm. Reservations necessary.

HIKING

Nature lovers will be impressed with the number of hiking trails in the greater metropolitan area. In addition to the **C&O Canal Towpath** and the **Mt. Vernon Trail** (see **Bicycling**), **Rock Creek Park** contains a network of hiking trails (282-1063 or 426-6829). The **George Washington Carver Nature Trail** starts from the Anacostia Museum, 1901 Fort Pl. SE (287-3369) and meanders for 7 mi. Virginia's **Great Falls Park** (703-285-2965) boasts 16 mi. of footpaths. Open daily in summer, 7am-dusk. Vistors center open daily in summer 9am-6pm. The small but scenic **Roosevelt Island** (703-285-2598) preserves wildlife and about 2 mi. of trails.

Shopping

Head to Georgetown for clothes, Adams-Morgan for ethnic groceries, and malls for more standard fare. The necessities of life are easy to find; drug stores and groceries abound in all parts of town, and the Yellow Pages can help you find the most convenient dry cleaner or newspaper stand.

■■■ SHOPPING MALLS

Georgetown would like to think that it has mastered the art of mall-building—the ritzy **Georgetown Park,** 3222 M St. NW, near Wisconsin Ave., shines even underground with lots of brass and 150 stores, including the likes of J. Crew and Williams Sonoma (298-5577; open Mon.-Sat. 10am-9pm, Sun. noon-6pm). The grandiloquent green Edwardian interior is a bit overwhelming, but waterfalls and air-conditioning create a climate-controlled oasis for weary travelers. Ask at the first-floor concierge office (next to the Martin Lawrence galleries) for a map or for parking validation. Glance up at the escalators; aside from leading you just where you don't want to go, they're the same ones Kevin Costner sprinted down in *No Way Out* before jumping on the fictitious Metro. To get to Georgetown Park, hop on any of the 30 buses which travel up Wisconsin Ave., or take the red Metro line to Friendship Heights. **Mazza Gallerie,** 5300 Wisconsin Ave. (966-6114; open Mon.-Fri. 10am-8pm, Sat. 10am-6pm, Sun. noon-5pm; Metro: Friendship Heights) and **Chevy Chase Pavilion,** 5335 Wisconsin Ave. (686-0937; open Mon.-Fri. 10am-8pm, Sat. 10am-6pm, Sun. noon-5pm; Metro: Friendship Heights), certainly give Georgetown a run for its money. (Don't be deceived, though; you'll probably find the same stores in all of them.) The **Fashion Centre at Pentagon City,** 1100 S. Hayes St. in Arlington (703-415-2130; open Mon.-Sat. 10am-9:30pm, Sun. 11am-6pm; Metro: Pentagon City) is another contender. The **Ballston Common Mall,** 4238 Wilson Blvd. between Stuart and Randolph St. (703-243-8088, open Mon.-Sat. 10am-9:30pm, Sun. noon-6pm), offers everything you need (and don't need) one block from the Ballston Metro. Two more clones are **Tyson's Galleria I and II,** 2001 International Dr., McLean, VA (703-827-7700; open Mon.-Sat. 10am-9pm, Sun. noon-6pm). Take the Metro to West Falls Church. A shuttle runs from the Metro to the mall Mon.-Fri. 6:40am-8:40pm (75¢). Mall-crazed Metro-users can also take the 23A or 23B bus to Tyson's from the Ballston stop, which might take over an hour. Both Tysons solicit shoppers at Rte. 7 and Rte. 123, off the Beltway at exit 10B or 11B. Finally, there's **White Flint Mall,** 11301 Rockville Pike, Rockville, MD (301-231-SHOP; open Mon.-Sat. 10am-9:30pm, Sun. noon-6pm. Metro: White Flint).

■■■ DEPARTMENT STORES

For those made paranoid by the mall revolution, a number of large department stores have maintained their independence (although some have settled in malls). Perhaps for the sake of solidarity, many have settled in Friendship Heights.

Woodward & Lothrop, 5400 Wisconsin Ave, NW (301-907-8311), directly across from Friendship Heights Metro. Open Mon.-Fri. 10am-8pm, Sat. 9am-8pm, Sun. 11am-6pm. Also at: 11th and F St. NW (347-5300). Metro: Metro Center. Open Mon.-Fri. 10am-8pm, Sat. 9am-8pm, Sun. noon-6pm.

Lord & Taylor, 5255 Western Ave. NW (362-9600), on the corner of Jenifer St. and Western Ave. near Mazza Gallerie. Open Mon.-Fri. 10am-9pm, Sat. 9am-7pm, Sun. 11am-6pm. Also at: White Flint Mall (301-770-9000). Metro: White Flint. Open Mon.-Thurs. 10am-9:30pm, Fri. 10am-10pm, Sat. 9am-9:30pm, Sun. 11am-6pm.

Filene's Basement at the Mazza Gallerie (966-0208). Open Mon.-Sat. 10am-9pm, Sun. noon-6pm. Also at: 1133 Connecticut Ave. NW (872-8430) Metro: Farragut North. Open Mon.-Sat. 9:30am-8pm, Sun. noon-5pm.

Hecht's, 12 St. and G NW (628-6661). Metro: Metro Center. Open Mon.-Fri. 10am-8pm, Sat. 9am-8pm, Sun. noon-6pm.

Nordstrom, 1400 S. Hayes St. in Arlington (703-418-4488). Metro: Pentagon City. Open 10am-9:30pm, Sun. 11am-6pm. Also at: 7111 Democracy Blvd. in Bethesda (301-365-4111). Open Mon.-Sat. 10am-9:30pm, Sun. 11am-6pm.

Macy's, 1000 S. Hayes St. in Arlington (703-418-4488). Metro: Pentagon City. Open Mon.-Sat. 10am-9:30pm, Sun. 11am-6pm.

Bloomingdale's at the White Flint Mall (301-984-4600). Open Mon.-Sat. 10am-9:30pm, Sun. noon-6pm.

■■■ BOOKSTORES

Another World, 1504 Wisconsin Ave. NW (333-8651), in Georgetown; entrance on P St. Comic recording gives a list of new comics (333-8650). Yes, Robin, there really *is* a Batman. And the comic books really came before the movies. Enjoy the latest Marvel, DC, and independent comic favorites without shame. Open Sun.-Tues. 11am-7pm, Wed.-Sat. 11am-8pm.

Atticus Books, 1508 U St. (667-8148), near 15th St. Metro: U St.-Cardozo. Used bookstore with a good selection of foreign-language and academic books. Paperbacks half off cover price. Open Mon.-Sat. 11am-7pm, Sun. 11am-6pm.

Booked Up, 1209 31st St. NW (965-3244), near M St. in Georgetown. As if you walked into someone's private library and felt underdressed for the occasion. Rare and antique books $15-20,000 each. Open Mon.-Fri. 11am-3pm, Sat. 10am-12:30pm.

Capitol Hill Books, 657 C St. SE (544-1621). Metro: Eastern Market. Right around the corner from Eastern Market. A small, dusty used book store covering all subjects, with strong gay studies and black studies sections. Check the carts out front for good paperback bargains. Open Tues.-Fri. 11:30am-7pm, Sat.-Sun. 10am-6pm.

Chapters, 1512 K St. NW (347-5495), in Old Downtown. High-quality downtown bookstore satisfies literati stranded in la-la-lawyer-land. You're encouraged to browse—they answer the phone at a whisper so as not to disturb you. Attractive half price book sales. Open Mon.-Fri. 10am-6:30pm, Sat. 11am-5pm.

Chuck and Dave's Books, Etc., 7001 Carroll Ave. (301-891-2665), in Takoma Park. Road atlases and maps, postcards of Yeats and Camus, newspapers like the *Village Voice,* a decent academic book collection, and a good selection of periodicals. Check out the remainers for some bargains— a semi-annual half price sale enables book buyers to practically walk off with the merchandise. Skylights make for cozy browsing. Open Mon.-Fri. 10am-8pm, Sat. 10am-7pm, Sun. 10am-5pm.

Idle Time Books, 2410 18th St. NW (232-4774), between Belmont and Columbia Rd. in Adams-Morgan. One of the largest used-book stores in the city, with three floors of shelves and great prices. Impressive art magazine section. Open Sun.-Thurs. 11am-10pm, Fri.-Sat. 11am-11pm.

Kramerbooks, 1517 Connecticut Ave. NW (387-3825). Metro: Dupont Circle. Every respectable city needs a late-night bookstore, and Washington has Kramerbooks, open all night Fri.-Sat. Browsers explore the extensive fiction and history sections before slipping past the cookbooks into **Afterwords Café** and bar in back. Open Mon.-Thurs. 7am-1am, Fri.-Sat. 24 hrs. (until Sun 1am closing).

Kulturas, 1741 Connecticut Ave. NW (462-2541), near R St. Metro: Dupont Circle. Piles up secondhand books, records, vintage clothing in friendly haphazardness. Paperbacks sell for half the original price. Note the paintings-of-the-month (by local artists) at the back of the store. Open Mon.-Sat. 11am-9pm, Sun. 11am-7pm.

The Lantern Bryn Mawr Bookshop, 3160 O St. NW (333-3222), near Wisconsin Ave. in Georgetown. Great big gobs of used books, from rare first editions to chintzy romance novels, all priced to move. Managed by charming grannies with a passionate love of books. Hardcover (from $6) and paperbacks (from $1) share shelf space with some old jazz and classical records ($1). Open Mon.-Fri. 11am-4pm, Sat. 11am-5pm, Sun. noon-4pm.

Logic and Literature Book Shop, 1222 31st St. NW (625-1668), between M and N St. in Georgetown. Used and rare books bought/sold. Specializes in history, science, and philosophy. Open Mon.-Tues. 11am-5:30pm, Wed.-Fri. 11:30am-6pm.

Luna Books, 1633 P St. NW (332-2543), on third floor above Café Luna and Skewers. Bookstore/coffeehouse moonlights as a "Democracy Center," which means your average patron is an activist and the major activity is political discourse. Come here to explore the discount nonfiction and political texts, and find out about the Center's many discussion groups. Open Mon.-Fri. 11am-6pm.

The Old Black Forest Bookshop, 3145 Dumbarton St. NW (965-3842), between 31st St. and Wisconsin Ave. in Georgetown. A small house full o' books; mostly general interest lit, history and art. Hardcovers downstairs, paperbacks upstairs, all at half the original price. Open Sun.-Mon. noon-6pm, Tues.-Sat. 11am-7pm.

Second Story Books, 2000 P St. NW (659-8884), at the corner of 20th. Metro: Dupont Circle. Thousands of perviously read paperbacks and hardcovers. A great place to hang out and browse. Open daily 10am-10pm.

United States Government Bookstore, 1510 H St. NW (653-5075), near 15th St. Metro: McPherson Square. Pamphlets galore: the most incredibly boring or most exciting reading material you've ever encountered. Open Mon.-Fri. 9am-4:30pm.

Yawa, 2206 18th St. NW (483-6805), between Kalorama Rd. and Wyoming Ave. in Adams-Morgan. Specializes in African and African-American literature; greeting cards, incense, cool jewelry. Open Mon.-Sat. 11am-9pm, Sun. noon-6pm.

Washington Project for the Arts, 400 7th St. NW (347-4813), in Old Downtown. **Bookworks,** the gift shop accompanying W.P.A.'s gallery, displays books and magazines for the contemporary *artiste.* Occasional evening performances and readings by local talent; check flyers or call for info. Open Tues.-Sat. 11am-6pm.

Yes!, 1035 31st St. NW (338-7874), near M St. in Georgetown. Alternative paths to health of body and soul: an affirmative experience for all who enter. Enormous selection of books on Krishna, acupressure facelifts, diet and nutrition, metaphysics and tarot, massage technique, astrology, martial arts, and Jungian studies. Also offers a nirvana-oriented music collection (not the band) featuring Gregorian chant and meditation music. Free coffee for browsers. Call 800-YES-1516 for free catalog. Open Mon.-Wed. 10am-7:30pm, Thurs.-Sat. 10am-8pm, Sun. noon-6pm.

Yesterday's Books, 4702 Wisconsin Ave. NW (363-0581), at Chesapeake St. Metro: Tenleytown. Plenty of used books (nearly 30,000) of every conceivable kind, from politics to literary criticism to gay studies. Also plenty of coffee, cake, and comfy chairs for your browsing pleasure. Open Mon.-Thurs. 11am-9pm, Fri.-Sat. 11am-10pm, Sun. 1-7pm.

■■■ CLOTHING STORES

If you're a young prepster looking for that perfect Polo shirt, you'll be in ecstasy over the number of collegic choices in Georgetown. All the old standbys are within walking distance from each other. **Benetton,** 1200 Wisconsin Ave. NW (625-0443). Open Mon.-Sat. 10am-10pm, Sun. 11am-8pm. **Banana Republic,** 3200 M St. NW (333-2554). Open Mon.-Sat. 10am-10pm, Sun. noon-8pm. **The Gap,** 1258 Wisconsin Ave. NW (333-2805). Mon.-Thurs. 10am-9pm, Fri.-Sat. 10am-10pm, Sun. 11am-8pm. **J. Crew,** 3222 M St. NW (965-4090). Open Mon.-Sat. 10am-9pm, Sun. noon-6pm. **Pantagonia,** 1048 Wisconsin Ave. NW (333-1776). Open Mon.-Fri. 10am-8pm, Sat. 10pm-6pm, Sun. 11am-5pm. **Urban Outfitters,** 3111 M St. NW (342-1012). Open Mon.-Thurs. 10am-10pm, Fri.-Sat. 10pm-11pm, Sun. 11am-8pm. The more original may be in the market for more unique shopping experience:

Clothes Encounters (...of a Second Kind), 202 7th St. SE (546-4004). Metro: Eastern Market. Across from Eastern Market, on the corner of North Carolina. Consignment shop for designer-brand women's clothing. Pick up nearly new dresses and accessories at a third of the new price. Open Mon.-Wed. and Fri. 11am-6pm, Thurs. 11am-7pm, Sat. 10am-6pm, Sun. noon-4pm.

Commander Salamander, 1420 Wisconsin Ave. NW (337-2265), near O St. in Georgetown. Drop in, tune in, turn on. Funky and offbeat clothing from traditional *Urban Outfitters*-esque grunge wear to outrageously extreme vinyl/plastic/ polyester fashions. Outfit yourself with style or frighten the conventional crowds of Georgetown. Open Mon.-Thurs. 10am-10pm, Fri.-Sat. 10am-11pm, Sun. 11am-8pm. On winter weekdays, it closes 1 hr. earlier.

Hats In the Belfry, 1237 Wisconsin Ave. NW (342-2006), across from Prospect St. in Georgetown. Hats average about $25, and go up to around $350! When the hot Washington sun beats down on Georgetown, they can charge as much as they want and still find a market. Open Mon.-Thurs. 10am-11pm, Fri.-Sat. 10am-midnight, Sun. 10am-9pm.

Man For All Seasons, 321 7th St. SE (544-4432). Metro: Eastern Market. On the same block as Eastern Market. Consignment shop for designer men's clothes offering stylish suits, shirts, and shoes for half of the new price. Open Tues.-Wed. and Fri. 11am-6pm, Thurs. 11am-7pm, Sat. 10am-6pm, Sun. 12:30-4:30pm.

Rainbow Artwear, 3001 M St. NW (333-3914), in Georgetown. Eclectic array of handcrafted clothing and accesories. Open Mon.-Tues. 10:30am-8pm, Wed.-Thurs. 10:30am-9pm, Fri.-Sat. 10:30am-9:30pm, Sun. noon-7pm.

Secondhand Rose, upstairs at 1516 Wisconsin Ave. NW (337-3378), near P St. in Georgetown. Consignment shop for designer women's clothing, shoes, and accessories. Look for merchandise by designers such as Donna Karan, Ralph Lauren, Yves St. Laurent, Chanel, and Anne Klein at less than a third of the original price. Open Mon.-Sat. 10am-6pm. Closed Mon. July-Aug.

■■■ GROCERY STORES

Addisu Gebaya, 2202 18th St. NW (986-6013), in Adams-Morgan. The smell of incense mingles with the smell of Ethiopian herbs and spices in this tiny grocery, which also stocks Ethiopian clothes, jewels, and magazines. Open Mon.-Sat. 9am-10pm, Sun. 9am-9pm.

Arlington Farmer's Market, at the Arlington Courthouse (Courthouse Rd. and Clarendon Blvd.). Metro: Court House. Farmers sell their fresh fruits, vegetables, flowers, and baked goods. All items must have been produced within a 100-mile radius, so you know it's the real stuff. Open Sat. 7am-noon.

Da Hua Market, 623 H St. NW (371-8888). Metro: Gallery Place-Chinatown. Chinese market with fresh vegetables as well as almost every canned and bottled good a Chinese kitchen would need. Look over the chicken feet, dried squid, and seaweed; tourists cooking on a budget will delight in the wide variety of Ramen noodle-type meals. Open daily 10am-8pm.

El Gavilan, 1646 Columbia Rd. NW (234-9260), between Ontario Rd. and Mozart Pl. in Adams-Morgan. A popular but small store; two aisles crammed with Latin, African, and West Indian groceries all the way up to the ceiling. Open Mon.-Sat. 9am-10:30pm, Sun. 9am-8:30pm.

Firehook Bakery, 106 N. Lee St. (703-519-8020), between King and Cameron St. in Alexandria. Metro: King St. Bread baked daily, in such off-beat flavors as green olive and sage ($4 per loaf). Loaves $1.50-5. Day-old bread ½ price on Mon. Open Mon. 7am-6pm, Tues.-Thurs. 7am-8pm, Fri.-Sat. 7am-10pm, Sun. 8am-7pm.

Merkato Market, 2116 18th St. NW (483-9499), near California St. in Adams-Morgan. Down a narrow flight of stairs. Look for the green sign. Named for the huge market in Addis Ababa, the Ethiopian capital. Small, airy store with 2 low-rise aisles stocked with Ethiopian food. Sniff around—you'll know they specialize in spices. Open daily 9am-10pm.

Middle East Market, 7006 Carroll Ave. (301-270-5154), in Takoma Park. Metro: Takoma. Noodles and cracked wheat in packages ($2). Spices and foodstuffs difficult to obtain elsewhere. Open Mon.-Fri. 10am-7pm, Sat-Sun. 10am-5pm.

Tiger Moon, 4811 Bethesda Ave. (301-951-9180). Metro: Bethesda. Don't miss the canned whole squid among the shelves of equipment and provisions for Southeast Asian cooking. Asian dishes such as Pad Thai are available for take-out at lunch and dinner ($4); they are also half-price (a steal!) 6-7pm. Open Mon.-Fri. 10am-7pm, Sat. 10am-5pm.

Tivoli Gourmet and Pastry, 2 locations, both in Arlington: 901 Stuart St. (703-528-5200), at the entrance to the Ballston Metro; and 1700 Moore St. (703-524-

8902), at the entrance to the Rosslyn Metro. Breathtaking pastry displays, quick quiches, pasta salads, and sandwiches at lunch time, as well as a beautiful selection of cheeses, fresh-baked crusty breads, wines, and meats. Things like sundried tomatoes sold in bulk. Gargantuan cookies $0.85-1.10 each, muffins 85¢. Open Mon.-Sat. 7am-8pm, Sun. 8:30am-3:30pm.

HEALTH FOOD

Cash Grocer Natural Foods, 1315 King St. (703-549-9544), near West St. in Alexandria. Metro: King St. Walk in past an overflowing bulletin board and piles of health-oriented pamphlets. Vitamins, hand-dipped candles, bulk nuts, and organic produce. Open Mon.-Wed. and Fri. 10:30am-6:30pm, Thurs. 10:30am-8pm, Sat. 9:30am-6:30pm.

Food For Health, 3804 Wilson Blvd. (703-524-4499), in Arlington. Metro: Virginia Sq./GMU. Vitamins and diet books line the walls; wheat germ ($2) and seaweed ($3) fill the shelves. Candy (ironically) at the counter. Open Mon.-Sat. 10am-7pm, Sun. noon-6pm.

Yes! Natural Gourmet, 1825 Columbia Rd. NW (462-5150), near 18th St. in Adams-Morgan. All manner of fat-free, meat-free, oil-free, salt-free, sugar-free concoctions. Open Mon.-Fri. 9am-8pm, Sat. 9am-8pm, Sun. noon-6pm. Also at: 3425 Connecticut Ave. NW (363-1559) Metro: Cleveland Park. Open Mon.-Sat. 9pm-9pm, Sun. 10am-8pm.

■■■ RECORD STORES

Atticus Books, 1508 U St. (667-8148), near 15th St. Metro: U St.-Cardozo. Used bookstore with a good selection of music. Records $1-20, $3-4 on average; CDs $3-9. Open Mon.-Sat. 11am-7pm, Sun. 11am-6pm.

CD Mania, 1083 Wisconsin Ave. NW (337-4979), upstairs at the corner of M St. in Georgetown. New, used, buy-sell-trade. They say they'll beat anyone's price on a new CD. Open Sun. noon-8pm, Mon.-Thurs. 11am-10pm, Fri.-Sat. 11am-11:30pm.

House of Musical Traditions, 7040 Carroll Ave. (301-270-9090) in Takoma Park. Metro: Takoma. Probably the top music shop in the D.C. area, the House boasts a superior collection of everything that ever went twang, wang, bong, boom, or shaka laka from Thailand to Portland; the staff might show you how to play the sturdier weird instruments. An international collection of folk, folk-rock, international, and bluegrass music, with tapes and CDs from Ireland, Britain, Hungary, and the Smoky Mountains (among others). Tickets for area folk concerts hang out here, making it the ideal starting point for folkies trying to get their D.C. bearings (prices vary; shows usually held at the Silver Spring Unitarian Church). They also repair instruments. Open Tues.-Wed. noon-7pm, Thurs.-Fri. noon-8pm, Sat. 11am-7pm, Sun. 11am-5pm.

The Record Mart, upstairs at 217 King St. (703-683-4583), between Lee and Fairfax St. in Alexandria. Metro: King St. Ascend a staircase plastered with an impressive collage of music posters to reach this shop jam-packed with music aficionados and great used music (mostly LPs). Pick up info here on monthly buy/sell/trade conventions. Open Mon.-Thurs. 10am-9pm, Fri.-Sat. 10am-10pm, Sun. 10am-7pm.

Smash!, downstairs at 3279 M St. NW (33-SMASH or 337-6274), near Potomac St. in Georgetown. Used to be a punk store; now it's a store that used to be a punk store. Fair assortment of local rock and "alternative" regalia. Open Mon.-Thurs. 11am-9pm, Fri.-Sat. 11am-midnight, Sun. noon-6pm.

12" Dance Records, 2010 P St. NW (659-2010), above the Subway restaurant. Metro: Dupont Circle. Budget some time to browse this house music heaven. Dim lights and a disco ball will make you want to stop awhile. Open Mon.-Thurs. and Sat. noon-9pm, Fri. noon-11:45pm, Sun. 1-6pm.

■■■ MILITARY SURPLUS

Sunny's Affordable Outdoor Store, a Baltimore-based chain with several Washington locations. All sorts of camping equipment and army-like outdoor clothing.
In **Old Downtown:** 917 F St. (737-2032). Metro: Gallery Place-Chinatown. Open Mon.-Sat. 8:30am-6:30am, Sun. 11am-5pm.
In **Georgetown:** 3342 M St. NW (333-8550). Open Mon.-Wed. 10am-7pm, Thurs.-Fri. 10am-8pm, Sat. 9am-7pm, Sun. 11am-5pm.
In **Farragut:** 1416 H St. NW (347-2774). Metro: McPherson Sq. Open Mon.-Sat. 8:30am-6:30pm, Sun. 11am-5pm.

■■■ SPECIALTY AND UNUSUAL STORES

CAPITOL HILL

Fairy Godmother, 319 7th St. SE (547-5474). Metro: Eastern Market. On the same block as Eastern Market. Sells games, books, and toys for the young and young at heart. Has blocks ($33) for budding architects, language tapes ($5-20) for budding diplomats, and a large social-studies section for budding senators. Open Mon.-Fri. 11am-6pm, Sat. 10am-5pm, occasional Sun. hours.

GEORGETOWN

Babbling Books, 1651 Wisconsin Ave. NW (342-1202), in Georgetown. Actually part of Washington Video. Books-on-tape for rent, essential for that long drive or ride. 3-day rentals $3.50-6, 7-day rentals $7-10. Return the tapes by mail for an additional $5; on Sun. rent 2 tapes for the price of 1. Open Mon.-Thurs. 10am-10pm, Fri.-Sat. 10am-11:30pm, Sun. noon-10pm.

Condom Rageous, 3212 M St. NW (337-0510), in Georgetown. 1-9 single condoms $1 each, 10-50 single condoms 75¢ each ("After that we'll talk"), as well as lots of condom humor. Open Mon.-Thurs. noon-9pm, Fri.-Sat. noon-11pm, Sun. noon-9pm.

Movie Madness, 1222 Wisconsin Ave. NW (337-7064), near M St. in Georgetown. As many movie and music posters as can fit into a 15-by-12-ft. room, from recent hits to old idols like Marilyn Monroe and James Dean. Postcards for the frugal. Prices $5-20. Open Mon.-Thurs. 11am-9pm, Fri.-Sat. 11am-10pm, Sun. noon-7pm.

The Pleasure Place, 1063 Wisconsin Ave. NW (333-8570), near M St. in Georgetown. Kinkier underwear than Frederick's of Hollywood and sex toys you'd expect to find on 14th St. Leave the kids at home and stock up on panties, pasties, and massaging oils. Cockrings $2. Over 18 only. Open Mon.-Tues. 10am-10pm, Wed.-Sat. 10am-midnight, Sun. noon-7pm.

S&A Beads, 3143 N St. NW (337-2204), in Georgetown. A spacious setting for a wide variety of domestic and imported beads. String your own. Open Mon.-Thurs. 11am-8pm, Fri.-Sat. 11am-9pm, Sun. 11am-6pm.

FARRAGUT

Capitol Coin and Stamp Co. of Washington, D.C., 1701 L St. NW (296-0400), Metro: Farragut North. This small store specializes in items of philatelic interest, political pins, posters, and banners. 96 of the 5000 buttons sell for $1 each. This is probably the only place you'll still be able to buy a Barry Goldwater doll ($45) or a Cuomo/Iacocca pin. Spoof paraphernalia abounds for the disenchanted. Open Mon.-Sat. 10am-6pm.

The Map Store, 1636 I St. NW (628-2608), across from Farragut Square. Metro: Farragut West. Maps ($2.50-13), globes, road atlases, and guides for the traveler. And (of course) *Let's Go* books galore. Stop here before hitting the road. Open Mon.-Fri. 9am-5:30pm, Sat. 10am-4pm.

DUPONT CIRCLE

Backstage, Inc., 2101 P St. NW (775-1488), at 21st St. Metro: Dupont Circle. A veritable caucus of rubber politicians greets thespians as they enter D.C.'s only theater store, which trafficks in everything from scripts and scores to costumes and criticism. Open Mon.-Wed. and Fri.-Sat. 10am-6pm, Thurs. 10am-7pm.

The Pleasure Place, 1710 Connecticut Ave. NW (483-3297), near R St. Metro: Dupont Circle. Lingerie, swimwear, edible underwear, dildos and vibrators await in this erotic novelty shop, which also offers a selection of gay and lesbian videos (for sale and for rent), books, and T-shirts ($3-20). Cockrings $2-7. Open Mon.-Tues. 10am-10pm, Wed.-Sat. 10am-midnight, Sun. noon-7pm.

SHAW/ U DISTRICT

Boutique Mikuba, 1359 U St. NW (483-6877), near 14th St. Metro: U St.-Cardozo. A crowded store specializing in African art, jewelry, and clothing. Open Mon.-Fri. 11am-8pm, Sat. 11am-8pm, Sun. 12:30-7:30pm.

ADAMS-MORGAN

Yawa, 2206 18th St. NW (483-6805), between Kalorama Rd. and Wyoming Ave. Bookstore specializing in African and African-American literature, greeting cards, and jewelry. Open Mon.-Sat. 11am-9pm, Sun. noon-6pm.

ALEXANDRIA, VA

Angie's Doll Boutique, 1114 King St. (703-683-2807) at Fayette St. Dolls, dolls, dolls: from the most exquisite to the latest Barbie. Beware of browsing with a 7-yr. old. Open Tues.-Sat. 11am-5:30pm.

Bavarian Alps, 924 King St. (703-683-3994), at Patrick St. The tackiest German gift store you've ever seen, and proudly so: wall-to-wall steins and nutcrackers. The red door is open Tues.-Sat. 10am-6pm, Sun. noon-5pm.

Birds in the Cage, upstairs at 110 King St. (703-549-5114), near Union St. A smattering (mess?) of vintage ball gowns, jewelry, antiques, pop art, and birds in cages. Clock repair. Hours are irregular; the owners change them all the time. In general, open Mon.-Thurs. 10am-9pm, Fri.-Sat. 10am-10pm, Sun. 11am-10pm, but call to make sure.

John Crouch Tobacconist/The Scottish Merchant, 215 King St. (703-548-2900), between Fairfax and Lee St. "If it's not Scottish, it's *crap!*" Kilts, pipes, clan memorabilia, smoking paraphernalia, and Scottish travel guides. Open Mon.-Thurs. and Sat. 10am-10pm, Fri. 10am-11pm, Sun. 11am-9pm.

The Washington Antiques Center, 209 Madison St. (703-739-2484), in Alexandria. More than 20 antique dealers in one place, all selling 18th- to early-20th-century doodads. Weekends mean free parking. Open daily 11am-6pm.

Bisexual, Gay, and Lesbian D.C.

Washington's bisexual, gay, and lesbian communities are exceptional for their diversity, visibility, and the comfortable geographic and legal positions they occupy within the city. D.C. law boasts a strong civil rights tradition which includes sexual orientation legal rights; the June 1995 ruling by the Court of Appeals in favor of adoption by gay couples is only one of the most recent examples of the openness of the city. Aided by this positive reinforcement, a number of gay neighborhoods have developed throughout the Washington area—most significantly around Dupont Circle and on Capitol Hill. Over 30 bars and clubs thrive, serving a gay population of almost 200,000. The men's scene transcends many of the professional, economic, and racial barriers that divide the rest of the city. At nearly every establishment, clean-cut yuppies and leather-clad centaurs can be seen enjoying the performances of drag queens and partying together. The lesbian scene is smaller and more sedate, but equally diverse where and when the socializing takes place.

Dupont Circle is the hub of gay activity in D.C. Easily accessible by Metro, the neighborhood offers whole blocks of gay and gay-friendly establishments from bars to bookstores. **P St.** is especially fruitful, where most bars ands restaurants cluster around **17th** and P St. between **21st** and **22nd.** Located on Connecticut Ave. half a block from the Metro, **Lambda Rising** (see p. 239) provides free maps and listings of area gay hotspots, and serves as a quasi-information center for travelers and locals alike. **Southeast** Washington contains upwards of 10 clubs and bars. Despite this area's commercial and social appeal, it is traditionally one of the city's most dangerous. Exercise caution and common sense if you choose to explore Southeast. Don't go alone at night and try to drive or take a cab home. Most clubs have free cab phones on the premises as well as parking lots, so use them.

There are a handful of gay publications in D.C. Most are free and widely circulated. The **Washington Blade** is the best source of news, reviews, and club listings; published every Friday, it's available in virtually every storefront in Dupont Circle. **MW,** a newer arts and entertainment weekly, contains brief public interest items, short fiction, extensive nightlife coverage, and is almost as easy to find as the Blade. Two rarer publications are **Woman's Monthly,** a lesbian periodical, and **Brown Sugar News,** a black gay men's weekly (50¢ on the newsstand).

All listings are near the Dupont Circle Metro unless specifically noted.

INFORMATION AND ADVICE LINES

Gay and Lesbian Switchboard: 628-4667. Separate lesbian number: 628-4666. Daily 7:30-10:30pm. Counseling, general information, and referrals.

Gay Deaf Assistance: TDD 628-4669.

Gay and Lesbian Hotline: 833-3234. Counseling and referral daily 7-11pm.

Gay Information and Assistance: 363-3881. 24 hrs. Counseling and information.

Gay Men's VD Clinic: 745-6129, general information 745-6125. Provides free routine testing for sexually transmitted diseases; men only. Walk-in hours Tues. and Thurs. 6-7:30pm at 1701 14th St. NW.

Gay and Lesbian Alliance Against Defamation: 2001 O St. NW, 429-9500.

Gay Men and Lesbians Opposing Violence: 2000 L St. NW, 452-7448. Call to report hate crimes; all calls are confidential and can be anonymous.

Sexual Minority Youth Assistance League: 333 Pennsylvannia Ave. SE, 546-5940. Metro: Eastern Market or Capitol South. Counseling and social programs for bisexuals, gays, and lesbians ages 14-21. Hotline staffed Mon.-Fri. 7-10pm; drop-in hours Fri. 6-8pm; Sat. youth groups meet noon-3pm.

■■■ ACCOMMODATIONS

Several D.C. hotels in the Dupont Circle area and in nearby Upper Northwest advertise as being especially gay-friendly. Among these are the Carlyle Suites Hotel, the Embassy and Windsor Inns, and the Kalorama Guest Houses. See **Accommodations** on p. 70 for details on these establishments.

The Brenton, 1708 16th St. NW (332-5550, 800-673-9042). 8 spacious rooms and bed-and-breakfast treatment in the Victorian splendor of a 16th St. townhouse. Gay men preferred. Singles $69, doubles $79. $10 each additional person. Includes continental breakfast and evening happy hour. Reservations suggested.

■■■ BARS AND RESTAURANTS

Since Dupont Circle is the nucleus of activity for D.C.'s gay community, most of the drinking and dining options congregate to the east of the Circle along 17th St. and west of it on P St. between 21st and 22nd. While some may not explicitly cater to gay clientele, they draw mostly gay patrons anyway. **Soho Tea and Coffee, Cafe Luna, The Pop Stop,** and **Trio** in the Circle all serve predominantly gay clientele. For more info., see **Food,** p. 98.

Starred entries are **Let's Go Picks,** the best of the best.

★**The Circle Bar,** 1629 Connecticut Ave. NW (462-5575). A 3-in-1 social emporium with a ground- floor restaurant, a top-floor bar, and an underground dance club. All three draw a young, professional, racially mixed crowd. Happy hour Mon.-Fri. 5-9pm drops Bacardi and Skyy Vodka prices to $2, while Sat.-Sun. happy hour 11am-10pm keeps all vodka prices $2. Wednesday is ladies' night. Open Sun.-Thurs. 11am-2am, Fri.-Sat. 11am-3am.

★**J.R.'s,** 1519 17th St. NW (328-0090). Upscale but downhome brick and varnished-wood bar, with wood floors, stained glass windows, and a DJ in a choir stall overlooking the tank of "guppies" (gay urban professionals). Happy hour Mon.-Fri. 2-8pm: $2 domestic bottled beer, Sat. noon-8pm and Sun. all day: 75¢ vodka. A relaxed neighborhood bar by day, at night it becomes *the* place for S&M (stand and model)—if you're into that sort of thing. Mon.-Thurs. 2pm-2am, Fri. 2pm-3am, Sat. noon-3am, Sun. noon-2am.

The Edge, 56 L St. SE (488-1200). Metro: Navy Yard. Around the corner from *Tracks*. Male entertainment warehouse with 6 bars, 2 dance floors, a snack bar, and game room. Crowd varies nightly. Wed. draws a racially diverse 20-thirty-something male crowd ($5 cover before 11pm, $8 after); Thurs. "Midweek Muscle" attracts buff men with a $3 cover and $1 drafts all night. Fri.-Sat. nights cater to a Black male crowd ($5 cover). Sun. "Pecs on the Deck" has no cover 4-7pm, and fills up fast with...er...pecs. Secure parking in nearby lots. Open Mon.-Thurs. 7pm-2am, Fri.-Sat. 7pm-4am, Sun. 4pm-2am.

The Green Lantern, 1313 L St. NW (638-5133). Metro: McPherson Sq. Enter through the rear (no pun intended). Cruisiest bar in D.C. boasts two floors of Levi/leather-clad studs looking at each other. Video bar downstairs. Happy hour Mon.-Sat. 11am-9pm offers $1.50 rails and domestic beers. 2-for-1 drinks Thurs. 9pm-2am and all day Sun. Open Sun.-Thurs. 11am-2am, Fri.-Sat. 11am-3am.

DC Eagle, 639 New York Ave. NW (347-6025). Metro: Mt. Vernon Sq. Busy leather bar whose faithful patrons come early to drink and stay late to dance. Happy hour Mon.-Fri. 6-9pm with $1.25 rails and domestic beers. 2 pool tables on 2 floors. Open Mon.-Thurs. 6pm-2am, Fri. 6pm-3am, Sat. noon-3am, Sun. noon-2am.

The Annex, 1415 22nd St. NW (296-0505). Enter at Badlands (same address). Video and pool room is the quieter cousin of one of D.C.'s hottest dance clubs. Located upstairs from Badlands. The obvious choice for those who like the clean-cut crowd but prefer the bar atmosphere. Fri. night karaoke led by a local drag queen. $5 cover. Open Fri.-Sat. 8pm-3am.

Remington's, 639 Pennsylvannia Ave. SE (543-3113). Metro: Eastern Market. A gay country-western nightclub and Top 40 video bar. Large dance floor on the first floor. Carpeted upstairs features posters of James Dean, a pool room and bar. Happy hour Mon.-Wed. 4pm-2am, Thurs.-Sun. 4-8pm. Free country-and-western dance lessons Mon.-Thurs. at 8:30pm. Cover $3 Fri.-Sat. after 9pm. Open Sun.-Thurs. 4pm-2am, Fri.-Sat. 4pm-3am.

Mr. P's, 2147 P St. NW (293-1064), near 22nd St.. Oldest gay bar in the Circle pleases die-hard regulars with free chips and salsa, $2 beers, and $2.25 mixed drinks. In the evenings, male patrons spill out onto the patio bar and head upstairs to the video bar to dance the night away. (Video bar 9pm-close.) 2-for-1 rails on Wed. and $5 unlimited drafts on Sun. after 4pm. Open Mon.-Thurs. 3pm-2am, Fri.-Sat. 3pm-3am, Sun. noon-2am.

Escalando!, 2122 P St. NW (822-8909). Amid neon lights, flashing mirrors, and walls emblazoned with colossal mulitcolored chili peppers, a predominantly Latino male crowd takes the floor for dancing and drinking. On the weekends, women join the fun. Free salsa and merengue lessons Mon. at 9pm; drag shows at midnight Sat.-Sun. Open Mon. 4pm-2am, Tues.-Thurs. and Sun. 11am-2am, Fri.-Sat. 11am-3am.

The Fireplace, 2161 P St. NW (293-1293). Casual bar is always crowded with men of all ages, styles and races. No food, just booze in this dark wood-walled saloon. $1.75 rails and domestic beers. Upstairs bar area has a reputation for getting cruisy on weekends. Open Sun.-Thurs. 1pm-2am, Fri.-Sat. 1pm-3am.

Trumpets, 1603 17th St. NW (232-4141), on the corner of 17th and Q. thirtysomething clean-cut and professional men use this restaurant and lounge more for eating and meeting than drinking or dancing. New Age decor with sheet metal bolted to the walls gives this place a little hipness to which its happy hour (Mon.-Fri. 4-8pm) adds $1 rails and domestic drafts and $3 imports and premiums. Daquiri bar on patio in summer. Wed. is women's' night. Wheelchair access on Q St. Open Sun.-Thurs. 4pm-1:30am, Fri.-Sat. 4pm-3am.

■■■ DANCE CLUBS

★**Tracks,** 111 First St. SE (488-3320). Metro: Navy Yard. One of the hottest straight dance clubs in D.C., Tracks becomes *the* hottest gay dance club in D.C. on Sat. nights. No cover 8-9pm, $5 9-11pm, $7 after 11pm. Two dance floors, three bars, patio, outdoor volleyball court. Opens Sat. 8pm with no set closing time. See p. 216 for more info.

★**Hung Jury,** 1819 H St. NW (279-3212). Metro: Farragut West. Believe it or not, no one's hung here. Lesbians from all over D.C. from 30something couples to singles scoping the scene spend their weekend nights bopping to Top 40. $5 cover. Men must be accompanied by a woman to enter; gay men are admitted but occasionally must "prove" they're gay. Shooter $1. Get a "grab bag" (whatever a bartender pulls out of a box) for $1.50. Open Fri.-Sat. 9pm-3:30am.

★**Fraternity House,** at 2122 P St. rear NW (223-4917), in the alley between 21st and 22nd St. The "Frat House" attracts an ethnically mixed crowd of young gay men. Ladies' night held once a month. Strobe lights, disco balls, videos, and hard-core house beats pump and flicker as the guys dance the night away amid mirrored walls. Happy hour (Mon.-Fri. 4-9pm) features $1.50 domestic beer. Specials every weeknight, like ½-price Tues. and $1 domestics on Wed. No cover for video bar; downstairs cover Mon., Wed., Thurs. $3; cover Fri.-Sat. $4. Open Mon. 4pm-3am, Tues.-Wed. 4pm-2am, Thurs. 4pm-4am, Fri. 4pm-5am, Sat. 8pm-5am, Sun. 8pm-2am.

★**Badlands,** 1415 22nd St. NW (296-0505), near P St. Enter the peach-colored monolith of a building where a young crowd serious about dancing moves to the beat of Top 40, dance, and house music. Tues. is ½-price night; a $2 cover goes to charity. Thurs. is college night; cover is $3. Cover Fri.-Sat. $5. Expect to wait in line Fri.-Sat. Open Sun.-Thurs. 9pm-2am, Fri.-Sat. 9pm-2:45am.

Phase One, 525 8th St. SE (544-6831). Metro: Eastern Market. Lesbian club with casual atmosphere draws women of all ages and styles for dancing. Pool tables, video bar, DJ. Beer $2.25. No cover Sun.-Thurs., $5 Fri.-Sat. Open Sun.-Thurs. 7pm-2am, Fri.-Sat. 7pm-3am.

Ziegfeld's, 1345 Half St. SE (554-5141). Metro: Navy Yard. Young and older gays and lesbians take turns attending Ziegfeld's nightly dance shows. Cover $6. Open Thurs. and Sun. 9pm-2am and Fri.-Sat. 9pm-3am.

■■■ SHOPPING AND SERVICES

Lambda Rising, 1625 Connecticut Ave. NW (462-6969), between Q and R. Largest selection of gay and lesbian literature in the world, including lots of gay and lesbian travel guides. T-shirts ($15-20) and novelty items also available. Serves as an information center and a ticket outlet for concerts and events in the gay and lesbian community. Helpful and friendly staff. Occasional book signings and live music. Open daily 10am-midnight.

GLIB BBS, a computerized information and communications service. Call 703-578-GLIB with your computer and a modem. Features on line chatting, Internet e-mail, message boards, and databases filled with info on bisexual, gay, and lesbian D.C. Free to those who are members of or financially support a gay community group, $60 per year otherwise. Definitely worth a look. Try a demo session at Lambda Rising.

Lammas, 1426 21st St. NW at P (775-8218). Extensive selection of feminist and lesbian literature. Wheelchair accessible. Generous bubble gum machine (25¢). Open Mon.-Sat. 10am-10pm, Sun. 11am-8pm.

The Leather Rack, upstairs at 1723 Connecticut Ave. NW (797-7401). All the leather gear you could possibly want, need, or imagine. A whole wall of whips ($7-26) and paddles ($20-30). 18+. Open daily 10am-10pm.

Outlook, 1706 Connecticut Ave. NW (745-1469). Novelty shop peddling everything from colored candles to clocks to cards. Wide selection of gay pride T-shirts and bumper stickers. Worth a browse even if you aren't buying. Open Mon.-Thurs. 10am-11pm, Fri.-Sat. 10am-midnight, Sun. 11am-10pm.

■■■ SPORTS & RECREATION

D.C. Strokes Rowing Club, P.O. Box 39076 (371-8897). Washington area group with competitive, recreational, and novice rowing programs for gay men and lesbians interested in the sport. Basically a bunch of young, fit gay men and women who love to row. Annual dues $30 or month long introductory ($50) and recreational ($60) programs. Call for further information.

Crew Club, 1321 14th St. NW (319-1333). Metro: McPherson Square. 24-hr. social recreation facility is a health club and gym for gay males looking to work up a sweat. Weight gym, lockers, showers, tanning, and game room. No alcohol. Admission is $12 6am-4pm and $18 4pm-6am. Half price Tues. 8am-midnight.

Daytripping from D.C.

The torrid sun and oppressive humidity of Washington summers can really zonk those unaccustomed to overexertion. If you are as fortunate as Congress and have some time off from work, try getting out of the sweltering city air, hop in a car, turn up the radio, and head out to the cool Atlantic or the shade of the Virginia countryside. For a change of urban pace, try Baltimore, Richmond, or Charlottesville. (A note to the hopelessly carless: most of these places can be reached by train or bus.)

Listed below are the D.C.-area getaways covered in this book. The more distant destinations might be considered weekend trips.

Annapolis, MD: 45 min.-1 hr. driving; 40 min. by bus.
Baltimore, MD: 45 min. driving; 30-40 min. by train; 55 min. by bus.
Fairfax County, VA: 30 min. driving; 1hr. by tourbus; 1½ hrs. by boat.
Shenandoah National Park, VA: 1 hr. and 10 min. driving.
Charlottesville, VA: 2½ hrs. driving; 2 hrs. and 15 min. by train; 2½ hrs. by bus.
Richmond, VA: 2 hrs. driving; 2 hrs. by train; 2 hrs. and 15 min. by bus.
Williamsburg, VA: 3 hrs. driving; 3 hrs. and 15 min. by train; 4 hrs. by bus.
Jamestown, Yorktown, and the James River Plantations: 3 hrs. driving.
Virginia Beach, VA: 4 hrs. driving; 5 hrs. by train; 6½ hrs. by bus.
Delaware Seashore: 2½-3hrs. driving; 3½ hrs. by bus.
Harper's Ferry, WV: 1½ hrs. driving; 1 hr. by train.

THE REST OF MARYLAND

Once upon a time, the Chesapeake Bay, a picturesque, shellfish-rich estuary, ruled the Maryland economy. On the rural eastern shore, small-town Marylanders captured crabs and raised tobacco. Across the bay in Baltimore, workers ate the crabs, loaded the ships, and ran the factories. Then the federal government expanded, industry shrank, and Maryland had a new, more slender core: not the bay, but the Baltimore-Washington Parkway. Suburbs grew up and down the corridor, Baltimore cleaned up its smokestack act and the Old Line State acquired a new, liberal urbanity. As D.C.'s homogenized commuter suburbs break the limits of Maryland's Montgomery and Prince Georges counties, Baltimore revels in its polyglot immensity and Annapolis, the capital, stays small-town. The mountains and mines of the state's western panhandle—geographic and cultural kin to West Virginia—are still largely undeveloped after all these years. If anything brings this state together, it may be a sense of proportion: forest and fields encompass but never overwhelm, rivers and islands aren't too big to explore, and cities—along with their problems—are too small to seem endless.

SUBURBAN MARYLAND

Every segment of Washington has its quieter suburban counterpart. Lower Montgomery County's parks rival Rock Creek Park in NW; NASA is Prince Georges' counterpart to NE Washington's spread-out installations like Catholic U. Where SE boasts Bolling Air Force Base, southern Prince Georges retaliates with Andrews Air Force Base. Much of the green on a Montgomery County map turns out to represent country clubs; the typical county resident shops at gourmet supermarkets, flaunts her children's school—private or public, high school or college—on an Audi or Saab, and golfs away the weekend. Of course, the county is more complicated than that, incorporating aging Silver Spring, high-tech Rockville, and neo-urban Bethesda along with ritzy Potomac. Prince Georges County is Montgomery's blue-collar cousin, with less dough and fewer executive homesteads.

GETTING THERE & GETTING AROUND

While it is possible to reach many Maryland destinations via D.C.'s Metro, it is not always entirely sensible. For instance, although Silver Spring and Bethesda border one another, the two are at opposite ends of the red line (which makes two stops that ought to be neighbors about 45 minutes apart). Elsewhere, idyllic farms, NASA, and other sights are totally inaccessible via public transportation. Travelers yearning to explore Maryland's suburbia should probably lay hold of an automobile.

Public transportation in the area is designed for people going to and from their cars. The Red Line follows Rte. 355, which starts in D.C. as Wisconsin Ave., turns into Rockville Pike (a strip mall enormity) after Bethesda, changes to Hungerford Dr., and finally settles on Gaithersburg Rd. The Capital Beltway links Montgomery to Prince Georges to Alexandria to Fairfax to Montgomery County again. The Baltimore-Washington Parkway cuts through Prince Georges, zipping past the Beltway and NASA in Greenbelt. U.S. 1 heads north as always through NE Washington, Prince Georges County, and College Park, home of the University of Maryland.

MONTGOMERY COUNTY

Wheaton Regional Park, 1400 Glenallen Ave., offers hikes, bicycle tours, canoeing, and crafts at the **Nature Center** (301-946-9071; open Tues.-Sat. 9am-5pm, Sun. 1-5pm). Guided horse tours leave every Sunday at 1, 2, and 3pm (301-622-3311; horse rides $15 per hour, by reservation only). Wheelchairs can traverse the paved bike trails, though these can get pretty steep. There's a children's playground complete with a small farm, a 1915 carousel, and a miniature train ride through 2 mi. of park (carousel and train open April-Aug. Mon.-Fri. 10am-5pm, train Sat.-Sun. 10am-6pm, carousel until 7pm; carousel or train tickets $1). To get to the park, take the Beltway (I-495) to exit 31 (Georgia Ave. or Rte. 97), then right onto Randolph Rd., then right again to Glenallen Ave. (Park admission free. Call for schedule Nov.-March 301-649-2703, April-Oct. 301-649-3640.)

The **National Capital Trolley Museum,** 1313 Bonifant Rd. in Wheaton (301-384-6088), lets you ride the original Washington and Maryland trolleys that were once the primary form of public transportation. The 20-minute ride includes a tour that explains the history of streetcars in D.C. and gives you the scoop on the particular streetcar you're riding. Trains run every half hour, so take a look at the museum while you wait for the next ride. To get to the Trolley Museum, take New Hampshire Ave. left onto Bonifant Rd., or on Saturdays, take the C8 bus from the Twinbrook Metro stop. (Open July-Aug. Wed. 11am-3pm, Sat.-Sun. noon-5pm; Sept.-June Sat.-Sun. noon-5pm; Memorial Day, July 4th, and Labor Day noon-5pm; closed Dec. 15-Jan. 1. Trolley rides $2, ages 2-17 $1.50.)

Glen Echo Park, just down MacArthur east of the Clara Barton House (301-492-6229 or 301-492-6282), is a turn-of-the-century amusement park; enjoy the relics. Pack a lunch and then picnic in the old Bumper Car pavilion, ride the restored 1921 Dentzel Carousel (May-Sept. Wed.-Thurs. 10am-2pm, Sat.-Sun. 11:30am-6pm; rides 50¢), or check out the wealth of local art at the gallery on-site (open April- Sept. Tues., Thurs., and Sat.-Sun. 10am-5pm, Wed. and Fri. 1pm-9pm; Oct.-March Tues.-Sat. noon-5pm). Kids can take in a puppet performance (320-6668; shows Wed.-Sat. 10am and 11:30am, Sun. 11:30am and 1pm; tickets $5).

Smaller than Great Falls Park on the Virginia side of the Potomac, Maryland's **Great Falls Park** (301-299-3613) includes part of the Chesapeake & Ohio Canal, whose towpath makes a perfect **jogging** and **biking trail** with a great view of the kayakers below. Pick up a **trail map** at the **Great Falls Tavern Museum** at the park, (open daily 9am-5pm). Only knee-deep water separates reasonable Maryland from the wild, green Virginia border. A 90-minute cruise of the canal on the mule-drawn *Canal Clipper*, including a demonstration of the lock system and a history of the canal told by guides in period costume, is more fun than it sounds and safer than

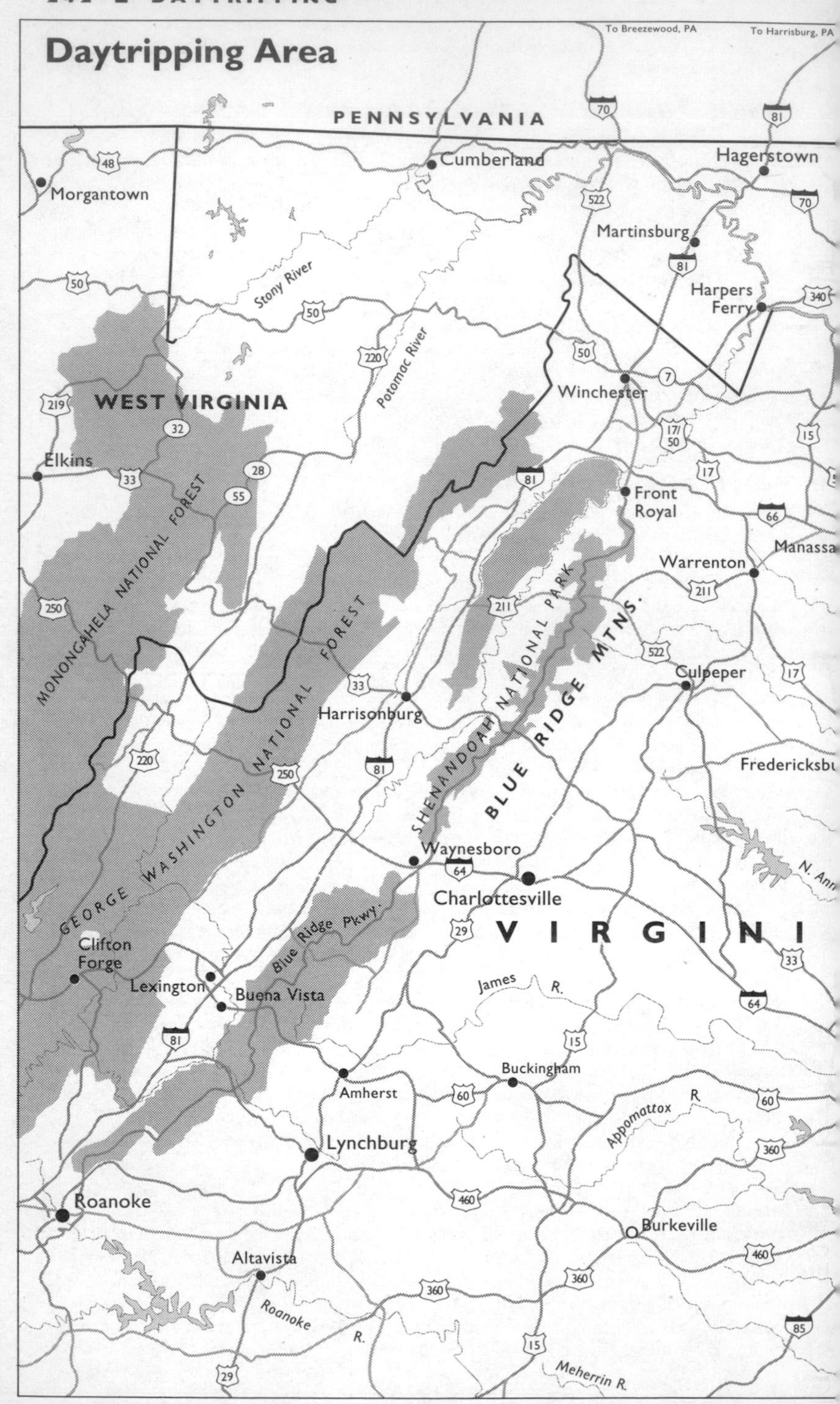
Daytripping Area
To Breezewood, PA
To Harrisburg, PA
PENNSYLVANIA
Cumberland
Hagerstown
Morgantown
Martinsburg
Harpers Ferry
Stony River
Potomac River
Winchester
WEST VIRGINIA
Elkins
MONONGAHELA NATIONAL FOREST
Front Royal
Warrenton
Manassa
GEORGE WASHINGTON NATIONAL FOREST
SHENANDOAH NATIONAL PARK
BLUE RIDGE MTNS.
Culpeper
Harrisonburg
Fredericksbu
Waynesboro
Charlottesville
VIRGINI
Blue Ridge Pkwy.
Clifton Forge
Lexington
Buena Vista
James R.
N. Ann
Amherst
Buckingham
Appomattox R.
Lynchburg
Roanoke
Burkeville
Altavista
Roanoke R.
Meherrin R.

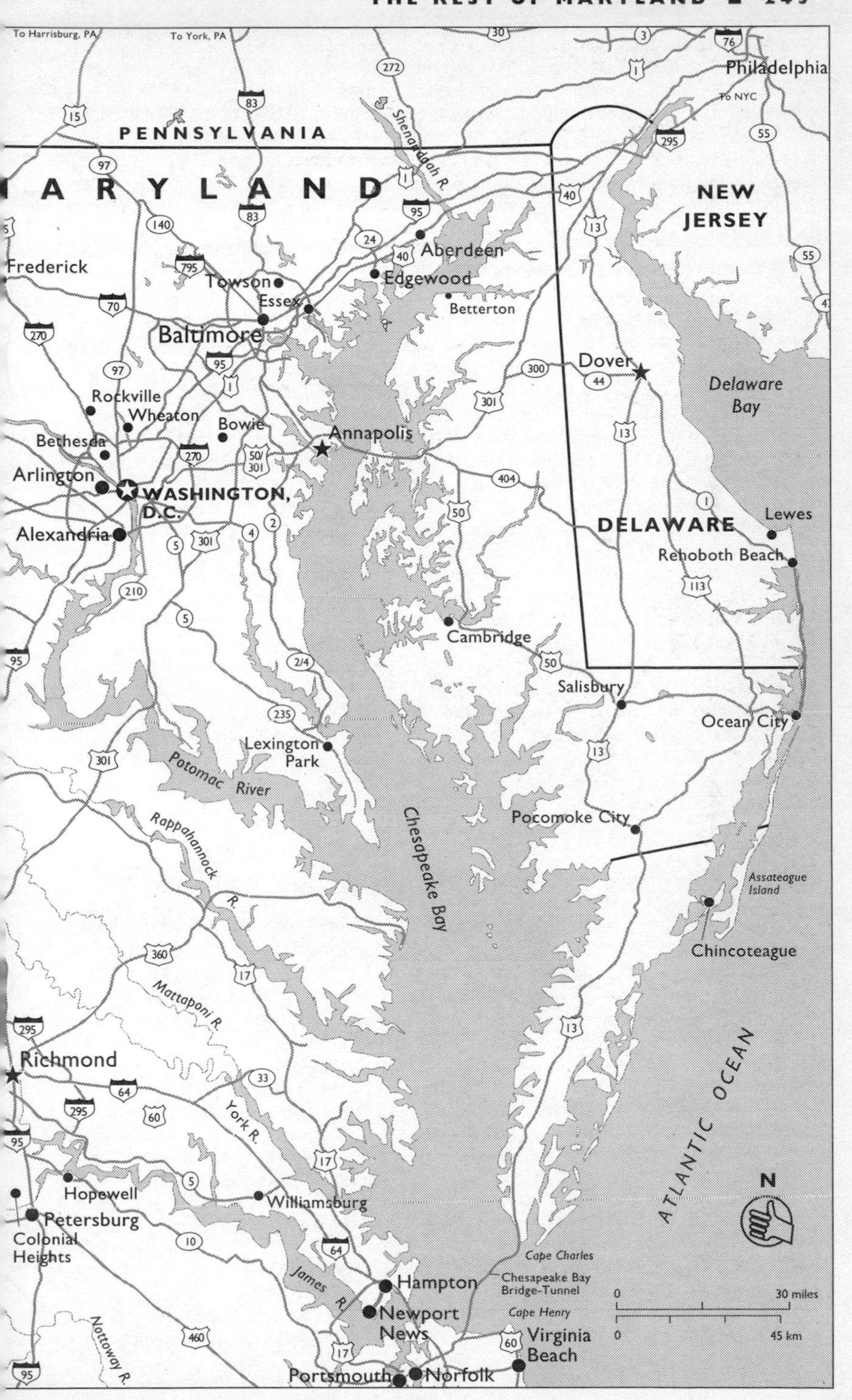
To Harrisburg, PA
To York, PA
Philadelphia
To NYC
PENNSYLVANIA
MARYLAND
NEW JERSEY
Shenandoah R.
Frederick
Towson
Essex
Aberdeen
Edgewood
Betterton
Baltimore
Dover
Delaware Bay
Rockville
Wheaton
Bowie
Annapolis
Bethesda
Arlington
WASHINGTON, D.C.
Alexandria
DELAWARE
Lewes
Rehoboth Beach
Cambridge
Salisbury
Ocean City
Lexington Park
Potomac River
Chesapeake Bay
Pocomoke City
Rappahannock R.
Assateague Island
Chincoteague
Mattaponi R.
Richmond
York R.
ATLANTIC OCEAN
Hopewell
Williamsburg
Petersburg
Colonial Heights
Cape Charles
James R.
Hampton
Chesapeake Bay Bridge-Tunnel
Newport News
Cape Henry
Virginia Beach
Nottoway R.
Portsmouth
Norfolk
N
0
30 miles
0
45 km

rock climbing. **Barge tours** leave from the Canal Museum at 11710 MacArthur Blvd., in Potomac, Wed.-Sun. 10:30am, 1pm, and 3pm. Tickets $5, seniors and children $3.50. Park open sunrise-sunset. Vehicle admission $4, pedestrians $2, seniors free. To reach Great Falls Park, take lovely MacArthur Blvd. westward until it ends.

At the very busy intersection of Rockville Pike (Rte. 355) and Viers Mill Rd. in Rockville, **F. Scott** and **Zelda Fitzgerald** lie in the graveyard of St. Mary's Church, surrounded by the graves of family members and 19th-century headstones. Admirers throw flowers beside *The Great Gatsby*'s famous last sentence: "So we beat on, boats against the current, borne back ceaselessly into the past."

PRINCE GEORGES COUNTY

Fort Washington Park (301-763-4600) gathers the requisite woods and grass to its military-historical bosom at the confluence of Piscataway Creek and the Potomac River. The two-waterway view will bliss you out; you can see Mount Vernon from the hill, and the 6-mi. trail along the water's edge provides a peaceful escape from the city. Rangers tour the fort in Civil War-era costume at 2, 3, and 4pm every weekend, and during the week by request. To reach Fort Washington Park, take South Capitol St., which becomes Indian Head Hwy., and turn right onto Fort Washington Rd. You can also take the Beltway I-95 to exit 3, turning right onto Indian Head Pkwy. Turn right off the parkway onto Fort Washington Rd. (Park open daily 8am-dark; fort open 9am-5pm; Visitors Center open daily 9am-5pm. Admission $4 per vehicle, $2 per pedestrian, biker, or motorcyclist; after 4:30pm weekdays and after 6:30pm weekends everyone gets in free.)

Space cases go ballistic at the **NASA/Goddard Space Flight Center** (301-286-8981). The tour covers, among other buildings in the complex, the Test and Evaluation Facility, the NASA Communications Network, and control centers for satellites. The Visitors Center itself has permanent exhibits reminiscent of the Smithsonian's Air and Space Museum. Hands-on activities show kids robotics, the mission of the Space Shuttle, the Hubble Space Telescope, and the uses of a space station. Don't bother with the drive unless you plan to take the tour. To get here take the Baltimore-Washington Pkwy. (I-295) and exit onto Greenbelt Rd. Follow the signs to the Visitors Center. (Open daily 10am-4pm. Free. Guided tours Mon-Fri. 11:30am, Sat. 11:30am and 2:30pm; also free.)

■■■ ANNAPOLIS

Annapolis walks the fine line between nostalgia and anachronism. Like an antique car with brand-new shiny parts, Annapolis both flaunts and hides its age. Though the major industry here is the government of Maryland, forget about office buildings and stuffed shirts; instead of a downtown, Annapolis has an historic waterfront district. Narrow streets flanked by 18th-century brick antique and gift shops run downhill to the bustling yet weirdly peaceful docks, where yachts relax on the water. Crew-cut "middies" (a nickname for Naval Academy students—midshipmen) mingle with longer-haired students from St. John's and affluent couples here on weekend getaways. If all the gardens and plaques get you down, walk down to the docks, buy some ice cream, and stare awhile at the soft bobbing of the masts.

Settled in 1649 with the rest of Maryland, Annapolis was declared the capital in 1694. All those fine Georgian houses once held colonial aristocrats (and their slaves). Annapolis made real history when the Continental Congress ratified the Treaty of Paris here in 1784, making the end of the American Revolution official. After its 1783-1784 stint as temporary capital of the U.S. (hot on the heels of Philadelphia, New York, and Trenton, NJ), Annapolis relinquished the national limelight.

PRACTICAL INFORMATION AND ORIENTATION

Emergency: 911

Visitor Information: Annapolis and Anne Arundel County Conference & Visitor's Bureau, 26 West St. (268-8687). Open daily 9am-5pm. On-the-spot ques-

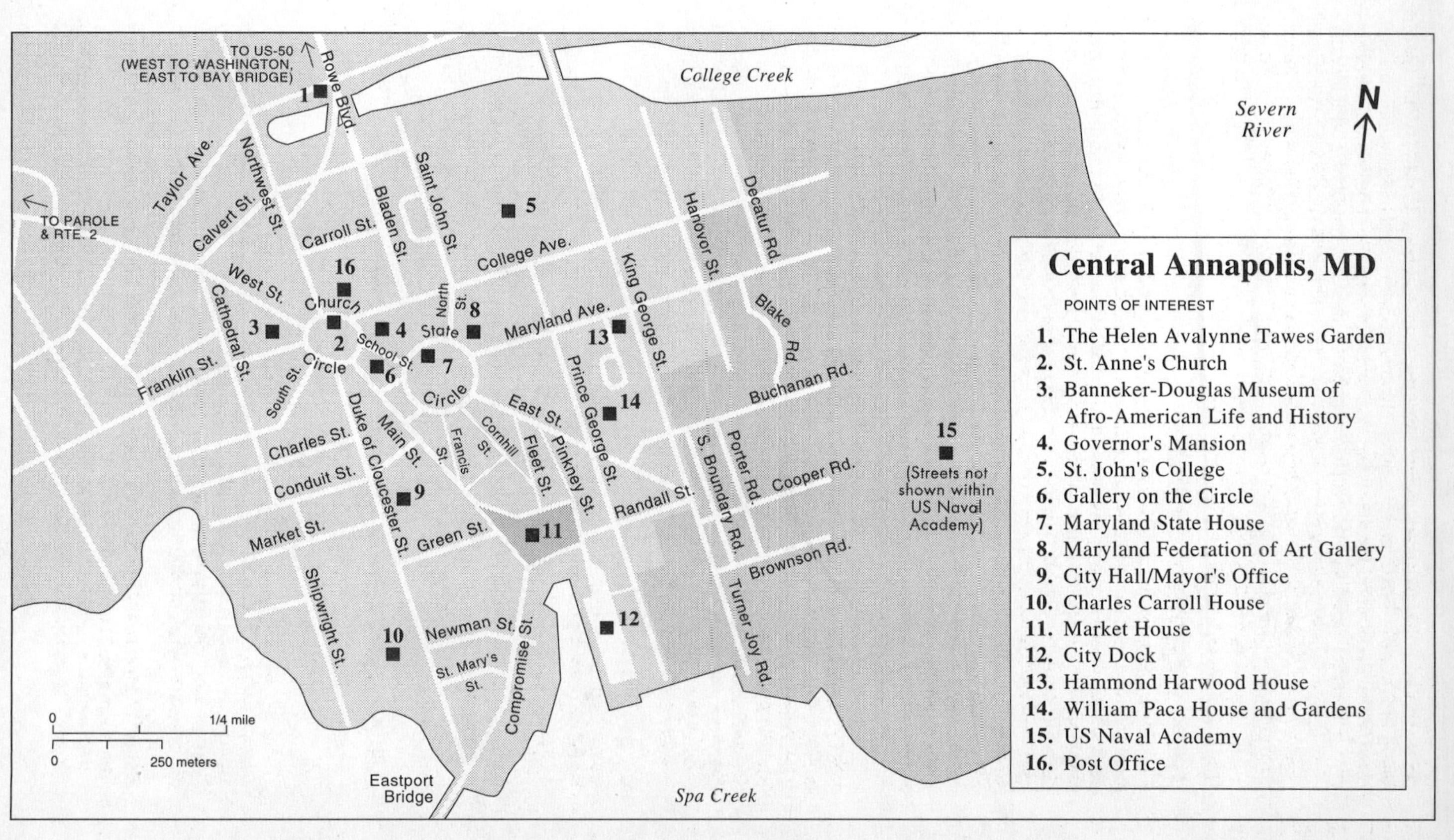
Central Annapolis, MD
POINTS OF INTEREST
1. The Helen Avalynne Tawes Garden
2. St. Anne's Church
3. Banneker-Douglas Museum of Afro-American Life and History
4. Governor's Mansion
5. St. John's College
6. Gallery on the Circle
7. Maryland State House
8. Maryland Federation of Art Gallery
9. City Hall/Mayor's Office
10. Charles Carroll House
11. Market House
12. City Dock
13. Hammond Harwood House
14. William Paca House and Gardens
15. US Naval Academy
16. Post Office
N
Severn River
College Creek
Spa Creek
(Streets not shown within US Naval Academy)
TO US-50 (WEST TO WASHINGTON, EAST TO BAY BRIDGE)
TO PAROLE & RTE. 2
Eastport Bridge
Rowe Blvd.
Decatur Rd.
Blake Rd.
Buchanan Rd.
Cooper Rd.
Brownson Rd.
Porter Rd.
S. Boundary Rd.
Turner Joy Rd.
Hanovor St.
King George St.
College Ave.
Maryland Ave.
Prince George St.
Randall St.
East St.
Pinkney St.
Fleet St.
Cornhill St.
Francis St.
North St.
State Circle
Saint John St.
Bladen St.
Carroll St.
School St.
Church Circle
Main St.
Duke of Cloucester St.
Green St.
Newman St.
St. Mary's St.
Compromise St.
Northwest St.
Calvert St.
Taylor Ave.
West St.
South St.
Cathedral St.
Franklin St.
Charles St.
Conduit St.
Market St.
Shipwright St.
0
1/4 mile
0
250 meters

tions can be answered at the **information desk** at the State House (841-3810). Desk open daily 10am-5pm.

Greyhound/Trailways: (800-231-2222). Buses stop at the MTA at the **football field** at Rowe Blvd. and Taylor Ave. Buy a ticket from the bus driver. Cash only. To: **Washington, DC** (2 per day, 1hr., $7.50); **Philadelphia** (2 per day, 7½hrs., $42); **Baltimore** (2 per day, 4hrs., $9).

Mass Transit Administration: (539-5000, call Mon.-Fri. 6am-9pm to speak to a disgruntled customer service rep.). To: **Baltimore** Express #210 runs Mon.-Fri. (1hr., $2.85); local #14 runs daily (90 min., $2.25). Call for times. Buses leave from St. John's and College Ave. and St. John's and Calvert St. Have exact change.

Public Transportation: Annapolis Dept. of Public Transportation (263-7964). Operates a web of city buses connecting the historic district with the rest of town. Buses run Mon.-Sat. 5:30am-10pm, Sun. 8am-7pm.

Taxi: Annapolis Cab Co. (268-0022); **Checker Cab** (268-3737).

Help Lines: Rape and Sexual Assault Crisis Center: 222-7273. **Youth Crisis Hotline:** 800-422-0009. **Poison Center:** 800-492-2414. All numbers are 24 hours.

Post Office: One Church Circle (263-9292). Open Mon.-Fri. 8:30am-5pm. **ZIP Code:** 2140.

Area Code: 410.

Annapolis lies southeast of U.S. 50 (also known as U.S. 301) 30 mi. east of Washington, D.C. and 30 mi. south of Baltimore. From D.C. take U.S. 50 east . (In D.C., 50 begins at New York Ave. and can be accessed from the Beltway.) From Baltimore, follow Rte. 2 south to U.S. 50 west, cross the Severn River Bridge, then take Rowe Blvd.

The city extends south and east from two landmarks: Church Circle and State Circle. School St., in a blatantly unconstitutional move, connects Church and State. Maryland Ave. runs from the State House to the Naval Academy. Main St. (where food and entertainment congregate) starts at Church Circle and ends at the docks. Those lost in Annapolis can reorient themselves by looking for the State House dome or St. Anne's spire. Annapolis is compact and easily walkable, but finding a parking space can be tricky; if you have the cash, save yourself a headache by parking in a lot or garage.

ACCOMMODATIONS

In this self-consciously quaint town, bed-and-breakfasts abound. Motels are harder to come by. After wandering around, you probably won't want to sleep in anything less cozy than a bed and breakfast anyway. The Visitors' Information Centers have brochures for B&Bs and hotels in the area. Try to reserve a room in advance, especially if you're traveling during the busy summer months. **Amanda's Bed and Breakfast Regional Reservation Service** (410-225-0001 or 800-899-7533; open Mon.-Fri. 8:30am-5:30pm, Sat. 8:30am-noon), can help you arrange for accommodations in Annapolis. Travel in pairs if you can, since two people share a room for only $5-15 more than the single rate in most of these establishments. Some rates fluctuate depending on demand; ask around and sound like you need convincing.

Gibson's Lodgings, 110 Prince George St. (268-5555). One block from city dock on Randall St. Spacious common parlors for elegant relaxing, as well as a patio between buildings. The 200-year-old Patterson House, with 6 rooms, is the cheapest of the 3 buildings. Complimentary continental breakfast. Free parking in the courtyard. Singles $58-98, doubles $68-113. Roll away beds for a 3rd person $15 extra. 40% discount during off season (Jan. 3-Feb. 28).

Scotlaur Inn, 165 Main St. (268-5665), atop Chick and Ruth's Delly. Ten guest rooms with A/C and private bath grace this homey "bed and bagel." Less fancy than some of the other B&Bs, but cheaper too. Mammoth breakfasts come from Chick & Ruth's (see below). Check-in 2pm; check-out 11am. Rates vary with room ($55-75, $5 per extra person).

Dolls House Bed and Breakfast, 161 Green St. (626-2028). One block off Main St. 3 rooms, each with a theme. Victoria and Sun rooms sleep 1 or 2 for $85. The Nutcracker Suite sleeps up to 6 for $120 ($105 as a double). Check or cash only.

Casa Bahia, 262 King George St. (268-8941), 4 blocks from Naval Academy. Modest townhouse offers 2 rooms for $85 each. $15 for each person after 2. Check or cash only. Full breakfast included. Not as quaint as some, but clean and casual.

FOOD

Middleton Tavern, 2 Market Space (263-3323), at Randall St. by the dock. Established in 1750 and frequented by members of the Continental Congress. Stuffed trophies, revolutionary war muskets, and a civil war uniform hang from the exposed beams. Excellent "appetizer" pastas easily make a full meal ($6.95). Delicious seafood lasagna $8; burgers and sandwiches $4.95-7.95. Nightly music gets the crowd rocking as they gulp down oysters from the raw bar. Open Mon.-Fri. 11:30am-2am, Sat.-Sun. 11am-2am. Fri-Sat. piano bar upstairs; Sun. local jazz and blues. Food served daily until midnight.

Chick & Ruth's Delly, 165 Main St. (269-6737). Brazen and petulant decor has helped make it an Annapolis institution, with dishes named, satirically, for local and national politicians. The all-day breakfast menu includes bottomless coffee (80¢), 18 kinds of doughnuts (55¢), hand-rolled soft pretzels, and foot-long cheeseburgers ($3). Milkshakes are thick and delicious; a "regular" comes with the mixing cup so you can refill your glass 3 times. Kosher food. Open 24 hrs.

New Moon Café, 137 Prince George St. (280-1956). The only place in Annapolis to find a creative cup of coffee, a healthful meal, and a Eurocafé atmosphere all under the same roof. Menu is organically inclined. Moon Burger (non-fat, all soy) $4.75. Turkey dog $3.75. Extensive coffee selection (95¢-$3). See nightlife for info. on live music and poetry readings.

Buddy's Crabs & Ribs, 100 Main St. (626-1100), on the 2nd fl. above Banana Republic. Bright, sterile, touristy warehouse o' seafood. On Sun., come for quantity; Buddy's boasts a breakfast buffet from 8:30am to 1pm ($6, children under 5 free). All-you-can-eat lunch buffet ($6; Mon.-Fri. 11am-2pm). All-you-can-eat crabs priced daily. Staunch and starving seafood lovers can belly up to the happy hour raw bar buffet (Mon.-Fri. 4-7pm, $7). Open Mon.-Thurs. 11am-10pm, Fri.-Sat. 11am-11pm, Sun. 8:30am-10pm.

City Dock Café, 18 Market Space (269-0969), at Pinkney St. Cool, calm coffeehouse adds sophistication to Annapolis with its Frank Lloyd Wright-esque interior and great espresso drinks ($1-3). Open Mon.-Thurs. 7am-10pm, Fri. 7am-midnight, Sat. 8am-midnight, Sun. 8am-10pm.

Carrol's Creek Bar & Café, 410 Severn Ave. (263-8102), in the Annapolis City Marina Complex, across the Eastport Bridge from Annapolis proper. Spectacular views of Spa Creek and the City Dock. Can be packed on weekends. Texas BBQ shrimp (from the Lite Fare menu) $8. Open Mon.-Thurs. 11:30am-4pm and 5-9:30pm, Fri.-Sat. 11:30am-4pm and 5-10pm, Sun. 10am-2pm and 3-9:30pm. Bar usually stays open until midnight. Happy Hour Mon.-Fri. 4-7pm.

Mum's, 136 Dock St. (263-3353), at the dock. This cutesy dinette sports a jukebox and $5-7 sandwiches. Wild mushroom and roasted garlic pizza ($5.75) and the cajun-style tuna steak sandwich ($7) are surprisingly well done. Open Mon.-Fri. 8:30am-2am, Sat.-Sun. 9am-2am. Nightly music (live band Sun.-Thurs., DJ Fri.-Sat.).

Storm Bros. Ice Cream Factory, 130 Dock St. (263-3376), offers a great view of the ships at the dock while you savor 39 flavors of ice cream and 3 flavors of yogurt. $1.15 for a scoop, $1.95 for 2, $2.35 for 3. Open Sun.-Thurs. 10:30am-11pm, Fri.-Sat. 10:30am-midnight.

SIGHTS

Inside the corinthian-columned **State House,** get Maryland maps and brochures at the information desk, where helpful volunteers are on hand to answer questions. Built from 1772 to 1779, it's the oldest working state house in the nation. The *Treaty of Paris* was signed here on January 14, 1784. Check out the history exhibits and silver collection, and watch the state legislature bicker if the senators and delegates are in session (from the 2nd Wed. in Jan. until mid-April). The State House gives free tours at 11am and 3pm. (Open daily 9am-5pm.)

From State Circle, follow Maryland Ave. to meet up with historic buildings. The **Hammond-Harwood House** hovers at 19 Maryland Ave., at King George St. (269-1714). This elegant 1774 building, the last one designed by Colonial architect William Buckland, keeps up period decor down to the candlesticks. (Open Mon.-Sat. 10am-4pm, Sun. noon-4pm. Tours on the hr.; last tour an hr. before closing. Admission $4, ages 6-18 $3. AAA discounts: admission $3.50, students $2.50. Uniformed armed service personnel free.) Enjoy the garden in back for free.

A right onto King George St., then another onto Martin St. reveals an unimposing parking lot and the sign for the **William Paca Garden,** 42 East St. (263-5553). Look to the end of Martin St. and admire the well-preserved fire department, then turn right onto East St., past the Brice House, and right again onto Prince George St. for the entrance to the companion museum, the **William Paca House,** 186 Prince George St. (263-5553). William Paca, an early governor of Maryland, was one of the signers of the *Declaration of Independence.* Visitors to his beautifully restored estate find a 1765 grandfather clock still ticking inside and trellises, water lilies, and gazebos outside. Preservationists rescued the garden from under a bus station and parking lot. Tours given whenever enough people gather; come at least an hour before closing. (House open daily 10am-4pm, Sun. noon-4pm; Jan.-Feb. Fri.-Sat. 10am-4pm, Sun. noon-4pm. Admission to house $4, garden $3. Both $6.) **Joint tickets** ($9) available for both the Hammond-Harwood and William Paca houses.

Follow the smell of food and the sound of tourists down Pinkney St. towards the **City Dock.** Restaurants and tacky tourist shops line the waterfront, a convenient **information kiosk** answers questions, and boats leave on maritime tours every hour during summer. Naval Academy ships (in summertime skippered by fresh-faced plebes) ply the waters. Watch the civilian yachtsmen congregate and flex—the docks easily earn their nickname, "Ego Alley."

Main Street, full of tiny shops and eateries, stretches from here back up to Church Circle. Stop by the **Maritime Museum** (268-5576), 77 Main St. at Compromise St., before heading up to the church. The building once served as a war supply center for the Continental army; today it houses temporary exhibits on 18th-century maritime Annapolis. Walter Cronkhite fans can also inquire about an audio tour of the town, narrated by the newscast king himself (open daily 9am-5pm, $7). The **Banneker-Douglass Museum** (974-2893), at 84 Franklin St. in an old church adjacent to Church Circle, houses temporary exhibits and photographs concerning African-American cultural history. (Open Tues.-Fri. 10am-3pm, Sat. noon-4pm. Free.)

From Church Circle, walk along College Ave. past St. John's St., and turn left onto the campus of **St. John's College** (founded in 1696 as King William's School). From the quad at St. John's, take College Ave. to King George St. and follow King George down to an institution whose name means Annapolis: the Naval Academy.

At the **U.S. Naval Academy,** harried, short-haired "plebes" (first-year students) in official sailor dress try desperately to remember the words of Navy fight songs while the rest of the undergraduates, "middies" (midshipmen), go about their business (which often includes bonking the plebes on the head and other, worse punishments). President Jimmy Carter graduated from Annapolis; more recently, the institution has made headlines for shamefully expelling its gay and lesbian students.

Bancroft Hall, an imposing stone structure about three blocks long, houses the entire student body, making it one of the world's largest dormitories. Its mammoth steps, stonework, and arched entryways suit its function as a cathedral of discipline. In the yard outside Bancroft Hall, witness the middies' noon lineup and formations. For good luck, kiss the bronze statue of Tecumseh that stands out front. (The rest of Bancroft Hall is closed to tourists.)

Walk to the north end of **Dahlgren Hall** to see a couple of Japanese torpedoes (they reside outside as a general reminder of enemy threat). Enter the hangar-like hall (where you'll find a gymnasium, ice rink, and café) and look up: a huge model sailing ship and a yellow water-landing biplane hang from the arched ceiling.

King Hall, the academy's gargantuan "mess," turns madhouse at lunchtime, serving the entire brigade in under four minutes. On summer Saturdays, watch wedding after wedding (sometimes one per hour) take place in the Academy's **chapel;** middies aren't allowed to marry before graduation. As the married couples leave the chapel, they walk beneath the raised swords of eight male classmates; and the woman, if she is a civilian, is greeted by a ninth with "Welcome to the Navy, Ma'am." (Open to visitors Mon.-Sat. 9am-4pm, Sun. 1-4pm.)

Elsewhere on campus, the Naval Museum in **Preble Hall** houses two rooms of naval artifacts (open Mon.-Sat. 9am-5pm, Sun. 11am-5pm; free). Walking tours of the academy begin at the **Armel-Leftwich Visitor's Center** (263-6933) located in the Halsey Field House at the end of King George St. (Call for info. on tour times. $5, seniors $4, students $3.) Throughout the summer, the academy provides entertainment for the general public, from parades and sporting events to movies and concerts. The schedule of events is published in the *Trident,* the academy's newspaper, which can be obtained for free at the visitors center.

NIGHTLIFE

Locals and tourists wander along City Dock or schmooze at local pubs. While some locals desert on the weekends for D.C. or Baltimore, other seem content to just sit on the dock of the bay. Theater-goers can check out **The Colonial Players, Inc.,**108 East St. (268-7373). Performances Thurs.-Sun. at 8pm, additional Sun. show at 2:30pm. Thurs. and Sun. $7 (seniors and students $5), Fri.-Sat. $10. Bars and taverns line downtown Annapolis, drawing crowds every night. The fact that you just had dinner at the **Middleton Tavern** shouldn't stop you from partying there later. The same is true for **New Moon Café,** where local jazz bands perform sporadically; Tuesday is poetry night 7pm-midnight ($4 cover). See **Food**, p. 247.

Ram's Head Tavern, 33 West St. (268-4545). Eclectic crowd shows up for 170 different beers and local music (Tues.-Thurs., Sat.). Open daily 11am-2am.

McGarvey's, 8 Garden St. (263-5700). Caters to a standard Annapolis mix of sailors (yum) and visitors. Open daily 11:30am-2am.

Armadillo's, 132 Dock St. (268-6680). Call their entertainment hotline at 626-1551 for info.; music starts nightly at 9:30pm. Open daily 9am-1:30am.

Marmaduke's Pub, 7th Ave at 3rd. 15 min. walk down Compromise St. across from the Eastport Bridge. Sailors flock here Wed. nights to watch videos of their races and enjoy the beer and burger special ($4.95). Open daily 11:30am-2am, weekend upstairs piano bar has $3 cover.

Buddy's Late Night Annapolis, 30 Hudson St. (266-5888). The first and only dance club in town boasts the biggest bar and dance floor in the state. Buddy's rocks to Top 40 tunes and attracts all ages and types. It's big, bright, and always busy. Nightly beer specials. 21+. Free before 10pm; cover: Wed. $3; Thurs. $3 for men (free for women), Fri.-Sat. $6. Open Wed.-Sat. 8:30pm-2am.

Sandy Point

If sitting on the dock and staring at dirty water starts to get old, hit the road (Rte. 50 to be exact) and head east for about 15 minutes (crossing the Severn River Bridge) until you see signs for **Sandy Point State Park**—it's exit 32, the last exit before the toll booth. During the summer months, for a $2 per person entrance fee, you can barbecue, picnic, swim, and rent jet skis. **Jet ski rentals** (410-757-7500) are $45 for ½ hr., $65 for a full hr. Rentals mid-May-mid-Sept., Mon.-Fri. 11am-5pm, Sat.-Sun. 10am-6pm. $250 deposit or credit card required. The Park is open every day of the year except Christmas and Thanksgiving. Call 410-974-2149 for more info.

■■■ BALTIMORE

Of the external embellishments of life there is a plenty there—as great a supply, indeed, to any rational taste, as in New York itself. But there is also something much better: a tradition of sound and comfortable living.
—H.L. Mencken, On Living in Baltimore, 1926

Although only 40 miles separate Baltimore and D.C., the two cities could be continents apart. While most sections of Washington have the groomed look of a great European city, Baltimore impresses the visitor with long rows of townhouses, as even, regular, and expensive as gold teeth in a broad smile. Maryland's famous crabs are everywhere, plastered on buildings, windows, posters, and billboards. And amidst the modern, industrial harbor are reminders of a distinguished past and a glorious present: historic stone drawbridges compete with new steel structures and the old Baltimore & Ohio Railroad contrasts with the sleek glass windowed skyline. Modern Baltimore still serves as Maryland's urban core, and old-time, shirtsleeve Bawlmer endures in the quiet limelight of Anne Tyler's novels and John Waters's films. Near the downtown skyscrapers, old ethnic neighborhoods like Little Italy front Baltimore's signature rowhouses, whose unique façades are microcosms of the larger city—polished marble stoops represent the shiny Inner Harbor, while straightforward brick fits the proud and gritty urban environs. After gaping at the National Aquarium's array of rays, be sure to explore the rest of Baltimore—the local events, the neighborhoods, and the people.

PRACTICAL INFORMATION AND ORIENTATION

Emergency: 911.

Visitor Information: Baltimore Area Visitors Centers, 300 W. Pratt St. (837-INFO or 800-282-6632), at S. Howard St. 4 blocks from Harborplace. Pick up a map, an armful of pamphlets, and a *Quick City Guide*, a quarterly glossy with excellent maps and events listings. Open daily 9am-5:30pm. An **information booth** on the west shoreline of the Inner Harbor, between the Light St. Pavilion and the Science Center, is often crowded. Open daily 9am-5:30pm.

Travelers Aid: 685-3569 (Mon.-Fri. 8am-4:30pm), 685-5874 (hotline staffed Mon.-Fri. 4:30-11pm, Sat.-Sun. 8am-11pm). Two desks are situated at the Baltimore-Washington Airport (859-7209; open Mon.-Fri. 9am-9pm, Sun. 1pm-9pm). Direct-line telephones are located at Penn Station and at the Greyhound terminal.

Baltimore-Washington International Airport (BWI): 859-7111. On I-195 off the Baltimore-Washington Expressway (I-295), about 10 mi. south of the city center. Use BWI as your gateway to Baltimore or Washington, D.C. Take MTA bus #17 to the N. Linthicum Light rail station. Airport shuttles to hotels (859-0800) run daily every ½ hr. 6am-midnight ($10 to downtown Baltimore). For D.C., **Washington Flyer** shuttles leave every 1½ hrs. 7am-8:30pm (Sat. every 2½ hrs. 8:30am-6:30pm) and drop passengers off at 16th and K St. NW (one-way $14, round-trip $25). Trains from BWI Airport run to Baltimore ($5; at $3, **MARC** trains are considerably cheaper but also slower and only run Mon.-Fri.). To Washington, D.C. ($10; MARC $4.50). BWI train office 410-672-6167.

Amtrak: Penn Station, 1500 N. Charles St. (800-872-7245), at Mt. Royal Ave. Easily accessible by bus #3 or #11 from Charles Station downtown. Trains run about every ½ hr. to: New York ($49-67, Metroliner $91), Washington D.C. ($12, Metroliner $17), and Philadelphia ($26, Metroliner $44). On weekdays, two **MARC commuter lines** connect Baltimore to Washington's Union Station (859-7400; 800-325-RAIL). The Penn line runs out of Penn Station (and stops at BWI airport), while the Camden line runs out of Camden Station, at the corner of Howard and Camden St. near Oriole Park. Both are $5.25 1-way, $9.50 round-trip. Ticket window open daily 5:30am-9:30pm, self-serve open 24 hrs. (credit card only).

Greyhound: 2 locations: downtown at 210 W. Fayette St. (752-0868, 800-231-2222), near N. Howard St.; and at 5625 O'Donnell St. (744-9311, 800-231-2222), 3 mi. east of downtown near I-95. Frequent connections to: New York (one-way

$23.50, round-trip $39), Washington, D.C. ($6, round-trip $12), and Philadelphia ($12, round-trip $20). Open 24 hrs.

Public Transport: Mass Transit Administration (MTA), 300 W. Lexington St. (recorded bus and Metro info. 539-5000, main office 333-3434, 800-543-9809), near N. Howard St. Operator available Mon.-Fri. 6am-9pm. Bus, metro, and light-rail service to most major sights in the city; service to outlying areas is more complicated. Some buses run 24 hrs. Metro operates Mon.-Fri. 5am-midnight, Sat. 6am-midnight. Light rail operates Mon.-Fri. 6am-11pm, Sat. 8am-11pm, Sun 11am-7pm. Base fare for all of these $1.25, but may be higher depending on distance traveled. Transfers 10¢. Bus #17 runs from the N. Linthicum light-rail to BWI.

Water Taxi (563-3901 or 800-658-8947), which makes stops every 8-18 min. (every 40 min. Nov.-March) at the harbor museums, Harborplace, Fells Point, Little Italy, and more, is an easy and pleasant way to travel to the main sights of Baltimore, especially in summer when service continues until 11pm or midnight. Price varies, but a pass for a full day of unlimited rides usually runs $3.25 for adults, $2.25 for kids 10 and under.

Taxi: Yellow Cab (685-1212); **G.T.P. Inc.** (to and from BWI airport $17; 859-1100).

Baltimore Trolley Tours: 752-2015. Tours and transportation to major sights in Baltimore. 1-day pass good for unlimited boarding along the 90-min. loop. Trolleys every 30 min. daily 10am-4pm in summer; limited schedule Nov.-March. Fare $12; children 5-12 $4.50, under 5 free.

Car Rental: Thrifty Car Rental, BWI Airport (859-1136), and 2042 N. Howard St. (783-0300), 9 blocks from Penn Station; also call 800-367-2277 (24 hrs.). Economy cars from $30 per weekday, $26-30 per weekend day, and $195 weekly. Unlimited mileage in MD and bordering states. Under 25 $10 extra per day. Must be 21 with a credit card. Airport branch open daily 6am-11pm.

Help Lines: Suicide Hotline (531-6677). **Sexual Assault and Domestic Violence Center** (828-6390). **Gay and Lesbian Switchboard** (837-8888). Gay bars, meetings, and special events; operators daily 7-10pm, recording all other times.

Post Office: 900 E. Fayette St. (347-4425). Open Mon.-Fri. 7:30am-9pm, Sat. 8:30am-5pm. **ZIP Code:** 21233.

Area Code: 410

Baltimore is plagued by one-way streets. Baltimore Street (which runs east a few blocks north of the Inner Harbor) and Charles Street (which runs north from the west corner of the Harbor) divide the city into quarters. Streets parallel to Baltimore St. get "West" or "East" tacked onto their names, depending on which side of Charles St. a given block is on. North-south streets get dubbed "North" or "South" according to their relation to Baltimore St. Interstates and signs deposit tourists at the **Inner Harbor,** near the corner of Pratt and Charles. The museum-heavy **Mount Vernon** neighborhood—reached by city buses #3, 9, and 11—exhibits itself up Charles St., north of the Inner Harbor, around Monument and Centre Ave. **Little Italy** hangs its hat a few blocks east of the Inner Harbor, past the Jones Falls Expressway; walk or drive east to Broadway, then turn right (south) and motor a few blocks to reach happening, bar-happy **Fells Point.**

Baltimore dangles in central Maryland, 100 mi. south of Philadelphia and about 150 mi. up the Chesapeake Bay from the Atlantic Ocean. The Jones Falls Expressway (I-83) halves the city with its southern end at the Inner Harbor, while the Baltimore Beltway (I-695) circles the city. I-95 cuts across the southwest corner of the city as a shortcut to the wide arc of that section of the Beltway. During rush hour, these interstates get slower than a whale on downers. Blue and green signs point drivers to tourist attractions. To drive from Washington, D.C. to Baltimore, take the Capital Beltway (I-495) to I-95 at exit 27 or to the Baltimore-Washington Expressway at exit 22. The two highways run roughly parallel. Take the Russell St. exit to reach the Inner Harbor. Without traffic, the trip takes less than an hour.

MOUNT VERNON
Madison Street
Monument St.
Centre St.
Hamilton St.
Franklin St.
Mulberry St.
Pleasant St.
Saratoga St.
Josephine St.
Lexington St.
Marion St.
Fayette St.
Baltimore St.
Redwood St.
Lombard St.
Pratt Street
Camden St.
Conway St.
Barre St.
Welcome St.
Lee St.
York St.
Hill
Hughes St.
Montgomery St.
Henrietta St.
Churchill St.
Warren St.
Key Highway
Dtuid Hill Ave.
Orchard St.
St. Mary St.
Pennsylvania Ave.
Linden Ave.
Howard St.
Cathedral St.
Saint Paul St.
Calvert St.
Park Ave.
Tyson St.
Eutaw St.
Jasper St.
Diamond St.
Liberty Street
Davis St.
Charles St.
Light St.
South St.
Commerce St.
Water St.
Greene St.
Paca St.
Penn St.
Emory St.
Washington Blvd.
Sharp St.
Peach St.
Leadenhall
Hanover St.
Russell St.
Greyhound Bus Terminal
Penn Station
LEXINGTON MARKET
CHARLES CENTER
M
Baltimore Arena
Camden Station
Orioles Stadium (Camden Yards)
Inner Harbor
83
395
1
2
3
4
5
6
7
8
9
14
15
19

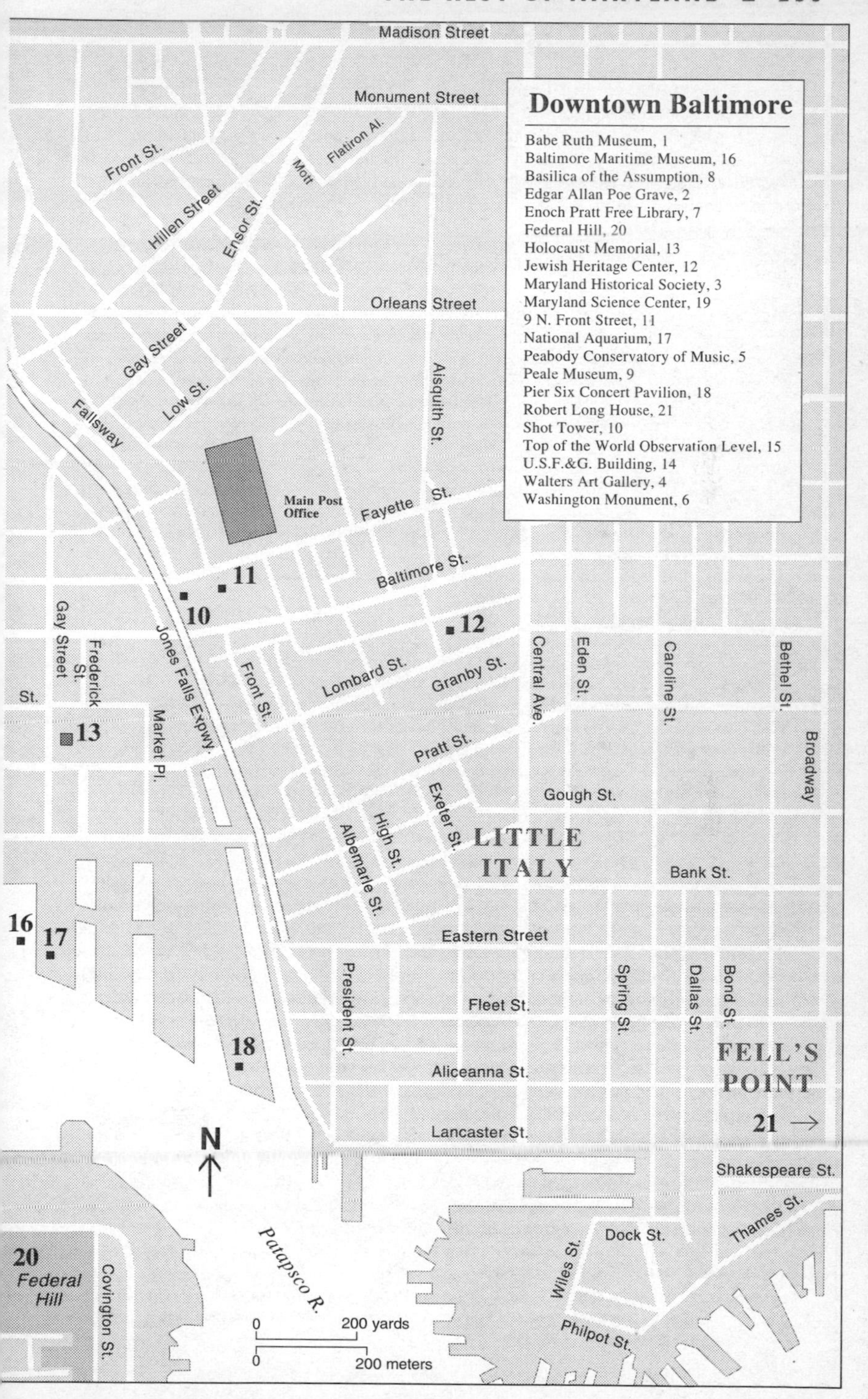
Downtown Baltimore
Babe Ruth Museum, 1
Baltimore Maritime Museum, 16
Basilica of the Assumption, 8
Edgar Allan Poe Grave, 2
Enoch Pratt Free Library, 7
Federal Hill, 20
Holocaust Memorial, 13
Jewish Heritage Center, 12
Maryland Historical Society, 3
Maryland Science Center, 19
9 N. Front Street, 11
National Aquarium, 17
Peabody Conservatory of Music, 5
Peale Museum, 9
Pier Six Concert Pavilion, 18
Robert Long House, 21
Shot Tower, 10
Top of the World Observation Level, 15
U.S.F.&G. Building, 14
Walters Art Gallery, 4
Washington Monument, 6
Madison Street
Monument Street
Front St.
Flatiron Al.
Mott
Hillen Street
Ensor St.
Orleans Street
Gay Street
Low St.
Fallsway
Aisquith St.
Main Post Office
Fayette St.
Baltimore St.
Gay Street
Frederick St.
Jones Falls Expwy.
Front St.
Lombard St.
Granby St.
Central Ave.
Eden St.
Caroline St.
Bethel St.
St.
Market Pl.
Pratt St.
Broadway
Gough St.
Exeter St.
High St.
Albemarle St.
LITTLE ITALY
Bank St.
Eastern Street
President St.
Fleet St.
Spring St.
Dallas St.
Bond St.
Aliceanna St.
FELL'S POINT
Lancaster St.
Shakespeare St.
Thames St.
Dock St.
Wiles St.
Philpot St.
Patapsco R.
Federal Hill
Covington St.
N
0 200 yards
0 200 meters
1
10
11
12
13
16
17
18
20
21

ACCOMMODATIONS AND CAMPING

Expensive chain hotels dominate the Inner Harbor; for more reasonable options, write to **Maryland Bed and Breakfast Association,** Box 23324, Baltimore, MD 21203 or call **Amanda's Bed and Breakfast Reservation Service,** 1428 Park Ave. (225-0001, 800-899-7533). The personalized service will match you with B&Bs in private homes, small inns, or yachts that suit your needs, whether you're allergic to cats or would like to have a private bath. Rates start at $50 a night. Reservations are recommended. (Call Mon.-Fri. 8:30am-5:30pm, Sat. 8:30am-noon.)

Baltimore International Youth Hostel (AYH/HI), 17 W. Mulberry St. (576-8880), at Cathedral St. in the historic Mount Vernon neighborhood. Near bus and Amtrak terminals. Take MTA bus #3 or 11 along Charles St. Elegant, centrally located 19th-century brownstone provides 48 beds in spacious dorm rooms, as well as full kitchen and laundry services. Linger in the lounge with marble fireplaces, a TV, and a baby grand piano. Friendly managers are a great source of information about Baltimore. Window-unit A/C in bedrooms and fans aplenty in common areas. Max. stay 3 nights, longer with manager's approval. Curfew 11pm, but house keys available for rent ($2). Members $13, non-members $16. Free baggage storage and linens. Mastercard and Visa accepted. Reservations recommended, especially in the summer. Don't walk alone near here at night.

Duke's Motel, 7905 Pulaski Highway (686-0400), in Rosedale off the Beltway. Don't worry about the bulletproof glass in the front office—all the motels around here have it. A gem amidst a slew of less desirable motels, and probably the only place worth staying at on the Pulaski Hwy. motel strip. Simple, clean rooms with A/C, carpeting, and cable. Suitable only for people with cars. Singles $41, doubles $46. $2 key deposit and ID required.

Quality Inn Inner Harbor, 1701 Russell St. (727-3400, 800-221-2222), near the Beltway in unfashionable South Baltimore, about 1 mi. from Inner Harbor. Standard rooms, free cable, and pool. Complimentary continental breakfast. Free parking. Don't walk here alone at night; best for people with cars. Singles $60, doubles $70. Weekend rates: singles $65, doubles $75. Occasional $40 tourist rate (with coupon—get one at the visitors center; subject to availability).

Mount Vernon Hotel, 24 W. Franklin St. (727-2000), near Cathedral St. in Mount Vernon neighborhood. Standard, comfortable rooms in a terrific location. A/C included. Singles from $70, doubles from $85. Parking $6 per day.

Capitol KOA, 768 Cecil Ave. (410-923-2771, 987-7477; fax 923-3169), near Millersville. Half-way between D.C. and Baltimore. See **Camping** on p. 76 for info.

FOOD

Virginia may be for lovers, but Maryland is for crabs—every restaurant, convenience store, diner, cafeteria, and mom (well, almost) serves crab cakes.

The **Light Street Pavilion** at **Harborplace,** Pratt and Light St. (332-4191), has multifarious foodstuffs to suit every tourist—that's why they all come here. **Phillips'** serves some of the best crab cakes in Baltimore; buy them cheaper from the cafeteria-style Phillips' Express line. (Open Mon.-Sat. 10am-9pm, Sun. 10am-6pm.)

Lexington Market, 400 W. Lexington (685-6169) at Eutaw St., provides an endless variety of produce, fresh meat, and seafood, as well as cheaper food stalls than at Harborplace. (Open Mon.-Sat. 8:30am-6pm. Take the subway to Lexington Station or bus #7.) **Cross Street Market,** between S. Charles and Light St. in South Baltimore, provides one of the best raw bars in the city along with produce and such. In Fells Point, the two-building **Broadway Market** sits square in the middle of S. Broadway St., about three blocks from the dock. (Open Mon.-Sat. 7am-6pm.) Old South Baltimore families still run many stalls: the sixth generation bakes fresh bread at **Muhly's Bakery,** 1115 S. Charles St., though no longer for 5¢.

Little Italy and Fells Point

Obrycki's, 1727 E. Pratt St. (732-6399), near Broadway; take bus #7 or 10. Arguably the most famous crab house in Baltimore, with some of the city's best crabs served any and every way—steamed, broiled, sauteed, or in crab cakes. Save up your pennies and an appetite and come feast on a dozen hard-shell crabs ($20-46 depending on size). Crab cakes $13.25. Expect lines on weekends. Don't walk here alone at night. Open Mon.-Sat. noon-11pm, Sun. noon-9:30pm.

Bertha's Dining Room, 734 S. Broadway (327-5795), at Lancaster. Obey the bumper stickers and "Eat Bertha's Mussels." Gorge yourself on the black-shelled bivalves ($7.50) while sitting at butcher-block tables, and don't miss the chunky vegetable mussel chowder (cup $1.75). Locals of all ages crowd in to hear jazz bands play Tues.-Wed. and Fri.-Sat. nights. 12 kinds of beer and ale ($1.50-6). Kitchen open Sun.-Thurs. 11:30am-11pm, Fri.-Sat. 11:30am-midnight. Bar until 2am. Entrance on Lancaster St. Wheelchair access.

Amicci's, 231 S. High St. (528-1096). The best bargain in Little Italy. Slick black-and-white walls hold up slick black-and-white photographs while paisley tablecloths hold up heaping portions of excellent Italian fare. The menu lists 11 pasta dishes under $10, and not a single dish over $13. Glow board announces daily specials ($9-12). Open Sun.-Thurs. noon-9pm, Fri.-Sat. noon-11pm.

Café Mundo, 1623 Thames St. (675-7105). The Eurodecor makes for a comfy dessert café with pastries made on the premises ($2-4). Cool down and caffeinate with an iced cappucino ($1.75) or snack on an elegant sandwich ($4-5). Open Sun.-Thurs. 10:30am-6pm, Fri.-Sat. 10am-midnight.

Luigi Petti, 1002 Eastern Ave. (685-0055), near S. Exeter. One of Little Italy's most attractive restaurants. Mama Marie's homemade pastas $11-13, shrimp scampi $7.50. Other entrees around $10. Outdoor patio and bar. Lunch menu available Mon.-Sat. until 3pm. Open Mon.-Thurs. 11:30am-11pm, Fri. 11:30am-1am, Sat. 12:30pm-1am, Sun. 12:30-10pm. Bar open daily until 2am.

Fells Point Diner, 435 S. Broadway (327-0715), at Eastern Ave. If you need a break from the more expensive restaurants in Fells Point, the pink booths and long pink counter of this clean, cheap diner will be a welcome sight. Daily specials from $6. Breakfast specials $2-5. Subs, sandwiches, as well as larger seafood and Middle Eastern entrees. Open Sun.-Fri. 6:30am-3am, Fri. and Sat. nights 24 hrs.

Lee's Homemade Ice Cream, 821 S. Broadway (276-4556), at the corner of Thames St. A Baltimore institution with a national claim to fame: they invented "cookies and cream." Cones $1.80. Skyscraping sundaes from $3. Open Sun.-Thurs. 11am-11pm, Fri.-Sat. 11am-1am. Winter hours may vary.

Mount Vernon

Mount Vernon manges to squeeze in a tremendous number of restaurants among its art galleries and conservatories, and virtually all are to be found on N. Charles St. within the blocks on either side of Baltimore's Washington Monument.

Hellmands, 806 N. Charles St. (752-0311). Don't let the white linen on the tables frighten you away: there's nary a thing on the menu over $10. Acclaimed by some local magazines as one of the ten best restaurants in the city, Hellmands serves exquisite Afghan dishes in which meat garnishes vegetables and yogurt sauces garnish all. To start, try the *kaddo borani,* pan-fried and baked baby pumpkin in a yogurt-garlic sauce. Open Sun.-Thurs. 5-10pm, Fri.-Sat. 5-11pm.

Buddies, 313 N. Charles St. (332-4200). Extensive salad bar with over 80 items ($3 per lb.; Mon.-Fri. 11am-2:30pm) and pile-driving sandwiches ($5-7). Jazz quartet draws in loyal locals and visitors of all ages (Thurs.-Sat. 9:30pm-1am). Domestic draft $1.70, mixed drinks $2.75. Happy hour Mon.-Fri. 4-7pm with 2-for-1 drinks. Wed. is Karaoke night (beginning at 8:30pm). Free delivery within a limited area ($10 min.). Open Mon.-Thurs. 4am-10pm, Fri. 11am-2am, Sat. 1pm-2am.

Kristo's, 206 W. Saratoga St. (727-3378) close to the AYH/HI hostel. Great, cheap restaurant mainly does takeout but has a small eat-in counter. An 8-in. personal pizza with 2 toppings and a coke only $3.50 (with coupon from takeout menu). Half-subs $3-5, whole $6-9. Sandwiches $2-4, pasta $4-6. Free delivery within a limited area ($6 min.). Be careful in this area at night. Open Mon.-Sat. 11am-2am, Sun. 11am-11pm.

Louie's Bookstore Café, 518 N. Charles St. (962-1222), just up the street from the youth hostel. In front, an upscale bookstore flaunts extensive sections on music and literature. In back, a lively café/bar/restaurant mixes well-tailored concert-goers with scruffy indie-rock tourists. Nightly live classical music (6:30-8:30pm). Lunch is cheap; the dinner scene is groovier. Sandwiches and burgers around $4-6. Entrees $8-10. Vegetarian dishes, too. Open Mon.-Fri. 11:30am-midnight, Sat. 11:30am-1:30am, Sun. 10:30am-midnight.

Buttery Restaurant, 531 N. Charles St. (837-2494), near E. Centre St. Great diner with cheap eats all day. Pancakes $2-4. Hamburger $1.40, sandwich platters $2.40-4.35. Open 24 hrs.

Akbar, 823 N. Charles St. (539-0944). Excellent Indian food served at not-so-excellent prices (entrees $10-15). For value, hit the $7 all-you-can-eat lunch buffet (Mon.-Fri. 11:30am-2:30pm). Wide selection of Indian breads ($1.50-2.75). Open Mon.-Thurs. 11:30am-2:30pm and 5-11pm, Fri. 11:30am-2:30pm and 5-11:30pm, Sat. noon-3pm and 5-11:30pm, Sun. noon-3pm and 5-11pm.

Farther Out

Ikaros, 4805 Eastern Ave. (633-3750), 2 mi. east of downtown; take bus #10. This spawn of East Baltimore's Greek community is perfect for cheapskate romantics. Try *avgolemono* soup (with egg, lemon, beef, and rice, $2.25) and spinach and feta pies ($2.85). Greek salads big enough for a meal ($6-6.75). Other specialties are *mousaka* ($8.50) and *kalamari* ($10.75). Open Sun.-Mon. and Wed.-Thurs. 11am-10pm, Fri.-Sat. 11am-11pm.

Bo Brooks, 5415 Belair Rd. (488-8144), exit 32a off the Beltway. Maybe this popular eatery does have Baltimore's "Best Steamed Crabs" ($15-40 per dozen) and crab cakes (from $6); but to see the tacky white dining room with orange plastic chairs, you wouldn't expect it. Bo knows marketing techniques, as the T-shirts ("Bo Knows Crabs") prove. Draft domestic $1.50. Open Mon.-Thurs. 11:30am-3pm and 5-10pm, Fri. 11:30am-3pm and 5-11pm, Sat. 5-11pm, Sun. 3:30-9:30pm.

Haussner's, 3242 Eastern Ave. (327-8365), at S. Clinton; take bus #10. An East Baltimore institution. 700 original oil paintings crowd the huge dining room, including some copies of Rembrandt, Gainsborough, Whistler, and Homer. Central European cuisine like fresh pig knuckle and *Sauerbraten* (meat stewed in vinegar and juices) $10.60, sandwiches $3.75-12; big portions. Try the strawberry pie ($3.75), or get other freshly baked goods to go. Long pants preferred after 3pm; lines for dinner on winter weekends. Open Tues.-Sat. 11am-10pm.

SIGHTS

Inner Harbor

Most tourists start at the Inner Harbor, and all too many finish there. Baltimore's generally gray and functional harbor terminates with a colorful bang in a five-square-block body of water bounded on three sides by the National Aquarium, Harborplace, the Maryland Science Museum, and a bevy of boardable old and new ships. A full-day **Water Taxi Pass** is ideal for a day of sightseeing in and around the harbor area. The **National Aquarium,** Pier 3, 501 E. Pratt St. (576-3800), makes the whole Inner Harbor worthwhile. More impressive than its similarly named sibling in D.C., this aquarium's multi-level exhibits and tanks show off rare fish, fat fish, red fish, and blue fish. Best of all, the museum's intelligent spiral lay-out means that it's impossible to miss any of the aquatic goodies as you ascend toward the 157-ft. glass-pyramid roof. As you enter, "Wings in the Water" lets you peer down on some 50 species of rays (including the playful manta) before you begin your ascent. Levels two, three, and four spiral over central tanks and through various aquatic communities, including Atlantic sea cliffs inhabited by cheeky puffins and a lush kelp forest. The Children's Cove on level four lets kids and adults handle intertidal marine animals in the Touching Pool. Level five (inside the glass pyramid) is a steamy tropical rainforest; piranhas, parrots, and a pair of two-toed sloths peer through the dense foliage. Exit down a remarkable four-story series of ramps inside a 13-ft.-deep, doughnut-shaped tank simulating a coral reef and inhabited by sharks of all shapes and sizes—it's like scuba-diving without getting wet. From ground level, proceed through an enclosed bridge to the Marine Mammal Pavilion, which contains dolphins and whales, with an amphitheater featuring performances à la Sea World. To avoid long lines for Aquarium tickets, arrive before 9am; on weekends and other busy days, you will have to buy a ticket from the booth outside and return at the time printed on the ticket (usually ½ hr. later, but up to 3½ hrs. in summer). Tickets can also be purchased in advance from TicketMaster (481-7328 before 3pm in Baltimore, 202-432-7328 in Washington, D.C.). Expect to spend three hours in the Aquarium. Excellent disabled access through separate entrance; call ahead. (Open March-Oct. Sun.-Thurs. 9am-6pm, Fri.-Sat. 9am-8pm; Nov.-Feb. Sat.-Thurs. 10am-5pm, Fri. 10am-8pm. Check aquarium lobby for slide shows and feeding times. Admission $11.50, seniors $9.50, children 3-11 $7.50, under 3 free; Oct.-March Fri. 5-8pm admission $3.50.)

Several ships bob in the harbor by the aquarium; most of them belong to the **Baltimore Maritime Museum** (396-3453), at Piers III and IV. Board the U.S.S. Torsk submarine—it sank the last Japanese combatant ships of WWII—the lightship Chesapeake, and the Coast Guard cutter Taney while you wait for your entry time at the Aquarium. (Open Mon.-Fri. 10am-5pm, Fri.-Sat. 9:30am-6pm; winter Fri.-Sun. 9:30am-5pm. Admission $4.50, seniors $4, children under 13 $1.75, active military free.) The musty frigate **Constellation** (539-1797) generally anchors in the Inner Harbor as well, showing walk-through visitors the joys and travails of life on an old sailing ship. The first commissioned ship of the U.S. Navy, the Constellation—whose sister ship is the Constitution, harbored in Boston—sailed from 1797 to 1945, serving in the War of 1812, the Civil War, and as a flagship of the Pacific Fleet during World War II. (Open daily 10am-5pm; winter 10am-4pm. Admission $2.50, seniors $2, ages 6-15 $1, active military $1, children under 6 free.)

If imitation is the sincerest form of flattery, **Harborplace** is Baltimore's most flattered building. When then-mayor Schaefer and developer James Rouse decided to make the Inner Harbor tourist-friendly, they started by building an air-conditioned shopping mall at the water's edge; Harborplace is the first and maybe the best of the pier-pavilions, which are now also in New York, Detroit, and San Francisco. Stop by Harborplace's Pratt Street and Light Street Pavilions, and the Gallery, across the street on the corner of Pratt and Light St., for a little wharfside shopping and air-conditioned bliss (332-4191; open Mon.-Sat. 10am-9pm, Sun. 10am-6pm).

At the Inner Harbor's far edge lurks the **Maryland Science Center,** 601 Light St. (685-5225), where children can learn basic principles of chemistry and physics cleverly disguised as hands-on games and activities. The Energy Place tires them out with pulleys and levers, while the Structures exhibit allows children to explore architecture and the arts of building. The IMAX Theater's five-story screen and planetarium stun audiences. Both are included in the price of admission. On summer weekends, come in the morning before the lines get too long. (Open Memorial Day-Labor Day Mon.-Thurs. 10am-5pm, Fri. and Sun. 10am-7:30pm, Sat. 10am-8:30pm; Sept.-May Mon.-Fri. 10am-5pm, Sat.-Sun. 10am-6pm. Admission $8.50, ages 4-17, seniors, and military $6.50, under 3 free.)

Some of Baltimore's best-restored homes lie to the west of Federal Hill. **Montgomery Street** gives perhaps the best example, with its grand façades and cobblestone. To the east along Key Highway, dilapidated warehouses loom along the shore. The former oyster cannery at 1415 Key Highway holds the **Baltimore Museum of Industry** (727-4808) in one of its warehouses. (Take bus #1 or the Water Taxi.) Guides will lead you through a working belt-driven machine shop, let you print a handbill on an 1880 press, and pass around a weighty pair of shears once used in Baltimore's dominant clothing trade. (Open Tues.-Fri. and Sun. noon-5pm, Sat. 10am-5pm; Sept.-May Tues.-Fri. 10am-5pm, Sat. 10am-5pm. Admission $3.50, students and seniors $2.50, families $12.)

Fort McHenry National Monument (962-4290), located at the foot of E. Fort Ave. off Rte. 2 (Hanover St.) and Lawrence Ave. (take bus #1), commemorates the fort's victory against British forces in the War of 1812, a triumph which inspired Francis Scott Key to write "The Star Spangled Banner." A flag flies over the fort all day, but *the* flag hangs in the Smithsonian Museum of American History in Washington. Take the #1 bus or a narrated cruise from Finger Pier in the Inner Harbor (round-trip $5, children 2-11 $3.75). (Open daily 8am-8pm; Sept.-May 8am-5pm. Admission $2, seniors and under 17 free. Wheelchair access; film close-captioned for the hearing-impaired. Ample parking.)

West Baltimore

A few museums dwell among the rowhouses west of the Inner Harbor. The **Babe Ruth Birthplace and Baltimore Orioles Museum,** 216 Emory St. (727-1539; take bus #31), off the 600 block of W. Pratt, remembers the "Sultan of Swat." Some exhibits pitch to diehards only, like the alcove recalling each of his 714 home runs. Others swing at a wider audience with Maryland baseball memorabilia, including a series of rotating exhibits on Baltimore's beloved Orioles. (Open daily 10am-5pm, on game nights until 7pm; Nov.-March 10am-4pm. Admission $5, seniors $3.50, ages 5-16 $2, under 4 free.)

Babe Ruth would be proud to call a shot or two at the sparkling new **Oriole Park at Camden Yards** (547-6234), just west of the Inner Harbor at Eutaw and Camden St. Flying in the face of the recent sporting trend to build large, impersonal stadiums on the outskirts of cities, Baltimore decided to put up an intimate, vintage-style stadium on an old industrial yard in the heart of downtown. If the O's aren't playing an afternoon home game, you can take a behind-the-scenes tour of the stadium, including the clubhouses, dugouts, press box, and scoreboard. (Tours leave hourly Mon.-Fri. 11am-2pm, Sat. 10am-2pm, Sun. at 12:30 and 2pm. Admission $5, seniors and children under 12 $4.)

Itself once a station for the Baltimore & Ohio Railroad, the **B&O Railroad Museum,** 901 W. Pratt St. (752-2490; take bus #31), looks out on train tracks where dining cars, Pullman sleepers, and mail cars park themselves for your touring frenzy. Inside the museum, three films chug through the history of railroads. The enormous Roundhouse captures historic trains and full-scale replicas thereof, including the 1829 "Tom Thumb," the first American steam-driven locomotive. Don't miss the extensive model-train display. (Open daily 10am-5pm. Admission $6, seniors $5, children 5-12 $3, under 5 free. Train rides on weekends cost an additional $2. Trains parked outside may always be toured for free.)

The **H.L. Mencken House,** 1524 Hollins St. (396-7997) near Gilmore St., reached by bus #2 or 31. Commemorative for the wit whose *American Spectator* improved the vocabularies and soured the outlooks of thousands of 1920s readers. (Open Sat. 10am-5pm, Sun. noon-5pm. Other times by appointment only. Tours Sat.-Sun. on the hour. Admission $2, seniors and children 4-18 $1.50, under 4 free.)

Cognac and Roses

A short-lived, mustached, opium-addicted 1830s author, Edgar Allan Poe virtually invented the horror tale and the detective story. His most famous works include *The Tell-Tale Heart* and *The Pit and the Pendulum.* He also penned macabre, extravagantly vacant poems like *The Raven* and *Annabelle Lee.* Poe wrote for money. He never envisioned his stories would be lauded as innovative and captivating; he considered them trash.

You probably won't hear a beating heart at the **Edgar Allan Poe Grave** where the divine Edgar sleeps evermore in the Westminster Churchyard (706-7228), at Fayette and Greene St. (Guided tours every 1st and 3rd Fri. evening at 6:30pm and Sat. morning at 10am. Reservations required. Tour $4, under 13 and seniors $2.) Every year on the anniversary of Poe's death (Oct. 7, 1849), a mysterious visitor dressed in black decorates his grave with cognac and roses. (Cemetery open during daylight hours.) Edgar Allan Poe came into this world at the **Edgar Allan Poe House** (396-7932), in a somewhat seedy area at 203 N. Amity St., near Saratoga St. (bus #15 or 23). The tour ushers Poe-heads through the writer's biography and around the tell-tale original furniture. (Poe house open Wed.-Sat. noon-3:45pm; Aug.-Sept. Sat. noon-3:45pm. Admission $3, under 13 $1.)

East Baltimore

In the eastern section of downtown, the **City Life Museums** line up in **"Museum Row"** at 800 E. Lombard St. (396-3523). On your way there, peer up at the **Shot Tower** at the corner of E. Fayette St. and Jones Falls Expwy. The Shot Tower looks like a huge smokestack; molten lead, dropped from the top, shaped itself into shotgun pellets as it fell and cooled. Enter the City Life complex through the first of the museums—**Carroll Mansion** (396-3523), which belonged to Charles Carroll, signer of the *Declaration of Independence,* depicts the lifestyle of a mid-19th-century upper-class family. In contrast, **1840 House,** the rowhouse next door, was home to a craftsman's family during the same time period. The **Center for Urban Archaeology** explores the methods archaeologists use to uncover the lipstick traces of a city's history. One of the center's more famous digs turned up the foundations of one of Baltimore's oldest and largest breweries—practically in the center's own backyard. You can visit the malty ruins in **Brewers Park,** right across Lombard St.; pick up an explanatory pamphlet at the center. (Open Tues.-Sat. 10am-5pm, Sun. noon-5pm; winter Tues.-Sun. 8am-4:30pm. Admission $5 to all Museum Row sites, children 4-18 and seniors $3.50, under 4 free. A $6 package includes admission to all Museum Row sights as well as the Peale Museum and Mencken House.)

Keep an eye out for City Life's new exhibition space, **The Balaustein Center.** Expected to open in April 1996, it features displays on Baltimore's social history.

A few blocks north of Museum Row sits a City Life straggler—the **Peale Museum,** 225 Holliday St. (396-1149). Portrait painter Rembrandt Peale built the museum in honor of his father Charles Wilson Peale in 1814, making it the oldest museum building in the U.S. A permanent exhibit of more than 40 portraits painted by the Peale family (Rembrandt was just the most famous son) as well as some traveling exhibits are housed there. (Open Tues.-Sat. 10am-5pm, Sun. noon-5pm. Admission $2, children 4-18 and seniors $1.50, under 4 free.)

The **Jewish Heritage Center** is a three-building complex located at 15 Lloyd St. (732-6400). On the left, the **Lloyd Street Synagogue,** built in 1845, was Maryland's first synagogue; the **B'nai Israel Synagogue,** the building on the far right, was founded in 1876 to preserve Orthodox religious practices; and between the two synagogues, the **Jewish Historical Society of Maryland** has established a library and museum to house documents, photographs, and objects reflecting the history of Maryland's Jewish community. The center makes its home in the heart of East Baltimore, where Maryland's first Jews settled. (Open Tues.-Thurs. and Sun. noon-4pm, other times by appointment. Library open by appointment. Admission $2, kids free.) A few blocks away on a hillside at Gay and Water St., the concrete **Holocaust Memorial** remembers the six million Jews who died in concentration camps during WWII. On the other side of the hill, facing Lombard St., a statue of flames engulfing the bodies of the Nazis' victims will shock you, especially after the less visceral symbolism of the memorial.

From Baltimore's historic districts, take bus #7 or 10 from Pratt St. to Albemarle St. to reach **Little Italy,** or ride the same buses to Broadway and walk down four blocks to **Fells Point.**

Mount Vernon

The Mount Vernon neighborhood, a mix of hip and stiff-upper-lip, is one of Baltimore's cultural cores. Its center is Baltimore's own **Washington Monument,** designed by Robert Mills, who later planned the more famous one in D.C. The older monument shows a 16-ft.-tall, toga-sporting General Washington resigning his commission as commander of the Continental Army. Vertiginously carved atop a 160-ft. column, the statue suggests that Washington never lost his poise. You may climb the 228 steps to the top for a view of the surrounding neighborhood and, in the distance, the Inner Harbor. (Open Wed.-Sun. 10am-4pm. Free. Take bus #3 or 31 up N. Charles St. to reach the sights in this area.) A few blocks south of the Washington Monument, the **Basilica of the Assumption** basks at the corner of Cathedral and Mulberry St. Benjamin Latrobe, who helped design the U.S. Capitol, planned the

Basilica in 1806. The first Roman Catholic church in the United States, it mixes Greek Revival lines with an octagonal base and Kremlin-style twin onion domes. No one knows how the domes got there, since Latrobe's original plans called for round towers. (Open Mon.-Fri. 7am-3:45pm, Sat.-Sun. 7am-6:30pm. Free tours available at noon on Sun. Call 727-3564 to arrange for other times.)

Baltimore's best museum, the **Walters Art Gallery,** 600 N. Charles St. at Centre (547-9000), keeps one of the largest private collections in the world, spanning 50 centuries in three buildings. The 19th-century collection—mostly paintings—congregates on the 4th floor of the 1974 building and includes a small but worthwhile Impressionist collection featuring Manet's *At the Café* and Monet's *Springtime.* The remaining floor space—and there's a lot of it—holds later additions to the collection, including a superb ancient art collection, two Fabergé eggs, and a 4th-century Byzantine vase carved from a single piece of agate. Like other museums of this scope, the Walters is too large to be seen in its entirety; pick up a map and trace out a battle plan. The museum's biggest deal is the Ancient Art collection on the second level, with sculptures, jewelry, and metalwork from Egypt, Greece, and Rome. Seven marble sarcophagi with intricate relief carvings are of a type found in only one other collection, that of the National Museum in Rome. The third floor holds medieval art, especially jewelry and metalwork, from the Byzantine, Romanesque, and Gothic periods. Paintings on the third and fourth floors give a nod to every European school between the 12th and the 19th centuries. Try not to miss the Hackerman House, the flashy addition to the Walters on the third floor. Rooms filled with dark-wood furniture, patterned rugs, and plush velvet curtains accumulate art from China, Korea, Japan, India, and Southeast Asia. The early Buddhist sculptures from China are very rare, as are the Japanese decorative arts of the late-18th and 19th centuries. Some of the finest examples of the often-copied Ming Dynasty Peachbloom Vases can be found here. The Gallery houses the **Walters Film House,** screening new and classic independent and foreign films on Fri. at 7:30pm. (Open Tues.-Sun. 11am-5pm. Admission $3, seniors $2, students and children under 18 free; free on Sat. before noon. Tours Wed. 12:30pm and Sun. 2pm.)

Mount Vernon's artistic and commercial communities join forces at **"First Thursdays,"** neighborhood festivals of public music, art, and extended shopping hours that occur 5-7:30pm on the first Thursday of every month.

The Johns Hopkins University

Approximately 3 mi. north of the harbor on N. Charles St. (bus #3, 9, or 11), **Johns Hopkins University** spreads out from 33rd St. The beautiful campus lies on a 140-acre wooded lot that was originally the Homewood estate of Charles Carroll, Jr., the son of a signer of the *Declaration of Independence.* Free tours of the campus are available at the Office of Admissions in Garland Hall. (Mon.-Fri. 10am, noon, and 3pm. Call 516-8171 to confirm times.) Two historic houses administered by the university also lie on or near the campus. **Homewood** (516-5589), the elegant house belonging to Carroll, displays 18th- and 19th-century furnishings, some original to the house; **Evergreen House** (516-0341), seated on 26 acres a mile north of the main campus at 4545 N. Charles St., shows the mansion, private theater, carriage house, and gardens of Ambassador John Work Garrett and family. (Homewood open Tues.-Sat. 11am-4pm, Sun. noon-4pm; admission $5, Hopkins students and under 12 free; tours hourly 10am-3pm. Evergreen open Mon.-Fri. 10am-4pm, Sun. 1-4pm; admission $5, Hopkins students free; tours hourly 10am-3pm.) The **Lacrosse Hall of Fame Museum,** 113 West University Parkway (235-6882), squats at the end of the Johns Hopkins Lacrosse fields. (Open Mon.-Fri. 9am-5pm; March-May Mon.-Fri. 9am-5pm, Sat. 10am-3pm. Admission $2, students $1.) A stone's throw from the lacrosse museum, on San Martin Dr., sits the **Space Telescope Science Institute,** where scientists navigate and monitor the oft-maligned (but recently redeemed) Hubble Space Telescope. There are no public tours—a gaggle of astronomers at computers is about all there'd be to see—but you can pop into the lobby and admire the scale model of the space scope as well as a monitor displaying its current orbital position and location.

To the west of campus at N. Charles and 31st St., the **Baltimore Museum of Art** (396-7100) picks up where the Walters leaves off, exhibiting a fine collection of Americana and modern art, including several pieces by Andy Warhol. The collection also impresses with works by Matisse, Picasso, Renoir, and Van Gogh. Two adjacent **sculpture gardens** of 20th-century art make wonderful picnic grounds. (Open Wed.-Fri. 10am-4pm, Sat.-Sun. 11am-6pm. Admission $5.50, students and seniors $3.50, ages 7-18 $1.50, under 7 free. Thurs. free. Metered parking available. Wheelchairs available.) In residence at the museum, the **Baltimore Film Forum** shows classic and current American, foreign, and independent films on Thursdays and Fridays at 8pm (admission $5, students and seniors $4); pick up a schedule at the museum or call 889-1993.

The Baltimore Zoo (366-5466) off of I-83, exit 7, is proud of its new Chimpanzee Forest exhibit with swinging monkeys and snapping crocodiles. It also features a spectacular Palm Tree Conservatory, and a lake surrounded by lush greenery. The zoo features elephants in a simulated savannah, Siberian tigers, and a waterfall. The Children's Zoo imports farm animals and animals from the Maryland wilds, like otters and crafty woodchucks. Children can also ride a carousel and a "zoo choo" train (rides $1.25). (Zoo open Mon.-Fri. 10am-4pm, Sat.-Sun. 10am-5:30pm; everything closes at 4pm in winter. Admission $7.50, seniors and ages 2-15 $4, under 2 free.)

ENTERTAINMENT & NIGHTLIFE

The **Pier Six Concert Pavilion** (625-4230) at—drumroll, please—Pier 6 at the Inner Harbor presents big-name musical acts at night from late July to the end of September. Get tickets at the pavilion or through TeleCharge (625-1400, 800-638-2444) during the summer ($15-30). Sit on Pier 5, near Harborplace, and eavesdrop for free. The **Baltimore Symphony Orchestra** plays at Meyerhoff Symphony Hall, 1212 Cathedral St. (783-8000), from Sept. to May and during their July Summerfest. (Tickets $15-45; box office open Mon.-Fri. 10am-6pm, Sat.-Sun. noon-5pm, and 1 hr. before performance.) The Lyric Opera House down the street at 140 W. Mt. Royal, near Cathedral St. (727-6000), hosts the **Baltimore Opera Company** from Oct. to April. Broadway hits get a tune-up from Oct. through July at the **Morris Mechanic Theatre,** 25 Hopkins Plaza at Baltimore and N. Charles St. (625-1400). All these venues are wheelchair-friendly.

The **Theatre Project,** 45 W. Preston St. near Maryland St. (752-8558), experiments with theater, poetry, music, and/or dance Wed. to Sat. at 8pm and Sunday at 3pm. (Ticket prices $5-14.) Box office open Tues. noon-5pm, Wed.-Sat. 1-9pm, Sun. noon-4pm. Call to charge tickets.) The **Arena Players** (728-6500), a black theater group, show musicals, comedies, drama, and dance at 801 McCullough St. at Martin Luther King, Jr. Blvd. The **Left Bank Jazz Society** (466-0600) sponsors jazz shows Sept.-May; call for schedules and information.

The **Showcase of Nations Ethnic Festivals** (837-4636, 800-282-6632) celebrates Baltimore's ethnic neighborhoods with a different culture each week from June through Sept. Though somewhat generic, the fairs are always fun, hawking international fare along with the inescapable crab cakes and beer. Most events happen at Festival Hall, at W. Pratt and Sharp St.

The beloved **Baltimore Orioles** now play at their new stadium at Camden Yards, just a few blocks from the Inner Harbor at the corner of Russell and Camden St. Bawlmer holds its breath for the yearly ups and downs of the O's with an attention very few cities can equal.

Bars and Clubs

Baltimore Brewing Co., 104 Albermarle St. (837-5000), just west of the Inner Harbor on the outskirts of Little Italy. Brewmaster Theo de Groen has captured the hearts and livers of Baltimoreans with his original and distinctive lagers, brewed right on the premises in the large brass tuns that loom behind the bar. The Weizen and Märzen styles are especially good, but keep an eye out for the spicy seasonals. Happy hour daily 4-7pm with $2 ½-liters of beer. Specializes in rib-sticking German fare ($7.25-13), although they offer a number of cheaper sandwiches and snacks. Open Mon.-Thurs. 11am-11pm, Fri.-Sat. 11am-midnight.

Cat's Eye Pub, 1730 Thames St. (276-9866), in Fells Point. *Playboy* thinks this is the best bar in Fells Point, and so do the regulars who pack it every night for live blues, jazz, folk, or traditional Irish music (beginning at 9pm). There's no cover, but drink prices rise when the band strikes it up. Over 25 different drafts and 60 bottled beers. Bands every night and twice Sat.-Sun. Happy hour 4-7pm brings slight price reductions. Live blues Sun. 3-8pm. Open daily 1pm-2am.

8 X 10, 10 E. Cross St. (625-2000). As the name implies, this bar is *small.* But, it's overflowing with locals. Progressive live rock every night. Cover ranges from $8 to $12. Open Mon. and Wed.-Sat. 9pm-2am.

Hammerjacks, 1101 S. Howard St. (659-7625). This is the place in Baltimore for big bands. Tickets, shows, and showtimes vary. Call for more information.

Orpheus, 1003 E. Praits St. (276-5599). This Art Deco establishment is a serious dance club. Tues. is Rave Night with a $7 cover; Thurs. is Gothic Night with a $5 cover, Fri. is house or alternative dance with a $5 cover; Sat. is 70s, 80s, and 90s dance mix with a $3 cover; Sun. is 18+ with deep house and a $5 cover. Open Tues. and Thurs.-Sun. 9pm-2am.

Louie/Louis, at the corner of Howard and Cross (727-2005). A hip crowd moves with the urban progressive and techno beats. Thurs. and Sat. are 18+ with an open bar. Cover: $6. Open Thurs.-Sat. 10pm-2am.

The Midtown Yacht Club, 15 E. Centre St. (837-1300), just off N. Charles in Mount Vernon, two blocks from the hostel. One of the only pub-style bars in the neighborhood draws locals with its daily food and drink specials, such as $5 domestic pitchers on Thurs. Happy hour (Mon.-Sat. 5-7pm, Sun. 9pm-2am) drops drink prices. 11 beers on tap. DJ and dancing on Sun. Open daily 11am-2am.

Green Turtle, 727 Broadway (342-4222). Popular with the Baltimore college crowd. Cheap $1.25 drafts are even cheaper (85¢) during happy hour (Mon.-Fri.4-7pm and all night Wed.). Open daily 11:30pm-1:30am.

Bohaeger, 515 S. Eden St. (563-7220) in Fells Point. Hopping bar becomes a happenin' dance club on the weekend. Chug $2.25 drafts on the huge outdoor patio. Happy hour (Fri. 5-7pm) takes 50¢ off all drinks and offers a free buffet. DJ music starts at 8pm Thurs.-Sat. Open Tues.-Fri. 11:30am-2am, Sat.-Sun. 3pm-2am.

Max's on Broadway, 735 S. Broadway (675-6297), at Lancaster St. in Fells Point. Maybe Max's has been listening to Prozac, because its personality has changed drastically of late. Once a grungy venue for alternative rock, country, R&B, reggae, and world beat, Max's is now one of Baltimore's best beer bars, boasting 24 taps and over 200 different bottled brews and a breathalizer at the door. Happy hour Mon.-Fri. noon-8pm brings $1-2 drafts. Open daily noon-2am.

Wharf Rat Bar, 801 S. Ann St. (276-9034), near Lancaster St. in Fells Point. A friendly bar with 29 beers on tap, including five of their very own "Oliver Ales." Stunning happy hour deal lets you quaff a ½-pint each of 3 different drafts for only $3. Mon.-Sat. 11:30am-1am.

John Steven, 1800 Thames St. (327-5561), near Ann St. in Fells Point. This acclaimed restaurant/bar, named after the owner's son's teddy bear, offers the expected sandwiches and seafood, as well as American sushi like the Bawlmer roll (backfin crab with avacado and scallions, $7.50). Beer $3, rails $2. Classical and jazz (on CD) are the genres of choice and are perfect for the shaded patio in back. Open Sun.-Thurs. 11am-11pm, Fri.-Sat. 11am- midnight.

Balls Sports Bar, 200 W. Pratt St. (659-5844), near Sharp St. 26 TVs and 3 satellite dishes make it possible to watch every sporting event in the country and most of the world. Students and businesspeople crowd in before and after baseball games at nearby Camden Yards. 18 beers on tap. Open daily 11:30am-2am.

Gay Bars and Clubs

The Hippo, 1 W. Eager St. (547-0069). Baltimore's largest and most popular gay bar, with pool tables, videos, and a packed dance floor. The first Sun. of every month is Ladies' Tea (6-10pm); Thurs. is Men's Night. Cover Thurs.-Fri. $3, Sat. $5. On Thurs., the $3 cover buys "drink chips" redeemable for $3 worth of drinks. Happy hour Mon.-Fri. 4-8pm. Saloon open daily 3pm-2am. Dance bar open Wed.-Sat. 10pm-2am. Video bar open Thurs.-Sat. 10pm-2am.

Allegro, 1101 Cathedral St. (837-3906), corner of Chase St. in the theater district. Popular gay nightspot. A young crowd gathers when the DJ starts at 9pm. Disco and house music nightly. Tues. is men's night; Thurs. is women's night; Wed. is "mixed energy" dance music; drag shows happen one Mon. per month. Sat. is always a theme night (like "Construction Party"). Cover Fri. and Sun. $3. Happy hour (Mon.-Sat. 6-10pm and Sun. 4-10pm) features ½-priced domestics and rails. Open Mon.-Sat. 6pm-2am, Sun. 4pm-2am.

Central Station, 1001 N. Charles St. (752-7133), on the corner of Eager St. A pub with pool tables downstairs and a beautiful restaurant upstairs—the place to be before the dance floors heat up elsewhere. Hamburgers and pizza $5 (5-11pm). Happy hour (daily 4-8pm) discounts drinks. Open daily 11:30am-2am.

Atlantis, 615 East Monument St. (727-9099). A typical run-of-the-mill gay bar. Happy hour Tues.-Fri. 4-7pm with ½-priced domestic drafts. On Sun. 4-8pm it's 2-for-1 drinks. Drafts $2. Open Tues.-Sat. 8pm-2am, Sun. 4pm-2am.

■■■ OCEAN CITY

Ocean City is a lot like a kiddie pool. It's shallow and plastic, but can be fun if you're the right age. This 10-mile strip of land packs endless bars, all-you-can-eat buffets, hotels, mini-golf courses, and tourists into a thin region between the Atlantic Ocean and the Assawoman Bay. Tourism is the town's only industry; in-season the population swells from 12,000 to 300,000, with a large migratory population of "June bugs," high school seniors that descend in swarms in the week after graduation. If you dig flashing lights, lots of action, and beer, this is the place to go. But if go-carts and boardwalks make you itch, head for quieter shores.

PRACTICAL INFORMATION

Ocean City runs north-south with numbered streets connecting the ocean to the bay. A good first stop is the **Ocean City Visitor's Center** (800-626-2326), 40th St. in the Convention Center (open Mon.-Thurs. 8am-5pm, Fri. 8am-6pm, Sat. 9am-5:30pm, Sun. 9am-5pm; Sept.-May daily 8:30am-5:30pm). **Carolina Trailways** (289-9307), at 2nd St. and Philadelphia Ave., sends seven buses per day to Baltimore (3 hrs., $22) and Washington D.C. (4 hrs., $36.50). (Station open daily 7am-8am and 10am-5pm; Sept.-May 10am-3pm.) Once in town, **the bus** (723-1607) is by far the best way to get around ($1 unlimited riding for the day). The bus runs 24 hrs. and travels the length of the town. **Parking** in Ocean City is a nightmare. You can park free during the day at the Convention Center, 40th St., or try to find a spot on the street.Ocean City's **post office:** 408 N. Philadelphia Ave. at 5th St. (289-7819; open Mon.-Fri. 9am-5pm, Sat. 9am-noon); **ZIP code:** 21842; **area code:** 410.

ACCOMMODATIONS AND FOOD

If you're going to stay in Ocean City, make every effort to secure a room at the **Summer Place Youth Hostel,** 104 Dorchester St. (289-4542), in the south end of town. This exceptional establishment houses two hip proprietors and tasteful southwestern decor, and gives you more bang for your buck than you're likely to find at most hostels anywhere. Private rooms come with access to kitchen, TV, common areas, deck, hammock, and grill. ($18 per person; no lockout, shared bath, reservations helpful but not required; open April-Oct.) If the hostel's full, try **Whispering Sands** (289-5759), 45th St. oceanside. The amenable owner rents out rooms, complete with kitchen access, to students for $15. (Open May-Oct.) You can also pitch a tent at **Assateague National Seashore** (641-1441) or **Assateague State Park** (641-2120). See Eastern Shore (p. 200) for details.

Dining in Ocean City is a glutton's delight. The streets are lined with seemingly identical restaurants hosting all-you-can-eat specials. Be sure to try Maryland's specialty: crabs. Locals favor **The Crab Bag** (250-3337), at 130th and Coastal Hwy., oceanside. It may look like a shanty, but the all-you-can-eat crabs ($15) are unbeatable. There's not much seating; plan to take out. (Open daily 4-9pm.) Pick up anything you could ever possibly want or need at the massive **Food Lion** (524-9039), on 120th St., bayside (open daily 6am-midnight).

SIGHTS AND ENTERTAINMENT

Ocean City's star attraction is its **beach,** and a beautiful beach it is. It runs the entire 10 mi. length of town and is wide and sandy the entire way. It's free and open 6am-10pm. When the sun goes down, hard-earned tans are put to work at Ocean City's league of bars and nightclubs. The most popular of the bunch is **Seacrets** (524-4900), on 49th St., bayside. This huge complex brings a taste of Jamaica to the mid-Atlantic. Barefoot barflies wander between floats to the strains of reggae. There are live bands every night. (Cover $3-5. Open Mon.-Sat. 11am-2am, Sun. noon-2am.) Seek refuge from the meat market at **Macky's Bayside Bar & Grill,** 5309 Coastal Hwy. (723-5565), bayside (no, really), behind Tio Gringo's. Macky's offers an all-wood interior and the opportunity to rub elbows with the locals (Open daily 11:30am-2am.

■■■ EASTERN SHORE

The long arm of land known as the Eastern Shore is claimed by Maryland in the north and Virginia in the south. Though the Chesapeake Bay is the only physical divide between the Eastern Shore and its mother states, the gulf between these areas is cultural as well. The Eastern Shore harbors a lifestyle last found in most of Virginia and Maryland decades ago. Peaceful hamlets and expansive fields punctuate the forests and dunes of this tranquil landscape. Here, tractors are more common than commuters on the roads, and wild ponies still go unpenned. For more information, contact the MD and VA visitors information centers.

ASSATEAGUE, MD AND CHINCOTEAGUE, VA

Local legend has it that horses first came to Assateague Island by swimming ashore after escaping a sinking Spanish galleon. Though less romantic, a more likely story is that a few centuries ago, several miserly mainland farmers put their horses out to graze on Assateague to avoid taxes and fencing expenses. Whatever their origins, the descendents of Assateague's original horses, the famous wild ponies, now roam free across the unspoiled beaches and forests of the island.

Assateague Island is divided into three parts. The **Assateague State Park** (410-641-2120), Rte. 611 in southeast Maryland, is a 2-mi. stretch of picnic areas, beaches, hot-water bathhouses, and campsites. (Park open daily April-Oct. 8am-sunset. $2 per person for day use, seniors free. Campsite registration 8am-11pm. Sites $20; reservations available only in one-week blocks, Sat.-Sat.) The **Assateague Island National Seashore** claims most of the long sandbar north and south of the park and has its own campground (sites $10, Nov.-mid-May $8) and beaches. The **ranger station** (410-641-3030) here distributes free back country camping permits, but only before 2pm; get there early. The **Barrier Island Visitors Center** (410-641-1441), Rte. 611, provides an introduction to the park and gives day-use information. (Visitors center open daily 9am-5pm. $4 entrance fee per car.) Meander down one of the ½-mile nature trails—the Forest Trail offers the best viewing tower, but the Marsh Trail (ironically) has fewer mosquitoes. Bring plenty of insect repellent. The mosquitoes are bad. Very bad. Oh, man. Bring gallons. Yeah.

The **Chincoteague National Wildlife Refuge** stretches across the Virginia side of the island. This refuge provides a temporary home for the threatened migratory peregrine falcon, a half million Canadian and snow geese, and the beautiful Chincoteague ponies. During slack tide, on the last Wednesday in July, the wild ponies are herded together and made to swim from Assateague Island to Chincoteague Island, where, on the following day, the local fire department auctions off the foals.

The adults swim back to Assateague and reproduce, providing next year's crop of ponies. Thus, the best time of year for pony sightings on Assateague Island is in mid-July, just before they're sold. To get more information on the refuge, swing by the **Chincoteague Refuge Visitor Contact Station,** on the island (804-336-6122; open daily 9am-5pm). The **Wildlife Loop** begins in the visitor's center parking lot and provides your best chance to see the ponies (open to people 5am-sunset; open to cars 3pm-sunset).

To get to Assateague Island, take **Carolina Trailways** (410-289-9307) to Ocean City, via daily express or local routes from Greyhound stations in Baltimore ($22) and Washington, D.C. ($36.50). From Ocean City, take a taxi to Assateague (289-1313; about $20). Carolina Trailways also buses from Salisbury, MD, and Norfolk, VA, stopping on U.S. 13 at **T's Corner** (804-824-5935), 11 mi. from Chincoteague. For more area info, call or write to **Chincoteague Chamber of Commerce,** P.O. Box 258 (6733 Maddox Blvd.), Chincoteague, VA 23336 (804-336-6161; open summer daily 9am-4:30pm, after Labor Day Mon.-Sat. 9am-4:30pm).

THE REST OF VIRGINIA

If Virginia seems obsessed with its past, it has good reason: the white settlement of North America, the shameful legacy of the slave trade, American independence, the aristocratic farsightedness of the early United States, and even the Civil War might all be said to have had their roots in Virginia. English colonists founded Jamestown in 1607; the New World's first black slaves joined them unwillingly 13 years later. While George Washington was still battling Native Americans in the French and Indian War, Thomas Jefferson wrote about religious and political freedom in the colonial capital, lavish Williamsburg. Virginian James Madison traveled to Philadelphia in 1787 with drafts of the *Constitution,* and Virginian George Mason led the campaign for a Bill of Rights. Meanwhile, eastern Virginia's Tidewater aristocracy dominated the state for a century with its rigid, gracious culture of slave-dependent plantations—a culture that exploded during the Civil War, when Union and Confederate armies pushed one another around the state on the way to Appomattox.

Virginia has mostly left the Old South it once led, but a host of Confederate street names, Robert E. Lee parks, fixed-up plantations, and battlefields exhibit to excess its antebellum days. In Richmond, where Patrick Henry boomed, "Give me liberty or give me death," nostalgia and horror compete in the Confederate Museum. Nostalgia climaxes in Colonial Williamsburg, where guides in 18th-century dress show sweating tourists around the restored capital.

■■■ FAIRFAX COUNTY, VA

What tourists see in Fairfax has little to do with the everyday lives of the people who live here. This largest of Washington suburbs prospered throughout the '80s as white- and blue-collar immigration transformed farms into suburbs, country roads into congested six-lane highways, and vacant lands into office complex upon shopping mall upon parking lot. Some feared uncontrolled development would turn Fairfax into a postmodern City of Quartz à la L.A. Democratic County Executive Audrey Moore, elected to beat back the real-estate moguls, has yet to placate the county's commuter voters in the face of a rough economy. Meanwhile, the people keep moving in. Reston, one of the nation's most successful "planned communities," now boasts its very own juvenile delinquents and an outdoor shopping plaza not unlike a sterilized Georgetown.

For visitors who aren't traffic engineers, though, the real sights of Fairfax belong more to the 18th than to the 20th century. When Philadelphia was still the nation's capital, aristocratic planters like George Washington and George Mason lived on Fairfax country estates and profited from Virginia's omnipresent cash crop, tobacco.

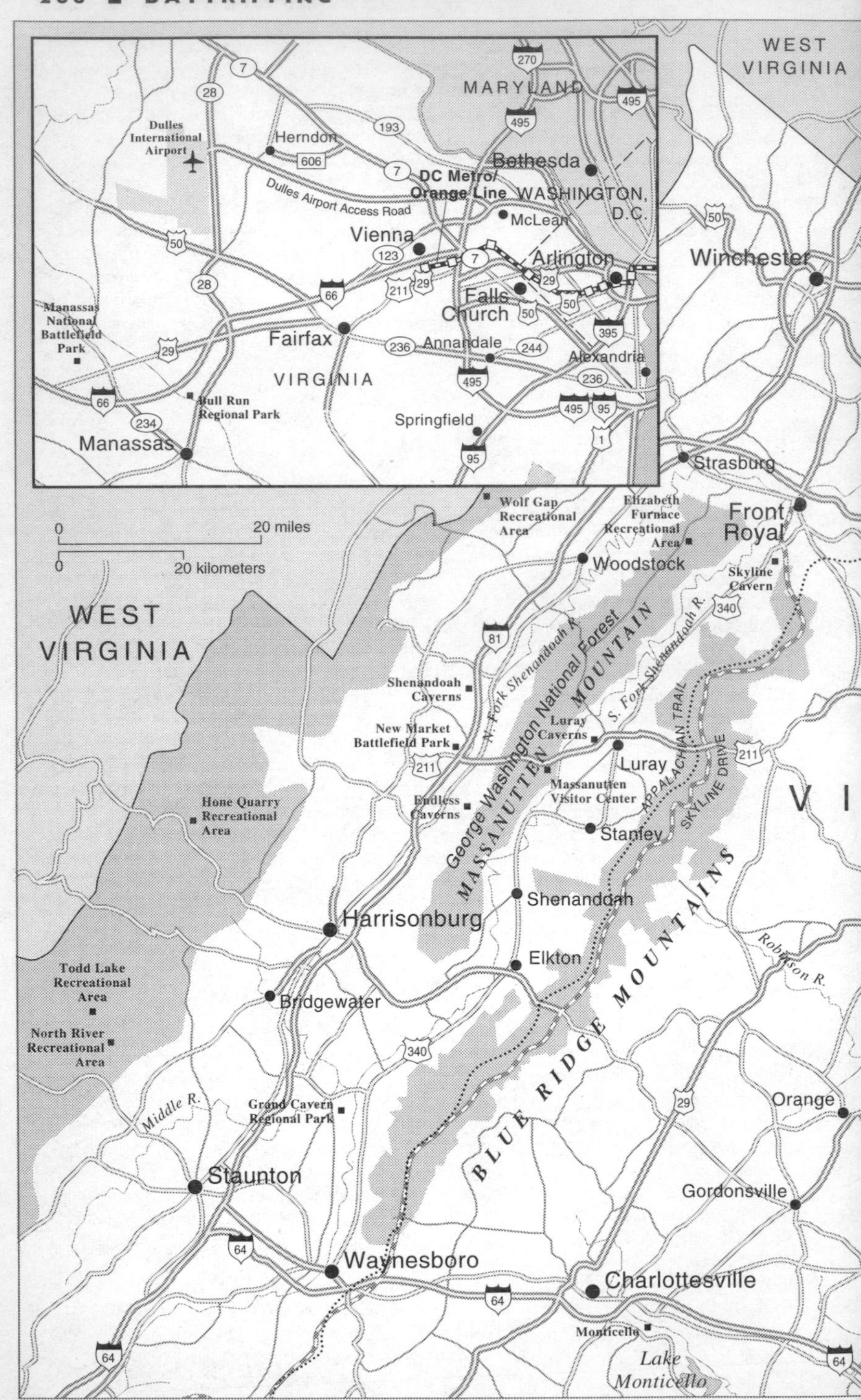

MARYLAND
WASHINGTON, D.C.
Dulles International Airport
Herndon
Dulles Airport Access Road
DC Metro/ Orange Line
Bethesda
McLean
Vienna
Arlington
Falls Church
Fairfax
Annandale
Alexandria
VIRGINIA
Manassas National Battlefield Park
Bull Run Regional Park
Springfield
Manassas
WEST VIRGINIA
Winchester
Strasburg
Front Royal
Wolf Gap Recreational Area
Elizabeth Furnace Recreational Area
Woodstock
Skyline Cavern
0 20 miles
0 20 kilometers
WEST VIRGINIA
N. Fork Shenandoah R.
S. Fork Shenandoah R.
George Washington National Forest
MASSANUTTEN MOUNTAIN
Shenandoah Caverns
New Market Battlefield Park
Luray Caverns
Luray
Massanutten Visitor Center
Endless Caverns
APPALACHIAN TRAIL
SKYLINE DRIVE
Hone Quarry Recreational Area
Stanley
Shenandoah
Harrisonburg
Elkton
BLUE RIDGE MOUNTAINS
Robinson R.
Todd Lake Recreational Area
North River Recreational Area
Bridgewater
Middle R.
Grand Cavern Regional Park
Orange
Staunton
Gordonsville
Waynesboro
Charlottesville
Monticello
Lake Monticello

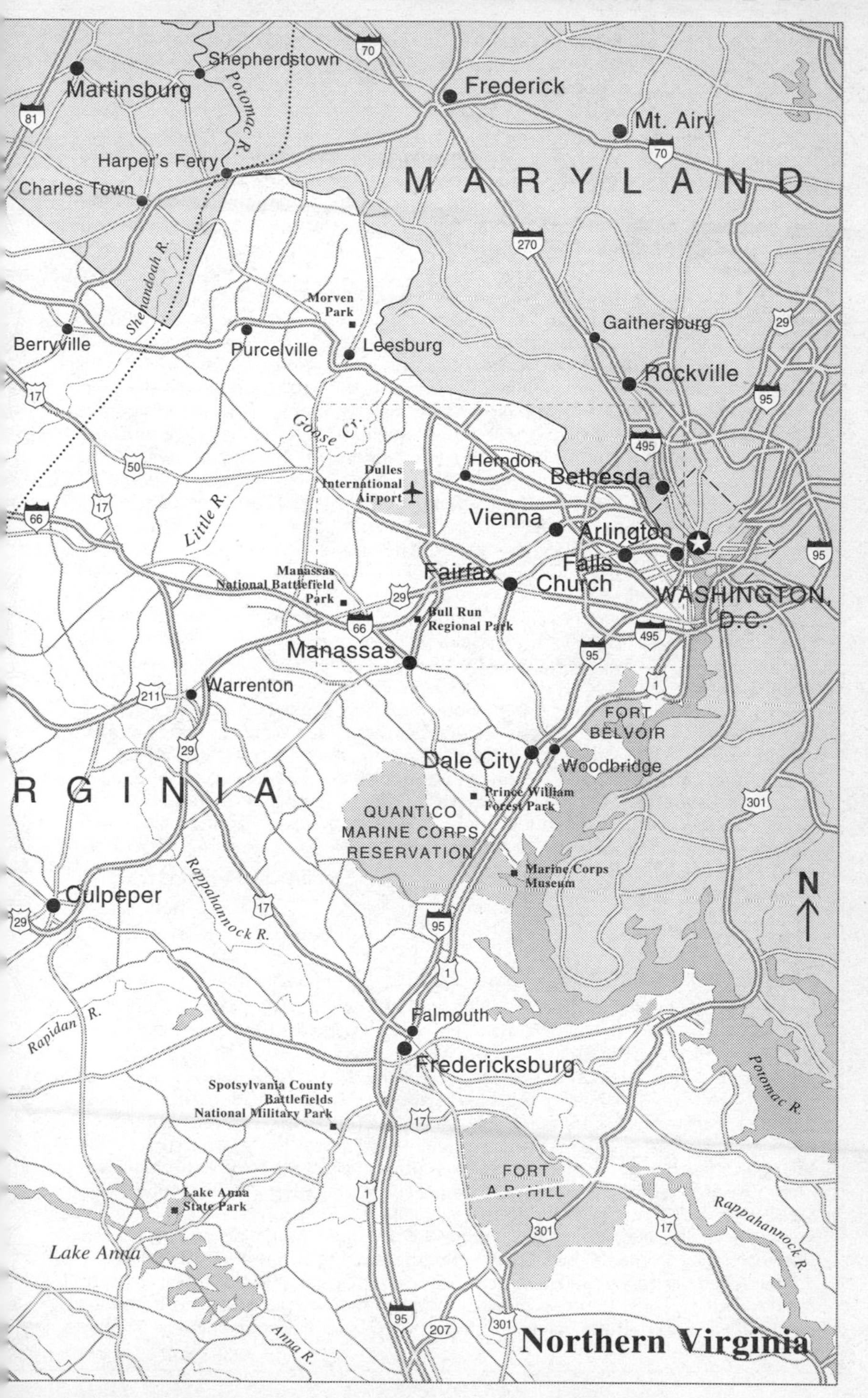
Martinsburg
Shepherdstown
Potomac R.
Frederick
Mt. Airy
Harper's Ferry
Charles Town
MARYLAND
Shenandoah R.
Morven Park
Berryville
Purcelville
Leesburg
Gaithersburg
Rockville
Goose Cr.
Herndon
Dulles International Airport
Bethesda
Little R.
Vienna
Arlington
Falls Church
Fairfax
WASHINGTON, D.C.
Manassas National Battlefield Park
Bull Run Regional Park
Manassas
Warrenton
FORT BELVOIR
Dale City
Woodbridge
RGINIA
Prince William Forest Park
QUANTICO MARINE CORPS RESERVATION
Marine Corps Museum
Culpeper
Rappahannock R.
N
Rapidan R.
Falmouth
Fredericksburg
Potomac R.
Spotsylvania County Battlefields National Military Park
FORT A.P. HILL
Lake Anna State Park
Lake Anna
Rappahannock R.
Anna R.
Northern Virginia

In the 1780s, the anti-federalist pressures that produced the Bill of Rights emerged first and most loudly from these Virginia slave-owners. One farm is even responsible for D.C.'s historically unpopular location. According to legend, George Washington, asked to pick a spot along the Potomac for the new national capital, chose the land closest to Mount Vernon, his home. Today, restored Colonial-era plantations compete for your tourist dollar with porticoes, porches, and patisseries. Few of these estates still produce crops, though the county's southern and western reaches preserve plenty of rural land. Some green space opens up to the public; parks and forests near the Potomac offer peace away from the sightseeing circuit.

GETTING AROUND

Fairfax doesn't exactly lack public transportation, but long distances and a scarcity of Metro stops make busing to Fairfax sights an adventure of up to two hours (see listings of individual sights for transportation information). Metrobuses are joined, or even replaced, by **Fairfax Connector buses** in much of the county (call 703-339-7200 for fare, route, and scheduling information). Arlington's George Washington Pkwy. winds speedily southward to an end near Mount Vernon, then becomes Mount Vernon Memorial Highway in southeast Fairfax. Rte. 1, the Jefferson Davis Highway, named for the president of the Confederacy, heads southwest from Arlington through Fairfax, then heads south, like the Union Army, on to Richmond. I-395 becomes I-95 beyond the Beltway; the northern Virginia leg, named the Shirley Highway, is sometimes called "the world's longest parking lot." Alexandria's Duke St. continues west to become the Little River Turnpike (Rte. 236). Lee Highway (Rte. 29) and Arlington Boulevard (Rte. 50) run east-west, joining Arlington to Fairfax City; after Fairfax City, Lee marches west to Manassas National Battlefield Park. Georgetown Pike, a cross-river continuation of MacArthur Boulevard in NW Washington, takes river rats northwest along the Potomac River to Great Falls Park. The Beltway (I-495 west of Springfield, VA, I-95 east of it) encircles Washington, while the Dulles Toll Road (Rte. 267) runs from the Beltway to Dulles Airport.

Driving in Fairfax County can be mighty confusing; if possible, call your destination and ask for detailed directions. Remember that Fairfax's roads, though numerous enough to stymie longtime Washingtonians, are still far too few to handle rush-hour traffic. On weekdays, don't drive here from D.C. between 4 and 7pm, or to D.C. from Fairfax between 6 and 9am. During these hours, parts of I-66 become HOV-3 or HOV-4, which stand for "High Occupancy Vehicle;" you're asking for a hefty ticket if you're caught in an HOV lane without the requisite number of people in your car (look for the backseat mannequins and inflatable dolls some desperate commuters use to circumvent this rule).

SIGHTS

Mount Vernon

George Washington slept here. He also ate here, bathed here, farmed here, and grew old here. He even died here. As Commander-in-Chief of the Continental forces and first President of the United States, Washington traveled extensively throughout the nascent nation, sometimes keeping away from Mount Vernon for years on end. But for all the time Washington spent in Philadelphia, New York, or on horseback at the head of an army, "home" never meant anything but Mount Vernon. An impeccable decorator and a courteous host, Washington spent his early and late years beautifying the interior of his mansion and sculpting the surrounding gardens for his own pleasure and for the comfort of his guests. Washington would be pleased to see that some 200 years after his death, the mansion is kept spotless and the gardens well-tended, all in the name of welcoming over a million visitors a year to his home.

Before you join the throngs filing through the mansion proper, grab a **map** of Mount Vernon's grounds at the entrance gate. The mansion is as good a place as any to start, but certainly don't stop there—the grounds merit at least an hour-long stroll. As you approach the mansion, stop to check out its Georgian exterior. From far away, the façade passes for stone; in fact, clever builders painted the pine boards and then sprinkled the wet wood with sand to give the house a stony face.

Once inside, attendants in each room will answer questions and do all they can to prod the line along. Pay close attention to the decor as you walk through the house: in Colonial America, men supervised the interior decoration, so you can judge George Washington's taste for yourself. Prussian-blue and vivid-green walls shine with their original hues, and much of the furniture and decorations in the house are the genuine belongings of Washington. When the lack of air conditioning gets you hot under the collar, you can look forward to the piazza in back of the house, where a superior view of the Potomac River accompanies a cooling breeze from the water.

The first room you enter once hosted the Washingtons' parties. Shuffle out the back door, across the piazza, and into the main hall, where a glass case protects the key to the Bastille, a relic of the French Revolution. Washington received it in 1790 from his close friend the Marquis de Lafayette (don't ask how Lafayette nabbed the key). Inside the common parlor, check out the harpsichord where Martha Washington's granddaughter Nelly Custis banged out the hottest hits of the 18th-century. Upstairs, bedrooms abound, including the room where George Washington actually did sleep—and die.

The tour ends downstairs in Washington's study, pantry, and kitchen. The pantry stored food for the whole household, its 300 slaves, and the Washingtons' house guests; if it seems too puny to have fed them all, it was—the main kitchen stood apart from the house so stove fires wouldn't burn them both down. Behind the kitchen, a gravel path leads to **George and Martha Washington's tomb;** consult your map, read the signs, and beware of poison ivy and disease-carrying ticks. Don't expect to get too close; George and Martha's stone sarcophagi are in a mausoleum behind a sturdy iron gate. Washington family members, like grandniece Bushrod, are also buried in the graveyard; nearby is the quiet, gravestone-less "slave burial ground," which now includes a long-overdue memorial to the slaves.

The estate also holds botanical gardens to peruse; the Mount Vernon fields once grew corn, wheat, tobacco, and, according to author Robert Anton Wilson, smokable marijuana. Only the corn remains at the **Mount Vernon Museum,** near the slave quarters' greenhouse to the left of the house; stop in for more Washingtoniana, including his swords, his toothbrush, her wedding slippers, and Houdon's 1785 bust of George Washington. Dig the exhibitions at the **Museum Annex** next door.

Crowds at Mount Vernon get out of hand in July and August; during those months, try to show up on a weekday morning. (Complex open daily 8am-5pm; Sept.-Oct. and March 9am-5pm; Nov.-Feb. 9am-4pm. Admission $7, over 61 $6, children 6-11 $3. Call 703-780-2000 for more information.)

Getting There

To **drive** to Mount Vernon, take the Beltway (I-495) to the George Washington Pkwy. on the Virginia side and follow the parkway to Mount Vernon's circular driveway. Parking in the Mount Vernon lot is free for four hours. The 18½-mi. Mount Vernon Trail for **bicycles** starts on Theodore Roosevelt Island and ends here (see **Sports,** p. 226). You can use public transportation, too: take the **Metro** to Huntington on the Blue/Yellow line and catch the Fairfax Connector 101 bus at the north end of the station (call 703-339-7200 for schedule information). If all else fails, you can get there by water. The **Potomac Spirit** runs from late March through October. The 75-minute trip takes you from Pier 4 on 6th and Water St. (a short walk from the Waterfront Metro) to the dock at Mt. Vernon. (Boat leaves Washington Tues.-Sun. 9am and 2pm from mid-June to late August. In early spring and fall, cruises depart only at 9am. Round-trip fare, including Mt. Vernon entrance fee, $21.50, senior citizens $19.25, children 6-11 $12.75. For information call 554-8000, or listen to the recording at 554-1542.)

Pope-Leighey House and Woodlawn Plantation

Two houses—one old, one new—sit on the grounds of Woodlawn Plantation, like book ends holding between them the span of American architectural history. The original Georgian-style Woodlawn mansion, completed in 1806, still anchors the 2000-acre lot, but it is now joined by Frank Lloyd Wright's simple and modern Pope-Leighey House, completed in 1940 and moved to this site in 1964.

From the main parking lot, a clear path points you to Woodlawn, but a sign for Pope-Leighey House directs you across the parking lot and into the woods. Take the road less traveled and admire Pope-Leighey first; plantations loiter on every Virginia street corner, but only one other Frank Lloyd Wright house of this kind is open to the public. Unfortunately, the house will be closed for renovations until March 1996. (The house is slated to shift a few feet because it was in danger of sinking.) Call ahead to make sure it's open when you visit.

The **Pope-Leighey** place is one of Wright's Usonian houses, designed for inhabitants of moderate means ("Usonia" was utopian author Samuel Butler's acronym for the United States of North America). The combination of history and genius provides a substantial attraction whose merits overwhelm the inconvenient pilgrimage by public transport which the terminally carless must resort to. Commissioned in 1939, the $7000 house held a family of four. When devious highway planners sent Rte. 66 through the house's original location in Falls Church, VA, Mrs. Robert Leighey rescued it by donating it to the National Trust for Historic Preservation in 1964. The 25 Usonian houses Wright built follow his famous design precepts in their organic unity with their environment: here cypress, glass, and brick blend with the surrounding forest. Note the house's modern form—unlike many of his contemporaries, Wright's houses never seem dated. Part of Wright's genius was his attention to detail: notice the kitchen cabinets, which all open away from the window to eliminate shadows on the shelves behind. Wright was also concerned with privacy: the windows along the house's façade are high up so as to let light in without affording a view of the interior.

The **guided tour** (every ½ hr.) probes the interior. Pope-Leighey covers only 1200 sq. ft., but Wright's design gives the impression of surprising roominess. Wright's interiors exemplify his "destruction of the box" with freely flowing space. Two patios and large windows at either end make the living and dining rooms seem to extend outdoors. Take a closer look at the modern geometric furniture: it's made of plywood. Wright intended it as furniture most people could afford to build for themselves. The two bedrooms also seem deceptively large because their closets hold, and hide, the bureaus. Seek no storage space under the house's flat roof; Wright considered attics and basements wasteful.

Woodlawn Plantation was a wedding present from George Washington to Nelly Custis, his adopted daughter, and Lawrence Lewis, his nephew. Custis lived with the Washingtons at Mount Vernon and she met Lewis when Washington asked him to come to Mount Vernon and serve as a secretary. Married by candlelight on February 22, 1799, George Washington's last birthday, the couple soon engaged William Thornton, the architect of the U.S. Capitol, to design and build a house on the land Washington had bequeathed them. Besides 2000 acres of his Mount Vernon lands, Washington's gift included his grist mill and a distillery.

Exquisitely preserved, Woodlawn's interior holds furnishings and paintings dating from the Federal period. Outside, well-tended lawns and well-pruned gardens invite a leisurely stroll. (Woodlawn open Feb.-Dec. daily 9:30am-4:30pm with the last tour at 4pm and the grounds closing at 5pm; admission $6, students through 12th grade and adults over 65 $4. Pope-Leighey open daily March-Dec. 9:30am-4:30pm; admission to Pope-Leighey House $5, students through 12th grade and adults over 65 $4. Wheelchair access limited; call 703-780-4000 for details.)

Getting There

To drive to Pope-Leighey House and Woodlawn Plantation, continue down Mount Vernon Hwy. from Mount Vernon until you reach Rte. 1, also called Richmond

Hwy. The driveway to the Woodlawn parking lot is right across the intersection. If you are coming from Gunston Hall, take Gunston Rd. and turn right onto Rte. 1. Then turn left at the light marking the intersection with Mount Vernon Hwy. By public transportation from Washington, take the yellow line to Huntington and catch the 9B Metrobus, which leaves approximately every half hour from the north end of the station. The bus will ultimately wind its way along Rte. 1; get off at the intersection with the Mount Vernon Hwy./Old Mill Rd.

Gunston Hall

Spend the extra 20 minutes on the road from Mount Vernon and stop by this well-preserved plantation. Thankfully skipped by the Tourmobile route, Gunston Hall (703-550-9220) gives a relaxed tour, which focuses as much on 18th-century living as on the plantation's one-time owner, George Mason. Especially for travelers with children, Gunston Hall will prove less crowded and at least as interesting as its more famous neighbor.

George Mason hung out with George Washington and James Madison, two other Virginia plantation aristocrats; but after they revolted against British rule, George Mason found the alternatives almost as revolting. With the outbreak of the American Revolution, the Second Continental Congress called for each colony to establish its own constitution. Mason prefaced Virginia's, the first of its kind, with his own document—the *Virginia Declaration of Rights.* Three weeks after the appearance of the Virginia Declaration, Thomas Jefferson used similar wording in the Declaration of Independence. Mason refused to sign the *U.S. Constitution* because it had no bill of rights; he helped convince Congress to add the first ten amendments (the *Bill of Rights)* to the *Constitution.*

While you're waiting for the guided tour to leave (it does every half hour), look around the **museum** in the visitors' building. The displays provide short, informative discussions about the life of the Mason family at Gunston Hall, using the family as a springboard from which to discuss 18th-century colonial life. An 11-min. video introduction to Mason's life plays continuously.

Behind the house, an English boxwood garden grows in formal geometric patterns. Stroll through the quiet garden or walk down to the wharf on the Potomac River. Because this area abuts the Mason Neck National Wildlife Refuge, it's a great place to bird-watch. In the meadow in front of the house, stunted sheep from Hog Island (in the Chesapeake Bay) haven't evolved much since the 18th century. Gunston Hall also sports the inevitable schoolhouse, kitchen, laundry, smokehouse, and dairy. A special celebration each year observes **George Mason Day,** Dec. 11. A **Kite Festival** in March numbers among other annual events here; call for more info.

Gunston Hall is open daily from 9:30am to 5pm with tours every half hour (except on Thanksgiving, Christmas, and New Year's Day); the last tour begins at 4:30pm and the grounds close at 6pm. (Admission $5, adults 60 and over $4, students grades 1-12 $1.50.) Gunston Hall is in the process of becoming wheelchair accessible; call to check on progress.

Getting There

The only practical way to reach Gunston Hall is by car. Follow the directions to Mount Vernon, and pick up Mount Vernon Memorial Hwy. where George Washington Memorial Pkwy. ends—at the circular driveway of Mount Vernon. Drive on Mount Vernon Hwy. until you hit Rte. 1, also called Richmond Hwy. You'll pass Fort Belvoir, but keep going until you hit Gunston Rd. (Rte. 242). A few miles down the road on your left is Gunston Hall. Parking is plentiful.

The Rest of Fairfax

Near George Mason's house, strain your neck bird-watching at the aptly named **Mason Neck National Wildlife Refuge,** a mile down Gunston Rd. (Rte. 242) from Gunston Hall (open 8am-dark; free). Hike through forest, grasslands, and marshes while trying to photograph bald eagles, great blue herons, beavers, and otters. No fires, camping, hunting, or fishing allowed.

The Wildlife Refuge may bore the skedaddle out of kids; take them instead to the **Pohick Bay Regional Park** (703-339-6100), also along Gunston Rd. The facilities include the largest swimming pool on the East Coast, a marina with sail- and paddle-boat rentals, an 18-hole golf course, miniature golf, picnic tables, a 4-mi. bridle path, and 200 campsites. (Open daily 8am-dark, swimming pool open only Memorial Day-Labor Day. Admission $4 per vehicle, $8 per vehicle with 10 or more passengers. **Swimming** fee $3.25, children 2-11 and adults over 59 $2.75. **Golf green** (339-8585) fees Mon.-Thurs. $19, Fri.-Sun. $23.)

Explore the same scenery the nation's founders savored at **Great Falls Park** (703-285-2966). Go **hiking** along the waterside paths and see what remains of the canal George Washington's Patowmack Company built in the late-18th century to transport goods to Georgetown. You can still see the thickly overgrown locks of the Patowmack and the ruins of Matildaville, a canal town that flourished here from 1790 to the 1820s. Hoof it to the **Visitors Center** for **hiking-trail maps.**

Some of the best **whitewater boating** east of the Mississippi rushes along this stretch of the Potomac River, but only experienced boaters should try it. Serious **rock climbers** get vertical on Great Falls's bare granite; the Park Service asks all climbers to register first at the Visitors Center. Many people enjoy scrambling over the rocks that line the river, though the Park Service would rather they kept to the paths; every so often someone tumbles sidelong into the Potomac. Park rules forbid any swimming in the Potomac, and for good reason—the churning river claims about seven lives a year. Special **ranger walks** are offered daily throughout the year; contact the Visitors Center for information.

If **fishing** lures you, come here to catch and eat catfish or carp; cast your line between the two overlook points to the right of the Visitors Center. Use cut herring, nightcrawlers, and clam snouts fished on the bottom for bait. Anyone over 16 must have a fishing license. Call the Visitors Center in advance for a list of locations in Virginia and Maryland where you can purchase one. Forget about taking a Metrobus here. To drive to Great Falls, take the Beltway I-495 to exit 13, then Georgetown Pike (Rte. 193) west. Turn right at Old Dominion Drive (Rte. 738). (Open daily dawn-dark, except on Christmas. Entrance fee $4 per vehicle, $2 per person without a vehicle, free for those under 16 and the disabled.)

Let your childhood dreams, or just your children, out at the **Reston Animal Park,** 1228 Hunter Mill Rd., Vienna VA (703-759-3636), where you can stroke and feed both commonplace and exotic animals—just try to do that at the National Zoo. Some animals, such as goats, a cockatoo, a pot-bellied piglet, and a buzzcockling, are loose in the courtyard. Ride Sukari the African elephant for $2.50, or jump on a free hayride and circle the bison-laden field. You won't have to pet them—promise. From Washington, take the Beltway (I-495) to the Dulles Toll Road (west); exit 5 will be Hunter Mill Road. From Great Falls, turn right onto Georgetown Pike (Rte. 193). After several miles, take a left onto Springvale Rd. After crossing Leesburg Pike (Rte. 7), turn left on Hunter Mill Rd. The park will be on the right. (Park open summer Mon.-Fri. 10am-5pm, Sat.-Sun. 10am-6pm; spring and fall Mon.-Fri. 10am-3pm, Sat.-Sun. 10am-5pm. Admission $8, seniors and children 2-12 $7. Mon.-Tues. $5.50 for everyone. Animal food 50¢ a cone.)

Among the fields and homes of suburban Langley is the most interesting Washington sight you'll never see. The new headquarters of the **Central Intelligence Agency,** which supervises Uncle Sam's spy network, is most emphatically closed to tourists. One in every $200 spent on new government buildings must pay for "public art;" though its grounds are hardly public, the CIA HQ's builders followed the rules by having sculptor Jim Sanborn create a flat, green wall-like sculpture stamped with thousands of letters and numbers. Only ex-CIA head William Webster and Sanborn know their secret meaning. Every two years or so, nonviolent mass protests block the CIA's driveways, keeping the spooks from driving to work.

■■■ SHENANDOAH NATIONAL PARK

Shenandoah National Park was one of our nation's first attempts at massive recyling. Before Congress established a national park here in 1926, the land was occupied by rocky formations and resourceful but reclusive mountain folk. Today, residents include not-so-reclusive deer, bears, and other critters who make their home in the lush forest that has reclaimed the area. Fields have given way to forest, transforming the park into a spectacular ridgetop preserve. A trip along its spine via Skyline Drive allows glimpses of the Blue Ridge Mountains, the fertile plains below, and quite possibly some of the park's furry and inquisitive inhabitants.

Shenandoah's natural beauty comes in the form of sweeping vistas and an abundance of life. On clear days, drivers and hikers can look out over miles of unspoiled ridges and treetops, home to more plant species than all of Europe. In the summer, the cool mountain air offers a respite from Virginia's oppressive heat and humidity. Early in June, see the blooming mountain laurel in the highlands. In the fall, Skyline Drive and its lodges are choked with tourists who come to enjoy the magnificent fall foliage. The narrow park stretches almost 75 mi. along the Blue Ridge Mountains, parallel to and south of the wilder George Washington National Forest.

PRACTICAL INFORMATION

Emergency (in park): 800-732-0911, or contact the nearest ranger.

Area Code: 540.

Park Information: 999-2243 (daily 8am-4:30pm), 999-3500 for 24-hr. recorded message. Mailing address: Superintendent, Park Headquarters, Shenandoah National Park, Rte. 4, P.O. Box 348, Luray, VA 22835.

Dickey Ridge Visitors Center: Mile 4.6 (635-3566), closest to the north entrance. Daily interpretative programs. Open April-Nov. daily 9am-5pm. **Byrd Visitors Center,** Mile 51 (999-3283), in the center of the park. Movie and museum explain the history of the Blue Ridge Range and its mountain culture. Open April-Oct. daily 9am-5pm. Both stations offer changing exhibits on the park, free pamphlets detailing short hikes, daily posted weather updates, and ranger-led nature hikes.

Shenandoah's technicolor mountains—bluish and covered with deciduous flora in the summer, streaked with brilliant reds, oranges, and yellows in the fall—can be ogled from overlooks along **Skyline Drive,** which runs 105 mi. south from Front Royal to Rockfish Gap. (Miles along Skyline Dr. are measured north to south, beginning at Front Royal.) The overlooks provide picnic areas for hikers; map boards also carry data about trail conditions. The drive closes during and following bad weather. Most facilities also hibernate in the winter. (Entrance $5 per vehicle, $3 per hiker, biker, or bus passenger, disabled persons free; pass good for 7 days.)

When planning to stay more than a day, purchase the *Park Guide* ($2), a booklet containing all the park regulations, trail lists, and a description of the area's geological history. Another good guide which doubles as a souvenir is *Exploring Shenandoah National Park* ($2).

Greyhound (800-231-2222) sends buses once per morning from D.C. to Waynesboro, near the park's southern entrance ($40 one-way), but no bus or train serves Front Royal. Rockfish Gap is only 25 mi. from Charlottesville on Rte. 64. You can also drive to Shenandoah from D.C.; take Rte. 66 west to 340 south to Front Royal.

ACCOMMODATIONS AND CAMPING

The **Bear's Den AYH/HI** (554-8708), located 35 mi. north of Shenandoah on Rte. 601 South, provides a woodsy stone lodge for travelers with two 10-bed dorm rooms and a room with one double bed and two bunk beds. Drivers should exit from Rte. 7 onto Rte. 601 South and go about ½ mi., turn right at the stone-gate entrance, and proceed up the hostel driveway for another ½ mi. No bus or train service is available. The hostel has a dining room, kitchen, on-site parking, and a laundry room. Ask the staff for activities information. (Check-in 5-10pm. Front gate locked and quiet hrs. begin at 10pm. Check-out 9:30am. $12, nonmembers $15. Camping $6 per person. Reservations recommended; write Bear's Den AYH/HI, Postal Route 1, Box 288, Bluemont, VA 22012.)

The park maintains two affordable lodges with motel-esque rooms in cabin-esque exteriors. **Skyland** (999-2211, 800-999-4714), Mile 42 on Skyline Drive, open April-Oct., lands brown and green wood-furnished cabins ($43-77, $5 more in Oct.) and slightly more upscale motel rooms ($78-82; open April-Nov.). **Lewis Mountain,** Mile 57 (999-2255 or 800-999-4714), also gets cabin fever with a set of its own ($52-55, $7 more in Oct.). Reservations are necessary, up to six months in advance.

The park service maintains three major campgrounds: **Big Meadows** (Mile 51); **Lewis Mountain** (Mile 58); and **Loft Mountain** (Mile 80). All have stores, laundry facilities, and showers (no hookups). Heavily wooded and uncluttered by mobile homes, Lewis Mountain makes for the happiest tenters. Sites at Lewis Mountain and Loft Mountain $12, at Big Meadows $12, $14 with reservation. Reservations possible only at Big Meadows (800-365-2267). Call a visitors center (see **Practical Information** above) to check availability.

Back-country camping is **free,** but you must obtain a permit at a park entrance, visitors center, ranger station, or the **park headquarters** (see Practical Information above) halfway between Thornton Gap and Luray on U.S. 211. Since open fires are prohibited, bring cold food or a stove; boil water or bring your own because some creeks are oozing with microscopic beasties. Illegal camping carries a hefty fine. Hikers on the **Appalachian Trail** can make use of primitive open shelters, three-sided structures with stone fireplaces, which are strewn along the trail at approximately 7-mi. intervals. At full shelters, campers often will move over to make room for a new arrival. These shelters are reserved for hikers with three or more nights in different locations stamped on their camping permits; casual hikers are banned from them. $1 per night donation. The **Potomac Appalachian Trail Club (PATC)** maintains five cabins in back-country areas of the park. You must reserve in advance by writing to the club at 118 Park St., SE, Vienna, VA 22180 (242-0693), and bring lanterns and food. The cabins contain bunk beds, water, and stoves. (Sun.-Thurs. $3 per person, Fri.-Sat. $14 per group; one member in party must be 21.)

HIKES AND ACTIVITIES

The **Appalachian Trail** runs the length of the park. Trail maps and the PATC guide can be obtained at the visitors center (see **Practical Information,** p. 271). The PATC puts out three different topographical maps (each $5) of three different parts of the park. When purchased as a package, the maps come with a trail guide, descriptions, and suggestions for budgeting time ($16). Brochures that cover the popular hikes are available for free. Overnight hikers should keep in mind the unpredictability of mountain weather. Be sure to get the park service package of brochures and advice before a long hike.

Old Rag Mountain, 5 mi. from Mile 45, is 3291 ft.—not an intimidating summit—but the 7.2-mi. loop up the mountain is deceptively difficult. This 6-8-hr. hike is steep, involves scrambling over and between granite, and at many points flaunts disappointing "false summits." Bring lots of water, energy food, and chutzpah. Camping is banned above 2800 ft. The **Whiteoak Canyon Trail** beckons from its own parking lot at Mile 42.6. The trail to the canyon is easy; the waterfalls and trout-filled streams below are spectacular. Waysides vend five-day fishing licenses ($7). From Whiteoak Canyon, the **Limberlost** trail slithers into a hemlock forest. At Mile 51.4, **Lewis Spring Falls Trail** takes only ¾-mi. to reach a gorgeous array of falls—the closest to Skyline Drive in the whole park. The trail descends farther (about an hour's walk) to the base of the falls, where water drops 80 ft. over the crumbling stone of an ancient lava flow. **Hogback Overlook,** from Mile 20.8 to Mile 21, bristles with easy hikes and idyllic views of the smooth Shenandoah River and Valley. At **Dark Hollow Falls,** Mile 50.7, a 1½-mi. hike takes you to the base of scenic cascades.

Take a break from hiking or driving at one of Shenandoah's seven **picnic areas,** located at Dickey Ridge (Mile 5), Elkwallow (Mile 24), Pinnacles (Mile 37), Big Meadows (Mile 51), Lewis Mountain (Mile 58), South River (Mile 63) and Loft Mountain (Mile 80). All have tables, fireplaces, water fountains, and comfort stations. When you forget to pack a picnic basket, swing by the **Panorama Restaurant** (999-2265 or 800-999-4714), at Mile 31.5, for a meal and a view. (Sandwiches $3-5, entrees $5-12. Open April-Nov. daily 9am-5:30pm.)

Blue Ridge Parkway

If you don't believe that the best things in life are free, this ride could change your mind. The 469-mi. Blue Ridge Parkway, continuous with Skyline Drive, runs through Virginia and North Carolina, connecting the **Shenandoah** and **Great Smoky Mountains National Parks** (in Tennessee). Administered by the National Park Service, the parkway joins hiking trails, campsites, and picnic grounds. Every bit as scenic as Skyline Drive, the Parkway remains much wilder and less crowded. From Shenandoah National Park, the road winds south through Virginia's **George Washington National Forest** from Waynesboro to Roanoke. The forest beckons motorists off the road with spacious campgrounds, canoeing opportunities, and swimming in cold, clear mountain water at **Sherando Lake** (Mile 16).

Nature trails range from the **Mountain Farm Trail** (Mile 5.9), a 20-minute hike to a reconstructed homestead, to the **Rock Castle Gorge Trail** (Mile 167), a 3-hr. excursion. At **Mabry Mill** (Mile 176.1) you can visit a mountain farm, and at **Crabtree Meadows** (Mile 339) you can purchase local crafts. **Humpback Rocks** (Mile 5.8) is an easy hike with a spectacular view. Of course, real go-getters will venture onto the **Appalachian Trail,** which will take you in scenic style all the way to Georgia. In addition to these trails, the Park Service hosts a variety of ranger-led interpretive activities. Information is available at the visitors centers.
The **Blue Ridge Country AYH/HI Hostel,** Rte. 2, P.O. Box 449, Galax 24333 (703-236-4962), rests only 100 ft. from the parkway at Mile 214.5. ($12 nonmembers, $15 members, which includes $3 stamp redeemable for membership.) Located in the world capital of old-time mountain music, this reproduction of a 1690 colonial building houses 22 beds. (Lockout 9:30am-5pm, curfew 11pm. Open Feb.-Dec.) There are nine **campgrounds** along the parkway, each with water and restrooms, located at Miles 61, 86, 120, 167, 239, 297, 316, 339, and 408. (Fee $9, reservations not accepted.) The cities and villages along the parkway offer a range of accommodations. For a complete listing, pick up a *Blue Ridge Parkway Directory* at one of the visitors centers.

For general info. on the parkway, call **visitor information.** For additional details call the park service in Roanoke, VA (540-857-2490), or in Montebello, VA (703-857-2490). For info write to **Blue Ridge Parkway Headquarters,** 400 BB&T Bldg., Asheville, NC 28801 (704-271-4779). Eleven **visitors centers** line the parkway at Miles 5.8, 63.8, 86, 169, 217.5, 294, 304.5, 316.4, 331, 364.6, and 382, located at entry points where major highways intersect the Blue Ridge. (Most open daily 9am-5pm, a few 9am-6pm.)

Outside the Park

The **Shenandoah Caverns** (477-3115) tout an iridescent panoply of stalactites and stalagmites, with Rainbow Lake and amusing Capitol Dome among the mimetic underground formations prospering in the year-round 56°F air. Take U.S. 211 to Newmarket, get on I-81 North, go 4 mi. to the Shenandoah Caverns exit, and follow the signs for the caverns—not the town of the same name. (Accessible to disabled persons. Admission $8, ages 8-14 $4, under 8 free. Open mid-April-mid-June and Labor Day-Oct. 9am-6pm, other times 9am-5pm.) **Skyline Caverns** (635-4545 or 800-635-4599) in Front Royal built a reputation on its anthodites, whose white spikes defy gravity and grow in all directions at the rate of an inch every seven thousand years. The caverns are 15 min. from the junction of Skyline Drive and U.S. 211. (Open mid-June-Aug. daily 9am-6pm; spring and fall Mon.-Fri. 9am-5pm, Sat.-Sun. 9am-6pm; winter daily 9am-4pm. Admission $10, ages 6-12 $5, under 7 free.) If a scenic paddle floats your boat, contact the **Downriver Canoe Co.,** Rte. 613 (Indian Hollow Rd.), Bentonville (635-5526). Trips stretch from 3 mi. to 120-plus mi. From Skyline Drive Mile 20 follow U.S 211 west for 8 mi., then north onto U.S. 340,14 mi. to Bentonville. Turn right onto Rte. 613 and go 1 mi. (Prices vary with length of trip. 3-mi. trips $29 per canoe; 3-day trip $122/canoe. 25% discount weekdays.

■■■ CHARLOTTESVILLE

The renowned jack-of-all trades Thomas Jefferson, when writing his own epitaph, was careful to point out his role as "father of the University of Virginia." The college he founded dominates Charlottesville economically, geographically, and culturally, supporting a community of writers such as Pulitzer Prize-winning poet Rita Dove—not to mention a community of pubs. Visitors are steered to Monticello, the cleverly constructed Classical mansion Jefferson designed. Even the friendly, hip, and down-to-earth population of the Blue Ridge foothills town seems to embody the third U.S. President's dream of a well-informed, culturally aware citizenry which chooses to live close to the land.

PRACTICAL INFORMATION AND ORIENTATION

Emergency: 911. **Campus Police:** dial 4-7166 on a UVA campus phone.

Visitor Information: Chamber of Commerce, 415 E. Market St. (295-3141), within walking distance of Amtrak, Greyhound, and historic downtown. Open Mon.-Fri. 9am-5pm. **Charlottesville/Albermarle Convention and Visitors Bureau,** P.O. Box 161, Rte. 20 near I-64 (977-1783). Take bus #8 ("Piedmont College") from 5th and Market St. Able to arrange same-day discount accommodations. Combo tickets to Monticello, Michie Tavern, and Ash Lawn-Highland ($17, seniors $15.50, under 12 $7.50). Open daily March-Oct. 9am-5:30pm, Nov.-Feb. 9am-5pm.

University of Virginia Information Center, at the rotunda in the center of campus (924-7969). Some brochures, a university map, and info. on tours. Open daily 9am-4:45pm. Students in **Newcomb Hall** (924-3363) provide a student locator service. Open daily 8am-10pm. The larger **University Center** (924-7166), off U.S. 250 west, is also home to the campus police—follow the signs. Transport schedules, entertainment guides, and hints on budget accommodations. Campus maps. Open 24 hrs.

Amtrak: 810 W. Main St. (800-872-7245, 296-4559), 7 blocks from downtown. To Washington, D.C. (1 per day, 3 hrs., $25), New York (1 per day, 7-8 hrs., $92), Baltimore (1 per day, 4 hrs., $42), and Philadelphia (1 per day, 5½ hrs., $62). Open daily 5:30am-9pm.

Greyhound: 310 W. Main St. (295-5131), within 3 blocks of downtown. To: Richmond (1 per day, 1½ hrs., $17), Washington, D.C. (3 per day, 3 hrs., $29), Norfolk (1 per day, 4 hrs., $32), Baltimore (4 per day, 4-5 hrs., $41), and Philadelphia (3 per day, 7-11 hrs., $48). Open Mon.-Sat. 7am-8:30pm, Sun. noon-8:30pm.

Public Transport: Charlottesville Transit Service (296-7433). Bus service within city limits. Maps available at both info centers, Chamber of Commerce, and the UVA student center in Newcomb Hall. Buses operate Mon.-Sat. 6:30am-6:30pm. Fare 60¢, seniors and disabled 30¢, under 6 free. The more frequent University of Virginia buses technically require UVA ID, but in practice, a studious look will usually suffice.

Taxi: Yellow Cab, 295-4131. 25¢ 1st sixth-mi., $1.50 each additional mile. To Monticello $8.

Help Lines: Region 10 Community Services Hotline, 972-1800. **Lesbian and Gay Hotline,** 971-4942. UVA-affiliated. Open Mon.-Thurs. 5-9pm.

Post Office: 513 E. Main St. (978-7610). Open Mon.-Fri. 8:30am-5pm, Sat. 10am-1pm. **ZIP Code:** 22902.

Area Code: 804.

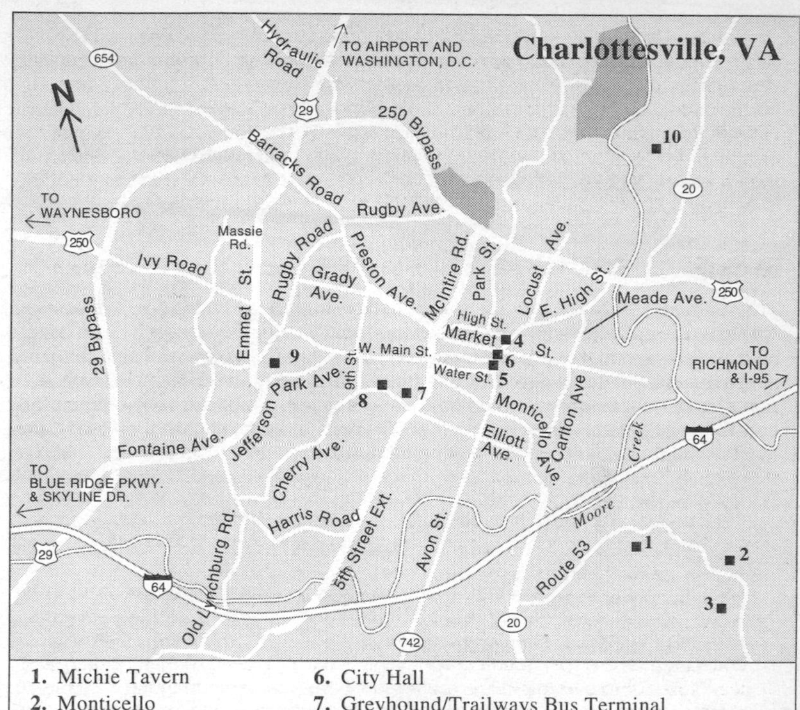

Charlottesville streets number east to west, using compass directions; 5th St. N.W. is 10 blocks from (and parallel to) 5th St. N.E. Streets running east-west across the numbered streets are neither parallel nor logically named. C-ville has two downtowns: one on the west side near the university called **The Corner,** and **Historic Downtown** about a mile east. The two are connected by **University Avenue,** running east-west, which becomes **Main Street** after the Corner ends at a bridge. Rte. 64, which runs east-west all the way to Richmond, is Charlottesville's main feeder.

ACCOMMODATIONS AND CAMPING

Budget Inn, 140 Emmet St. (U.S. 29) (293-5141), near the university. 40 comfortable, hotel-quality rooms. TV, A/C, private baths. Singles $33, doubles $36. $1 off in winter. Each additional person $5. Senior discounts. Office open daily 8am-midnight.

Econo Lodge, 400 Emmet St. (296-2104). 60 predictable rooms and a pool. Singles $39, doubles $46. Office open 24hrs.

Charlottesville KOA Kampground, Rte. 708 (296-9881 for info., 800-336-9881 for reservations). From Charlottesville, take U.S. 29 south to Rte. 708 southeast. All campsites are shaded. Recreation hall with video games, a pavilion, and a pool (open daily 10am-8pm). Fishing (not wading or swimming) allowed. Sites $17, with water and electric $21, full hookup $23. Open March 15-Nov. 15.

FOOD

The Corner neighborhood near UVA boasts bookstores and countless cheap eats, with good Southern grub in C-ville's unpretentious diners.

The Hardware Store, 316 E. Main St. (977-1518), near the middle of the outdoor "mall." Bar atmosphere, but slightly off-beat: beers served in glass boots, appetizers in microcosmic basketball courts, and condiments in toolboxes. American grille and an eclectic set of entrees, from *ratatouille gratinée* ($5.75) to crepes both sweet ($2-5) and savory ($6-7). Sandwiches ($3-7). Quality desserts. Open Mon.-Thurs. 11am-9pm, Fri.-Sat. 11am-10pm.

Macado's, 1505 University Ave. (971-3558). Great sandwiches ($4-5), a handful of entrees ($5-7), and home-made desserts are surrounded by walls full of UVA memorabilia (somewhat heavy on the football). Pinball machine and candy store. Upstairs is a rockin' bar where Edgar Allen Poe once lived. Listen to the tell-tale jukebox. Open Sun.-Thurs. 9am-1am, Fri.-Sat. 9am-2am.

Littlejohn's, 427 University Ave. (977-0588), 2 doors down from Macado's. Deli serves students (and you) great sandwiches ($3-6), soups, and gigantic muffins ($1.10). The Nuclear Sub ($4) is a potent combo of barbecued beef, coleslaw, and melted cheese calculated to cause internal meltdown. Open 24 hrs.

Coupe DeVille's, 9 Elliewood Ave. (977-3966). College students cross the road for chicken, the house specialty (½ rotisserie chicken $6.50). Open Mon.-Fri. 11:30am-2pm and 5:30-10pm, Sat. 5:30-10pm. Pub open Mon.-Sat. 10pm-2am.

SIGHTS

Most activity on the spacious **University of Virginia** campus clusters around the **Lawn** and fraternity-lined **Rugby Road.** Jefferson watched the university being built through his telescope at Monticello; return the gaze with a glimpse of Monticello from the Lawn, a terraced green carpet which is one of the prettiest spots in American academia. Professors live in the Lawn's pavilions; Jefferson designed each one in a different architectural style. Lawn tours, led by students, leave on the hour at the Rotunda from 10am to 4pm; self-guided tour maps are provided for those who prefer to find their own way. **The Rotunda** (924-7969) once housed a bell which was shot for the crime of waking students up early. (Free tours daily; call for times. Open daily 9am-4:45pm.) The **Bayley Art Museum,** Rugby Rd. (924-3592), features visiting exhibits and a small permanent collection including one of Rodin's castings of *The Kiss.* (Open Tues.-Sun. 1-5pm.)

The **Downtown Mall,** about five blocks off E. Main St., is a brick thoroughfare lined with restaurants and shops catering to a diverse crowd. A kiosk near the fountain in the center of the mall has posters with club schedules.

Jefferson oversaw every stage of the development of his beloved **Monticello** (984-9800), a home which truly reflects the personality of its creator. The house is a Neoclassical jewel loaded with fascinating innovations compiled or conceived by Jefferson. A unique all-weather passage links the kitchen with the dining room so that neither rain nor snow nor gloom of night could keep dinner from its appointed rounds, while an indoor compass registers wind direction using a weathervane on the roof. The cleverly laid-out grounds afford magnificent views in every direction and entertain the eye with orchards and flower gardens. Tours of Monticello are offered daily; arrive before 9am to beat the heat and the crowds. Wheelchair accessible. Open daily March-Oct. 8am-5pm; Nov.-Feb. 9am-4:30pm; tickets $8, seniors $7, ages 6-11 $4, students $3, Nov.-Feb $1.

Minutes away (take a right turn to Rte. 795) is **Ashlawn** (293-9539), the 500-acre plantation home of President James Monroe—a close friend of Jefferson. (Open daily 9am-6pm; Nov.-Feb. daily 10am-5pm; tour $6, seniors $5.50, children 6-11 $3.)

Down the road from Monticello on Rte. 53 is **Michie** (Mick-ee) **Tavern** (977-1234), with an operating grist mill, a general store, and a tour of the 200-year-old establishment (open daily 9am-5pm; $5, under 6 $1). Mega-touristy.

ENTERTAINMENT AND NIGHTLIFE

The town loves jazz, likes rock, and has quite a few pubs. Around the Downtown Mall, ubiquitous posters and the free *Charlottesville Review* can tell you who plays where and when. In the **Box Gardens** behind Ashlawn June-Aug., English-language opera and musical theater highlights the **Summer Festival of the Arts** (293-4500, open Tues.-Sun. 10am-5pm; call for shows and ticket prices). Ashlawn hosts **Music at Twilight** on Wed. evenings ($10, seniors $9, students $6), including New Orleans jazz, Cajun music, blues, and swing.

The Max, 12 11St. SW (295-6299). One of the largest and most popular bars in the city. Tues. features Top-40 DJ and dancing (cover: men 21+ $4, women 18+ $3); Wed. is 2-steppin' with free lessons until 9:30pm ($4 cover); Fri.-Sat. brings live bands (and a $5 cover for men). Drafts $1.85. Open Tues., and Thurs.-Sat. 8pm-2am, Wed. 7pm-midnight.

Outback Lodge, 917 Preston Ave. (979-7211). Happenin' pub with a pooltable, foosball, and a jukebox. Popular live music Wed.-Sat. with a cover averaging $10. Call for bands, times, and exact cover. Open Mon.-Fri. 11am-2am, Sat.-Sun. 5pm-2am.

Eastern Standard, 102 Old Preston Ave. (295-8668), at the Downtown Mall near the Omni Hotel. Drafts $2.75. DJ house beats Sun., beginning at 11:30pm ($2 cover). Open Tues.-Thurs. 5pm-midnight, Fri.-Sat. 5pm-2am, Sun. 5pm-2am.

Dürty Nelly's, 2200 Jefferson Park Ave. (295-1278). Bar/deli. Domestic drafts $1.50, $1.10 during happy hour (Mon.-Fri. 4-7pm). Occasional live music with a $2-4 cover. Open Sun.-Thurs. 11am-10pm, Fri.-Sat. 11am-midnight.

Miller's, 109 W. Main St. (971-8511). Jazz bar. The music begins at 10pm. Open daily 5pm-12:30am.

Tryangles, 212 W. Water St. (246-8783). The only gay bar in the city. To get in you need to buy a $25 membership which entitles you to free admission Sun.-Thurs. Fri.-Sat. features a DJ and dancing ($3 cover). Domestic drafts $1.25. Open Sun.-Thurs. 9pm-1am, Fri.-Sat. 9pm-4am.

■■■ RICHMOND

Once the capital of the rebel Confederacy, Richmond is by no means reluctant to display its history. Civil War leaders Robert E. Lee and Stonewall Jackson are worshipped through Richmond's numerous museums and restored homes, which showcase anything and everything Confederate. But Richmond is not mired in its own history; with districts like the sprawling, beautiful Fan and formerly industrial Shockoe Bottom, this state capital shows its kinder 20th-century face.

PRACTICAL INFORMATION AND ORIENTATION

Emergency: 911.

Visitor Information: Richmond Visitors Center, 1710 Robin Hood Rd. (358-5511), exit 78 off I-95/64, in a converted train depot. Helpful 6-min. video introduces the city's attractions. Walking tours and maps of downtown and the metro region. Can also arrange for same-day discounted accommodations. Open Memorial Day-Labor Day daily 9am-7pm; off-season 9am-5pm.

Amtrak: far away at 7519 Staple Mills Rd. (264-9194, 800-872-7245). To: D.C. (4 per day, 2 hrs., $18-23), Williamsburg (8 per day, 1¼ hr., $9-10), Virginia Beach (2 per day, 3 hrs., $16-19, the last 3rd of the trip is on a shuttle), New York City (8 per day, 7 hrs., $81), Baltimore (5 per day, 3 hrs., $26-31), and Philadelphia (5 per day, 4¾ hrs., $38-48). Taxi fare to downtown $12. Open 24 hrs.

Greyhound: 2910 N. Boulevard (254-5910 or 800-231-2222). 2 blocks from downtown; take GRTC bus #24 north. To: D.C. (16 per day, 2½ hrs., $10), Charlottesville (2 per day, 1½ hrs., $18), Williamsburg (8 per day, 1 hr., $9), Norfolk (10 per day, 3 hrs., $16), New York City (26 per day, 6½ hrs., $53), Baltimore (8 per day, 3½ hrs., $22) and Philadelphia (9 per day, 7 hrs., $40).

Public Transport: Greater Richmond Transit Co., 101 S. Davis Ave. (358-4782). Maps available in the basement of City Hall, 900 E. Broad St., and in the

Yellow Pages. Buses serve most of Richmond infrequently, downtown frequently; most leave from Broad St. downtown. Bus #24 goes south to Broad St. and downtown. Fare $1.15, transfers 15¢. Seniors 50¢ during off-peak hours. Free trolleys provide dependable, if limited, service to downtown and Shockoe Slip daily 10am-4pm, with an extended Shockoe Slip schedule 5pm-midnight.

Taxi: Colonial Cab (264-7960); Town and Country Taxi (271-2211).

Help Lines: Traveler's Aid, 643-0279 or 648-1767. **Rape Crisis Hotline,** 643-0888. **Psychiatric Crisis Intervention,** 648-9224. **Gay Information,** 353-3626. **AIDS/HIV Info.,** 359-4783. Mon.-Fri. 8am-6pm, Sat. noon-5pm, Sun. noon-8pm.

Post Office: 1801 Brook Rd. (775-6133). Open Mon.-Fri. 7am-6pm, Sat. 10am-1pm. **ZIP Code:** 23219.

Area Code: 804.

Imaginative locals have come up with novel names for Richmond's neighborhoods. **Carytown** is an upscale district in the northwest between Thompson St. and the Boulevard. The **Fan** neighborhood, bounded by the Boulevard, I-95, Monument Ave., and Virginia Commonwealth University, holds many of Richmond's oldest homes and is named for its dubious resemblance to a lady's fan. **Jackson Ward,** in the heart of downtown (and surrounded by Belvedere, Leigh, Broad, and 5th St.), and **Shockoe Slip** and **Shockoe Bottom** further to the east are more urban sections of town. **Broad St.,** not Main St., is the city's central artery, and the numbered streets that cross it ascend from west to east. Both I-95, leading north to Washington, D.C., and I-295 encircle the urban area.

ACCOMMODATIONS AND CAMPING

Budget motels in Richmond cluster on **Williamsburg Rd.,** on the edge of town, and along **Midlothian Turnpike,** south of the James River; public transport (see Practical Information above) to these areas is infrequent at best. As usual, the farther away from downtown you stay, the less you pay. The **visitors center** (see **Practical Information,** above) can reserve accommodations, sometimes at $10-20 discounts.

Massad House Hotel, 11 N. 4th St. (648-2893), 4 blocks from the capitol, near town. Shuttles guests via a 1940s elevator to clean rooms with shower, A/C, and TV. The only inexpensive rooms downtown. Singles $38, doubles $40.

Cadillac Motel, 11418 Washington Highway (798-4049), 10 mi. from the city. Take I-95 to exit 89. Offers sparse but economical rooms. Singles $38, doubles $45.

Red Carpet Inn, 5215 W. Broad St. (288-4011), 3 mi. from center of town; take bus #6. Offers grand (by motel standards) but slightly faded rooms and a pool/health club. Singles $42, doubles $46.

Pocahontas State Park, 10301 State Park Rd. (796-4255), 10 mi. south on Rte. 10 and Rte. 655 in Chesterfield. Offers showers, biking, boating, lakes, and a huge pool. (Sites $10.50. No hookups. Pool admission $2.25, ages 3-12 $1.75.) Open year-round. For free reservations, call 225-3867 or 800-933-PARK.

FOOD

At once a college town and a Southern capital, Richmond offers cheap student eateries and affordable down-home fare. At the **farmers market,** outdoors at N. 17th and E. Main St., pick up fresh fruit, vegetables, meat, and maybe even a pot swine. For student haunts, head for the area around Virginia Commonwealth University (VCU), just west of downtown; for fried apples, grits, and cornbread, try downtown itself.

Coppola's, 2900 W. Cary St. (359-6969). A popular deli and food mart crowded with happy people and Italian food. Dinners ($5-7) and fantastic sandwiches ($3-6). Outdoor seating available. Open Mon.-Wed. 10am-8pm, Thurs.-Sat. 10am-9pm.

3rd St. Diner, at the corner of 3rd and Main (788-4750), is a taste of Richmond day or night. Enjoy the $2.25 breakfast special (2 eggs, biscuit or toast, and homefries,

RICHMOND

Downtown Richmond

POINTS OF INTEREST

1. Bell Tower
2. Farmer's Market
3. Festival Park
4. Governor's Mansion
5. John Marshall House
6. Maggie Walker House
7. Money Museum at the Federal Reserve
8. Edgar Allen Poe Museum
9. Richmond City Hall
10. State Capitol
11. To Richmond National Battlefield Park
12. To St. John's Church
13. Valentine Museum
14. White House and Museum of Confederacy

grits, or Virginia fried apples) on the mint-green balcony. Old-time locals served by tatooed waitresses in combat boots. Open 24 hrs.

Texas-Wisconsin Border Café, 1501 W. Main St. (355-2907). Stetson-sporting stuffed steer survey a selection of specialties ranging from salsa to sauerkraut. At night the café secedes to become a popular bar. Lunches and dinners $4-8. Open daily 11am-2am.

The Ocean Restaurant, 414 E. Main St. (643-9485), serves excellent, filling breakfasts and lunches. All items under $5. Open Mon.-Fri. 6:30am-3pm, Sat. 9am-3pm.

Bottom's Up, 1700 Dock St., at the corner of 17th and Cary. This popular hangout serves the best pizza in Richmond ($8, will feed two) and will ply you with drinks after dark. Open Sun.-Wed. 11am-11pm, Thurs. 11am-midnight, Fri.-Sat. 11am-2am.

SIGHTS

Ever since Patrick Henry declared "Give me liberty or give me death" in Richmond's **St. John's Church,** 2401 E. Broad St. (648-5015), this river city has been quoting, memorializing, and bronzing its heroes. Sundays in summer at 2pm, actors recreate the famous 1775 speech. You must take a tour to see the church. (Tours Mon.-Sat. 10am-3:30pm, Sun. 1-3:30pm; $3, seniors $2, students under 18 $1.) The Thomas Jefferson-designed **State Capitol,** at 9th and Grace St. (786-4344), is a Neoclassical masterpiece that served as the home of the Confederate government during the Civil War and today houses the only statue of George Washington that the first President ever actually posed for. (Open daily 9am-5pm; Dec.-March Mon.-Sat. 9am-5pm, Sun. 1-5pm.) For a trip down Richmond's memory lane, follow Franklin Ave. from the capitol until it becomes **Monument Avenue,** a boulevard lined with trees, gracious old houses, and towering statues of Confederate heroes. Robert E. Lee faces his beloved South; Stonewall Jackson scowls at the Yankees.

The **Court End** district stretches north and east of the capitol to Clay and College St. and guards Richmond's most distinctive historical sights. The **Museum of the Confederacy,** 1201 E. Clay St. (649-1861), is the world's largest Confederate artifact collection. The main floor leads visitors through the military history of the Great War of Northern Aggression; the basement displays guns and flags of the Confederacy; and the top floor houses temporary exhibits on such topics as slave life in the antebellum South. The museum also runs one-hour tours through the **White House of the Confederacy** next door (ask at the museum desk). Statues of Tragedy, Comedy, and Irony grace the White House's front door. (Museum open Mon.-Sat. 10am-5pm, Sun. 1-5pm; tours of the White House Mon., Wed., and Fri.-Sat. 10:30am-4:30pm, Tues. and Thurs. 11:30am-4:30pm, Sun. 1:15-4:30pm. Admission to museum $5, seniors $4, students $3, under 6 free; for the White House $5.50, seniors $4.50, students $3.50; for both: $8, $5, $3.50.)

The **Valentine Museum,** 1015 E. Clay St. (649-0711), enamors visitors with exhibits on local and Southern social and cultural history. Admission price includes a tour of the recently renovated **Wickham-Valentine House** next door. (Museum open Mon.-Sat. 10am-5pm, Sun. noon-5pm; house tours on the hr., 10am-4pm. Admission $5, seniors and students $4, children 7-12 $3.) Combination tickets to the Museum of the Confederacy, White House of the Confederacy, Valentine Museum, and **John Marshall House**—all within easy walking distance of each other—are $11, seniors and students $10, ages 7-12 $5 (tickets available at any of the sights). John Marshall House, at 818 E. Marshall St. (648-7998), is open Tues.-Sat. 10am-5pm, Sun. 1-5pm.

East of the Capitol, follow your tell-tale heart to the **Edgar Allan Poe Museum,** 1914 E. Main St. (648-5523). Poe memorabilia stuffs five buildings, including the **Stone House,** the oldest extant structure within the original city boundaries. (Open Tues.-Sat. 10am-4pm, Sun.-Mon. 1-4pm. Admission $5, seniors $4, students $3.)

Four blocks from the intersection of Monument Ave. and N. Boulevard reposes the Southeast's largest art museum, the **Virginia Museum of Fine Arts,** 2800 Grove Ave. (367-0844; open Tues.-Sat. 11am-5pm, Thurs. 11am-8pm in the North Wing Galleries, Sun. 1-5pm; $4 donation requested).

The **Maggie L. Walker National Historic Site,** 110½ E. Leigh St. (780-1380), commemorates the life of an ex-slave's gifted daughter. Physically disabled, Walker fought for black women's rights and succeeded as founder and president of a bank. (Tours Wed.-Sun. 9am-5pm. Free.) The **Black History Museum and Cultural Center of Virginia,** 00 (yes, 00) Clay St. (780-9093), showcases rotating exhibits. (Open Tues. and Thurs.-Sat. 11am-4pm. $2, children $1.)

To the west lies the hands-on **Science Museum of Virginia,** 2500 W. Broad St. (367-1080). The museum houses the **Universe Theater,** which doubles as a planetarium and an Omni theater. (Museum open Mon.-Fri. 9:30am-5pm, Sat. 9:30am-9pm, Sun. noon-5pm. Planetarium and Omni shows daily; call for times. Admission $4.50, seniors and children 4-17 $4. $2-3 extra for shows.)

The **Shockoe Slip** district from Main, Canal, and Cary St. between 10th and 14th St. features fancy shops in restored and newly painted warehouses, but few bargains. **Cary St.,** from the Boulevard to Thompson St., is crowded with vintage clothing stores, antique boutiques, and entertaining crowds.

ENTERTAINMENT AND NIGHTLIFE

One of Richmond's most entertaining and delightful diversions is the marvelous old **Byrd Theater,** 2908 W. Cary St. (353-9911). Buy your ticket from a tuxedoed agent, then get ushered into an opulent, chandeliered theater and treated to a pre-movie concert, played on an ornate and cavernous Wurlitzer organ that rises out of the floor. All shows 99¢; on Saturdays the balcony opens for $1 extra. **Free concerts** abound near the farmers market at N. 17th and E. Main St. in the summer; check *Style Weekly,* a free magazine available at the visitors center. Nightlife enlivens Shockoe Slip and sprinkles itself in a less hectic manner throughout the Fan.

Tobacco Company Club, 1201 E. Cary St. (782-9555), smokes with top 40 music. (Open Tues.-Sat. 8pm-2am; rarely a cover.)

Matt's British Pub and Comedy Club, at 1045 12th St. (643-5653), pours out a bit of Brit wit Fri. at 8 and 10:30pm and Sat. at 8 and 11pm. Microbrews and drafts $2.75-$3.60, rails $3.40. Open Mon.-Sat. 1:30pm-2am, Sun. 4pm-2am.

Penny Lane Pub, 207 N. 7th St. (780-1682). Unusually authentic Irish tavern with traditional live Irish music on Fri. and local bands other nights. Open Mon.-Sat. 11am-2am, Sun. 4pm-2am.

Flood Zone, 11 S. 18th St. (643-6006), south of Shockoe Slip, hosts both big-name and off-beat rock bands. (Ticket office open Tues.-Fri. 10am-6pm. Tickets $6-20, depending upon the show.)

Paramyd, 1008 North Blvd. (358-3838). One of Richmond's few gay bars is a gay dance club on weekends. Happy hour Mon.-Fri. 6-9pm. Drafts $2. Fri.-Sat. cover varies, Sun. $4.

Broadway Café, 1624 W. Broad St. (355-9931). Gay watering hole with cheap beer. Drafts $1.35-1.45. Appetizers hover around $4. Open Mon.-Sat 6pm-2am, Sun. 7pm-2am.

■■■ WILLIAMSBURG

At the end of the 17th century, when women were women and men wore wigs, Williamsburg was the capital of Virginia. During the Revolutionary War, the capital moved to Richmond, along with much of Williamsburg's grandeur. The depressed city was rescued in 1926 by John D. Rockefeller, Jr. who showered the troubled spots with money and restored a large chunk of the historical district as a colonial village. His foundation still runs the restored section, a five-by-seven-block town-within-a-town called **Colonial Williamsburg,** where fife-and-drum corps march in the streets and cobblers, bookbinders, and blacksmiths go about their tasks using 200-year-old methods.

Street-side performers, evenings of 18th-century theater, and militia reviews are just part of everyday business in Williamsburg. But although the ex-capital claims to be a faithfully restored version of its 18th-century self, don't look for dirt roads, open sewers, or African slaves. Williamsburg also prides itself on **William and Mary,** the second-oldest college in the United States. Outside Williamsburg, Virginia's other big tourist sights (**Jamestown, Yorktown,** and **Busch Gardens**) lie in wait.

PRACTICAL INFORMATION AND ORIENTATION

Emergency: 911.

Visitor Information: Williamsburg Area Convention & Visitors Bureau, 201 Penniman Rd. (253-0192), ½ mi. northwest of the transportation center. Free *Visitor's Guide to Virginia's Historic Triangle*. Open Mon.-Fri. 8:30am-5pm. **Tourist Visitors Center,** 102 Information Dr. (800-447-8679), 1 mi. northeast of the train station. Tickets and transportation to Colonial Williamsburg. Maps and guides to historic district, including a guide for the disabled, upstairs. Information on prices and discounts on Virginia sights, available downstairs. Open daily 8:30am-8pm.

Transportation Center: 408 N. Boundary St. across from the fire station at the end of the road. **Amtrak,** 229-8750 or 800-872-7245. To: New York (1 per day, $56, 7½ hrs.), Washington, D.C. (1 per day, $26, 3½ hrs.), Philadelphia (1 per day, $40, 6 hrs.), Baltimore (1 per day, $30, 6hrs.), Richmond (3 per day, $9, 1½ hrs.), and Virginia Beach (2 per day, $12, 2 hrs.). Open Fri.-Mon. 7:15am-9:30pm, Tues.-Thurs. 7:15am-2:45pm. **Greyhound/Trailways,** 229-1460. Ticket office open Mon.-Fri. 8:30am-6pm, Sat.-Sun. 8:30am-2pm. To: Richmond (7 per day, $9, 1 hr.), Norfolk (8 per day, $13, 2 hrs.), Washington, D.C. (7 per day, $35, 4 hrs.). **James City County Transit (JCCT),** (220-1621). Service along Rte. 60, from Merchants Sq. in the Historic District west to Williamsburg Pottery or east past Busch Gardens. Operates Mon.-Sat. 6:15am-6:20pm. Fare $1 plus 25¢ per zone-change; exact change required.

Bike Rentals: Bikes Unlimited, 759 Scotland St. (229-4620), rents for $10 per day, with $5 deposit (includes lock). Open Mon.-Fri. 9am-7pm, Sat. 9am-5pm, Sun. noon-4pm. **Bikesmith of Williamsburg,** 515 York Rd. (229-9858), rents single-speed bikes at $8.50 for 4 hrs., $11.50 a day. Open Mon.-Sat. 10am-6pm.

Taxi: Williamsburg Limousine Service (877-0279). To Busch Gardens or Carter's Grove $6 round-trip. To Jamestown and Yorktown $15 roundtrip. Call between 8:30am-10pm.

Post Office: 425 N. Boundary St. (229-4668). Open Mon.-Fri. 8am-5pm, Sat. 10am-2pm.

ZIP Codes: 23185 (Williamsburg), 23690 (Yorktown), and 23081 (Jamestown).

Area Code: 804.

Williamsburg lies some 50 mi. southeast of Richmond between Jamestown (10 mi. away) and Yorktown (14 mi. away). The Colonial Parkway, which connects the three towns, has no commercial buildings along its route, helping to preserve an unspoiled atmosphere. Travelers should visit in late fall or early spring to avoid the crowds, high temperature, and humidity of summer. Signs lead to the Visitors Center, which offers information, tickets, and free parking.

ACCOMMODATIONS AND CAMPING

Budget motels line Rte. 60 west and Rte. 31 south. Avoid the hotels operated by the Colonial Williamsburg Foundation; they're expensive. A cheaper, friendlier, and more comfortable alternative is guest houses. Some don't require reservations, but all expect you to call ahead and most expect customers to avoid rowdiness and behave like house guests.

Only five minutes from the historic district, **Lewis Guest House,** 809 Lafayette St. (229-6116), rents several comfortable rooms, including the upstairs unit with private entrance, kitchen, and bath as a single (for $25) or double (for $30). The friendly proprietor keeps a very short dog. A few doors down is the **Carter Guest House,** 903 Lafayette St. (229-1117). Two spacious rooms, each with two beds and a shared bath. (Singles $25, doubles $26-30.) Be forewarned: Mrs. Carter will not let unmarried men and women sleep in the same bed. Hotels close to the historic district, especially chain- or foundation-owned hotels, do not come cheap. The **South-**

ern Inn, 1220 Richmond Rd. (229-8913), a 10-minute walk from William & Mary, has clean, ordinary rooms with colonial-looking façades and a pool. (Singles $30-35. Doubles $35-40.)

Several campsites blanket the area. **Anvil Campgrounds,** 5243 Moretown Rd. (565-2300), 3 mi. north of the Colonial Williamsburg Information Center on Rte. 60, boasts 73 shaded sights, a swimming pool, bathhouse, recreational hall, and store. (Sites $17.50, with hookup $24.50.)

The closest hostel, **Sangraal-by-the-Sea Youth Hostel (HI/AYH),** Rte. 626 (776-6500), near Urbanna, is 30 mi. away. It does provide rides to bus or train stations during business hours, but don't expect a daily ride to Williamsburg. (Singles $15, nonmembers $18.)

EATING AND DRINKING

Avoid the authentic-looking "taverns"—most are packed with sweaty tourists and priced accordingly. For a fraction of the price, you can still enjoy a colonial culinary experience by fixing a picnic with food from the **Williamsburg Shopping Center,** at the intersection of Richmond Rd. and Lafayette St. Rte. 60 also contains a bevy of fast-food places and far more pancake houses than any sane person might expect.

Greenleafe Café, 465 Scotland St. (220-3405), next door to Paul's Deli. Always mellow, Greenleafe cultivates a subdued atmosphere while serving sandwiches and salads ($3.50-5.50) and swaying on Tues. (after 9pm; cover $2) to the quiet sounds of live folk music. The café's slogan is "Life's too short to drink bad beer." You won't get any here: 15 yummy brews on tap ($2.95 per pint, $3.25 for bottles). Locals and students eat at a 20% discount. Open daily 9am-2am.

Beethoven's Inn, 467 Merrimac Trail (229-7069). Great sandwiches, subs, and other light fare with music-related names. Try the Titanic Sub, a combination of turkey, roast beef, grilled veggies, and feta cheese ($5.50). Play a variety of board games while you wait for your food. Open Mon.-Sat. 11am-9pm, Sun. noon-8pm.

Paul's Deli Restaurant and Pizza, 761 Scotland St. (229-8976), a lively summer hangout for errant, leftover William and Mary students, sells crisp stromboli for 2 ($6.15-9) and filling subs ($4-5). Great jukebox. Open daily 11am-2am.

College Delly Restaurant, 336 Richmond Rd. (229-6627), faithfully delivers sandwiches and subs. The "Holly" (a bacon, roast beef, and turkey sub) can serve 1 hungry person or 2 delicate ones for $4. Free delivery within limited area 6pm-1am. Open daily 10:30am-2am.

The Old Chickahominy House, 1211 Jamestown Rd. (229-4689), rests over a mile from the historic district. Share the antiques and dried-flower decor with pewter-haired locals whose ancestors survived "Starvation Winter" in Jamestown. Miss Melinda's "complete luncheon" of Virginia ham served on hot biscuits, fruit salad, a slice of delectable homemade pie, and iced tea or coffee will fill you up for hours ($4.95). Expect a 20-30-min. wait for lunch. Open daily 8:30-10:15am and 11:30am-2:15pm.

Sakura, 601 Prince George St. (253-1233) is popular with William and Mary students. And why not? Weeknights they get 2-for-1 with their IDs; if you can't scare up a student, try the affordable lunch options ($5-6.50). The chicken and steak combination ($5.50) comes highly recommended. Open Mon.-Fri. 11:30am-2pm and 5-9pm, Sat.-Sun. 5-10pm.

Chowning's Tavern, Duke of Gloucester St. (229-1000, ext. 2816). If you absolutely insist on eating in the historic district, you can wait in line for stew, sandwiches, or the misleading "Welsh Rabbit," bread in cheese and beer sauce with ham (lunch entrees from $5.95, dinner from $15.25). Miss the prohibitively expensive dinner here and instead join in the gambols after 10pm: costumed waiters serve mixed drinks and sandwiches, sing 18th-century ballads, and teach patrons how to play outdated dice and card games. Open daily 11am-midnight.

SIGHTS

Unless you plan to apply to W&M, you've probably come to see the restored gardens and buildings, crafts, tours, and costumed actors in the historic district also known as **Colonial Williamsburg.** The Colonial Williamsburg Foundation (CWF) owns nearly everything in the historic district, from the **Governor's Palace** to the lemonade stands and even most of the houses marked "private home." A **Patriot's Pass** allows two days of unlimited admission to sights (good for 1 year; $30, kids 6-12 $18). A one-day **Basic Admission Ticket** allows unlimited admission for one day ($25, kids 6-12 $15). Buy them at the **CWF Visitors Center** (220-7645). Open daily 8:30am-8pm.

"Doing" the historic district without a ticket definitely saves money; for no charge you can walk the streets, ogle the buildings, march behind the fife-and-drum corps, lock yourself in the stocks, and even use the restrooms. Some old-time shops that actually sell goods—notably **McKenzie Apothecary,** by the Palace Green—are open to the public. Two of the buildings on the CWF map, the **Wren Building** and the **Bruton Parish Church**—are made to look like regular exhibits but in fact are free. Outdoor events, including a mid-day cannon-firing, are listed in the weekly *Visitor's Companion,* given away to ticket-holders—many of whom conveniently leave it where non-ticket-holders can pick it up.

Take one of the **guided walking tours** trampling Colonial Williamsburg night and day. The fascinating "Other Half" tour relates the experience of Africans and African-Americans (tours March-Sept.; separate ticket ostensibly required).

Those willing to pay shouldn't miss the **Governor's Palace,** on the Palace Green. This mansion housed the appointed governors of the Virginia colony until the last one fled in 1775. Reconstructed Colonial sidearms and ceremonial sabers line the reconstructed walls, and the extensive gardens include a hedge maze. (Open daily 9am-5pm. Separate admission $17.) Most sights in town are open 9:30am-5:30pm; a complete list of hours is provided in the *Visitor's Companion.*

Spreading west from the corner of Richmond and Jamestown Rd., the other focal point of Williamsburg, **The College of William & Mary,** is the second-oldest college in the U.S. Chartered in 1693, the college educated Presidents Jefferson, Monroe, and Tyler. The **Sir Christopher Wren Building,** also restored with Rockefeller money, is the oldest classroom building in the country. Nearby, the shops at **Merchant Square** sprawl a hair's breadth from the historic district. Park here and walk straight into the restored town proper.

BUSCH GARDENS, WATER COUNTRY: USA, AND THE ANHEUSER-BUSCH BREWERY

When you've filled your colonial quotient, head to **Busch Gardens: The Old Country** (253-3350), 3 mi. east of Williamsburg on Rte. 60. You'll be flung, splashed, and throttled by the various shows and rides. Each section of the park represents a European nation; trains and sky-cars connect the sections. Recently opened is **Escape from Pompeii,** a water coaster ride. **Questor** brings roller coasters into the video age, while **Drachen Fire** provides timeless thrills. The **Loch Ness Monster** roller coaster is another enduring classic. Williamsburg Limousine serves Busch Gardens (see **Practical Information** above). (Open April-mid-June daily 10am-7pm; mid-June-Aug. Sun.-Fri. 10am-10pm, Sat. 10am-midnight; Sept.-Oct. daily 10am-7pm. Admission $29, children 3-6 $24. $5 off after 5pm. Parking $4.) Owned and operated by Busch Gardens (and about 2 mi. away) is **Water Country: USA,** a mammoth water park to end all water parks. Open weekends in May and June-Sept.10 10am-dusk. Admission $20, kids 3-6 $16. After 3pm, $12 for all.

A free monorail from Busch Gardens takes you to the **Anheuser-Busch Brewery** (253-3036). The Brewery is under renovation through 1996; call ahead to see if any tours are being given. Even if you can't get into the actual brewery, you can still get **two free cups of Busch beer** at the **Hospitality Center.** Accessible from I-64. (Open daily 10am-4pm. Free.)

■ JAMESTOWN, YORKTOWN AND THE JAMES RIVER PLANTATIONS

Jamestown and Yorktown are both part of the U.S. colonial story. The National Park System provides free, well-administered vistors guides to the two areas. **Williamsburg Limousine** (877-0279) offers daily round-trip transportation from Williamsburg to Jamestown, Yorktown ($15) and Carter's Grove ($8), but if you can, bike from South England St. in Colonial Williamsburg along the one-way, 7-mi., wooded **Carter's Grove Country Road** to Carter's Grove and the other James River plantations. The unlined **Colonial Parkway** to both Jamestown and Yorktown makes a beautiful biking route.

JAMESTOWN

Early American history buffs and anyone interested in dispelling Disney's latest myth should head to Jamestown. While there is no longer a city that bears this name, there is a national historic site to commemorate the first permanent settlement in North America.

Accommodations

You'll be hard pressed to find a place to stay any closer than Williamsburg unless you sleep in the forest, but **Carrot Tree Kitchens and Lodging,** 1782 Jamestown Rd. (229-0957), is the exception. Fancifully decorated and comfortable rooms and 30 wooded camp sites out back ($30-45). In the morning guests get free goodies from the bakery next door.

Sights

At the **Jamestown National Historic Site** you'll see the remains of the first permanent English settlement (1607) as well as exhibits explaining colonial life. At the **visitors center** (229-1733), skip the hokey film and catch a 30-min. "living history" walking tour (free with admission to the site), on which a guide portraying one of the colonists describes the Jamestown way of life. Among other sights, you'll visit the **Old Church Tower,** built in 1639 and the only 17th-century structure still standing. Also featured is a statue of **Pocahontas** (see graybox on p. 285). Call ahead for tour info. since "living history" guides get occasional off-days.

After the tour, you may want to explore on your own. You can rent a 45-min. **audio tape** ($2) and drive or hike the 5-mi. **Island Loop Route** through woodlands and marsh. In the remains of the settlement itself, archeologists work to uncover the original site of the triangular **Jamestown fort.** Over 50,000 artifacts have been unearthed already, some of which are on display at **Dale House.** Glassblowing goes on at the **Glasshouse** (open daily 8:30am-6pm), where workers dressed in 17th-cen-

Pocahontas

You've seen the movie, but that's not the real story. Pocahontas (meaning "little playful one") was actually only about 12 years old when she met Captain John Smith, a member of an English scouting voyage to America. She was not the buxom 17- or 18-year-old beauty Disney portrayed in its 1995 animated film that bears her name. Pocahontas did save Smith's life, but historians speculate that this may have been part of a Native American ritual of adoption. After the incident, Smith was made a subordinate chief of the tribe. There is no evidence of the supposed romance between Smith and Pocahontas, but when one of the settlers at Jamestown kidnapped her to gain leverage with her father, Chief Powhatan, she was detained in the Jamestown settlement for a year. During that time, she learned English, met and married John Rolfe, was baptized a Christian, and took the English name Rebecca. In 1616 she sailed with her husband and her son John to England. She was presented to the Queen, and shortly thereafter died of smallpox at the age of 22.

tury garb work in an attempt to replicate the glassworks that were briefly produced on the settlement. The remains of the original glasshouse are nearby.

The National Historic Site is open daily 9am-6pm; off-season 8am-5:30pm. The park opens and closes a half hour before the visitors center. Entrance fee $8 per car, $3 per hiker or bicyclist.)

Sniff around at the nearby **Jamestown Settlement** (229-1607), a museum commemorating the settlement with changing exhibits, a reconstruction of James Fort, a Native American village, and full-scale replicas of the three ships that brought the original settlers to Jamestown in 1607. The 20-min. "dramatic film" lives up to its name and fills tourists in on the settlement's history, including an embarrassed treatment of settler relations with the indigenous Powhatan tribe. (Open daily 9am-5pm. Admission $9, kids 6-12 $4.25.

JAMES RIVER PLANTATIONS

Built near the water to facilitate the planters' commercial and social lives, these country houses buttressed the slave-holding Virginia aristocracy. Tour guides at **Carter's Grove Plantation,** 6 mi. east of Williamsburg on Rte. 60, show off the restored house and fields. The last owners doubled the size of the original 18th-century building while trying to keep its colonial "feel." The complex also includes reconstructed 18th-century slave quarters and, in front of the house, an archaeological dig. The brand-new **Winthrop Rockefeller Archaeological Museum,** built unobtrusively into a hillside, provides a fascinating case-study look at archaeology. (Plantation open Tues.-Sun. 9am-5pm; Nov.-Dec. 9am-4pm. Museum and slave quarters open March-Dec. Tues.-Sun. 9am-5pm. Country Road open Tues.-Sun. 8:30am-4pm; Nov.-Dec. 8:30am-3pm. $13, kids 6-12 $9, free with CWF Patriot's Pass (229-1000 for info.).

Berkeley Plantation (829-6018), halfway between Richmond and Williamsburg on Rte. 5, saw the birth of President William Henry Harrison. Union Soldiers camped on the grounds here in 1862; one of them wrote the famous bugle tune *Taps.* Pause at the terraced box-wood gardens which stretch from the original 1726 brick building to the river. (House open daily 9am-6pm; grounds open daily 8am-5pm. House and grounds $8.50, seniors $6.65, ages 6-12 $9. Grounds only $5, seniors $3.60, ages 6-16 $2.50.)

Shirley Plantation (829-5121). Follow Rte. 5 west from Williamsburg, or east from Richmond. Surviving war after war in colonial times, and, incredibly, Reconstruction, this 1613 plantation has a Queen Anne-style mansion unrivaled by the other area plantations. Admission $7.50, 13-21 $5, 6-12 $3.75, over 60 $6.50. Open daily 9am-5pm.

YORKTOWN

The British defeat at **Yorktown** signaled the end of the Revolutionary War. British General Charles Lord Cornwallis and his men seized the town for use as a port in 1781, but were stranded when the French fleet blocked the sea approaches. Colonists and French troops attacked and the British soldiers surrendered, dealing a devastating blow to the British cause. The Yorktown branch of **Colonial National Park** (898-3400) vividly recreates this last significant battle of the war with an engaging film, dioramas, and a smart-looking electric map (behind the information center). Take a 7-mi. automobile journey around the battlefield; you can rent a tape cassette and recorder for $2 at the visitors center to listen to while you drive (**visitors center** open daily 8:30am-6pm; last tape rented at 5pm). The **Yorktown Victory Center** (887-1776), one block from Rte. 17 on Rte. 238, offers a museum brimming with Revolutionary War items and an intriguing "living history" exhibit: in an encampment in front of the center, a troop of soldiers from the Continental Army of 1781 takes a well-deserved break from active combat. (Open daily 9am-5pm. $6.75, kids 6-12 $3.25.)

■■■ VIRGINIA BEACH

After years of attracting a cruising, college crowd, Virginia Beach is shedding its playground image and evolving into a family-oriented vacation spot. While the beach and boardwalk still draw hundreds of students, nightlife venues are being systematically pushed off the main drag by the town's inhabitants; residents of Virginia Beach have become so concerned about crime and youthful irreverence that they recently had security cameras installed on the boardwalk. However, be assured that Virginia Beach is no retirement community; it remains a beach town, with the usual menagerie of surf shops, fast-food joints, and motels, which often fill seaside towns.

PRACTICAL INFORMATION

Tourist Office: Virginia Beach Visitors Center, 22nd St. and Parks Ave. (437-4888 or 800-446-8038). Information on budget accommodations and area sights, as well as the Virginia Beach Bikeway Map. Open daily 9am-8pm; Labor Day-Memorial Day 9am-5pm.

Trains: Amtrak, (245-3589 or 800-872-7245). The nearest station, in Newport News, provides free 45-min. bus service to and from the Radisson Hotel at 19th St. and Pavilion Dr. in Virginia Beach, but you must have a train ticket to get on the bus. To: Washington, DC (6hrs., $42); New York City (10hrs., $85); Philadelphia (8½hrs., $70); Baltimore (7hs., $49); Richmond (4hrs., $18); Williamsburg (2hrs., $13).

Buses: Greyhound, 1017 Laskin Rd. (422-2998 or 800-231-2222). Connects with MD via the Bridge Tunnel. To: Washington, DC (6½hr., $35); Richmond (3½hr., $23); Williamsburg (2½ hrs., $14).

Public Transportation: Virginia Beach Transit/Trolley Information Center (428-3388) provides info. on area transportation and tours, including trolleys, buses, and ferries. The **Atlantic Avenue Trolley** runs from Rudee Inlet to 42nd St. (in summer daily noon-midnight; 50¢, seniors and disabled 25¢). Other trolleys run along the boardwalk, the North Seashore, and to Lynnhaven Mall.

Bike/Moped Rental: Atlantic Convenient Mart (491-6143), at 28th St. and Atlantic Ave. Bikes $3 per hr., $13 per day. In-line skates $5 per hr., $15 per day. Open daily 7am-midnight. **Moped Rentals, Inc.,** 21st St. and Pacific Ave. Mopeds $23.50 per 1½hr. Open in summer daily 10am-midnight.

Emergency: 911.

Post Office: (428-2821), 24th St. and Atlantic Ave. Open Mon.-Fri. 8am-4:30pm.

ZIP Code: 23458.

Area Code: 804.

Virginia Beach is hard to get to, but easy to get around. Drivers from the north can take I-64 east from Richmond through the Bay Bridge Tunnel into Norfolk, then get on Rte. 44 (the Virginia Beach-Norfolk Expressway, toll 25¢), which will deliver them straight to 22nd St. and the beach. In Virginia Beach east-west streets are numbered; north-south avenues parallel the beach.

ACCOMMODATIONS

The number of motels in Virginia Beach is unreasonably high; unfortunately, so are most of the rates. Atlantic Ave. and Pacific Ave. buzz with activity during the summer and boast the most desirable hotels; reserve as far in advance as possible. If you're traveling in a group, look for "efficiency rate" apartments, which are rented cheaply by the week (see below).

Angie's Guest Cottage-Bed and Breakfast and HI-AYH Hostel, 302 24th St. (428-4690), ranks as the best place to stay on the entire Virginia Coast. Barbara Yates (a.k.a. "Angie") and her team welcome guests with exceptional warmth. (Check-in 10am-9pm. Memorial Day-Labor Day $11, nonmembers $14. Off-season: $8.50, nonmembers $11.50. Overflow camping at off-season rates. Kitchen and lockers available. Linen $2. Reservations helpful, but not required. Open April 1-Oct. 1, March with reservations.) In the bed and breakfast, breakfast is (duh) included (doubles $48-72). Accommodations at the **Ocean Palms Motel** (428-8362), 30th St. and Arctic Ave., consist of 2-room apartments with refrigerators ($30-45 per night). Right next door, the **Cherry Motel,** 2903 Arctic Ave. (428-3911), rents tidy one- and two-bedroom apartments by the week, each with four beds and a kitchen. (May 15-June 15 one-bedroom $300, two-bedroom $375; June 16-Labor Day $375/$525.)

Camp at the **Seashore State Park** (481-2131, reservations 490-3939), about 8 mi. north of town on U.S. 60, where choice sites go for $19. Because of its desirable location amid sand dunes and cypress trees, the park is very popular; call two to three weeks ahead (during business hours) for reservations. (Park open 8am-dusk. Take the North Seashore Trolley.) **KOA,** 1240 General Booth Blvd. (428-1444 or 800-665-8420), runs a quiet campground with open sites and free bus service to the beach and boardwalk. The campground may be hard to find; keep your eyes peeled for the red and yellow KOA sign. (Sites $24, with electricity $26, with full hook-up $33; comfortable and spacious 1-room cabins $46.)

FOOD AND NIGHTLIFE

Junk-food aficionados will love Virginia Beach, thanks to the jumble of fast-food joints along the boardwalk and the major thoroughfares. Beyond the neon glare, **The Jewish Mother,** 3108 Pacific Ave. (422-5430), dotes on her customers with quiche, omelettes, crepes ($5-9), deli sandwiches ($4-6), and desserts ($2-4). At night the restaurant becomes a popular (and cheap) bar with live music. The grill stays open until 2 or 3am on the weekends, feeding the "lush rush," an influx of drunkards who appear when other bars shut down. (Cover $3-5; no cover for "ladies" on Thurs. Open Sun.-Thurs. 9am-2am, Fri.-Sat. 9am-3am.) **The Raven,** 1200 Atlantic Ave. (425-1200), lays out tasty seafood and steaks in a tinted-glass greenhouse, or outdoors when it's warm. (Sandwiches and burgers $5-7, dinners $12-17. Open daily 11:30am-2am.) **Giovanni's Pasta Pizza Palace,** 2006 Atlantic Ave. (425-1575), serves tasty Italian pastas, pizzas, and hot grinders. (Lunches and dinners $5-8. Open daily noon-11pm.)

For organic produce and vegetarian goodies try **The Heritage Store,** 314 Laskin Ave. (428-0100). The Garden Burger is particularly tasty ($5). (Open Mon.-Sat. 10am-7pm, Sun. 12-6pm.) At 31st St. (Luskin Rd.) and Baltic Ave., the **Farm Fresh Supermarket** salad bar, stocked with fresh fruit and pastas ($3 per lb.), is a cheap alternative (open 24 hrs.).

In darkness the beach becomes a haunt for lovers. **Chicho's** (422-6011), on Atlantic Ave. between 20th and 21st St., is one hot spot left from the days when bars clustered near the water. (Dress code: T-shirts, shorts, tight dresses, tanned skin.) Bartenders shout to one another while videos of surfing competitions and bungee jumping play on screens above their heads and hopeful patrons ogle their neighbors. (Open Mon.-Fri. 5pm-2am, Sat.-Sun. 1pm-2am; no cover charge.) Increasingly, the bar scene has retreated from the main arteries to places like **H_2O,** 1069 19th St. (425-5684). Massive columns filled with burbling blue water flank the walls and give the club the atmosphere of a posh, tasteful fish tank. Mingle with other tanned and well-groomed fishes for a $3-5 cover. (Open daily 11am-3pm for lunch, 5pm-10pm for dinner, 5pm-2am for drinks. Live DJ and a dance floor.) Across the way, at 1900 Pavilion Dr. (on the first floor of the Radisson Hotel), **The Bayou** (422-8900), will drown you in the deafening sounds of live alternative bands 5 nights a week (cover $3-5; open daily 6pm-2am).

OTHER DAYTRIPS

■■■ DELAWARE SEASHORE

Lewes Founded in 1613 by the Zwaanendael colony from Hoorn, Holland, **Lewes** (LOO-IS) touts itself as Delaware's first town. More than 350 years later, the town is still just a sleepy burg on the Delaware Bay. Lewes' history and its calm shores attract an annual influx of antique hunters and vacationing families, who seek a safe retreat from the rough Atlantic waters. The atmosphere in Lewes is upscale and reserved, but well-kept beaches and welcoming natives make the town inviting for budget travelers as well.

The **Lewes Chamber of Commerce** (645-8078) operates out of the Fisher Martin House on King's Hwy. (open Mon.-Fri. 10am-4pm, Sat.-Sun. 10am-2pm). East of Lewes, on the Atlantic Ocean, the secluded **Cape Henlopen State Park** (645-8983) is home to a seabird nesting colony, sparkling white "walking dunes," and a beach with a bathhouse. ($5 per car, bikes and walkers free; open daily 8am-sunset.) Sandy campsites are available on a first-come, first-served basis. (645-2103; sites $15; open April-Oct.) Enjoy a sandwich ($2-4) and a fat-free, caffeine-free Vanilla Dream ($1.25) at the aromatic **Oby Lee Coffee Roasters and Café,** in the **Lewes Bake Shoppe,** 124 2nd St. (open Sun.-Fri. 7:30am-10pm, Sat. 7:30am-11pm).

Carolina Trailways (227-7223 in Rehoboth for ticket info.) serves Lewes, from the Ace Hardware on Rte. 1, with buses to Washington DC (3½hr., $31), Baltimore (3½hrs., $27), and Philadelphia (4hrs., $29). Lewes makes up one end of the 70-min. **Cape May, NJ/Lewes, DE Ferry** route (Lewes terminal 645-6313). The Delaware Resort Transit (DRT) **shuttle bus** (226-2001 for schedules) runs from the ferry terminal, through Lewes, and to Rehoboth and Dewey Beach, approximately every ½-hr. ($1 good for all day; Memorial Day-Labor Day daily 7am-4am.)

Rehoboth Beach A youthful gay minority has found a home in **Rehoboth Beach,** leaving its mark both on the town's social life and its business activities. Unlike some towns which simply host a gay social scene, Rehoboth is fostering a settled gay community. Of course, visitors of all orientations come to Rehoboth to tan, mix, and mingle on summer weekends at the beach. Follow Rehoboth Ave. until it hits the water at Rehoboth Beach, or follow Rte. 1 south to **Dewey Beach.**

For more info., visit the **Rehoboth Beach Chamber of Commerce,** next to the lighthouse at 501 Rehoboth Ave. (800-441-1329 or 227-2233; open Mon.-Fri. 9am-5pm, Sat. 9am-noon). Rehoboth's **post office:** 179 Rehoboth Ave. (227-8406; open Mon.-Fri. 9am-5pm, Sat. 8:30am-12:30pm); Lewes and Rehoboth's **ZIP code:** 19971; **area code:** 302.

For inexpensive lodging, try **The Abbey Inn,** 31 Maryland Ave. (227-7023), where there's always a local and a conversation waiting on the porch. Call for reservations at least one week in advance, especially in summer. (2-day min. stay. Singles from $32, doubles from $40; 15% surcharge on weekends.) **The Whitson,** 30 Maryland Ave. (227-7966), sits right across from The Abbey, and offers plush rooms for a bit more money. (2-day min. stay on weekends, 3 on holidays. Singles $43-53, doubles $58-63.) Located just one block from the boardwalk, **The Lord Baltimore,** 16 Baltimore Ave. (227-2855), has clean, antiquated, practically beachfront rooms, TV and A/C. (Singles and doubles $30-65. Call ahead; it's popular.) The **Big Oaks Family Campground,** P.O. Box 53 (645-6838), sprawls at the intersection of Rte. 1 and 270. The campground itself is secluded but the sites are open. (Sites with hookup $21.50.)

Practice your French and enjoy a Grand Marnier crepe ($4) at **Cafe Papillion,** 42 Rehoboth Ave. (227-7568), in the Penny Lane Mall. The croissant sandwiches (about $5) are wicked good. (Open Mon.-Fri. 8am-midnight, Sat.-Sun. 9am-midnight.) **Thrasher's** has served fries and only fries, in enormous paper tubs ($3-6) for over 60 years. Don't expect ketchup; these fries come with vinegar and salt. Locations on both sides of the main drag, at 7 and 26 Rehoboth Ave., make it easy to find. (Open daily 11am-11pm.) The **Blue Moon,** 35 Baltimore Ave. (227-6515), rises at 4pm daily and rocks a predominantly gay crowd until 1am (no cover). Live music, Irish on the weekends and rock during the week, awaits at **Irish Eyes,** 15 Wilmington Ave. (open Mon.-Fri. 5pm-1am, Sat.-Sun. noon-1am).

Carolina Trailways, 251 Rehoboth Ave. (227-7223), runs through Rehoboth Beach. Buses go to: Washington, DC (3½ hrs., $31), Baltimore (3½ hrs., $27), and

Philadelphia (4 hrs., $29). To get around within Rehoboth, use the DRT **shuttle bus** (226-2001), which runs from the ferry terminal in Lewes to Rehoboth and Dewey Beach, approximately every ½-hr. ($1 good for all day; Memorial Day-Labor Day daily 7am-4am.)

■■■ HARPER'S FERRY, WV

Harper's Ferry's stunning location—at the junction of the Potomac and Shenandoah rivers—has time and again provided a beautiful backdrop to the events of history. This town witnessed John Brown's famous 1859 raid on the U.S. Armory—an attempt to start a war to liberate the slaves. (Although he failed to end slavery himself, and paid for his actions with his life, Brown's raid fanned the smouldering fires which soon blazed into the Civil War.) No longer a revolutionary hotbed, Harper's Ferry today provides excellent hiking, biking, canoeing, rafting, and surveying nature's beauty. Thomas Jefferson called the view from a Harper's Ferry overlook "worth a voyage across the Atlantic," and while that may seem a strong statement, if you're already across it's certainly worth the journey.

PRACTICAL INFORMATION

Emergency: 911 or contact a ranger at 535-6455.
Area Code: 304.
Park Information: 535-6223. Mailing address: Harper's Ferry National Historical Park, P.O. Box 65, Harpers Ferry, WV 25425.
Visitors Center: (304-535-6298) just inside the park entrance off Rte. 340. Open daily 8am-5pm, Memorial Day-Labor Day 8am-6pm. Admission fee $5 per car, $3 per hiker or bicyclist; good for 7 consecutive days.) If you drive, park near the Visitors Center; you'll get ticketed any closer to town. The shuttle bus between the parking lot and town shuttles every 15 min.
West Virginia Welcome Center: (535-2482), across the street from the entrance to Harpers Ferry, unaffiliated with the town but great for in-state travelers; get information on accommodations, restaurants, and activities such as white-water rafting. Open daily 9am-5pm.

Harper's Ferry makes a convenient daytrip from Washington. The drive from D.C. takes an hour and a half by car. Take I-270 north to Rte. 340 West. **Amtrak** (800-872-7245) goes to Harper's Ferry (station is on Potomac St.) from D.C. only in the afternoon and back to D.C. in the morning. Reservations *required* ($15 one-way, $24 round-trip, depending on availability). The **Maryland Rail Commuter (MARC)** (800-325-7245) trains offer a cheaper and more frequent rail-ride; on Mon.-Fri., 2 trains run to Union Station in D.C. and 3 return to Harper's Ferry. ($6.75, seniors, disabled travelers, and children 5-15 $3.50. Ticket office open Mon., Wed., and Fri. 6am-9pm, Tues. and Thurs. 5am-8pm. You can also buy tickets on the train, for $3 extra if the ticket window is open.) The closest **Greyhound** bus stations are half-hour drives away in Winchester, VA, and Frederick, MD.

ACCOMMODATIONS

Hikers can try the **Harper's Ferry AYH/HI Hostel,** 19123 Sandy Hook Rd. (301-834-7652), at Keep Tryst Rd. in Knoxville, MD, for cheap accommodations. Meet a rugged through-hiker or two about halfway along their 2020-mi. Appalachian Trail odyssey. This renovated auction house, standing high above the Potomac, has 36 beds in two dormitory rooms. Train service is available to Harper's Ferry, 2 mi. from the hostel, and Brunswick, 3 mi. away. (Lockout 9:30am-5pm. Check-in 7:30am-9am and 5-9pm; curfew 11pm. Limited parking. Members $9, non-members $12. Sleepsack $2. Camping $4 per member or ATC hiker, $7 per non-member; includes use of hostel kitchen and bathrooms. Max. stay 3 nights. 50% reservation deposit.)

The **Hillside Motel,** 340 Keep Tryst Rd. (301-834-8144) in Knoxville, MD, has 19 rooms. Singles $30, doubles $35.

You can **camp** along the C&O Canal, where sites lie 5 mi. apart, or in one of the five Maryland state-park campgrounds lying within 30 mi. of Harper's Ferry. **Greenbrier State Park** (301-791-4767) lies a few miles north of Boonsboro on Rte. 66 between exits 35 and 42 on I-70 ($16; open April-Nov.). Far closer is the commercial **Camp Resort,** Rte. 3, Box 1300 (304-535-6895), adjacent to the entrance to Harper's Ferry National Park (sites $25 for 2 people, with water and electric hookup $28; each additional person $4, under 17 $2; registration fee $3 per person). They also rent cabins: $75 for a two-room cabin that sleeps eight.

HIKES AND ACTIVITIES

Park rangers at the visitors center provide free 45- to 60-minute tours, daily from 10:30am to 4pm throughout the summer. Also, keep your ears open for evening programs during that season.

The bus from the parking lot stops at **Shenandoah Street.** Browse through the renovated blacksmith's shop, ready-made clothing store, and general store. Wince as the blacksmith hammers at real iron fired in a furnace; the stores contain replicas of 19th-century goods. Guides in period costume explain the vagaries of the Industrial Revolution. A turn onto High St. reveals many of Harper's Ferry's most interesting exhibits. **Black Voices from Harper's Ferry,** on the corner of High and Shenandoah St., is an exhibit on the history of local African-Americans from slavery to Storer University. Also on High St., the **Civil War Story** chronicles the town's role in the national conflict through displays and a 20-foot time line.

High St. also offers more "olde time" crafts, West Virginia t-shirts, and books on Harper's Ferry than should be legal. The restaurants here are also predictable; walk down Potomac St. instead. Here you'll find the **Little Ponderosa** (535-2168), which dishes out barbecue sandwiches and platters ($5-10) in an old train car. (Open Mon.-Thurs. 8am-5pm, Fri. 8am-8pm, Sat.-Sun. 7:30am-6pm.) The **Back Street Café** (304-725-8019), also on Potomac St., doubles as a burger joint (burgers and hot dogs under $2.25) and an offbeat guide service; "Ghost Tours" of the town are offered weekend nights. (Tours May-Nov. 8 Fri.-Sun. 8pm; reservations recommended in Oct; tours cost $2. Call Shirley at 725-8019. Café open daily 10am-5pm.) A few three-speed bikes are for rent near the Back Street Café ($3 per hr. and $15 per day).

Uphill, stairs on High St. follow the Appalachian Trail to **Upper Harper's Ferry.** The way up passes **Harper's House,** the restored home of town founder Robert Harper, **St. Peter's Church,** where a sagacious pastor flew the Union Jack during the Civil War to protect the church, and **Jefferson's Rock,** where you-know-who had his Atlantic crossing inspiration. At the top of the climb moulders **Storer University,** one of America's first black colleges (closed now for over 20 years).

Those who prefer to combine history with nature have several options, including hiking and boating. The **Maryland Heights Trail** offers some of the best views in the Blue Ridge Mountains and winds past cliffs worthy of experienced rock climbers. Climbers must register at the Visitors Center. The **Bolivar Heights Trail** follows a Civil War battle line and features trailside exhibits and a 3-gun battery. The **Appalachian Trail Conference Headquarters** (304-535-6331), at the corner of Washington and Jackson St., offers catalogues to its members featuring good deals on hiking books, as well as trail information and a maildrop for hikers. (Open May-Oct. Mon.-Fri. 9am-5pm, Sat.-Sun. 9am-4pm; Nov.-mid-May Mon.-Fri. 9am-5pm. Membership $25, seniors and students $18. Write to P.O. Box 807 or call.) The less adventurous can walk along the **Chesapeake & Ohio Canal Towpath,** off the end of Shenandoah St. and over the bridge. The Towpath is also popular with bikers.

Water fanatics should contact **Blue Ridge Outfitters** (304-725-3441), a few miles west of Harper's Ferry on Rte. 340N; they arrange excursions ranging from four-hour canoe trips on the Shenandoah to three-day white-water raft rides on Virginia's toughest waterways. On weekdays, prices start at $45 for either a canoe or a seat on a half-day raft trip. (Open daily 8am-7pm.) **River & Trail Outfitters** (301-834-9950), 604 Valley Rd. at Rte. 340 at the blinking light, rents canoes, inner tubes, and rafts in addition to organizing guided trips (canoes $45 per day per, raft trips $45 per person, tubing $28.50 per day). It also organizes cross-country skiing weekends ($199) and day trips ($60). Call ahead for reservations. Open daily 9am-5pm.

Antietam National Battlefield

A few miles north of Harper's Ferry, the bloodiest one-day battle of the Civil War was fought after skirmishing at Harper's Ferry. On September 17, 1862, 12,410 Union and 10,700 Confederate soldiers lost their lives as Confederate General Robert E. Lee tried and failed to overcome the army of Union General George B. McClellan. McClellan's typical failure to follow the retreating Confederates and crush them decisively tainted the victory, but the nominal Union triumph provided President Lincoln with the opportunity to issue the Emancipation Proclamation, freeing all slaves in those states still in rebellion against the United States on January 1, 1863. The **visitors center** (301-432-5124) has a museum of artifacts used in the battle, free maps for self-guided tours of the battlefield, tapes for rent ($5) with a detailed account of the battle, and an introductory film on the battle (film 9am-5pm on the hr.; center open daily May-Sept. 8:30am-6pm, Oct.-April 8:30am-5pm; battlefield fee $2, family $4). To get to Antietam from Harper's Ferry, take Rte. 340 N. to Rte. 67 heading toward Boonsboro. Stay on Rte. 67 N. until you reach Rte. 65; follow 65 to Antietam.

Appendix

SPECIAL EVENTS

D.C.'s seasons brim with special events; in spring and summer, periodic parades, marches, and festivals block off streets and clog the Mall with booths and banners.

Remember that some of the best (and, by definition, the most spontaneous) special events don't get planned a year in advance and can't be listed in *Let's Go.* Outdoor rock concerts, demonstrations, marches, and rallies, promoted by street posters and word of mouth, can leap into existence only days after the news events that inspire them.

THE FOURTH OF JULY

On the nation's birthday, the capital throws an all-day bash. In mid-morning, "colonial" troops carry out military maneuvers while patriotic music plays, and a costumed orator reads the country's birth certificate, the *Declaration of Independence,* from the steps of the National Archives at 7th St. and Constitution Ave. NW (501-5000). A noisy demonstration of Colonial-era militia segues at noon into the old-fashioned **Fourth of July parade** (789-7000), along Constitution Ave. to 17th St. NW. (Tourists line the sidewalks by 11:30am; arrive early.) High school bands, veterans, baton twirlers, horses, and marchers from as far as South America celebrate the country's existence.

The **National Symphony** (416-8100) plays on the Capitol's West Lawn from 8pm on, but sitting there won't afford a good view of the 9:20pm **fireworks,** best observed from the grounds of the Washington Monument. Bring friends and a blanket, arrive by 6:30pm for a decent spot, and face west (away from the Capitol, towards the Lincoln Memorial). For a memorable if slightly guilty pleasure on Independence Day, **befriend a White House intern** and squeeze an invitation to the White House Lawn; spread out in front of the balcony for a front-row view of the Clintons. If none of these options pans out, try the Jefferson Memorial: your view is less likely to be obstructed there than at the Mall.

SUMMER-LONG EVENTS

Marine Corps Tuesday Evening Sunset Parades, at the Iwo Jima Memorial, with the U.S. Marine Drum and Bugle Corps and Silent Drill team. Metro: Arlington Cemetery. Tues. 7-8:30pm. Free shuttle service from Arlington Cemetery Visitors Center 5-7pm and 9pm return service. Free.

Marine Corps Friday Evening Parades (433-6060), May-Aug. at the Marine Barracks, 8th and I St. SE. Metro: Eastern Market. The Eighth and Eye Marines strut their pomp at 8:45pm sharp: Marine Corps Band music, a procession of soldiers, the Marine mascot (a bulldog), and a spotlit figure bugling *Taps* into the night. Free, but be sure to reserve over three weeks in advance.

Military Bands Summer Concert Series, June-Aug. at the Washington Monument and U.S. Capitol. Call for exact dates and locations: Army (703-696-3399), Navy (433-2525), Air Force (767-5658), Marines (433-4011). 8pm. Free.

Navy Band Concerts, (737-2300). Metro: Archives-Navy Memorial. Daily in the summer at the U.S. Navy Memorial. Call for schedule.

ANNUAL EVENTS

Martin Luther King Jr.'s Birthday, observed Jan. 20 (619-7222). Wreaths laid and the "I Have a Dream" speech re-spoken at the Lincoln Memorial. Choirs, guest speakers, and military color guard. 11am. Free.

Robert E. Lee's Birthday, Jan. 22 (703-548-8454). Metro: Arlington Cemetery. At Arlington House, Lee's former residence. 19th-century music, birthday cake, and a show of the house. 3-5pm. Admission $3.

Abraham Lincoln's Birthday, observed Feb. 12 (619-7222). Laying down of wreaths and booming out of the Gettysburg address from the cold steps of the Lincoln Memorial, starting at noon. Free.

Chinese New Year Parade, mid-Feb., down H St. NW between 5th and 8th St. Metro: Gallery Place. Firecrackers, lions, drums, and dragons make the normally tame streets of Chinatown—all 6 of them—explode with delight. Free.

Mount Vernon Open House, Feb. 19 (703-780-2000). Free admission to Mount Vernon, fife and drums on the green, and the obligatory wreath-laying. Don't take any wooden teeth. 9am-4pm. Do a little dance.

George Washington's Birthday Parade, Feb. 19, through Old Town Alexandria (703-838-4200). Metro: King St. Rather self-explanatory. Free.

U.S. Army Band Anniversary Concert, Jan. 30 at 8pm, at the Kennedy Center (703-696-3399). Metro: Foggy Bottom/GWU. Top brass, so to speak; also choral music. Free.

Festival of St. Patrick, mid-March (347-1450). Irish culture proliferates at 924 G St. NW, with books 'n' musicians 'n' dancers. Metro: Gallery Place. Free.

St. Patrick's Day Parade, March 17, downtown on Constitution Ave. NW. A celebration of things green. Dancers, bands, bagpipes, and floats start at 1pm. Free.

U.S. Botanic Gardens' Spring Flower Show, March 23 to April 21 (225-8333). Metro: Federal Center SW. Colorful. Refreshing. Free.

Smithsonian Kite Festival, March 30 (357-3244). Metro: Smithsonian. Go fly a kite or watch designers of all ages at the Washington Monument grounds compete for prizes and trophies from 10am-4pm. Free.

National Cherry Blossom Festival, March 25 to April 9, all over town; contact the festival committee (737-2599), the Convention and Visitors Assn. (789-7000), or just read the *Washington Post.* Official Washington goes bonkers over the Japanese blossoms, expected to appear during these weeks. April 9 parade down Constitution Ave. NW from 7th to 17th St. Other events (some free) include fireworks, a fashion show, free concerts in downtown parks, the Japanese Lantern Lighting Ceremony, the Cherry Blossom Ball, and annual Marathon Race.

Save the Children/Marvin Gaye Day, April 24. Metro: Gallery Place. Go-go, jazz, and gospel music with food and festing in the outdoor "downtown mall" on F St. NW, between 7th and 9th St. and behind the National Museum of American Art.

Easter Sunrise Service, on Easter Sun., at Arlington Cemetery (475-0856). Free.

White House Easter Egg Roll, on Easter Mon. on the White House South Lawn (456-2200). Metro: McPherson Sq. or Metro Center. For kids 6 and under. Famous egg roll usually brings out the president and the press for perfect photo opportunities with all-American kids; you'll have to stand in line. Eggs provided; entertainment scheduled. Enter at the southeast gate of the White House on East Executive Ave. Call for hours. Free.

American College Theater Festival, April 15-23, at the Kennedy Center (416-8000). Metro: Foggy Bottom-GWU. A jury chooses the nation's best college shows, which go on at the Kennedy Center. All shows are free; line up the Friday before at 10am in the Kennedy Center's Grand Foyer, or just show up that night.

Smithsonian Craft Show, April 25-28, at the National Building Museum (357-4000). Metro: Judiciary Square. A sales exhibition of fine hand crafted objects; 100 exhibitors in fiber, ceramics, glass, jewelry, leather, metal, paper, textiles, and wood, chosen by cunning experts. Entrance fee about $6.

Duke Ellington Birthday Celebration, April 20 at Freedom Plaza, 13th St. and Pennsylvania Ave. NW (331-9404). Metro: Federal Triangle. The late D.C.-born jazz legend deserves this celebration, which prominently showcases his music. Noon-6pm. Free. Special events and workshops continue through the week.

Shakespeare's Birthday Celebration, April 20 at the Folger Shakespeare Library, 201 E. Capitol St. SE (544-7077). Metro: Capitol South. Exhibits, plays, Elizabethan music, food, and children's events. 11am-4pm. Free.

Department of Defense/Joint Services Open House, mid-May; call for exact dates (301-568-5995, 301-981-4424). The Andrews Air Force Base, in Camp Springs, MD, opens up for visitors and aerobatics. Army parachutists plummet and recover; Blue Angels and Golden Knights demo teams zoom and swerve under the clouds. Don't try this at home, kids. To reach the base, take the Beltway I-95 to exit 9. Turn right onto Allentown Rd. and follow the signs. Free.

Greek Festival, May 19-21 and Sept. 16-18, at Saints Constantine and Helen Greek Orthodox Church, 4115 16th St. NW (829-2910). Greek food, music, dance, etc. Noon-9pm. Free.

Malcolm X Day, May 21 in Anacostia Park along the Anacostia River in SE (fax 543-1649). A day-long festival honoring the slain black leader. Food, speakers, and "Harambe Village" (three tents of exhibits) complement gospel, African, Caribbean, blues, and go-go music. Noon-7pm. Free.

National Symphony Orchestra Memorial Day Weekend Concert, May 27 on the West Lawn of the U.S. Capitol (416-8100, 619-7222). Free.

Memorial Day Jazz Festival, May 27, in Old Town Alexandria, VA (703-838-4844). Local big bands. Noon-7pm. Free.

Memorial Day Ceremonies at Arlington Cemetery, May 27 (475-0856). Metro: Arlington Cemetery. Wreaths at John F. Kennedy's tomb and at the Tomb of the Unknown Soldier, and services in Memorial Amphitheater. Free.

Memorial Day Ceremonies at the Vietnam Veterans Memorial, May 27 (619-7222). Wreath-laying, speeches, bands, and a keynote address. 11am. Free.

Dupont-Kalorama Museum Walk Day, early June (667-0441). Metro: Dupont Circle. 8 museums north of Dupont Circle seek publicity, including the Textile Museum, Anderson House, and the Fondo del Sol Arts Center. Music, historic house tours, food, crafts, etc. Noon-4pm. Free.

Gay Pride Day, in June. Metro: U St.-Cardozo. Huge march through downtown for gay and lesbian consciousness, visibilty, and rights. Starts at 16th and W St.; ends in a festival at the Francis School, 24th and 25th St. Check *The Washington Blade* for exact dates and related events. Fabulous and free.

Philippine Independence Day Parade and Fair, June 3 (call the Philippine Embassy at 467-9300). Parade: Pennsylvania Ave. NW from 4th St. to 13th St. Fair: Freedom Plaza at 13th St. and Pennsylvania Ave. Hey, it's free.

Dance Africa D.C., mid-June at Dance Place, 3225 8th St. NE (269-1600). Metro: Brookland-CUA. Hourly free traditional dance performances from all over Africa, accompanied by an outdoor food and crafts market.

Bloomsday Marathon Ulysses Reading, begins June 15 at Kelly's Irish Times pub, 14 F St. NW (543-5433). Metro: Union Station. Annual read-through of Joyce's 2nd published novel draws crowds of literary and Irish notables. Starts around 11am on Saturday morning and continues through the night. Hear the final gasps of "yes I said yes I will yes" sometime around 10pm on Sunday. Bring along a copy of the novel to follow along. Yes, it's free, yes it's free, yes.

Festival of American Folklife, the first 2 weekends in July on the Mall (357-2700). Huge Smithsonian-run fair demonstrates the crafts, customs, food, and music of a few selected states, and foreign countries to over a million visitors, with musicians, performers, and craftspeople imported from the featured regions. Free.

Bastille Day Waiters' Race, July 14, starting at Pennsylvania Ave. and 20th St. NW. Metro: Foggy Bottom-GWU. Waiters carry champagne glasses and splits of champagne on trays and demonstrate their juggling abilities for a grand-prize trip to Paris. Dominique's Restaurant (452-1132) sponsors. Usually at 2pm. Free.

Virginia Scottish Games, July 27-28, 3901 W. Braddock Rd. in Alexandria, VA, on the grounds of Episcopal High School (703-838-4200). Free shuttle from King St. Metro back to the games. 2-day annual Scottish festival is one of America's largest, with Highland dancing, kilts, tartans, sheepdogs, bagpiping, national professional heptathlon, animal events, fiddling and harp competitions, and Scottish foods, goods, and genealogy. Advance tickets $9 for 1 day, $15 for 2. Regular tickets $10 for 1 day, $17 for 2. Ages under 15 free with adult, $1 without.

Latin American Festival, in late July on the Washington Monument grounds; call for exact date (347-2873). Metro: Smithsonian. Free food, music, dance, and theater from 40 Latin American nations.

Latin and Jazz Festival, in late June at Freedom Plaza, 13th St. and Pennsylvania Ave. NW (331-9404). Metro: Federal Triangle. Continuous live jazz and ethnic food. By the same people who organize the Duke Ellington Birthday Celebration.

Civil War Living History Day, mid-Aug., at Fort Ward Museum and Historic Site, 4301 W. Braddock Rd., Alexandria, VA (703-838-4848). Torchlight tours of soldiers' camps in the evening. Soldiers reenact camp life and perform artillery drills during the day. Suggested donation $2.

Navy Band Children's Lollipop Concert, mid-Aug. on the Washington Monument grounds (433-2525). Metro: Smithsonian. 8pm. Free.

National Frisbee Festival, Sept. 7, noon-5pm, on the Washington Monument Grounds (301-645-5043). Metro: Smithsonian. The largest non-competitive frisbee festival in the U.S., with frisbee studs and disc-catching dogs. Free.

African Cultural Festival, early Sept. at Freedom Plaza, 14th St. and Pennsylvania Ave. NW. Metro: Federal Triangle. African cooking, sounds, and stuff. Noon-7pm.

D.C. Blues Festival, Sept. 9 at the Carter-Barron Amphitheatre near Rock Creek Park (828-3028; call for exact date). Blues people twang, wail, and moan. Free.

Black Family Reunion, early Sept. on the Mall (628-0015; call for exact date). "Celebration of the black family" with music, food, exhibits. Free.

National Symphony Orchestra Labor Day Weekend Concert, Sept. 3 on the West Lawn of the U.S. Capitol (in the Kennedy Center if it rains; 416-8100 or 619-7222). Metro: Federal Center SW. 8pm. Free.

Kennedy Center Open House, mid-Sept. (467-4600). Metro: Foggy Bottom. A 1-day hodgepodge of classical, jazz, folk and ethnic music, dance, drama, and film from D.C. performers including members of the National Symphony Orchestra. Free.

Adams-Morgan Day, traditionally the first Sunday after Labor Day, unrolls along 18th St. between Columbia Rd., and Florida Ave. NW in its namesake neighborhood (332-3292). Live music on 3 stages, stuff for sale, and the wondrous kaleidoscope of ethnic food for which Adams-Morgan is justly famous. Free all day, always jammin', and consequently always jammed.

Saints Constantine and Helen Greek Orthodox Church Bazaar, third weekend in Sept. at 4115 16th St. NW (829-2910). Greek food, crafts, and dancing.

White House Fall Garden Tours, mid-Oct. (619-7222). Like the spring garden tours, but this time with military-band music. Free, but fills up fast; call ahead.

Veteran's Day Ceremonies, Nov. 11, around Arlington Cemetery (475-0843). Metro: Arlington Cemetery. Solemn ceremony with military bands honors the nation's fallen soldiers. The president or a substitute lays a wreath at the Tomb of the Unknown Soldier. Ceremonies begin at 11am. Free. Vietnam Veterans Memorial (619-7222) holds ceremonies at 1pm. Free.

Kennedy Center Holiday Celebration, throughout December (467-4600). Musical events colonize the Kennedy Center from Dec. 1 to the New Year. Free performances include classical chamber, choral, cello, and "Tubachristmas" concerts, a gospel music concert (tickets given away a few weeks in advance), and the hugely popular sing-along to Handel's *Messiah*.

Woodlawn Plantation Christmas, at Woodlawn Plantation, 9000 Richmond Highway, Alexandria, VA (703-780-4000). Recreates an early-1800s Christmas; log fires, lighting, and libations. Dec. 2-10; call for hours and to make reservations. Tickets at the door. $6, $4 for students and seniors.

People's Christmas Tree Lighting (224-6645), in mid-Dec. on the Capitol's West Lawn. Metro: Federal Center SW. Congress lights its own Christmas tree while the military band plays on. 5pm. Free.

National Christmas Tree Lighting/Pageant of Peace, on the Ellipse south of the White House (619-7225). Metro: McPherson Sq. The President switches on a Christmas tree and a Hanukkah Menorah on a Thurs. in mid-Dec.; the Ellipse hosts choral music, a Nativity scene, a burning yule log, and lit-up trees from the 50 states until the New Year crashes in. Free.

Washington National Cathedral Christmas Celebration and Services (537-6247), Dec. 24-25 at the Cathedral, Massachusetts and Wisconsin Ave. NW. Christmas carols and choral music during the day, but the nighttime service is more famous. Dec. 24: pageant 4pm, service 10pm. Dec. 25: service 9am. Free.

White House Christmas Candlelight Tours (619-7222). See Bill and Hillary's Christmas decorations between 5-7pm, generally on the 3 days immediately following Christmas. Call for exact dates. Free.

Index

C

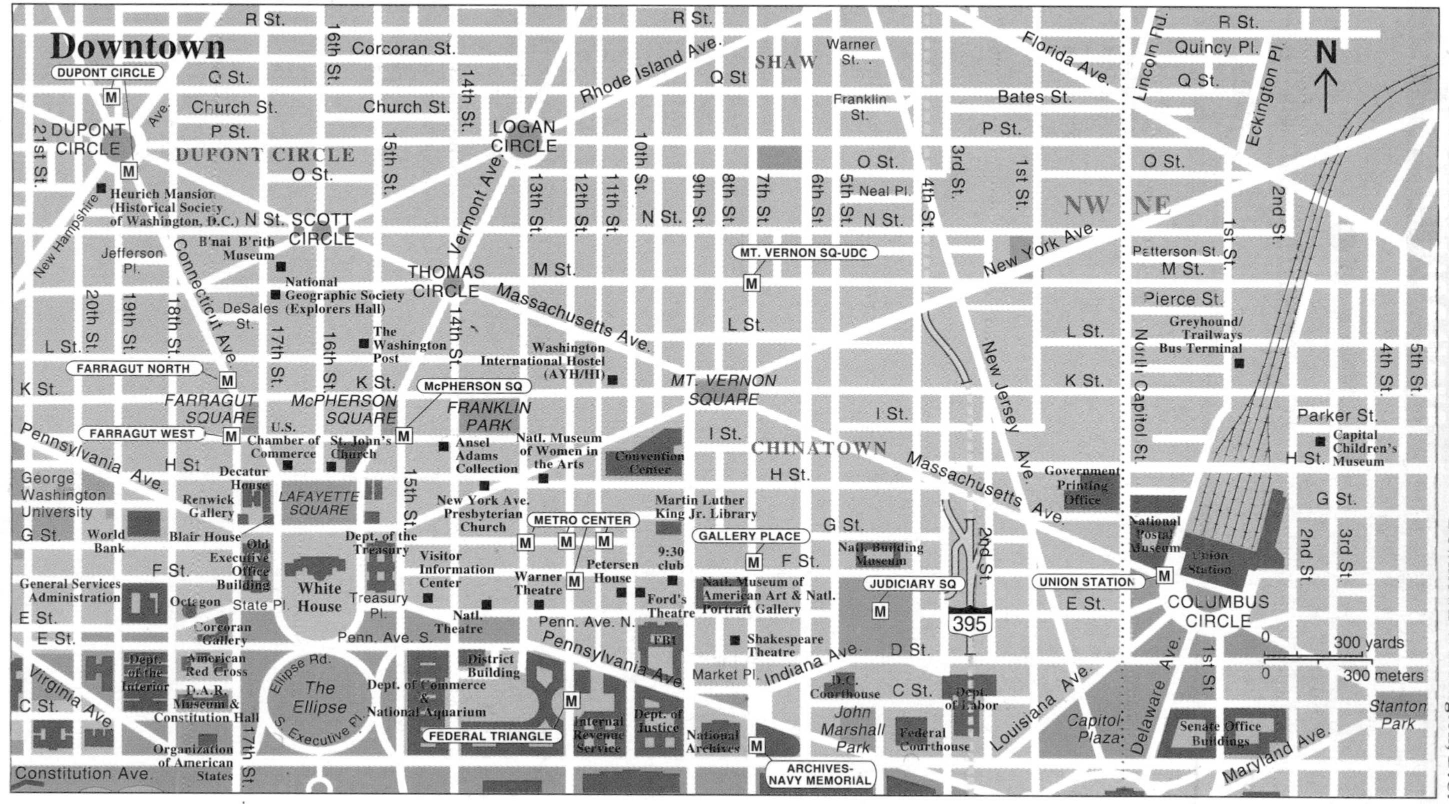
Downtown
N
DUPONT CIRCLE
DUPONT CIRCLE
SCOTT CIRCLE
THOMAS CIRCLE
LOGAN CIRCLE
SHAW
CHINATOWN
NW
NE
FARRAGUT SQUARE
McPHERSON SQUARE
FRANKLIN PARK
MT. VERNON SQUARE
LAFAYETTE SQUARE
John Marshall Park
Capitol Plaza
Stanton Park
COLUMBUS CIRCLE
The Ellipse
FARRAGUT NORTH
FARRAGUT WEST
McPHERSON SQ
MT. VERNON SQ-UDC
METRO CENTER
GALLERY PLACE
JUDICIARY SQ
UNION STATION
FEDERAL TRIANGLE
ARCHIVES-NAVY MEMORIAL
395
Heurich Mansion (Historical Society of Washington, D.C.)
B'nai B'rith Museum
National Geographic Society (Explorers Hall)
The Washington Post
Washington International Hostel (AYH/HI)
Natl. Museum of Women in the Arts
Ansel Adams Collection
New York Ave. Presbyterian Church
U.S. Chamber of Commerce
St. John's Church
Decatur House
Renwick Gallery
Blair House
Old Executive Office Building
White House
Dept. of the Treasury
Visitor Information Center
Warner Theatre
Natl. Theatre
Convention Center
Martin Luther King Jr. Library
9:30 club
Petersen House
Ford's Theatre
FBI
Natl. Museum of American Art & Natl. Portrait Gallery
Shakespeare Theatre
Natl. Building Museum
Government Printing Office
National Postal Museum
Union Station
Greyhound/ Trailways Bus Terminal
Capital Children's Museum
Senate Office Buildings
Dept. of Labor
Federal Courthouse
D.C. Courthouse
National Archives
Dept. of Justice
Internal Revenue Service
District Building
Dept. of Commerce & National Aquarium
Corcoran Gallery
Octagon
American Red Cross
D.A.R. Museum & Constitution Hall
Organization of American States
Dept. of the Interior
General Services Administration
World Bank
George Washington University
Connecticut Ave.
New Hampshire Ave.
Massachusetts Ave.
Rhode Island Ave.
Vermont Ave.
New York Ave.
New Jersey Ave.
Florida Ave.
Pennsylvania Ave.
Indiana Ave.
Louisiana Ave.
Delaware Ave.
Maryland Ave.
Virginia Ave.
Constitution Ave.
Penn. Ave. N.
Penn. Ave. S.
North Capitol St.
Eckington Pl.
Lincoln Rd.
Quincy Pl.
Patterson St.
Pierce St.
Parker St.
Bates St.
Franklin St.
Warner St.
Neal Pl.
Corcoran St.
Church St.
Jefferson Pl.
DeSales St.
Market Pl.
Treasury Pl.
State Pl.
Ellipse Rd.
S. Executive Pl.
R St.
Q St.
P St.
O St.
N St.
M St.
L St.
K St.
I St.
H St.
G St.
F St.
E St.
D St.
C St.
1st St.
2nd St.
3rd St.
4th St.
5th St.
6th St.
7th St.
8th St.
9th St.
10th St.
11th St.
12th St.
13th St.
14th St.
15th St.
16th St.
17th St.
18th St.
19th St.
20th St.
21st St.
0
300 yards
0
300 meters

Central Washington, D.C.

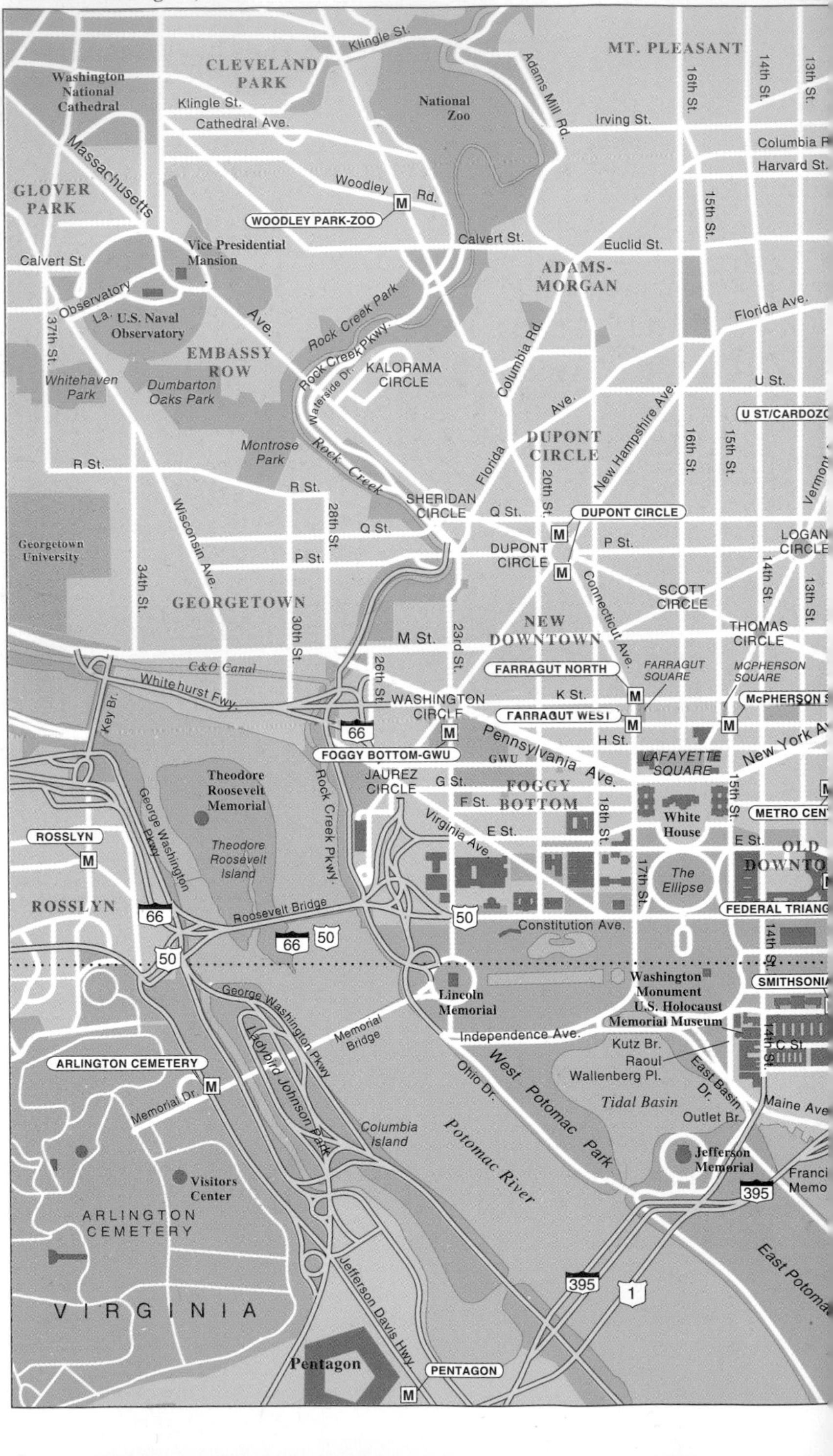

CLEVELAND PARK
MT. PLEASANT
Washington National Cathedral
Klingle St.
Cathedral Ave.
National Zoo
Adams Mill Rd.
Irving St.
16th St.
14th St.
13th St.
Columbia Rd.
Harvard St.
GLOVER PARK
Massachusetts Ave.
Woodley Rd.
WOODLEY PARK-ZOO
15th St.
Vice Presidential Mansion
Calvert St.
Euclid St.
ADAMS-MORGAN
Observatory La.
U.S. Naval Observatory
37th St.
Rock Creek Park
Rock Creek Pkwy.
Florida Ave.
EMBASSY ROW
KALORAMA CIRCLE
Waterside Dr.
Columbia Rd.
Whitehaven Park
Dumbarton Oaks Park
U St.
U ST/CARDOZO
New Hampshire Ave.
DUPONT CIRCLE
Montrose Park
Rock Creek
Vermont
R St.
SHERIDAN CIRCLE
Q St.
20th St.
28th St.
Wisconsin Ave.
P St.
Georgetown University
LOGAN CIRCLE
34th St.
GEORGETOWN
Connecticut Ave.
SCOTT CIRCLE
30th St.
NEW DOWNTOWN
M St.
23rd St.
THOMAS CIRCLE
C&O Canal
FARRAGUT NORTH
FARRAGUT SQUARE
MCPHERSON SQUARE
Whitehurst Fwy.
26th St.
K St.
WASHINGTON CIRCLE
FARRAGUT WEST
McPHERSON SQ.
Key Br.
66
H St.
New York Ave.
FOGGY BOTTOM-GWU
Pennsylvania Ave.
GWU
LAFAYETTE SQUARE
Theodore Roosevelt Memorial
JAUREZ CIRCLE
G St.
FOGGY BOTTOM
George Washington Pkwy
Rock Creek Pkwy.
F St.
White House
METRO CENTER
ROSSLYN
Theodore Roosevelt Island
Virginia Ave.
E St.
18th St.
17th St.
OLD DOWNTOWN
The Ellipse
ROSSLYN
Roosevelt Bridge
50
FEDERAL TRIANGLE
Constitution Ave.
Washington Monument
SMITHSONIAN
Lincoln Memorial
U.S. Holocaust Memorial Museum
George Washington Pkwy
Memorial Bridge
Independence Ave.
Kutz Br.
C St.
Ladybird Johnson Park
Raoul Wallenberg Pl.
ARLINGTON CEMETERY
Ohio Dr.
West Potomac Park
East Basin Dr.
Memorial Dr.
Tidal Basin
Maine Ave.
Outlet Br.
Columbia Island
Potomac River
Jefferson Memorial
Visitors Center
395
Franklin Memorial
ARLINGTON CEMETERY
East Potomac
Jefferson Davis Hwy
1
VIRGINIA
Pentagon
PENTAGON

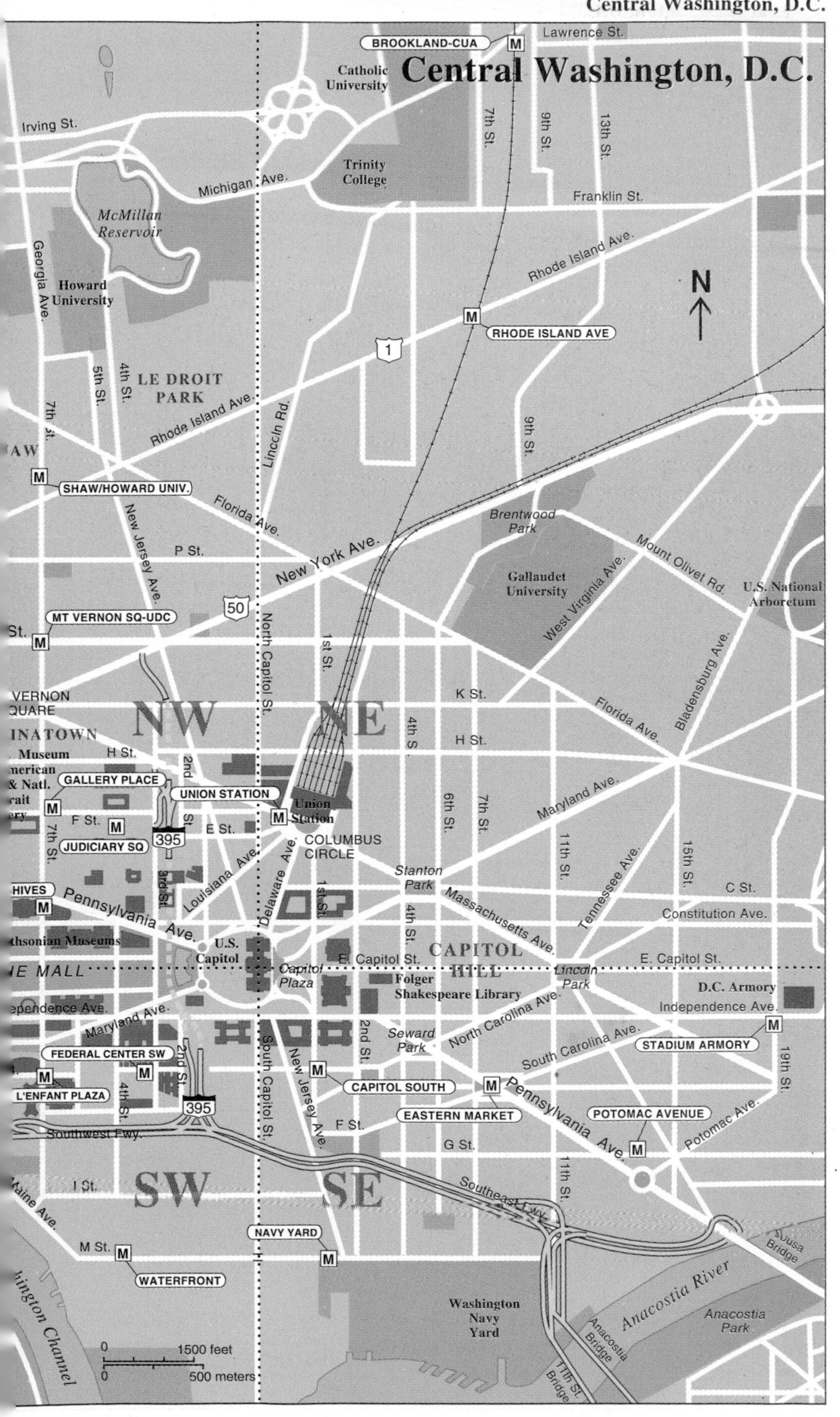
Central Washington, D.C.
BROOKLAND-CUA
Lawrence St.
Catholic University
Irving St.
Trinity College
Michigan Ave.
7th St.
9th St.
13th St.
Franklin St.
McMillan Reservoir
Georgia Ave.
Howard University
Rhode Island Ave.
N
RHODE ISLAND AVE
1
LE DROIT PARK
5th St.
4th St.
7th St.
Lincoln Rd.
SHAW/HOWARD UNIV.
Florida Ave.
New Jersey Ave.
Brentwood Park
P St.
New York Ave.
Gallaudet University
Mount Olivet Rd.
West Virginia Ave.
U.S. National Arboretum
50
MT VERNON SQ-UDC
North Capitol St.
1st St.
Bladensburg Ave.
K St.
NW
NE
Florida Ave.
H St.
4th St.
GALLERY PLACE
UNION STATION
Union Station
2nd St.
6th St.
Maryland Ave.
F St.
E St.
395
JUDICIARY SQ
COLUMBUS CIRCLE
Louisiana Ave.
Delaware Ave.
11th St.
Tennessee Ave.
15th St.
Stanton Park
C St.
3rd St.
1st St.
Massachusetts Ave.
Constitution Ave.
Pennsylvania Ave.
U.S. Capitol
4th St.
CAPITOL HILL
E. Capitol St.
Capitol Plaza
Folger Shakespeare Library
Lincoln Park
D.C. Armory
Independence Ave.
Maryland Ave.
North Carolina Ave.
Seward Park
STADIUM ARMORY
FEDERAL CENTER SW
2nd St.
South Capitol St.
New Jersey Ave.
2nd St.
South Carolina Ave.
19th St.
L'ENFANT PLAZA
4th St.
CAPITOL SOUTH
Pennsylvania Ave.
EASTERN MARKET
POTOMAC AVENUE
395
F St.
Southwest Fwy.
G St.
Potomac Ave.
SW
SE
Southeast Fwy.
11th St.
NAVY YARD
Sousa Bridge
M St.
WATERFRONT
Anacostia River
Washington Navy Yard
Anacostia Park
Anacostia Bridge
11th St. Bridge
0 1500 feet
0 500 meters

The Mall Area, Washington, D.C.

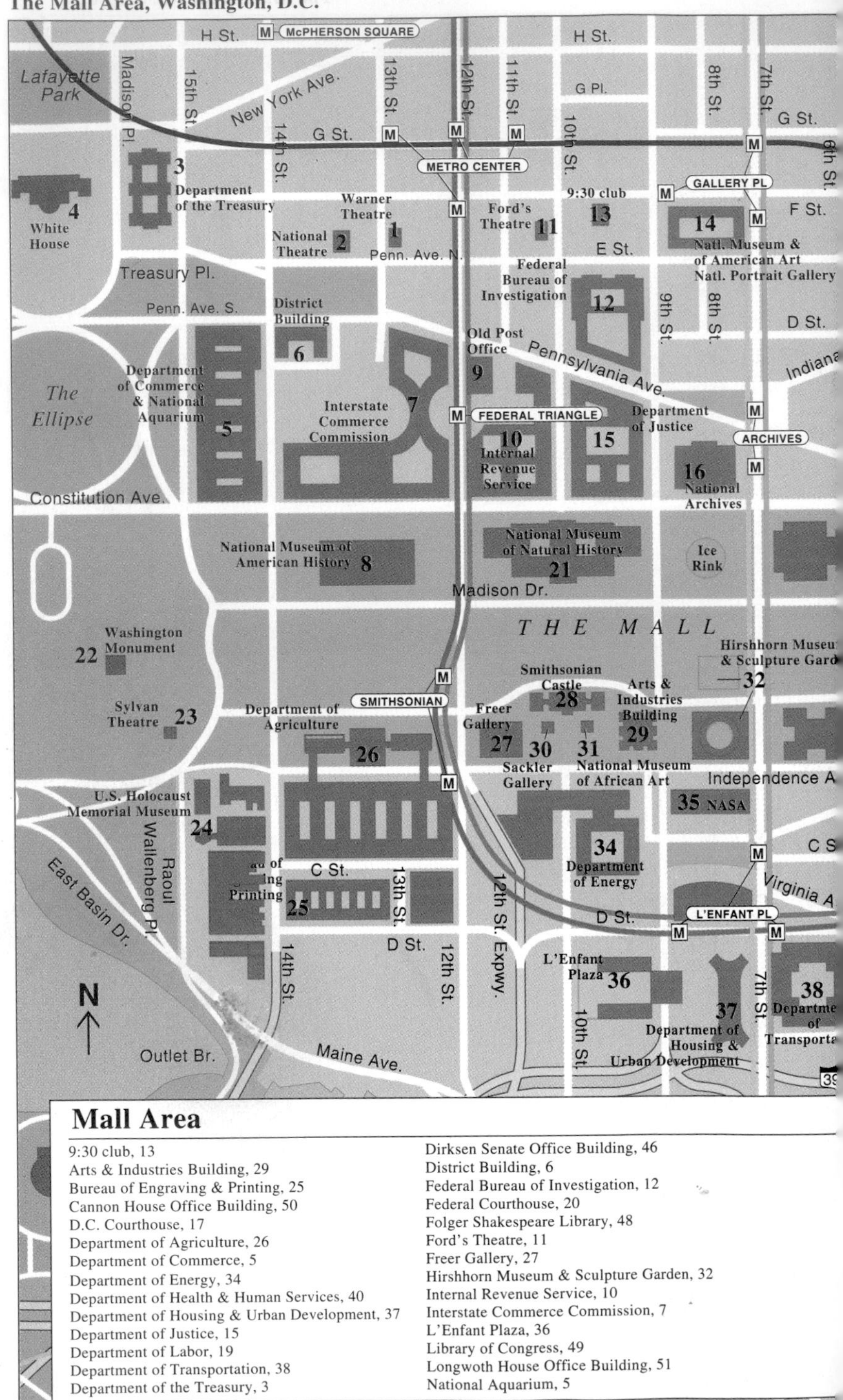

Mall Area

9:30 club, 13
Arts & Industries Building, 29
Bureau of Engraving & Printing, 25
Cannon House Office Building, 50
D.C. Courthouse, 17
Department of Agriculture, 26
Department of Commerce, 5
Department of Energy, 34
Department of Health & Human Services, 40
Department of Housing & Urban Development, 37
Department of Justice, 15
Department of Labor, 19
Department of Transportation, 38
Department of the Treasury, 3
Dirksen Senate Office Building, 46
District Building, 6
Federal Bureau of Investigation, 12
Federal Courthouse, 20
Folger Shakespeare Library, 48
Ford's Theatre, 11
Freer Gallery, 27
Hirshhorn Museum & Sculpture Garden, 32
Internal Revenue Service, 10
Interstate Commerce Commission, 7
L'Enfant Plaza, 36
Library of Congress, 49
Longwoth House Office Building, 51
National Aquarium, 5

The Mall Area, Washington, D.C.

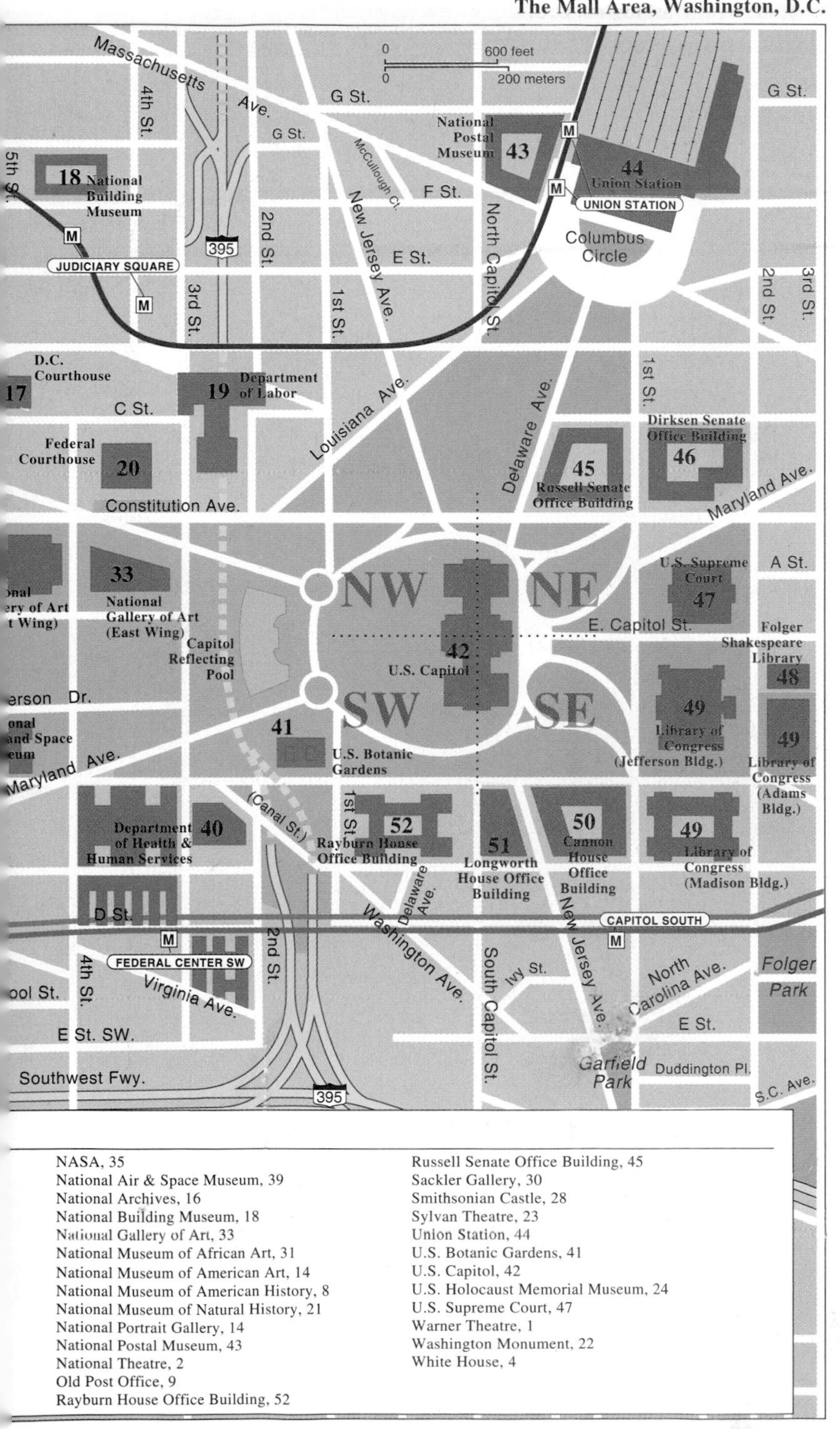

NASA, 35
National Air & Space Museum, 39
National Archives, 16
National Building Museum, 18
National Gallery of Art, 33
National Museum of African Art, 31
National Museum of American Art, 14
National Museum of American History, 8
National Museum of Natural History, 21
National Portrait Gallery, 14
National Postal Museum, 43
National Theatre, 2
Old Post Office, 9
Rayburn House Office Building, 52
Russell Senate Office Building, 45
Sackler Gallery, 30
Smithsonian Castle, 28
Sylvan Theatre, 23
Union Station, 44
U.S. Botanic Gardens, 41
U.S. Capitol, 42
U.S. Holocaust Memorial Museum, 24
U.S. Supreme Court, 47
Warner Theatre, 1
Washington Monument, 22
White House, 4

White House Area, Foggy Bottom, and Nearby Arlington

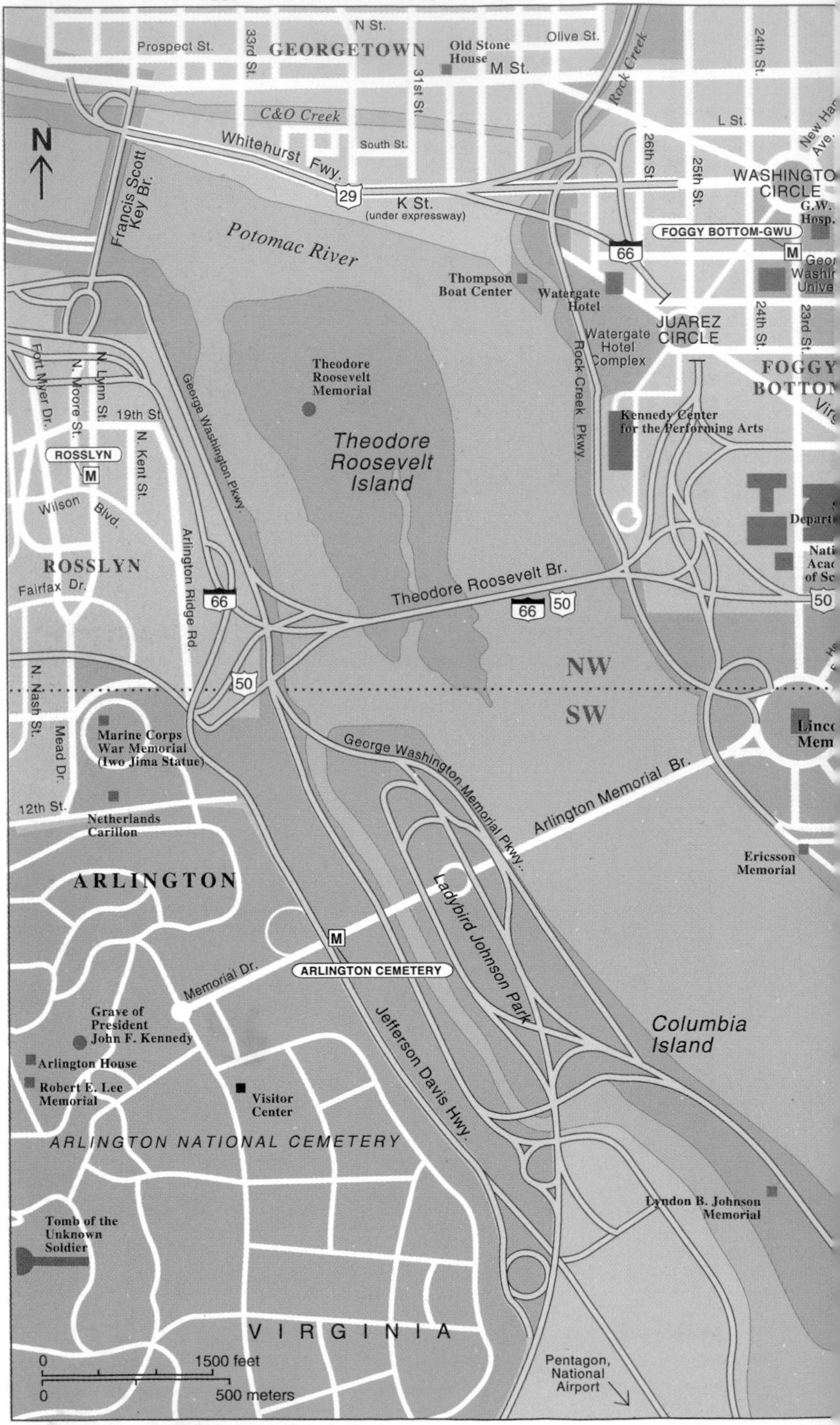

N St.
Prospect St.
33rd St.
GEORGETOWN
Old Stone House
M St.
Olive St.
31st St.
Rock Creek
24th St.
C&O Creek
L St.
South St.
Whitehurst Fwy.
N
Francis Scott Key Br.
29
K St.
(under expressway)
26th St.
25th St.
WASHINGTON CIRCLE
G.W. Hosp.
FOGGY BOTTOM-GWU
M
Potomac River
66
Thompson Boat Center
Watergate Hotel
JUAREZ CIRCLE
Watergate Hotel Complex
24th St.
23rd St.
FOGGY BOTTOM
Fort Myer Dr.
N. Moore St.
N. Lynn St.
19th St.
George Washington Pkwy.
Theodore Roosevelt Memorial
Theodore Roosevelt Island
Rock Creek Pkwy.
Kennedy Center for the Performing Arts
ROSSLYN
M
N. Kent St.
Wilson Blvd.
Arlington Ridge Rd.
ROSSLYN
Fairfax Dr.
66
Theodore Roosevelt Br.
66
50
50
NW
SW
50
N. Nash St.
Mead Dr.
Marine Corps War Memorial (Two Jima Statue)
George Washington Memorial Pkwy.
12th St.
Netherlands Carillon
Arlington Memorial Br.
Ericsson Memorial
ARLINGTON
Ladybird Johnson Park
M
ARLINGTON CEMETERY
Memorial Dr.
Grave of President John F. Kennedy
Jefferson Davis Hwy.
Columbia Island
Arlington House
Robert E. Lee Memorial
Visitor Center
ARLINGTON NATIONAL CEMETERY
Lyndon B. Johnson Memorial
Tomb of the Unknown Soldier
VIRGINIA
0
1500 feet
0
500 meters
Pentagon, National Airport

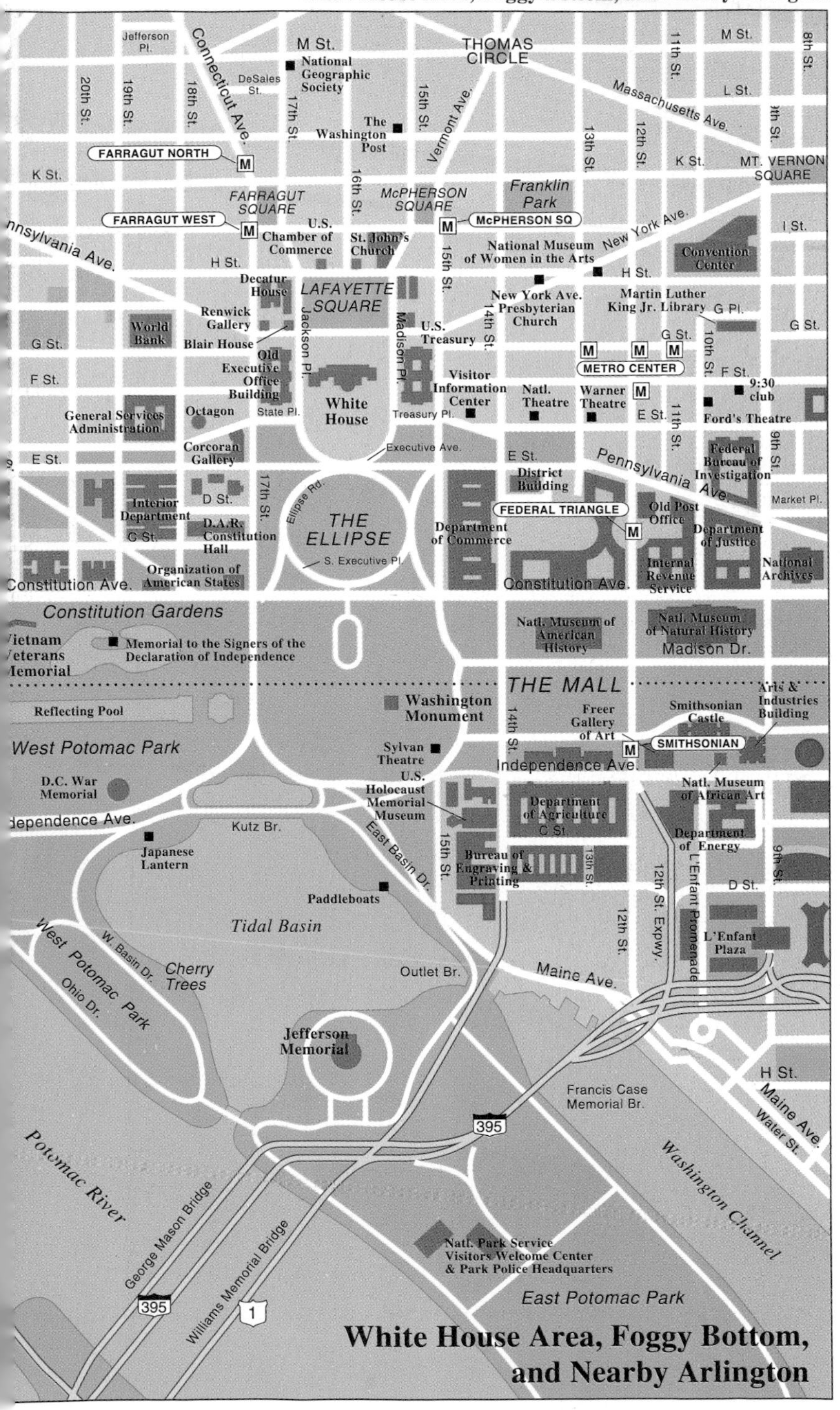
White House Area, Foggy Bottom, and Nearby Arlington
THOMAS CIRCLE
National Geographic Society
The Washington Post
FARRAGUT NORTH
FARRAGUT SQUARE
FARRAGUT WEST
McPHERSON SQUARE
McPHERSON SQ
Franklin Park
MT. VERNON SQUARE
U.S. Chamber of Commerce
St. John's Church
National Museum of Women in the Arts
Convention Center
Decatur House
LAFAYETTE SQUARE
Renwick Gallery
World Bank
Blair House
U.S. Treasury
New York Ave. Presbyterian Church
Martin Luther King Jr. Library
METRO CENTER
Old Executive Office Building
White House
Visitor Information Center
Natl. Theatre
Warner Theatre
9:30 club
Ford's Theatre
General Services Administration
Octagon
Corcoran Gallery
District Building
Federal Bureau of Investigation
Interior Department
D.A.R. Constitution Hall
THE ELLIPSE
FEDERAL TRIANGLE
Old Post Office
Department of Commerce
Department of Justice
Organization of American States
Internal Revenue Service
National Archives
Constitution Gardens
Vietnam Veterans Memorial
Memorial to the Signers of the Declaration of Independence
Natl. Museum of American History
Natl. Museum of Natural History
THE MALL
Reflecting Pool
Washington Monument
Freer Gallery of Art
Smithsonian Castle
Arts & Industries Building
SMITHSONIAN
West Potomac Park
Sylvan Theatre
D.C. War Memorial
U.S. Holocaust Memorial Museum
Department of Agriculture
Natl. Museum of African Art
Department of Energy
Japanese Lantern
Bureau of Engraving & Printing
Paddleboats
Tidal Basin
L'Enfant Plaza
Cherry Trees
Jefferson Memorial
Francis Case Memorial Br.
Washington Channel
Potomac River
George Mason Bridge
Williams Memorial Bridge
Natl. Park Service Visitors Welcome Center & Park Police Headquarters
East Potomac Park
White House Area, Foggy Bottom, and Nearby Arlington

Metrorail System, Washington, D.C.

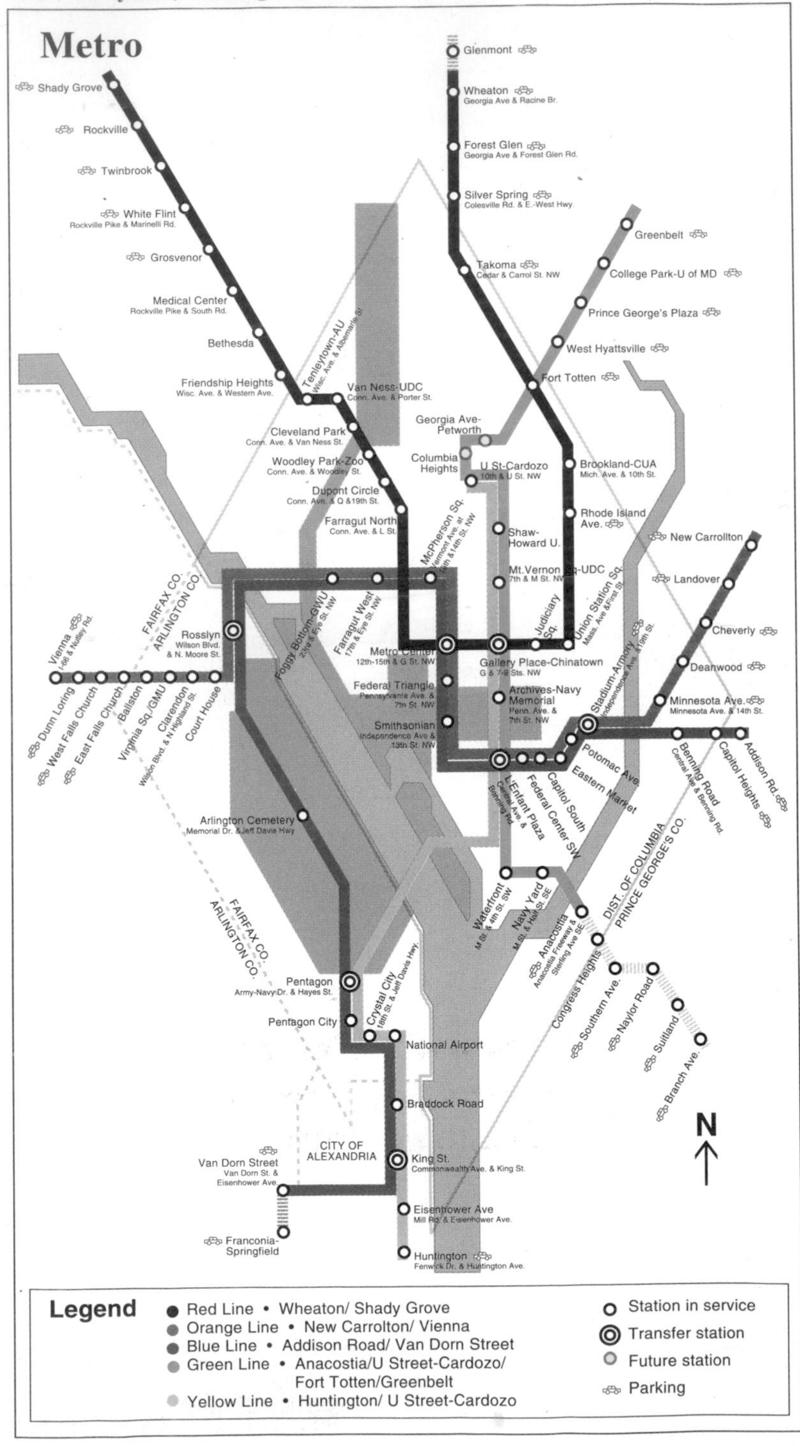